Real-Time Strategy Game Programming Using MS DirectX 6.0

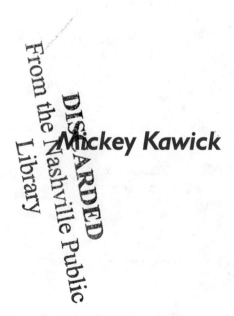

Mickey Kawick

Wordware Publishing, Inc.

Library of Congress Cataloging-in-Publication Data

Kawick, Mickey
    Real-time strategy game programming using MS DirectX 6.0 / by Mickey Kawick.
       p.   cm.
    Includes index.
    ISBN 1-55622-644-6 (pbk.)
    1. Computer games--Programming.   2. DirectX.   I. Title.
    QA76.76.C672K39   1999
    794.8'15268--dc21
                                                     99-17905
                                                        CIP

ISBN 1-55622-644-6
10 9 8 7 6 5 4 3 2 1
9903

Product names mentioned are used for identification purposes only and may be trademarks of their respective
companies.

All inquiries for volume purchases of this book should be addressed to Wordware Publishing, Inc., at
the above address. Telephone inquiries may be made by calling:

(972) 423-0090

Dedication

To Mr. Richard Warner, my high school physics/electronics/
computer science teacher.

Acknowledgments

Thanks to my mom, my sister Marie, and my little sister, Becky.

Special thanks to Robin, my wife, for keeping things going while I was away at my computer for months on end, my son Cedric for expanding my understanding of AI, and my son Drake (now 19 months old) for periodically turning off my computer when I wasn't looking.

Contents Summary

Chapter 1   *Welcome*   1
Chapter 2   *Gameplay*   9
Chapter 3   *Getting Started on Your Game*   15
Chapter 4   *Documents*   65
Chapter 5   *Development*   71
Chapter 6   *Standard Macros and Data Types*   85
Chapter 7   *Background*   105
Chapter 8   *Great Ideas*   123
Chapter 9   *Working with DirectDraw*   155
Chapter 10   *How to Draw as Easy as 1, 2, 3*   211
Chapter 11   *How to do Your ABC's*   245
Chapter 12   *The Drawing Manager*   277
Chapter 13   *Loading Graphics*   291
Chapter 14   *The Black Space and the Wild Void of Life* . . .   355
Chapter 15   *Animation*   379
Chapter 16   *The Landscape*   421
Chapter 17   *The Interface*   485
Chapter 18   *Objects and Creatures in the World*   521
Chapter 19   *Pathing*   603
Chapter 20   *DirectSound*   687

Index   705

Contents

Chapter 1   **Welcome**   1
   Introduction.   1
   What is a Real-time Strategy Game?   2
      Real-time Strategy vs. Real-time Tactical   3
      The 3 ~~Stooges~~ Stages.   4
         The Beginning Game   4
         The Mid Game   5
         The End Game   5
         Completion.   5
   What is DirectX?   5
   What is This Book About?   6
   Required Tools   7
   The Web   7

Chapter 2   **Gameplay**.   9
   Strategy   9
   Tactics.   10
   Mood   11
   Elevation   12
   Terrain.   12
   Where to Build   13
   Resources   13

Chapter 3   **Getting Started on Your Game**   15
   The Design   16
   The High-Level Design   17
      Planning to Go   17
      Break It Up   19
      Volatility.   21
      Building a Paradigm.   27
      Defining the Framework   30
      Creating the Schedule   31
   The Development Cycle   31
   Programming and Programming Style   33
   Coding Style   39

Contents

Caps every word, no caps first word and caps all others,
underscores between... 39

Member variables should have a designation so you can tell... 40

Where should I put my braces?. 40

Macros or templates?. 41

Whitespace, comments, filler, and FDA approval 41

Should I use shorthand names to cut down on my typing? 42

The Library 43

A Note about Your Coding Environment. 43

Setting Up the WinMain and the MessageHandler 45

What Exactly is a Message Handler Anyway? 52

This is your queue... 54

Chapter 4   **Documents** 65

The Design Doc. 65

The Technical Design Doc. 68

Chapter 5   **Development** 71

The Cycle 73

Code Design. 75

Engine Design 77

Reusability 78

Which Tools to Use 79

Hardware Considerations. 79

Designing a Schedule for Your Code 80

Expectations. 80

Competition and Sales 81

Optimism 81

Backing Up. 81

Sharing Code and Source Control 82

Chapter 6   **Standard Macros and Data Types** 85

Chapter 7   **Background** 105

Installation and Good Directory Setup 105

Install with the Help Files. 106

Getting Used to Hot Keys 106

Rearranging the Desktop 107

Starting a New Project 111

Project Settings 113

Creating Your Project 115

Building a Test Bed 118

A Long Word about How to Set Up Headers for Efficiency 119
Files to Delete 121

Chapter 8   **Great Ideas** 123

Chapter 9   **Working with DirectDraw** 155
Introducing DirectDraw 156
The DirectDraw File Structure 158
Data Types 159
Broad Concepts 162
    Double Buffering 163
    Offscreen Buffer or Back Buffer 164
    Blitting 164
    Flipping the Screen 165
    Graphics Device Interface (GDI) 165
Color Modes 165
    8-bit 165
    15-bit 166
    16-bit 167
    24-bit 167
    32-bit 168
Color Models 169
    RGB 169
    CMYK 169
    YUV 169
    HSV 169
    15-bit vs. 16-bit 170
DirectDraw Class 171
Integrating the DIRECT_DRAW_MANAGER 203

Chapter 10   **How to Draw as Easy as 1, 2, 3** 211
The Screen Layout and Pixels 212
Color, Anyone? 214
Horizontal Line Drawing 216
Vertical Line Drawing 219
Introducing Bresenham's Line Drawing 222
Clipping 224
Optimizing Line Drawing 227
Rectangle Filling 232
Rectangle Outlining 234
Better Line Clipping, Rectangle Clipping, and Safety Measures 236
Tough Clipping 239

A Faster Bresenham's Line Algorithm 242

Chapter 11   **How to Do Your ABC's** 245
  Characteristics of Characters 246
  Building an Alphabet Manager 247
  The Alphabet Editor 259
  Optimized Letter Drawing 260
  Basic Graphics Blitting 262
      Creating a Fake Graphic 264
      Blitting a Simple Graphic 265
      Optimizing Blit Routines 268
      A Better Optimization 269
  Clipping Graphics 270
  Clipping Text 275

Chapter 12   **The Drawing Manager** 277

Chapter 13   **Loading Graphics** 291
  How to Load a Targa 292
  Stringy Strings 293
  The Load Targa Function 300
  Typical Graphic Storage 301
  Converting 24-bit to 16-bit 303
  How to Draw 305
  Storage and Reindexing 306
      The SCREENOBJECT Portion of a Graphic 307
      Filenames 308
      The GRAPHIC Class Definition 309
      The GRAPHIC.CPP Listing 312
  Using Our New LLE 331
  Span Lists 334
  Full Offscreen Buffer 352
  An Alternative to Span Lists 353
  Particle Systems 353

Chapter 14   **The Black Space and the Wild Void of Life** 355
  LLE Compression 357
      The LLE Compression Format 361
  Drawing with LLE 369
  Clipping with LLE 372

Chapter 15 *Animation* 379
   The Cycle and the Sequence 380
   Preparing the Art 380
   3-D Art Packages 382
   Mirroring. 382
   Establishing the Need for Animation 385
   A First Look at Graphics Maintenance 386
       The FRAME Structure 388
       The Animation Data Structure 391
       The Encapsulated Approach 398
   Putting All Eight Directions Together 400
   Animated Backgrounds 405
       Flowing Lava and Water 406
       Moving Trees 406
       Shifting Sands and Shifting Landscape 407
       Twinkling Stars 408
       Rain and Weather 408
   Reacting to Action 409
   Preparing Animation for Each State. 409
   Independent Entities and Animation 410
   Skipping Frames 411
   The Simple Act of Turning Around 412
   The Remains and the Resources 413
   Animated Buildings 414
   Effects 415
   Animated Overlays 415
   Animating Death. 416
   Blending Color with Backgrounds for Cool Explosions 419

Chapter 16 *The Landscape* 421
   What Does the Landscape Look Like? 422
   The Concept of a Tile 422
   What Do You Put on the Landscape? 430
   Can the Landscape be Damaged? 431
   3-D Texturing vs. 2-D Blit 432
   Resources 432
       Permanent or Declining. 432
       Types and Availability 433
   Background and Ambience 434
   Passable and Impassable Terrain 436
   Landscape Elevation 436

Contents

Rendering the Landscape and Overdraw 455
Cliffs 457
Mountain Passes and Other Graphics Overlays 458
Elements of Pathing 459
Random vs. Fixed Maps 460
Random Starting Locations 463
Pointers to Graphics vs. Indexing 466
Pointers to Entities 466
The Minimap 467
Map Size Considerations 467
Fog of War 468
Tile Grouping 469
Tile Size—51x25 vs. 48x24 472
World Coordinate System 472
Map Coordinate Systems 474
Graphic Storage for a Map System 477
The Map Editor 477
Other Considerations 477
    Seasons 477
    Animated Landscape 478
    Trap and Mine Management 478
    Hot Points and Triggers 479
    Specialized Equipment 479
    Kingdoms and Region Definitions 480
    Walls and Trenches 481
    Decaying Bodies 482
The Update Cycle 482

Chapter 17   **The Interface** 485
Utility vs. Beauty 486
Make it Easy to Understand and Intuitive 487
Feedback and Tracking Progress 487
Passing Messages via Windows 488
Selections 495
Scrolling 496
Cursors 496
Windows and Buttons 497
The Mouse 516
Buttons 516
A Selected Creature 517
Networking and Making Sure All Players Get the Same Data 518

Interface Color Choices. 519
Different Player Colors 519

Chapter 18   **Objects and Creatures in the World** 521
Defining an Entity 521
   What Does an Entity Do?. 521
   How Does an Entity Live? 523
   Where Do Entities Fit into the Design? 524
   Basic Entity Characteristics. 525
   What Kind of Group Behavior Does an Entity Exhibit? 525
   What Kinds of Actions are Available to the Average Entity? 526
   Who Owns an Entity?. 526
   How Do Entities Communicate? 527
   How Do Entities Think? 527
   How Do Entities Remember?. 528
Creature Definition 528
   Where Does an Entity Get His Default Values? 546
   Selectable Entities. 547
   Resource Entities 548
   Goals 550
   Queued Entities. 555
   The Event 559
   Moving Entities 560
   Construction Entities 562
   Peon and Resource Gathering Entities 565
   Fire and Consumption Entities 568
   Soldier Entities 569
   Transport Entities 575
   Missile Entities 576
   Missile Firing Entities 577
   Flying Entities 577
   Explosion Entities 578
A Final Note on Entities. 578
Memory Management. 579
Calculating Screen Position Based on World Position 598
Resources and Gathering 600
Area and Build Area 600

Chapter 19   **Pathing** 603
Simple Terrain 603
Blocking Terrain 607

Contents

Tough Terrain 609
The Destination 609
Finding Your Way 611
  BFS 611
  Estimating Distance Remaining 612
  DFS 612
  A* Described 612
      The TAG_LIST Again 629
  A* Described Continued.... 637
  Ray Cast Pathing 646
Managing Multiple Paths Simultaneously 650
Adding Elevation to the Mix. 650
Simple A* Implementation 651
Waypoints and Partial Paths 675
Sources 676
Groups. 676
The Entities-Trying-to-Get-Around-Each-Other Problem 678
How to Keep Track of Paths Passed 678

Chapter 20 *DirectSound* 687
The ALLOCATOR Class 687
Header Files 688
Implementation 692

Index 705

Preface

Welcome, reader. Games are my life. I live and love them, but no game shapes and stirs my soul like real-time strategy. The involvement, planning, forethought, and strategy combine with beautifully rendered graphics to create an experience of being a great general or king. These games come in all shapes and sizes, but a big commitment must come from the player to learn them. The learning curve is always steep, and strategies that may work in one game may not work in another. Mastery of these games comes only after hundreds of hours of playing. Luckily, this isn't difficult since very few real-time strategy games can be played in under two hours, particularly in multi-player mode. I once played a game of Age of Empires with Mike Maynard, Russ Hughes, Noel Stephens, and John Romero from about 10 p.m. to 3 a.m., about five hours. My partners all died off early, and that left me, John, and Noel. I was separated from all resources, so all I could do was hold them off for two hours. They finally found a tree in a forgotten corner of the map, built a boat, and starting racking up gold using docks between them. They would have won but in a cheesy way, and since I had run out of resources, I couldn't hold them off forever, and I could never win ... so I surrendered. After five hours—on a single game—I went home.

This book is my attempt to provide a broad, general overview of programming a real-time strategy or real-time tactical game. Many of the baseline subjects are covered in some detail and there is a particular emphasis on DirectDraw and graphics. The code is extensive and the Library directory on the CD contains over 140,000 lines of original code that you are welcome to use or modify. The number of lines of code is an almost worthless measure, but the code is stable and tested. It works in many different situations. Much of that code is well explained in this book, but most of it is left up to the reader to peruse and enjoy.

I have a lot of code in the book to simplify the understanding of concepts I discuss, but that simply isn't enough. Plan on having a code editor up and running at all times while you read this book to look over the code and hopefully follow along. Cross-references and multiple files may need to be examined to understand the full extent to which the code interacts and how all of the code works.

There is code for basic Windows and basic DirectDraw, including a class that fully encapsulates all DirectDraw stuff and makes your life much easier. I have included some material on DirectSound with a neat little sound loading and management scheme that makes sound management a breeze. All basic concepts of line drawing, alphabet management, clipping, rectangle drawing and filling, and bitmap drawing are covered. Blitting graphics and compressing graphics to eliminate black space are detailed. Then we get into entity management and basic AI concepts, with quite a bit of code. Interface management and button creation are also here, along with windows management and passing messages. We even talk extensively about pathing in a real-time strategy map, along with extensive detail about the maps themselves.

Things notably missing are coverage of Direct3D and any meaningful discussion on DirectPlay and networking in general.

The CD contains a number of directories that correspond to individual chapters. In addition, there is my Alphabet editor, a pretty cool tool if you ask me. You'll also find a cheesy tile system example, and most importantly the library. The library contains all of the base files for the book and a daunting amount of code. Don't worry… it is mostly readable and fairly well-documented. Be sure to copy the Library directory to your C drive as C:\Library. All of the code refers to it being in that base directory.

Pick up a copy of Visual C++. I saw a "Standard" version the other day for $99, but you can probably get it cheaper at a university bookstore, especially if you are a student. I highly recommend getting a copy of Borland C++ Builder too. This product is unequaled and simplifies tool development. All Windows-based tools I do for various games are done with this product. The "Standard" version is also $99 and you can even do DirectX stuff with it. It even comes with OpenGL support in case you're keen on that idea.

I wish you luck in your endeavor to create a real-time strategy or real-time tactical game. I hope you succeed, because that'll be another game to play and it'll expand the life of this beautiful genre. Specific questions I'll answer at MKawick@sprintmail.com.

Chapter 1

Welcome

Games are the lifeblood of any gamer. We live and die playing games. They challenge our minds, our dexterity, our intuition, our spatial acuity, our pocketbooks, and even our time management. I heard back in 1994 that Tennessee state workers were so busy playing the Windows 3.1 version of Solitaire that they started a support group to help people with their addiction.

Games take a lot of effort to play. There are controls to master, keyboards to configure, and dozens of game-related terms to learn. The best games can be played intuitively, with very little time spent mastering the controls; requiring over 60 different keystrokes makes for a bad game.

Most people (in the industrialized world) have played some form of computer game. Many people play Microsoft Solitaire or Windows Minefield. Some actually buy games. One common thread that has helped in the last eight or nine years is the mouse. It is the primary input device these days. Unless you are a writer or programmer, it is unlikely that you use the keyboard more than the mouse.

But most people do not consider the work that goes into a game. Even a mediocre game takes about 21,000 hours to develop, while the big ones, like Final Fantasy VII, take about 600,000. Most Americans work about 2,000 hours a year, but game programmers and associated staff work more than 2,500, often reaching 3,000. Well-known game programmer John Carmak works around 4,000 hours a year. Many consider him a workaholic, but he "cranks" out the games. He wrote almost all of the code for Quake and Quake II himself, including the tools. Since Quake took two years or so, he spent over 8,000 hours—just himself—on the game. There were also a bunch of level designers, artists, producers, and so on.

Introduction

New landscapes have arisen. The world of war will never be the same after brilliant real-time strategy and real-time tactical games have given us new abilities: playing the part of commander, general, or even God. The strategic landscape is strewn with the slowly decomposing bodies of enemies not controlled well enough by your rival, your friend on the other end of the TCP/IP connection. Computers have taken the place of real bullets, and orcs come across portals with the intention of killing off every last human. Unlike first-person shooters or turn-based strategy games, armies roll across landscapes in real time, built by the computer whiz kid and his trusty mouse. The player who can maintain production, staff his armies, control resource production, and the "winning-est" tactician will always prevail. The only problem is maintaining everything at the same time and remembering where all of your troops are.

These are the most challenging games to play today. Their ranks include a small group of great games and quite a few losers. A few of the best are (in no particular order): Warcraft II, Command and Conquer, Dungeon Keeper (a little different), Age of Empires, Total Annihilation, and Dark Reign. They allow the player to do so many different things at once. The level of management varies in each game, but all are a lot like running a major corporation. These games are intense and require nerves of steel. Many of my friends who play Quake on a regular basis find real-time strategy/tactical games much more intense and difficult to master.

From a creative standpoint, these games are the most challenging to create. They require good ideas, number one. Many other good games have very little story line or concept to them. Most RTS/RTT (real-time strategy/real-time tactical) games need a lot of story, but even without a good story, they seem to take on a life of their own as we watch the soldiers march off to war. Seeing the armies from a bird's-eye view adds a lifelike quality to the games. Number two, these games require a lot of forethought. Planning for a game like this is very difficult, probably among the most difficult of any type of project management. Drawing a rough outline and sticking to it is nigh impossible. As you go through the development process, new ideas emerge or other games are released with things "we just gotta add." Lastly, the level of talented personnel is about the highest in the games industry. You need a highly qualified art team, highly qualified designers, highly qualified musicians, and highly qualified programmers.

This book will take you through the entire production cycle, introducing you to the game design doc, the technical design doc, basic art concepts, graphics systems, tile-based systems management, landscapes, buildings, pathing, simple and complex behaviors, group behaviors, interface design, and a set of principals for good, reusable code.

The programming world is slowly migrating to C++. All libraries in this book are in C++. All code is free to use, and any methodologies discussed are public domain to the best of my knowledge. This is meant to be a technical programming manual that will familiarize you with many aspects of the game development cycle. It is not all-inclusive. You will not find anything on 3-D, networking, code management, code delivery, or debugging. There are so many books dedicated to these topics that it doesn't seem appropriate to rehash them here.

This is a big book. Take it slowly. Try every example. Mostly, enjoy yourself.

What is a Real-time Strategy Game?

That is a big question. In terms of gameplay, these are truly the most complicated games to play and probably will be for the foreseeable future. These games force you to play a huge chess game in real time with no breaks. You command armies, or at least small groups of soldiers and tanks, in a real-time combat simulation. *Real time* means that the action continues whether the player participates or not. Things are happening and creatures are moving around the screen like in any action game; action abounds and the player needs to be constantly alert.

A player needs to have city construction abilities to play these games, and a sense of which buildings will be important to overall strategy. The ability to build and run a city is probably the hardest part of these types of games. Managing which building to construct next, which building to upgrade, which resources are collected, and how many of each building to construct involves planning and a little intuition.

Players need to balance resources. Most real-time strategy games have limited resources during any game session. These could be steel, energy, food, and the like. If you build too many buildings, you may not be able to afford upgrades or more combat units.

Players need to be able to time events. Three buildings are constructing new units, an army of soldiers has just come knocking, your army is away attacking someone else, and your peons are being killed by lions. What do you do?

These games all have a feel, or mood, to them. This makes the game feel different from all other games in that genre. They also have a theme or focus: combat, diplomacy, resource management, building, collecting, technology improvements, just to name a few. These games all have a setting: space, underwater, forests, old west, post modern, medieval, fantasy (orcs, hobgoblins, dragons, fairies, etc.), capitalism, and so on.

Real-time Strategy vs. Real-time Tactical

Strategy and tactics are important elements of any real-time strategy game. No real-time strategy game can exist without both. You'll see a lot of overlap where these definitions merge into a coherent, playable game. "Real-time tactical" is a new term, and most people still use the rather generic term "real-time strategy" when referring to games of this type.

Strategy involves logistics, construction, and resource management. According to Webster's Web site (**http://www.m-w.com/netdict.htm**), strategy is:

> **1 a** (1) : the science and art of employing the political, economic, psychological, and military forces of a nation or group of nations to afford the maximum support to adopted policies in peace or war (2) : the science and art of military command exercised to meet the enemy in combat under advantageous conditions **b** : a variety of or instance of the use of strategy
>
> **2 a** : a careful plan or method : a clever stratagem **b** : the art of devising or employing plans or stratagems toward a goal
>
> **3** : an adaptation or complex of adaptations (as of behavior, metabolism, or structure) that serves or appears to serve an important function in achieving evolutionary success <foraging *strategies* of insects>

Strategy uses whatever means necessary to build up a civilization. This means collecting taxes, building infrastructure, constructing spaceports, collecting resources, and basic city management.

Tactics involves military usage to build up a civilization. Webster's Web site reads simply:

> **1** : a device for accomplishing an end
>
> **2** : a method of employing forces in combat

Most tactics involve attacking an enemy, conquering an enemy, destroying a building, routing a group of cavalry, three players attacking simultaneously from three different directions, setting a battalion for a charge, launching interceptor aircraft, etc. Tactics normally is a term of offense, not defense, but building a good defense of attack units can be regarded as deployment, which also falls under the tactics umbrella.

PC Gamer magazine first made the distinction between real-time strategy (RTS) and real-time tactical (RTT) games. Although there is more overlap than distinction between these two classes of games, it all depends on focus. If your game makes building very easy and resource gathering very simple, then the gamer can focus on fighting and tactics, meaning that your game would be an RTT game. However, if there is a long period of buildup, you might be more inclined to call it an RTS game. Other RTS characteristics include: one building type can't be built until another is finished, resource collectors will need to be reassigned from time to time, and there is quite a bit of micromanagement. If these are true of your game, it is safe to say that you are developing an RTS game.

All RTS/RTT games have some strategic elements. Most provide for needing construction, managing resources, establishing factories, and unit construction facilities. All RTS/RTT games have some tactical elements. They all have unit movement and deployment, management of small armored divisions, and unit upgrades for increased performance or defense.

The 3 ~~Stooges~~ Stages

These RTS/RTT games are continuous, where all players start roughly equally and one eventually crushes the other. There are three distinct stages to these games.

The Beginning Game

Getting started takes the longest. You only have enough resources for building the cheapest, cheesiest units that are almost useless in later stages of the game. Basically, you can build a support building (a house or hatchery), a few peons (resource gatherers or collectors), and a barracks (a training center or factory for building simple units). You need to immediately build units for collecting resources, and then start finding resources. They can normally be found near the starting location of each player. Assign as many resource gatherers to these resources until you have 10 to 13 resource gatherers. You may ask, "How do I know how many to assign? Isn't each game different?" Well, yes, but they all seem to need about the same number of peons in the beginning game. The only real exception I can think of is Total Annihilation.

Next, as soon as about six to eight peons are built, start construction on a barracks; you should have enough resources by now. Just use one peon for this process. Next, start to think about defense. Get all of the peons up to snuff, build a few soldiers, upgrade all of your units, and build all remaining basic structures (basic buildings usually all need to be built). Depending on the game, this usually takes 10 to 20 minutes.

The Mid Game

You have four or five buildings, reasonable resources, some upgraded units, and a small army, and you are feeling a little powerful. Now is the time for full concentration. Depending on how you play, you can control how the whole rest of the game is played. If you play defensively, you'll start building walls, towers, and a defense perimeter. If you play offensively, you start building legions of units and prepare them for your first attack, which will come soon. If you play expansionistically, then you send a few peons off to build another home base or whatever on another part of the map. If you play technologically, you'll build minimal defenses and concentrate on expanding research and science so that you will have the technological advantage, which means being able to build tougher starships.

This is where most of the fighting takes place, where you are always scrambling for more resources to build units to fight off invaders, and you are trying to get a leg up on your opponent. One player usually establishes himself as dominant. In most games, you'll need to "uncover" the fogged map, and most of that happens at this stage.

The End Game

This is the rough part, where you and your opponents kind of have an idea of who will win. The resources are getting very hard to find and nobody has very many units left. Everything is now strategically important and strikes against your opponent are more well thought out. The map is close to fully revealed from the fog. There will be a few epic battles, but most players don't have many resources left, so all players are essentially "stuck" at whatever technology level they finished with in the mid game. The end game is usually equal to the beginning game in length.

Completion

There will always be a few units left. The other players have already lost any ability to compete for resources or build new units. Be careful; some players send a sole unit into some hidden corner and rebuild, coming from behind to win the game. Usually, all players have exited the game and you are left there to clean up the few remaining units. For this reason, this is not considered a real stage in gameplay.

What is DirectX?

One of the best things about Microsoft is its ability to take over new fields, one of which is game APIs. An API is an *application programming interface,* or a group of functions that are related to one another. There used to be a number of very small companies that provided reasonable APIs for a nominal fee. Now Microsoft owns this market but only charges $11 for the development tools, via mail, for DirectX 6 on CD-ROM. It's an easy install, but you'd better have a lot of hard drive space.

DirectX is basically five products in one. DirectDraw handles all of the basic graphics management that used to be so difficult. Since the advent of VESA 2, the memory location of the screen is one continuous block, unlike the old days of video memory segmentation. Basically, the pointer returned from DirectDraw is a pointer to the video buffer to which you can begin plotting pixels. It's a major improvement over the old days.

DirectSound handles sound. Simple. You load a WAV file into a buffer and tell DirectSound to play the sound. It is trivial to implement. This is covered in Chapter 20.

DirectPlay is an interface for handling networking computers together. Since DirectX 5, this is a stable means of communicating via network. I've heard that there have been major improvements in packet size in version 6, whereas version 5 had an 80-byte overhead per packet. Also, sync objects have been introduced and guaranteed packets are now supported for IPX, a network protocol that will probably go the way of the horse and buggy very soon. DirectPlay does not have the smoothest interface and can be a bit difficult to work with.

DirectInput handles IO, but its biggest benefit is joystick management. IO still goes on while your game is running, in terms of keyboard and mouse input. Since no real-time strategy game has used a joystick yet, this isn't particularly helpful in this book.

Direct3D is perhaps the biggest benefit of the DirectX family right behind Direct-Draw. It provides a decent interface to all (well, almost all) video cards for 3-D rendering. Some people think that OpenGL is better, and for the most part they are right. DirectX 5 and later introduced a new function—DrawPrimitive—to the API, which makes DirectX draw whatever you want right then. There used to be a nightmare object called the Execute Buffer, which made DirectX programming no fun at all. Now things are different, and while DirectX still has its problems, what API doesn't? It works, and all video card vendors are supporting it.

What a short and tumultuous history! DirectX version 1 came out in January of 1996 and in less than three years, Version 6 became the common version available. Now Microsoft is working on version 7, so keeping up with the constant changes is nigh impossible.

What is This Book About?

This book will get you started on the trek to the most challenging programming field around. A simple game involves seven or eight areas of expertise in programming. Many people spend their entire programming lives studying just one of these areas, so you must learn a lot. My intention is to give you most of the difficult basics in getting your RTS/RTT game going. I cover graphics in great detail, path finding, AI, tile systems, engine organization, and interface management. I do not cover networking, joystick usage, or 3-D.

You will get to know quite a bit about getting a full game engine going and a lot about games in general.

Required Tools

In order to get started, you'll need DirectX version 6 or later. This book makes a few references to DirectX 6 function calls that simply will not work with previous versions. Check out:

http://www.microsoft.com/directx/default.asp

for a download of the latest version of DirectX.

You'll need a compiler. For building your program and debugging, Visual C++ 5.0 or later is probably the best tool. For the final release, Watcom 11.0 is undeniably the best tool for building the most solid, stable code. It never makes compile mistakes, which Visual C++ does on occasion. For developing Windows-based tools or applications, forget Microsoft and use Borland C++ Builder. What an awesome product—probably the best product I've ever seen from Borland.

You'll need programming experience. Study and master the programming language C. Next, study and understand all of the basics of C++, and you're ready. For some of the more complicated areas, you'll need a better understanding of C++-like templates and dynamic_cast, but we'll get there later.

Start buying programming books now. It will be a long time before you finish writing your game and putting all of the pieces together.

The Web

There are hundreds of Web sites with AI, graphics, sound, DirectX, networking, and whatever. Do a Web search for game programming. I like the following site, but you can find hundreds just like it:

http://www-cs-students.stanford.edu/~amitp/gameprog.html

Chapter 2

Gameplay

This chapter contains a list of gameplay issues that will be covered in this book. This laundry list covers all of the basic questions for design. It is by no means all-inclusive or exhaustive. It has a lot of considerations that you may have forgotten and will help you get started. Most elements here will be detailed later in the book.

The importance of gameplay and great design cannot be understated. As important as these are, most people do not think about these roles in creating a great game. But they hold the keys of success to a popular and enthralling game, one that magazines and people talk about for years. The things to think about are how the design facilitates the game, how it creates resources for the player, how the elevation affects gameplay, and how the overall strategy works based on the landscape. Below are a series of questions you should pose about your game that will help complete what your world does and help define the key points of your game. Do not skip these; they will help you design a better game.

Good design brings variety and flavor to a game, often giving the game its long-term playability. Design is an evolution. Anyone can sit down with a couple of cool ideas and claim that he has a good design. Good design has the flexibility to evolve as the development of the project continues and yet enough consistency to remain essentially the same game from conception to store shelves.

Here are a few good morsels for thought:

Strategy

How many types of buildings are enough?

Keep It Simple, Stupid (KISS). The best RTS/RTT games all have fewer than 15 building types. There is usually a town center or home from which peons/workers are created, and resources can always be returned to the town center in RTS games. Then there are usually support buildings—a farmhouse or the like. Most RTS games require one of these structures per four or five military units. Then there are various factories, science facilities, storage facilities, and resource support facilities as well as towers, walls, generators, and so on.

How detailed should the tech tree be?

It should contain only a few levels of detail. Levels are chances for an upgrade like footman to soldier to infantry to heavy infantry to phalanx. Three or four levels are enough. The tech tree should also be broad. There should be the ability to upgrade almost every unit on the field and each upgrade should cost plenty. This forces players to choose a plan of action in upgrading rather than just upgrading everything in their arsenal. RTT games don't offer much in the way of upgrades. Total Annihilation won't even let you upgrade units; the units upgrade themselves by becoming "veterans" after killing five opponents.

What level of micromanagement is enough? Too much?

Micromanagement can be a pain for the player. Avoid it. Upgrades should apply to all units of the upgrade type. WarWind forced a player to upgrade each unit individually. Wow, was that tedious! Units should group intuitively. The interface should be simple. Don't make the players learn 50 steps for something that should only take two or three.

How many types of units should be available?

From a strategic view, there should only be a few strategic units. Perhaps a few different construction units, a few different construction workers, and a repair unit or healer would be enough. Too many merely complicates things and adds nothing to your game.

How much should units cost?

Basic units should cost almost nothing, while upgraded units should be more expensive. Some people argue that the upgrade that you pay for makes all future units cost the same as the old unit. Forget it. It is evident that if you pay for research and development, the newly developed object will cost more. You can make future units decrease in cost due to economies of scale, but that is probably too much trouble. Just charge 20 to 50 percent more than the original unit for upgraded units and continue cost increases for each subsequent generation of upgrade. In any case, the best way to choose an initial cost is to take the cost of a house or farm and divide it in half. That is the cost of a basic soldier. They should be fairly expensive.

How can I use landscape for strategy elements?

A cove or hidden area is great from a strategic standpoint, making it difficult for the opposition to find you. The top of a hill is even better. An area surrounded on three sides by forest makes an easy place to defend. Just make sure that your maps have these elements.

Tactics

How many tactical units should I have?

These days, it seems, the more tactical units, the merrier. Total Annihilation started with 75 different units for each side and added about 30. Age of Empires has about

50 units per side, while Starcraft has a measly 25 or so. I say, the more you have, the more a player will want to play the game to try using different combinations of units. However, this also causes the problem of game balance, as it is hard to make sure that all sides are roughly equal with hundreds of different units.

How does the landscape affect movement?

Units moving up a hill should move slower than on flat land; when descending, they should speed up. Trees should block movement, as should a deep pit. Lakes need to be crossed and rivers forded.

How can I use landscape for tactical elements in the game?

High points on the map from which to attack can provide attack benefits. Flying units should be able to move over any type of terrain and amphibious vehicles should be able to move between water and land with ease. Players might be able to rip down trees in enclosures and hide behind them to block attackers while the player lobs missiles into the fray. Your game should accommodate most of these types of things.

How do I manage groups?

By dragging the mouse over a bunch of military units, a player should be able to easily select a group of units to march against an opponent. The units need to path to their destination and around each other. Groups should be assignable. You should be able to take any two units and assign them to a number or letter on the player's keyboard for instant selection.

Mood

What kind of mood does the world create?

Dark tiles with an occasional skull and a lot of dead or rotting vegetation create a mood of death. Lots of green and forests with large trees and rivers create a mood of a healthy world where most creatures can live. Floating platforms with turtles and bees create a mood of Mario Bros. Be innovative when creating your game's mood.

How real should the world be?

If you can create a realistic, yet different, world that is convincing, you are on the road to success. Create realism, but don't add steps that take the player a long time to do like collecting the tire, engine, frame, and transmission in order to make a car. If you make the interface easy, and also make the world seem like it has a life of its own, people will like your game.

Does mood really matter?

Gameplay is more important, but mood counts more than most other elements. It does matter and is something the designer should think about before the start of production. Then it becomes easy to guide the art and gameplay to meet that mood. Most of the mood is set by art and sound anyway and rarely affects the actual gameplay. Mood makes the difference between a good game and a great game.

Elevation

Should I go through the effort to support elevation?

Pros: great strategic element, adds a nice look to the game, great game depth item. Cons: difficult to implement, takes up to 24 times as much art, need to program creatures walking slow uphill and fast downhill, major effort.

How much elevation is good?

Just a few levels is probably best. This allows strategic elements to be the focus and provides a good balance of variety of landscape and manageability for the player's buildings. Too many levels make creatures on the top of a hill clip off the top of the screen, and the base of a tall hill takes up a huge section of the map. Too few levels aren't worth the effort. And the worst part is that too much variation in land height makes most of the land hillsides, and it is usually impossible to build on a hillside.

Should I fake elevation?

Probably. This is an easy implementation where you simply place a graphic overlay that looks like a hill or cliff. However, it doesn't have the visual effect nor can you slow down a creature walking up it.

What can I do when players try to build on the side of a hill?

You should have an icon or colored box that changes to green when an area is safe to build on. The icon should change color in real time, which will probably take close to no time at all.

Should I allow the change of elevation during gameplay?

Unless you have gods or wizards in the game, the answer is probably no. Also, too many problems arise from this including what happens to buildings, rivers, wheeled vehicles, etc. This makes the problem almost unmanageable unless you are prepared to answer all of these questions. Keep elevation changes in the random map generator and level editor.

If I fake elevation, how do I give an attack bonus to units on the "higher" ground?

You'll need to create a height overlay for every terrain overlay. When the map is saved from the editor, those height values should be stored on the underlying map. When a unit fires, you simply grab the height value of the tile it is on.

Terrain

How many types of terrain should I support per map?

Do yourself a favor and limit it to two or three types. The problem is one of memory, border tiles, and good level design. Age of Empires is the only game I've seen do more than three types of terrain on a single map right. It also took 2½ years to complete, not for that reason alone, but certainly that helped.

How uneven should the terrain be?

Not very. Players need to build and since you can't build on uneven terrain, this makes much of the land unusable. Also, uneven terrain should slow units down as they cross it, which can be a strategic element.

How colorful should the terrain be?

Stick to dull colors. Leave bright colors for the creatures, which should have a few brightly colored spots as markings for player identification. Bright colors hurt your eyes and make it impossible to find the creatures.

Where to Build

Should I allow players to build anywhere or restrict building?

In the real world, you are limited as to where you can build. Building should be limited to a few small areas on the map; make the players fight for these areas. Forests are great because players have to chop down the trees before they can build in those areas. On any given level, only 50 to 60 percent of the land should be readily available for construction. The rest should have lakes, trees, mountains, rivers, boulders, pits, and lava flows, or be dangerous lairs of orcs, goblins, dragons, and other creatures.

How do I allow players to build on uneven ground?

Don't—the amount of extra work involved, including all of the extra art for a building on the side of a hill, makes this prohibitive.

What if a player wants to build on an area where a tree is?

As the player moves his construction cursor over the map, it should be reddish until it is over clear, even tiles. Say the building is 3x3 tiles in size. As the cursor shaped like the building moves over the map looking for a spot, the building should be polling the map at all nine points to see if anything is on the tiles. If so, the cursor remains reddish; otherwise it turns color, signaling the player that the building can be placed.

Resources

How should resources be dispersed?

As equally as is possible. You want all players to be fairly equal at the start. An unbalanced game is fun for nobody.

How much should each player start with?

The minimum is to start each player with enough resources to buy six to ten peons for all very basic resource gathering. Then you'll want to include enough extra resources to build one or two of the first buildings that he'll need. Maybe a bit more. Too much more makes the beginning game too easy and too much less makes your game tedious for collecting resources.

Should I put a lot of resources all over the map or restrict them to a few areas?

Resources are a key element of the game. As long as all players start with the same amount near their starting locations, I say put a lot out in the world to fight over. Also, give the players enough to work with at the beginning. Nothing is more frustrating than always struggling to find resources. It is also helpful to make each resource "cache" provide a lot of resources, enough to keep the peons busy for ten minutes or more.

Keep these ideas in mind for your game when in the design phase. Again, these are here to get you started.

Chapter 3

Getting Started on Your Game

Getting into the cycle of development is the most difficult part. Where to begin? The more you look at the big picture of creating a game from scratch, the more daunting it seems. Which model do I use? Should I use MFC or straight Windows? How about DOS? Maybe I should forget DirectDraw and code everything myself in DOS. Will this be a multiplayer game? If so, how do I handle networking? Is sound a tough business? Oh, my god, what am I getting myself into?

Actually, these are valid concerns. Creating a game from scratch is probably one of the most difficult things you can do in life. It rates up there with getting your bachelor's degree. I don't think that I ever put as much time into my college coursework as I've put into creating even a single game. You can expect to work 9 to 12 hours a day for 12 to 18 months with the last two months working 18-plus hours a day. Since you get few, if any, breaks and vacations are rare, this is a period of intensity and hard work. Starting with a solid foundation and know-how is critical if you are to reach the shipping date.

The most important skill you need is perseverance. I don't care what level of skill you have; if you don't have long-term dedication and a lot of tenacity, your project will fail. Programming skill is also vital, as are fantastic debugging skills, full awareness of C/C++ capabilities to make your code solid, and strong design skills. Organization skills help a great deal as well. Now that you are ready, where do you begin?

Planning will get you halfway to your destination. You must spend the time, up front, fleshing out design concepts and trying to break the game into a set of small, easily managed projects. It does you no good to constantly worry about the entire design while you are coding. Your design must be predefined but flexible. This allows for a strong code base that will provide you with tools to reduce the time investment on future projects.

The structure of your code will determine how flexible it is. You'll need it to be flexible. The game design will change, and you may wish to reuse your code base in another game, or maybe even version 2. Like an artist standing before a white canvas, you have a lot of planning and forethought ahead before you decide to put paint on your palette. The canvas will come later.

The programming aspects will be covered later, but first you need to create the structure that will carry the game from the idea stage to the retail shelves.

The Design

This design is the way your program will work. The game design should already be written and some art should have been completed before you ever reach this part. We don't care about the game design other than it better have some new twists, great creature interaction, a lot for the player to do, and a cool story line. We're mostly concerned here with what makes the program tick. How do you design the "engine" behind the game? It may surprise you to know that the specifics of the game are just as important as the overall design. A simple effect like shadows on creatures can hold up a project for weeks if it isn't put into the game design doc. Just redoing the art for the shadows is time consuming and tedious. Any additions to the game must be accounted for, even if they may not actually make it into the game.

Start by making sure that you understand the game fully before writing one line of code. If you start coding and don't fully grasp what the game is, you are in trouble. It has happened to my colleagues and me. Let's say a game designer has a pretty good idea that he writes down on paper. When you begin asking questions, he says that he knows he wants a 2D-tile system that allows creatures to walk around on it. He's not sure about everything, but most of it is easy and you should get started right away. Doom is approaching.

Without fully understanding the game design, we lost months recoding code that was really great in the first place. What a bummer. We went ahead with it anyway, trusting that the final design wouldn't be much different than what we already had. So we created this really powerful graphics subsystem, a creature subsystem, a file loading subsystem, a sound subsystem, some Windows-based tools to help the artists, etc., etc., etc. The designer then came back and said that he wanted to try a different graphics subsystem, and that the file loading system we had painstakingly developed wasn't user friendly. So back to work we went. We didn't know that we needed a user-friendly file system, nor was the 2D-tile system well defined.

As unlikely as this may sound, this happened to me five times on a single product once. I actually had to start coding from scratch three times over the course of ten months. Over six months of work was completely wasted. Another programmer and I, along with a team of 12 artists, were paid for six months of work on a system that was scrapped. I could blame myself, but in this case, the designer couldn't make up his mind. The code we wrote was to specifications and beat all time estimates by a large margin.

This brings up two important points. First, once you have a design, you should hold a designer to it as if he had given you his word that it wouldn't become a different game altogether. This is so common as to not be funny (well, the cliché is annoying, so I reworded it). Often, a designer will inform you, after you have spent three months designing a perfect 3-D editor, that it now needs to be more like 3D Studio. Now you desperately search for ways to salvage the 3-D code you've written and make that three months count for something. Unfortunately, the salvaging process takes time, and does not fit within the design of a 3-D editor written like 3D Studio, and so ultimately your product fails or performs badly. Once a designer makes a decision, don't let him weasel out of it.

Secondly, and more importantly, you need to realize that the game design will change. There is no way to avoid it. Your code must be flexible. Code modules should never rely too heavily on one another. Each should stand as a strong, separate piece of code. You should design with the idea of ripping out the guts of your code and using it for another game. The code must be tested and thorough.

A house is built of bricks. So is a program. As you build a foundation of code, the bricks you make must be reliable. You have to build thousands of small parts that together make up a game. Each function is a brick in that game. You should develop good habits of testing early on. But if you don't test well early in development, it will exponentially increase other forms of debugging later. I cannot stress it enough: Debug each group of code as you develop it. Create test beds that allow precise data manipulation and trace through every conceivable possibility to make sure that it works.

Sidebar: Your interface buttons keep crashing your program. So you trace into the code and find that the interface element runs perfectly. Everything is in order. After a full day of hacking at it, it looks like your pointer to the text was lost. So you spend a day and a half looking at the text subsystem, and find no problems. So then you spend a week to find out that the graphics you load overwrite their memory bounds by 2 bytes, stepping on the memory of your text. Ouch, a week and a half. If you had only spent three or four more hours making sure that your graphics subsystem was perfect…

The design is tricky and takes patience. Do not shortchange yourself here. Take two weeks to think about it thoroughly and rely on your colleagues to read your design and critique it. Better to swallow your pride in the beginning, than when your product is two months late and no end is in sight. Start with the overview: the high-level design.

The High-Level Design

Planning to Go

Deciding on a good code design is tough. Once you have the game design, you're ready to begin. The question is, Where do you start? Well, what do you want to accomplish? How much data should be global? What is the maximum size you should let the modules reach? How many files should be in your project? How should you structure your class hierarchies? Ad infinitum…

The biggest difficulty is understanding the big picture. The definition of the problem domain lends itself to a design and begins to define a program structure. Since we are making a real-time strategy game, the domain of the questions is somewhat limited, but a huge task still awaits. Don't take the beginning lightly. A good beginning is the most important step and all critical mistakes will be made here. Some of the questions that help flesh out your game are:

➤ How many creatures will be in the game? What types?

➤ How will the landscape be defined? Will maps be pregenerated or randomly generated at run time?

➤ What types of differences will exist between the enemies involved?

➤ How are projectiles supposed to work?

➤ What kinds of things will be animated? How many frames of animation per creature?

➤ Will everything move in eight directions, 16, 32?

➤ How will building work? Will there be peons to do the resource gathering?

➤ How many resources and what types will be involved?

➤ What are the minimum hardware requirements?

➤ What is the development time frame?

➤ How many programmers are available?

➤ How much is the design likely to change during the course of development?

➤ Describe the interface. How does it work? What kinds of graphics are on it? What kinds of information will it tell the player?

➤ Describe how the mouse will be used. What can be clicked on? How will menus work?

➤ Can games be saved while in progress?

➤ Is there a story to the game? Does it affect gameplay?

➤ How are colors used to identify the players?

➤ Will there be network play? Who will program it? What will be different about that than playing against the computer?

➤ How do units move? In groups?

➤ How good are the computer opponents supposed to be? Will they have different personalities? Will they vary in difficulty?

➤ Describe technology and how the player progresses from one level of technology to another.

➤ How should the game be balanced?

➤ What kinds of eye-candy will be in the game?

➤ Will there be hot keys? If so, what will they be?

➤ What video resolution depths will the game support?

➤ What are the levels of difficulty?

Many more questions will be asked, but each of the above is important in terms of programming time and design. The more complex the landscape, the more time it takes; the more creatures that are in the game, the longer it takes. More frames of animation mean more memory is used and the harder it is to manage, etc.

Each of the questions will probably equate to a different code module and most will equate to half a dozen structures or so. You should have an animation.cpp, an interface.cpp, and a techtree.cpp. Be careful about long filenames. Some machines may not accept them, and their DOS equivalents are always strange (i.e., animat~1.cpp). Also expect a struct ANIMATION, a struct INTERFACE, and a struct TECHTREE. Of course the names are arbitrary and you can pick your own, but I highly recommend calling a duck a duck, a tree a tree, and so on. Don't waste time trying to come up with clever names that will ultimately be difficult to remember.

Try to get as much detail as you can about each question. Not only *how many* creatures but also their abilities. Will they have a walk sequence or talk sequence? Will they attack, run, dodge, climb, duck, fire projectiles, block attacks, or perform similar motions? Do they have special abilities that may require special programming? How about that lightning bolt spell? Can they destroy buildings? How about build buildings? Can they enter a transport vehicle? How smart are they? How far can they see? The list is long. Keep asking questions and the game design will be easier.

Once you've gathered all of your info, you are closer to the design you'll need to begin coding your game. Find out about technology. Will the game require P450s or better, 4x AGP, 48x CD-ROM, 1 gig of hard drive space, and 256 MB of RAM? Or will it require much less? This will tell you how much attention you will need to pay to such things as optimization and game speed.

Now, how many people will be working on code with you? How will their skills be utilized? Who will manage everyone? How much effort will be required to find appropriate tasks for everyone involved? Is everyone a self-starter? These factors are important to consider when evaluating your design.

Now you have all of the major pieces in one place. You are ready to begin with your design.

Break It Up

Expect the code base to be enormous, and break it apart early. Outline the code by functionality. Do not avoid this step and start coding the easy stuff first. That is always a big mistake. Too often a team starts with very little information. Then they decide that the graphics code is standard and easily modifiable. After a few weeks, they discover that the graphics must be shrunk when read in and color reduced. Then they must restart the graphics code.

You will invariably recode a good portion of what you just did if you avoid the outline stage. You must outline the stages of development and what you hope to accomplish at each stage. The statistics show that for each hour of proper planning in the beginning, you save two hours of redesign, five hours of recoding, ten hours of code massaging, and 30 hours of debugging. The figures may vary from source to source, but if you spend the time to fully define the problem domain before the first line of code is written, you will save a lot of time in the long run.

Diagram your design as shown in Figure 3.1.

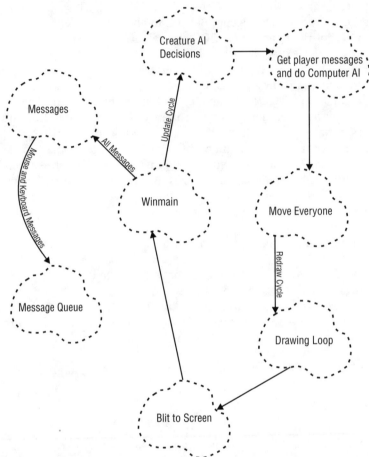

Figure 3.1
Basic diagram of computer game design

The sample here is a very rough design. Although it is basic, this might be how you want your program to flow. This is a good high-level design that will be improved on once you understand more about what you are doing and all the basics are out of the way.

Figure out code flow. How will messages be passed around inside your program? How about between the different players' machines? Will AI be part of every update cycle or will you simply set up a second thread? How does a creature know if his path is blocked? Does everybody in the game see the map? Should it be global data? How do you respond when a player clicks on an interface button? The code flow and data flow are critical, and you should spend hours contemplating exactly how this occurs.

Definition: Threads are like a second program running in the background behind your program. Windows will automatically allot time for them when your program is idle. Threads to run the graphics system are a bad idea and I have found them to be ineffective. Use them for secondary systems only, and make sure that they do not need a lot of processing time because they won't get it.

Outline your modules in pseudo code. Figure out which variables are passed to each module and how. If a lot of data is being passed, consider using structures for passing data. Which areas will be frequently accessed? Which areas will need to be optimized?

This is a chance for you to see the overall picture and plan for problems down the line. Breaking the problem domain into smaller chunks will dramatically reduce the complexity of your program and therefore reduce debugging time. Coding will be much simpler. The entire project is much more likely to stay on schedule and maybe under budget. Spend at least a week just planning, outlining, and breaking it up. I recommend two weeks, but this can be a bit tedious at times. A little test code now and then is helpful.

Make sure that the entire team understands the approach you will be taking. Make sure that everyone is clear about the design and that they see how the different portions integrate with the rest of the program. Draw a series of Booch diagrams to define the role of different sections of the code and their subsections.

Now that you've decided what needs to be done—and by now you will have around 200 items on your task list—you must decide who does what. There are really only two criteria when deciding who gets which tasks: willingness and skill.

The people who get each section/subsection must have an idea of what they are doing, or at least have somebody to rely on for advice and help. Secondly, and maybe more importantly, is a willingness to take on the tasks. Personally, I will take on any task, but I really love graphics, low-level optimization, and AI. You won't catch me doing networking, sound, or a host of other things, simply because they are either too easy or they don't interest me. Everyone you work with will have different preferences and you must be willing to work with those who may not want to do certain things. There are tasks that nobody likes, like file management. Too bad; somebody will have to do it. Maybe not you, but somebody. That is part of the cycle. Just make sure that it is done right.

Volatility

When designing, account for change. These "volatile" areas will cause you problems if you don't make room for the change in the original design. Without a doubt, the game design will change or a certain way of doing something that you designed will prove impossible. It is simply not possible to predict exactly where change will occur, but you will find it worthwhile to sit down and discuss where change is likely to occur in the game. Perhaps more creatures will be added. The technology tree is guaranteed to change.

Areas that are likely to change I call volatile. Plan for change by testing them as individual entities and treating them as lepers in the rest of the code—that is, access them in generic ways and as infrequently as possible. The types of things you'll need are nonspecific naming and generic functions like GetWidth or OpenFile. Do not create code that you'll need to change often; stick to the C++ ideal of centralizing code. Create a function to do a whole bunch of things rather than recoding that functionality every time you need it. Centralizing code is key to writing less code and having less volatile code.

The more specific this volatile code is, the harder it will be to change or remove it when the game design changes come. Also, call the functions therein as infrequently as possible. The more integrated it is into the rest of the program, the more difficult it will be to replace. This is a good rule of thumb anyway. This is a concept called coupling. *Coupling* is the amount of activity that happens between modules. Instead, you want your module to be highly cohesive. C*ohesion* is the amount of activity that happens inside of a single module. This means that all you should ever need to do is say Creature->Draw (), and the creature should handle all setup and display properties, it should know where it is, and you should see it on the screen. You shouldn't need to do very much work to get it to draw. That way, when the entire engine changes the way it draws, nothing in the rest of the code will change.

Most of the functions you call should be within a module, not between modules. The concept is to keep data and functions together and not make other modules highly reliant on them. "Loosely coupled, highly cohesive" should be your motto. Remember it—it will save you hundreds of programming hours rewriting code. I guarantee it.

You may also want to make these volatile areas data driven. Make a database that the game designer can modify and let him tinker with it while you go on and code something else. To do this:

1. Create a series of functions that read data from a text file.
2. Design a database or spreadsheet that formats that data how you need it.
3. Export the data in a text format (usually in the file menu under Export...) so that your program can read it in.

Data-driven code is harder to write, but well worth the effort when the deadline is two weeks away and you can easily change a number in the database and rerun the program. Recompiling is a pain and changing the right variable is difficult and time consuming. It may also take a while to find. By the way, you should make as much of your game data driven as possible. Obviously, making sound or graphics data driven may be silly, but the sound filenames and graphic filenames could easily be part of the database as well as behavior, creature variables, etc.

Also, data driven doesn't just mean having a database or spreadsheet to maintain your data. The best way (in my humble opinion) is to create tools that allow you to work on a single creature or object at a time and then export all of the data as a single file. A single file that contains all of the animation data, behavior, skills, armor values, and so on is the easiest way to work with data and create a solid data-driven model. See Figures 3.2, 3.3, 3.4, and 3.5.

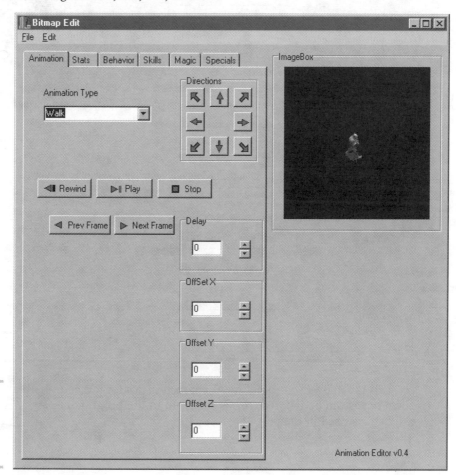

Figure 3.2
*Bitmap Edit |
Animation tab
for setting
animation data*

Figure 3.2 shows part of the editing tool that allows you to set animation data for a unit. The offsets allow you to control how many pixels a creature offsets his screen position when moving. The pull-down list allows you to select which animation sequence you are editing. Delay is how long to pause before the next frame of animation. The Directions area allows you to view the animation in each of the eight directions. All of the button graphics are programmer art.

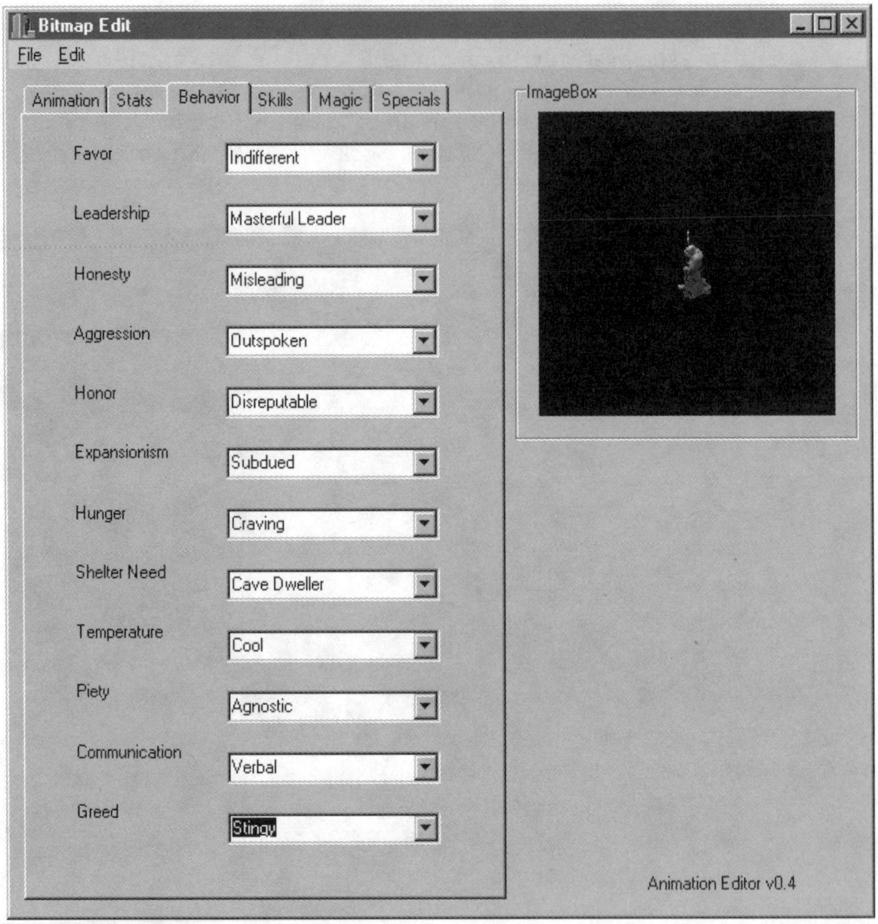

Figure 3.3
Bitmap Edit |
Behavior tab for
defining AI
characteristics

This tab allows you to define AI characteristics for a creature. Many of the pull-down boxes can be ignored; this is really up to the programmer and designer. These will be discussed in Chapter 18.

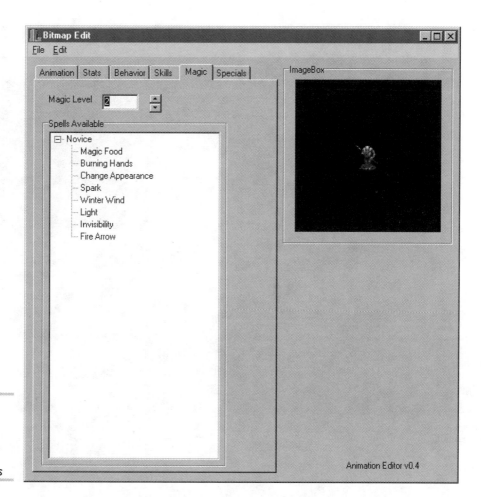

Figure 3.4
Bitmap Edit |
Magic tab to
define magic
characteristics

This selection allows you to define magic for creatures. In the example, each level of magic gives you four more predefined spells. This creature has eight spells.

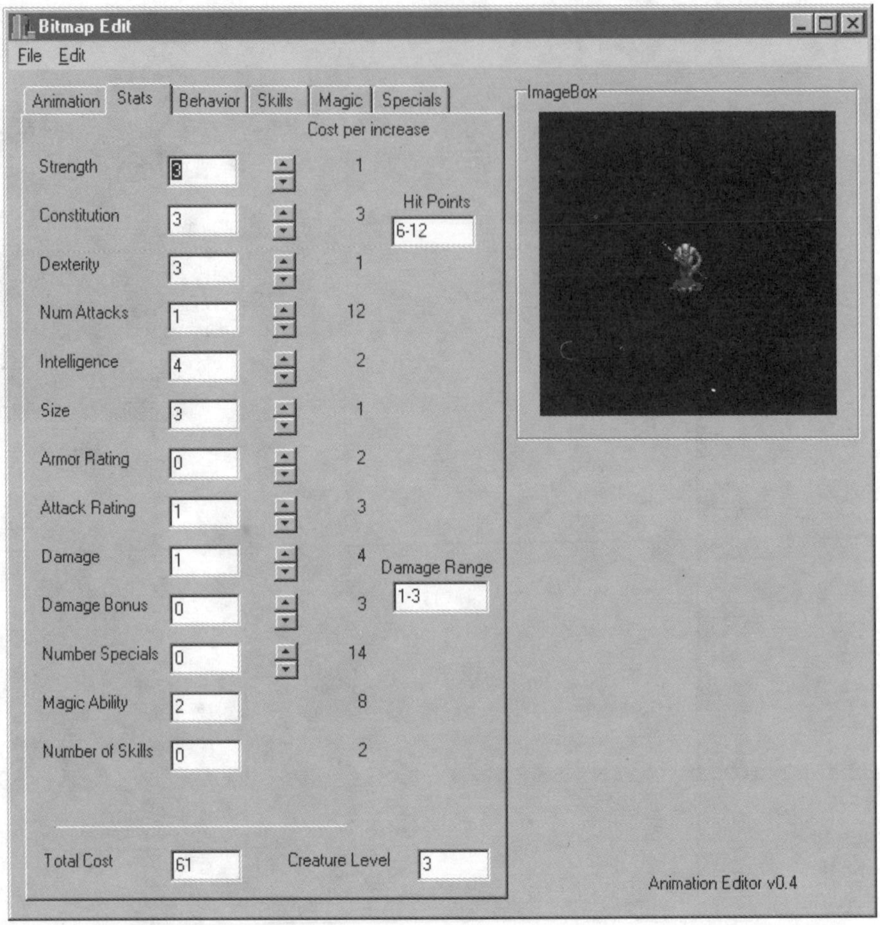

Figure 3.5
Bitmap Edit |
Stats tab

This tab contains a lot of information. Let's use Constitution as an example. Say I increase Constitution by 1. That costs 3 points, as noted in the Cost Per Increase column. That cost affects the Total Cost. For every 10 points of cost above 40, the creature level increases. This level is used in game balancing to make sure that every race has the same number of levels among its creatures. Spell levels from the Magic tab also affect total cost, listed here under Magic Ability. Lastly, Hit Points are given in a range so as to be somewhat random. After all, no two people are quite the same. This range is directly affected by Constitution. For every point of Constitution, the range of hit points increases slightly.

Another thing about areas that are likely to change: Make volatile areas of your code really flexible. Include extra variables that you may never use, just in case. These types of variables are normally called pads (as in padding). Put in extra functionality that will probably be helpful. Talking in depth with the game designer about how things might change will help you decide how to build the volatile areas of the program. Be sure to write the word "volatile" on any 3x5 card (see the Creating the

Schedule section later in this chapter) that may need extra attention. Save files should always have a floating-point number at the beginning of them to provide version control. This affects the way you read in the data. You can (usually) read in any old data and then when you save, you simply write all of the updated data. The read file looks something like this:

```
void  Load (FILE*)
{
        FILE->Load (&Version, sizeof (float));
        FILE->Load (&ArmorVar, sizeof (int));
        If (Version >0.02) FILE->Load (&StrengthVar, sizeof (int));
        If (Version >0.50) FILE->Load (&AgeVar, sizeof (int));
}
```

This example works for any data loading routine, where the types of data saved and read is likely to change.

Building a Paradigm

Coming up with good design methodologies and then building a paradigm around it is difficult. Without this step, you will probably flounder and ultimately fail. How will I manage processor time? How will modules get their messages from the queue? Where is the glue that keeps everything running? Can I use an existing design paradigm? How does the code flow? After I finish drawing in every frame, then what? Which messages go to the network?

Defining all of this will help you succeed in your endeavor and ensure that the game is playable. The paradigm/structure ultimately affects everything related to game performance, expandability, etc. Some of the really big decisions are listed below along with their impacts. This table is meant to give you perspective, not answer all of your questions. The fact is, I can't give you all of the effects and side effects of everything you do in your game. The table is simply to demonstrate how you might want to analyze the pros and cons. After creating a similar table for the management of your particular project, show them what you're up against and then work with them. Management will have certain expectations, so make sure they understand the full impact of the decisions they make. Making a table similar to this will help outline the entire project and, ultimately, save you hundreds of hours in planning your project. This also sets you up for building a good paradigm. Once you've made decisions about the nitty-gritty of your problem domain, you will be prepared to actually design your game engine.

Question	Choice	Comments
Should I use a lot of global data, or should I rely on data hiding?	Lots of global data	Competition for reading and writing data at the same time—especially in a multithreaded game. Sloppy coding, too much data on the stack, and a tendency for competing resources, i.e., crash.
	Some global data	Balanced and useful. Keep global data within a single module where possible.

Question	Choice	Comments
Should I use a lot of global data, or should I rely on data hiding? (Cont.)	Little or no global data	Too many access routines, too hard to access data sometimes.
What should happen in a frame per second?	Network input	Get input back from the network queue.
	Input	Any mouse movement or keys that were pressed should be sent to the network queue so that everyone in the game can process the message.
	Output	Any buttons that were pressed should highlight and text should be displayed for any item on which the mouse is now resting.
	Sound	A queue for sounds will be played.
	Graphics	Scroll the map, and redraw the landscape, buildings, and all the creatures.
	Creature movement	Creatures wanting to move will now be processed.
	Creature AI	Creatures will have a little time to make some decisions.
	Group AI	Creature groups will receive a little time to think.
	Computer opponent AI	The computer opponent will get a lot of time for assessments and decision making.
	Damage assessment	All creatures that were attacked during this frame will now take their damage; some will die and some will live.
	Tally sheet	Scores updated, resources added, new units finished, units heal slightly, weapons repaired, etc.
	Random events	Earthquakes, tornadoes, buffalo stampede, flood.
	Graphic effects	Fog of war adjusted, map updated, mini-map updated, slowly rotting bodies deteriorate.
How can I keep my game within 30 frames per second? (This means making the game run at a reasonable speed.)	Strategy one	Make sure that your graphics engine is running at 90 frames and the rest will take care of itself.
	Strategy two	When in the update cycle, make the call timeGetTime(), which returns time to the nearest millisecond, and force a return after 8 milliseconds.
	Strategy three	Keep the screen resolution low.
	Strategy four	Only update objects on the screen.
	Strategy five	Significantly limit the number of units per player.
	Strategy six	Try to use hardware support to draw some items, such as interface items.
	Strategy seven	Try to keep all data cached in memory and save the amount of time it takes to access the hard drive.
	Strategy eight	Limit the amount of animation; this saves memory and hence speeds access.

Question	Choice	Comments
How can I keep my game within 30 frames per second? (Cont.)	Strategy nine	Try to do as little as possible in each frame of animation and schedule update cycles for all of the creatures in the game so that everyone gets a turn every five or so frames.
	Strategy ten	Let group AI make decisions for a group and simply let the members follow orders.
Should I use dynamic memory?	Use	Easy to program and speeds development time as long as memory leaks are tracked well. Memory allocation will slow down your program. Memory fragmentation may cause a long-playing game to slow to a crawl.
	Don't use	Little or no memory fragmentation. The problem of speed loss due to allocation can be reduced to almost zero. Longer development time. Not very flexible.
	Limited use	Flexibility when needed. Speed can be increased when a lot of allocation is occurring. Longer development time than full use. May be best solution.
How should I handle file reading and writing?	fread, fwrite	Too verbose since it requires everything to be in quotes. However, it's simple and everyone knows how to use it.
	iostream	Somewhat cryptic and sometimes difficult to format. Great for reading in streams of text and parsing them.
	read, write	Good option, but old school; some might think your code is old.
	ReadFile, WriteFile	Good Windows API. I found a bug, however. It seems that in the middle of a huge data file, I told it to write a 4-byte int and it wrote a 2-byte short. No explanation, but after three hours I gave up and started using read and write.
	proprietary	I recommend hiding the actual method you use in an internal set of routines that allows you to change the method you use at any time without needing to go through and change files.

You could use this table to help you make decisions about everything in your game, and we'll go through recommendations as this book progresses. The thing to remember is that you should outline the difficulties that you expect in your game and then make a table of possible solutions like the one above. Then you should follow with suggestions, recommendations, and concerns. This may be the most important thing you do toward the eventual success of your project.

Now, how do you use the answers in the table to build a successful paradigm and ultimately create a kick-ass game? Let's start with a simple example. Say that you decide to create your own proprietary file reading and writing class. I happen to think that this is the most flexible and is not notably slower. How does it impact the way you pass file handles? You're now not passing a void* as in fopen, but now you need to pass a pointer to a file management class or at least some kind of data structure. This means that all files that will do any reading or writing will need to include the header for this class. You should make this header a simple framework and not include any other headers within it. How should you use such a class? Probably like fopen where you pass a few parameters that tell the new class what you want to do, such as read a file. This should probably be generic and not rely on any other header files since you may want to replace the method that this FILE_MANAGER uses. What should happen when the FILE_MANAGER falls out of scope or is deleted? It probably should automatically close the file that it opened upon instantiation. Should it have an open function or simply open the file as a passed parameter in the constructor? You might want to allow both and have a bunch of flags to tell if the file was opened properly. You will also need at least a small amount of error checking, maybe returning 0 if there were no errors and –1 for all other errors.

This analysis will structure the program for you. This is a building block that provides a firm foundation and will simplify your code later if your design is to be easy to use in the first place.

Now, on to bigger issues. You have solved a small problem and defined a small portion of the paradigm. What about the big picture? Sometimes you have to break a big picture down into a series of smaller pictures. This is how you solve the big picture issue. Start by solving critical areas like file management, graphics handling, animation, etc. If you are very careful about designing these areas and making them consistently easy to use, the big paradigm picture will fall into place. The entire problem domain is too complex to solve all at once, and unless you are a grand super ultra genius, breaking the paradigm down into a series of powerful, flexible, and stable paradigms is the best possible solution.

So start with the table and define at least three solutions to every problem with pros and cons for each. Then start by further examining how the different areas fit together and interact. Then write some pseudo code showing interactions between modules and data in different parts of your program. This will define your paradigm for you, almost magically.

Defining the Framework

It is probably much too early for you to start defining the framework considering that we haven't even explored different frameworks, structures, class definitions, code definitions, etc. However, we can at least formulate a game plan. You have a pretty good idea of what you want your game to do—at least I hope that you do—and so now you need to begin thinking about how you will store data, handle mouse events, distribute messages to other players in a network game, draw graphics, and so on. Because the code or code alternatives haven't been fully defined, we'll come back to the framework question again and again as we move through coding a simple game engine. You will eventually make some framework decisions, and go on your own path.

In the meantime, I suggest that you formulate a list of questions:

> ➤ How will I draw graphics?

> ➤ How will creatures find their own way across the map without running into things?
> ➤ What are some good methods for creating creature interaction?

Much like in the Building a Paradigm section, you should explore alternatives in your mind and write some of them down. These issues, and hundreds of others, will be discussed as the book progresses.

Just remember: I will be trying to help you focus on the big picture—the framework—throughout the rest of this text. The methods for achieving results of any kind are plentiful, and so picking a good solid framework for your game is an art, not a science. Good luck.

Creating the Schedule

Each person should divide up his or her own tasks into a priority schedule. It helps to put each task on a 3x5 card with details about the task. First, each person should look at other peoples' tasks and see which ones must be completed for other programmers to progress with their work. You don't want to hold others up. You also need to think of natural progression. You can't very well do a graphics engine without DirectDraw (or some other viewing method) up and running. So you need to create a base graphics engine before you can even get started, let alone worrying about whether or not you are holding up other people. They will simply need to work around you.

This prioritizing method involves giving each task a letter value. Important tasks that must be completed first are given an "A" designation. Those that can wait a few months, like sound, are given a "B." Those that can be done right before the end of the project, like burning the CD, or omitted altogether are given a "C" designation. Now forget the B's and C's and start prioritizing the A's.

Once each task is prioritized, you are ready to write in time schedules. How long will each one take to accomplish? Remember that you already know which ones are most important and which could hold up others; those were at the top of the pile. Now you are simply putting a best guess estimate on the time for each. After you finish this (simple?) task, you are ready for a revision of your estimates.

Go through all of your time estimates and add a little. If you are experienced in the game industry, add 50 percent to your estimates. If you are fresh out of college, double your estimate. These revised estimates will be much closer to the actual time it takes, including debugging, research, and testing. You can count on it. Do not revise these estimates after the new increase. In the end, it will add up to this number.

Now you can create a schedule and a list of milestones. This helps everyone track your progress and helps keep you on schedule.

The Development Cycle

Long hours, long weekends, hard-as-hell algorithms, pain-in-the-ass managers, crashing networks, self-formatting hard drives, lazy designers, dumb artists, whiteboard after whiteboard, recoding for design changes, sleeping at work under your desk, pizza every night at 7 o'clock, tight deadlines, relatively low pay, and old hardware.

Everything listed will either slow you down or eat at you when working for just about any game company.

The development cycle will whittle away at your days, and you can expect a long year or two of grueling hours and great work. Other than working at NASA Jet Propulsion Labs or in Special Development at Xerox, there are very few jobs in the real world as mentally challenging as game development. Applications, UNIX, Linux, Windows NT, COBOL, and the like do not hold a candle to game development in terms of challenge. Biophysicists, biochemists, astrophysicists, oceanographers, and those in most research fields do not touch the level of thinking that must take place in real-time strategy games. It takes tremendous effort to move an army of virtual goblins from one side of the map to the other, attack your opponent's city, collect the spoils, and return in time to defend your city. Considering the average level of education of most game programmers, it is amazing that games can do what they do. Some of the best game programmers have one year of college or less. Amazing, if you ask me. Yet most understand the details of assembly programming, the characteristics of light, memory management, the writings of Emmanuel Kant, how to play piano fantastically, how to program for post-calculus linear algebra, the process to make characters dance using inverse kinematics, or the utilization of program interrupts.

Now when you consider how much goes into a game, it is truly amazing that games ever get completed. When you are asked how long it will take to complete the game you are working on, take your best estimate, and add 50 percent. This is a conservative value. Many pundits say double the value, so I may be a little optimistic myself. Programmers always underestimate the length of time that the development of a game will take. ALWAYS. Better to overestimate, and then begin cutting out unnecessary things. You can add them later if you have time, which you won't.

The development cycle has about ten stages. Here is the basic framework, although you can expect variations:

1. Idea. Develop an idea and write it down into a cohesive story and game plan. 1 to 4 weeks ideally.
2. Approval. You need money and time and permission and people and computers and software and other hardware and … 4 to 8 weeks hopefully; can take significantly longer.
3. Setup. Assemble your team, gather equipment, find a place to develop, get your whiteboard, familiarize the team with the concepts, get computers running and networks up, make sure that all software is working and everyone is properly prepared to do the jobs assigned. 4 to 6 weeks if all goes well; most of the time this takes a little longer.
4. Begin coding and research. Find good asset delivery methods, start tools work, begin simple program testing, establish game engine framework, make sure you have the latest version of DirectX, spend time on the Web looking up pathing, etc. 8 to 12 weeks.
5. Code. You will need to develop many of the tools yourself, but you need to design them such that you can rely on them. You will be subject to "feature creep" here,

so expect delays. Depending on your game, this can take as little as six weeks for a simple game or as long as 72 weeks. 40 to 56 weeks normally.

6. Cleanup. This is when the end is in sight. Most of the game basics work and now you'll do a code review and lock down features. Don't add any new features. Fix bugs and prep for Alpha. 6 to 8 weeks.

7. Alpha. Send out Alpha and start getting all of the levels in the game fully tested. Put all creatures in the game in situations where they need to think and make sure you have no crashes. Prep for Beta. 4 weeks or more. Alpha almost always take the same amount of prep time in RTS games unless your management is disorganized.

8. Beta. The game should be done and have fewer than 100 bugs. You need to concentrate fully on crushing bugs and let the level designers test the last few levels by themselves. You are almost done. 3 to 6 weeks.

9. Prep to ship. Prepare the install routines. You might be preparing for internationalization and testing on different hardware. 2 to 3 weeks.

10. Ship. Get some sleep, take a vacation, make love to the woman you used to call your wife until you didn't come home for three months, etc. Catching up on reading is good here too.

That about does it. For a programmer, this is almost always the same year and a half routine.

Programming and Programming Style

It seems that the most pervasive argument in the game industry has nothing to do with hardware, which development environment to use, which tools to use, or anything really important. People seem unable to decide on whether or not to use C++. What a no-brainer! C++ is as fast as C and in some cases, a lot faster. You get better design, the code almost designs itself, and data and functions all work together better. I will defend this for a few pages, and then move on to the actual code.

This is where we talk about the actual programming of your game. We'll look at a few different game engine models and then do a lot of code. Everything will be in C++ style with a few twists. I fully expect that you will love some of what we discuss here. Other parts will make you feel somewhat less fuzzy inside. But before I begin, let's discuss your and my favorite: Why C++?

 Definition: An engine is a bunch of code that can easily be modified to create games. An engine is difficult to create and takes many years of experience just to finally make the engine breakthrough. A good example of an engine is the Quake engine. This engine was made into the popular first-person shooter Quake. For about $500,000 to $1,000,000 you can license this game engine. It has a lot of tools, which aren't great, but the engine is.

C++ is really the best of all worlds (in my opinion). You get very close to the metal, that is to say, your code translates almost directly into machine assembly without much overhead or garbage. Almost any single line of code you do in C/C++ becomes two to six lines of assembly. This means that C/C++ is nicely translated. Visual Basic can become dozens of lines of assembly code. You definitely don't want that. C/C++ code generally generates the fastest executable other than if you had written it in assembly. In fact, you could say that when you need speed, C/C++ is the way to go.

But why not just program directly in assembly? There are quite a few reasons. Assembly is notorious for being difficult. There are no variables, per se, and no functions. Debugging is very difficult and since there can be no random organization (like any C/C++ file), things must be ordered and ordered well. Time is actually the key factor. Writing good assembly code to accomplish a particular task most often takes five to ten times longer than doing the same task in C, depending on what you hope to accomplish and the talent of the programmer. Since C/C++ is very fast anyway, most of the time assembly is not necessary in the vast majority of your program. Most people agree that assembly programming should be reserved for speed bottlenecks and some people say that you should avoid assembly programming altogether (those people would also be idiots). When your code is slow in a particular area and you are sure that the bottleneck is in that area, you should consider recoding it in assembly. My advice: Save the programming hours and make your life easy by sticking to C/C++ most of the time and leave the assembly for optimization.

By the way, it is important to note that if you have the willingness and ability to do assembly programming, I highly recommend it. I find it a rewarding experience to take a function that is holding up the rest of the program for any reason and optimize it. I enjoy watching the frame rate gain 10 percent or, sometimes, double. It can be very rewarding but also very time consuming.

Let's not neglect other languages. Why not Pascal? Good question. These days Object Pascal/Delphi is as good as C/C++. It is about as fast in terms of run time and compiles three to four times faster. So why not? I'll tell you why: BEGIN and END. Every code block in Pascal must begin and end with those capitalized words, which are a pain to type and make your code messy. C/C++ looks clean. Easy to read means easy to program. Other than that, I see no reason whatsoever not to use Pascal, although it does have the declaration problem. Every declaration needs a colon following, which is a minor nuisance. For example:

```
int:    iType;
```

Pascal has pointers (a critical reason to not use languages like Fortran, COBOL, and Basic), and can call hardware interrupts and do inline assembly. You may get perfectly good games out of it. If you are willing to translate the code in this book into Pascal, it may be worth the effort. Incidentally, C/C++ and Pascal are coded in much the same way, use a lot of the same conventions, and have executables that come out to be about the same size.

The best alternative to C++ or C seems to be Java. Although it may be a bit slower for Windows-based stuff and interface things, you'll hardly use any of that functionality. Pure Java code runs just about as fast as C or C++ and can be more reliable and certainly more flexible. If you are looking for a programming language to branch off into, try Java. It is a great language.

Now comes the hard question. C++, am I mad? C++ is slower than C. What about all of those warnings about "assigning long to int: possible loss of data" and who ever thought about function overloading? I've heard all the arguments. The fact is nothing beats being able to put variables and functions in one nice neat package. Game coders using C will come up with something like the following:

```
struct Creature
{
int intelligence;
int strength;
int armor_rating;
int creature_type;
    ...
};
```

Then they will create a bunch of functions that modify or act on that data:

```
void CreatureDecideWhatToDo (Creature* c);
void CreatureAttack (Creature* c, Creature* attacked);
void CreatureDeathSequence (Creature* c);
...
```

Every function name contains the prefix "Creature," telling a little about what it does and keeping the function names unique for the program. What a pain, if you ask me.

What do you think of this model?

```
struct Creature
{
int     intelligence;
int     strength;
int     armor_rating;
int     creature_type;

void    DecideWhatToDo ();
void    Attack (Creature* attacked);
void    DeathSequence ();
};
```

Notice how it's all together. Also, the functions have fewer passed variables. This makes a function call faster. True, this is pushed on the stack, but then all variables are read directly from memory rather than from a pointer. Let me show you what I mean.

This was compiled in Visual C++ version 5.0 using the C compiler and the C++ compilers, respectively. Disassembly was obtained by putting in a breakpoint and when the program halted at my breakpoint, I hit Ctrl-Tab.

First, let's look at plain C:

```
void    IncreaseIntelligence (Creature* c)
{
c->intelligence += 100;
```

```
}

void   main ()
{
Creature c;
IncreaseIntelligence (&c);
}
```

The function call from main looks like this:

```
lea    eax,dword ptr [c]
push   eax
call   @ILT+10 (?IncreaseIntelligence@@YAXPAUCreature@@@Z)(0x0040100a)
add    esp,4
```

and the function itself, IncreaseIntelligence (), looks like this:

```
push   ebp
mov    ebp,esp
mov    eax,dword ptr [c]
mov    ecx,dword ptr [eax]
add    ecx,64h
mov    edx,dword ptr [c]
mov    dword ptr [edx],ecx
pop    ebp
ret
```

This takes eight clock cycles (a lot of pipeline stalls). The call from main takes six cycles for a total of 14 in this simple function call. In C++, we'll pay only slightly more. Using this structure:

```
struct Creature
{
int    intelligence;
int    strength;
int    armor_rating;
int    creature_type;

void   IncreaseIntelligence ()
{
intelligence += 100;
}
};

void   main ()
{
Creature c;
c.IncreaseIntelligence ();
}
```

the function call in main looks like this, taking five clock cycles:

```
lea    ecx,dword ptr [c]
call   @ILT+0 (?IncreaseIntelligence@Creature@@QAEXXZ)(0x00401000)
mov    esp,ebp
```

The member function IncreaseIntelligence takes 11 clock cycles for a total of 16:

```
push    ebp
mov     ebp,esp
push    ecx
mov     dword ptr [ebp-4],ecx
mov     eax,dword ptr [this]
mov     ecx,dword ptr [eax]
add     ecx,64h
mov     edx,dword ptr [this]
mov     dword ptr [edx],ecx
mov     esp,ebp
pop     ebp
ret
```

So C++ is slower than C, right? Well, not really. In some cases, yes; in some cases, no. The next example is so lengthy that I will reserve it to code and avoid the assembly. You'll have to trust that my numbers are correct and you will see that C++ is faster. This is pretty typical for a C-written brancher. You have a list of creatures and when you are in an update cycle, you call this function repeatedly.

```
void    UpdateCreature (Creature* c)
{
        switch (c->creature_type)
        {
            case YETI:
            CreatureUpdateYeti ();
            break;

            case POTSMOKER:
            CreatureUpdatePotSmoker ();
            break;
            ...
        }
}
```

There are two slowdowns here. You have to call a function, the brancher function above, just to find out which function to actually call, i.e., CreatureUpdateYeti (). The second is the switch statement. It is not a jump table. Au contraire, it becomes a series of if...else's. Boy, is that slow! In fact, you really couldn't make that chunk of code much slower if you tried. If the creature is a YETI, the above code takes 24 clock cycles just to call the correct function; a little less in the case of a POTSMOKER. This breaks down to six for the entry into UpdateCreature, six for the function call CreatureUpdateYeti, and 12 for various pops, cmps, bnes, etc.

In C++, it looks like this (don't worry if it looks convoluted; it is actually a better way):

```
struct Creature
{
            int intelligence;
            int strength;
            int armor_rating;
            // int creature_type; not needed in C++, well
```

```
                   // not always. We're waiting for RTTI which is now in
                   // standard C++ but still a pain to use
                   virtual void  Update ()    // the word virtual sets up a jump
                                              // table. Very fast.
         {

                   intelligence += 100;
         }
};

struct YETI: public Creature
{
         void  Update () // we are helping the compiler to create a
                         // jump table
         {

                   intelligence += 100;
         }
};

struct POTSMOKER: public Creature
{
         void  Update () // continuing with the jump table
         {

                   intelligence += 100;
         }
};

void main ()
{
Creature* c = new YETI;
c->Update ();
delete c;
}
```

Notice main has the keywords new and delete. These operators allocate memory and call the constructor and destructor, among other things. The phrase "Creature* c = new YETI;" could be replaced by "Creature* c = new POTSMOKER;" or any other, including just plain "Creature." The program knows which function to call based on its type. The above function call costs only six cycles. It's four times as fast. Try it out and you'll see. C++ can be a lot faster than C. It really depends on the situation and how good a coder you are.

You may not understand C++ very well and that's okay. I recommend:

Object Oriented Programming in C++ by Robert LaFore (The Waite Group). It's a great book for beginners.

The C++ Programming Language by Bjarne Stroustrup (Addison Wesley). Very technical and informative but not for the faint of heart. This is not a user's guide but more of an encyclopedia.

The most difficult text, or at least the most advanced, is *C++ Primer* by Stanley B. Lippman and José Lajoie (Addison Wesley). This book is challenging, even after many years of programming C++. If you think you're a stud, give it a shot.

> **Note**: Whether or not you like C++, the world is slowly migrating toward it, and more than half of all game programmers use it. Most all real-time strategy games use it. Since C++ and C are most always the same speed, there is no benefit to using C over C++. You might as well learn to enjoy its many benefits. My advice: Get used to it.

Coding Style

Style is so arbitrary, it is almost like dressing every morning. What you wear on a regular basis is purely a matter of taste and flair, and so is the way you code. Good coders make clean, solid code, but if you ask anyone who has ever worked on the Quake engine, code doesn't need to be clean at all as long as it's fast and efficient. Naming conventions are usually a good idea. Separating .cpp files by the type of code inside is helpful. Typing comments is almost always better than trying to finish the code without them, regardless of the time it takes. It is usually a good idea to put all of your common macros into a single file that all of your files include. How you indent inside of braces speaks for style. At Ensemble Studios, programmers used to fight over whether to use three or four spaces for the indent inside of braces. It may sound petty, but editing and quickly reading your code is essential, especially when it comes to crunch time. Indents can be important.

The best way to deal with these issues is to pick a way of doing things and stick to it. Programming is 10 percent technical prowess, 30 percent programming knowledge, 10 percent debugging and analysis, 10 percent math, and 40 percent art. Your figures may vary but it's pretty close to that. The art, the creative intellect it takes to continue designing good solutions, can be one of the most difficult challenges. I'll give a rough overview that covers a few important areas.

Caps every word, no caps first word and caps all others, underscores between...

Who would argue about such a thing? How would you name a function that draws an animation frame?

1. `DrawFrame ()`
2. `drawFrame ()`
3. `drawframe ()`
4. `draw_frame ()`
5. `df ()`
6. `m_fDrawFrame ()`

Note: Here and pretty much throughout my code, I put a space between the function name and the parameter list. I think it is more readable. You do whatever you like.

Actually it doesn't matter. I recommend not using No. 5, but it's completely up to you. No. 4 is probably the most readable, but also the toughest to type. I prefer No. 1, and all of my code features it. The choice is yours.

Who dreamt up No. 6? A lot of MFC and other "gurus" came up with this system. It is difficult to read and tells you absolutely nothing. I'll deal with this more in the variable naming section next, because that is where this naming convention started. If you are trying to get in the habit of using this standard, do us all a favor: Don't.

Member variables should have a designation so you can tell...

I disagree with the above statement. I cannot read variables like:

```
char*       m_cpString;         // member char pointer
int         m_iVariable;        // member int
```

This looks awful, it's difficult to type, and it's not particularly helpful. If you must do this, use suffixes:

```
char*       String_cpm;         // char pointer member
int         Variable_im;        // int member
```

I avoid this designation with a passion. Use it if you must. Because a well-designed C++ program uses almost no global variables, most variables are members or are at least local. What is the point of having the m_ designation anyway? All variables not declared locally must be member variables. As far as the i, c, l, etc., you decide.

Where should I put my braces?

I prefer matching braces, but I know two people who do not. Some people have no method to the way they use braces—they are usually terrible programmers. Your options are:

```
void Foo () {                   // this saves space
        if (x == 3) {
                y = 100;
        }
}

or

void Foo ()                     // this is more readable… to me
{
        if (x==3)
        {
                y = 100;
        }
}
```

Macros or templates?

These are not mutually exclusive. Macros are important and should be used whenever possible. Templates are ideal as containers or memory managers. Templates do not generate macros (anymore) and macros cannot touch the power of a template. Templates used to cause code bloat, but now they create reasonably sized versions of the specific code that they were designed to replace. Here are a couple of macros:

```
#define  ABS (a)          (((a) < (0)) ? - (a) : (a))
#define  SWAP (a, b)      {(a)^=(b)^=(a)^=(b);} // xor
#define  LIMIT (val, l, h) ((val)<(l) ? (l) : (val) > (h) ? (h) : (val))
```

You use these like functions. SWAP is very cool. I found it in *Graphics Gems* years ago and still love it. LIMIT keeps a number within a range.

Below is a good template. We'll see the code later.

```
template <class type>
class QUEUE
{
public:
enum   {MAXENTRIES = 128};
protected:
      type*      array;
      int        Max, Begin, End;
int    OverWriteFlag;/* a flag to overwrite old data as new data is pushed onto
the queue, otherwise new data does not go on the queue until old stuff is
popped*/
      int        LastItemFlag;   // used to make the last item useful
void  InitArray ();
void  CleanupArray ();

public:
      QUEUE ();
      QUEUE (int num);
      ~QUEUE ();
      //**********************
void  Push (type* obj);
type* Pop (void);
      //**********************
void  Clear (void);
      //**********************
      //**********************
};
```

Whitespace, comments, filler, and FDA approval

Whitespace is good. It makes a huge difference in the readability of your code. Put ten lines (or however much you like) of whitespace between every function and use a row of asterisks:

```
//*********************************************
```

This is the world's best separator for helping the readability of your code. Each function can be preceded by a description of what types of variables it accepts and what it will return. If you use built-in C++ type checking, you couldn't possibly need it, but it's always a good idea.

```
//****************************************************
// this function accepts an int for a multiplier and another int as the
// second multiplier
// it returns the result of a simple multiply
//****************************************************

int  Multiply2Numbers (int x, int y)
{
        return x*y;
}
```

The trick here is to not overdo it.

 Note: Make good comments that are helpful, but remember that you are not writing a book. The idea is to help the reader. Also, a good approach to take is to consider that someday you might want to license this engine to somebody else, and unless you want to be at that person's office 24 hours a day... (did I mention game programmer hours?). Think about somebody else trying to figure out what you just did, and remember that three months from now, you will be that somebody else.

Should I use shorthand names to cut down on my typing?

NO! NO! NO! Do yourself a favor—learn to type. I would rather type than talk. I can type two to three times faster than I can talk. You should be able to accomplish this simple feat as well. Make your code readable. A beginning programmer should be able to look at your code for the first time and make heads or tails of it. I recently had to read someone else's code that looked like this:

```
dmPr = (LayDim*) obPr->L ();
```

After two hours, I discovered that I needed to rewrite it so that I could read it. It came out to:

```
LayerDimPtr = (LayerDim*) PalletPtr-> GetLayerLength ();
```

It still doesn't make a whole lot of sense, but at least I can read it. The most critical part of writing code is to make it self documenting. If anything about coding can be said to be the most important, choosing names that make the code explain itself is it. Comments are great, but when you use readable names in the first place, comments become nearly unnecessary. I realize that the following code is a little unrealistic and that you would never need to pass *x* and *y* to an object that draws itself, but I am trying to illustrate the naming convention under discussion.

```
void foo (CREATURE_STRUCT* Creature, int NumCreatures)
{
     int i = NumCreatures;

     while ( i--)
          {
          int  x = Creature[i]->x, y = Creature[i]->y;
               int  width = Creature[i]->width, height = Creature[i]->
                         height;
               Creature[I]->Draw (ScreenPointer, ScreenWidth,
                         ScreenHeight, x, y, width, height);
          }
}
```

Unlike you have seen in other places, my conventions are easy to read and do not follow any Microsoft standards. There is simply no excuse for Hungarian notation. After all, what is a LPSTR, LPCCHOOKPROC, or a LPCVARIANT? It is simply silly to come up with something like LPSTR, which is exactly the same thing as a char*.

Coding style is a difficult thing to establish, but once you do it, no other style seems correct. I am not saying that I am inflexible; I just hate conventions that slow me down, and Hungarian notation slows me down.

The Library

You will develop a library of common files that you will use for starting nearly every game project. This is a command: You will develop a library! The idea of starting your game from scratch is ludicrous these days. Still, most game programmers want to write a new engine every time. We don't live long enough. You simply don't have time. Make your code modules versatile and extensible. They should be loosely coupled with the other modules in your library and strongly cohesive.

A string class file that parses filenames is a must. Template-based linked lists, queues, and memory managers are important. Save everything that you write somewhere. If it's important to you, you'll remember where you last left it. Otherwise, forget it. But having a library is very important to the long-term success of your games and your game-writing career.

Also, developing a common set of dynamic-link libraries can be useful. These are libraries that you link in at run time that provide certain common functionality. You might develop a graphics layer that you can then abstract to a DLL or maybe a network layer. Anyway, the thinking involved in abstracting your code into separate modules will help you manage your code more effectively and ensure the code's success.

A Note about Your Coding Environment

This is where the code writing begins. This book is dedicated to writing DirectX code, in particular DirectDraw. The DirectX API is available only in Windows, so in order to use it you need to know something about Windows.

You should be familiar with the "main" function in any standard code. In Windows, you have WinMain. It's the entry point for a Windows executable and has a continuous loop that repeats until the program ends or Windows crashes, whichever comes first. (Provided that you write solid code, it will probably be Windows crashing. This may not be your fault; it's just that Windows is never as stable as UNIX, Linux, OS/2, MacOS, or a host of smaller operating systems. It's just something that you have to get used to.)

In case you love MFC, forget it. It is slow. It works fine for simple stuff, but if you want to do a game, it has a ridiculous amount of overhead. It will make your compile times unacceptable, sometimes taking over 20 times longer to compile an executable. If you don't know why, look at stdafx.h sometime and see how many headers are compiled each time you recompile a single line of code. Precompiled headers should alleviate this, but in practice, it only has an effect 20 to 30 percent of the time—in my experience. The fact is that MFC is not as useful as it used to be. If you need to create powerful apps quickly, use Borland C++ Builder. MFC just feels like a series of kludges to me. It had its place a few years ago when nothing else was available, but Borland is back on top now. For all of your tool development, or any Windows app for that matter, forget Visual C++ and go to Borland; they rock. In addition, you'll save literally hundreds of hours on simple apps that are easy to use and yet more then enough for the average programmer.

For the game itself, I use Visual C++. The debugger is excellent and the development IDE is fantastic. I wish that it allowed a little more control over window placement and the assembly code it generates is questionable at times, but overall it gives very good results. I understand that Borland C++ Builder is just as easy for doing DirectX stuff, but game systems should simulate a real DOS system and so I prefer Visual C++. Plus, Borland C++ Builder is a high-level language, fourth generation, and as such suffers from some of the same overhead problems that MFC has. The WinMain/low-level system seems to be simpler and you can control every aspect of the code, which is necessary in game coding. This highlights another reason MFC is unacceptable. By the way, trying to code a game in Visual Basic is ludicrous. It might be possible, but VB is worse than MFC on speed. Games require all the horsepower you can give them, so stay clear of compilers that generate slow code.

For my examples and testing I have been using VC 5.0 or what Microsoft calls Visual Studio 97. The assembly it produces seems to be somewhat better than VC 4.2 or earlier. I don't remember, but I think that using the __fastcall keyword in VC 4.2 or earlier gave no better results. These days, it is the equivalent of passing by register. For those of you out of the optimization loop (pun intended), this means that items are not pushed on the stack before calling another function. For commonly called functions, this can provide a small increase in speed. Most of the time you may not notice the difference. The trick is that you must be passing three or fewer variables. Don't forget to include in your count the hidden this parameter passed to function calls belonging to a class.

The VC 5.0 interface is much easier to use. I especially like the fact that you can right-click on the project window to add files or change files to your project. You can also put files into folders so that you can separate your .cpp files into discrete sections. Overall, it is a good working environment except when it comes to making tools.

Setting Up the WinMain and the MessageHandler

There are two primary sections in a Windows program. These are the WinMain and the MessageHandler. The WinMain handles the setup and closing of your program as well as maintenance through updates/messages. The MessageHandler provides a simple way to process things like mouse moves and key presses. We can also send messages to the MessageHandler, which is another story altogether but a useful tool nonetheless. See Figure 3.6.

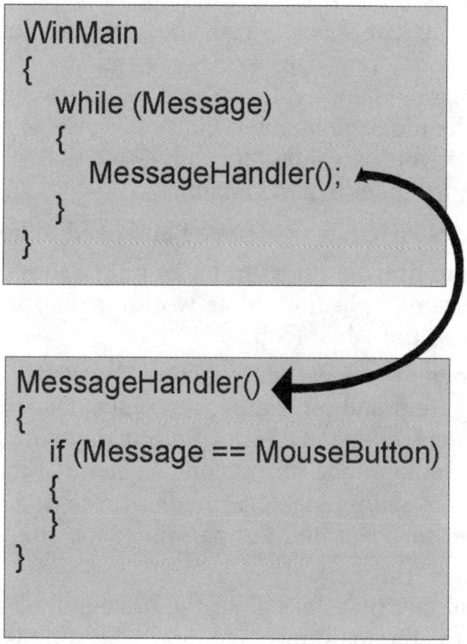

```
WinMain
{
    while (Message)
    {
        MessageHandler();
    }
}


MessageHandler()
{
    if (Message == MouseButton)
    {
    }
}
```

Figure 3.6
Program control diagram

All Windows programs have this structure. Using MFC makes no difference because MFC encapsulates or hides all of the muddy details. Visual Basic, Borland C++ Builder, and Turbo Pascal all do exactly the same thing behind the scenes (with trivial differences). So once you understand the basics of Windows programming, programming a game will seem easy. Windows is a confusing API with Hungarian notation and strange naming conventions. The Windows developers also took many of the good names for their functions. MoveTo and LineTo are Windows API function calls, so don't even think of using them. PlaySound, DestroyWindow, and SendMessage are also taken. This can make Windows programming difficult. I recommend that you limit the files that use Windows API calls to three files. This means that most of your .cpp files will not include windows.h. The only files that should include it are: the WinMain file, which you should probably name

WinMain.cpp; the MessageHandler file, which I like to call message.cpp; and the DirectDraw handler, which I usually call screen.cpp.

In WinMain, you initialize all of the variables necessary to create a window. Windows will handle the rest when you make a call to CreateWindow, which is a standard Windows API call. Windows 95 introduced a new function call—CreateWindowEx, which is essentially the same, with a few new parameters passed. This function, CreateWindowEx, accepts a structure, whose variables you define, and returns an HWND variable. This HWND variable happens to be an unsigned long. Windows knows what the value of this variable means, but good luck finding any interpretation of it in any book or resource. You will use this returned variable often and it is a good candidate for a global variable. If CreateWindowEx returns a valid number (a number below 0x1000, or so, and not equal to 0), then the program is off and running. Otherwise the program exits; this is very unlikely, but it can happen. Now you need to tell Windows to dispatch each message it receives to your message handler. Set up a "while" loop that sees if there are any messages to process and if so, tell Windows to dispatch that message to the message handler. Refer back to Figure 3.6.

The Windows kernel calls the message handler. That's because as part of the initialization of the variables above, you pass a pointer to the function used for handling messages. What happens in the while loop of WinMain is:

1. We test to see if any messages have been processed and need to be processed.

2. If no messages, we prepare to draw the next frame of animation, process any network messages, update everyone's position in the world, make some AI decisions, draw the frame, and return to the while loop.

3. If there is a message, we immediately call the function TranslateMessage and then DispatchMessage. Microsoft Help and most other reference material is not very clear as to what these functions do, so good luck finding any data on the subject. TranslateMessage performs some minor conversions on some of the messages. DispatchMessage has the effect of calling MessageHandler through a circuitous route through the kernel, and over the river and through the woods to grandmother's house we go.

Below is a typical basic WinMain that does all of the basic initialization and starts the program running. After that is the main message loop. The code is discussed after the listing.

```
//********************************
// winmain.cpp


#include <windows.h>

int ActiveApp = false;          // global flag that tells us if this
                                // program is in the foreground or if it's
                                // behind some other program, look for the
                                // change in the message handler

LRESULT CALLBACK MessageHandler (HWND hwnd, UINT message, WPARAM wParam,
```

```
    LPARAM lParam);                         // prototype

//*******************************

int WINAPI WinMain (HINSTANCE hInstance, HINSTANCE hPrevInstance,
        LPSTR lpCmdLine, int nCmdShow)
{
        MSG         msg;                    // a Windows structure
        HWND        WindowHandle;           // an unsigned int
        WNDCLASS    wc;                     // a Windows structure
        char ClassName[] = "Basic Windows"; // just a string with a name I picked

        hPrevInstance = hPrevInstance;      // this avoids a compiler warning –
                                            // variable not used

        wc.style = CS_HREDRAW | CS_VREDRAW; // horizontal or vertical
                                            // redraw if the window size
                                            // is changed
        wc.lpfnWndProc = MessageHandler;    // pointer to the function below
        wc.cbClsExtra = 0;                  // any extra bytes in this structure,
                                            // who knows why this is here?
        wc.cbWndExtra = 0;                  // extra bytes in the windows definition
                                            // of this program; useful in dialog boxes
        wc.hInstance = hInstance;           // Windows has an index list of each
                                            // program it instantiates and this
                                            // number is passed in this structure
        wc.hIcon = LoadIcon (hInstance, IDI_APPLICATION); // an icon that
                                            // is loaded to appear in the taskbar
        wc.hCursor = LoadCursor (NULL, IDC_ARROW);        // a mouse cursor; it
                                            // probably won't be used in a game but
                                            // Windows needs it
        wc.hbrBackground = NULL;            // a Windows definition for a brush; it
                                            // is used for repainting a window
        wc.lpszMenuName = ClassName;        // naming our program in the taskbar
        wc.lpszClassName = ClassName;       // the window class name

        RegisterClass (&wc);

        WindowHandle = CreateWindowEx ( // here we create the window
          WS_EX_TOPMOST,
          ClassName,
          ClassName,
          WS_POPUP,
          0,                                // upper left
          0,                                // upper right
          640,                              // width
          480,                              // Height
          NULL,
          NULL,
          hInstance,
          NULL);
```

3

Chapter

```
            if (!WindowHandle) return FALSE; // this means that Windows had a problem


    ShowWindow ( WindowHandle, nCmdShow );
    UpdateWindow ( WindowHandle );
    SetFocus    ( WindowHandle );
    ShowCursor ( FALSE );                    // turns off the cursor; useful for full-
                                             // screen games; normally this would be
                                             // TRUE in standard Windows

while (1)                                    // infinite loop
    {
int t = PeekMessage (&msg, NULL, OU, OU, PM_NOREMOVE);// do we have a message
    if (t)
        {
        if (!GetMessage (& msg, NULL, 0, 0))      // get the message
        return msg.wParam;
        TranslateMessage (&msg);   // conversion of some values
        DispatchMessage (&msg);    // call the MessageHandler
        }

        else if (ActiveApp)          // this is important here
            {
                RedrawScreen ((LPVOID) NULL);
                UpdateProc ((LPVOID) NULL);
                HandleEvents ((LPVOID) NULL);
            }
        else if (!ActiveApp)          // if the program goes into the background
                                      // behind some other program then suspend
                WaitMessage ();       // messages
    }
return msg.wparam;             // return the final message, not particularly useful
}


// ************************** MessageHandler *****************************

LRESULT CALLBACK MessageHandler (HWND hwnd, UINT message, WPARAM wParam, LPARAM
lParam)
{
    int mousex, mousey;

    switch (message)
    {
        case WM_ACTIVATEAPP:
            ActiveApp = wParam;
        break;

        case WM_CREATE:
        break;

        case WM_TIMER: // we can set a timer to automatically create an event
```

```
                         // break every so often; not real great for a game but
                         // you might use it to keep time or something; timers
                         // are limited to about once every 55 milliseconds
break;

case WM_MOUSEMOVE:
            mousex = lParam&0xffff;      // how Windows passes location
            mousey = (lParam&0xffff0000)>>16;
            if (wParam & MK_LBUTTON)     // make sure that the left button
                                         // is pressed
                DragMouse(mousex, mousey); // my own function
break;

case WM_KEYDOWN:             // VK_ precedes all key presses. For alphabet
                             // or numbers use case 'A':
        switch (wParam)
        {
            case VK_ESCAPE: // the Esc key closes down the program
                DestroyWindow(hwnd);
        break;

            case VK_SPACE:
            break;

            case VK_END:
            case VK_DOWN:
                ZoomOut ();              // my own function
            break;

            case VK_HOME:
            case VK_UP:
                ZoomIn ();               // my own function
            break;

            case VK_LEFT:
                RotateLeft ();           // my own function
            break;

            case VK_RIGHT:
                RotateRight ();          // my own function
            break;
        }
      break;

case WM_LBUTTONDOWN:                    // mouse left button down
{
     int x = LOWORD (lParam);
     int y = HIWORD (lParam);
     LeftMouseClick (x, y);             // my own function
}
break;
case WM_RBUTTONDOWN:                    // mouse right button down
```

```
        {
            int x = LOWORD (lParam);
            int y = HIWORD (lParam);
            RightMouseClick (x, y);     // my own function
        }
        break;

        case WM_DESTROY:
            ShowCursor (TRUE);          // restore mouse cursor
            PostQuitMessage (0);
        break;

        default:                        // most regular Windows messages we don't need
        return DefWindowProc (hwnd, message, wParam, lParam);
    }
    return 0L;
}
//***********************************
```

WinMain accepts a few parameters. WinMain is actually a regular function that is called by main. Where is main, you ask? It's hidden, really. Compilers conveniently hide the main. It is still there and it is the entry point for the program. It calls some Windows functions and then calls your WinMain, passing some variables. The hInstance is an identifier for the program that Windows uses when allocating time for a program to run. Think of it as an index number in an array. The hPrevInstance is an old variable used in Win16 to keep track of other instances of the program running concurrently. This variable is now always set to NULL. The next parameter—lpCmdLine—is important. This variable is a string to any parameters that will be passed to the program. For example, at the DOS prompt, you might enter "run.exe –l –m hello". The run.exe is the program and the parameters tell the program how you would like to initialize. This is great for determining default screen resolution, files to load, number of characters in the game, whether or not to run in windowed mode or full-screen, etc. The last variable passed is nCmdShow. It tells the program how to run—maximized, normal, hidden, etc. This variable is normally useless to a game program and to most other Windows programs in general; ignore it.

The MessageHandler is the way Windows handles IO. There are some good things about the way it works and some bad. It is encapsulated and easy to maintain. The switch statement probably isn't the fastest method of handling important messages, so we'll come up with a slightly better model later. Regardless of any other method you might devise, you have to live with the Microsoft model for now. The worst part is that we need to take these messages from the windows and store them in our own queue, which we'll discuss in a while. We need to store the messages and then process them when we see fit. This allows us to send them over a network, look for specific messages, or just keep things tidy while we do other things.

The code you see above is a minor variation on the code you will find in the book *Programming Windows 95* by Charles Petzold. This is the classic Windows programming book that all Windows programmers probably have and one that you should buy. Things that you will need, such as keystroke messages, are in this book, and it is a must for anybody wishing to learn Windows programming or refine his or her skills.

Advanced Windows by Jeffrey Richter is a good resource for multithreading and multi-tasking as well as a better explanation of the Windows kernel.

Note: Windows programming is not intuitive. Don't even think it. When learning Windows for the first time, forget about game programming and spend about two months trying to bring up a window, display text, handle various messages, draw bitmaps, etc. Once you understand that, Windows game programming may not be so bad. Otherwise, you will always be confused. Take it from me....

The middle section that handles the regular game loop is interesting. We check to see that the ActiveApp flag is set so we know that the game should be processing. Of course, we've already processed any messages beforehand. The "if—else if—else if" format ensures that in this loop, all Windows messages have priority over any other computer processing. This means that we're ready to control game flow and here we do.

There are three functions here that are not part of the Windows API: RedrawScreen, UpdateProc, and HandleEvents. These functions are to be declared later but they form the thrust of your future game engine. Most DirectX-based game engines use something similar to this. The program will not compile as it is; you will need to define these three functions. The program won't do much right now anyway, but you might want to try to compile it. Just define these functions as void RedrawScreen (void* struct){} and do the other two functions similarly before the WinMain in the listing and it should compile. You will also need to comment out the function calls in the MessageHandler. For now, let's not compile. We'll get to that later, after an overview and a little comprehension.

The RedrawScreen function is called first. For now we'll pass a NULL to it (and all other special functions), although eventually we'll pass a structure that will take care of everything. This function will have all of the necessary means to determine what is on the screen and what should be drawn. It will have pointers to all tiles, buildings, trees, creatures, mouse pointers, interface elements, explosions, dying creatures, and tanks. It will be able to tell each screen object to draw itself by passing a pointer to the screen for drawing in a function like Obj->Draw (ScreenStruct). We'll see this code much later.

UpdateProc has pointers to all objects in the world that can be changed and offers each an opportunity to update. UpdateProc is also aware of the time and will limit itself to no more than 8 milliseconds. This ensures that no matter how many objects are in the world, that frame rate never drops. It also has a pointer to where it leaves off so that the next time it is called it can continue. It will allow each creature to path across the world, gazelles to run away, buildings to create resources, trees to burn, peons to collect wood, new units to be built, etc. It may also update the information in the minimap. The update cycle is where the action happens in the game. If the computer is fast and the drawing time is acceptable, the update cycle time limit can be larger. The ideal is to make sure that the drawing cycle and the update cycle combined never take longer than 33 milliseconds to ensure 30 frames per second. We'll discuss strategies for achieving this. For now, keep 30 fps and 33 milliseconds in the back of your mind until we get there.

The HandleEvents function handles pulling items off of the message queue and processing them. In a network game, this also means interpreting what the other players' events mean. The queue will store all messages equally. This part of the processing is the fastest in the game loop and will take so little time as to be unmeasurable. It should take about 0.03 milliseconds on a P133 just for argument, but it really is not a large amount of time. An event can be a mouse click on a building to select that building, change the interface, and play a click sound. An event can also be pushing a key and recognizing that it is a hot key and jumping the screen location on the map back to base.

This is the primary part, the guts, of the game engine. Although we haven't looked at any code, you get to see the best way to handle it in Windows. The last section, WaitMessage, is a Windows API call that tells the application to suspend any action while the application is in the background. The ActiveApp flag controls whether this is called; it generally is not.

The ActiveApp flag is modified in the MessageHandler when the application receives a WM_ACTIVATEAPP message. This message happens when the application goes to the front of all other applications. It will be helpful when we begin debugging. You cannot debug in full screen mode, that is, not without crashing the computer. What the DirectDraw API does is lock out all other programs so that when you run the game, it will achieve maximum results. Unfortunately, this has the nasty effect of locking out the debugger and when a breakpoint is reached, the program locks; the computer is then 100 percent locked. Ctrl-Alt-Delete does nothing.

What Exactly is a Message Handler Anyway?

The MessageHandler is simple. Windows calls it when you call the function DispatchMessage, which makes Windows go through a series of tasks, eventually sending messages and parameters to the MessageHandler. In case you are wondering, most other reference books call this function WndProc. Charles Petzold also follows this convention. I think that you should call a horse a horse and a duck a duck. WndProc means absolutely nothing to me. MessageHandler is more descriptive, and you should always try to make your code as intuitive as possible. Use names that make your code readable so that when you come back to the code in three months, you can read the code, not have to interpret it. Interpretation takes way too long and borders on full-blown analysis. In a game with tight deadlines, you cannot afford to choose bad names for functions. Most Windows programmers apparently don't care about this—WndProc is a case in point.

Windows registers events. This means that when the user does something, Windows registers that and passes it along to your application. The MessageHandler is basically the way that you tell Windows what to do with each type of message it receives. The switch statement allows you to control code flow based on whatever the message passed to it is. In a game, unlike a regular Windows app, the program is not "event driven." Windows has this concept of being "event driven," which means that an application should be idle until the user does something. Then the app can respond to it. Games have to keep running whether or not the user does anything. Creatures still march, buildings still produce units, enemies still attack, so the "event-driven" concept is limited. The event-driven model is only a means to an end; it tells you when the player does something.

Windows sends a lot of different messages to your MessageHandler. Some of these are relatively meaningless to the average game programmer. Some of them tell you when the application is first starting, when the main window is being created, when the window is resized, when a CD is inserted, etc. All of the program initialization will happen right after the main program has successfully called CreateWindowEx (which we'll discuss in a while), so we don't care about the event for starting the application. The main window will never need to be created since we'll have a blank background for the game. Most of the Windows type events are not helpful and the ones that are, are listed in MessageHandler.

Several parameters are passed to MessageHandler. The first parameter is a handle to the main window. In the case of the MessageHandler, this will almost never be used in games. The second parameter is the message as defined by <winresrc.h>, which has all of the possible messages #defined. These will be evaluated in the switch statement. The next parameter is wParam, which is a naming convention I have chosen to follow since no other name seems obvious. It usually holds additional data like which key was pressed when responding to a WM_KEYDOWN message. The last parameter, Param, is not often used, but it still is used by other Windows messages. Notice how it is used by WM_LBUTTONDOWN and WM_RBUTTONDOWN. The mouse location at the time the left mouse button is pushed is stored as a single parameter where the high 16 bits are the *x* position of the mouse and the low 16 bits are the location of *y*.

The only important events for our game are WM_ACTIVATEAPP, WM_CREATE, WM_TIMER, WM_MOUSEMOVE, WM_LBUTTONDOWN, WM_RBUTTONDOWN, WM_KEYDOWN, and WM_DESTROY. They are relatively self-explanatory but we'll briefly discuss each one.

A WM_ACTIVATEAPP event is processed when your application is moved from front to back or vice versa. The value of wParam is TRUE or FALSE. TRUE means other applications are in the background. FALSE means your application is in the background. You'll see that we test for this in the main loop of WinMain.

WM_CREATE and WM_DESTROY are good points for initialization and cleanup if you choose to do it within the MessageHandler. WM_TIMER requires that you call a couple of API functions to set up a timer, but then this message is automatically triggered every so often. You determine the amount of time between events but it is limited to a minimum of something like 55 milliseconds, or about 18 times per second.

WM_MOUSEMOVE tells you the new position of the mouse, which usually serves no purpose other than to allow you to redraw the mouse pointer in a new position. Some games allow you to move the mouse pointer over a unit and display properties about the creature over which the mouse position has stopped. You would perform all of that functionality here. WM_KEYDOWN captures keyboard events. WM_LBUTTONDOWN and WM_RBUTTONDOWN tell you where the player has clicked the mouse. In a real-time strategy game, this may be your most important user event.

There are other ways to handle events. Rather than processing them directly, we can put them into a queue and store that data until later. Notice in the WinMain that we have a function called HandleEvents. This is reserved for just such an occasion. This leads us to the next important question—What is a queue and how is it used?

This is your queue...

You may be asking, "How will a queue help me?" For those old hands at programming, this is a ridiculous question. But many people don't often use them. A queue is probably the most important item in programming behind the "stack." What it allows us to do is save the messages temporarily until we decide we want to process them instead of doing it when Windows gives them to us. This helps a lot when doing networking, because the only packets we need to send on any given frame are those that give us player input. Everything else in a real-time strategy game is calculated; even the random numbers are predictable. So creature position, building state, creatures attacking, etc., are maintained by a series of algorithms that keeps network traffic to a minimum. This ensures that the game runs at a reasonable speed and the game on everyone's machine is kept in sync.

A *stack* is like a pile of plates. You put a plate on top of the pile and the only way to remove a plate (safely) is to remove it from the top. These are like plate stackers found at restaurants. They are spring loaded and hold about 80 plates. As you put plates on top, the stack is pushed down. This functionality is known as first in, last out, or FILO.

A *queue* is like a line at the bank. The first person in line gets served first. This is how we drive, how we pick up paychecks on Friday, and how air traffic works. This concept is called first in, first out, or FIFO. This is what we'll be doing with our messages, storing them in the order in which they come in.

First, let's define a structure and talk a little about it:

```
struct EVENT
{
        int   Event;
        int   Time;
        int   MouseX, MouseY;
        char Key;
        char Alt, Ctrl, Shift;
}
```

The Event variable is used to simply store the message passed to the MessageHandler. Time is used, later, to prioritize events based on when they occurred. The MouseX and MouseY variables are used to store the mouse position in cases where the mouse is used. The Key variable holds the value of the key in cases where the key is pressed. Alt holds the state of the Alt key, which is commonly used in games these days. Ctrl and Shift are the same. The state of these keys is retrieved by calling the Windows API function GetAsyncKeyState (), which takes a single parameter. Pass it either VK_SHIFT, VK_CONTROL, or VK_MENU. The VK_MENU item means the Alt key. You'll do this before you put the item in the queue, so you need to call this function three times.

The queue must have a mechanism for storing events and for removing them. I'll show you a dynamic model and eventually discuss the static model. Below you'll find the queue class, which will store the above structure. It should know nothing about windows or the actual messages. It simply stores the data and maintains it until retrieved. In the tradition of my forefathers, I will use the convention of "push" to put an item into the queue and "pop" to remove an item from the queue. This convention is as old as programming itself. You may use function names like "store" and "retrieve" or "get." Those names make more sense but they don't follow the long-established convention. You decide. One thing I'd like to point out—there are at least four recognized methods of implementing a queue. Below is a fairly simple one that I made from scratch. Bjarne Stroustrup has a simpler one in *The C++ Programming Language* (Addison Wesley). You might also glance through *Algorithms, Data Structures, and Problem Solving with C++* by Mark Allen Weiss (Addison Wesley). As for me, I like this implementation. There are dozens of different ways to manage this and we'll discuss another in Chapter 16.

```cpp
//***********************
//***********************

struct EVENT
{
        int    Event;
        int    Time;
        int    MouseX, MouseY;
        char   Key;
        char   Alt, Ctrl, Shift;

        EVENT*  next;                     // standard for a linked list

        EVENT () {Clear ();}              // standard constructor
        EVENT (int event, int time, int x, int y, int key, int alt, int ctrl,
             int shift)
        {
             Event = event, Time = time, MouseX = x, MouseY = y, Key = key,
             Alt = alt, Ctrl = ctrl, Shift = shift;

             next = NULL;
        }
        void Clear () {Event = Time = MouseX = MouseY = Key = Alt = Ctrl =
             Shift = 0; next = NULL;}
};

//***********************
//***********************

class EVENT_QUEUE                         // nothing should be deleted externally
{
private:                                  // being verbose
        EVENT* Back, * Front, * Temp;     // temp will be used for a return value

public:
```

```
            EVENT_QUEUE () {Back = NULL, Front = NULL, Temp = NULL;}
            ~EVENT_QUEUE ()
            {
                while (Front != NULL)
                {
                    pop ();                  // we don't need to save the value and
                                             // temp is automatically deleted as the
                                             // pointer is advanced
                }
                if (Temp) delete Temp;       // for the last item
            }
        void  push (int event, int time, int x, int y, int key, int alt, int
            ctrl, int shift);
        EVENT* pop ();
};


//***********************
//***********************
//***********************

void EVENT_QUEUE :: push (int event, int time, int x, int y, int key, int alt,
int ctrl, int shift)
{
        if (Front == NULL)              // 1st value stored
        {
            Front = new EVENT (event, time, x, y, key, alt, ctrl, shift);
            Front->next = NULL;
            Back = NULL;
        }
        else if (Front->next == NULL)   // 2nd val which is somewhat tricky
        {
            Back = new EVENT (event, time, x, y, key, alt, ctrl, shift);
            Back->next = NULL;
            Front->next  = Back;
        }
        else                            // normal
        {
            EVENT* QueueTemp = new EVENT (event, time, x, y, key, alt, ctrl,
                shift);
            QueueTemp->next = NULL;
            Back->next = QueueTemp;
            Back = QueueTemp;
        }
        if (Temp) delete Temp; Temp = NULL;
}


//***********************

EVENT*  EVENT_QUEUE :: pop (void)
{
            if (Front == NULL) {Back = NULL; return NULL;} // no items in
                                        // queue, this is an error code
```

```
    if (Front->next == NULL)        // only 1 item in queue
    {
        Temp = Front;
        Front = NULL;
        Back = NULL;
        return Temp;
    }
    if (Temp) delete Temp;          // from before
    Temp = Front;
    Front = Front->next;            // advance the pointer
    return Temp;
}
```

You can test it using the following code:

```
//***********************
EVENT_QUEUE Events;
EVENT* ptr = Events.pop ();
cout<<ptr<<" "<< endl;
ptr = Events.pop ();
cout<<ptr<<" "<< endl;

for (i=0; i<20; i++)
{
    int e = rand () %100;
    int t = rand () %100;
    int x = rand () %100;
    int y = rand () %100;
    int k = rand () %100;
    int a = rand () %100;
    int c = rand () %100;
    int s = rand () %100;
    Events.push (e, t, x, y, k, a, c, s);
    cout<<e<<" ";
}
cout<<endl;

while (1)
{
    ptr = Events.pop ();
    if (ptr == NULL) break;
    x =ptr->Event;
    cout<<x<<" ";
}
cout<<endl;
cout<<endl;                         // make sure that the text is all output
getch ();

//***********************
```

One thing that every queue must have is a Clear function. In fact, I include void Clear () in every class I make as a matter of course. It is very convenient. Say I have a linked list of items, and use Clear as in the following code:

```
EVENT_QUEUE :: EVENT_QUEUE () {Back = NULL, Front = NULL, Temp = NULL;}
EVENT_QUEUE :: ~EVENT_QUEUE () {Clear ();}
void EVENT_QUEUE :: Clear ()
{
      if (Back) delete Back; Back = NULL, Front = NULL, Temp = NULL;
}
```

Here, a few problems are solved. First, notice that we initialize all variables to NULL. Then the destructor calls Clear, which deletes the top of the queue, which in turn deletes the next item, and so on. By calling Clear on a linked list this way, the entire list is cleared with a single function call. Well… a single function call that you have to make anyway.

Networking is where we'll be looking eventually, at least the proper models for it. DirectPlay is not worth considering. Networking provides an 80-byte (or so) overhead on every packet passed, making networking a pain. DirectX 6 has reduced that to 24 bytes per packet, so there is something to be said for progress. Learn WinSock, which is basically like using fread when you have an open file. It might be a good alternative to the sometimes kludgy DirectPlay. The important point is to only pass messages onto the network that change the behavior of one or more units. We'll define all of this later, but it is something to keep in the back of your mind until we start talking about this advanced topic.

Now what we have is a perfect beginning model for a game engine. Don't sweat the small stuff; we're getting there. Just sit back and relax. We'll work out the Direct-Draw graphics in Chapter 9. Figure 3.7 shows our model so far. The entire right side will be finished later. But this chapter defined, for the most part, the left side.

I prefer the template class coming up. This QUEUE class is robust. It is short and clean and has a fixed memory size. This prevents memory fragmentation. The template is efficient and generally fast. I have improved its speed by creating a small bit array, which tells me which items are in use. I then use a string search to find an item in that "tag list" to find an item without a tag (a tag is simply a 1, not a 0). This can be faster. The following below is plenty fast though, and in random tests, it proves to be about eight times faster than the EVENT_QUEUE model (results may vary).

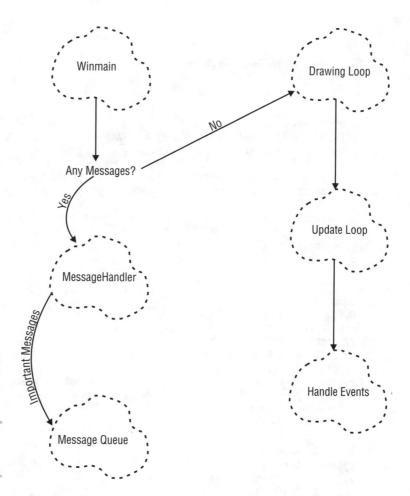

Figure 3.7
The graphics game model

```
// queue.h
#if _MSC_VER >= 1000
#pragma once
#endif                          // _MSC_VER >= 1000


#ifndef __QUEUE_H_
#define __QUEUE_H_

// queue.h
#include <string.h>

#define FC __fastcall

//*************************************************************
//*************************************************************
template <class type>
class QUEUE
```

```
        {
        public:
                enum    {MAXENTRIES = 128};

        protected:

                type* array;
                int   Max, Begin, End, SearchBegin, SearchEnd;
                int   OverWriteFlag;
                        // a flag to overwrite old data as new data is pushed onto the
                        // queue, otherwise new data does not go on the queue until old
                        // stuff is popped

                int   LastItemFlag;                    // used to make the last item useful

                void InitArray ();
                void CleanupArray ();

        public:
                QUEUE ();
                QUEUE (int num);
                ~QUEUE ();
                //***********************
                void FC  Push (type* obj);
                type* FC Pop ();
                type* FC Peek ();                  // look at the bottom item
                type* FC Push ();                  // get an item to use
                //***********************
                void FC  Clear ();
                //***********************
                type* FC  GetNext ();
                type* FC  GetFirst ();
                //***********************
                int   FC  Count ();
        };



        //*************************************************************
        //*************************************************************
        //*************************************************************
        //*************************************************************

        template <class type>
        QUEUE <type> :: QUEUE ()
        {
                Max = MAXENTRIES;
                InitArray ();
        }


        //**********************************

        template <class type>
```

```
QUEUE <type> :: QUEUE (int num)
{
     Max = num;
     InitArray ();
}


//**************************************

template <class type>
QUEUE <type> :: ~QUEUE ()
{
     CleanupArray ();
}


//****************************************************************
//****************************************************************

template <class type>
void  QUEUE <type> :: Push (type* obj)
{
     if (LastItemFlag == 1) return; // in case we've already used the last item
     if ((End+1 == Begin) || (End+1>=Max && Begin == 0))
               LastItemFlag = 1;                // do not overlap old data

     memcpy (&array[End], obj, sizeof (type)); // copy data
                                               // in case it changed so we
                                               // don't advance the index
     if (LastItemFlag == 1) return;

     End++; if (End>=Max) End = 0;             // the wrap around
}


//**************************************

template <class type>
type* QUEUE <type> :: Push ()                  // get an item to use
{
     if (LastItemFlag == 1) return NULL;       // in case we've already used
                                               // the last item
     if ((End+1 == Begin) || (End+1>=Max && Begin == 0))
               LastItemFlag = 1;               // do not overlap old data

     /*memcpy (&array[End], obj, sizeof (type)); // copy data*/

     // in case it changed so we don't advance the index
     if (LastItemFlag == 1) return &array[End];

     End++; if (End>=Max) End = 0;             // the wrap around
     return &array[End];
}


//**************************************
```

```
template <class type>
type* QUEUE <type> :: Pop ()
{
      if (Begin == End) return NULL;           // no data
      int temp = Begin;                        // store this value
      Begin++; if (Begin>=Max) Begin = 0;      // advance the pointer
      LastItemFlag = 0;                        // reset flag
      return &array[temp];                     // return the queue value
}


//***********************************

template <class type>
type* QUEUE <type> :: Peek ()                  // look at the top item
{
      if (Begin == End) return NULL;           // no top item
      return &array[Begin];                    // return the queue value
}


//*************************************************************
//*************************************************************

template <class type>
type* QUEUE <type> :: GetNext ()
{
      if (SearchBegin == SearchEnd) return NULL;       // no data
      int temp = SearchBegin;                          // store this value
      SearchBegin++; if (SearchBegin>=Max) Begin = 0;  // advance the pointer
      LastItemFlag = 0;                                // reset flag
      return &array[SearchBegin++];                    // return the queue value
}


//***********************************

template <class type>
type* QUEUE <type> :: GetFirst ()
{
      SearchBegin = Begin, SearchEnd = End;
      if (Begin == End) return NULL;           // no data
      return &array[SearchBegin++];            // return the queue value
}
//*************************************************************

template <class type>
void  QUEUE <type> :: Clear ()
{
      Begin = 0; End = 0; LastItemFlag = 0;
      memset (array, 0, sizeof (type)*Max);
}


//*************************************************************
```

```
template <class type>
void  QUEUE <type> :: InitArray ()
{
      array = new type[Max];
      Clear ();
}


//************************************

template <class type>
void  QUEUE <type> :: CleanupArray ()
{
      delete array;
}


//************************************
template <class type>
int  QUEUE <type> :: Count ()
{
      int count = 0;
      if (Begin > End)
      {
            count += Max-Begin;
            count += End;
      }
      else
      {
            count += End-Begin;
      }
      return count;
}
//*************************************************************
#undef FC

#endif
```

One concern many programmers have about templates is "code bloat." A template creates or duplicates the same code for every "type" that uses it. It really doesn't make that much difference, and these days Visual C++ can optimize well enough where code bloat is kept to a minimum.

Clearly, initializing the variable each time becomes necessary and storing variables in the EVENT structure is a matter of manually passing values rather than the "push" method we used before. There are tradeoffs, but overall, a well-oiled machine like the template above is worth it.

Good luck, and I'll see you in Chapter 4.

Chapter 4

Documents

In preparing your game for approval, there is the requirement of producing a document that states how your game project will proceed. It includes your projection, estimates, costs, level of difficulty, and so on. Be thorough here. This is where you will be judged about your game before it is even written.

The Design Doc

The design document describes the game. It tells what the game is about and discusses creatures, interfaces, vehicles, weapons, landscape, networking, and the general mood of the game. Most importantly, it describes the gameplay, such as how the game works, what a player can expect, how many players can play at a time, how technology in the game affects gameplay. This really isn't your job as a programmer to do. But you should at least know what to expect from the designer and what to demand.

First of all, this is a document. Ideas are just ideas and unless you can express them in a document, you can rarely sell the idea to anyone. It must be fairly long; I've seen some documents 10 pages and I've seen some 450 pages (Tom Hall). It must be written down and it must make sense. Let's assume that the designer has gotten past the idea phase.

All design docs need a story, even if it's only a two-paragraph story of ten sentences. Anything less shows a lack of forethought and the tendency of the designer to be lazy and cut corners. Most designers will give you 20 pages of story. Be sure to read the story because it sets a mood, a theme. A lot of designers will write a great story, and then make a game that isn't related in any way.

Don't let the designer hand you a half-cocked design doc and then ask you to get started on the product. Often (most of the time), the game design will change so significantly that all of the initial code you write will need to be rewritten. When I was working on Doppelganger, I was handed an idea/design doc for a real-time tactical game. Mike Maynard coded a great tile engine and I began the code for the AI. Within a month and a half, we had it all working, in a rudimentary sort of way. We suggested to our designer that we use 3-D landscape, which we got working in a week or so. He didn't want to use 3-D. I think this is also when our designer insisted that 3-D in software runs just as fast as with a 3-D accelerator because he had seen Quake running in software and in hardware, and they ran the same frame rate.

What the designer failed to note was that hardware was running in 1024x768 but software was running in 512x480. Basically, we couldn't convince him otherwise and he walked all over us. It didn't matter—he didn't want 3-D landscape. In fact he wanted a bigger change. Our designer changed the game to include a Voxel engine from Animatek for all of the creatures in the game. The engine was great and it made fantastic-looking creatures that could rotate in any direction, but it was slow. We couldn't put more than five or six creatures on the screen at a time. That doesn't work well for RTT games, which often need 40 to 60 creatures on the screen at a time, so we were no longer doing an RTT game. The idea/design doc changed to an adventure game.

We threw out everything and started over. Then the designer wanted different landscape, then tried to throw that out (Mike wouldn't let him), and made huge changes in design. I was doing tools, AI, pathing, interface, color mapping (it started in 8-bit graphics, went to 16-bit, then the designer wanted to support both 8- and 16-bit), and drawing routine, and I ended up recoding the entire section of code four times in nine months. We had an alpha complete with nine levels (I think) after nine months but I had worked 12 to16 hours a day for the entire nine months. And still there were more design doc changes.

The problem was the design doc, partially. The doc contained 60 pages of creatures, 10 pages of weapons, 16 pages of interface stuff, and about two pages of actual gameplay and engine discussion. If we'd had more talk about engine or gameplay, I think that would have locked the designer down and prevented all of the extra work that Mike Maynard and I did.

Anyone can be a victim of this. If the designer is allowed free rein, he will make huge changes in the interest of the game. He wants to make the game better, and rightfully so. He wants to improve sales and make a cool game with his name on it. Who doesn't? But there has to be a bit of control as to the changes. Every team has an engine architect, someone who oversees the production of the game, and he has to decide what is easy to add to or change about a game. He also needs to ensure that the designer doesn't get too far off of the design doc.

A design doc is not a restraint for the designer but rather a strong guide. He should stick to the design, mostly because the programmers and artists are making the game to fit that vision. The only way a designer should significantly change a design is to hold meetings with the staff and find out what is doable within the time frame and what isn't.

Below is an example of what the design doc should contain:

➤ Minimum Hardware Requirements: Pentium 300, NVidia Riva video card, 128 MB, joystick, etc.

➤ Game Genre: Real-time tactical (or shoot 'em up)

➤ Similar Games in Genre: Age of Empires, Dark Reign, Quake

➤ Number of Players: 4, 8, 12, 16 (groups of 4 is good)

➤ Purpose of Game: Conquer the world by balancing resource gathering and crushing all enemies with huge armies.

➤ Brief Summary: In 2304, genetically engineered humans, who have begun killing off humans because of their inferiority (sort of a reverse racism), have dominated the world. You get to act as commander of either the humans or the genetically enhanced humans as they wage war for conquest of the world. New weapons and tanks are available to you as you research technology. This will be a bloody battle for the earth.

➤ Look: Post-industrial era/beginning of an apocalyptic era. Lots of burned buildings and newer-looking technology.

➤ Feel: A lot of outdoor gameplay, but creatures can go indoors like in XCOM.

➤ Sound: A soundtrack like in *Starship Troopers*; heavy-sounding explosions and very high-tech sounding.

➤ Engine Type: Typical real-time tactical game, minimap, assigning waypoints to units, slick interface. Different interface for humans and genetically engineered humans. Land types include grass, forest, hilly, and rocky. The land can be only one of these types for any given level. Resources are infinite, but characters must find the rocks and energy sources that provide this infinite resource. Very much mouse-driven with hot keys. 40 different units per side, 12 different buildings per side. Some of the genetically engineered humans do not move like humans.

➤ Landscape and Background: Rectangular isometric tiled landscape with earth-like features, trees, rivers, etc. A few new creatures genetically enhanced from previous generations.

➤ Graphics: 16-bit pre-rendered animated sprites.

➤ Estimated Number of Staff: 3 programmers, 6 artists, 1 designer, 1 producer, support staff.

➤ Staff Hardware Requirements: 11 PCs with 128 MB of RAM, 6 Watcom tablets, 11 monitors.

➤ Staff Software Requirements: 3 copies of 3D Studio, 3 copies of Alias, 3 copies of Borland Builder, 3 copies of Microsoft Visual C++, 3 copies of Watcom compiler, 1 copy of MS Project.

➤ Schedule: 19 months.

➤ Estimated Cost: $1,200,000.

➤ Estimated Sales: 200,000 units.

➤ Game Description: This is where the full description of the game goes, perhaps 8 to 10 pages.

The part you need to pay most attention to is the engine type. This gives you (ideally) a lot of information on how a programmer should proceed. You should have enough details to get the idea of scope, how much you'll need to do in order to finish.

Another issue is quality. A designer always wants the best quality. But as any good project manager will know, the only three things affecting the cost of a project are quality, scope, and time. If the project emphasis is on quality, then the scope will change and so will the time, usually with increases. If the emphasis is on scope (limiting the scope to include everything in the design doc), then time will slip and quality may as well. And, of course, if time is your priority (completing within the scheduled time), then scope will be affected—you'll have to cut out items, and the quality may suffer—and you may not be able to spend enough time game balancing.

When games have no limits on these three factors, the cost runs out of control and the game rarely ships. Games do best when the emphasis is on quality. Every major best seller, in any game genre, has not had to worry about time limits or scope limits. The only worry is quality. Since money is always a big issue, and since the longer you take the more it will cost, very few people get the luxury of emphasizing quality. Still, you should consider it.

The designer should inform you, in the design doc or in a meeting where everyone can hear, what emphasis the game is taking. Be sure to explain the ramifications to him. Most designers, the guys who are supposed to write the schedule, rarely understand the balance of scope, quality, and time in designing a schedule. You will probably have to explain it to your designer and give him a day or two to think about it.

The Technical Design Doc

The technical design doc is your responsibility. If you understand the scope, schedule, and your resources, you are ready to start preparing technical design docs. Do not even think about doing this document until you understand all three. The scope defines approximately how much you, as a programmer, will have to do. The schedule tells you, in no uncertain terms, when you are to be done and how flexible that time is. Your resources define the hardware and the people you'll have for the project. Once you have all of this information, you can make a rough estimate as to whether or not you'll be on time.

I hate writing technical design docs; if you have half a brain, you will too. Basically, management wants to see how you schedule your time for completing the entire project. They want to be sure that you know how to carry a project from drawing board to completion. Also, this document can help any new programmers you hire understand the rough format of how the program will work.

The tech doc contains a breakdown of the project, schedule information, a timeline, areas of research, possible delays, extra resources needed, technologies to explore, time-saving ideas, possible areas to cut, and program diagrams. I won't give you too many examples, but I will explain all of these.

The project breakdown divides the project into dozens of small projects. Each of these small projects is assigned to someone based on his or her skill and desire. An approximate time is assigned to each small project of something like 1 week, 2 weeks, 3 days, and the like. No small project should ever be so small as to take less than a day. Also, a project breakdown should never have more than a hundred or so items. Most should have fewer then 40.

The schedule tells you when the last small item in the project breakdown will be done. This doesn't include the debugging schedule or the game balancing. It also defines milestones, which help provide structure to the development of the game.

The timeline defines the dates when you will have the basic engine working, when you will have the level editor done, when alpha will ship, when beta will ship, when game balancing will end, when final debug will be done, and when shipping will begin. The timeline defines specific milestones, always big ones, for measuring the progress of the game schedule.

It is not always easy to gauge what you don't know, and that is why you need areas of research. This defines things that you aren't completely sure about. Say you have to do a 3-D landscape, and you have done a Doom-like game before. Well, you've done 3-D but not landscape, and a BSP tree probably won't work well for a large number of polygons in open terrain. You need to find a better method of presorting the polygons. This is the time to wave the areas-of-research card. This card buys you a little more time to think of a good way to do a task.

When you don't have the latest video cards and they are on back order or you need the latest Quake library to handle animation coming from Lightwave, you run into possible delays. Possible delays usually refers to something beyond your control like waiting for the latest installment of DirectX or something else. Other possibilities include: drivers, libraries, new video cards for testing, waiting for more programmers to join the team, the company is changing offices in three months, etc.

Do you have all of the people you need? Do you have all of the programming books and software that you need? Extra resources needed just tells the management what you need to complete your job. Make sure that you distinguish items you need from items you'd like or you want. You might just want to make out a wish list and hand it to the management separately.

Technologies to explore offers alternatives and different ideas. You've already suggested how the company should proceed, but what about that engine that you could license? What about 2-D landscape instead of 3-D landscape? What if you were to support 3-D sound? You think that it would be cool to offer 12 players in the multi-player game instead of just 8. This is a wish list for the programmers as to things that might make the game more interesting or fun.

If you pour your time into a different technology, you might be able to reduce development time. This falls under the umbrella of "time-saving ideas." You can offer dozens of time-saving ideas including using different methods to accomplish the same goals, hiring more programmers, having a line manager help with code design, buying some sections of code rather than reinventing the wheel, trying to reuse old code, and so on. Managers appreciate these and it shows that you've got a good head on those shoulders of yours. Plus, if you can save time, you can spend more time tweaking and perfecting your game for increased sales, which management loves.

When looking at the design, you will have to identify possible areas to cut. These are areas that are slow to develop, may not do very much for gameplay, and really add questionable value to the game as a whole. Every game design has a few of these and some game design docs have nothing but these. Outline these as areas you are likely to program last and that you may not do because the game gets so little "bang for the buck."

Program diagrams are the Booch diagrams of the world. They are rough diagrams showing the overall structure of the program and some of the communication

4

Chapter

between the various parts. These are very helpful to the programmers and newbies who come along in the middle of the project. They also help you program your specific area and help you stick to the design. Believe me, it is way too easy to start programming for everything at once rather than concentrating on a single module or two.

A technical design doc also can produce ideas on technologies. If you have devised cool methodologies or a great way of managing the data in the game, something unique, then that should go into the design doc as "technologies." There is usually time associated with new technologies and a risk factor that says, "How likely is this to work and how hard is it to program?" You'll also want to weigh benefits and detriments on any new technologies.

The technical design doc isn't too bad, although it does ask you to make estimates about things with a lot of unknowns. Most designers and developers think of it as a commitment to how tasks will ultimately be done, so be careful about what you say. The interesting thing about that is a designer rarely assumes that his design doc is set in stone, but everyone assumes that the technical design doc is. Just remember that when the designer changes the design doc, you'll need to remind him that the technical design doc no longer applies.

The technical design doc should take two to three days, and it'll be rather tedious. Never write it without consulting the other programmers. When they tell you how their schedules will work, make them write a technical design doc that describes their schedules in detail. Let them skip the rest; you just want a rough commitment from them about completing tasks on time. This is called covering your own ass.

When you submit this document, make sure you say that it does not include time for testing or game balancing, only writing code, and make sure that you write that into the document in several places. Often, managers think that the done date means fully debugged, which it doesn't.

Chapter 5

Development

The following list is not all-inclusive, but this foundation is enough to make almost any development group moderately successful. To be a successful game programmer, the following words of advice can be valuable. These are not just good rules of thumb, but good ways of managing time and resources. Although your success as a programmer will depend more on you understanding how *you* work best than by following my list, if you don't already have these habits, maybe you should try to pick up a few of them. The more of these you can perform, the more successfully you'll fit into any development team.

➤ Plan on long hours. Programmers typically work the longest hours of anybody else in the game development world, except maybe designers who take their job seriously. Since some designers do not take their job very seriously, programmers generally work far longer hours than anyone else. Normal hours are nine-hour days in the beginning. Crunch time brings about the dreaded 72-hour day. Get used to it. It can be rewarding.

➤ Program in spurts. The very best programmers leave programming to intense bursts. They wander around the office for 20 minutes and then program intensely for three hours. These breaks allow for creative cognition and better design decisions to coalesce. Getting up from your desk just to shoot the breeze, on occasion, is a great stress reliever and helps clear the mind. Not only that, it gives you a chance to talk to your coworkers about ideas or problems that you are working on. You will produce better code; I guarantee it. But watch out for programmers who spend too much time on breaks, especially if they are not in design.

➤ Never leave work in the middle of debugging or in the middle of a code section. Once you get "on a roll," as we call it, stay on that roll until you finish. At the end of it, you'll feel like you've accomplished more than in the previous three days combined. If you break up the rhythm of a roll, it is almost impossible to pick up where you left off.

➤ Take notes. Make a list of your goals—a to do list—every morning. This will help you focus. Make the list short and easy. Once you finish it, work on something you'd like to be working on. This way, you complete sections of the grunt or non-fun code every morning, and you reward yourself by doing the more interesting stuff in the afternoons. This is a productivity tool and will decrease the time it takes for you to complete your game.

➤ Make an evening list. Every night before you leave work, make a list of where you left off, which files were being edited, which bug you were working on, and any other tasks left hanging. If you were working on fun stuff, schedule that for the next afternoon. If it is boring grunt stuff, do it first thing in the morning when you have the willpower to tackle it.

➤ Write down variable values while debugging. Not every value, just a few for a baseline and then the exceptions. This will decrease debugging time.

➤ Read, read, read. There are so many good books on coding styles, beginning C++, algorithms, and object-oriented design that you could read for the rest of your life and not read them all (ignoring the fact that more are being written all the time).

➤ Get a source control program, even if you are the only programmer. It backs up all of your files, so that if you change a file and something breaks, you can grab the earlier version. Visual Source Safe, which comes with Visual C++, is just fine.

➤ Spend time designing your code; try to figure out and fully understand your coding style. This will make it easier for you to decipher later and for others to work with you, since you can explain why you do a particular thing.

➤ The design phase will always be ongoing, but a lot can be done up front. Every (product) hour spent in initial code design can save you 200 hours on the back end (statistically). A number of studies have shown that good early design will save a lot of development hours. The numbers actually vary a lot from study to study. Some say you will save about 60 and some go as high as 200. Spend the time to fully flesh out how data will be shared and accessed, and how you will store graphics, sound, and characteristics in the data file and in memory.

➤ Books about code design will help you, even if they are bad books. They cause you to think seriously about your own coding style and design and break down any mental blocks that you may have developed over the years.

➤ Break your code down into small chunks. These code particles will be the most reusable parts of your code. For example, I am creating a class that loads BMPs, formats the data into 16-bit graphics, and displays it on the screen. Well, I need a screen object class for things that will be on the screen. I can inherit this graphic class from it. I need an encapsulation of file loading to simplify loading and I can have multiple inheritance from that. I am creating common functionality and encapsulating it. Spending time doing this will double the amount of code that you will be able to reuse.

➤ Do not ignore compiler warnings; they tell you something important. You should try to get zero compiler warnings with the compiler warnings set to the highest level. The most common warning is a cast situation where you are using one structure like another or an int from a float. Just cast the one type into the other.

> There is nothing new under the sun. This is from the Bible, but in the world of programming, nothing could be truer. We always like to pat ourselves on the back when we develop a new algorithm for drawing a gouraud shaded polygon, only to find out that it has been done that way for 45 years. You are very unlikely to develop anything that hasn't been done before, but if you do, make it public domain and add to the pool of knowledge that we all use. (By the way, gouraud shading is a method of drawing a polygon that blends different colors across the face of the poly.)

The Cycle

The cycle is a long one. Most games these days take 12 to 18 months. Some can use existing technology to create a game in as little as four months, but that is less than one game in a thousand. Some games, like Final Fantasy VII, take 3½ years, about 100 people doing various things (mostly PR and sales type stuff in this case), and an enormous budget. You probably don't have that much time or patience, let alone that kind of budget.

Still, 16 to18 months is more standard. Real-time strategy takes a bit longer. The AI alone can take well over a year. The graphics engine can take six months and then a year of tweaking. The tile engine can take a long time too. Then there's the question of art. You are likely to try at least three types of art delivery during the course of your game. There is also the cinematic.

The development cycle is mostly tumultuous. Give up on complete predictability now. Even the best plans run into simple problems:

> The art staff thought you wanted everything palettized and so did all of the art in a 256-color optimized palette. They now need to completely re-render everything in 16-bit color. Is that true 16-bit or 15-bit?

> The network was never meant to handle anything more than file serving and now needs to be replaced as you begin your programming for a network game. Oh no, the server has lost all of its data during the upgrade...

> A new game on the store shelves looks exactly like yours but a little slicker. What can you do to compete? What can you add to your game three months before it's supposed to ship? The publisher is on the phone about that new game...

> The lead programmer just quit...

> The lead designer decides that you need to add a new race of beings to the game. Is the engine able to handle more or is everything hard-coded?

> Your investor (probably a publisher) is low on money and cannot afford to provide funding for the next four months.

Good luck planning for these. The best that you can hope for is that your company is stable and the people like it enough to want to stay through the end of the project.

5

Chapter

There are a few definable stages through which a project will go. The clock usually doesn't begin until the word go. So there is a little time period in which you are waiting for funds, approval, design docs, and so on. This is the worst stage because no one knows what will happen and any work you do today may be trashed tomorrow. Still, people have to give you the go-ahead, and it doesn't help to own your own company. Most game company owners rely heavily on advance royalties to fund them through the end of the project. That means that the current project they are doing has to be approved by committee, which can take as much time as a glacial flow.

Once the project is approved, then your publisher/boss will expect to see immediate success, including demos and screen shots of a game that is barely started. How you are supposed to manage this is anybody's guess, but there will be press releases and parties. You will work at an even more maddening pace up until crunch time, when you can expect to work 72-hour days. I am not joking. Crunch time will not be the most pleasant time for you and you will spend more time smelling bad than good. Then comes the release, the end, the elation.

Here are the steps:

1. Idea comes to mind.

2. Write it down and create a design document.

3. Pass the design doc around and have everyone edit it, find mistakes, add new ideas, and give it back.

4. Finalize design and submit it. Try to include code, drawings, concept art, a demo, etc.

5. Wait, twiddle thumbs, write some code, practice your golf swing, etc.

6. Design doc comes back for revision; go to step 2.

7. Once the design is approved, you'll need to do a budget. You may have done it before you got to this step, but it definitely needs to be done now. Submit everything in one package. You'll need a list of people on your team, and maybe short biographies of everyone on the team. This helps the management know who you are.

8. Wait until you get final approval or it's rejected. If it's rejected, go to step 1.

9. Now you have funding and you can proceed. Draw up code design and start planning a schedule. Figure out each person's responsibilities and make deadlines for specific tasks to keep the project on schedule.

10. Hold design meetings at least once a month and when otherwise needed. This keeps everyone thinking and on track. Even if you think that everyone is on the same page, you will be surprised at how differently everyone else is thinking about the same issues that you've already found a solution to.

11. Plan out your code far ahead and accept the fact that the design may change the way you need to do everything. Plan for change and make everything you can extensible. This will save you hundreds of hours in the long run but cost a little more in the short run.

12. You are working toward alpha. This is basically a playable demo. All of the basics are in place, but maybe only one race exists, the AI is really dumb, the interface

elements are black blocks with writing on them, and there is no sound. Alpha is completely arbitrary, so you can determine what it is. It should at least show all of the basics of the final game.

13. Concentrate on framework, not details. This is probably the hardest task. I always want to do things right the first time, but alpha is usually a more important goal since continued funding usually rests on whether or not you get alpha to your funding group. Build a rough framework that is stable and fill in the details as art becomes available. This allows you to keep working without waiting on art. Build the entire game in such a way that if the art for a particular aspect does not exist, text is in its place or maybe even programmer art. This is a great way to demo a product when the artists are behind (which happens fairly frequently).

14. Once you start approaching alpha deadline, hopefully the game works and is fairly stable. Now save your work. Back it up because the next month will be dedicated to mucking it up. You will be creating one hack after another and you will have long hours. It is a rewarding time and in the unlikely chance that you make the deadline, you will be quite proud of yourself. This is a time to plan ahead. Alpha will need to be delivered to somebody. Plan out how you will ship it to this person. Will a readme file accompany the demo or will you simply have an executable? How will the art be delivered? Will you put it on a CD or is all of it small enough to fit on a floppy? What about compression? You need to plan on delivery.

15. What is necessary and what can be eliminated from the alpha? This applies throughout development, but in the alpha release, this is more obvious. Eliminate small items and focus on the important aspects of the game. Focus on what people will see. Forget what you promised; if the show and fanfare are good, they will forgive the rest. What your funding group wants to see is firm progress. Two weeks before alpha is a good time to update them. Call them and tell them where you cut stuff out of the design and what you will actually be delivering. Ask if they have any special requests. This simple call will be enough to prepare them for what to expect. They usually don't know what to expect even though you agreed to it eight months earlier. They have typically forgotten.

16. One week before, lock the art. Unless the game is still waiting on critical art, lock down the art with no more changes. Tell the artists to save to their local drives and to not disturb the network.

Code Design

Your first draft of the whole game, once you get an initial game design, should be based on as much information as possible. Ask for details in the design. The designer won't want to give them but keep asking anyway. All details you understand up front will probably save you many hours in fixing code that could have been designed better had you known in the first place.

Now that you have the design in hand, look at what the game is. Now you need to imagine that you are the designer. What features will he probably add? This helps if you have worked with a certain designer for a period of time, but you can still make some assumptions. Add these predictions to the things you are programming for. Now look at other games in your genre and start making comparisons. What do they have that you don't and which of those things do you think needs to be added to your game? Add those to your design specs and begin planning your schedule. This process should take two to five days, so don't skimp. You can be doing other things while you think about it, but you should give yourself at least a few days before you begin the code design.

It will become immediately apparent which basics will need to be done for the game. First, commit to memory all of the major points of the game design and then just let it sit in your brain. Your entire programming staff should be doing the same. Once you are ready, begin doing other tasks like programming a file management class or a new interface class. Read a good book on graphics programming or maybe something on DirectX. While you are doing these other tasks, thoughts will come to you about the design of the code. Write them down. In a few days, get together with your programming colleagues and start outlining your game plan.

Before you start the meeting, check with the designer and pick up the latest game changes. There will be some, even though only a few days have passed. Examine the changes and see how they impact the game. Now you are ready.

Preparing for a large design is never an easy task. Breaking a task, a huge one really, into smaller components that somehow interact is one of the biggest challenges in software development. There are entire college courses dedicated to software design because this can be such a major undertaking.

Break apart the game design into little pieces. This is a long process. The best way to do it is to identify major parts and then break those apart. Graphics, sound, networking, tile engine, unit AI, pathing, interface, unit definition, level development, tool development, graphics management, database management, file management, computer decision making, computer opponent AI, etc.: These are all major areas, which almost all computer games have. Now who does these? You'll have to assign these tasks. Once people choose what they're willing to do, you are able to break these tasks into subtasks and plan delivery better.

Of course, some areas are bigger than others. Make sure that everyone has his share of tasks. The time each of these tasks takes will depend on the talent of the programmer and the size of the task, but divide these tasks up as evenly as possible to save on development time. Time is everything, and also remember that every programmer will underestimate the time it takes for him to finish a task.

Design meetings are the hardest. Picking apart the overall design can be time consuming and then deciding who gets which task is arbitrary. All things considered, just getting through these meetings with a true consensus is hard. There are conflicts of ideas, schedules, methodologies, and so on. And then there are the unknowns: How long will it really take to perfect the graphics engine? How do creatures in the game access the tiles on the map? How do we keep the game in sync over the network?

Design methodologies are in abundance. Use whatever makes you comfortable. When designing modules or code in general, keep a few things in mind. How do the sections of code communicate with each other? Which module owns which data? When is it helpful to create a parent class and then use polymorphism to your advantage? How do you reduce the amount of code you have to write? How do you make your code more reusable?

Those questions are the primary keys to any design methodology. Don't focus too much on details, just outline the framework. The details will come as the design is fleshed out and as the game is completed.

Reusability is a beautiful thing. Unfortunately, most game designers do not plan for it. If you don't plan for it, it'll never happen and you will end up rewriting every game from scratch. Bummer. It is a lot better to pull out common areas that you will plan to use for any type of game and declare these as areas for reusability. Then there is the area for RTS/RTT games. You'll want to identify these areas and separate them as well for future RTS/RTT games. We'll talk about this a bit more later.

Good structure is hard to come by. It is easy to design a class, but making it interact well with other classes in your game can be hard. Stick to simple designs. Encapsulation is your friend, so spend the time necessary to plan which classes will end up with which data and how they will share it with other classes.

Less code is more. You will want to try to reuse as much code as possible during the development of your game. Set up and plan for hierarchies of classes, particularly in the AI portions of the code. There is a lot of code in AI that can be reused. A dragon should have the same basic characteristics as a human, a space ship should have the same hull characteristics as a cargo ship, and a sheriff should have the same type of definitions as an outlaw. All of this comes with good design and productive design meetings. Plan for success.

Engine Design

Defining an engine is difficult but here goes: An *engine* is the core code that can be used to make a similar game in less time. The key components to an engine are the concept of a core code module, reusability of that code with minor changes in a new game, and easily replaced assets. Assets are the parts of the game that are non-code based—art, sounds, creatures, buildings, weapons, etc.

Unfortunately, most games end up not being engine based. A lot of assumptions are made in the development of a game and a lot of things are hard-coded into the game. These things make the engine less reusable. The more general you can make the code, and the more you rely on tools, databases, and scripts to define general game behavior, the better your engine will be.

Engines should be able to read in a creature definition from some sort of file, and know how to set the creature's characteristics and behavior, and make it perform logically in the context of the game. This is called a data-driven engine. This is not easy to do, but it is a requirement to make a true engine.

Why put something into an engine and not just into code? Well, generally, code is designed for a specific purpose and most code is not generalized enough to work in all contexts. Once code is designed to operate in a specific way, getting it to operate in different ways is often difficult, tedious, and rarely successful. Most programmers would rather start all over and only copy code from an old game if they think it's necessary.

This problem can cost a lot of money. By designing your game as an engine, you can plan on expansion, and hence more income. If you plan to do several versions and upgrades and expansion packs and level packs and secret levels and post new races and creatures on your Web site, you had better plan on making a general engine that is expandable by introducing new files of monsters, levels, and such. Many games these days make as much money with the expansion packs as with the game. There are two reasons for this. First, the engine already works so programmers will be working on other things and they do not affect the cost. Secondly, expansion packs generally take about one-third to one-eighth the development time as a full game, so costs are reduced significantly.

The biggest problem is cost. For a good engine, you can expect to spend 25 to 33 percent longer developing it. However, it should cut 33 to 60 percent off the development time for the next version. So you need to be sure you will use the engine and that you will have another game before you plan for it. The second biggest problem is finding talent. Most beginning and inexperienced programmers do not understand the concept of an engine or how to design and code it. Experience and talent are the two biggest problems facing the game development industry, so good luck with this one.

Reusability

Reusability comes in all shapes and sizes. There is code reusability, engine reusability, asset reusability, function reusability, and design reusability. Code reusability means designing code so that a class or .cpp file can be used in multiple projects and at almost any time, for anything. Engine reusability allows you to design the code for a game, and then reuse almost all of that code, with few changes, for a new game or a new version of the same game. Asset reusability is rare but means reusing art or graphics from one game to the next or in multiple situations. Function reusability is the most basic form of reusability and basically means having a few functions that can be used in many situations, kind of like a library of functions. Reusing a program design is rarely possible, but if it can be reused, most of the code, functions, and engine will also be reusable. A good example of this is the Quake engine that has been licensed to dozens of different game companies. Reusability usually means the code structure can be reused.

How reusable is most code? Most general code is reusable. Most code for tile definitions, creatures, interfaces, and so on is not reusable unless designed specifically for that purpose. How do you design for reusability? You don't and you do. Following a few specific rules makes the code reusable, but planning for reuse is like trying to read the future.

➤ Plan to make classes. Classes, by their very nature, are more reusable than the specific code required in C to work on different structures. Avoid the generic lure of a C-like structure that seems so helpful. Classes keep all variables, loading, saving, behavior, graphics, and functionality together in one file, making this the logical choice to help with reusability.

➤ Make the classes robust. Add all of the access routines that you may need, and all of the possible interface elements to the class. This makes the class robust, making it easy to work with and hence more likely to be reused.

➤ Plan on using inheritance. A parent class, designed well, can make using all of its children very easy to use, and therefore makes a programmer more willing to reuse the code.

➤ Think encapsulation. Keep everything together—data, functions, and definitions—and everyone will want to reuse the code.

➤ Make the directory structure easy to read. Make the filenames logical and arrange the files into logical folders.

Now you'll have reusable code.

Which Tools to Use

Everyone has a preference or an idea about which programming and development tools are best. If you can get the tools you like, and management agrees to get those tools, get them. Management decisions will often interfere with your preferences, however. They have ideas about which tools are best and you are often stuck with that decision. And if that isn't bad enough, cost may play an important factor. Actually, programming tools are often cheap when compared to the cost of art tools, hardware, software, and labor. But many managers say things like, "We can't afford that $300 development tool. You'll just have to develop your level editor using MFC and spend the extra three weeks that it'll take." I wonder how much that costs in labor.

The best development tools are the way to go. Microsoft's Visual C++ is the best for debugging since it is easy to use and integrated into the IDE. Watcom has a good debugger too. Once you have your code in good shape, Watcom has the best compiler and it produces the most solid code overall. Best to compile the final release in Watcom. For Windows development like tools and graphics management tools, use Borland Builder. It is C++ with the best programming for Windows that I have seen. Most things you can do in MFC can be done better, faster, and more reliably in Builder, and for about $300 you'll save a lot of development time. The debugger, however, could use a little work.

Hardware Considerations

Take the cheap-o model computer on the day you start development. Consider this your base machine. Today, if you start developing a game, make your minimum machine a P450 because a year and a half from now, the standard machine will be a P800 or something. Other hardware considerations don't matter too much. A 3-D card won't help you much unless you are planning your game to be a Direct3D RTS/RTT game. If that is the case, go with a current model, maybe a Riva or Glide-based card. It is hard to predict the future of 3-D cards since Intel will start making them and a bunch of others are trying to squash the competition. Memory on the computer should be 64 MB or more. Anything less is just plain silly. The future of PCs seems to be 128 in the next year or so, but by 2000, most PCs will probably ship with 192 or 256 MB.

Designing a Schedule for Your Code

No great answers to this issue. Scheduling is a matter of choice and preference. But you should plan for milestones. These are specific dates when a certain amount of the game should be working. Every game should have enough of a schedule to be able to make milestones for the following:

➤ Initial design completed
➤ Graphics engine implemented
➤ Networking basics completed
➤ Interface completed
➤ Level editing and loading ready
➤ Basic game structure completed
➤ Alpha and testing
➤ AI finished
➤ Full game completed
➤ Beta and testing
➤ Load sequence
➤ Install program
➤ Internationalization
➤ Shipping and delivery

Outline the flow of things, what needs to be developed first to complete each of the stages listed. The schedule should be worked on by the programming staff in bits and pieces. You should also remember that this is a research and development group and that the research can often take a great deal of time.

Avoid scheduling just to schedule. A lot of people just like to write a schedule or plan a Gantt chart. Forget it. Write the schedule as a guideline, not as something to be written in stone. As such, you should write it to be helpful. It is supposed to give everyone an idea of what comes next.

Expectations

Everyone wants more from a programmer than from anyone else. That's why they pay you more. They expect expert opinions, so stay informed, although most game companies ignore expert opinions offered by programmers. They expect the game completed on time, which rarely happens, but they expect it nonetheless. They expect long hours from their programmers, and they expect their programmers to accept offerings of pizza. Expectations are high, but programmers are usually treated better than most others, so you won't mind all of the expectations.

Competition and Sales

There is a lot of competition. In 1995, almost 4,000 games were released. Many game industry gurus still claim that 4,000 games are released every year. That number is probably lower these days with distribution being handled by fewer companies and the big companies taking fewer risks. Still, the number of RTS/RTT games released at Christmas of 1997 was 40, with about the same for 1998. The competition is fierce, so make your game the best that you can.

Don't expect too much in terms of sales. Most games don't do that well. RTS/RTT games have been doing better than the average, but even so, you shouldn't expect more than about 100,000 in sales. There are hundreds of things you can do to improve your sales; we'll discuss those throughout the rest of this book. For basics, you'll need, in order of importance:

➤ Great gameplay
➤ Usable and informative interface
➤ Interesting characters and creatures
➤ Easy-to-instruct and intelligent units
➤ Strong and selectable level AI
➤ Great graphics
➤ Great sound
➤ Great cinematics

Focus on these, in order of importance, and you'll have a million seller.

Optimism

You will be overly optimistic on your schedule. Not only that, you will be late on your optimistic schedule. Every programmer tries to predict the future, but only the most conservative and clairvoyant programmer will ever guess correctly. The rule of thumb is to take your best guess on the time it takes to complete the game and add 50 percent. That is your best guess. If you want a little extra time left over for debugging and so on, double your estimate. Plan on being late and you will not be disappointed.

Backing Up

Backing up is critical to your success. You will lose data. You will lose code. Intel-based machines are not reliable, especially compared to mainframes, and that rare crash can ruin a month's work. Backing up is just good sense. Plan on a backup every Friday at 3 o'clock. Just begin backing up everyone's code. Copy it all to a CD or to a network drive. You can even rely on Visual Source Safe to back up all of the code because it backs up every file that you check in.

5

Chapter

You should also back up every release like demos, alphas, betas, and so on. If someone shows you a bug, it will probably be from a previous release and it'll be much easier to find with that code rather than the newly modified code.

Sharing Code and Source Control

Sharing code is hard. You and another programmer are working on a network on your game. You'll make a change to a file and then he will make a change to that same file. You save your changes and then he saves his. His save will overwrite yours, losing all of your changes. This is where source control comes in. But before we go there, let's talk about how to share code in the first place.

This is simpler than most people make it. Follow the simple rule of having an interface to all sections of code. This is part of what is called "loosely coupled" code and modules. You must design your modules and classes to be as loosely coupled as is possible. That means that their reliance upon one another should be minimal. Each class should be able to stand on its own and do its own work. (That sounds like the speech my father gave me when I was 17 years old.)

A class should not need to know much about another class in order to use it. A simple interface to a class helps the entire code cycle by reducing errors and code bloat. It centralizes functionality to within a class. Below you'll find an example of a "tightly coupled" section of code. Notice how much information we need to know about the Object in order to use it:

```
QueueItem* Item;

Object->SetVelocity (Object->VelocityX+Object->VelocityChangeX,
        Object->VelocityX+Object->VelocityChangeY);
Object->SetPosition (Object->PosX+Object->VelocityX,
        Object->PosY+Object->VelocityY);
while ((Item = Object->Queue->next ()) != NULL)
{
        Object->ProcessQueueItem (Item);
}
Object->Draw (&screenstruct);
```

Boy, is that awful. This is what happens when a C programmer first gets hold of C++. This bit of code is way too complex, hard to read, and probably prone to duplication. The code depends too much on knowing the members of the Object here, which should probably not be accessible except by the class itself.

You will need to do this same thing throughout the code, probably in many places, so lots of code will need to be duplicated. When you need to make a change, it will all need to be updated, and the walls of your city of Jericho will come crashing down when you realize how much you need to do. Whatever happened to encapsulation? All implementation details should be hidden. We're going to do just that:

```
Object->UpdateVelocity ();
Object->UpdatePosition ();
Object->ProcessQueue ();
Object->Draw (&screenstruct);
```

Wow, is that easier to read! This will make your coding job so much easier. Of course, the same thing is being done behind the scenes, but other modules in your project do not need to know much about this Object. This prevents duplication, simplifies your code base, and drastically reduces debugging. Coding errors are much less likely and this code is highly maintainable because the functionality all exists in one place.

Now that we've cleared that up, back to sharing code. Another must is dividing up responsibilities. Once you have clearly defined who does what, hopefully based on interest and skill, you should stay out of other programmers' modules and they should stay out of yours. You need only look at headers, and if you need a special functionality, ask the other person to implement it for you. If he doesn't have the time, it is usually better to wait and have him do it for you than to guess how you should proceed. Of course, access routines like GetColor () you can do yourself, but any slightly more difficult functions should be implemented by the "owner" of that particular module.

This is a team effort; if you stress the importance of a change, your team should be responsive enough to do it immediately for you.

Since your team never works on the same .cpp files at any given time, who needs source control? That is a valid point if you manage your project correctly from the get-go. But source control does back up your files every time you check out a module. This means that you can easily go back to a previous version of your code in case you break something and you're not quite sure what. It keeps dates on updates of code files. There are lots of reasons to use it and practically none to avoid it, other than maybe a little time to set it up.

Also, no matter how hard you try, you will occasionally have a few programmers with the same files open, and without source control, you will lose work.

Chapter 6

Standard Macros and Data Types

Before we get any deeper into programming and setting up our engine, we need to cover a few basics like common data types. For example, in a 16-bit graphics world, it might be helpful to have a class that manages color in 24-bit and allows you to manipulate it into 16-bit and vice versa. How about a 16-bit data type?

When considering what depth of code to include in this book, I thought keeping it simpler might be the best approach, but for this particular file, I've decided to include the beautiful artisanship of well-defined code (or so my self-delusional state would have me believe).

I wanted to submit a list of common expressions, in macro form, that everyone can use. Granted, macros can be a pain to debug, but if you have a standard list that works in most situations and you don't use macros for every possible solution, you'll never really have a problem.

Also included in the file are constants. Most of these are not included in any library that I've seen and I'm not quite sure why. The constant for natural log is very long and I'd like to thank Borland for the level of detail they paid to their constants. I borrowed it here.

Macros go against the grain of most C++ programmers. They are not object oriented, not part of any subsystem, and somewhat confusing to read. If you hate them, then replace them with functions, but I like them and although I don't use them every day, they always seem to find a home somewhere in my code. Granted, some of these I have never used, but most are useful and some are very cool.

Let's look at the constants first. PI is obvious and it is defined well in math.h as M_PI as well as in Borland headers. I have no idea why Microsoft chose not to include PI in this header, but it is defined here. PI2 is simply pi times 2. PIdiv2 and PIover2 are the equivalent of 90 degrees. In case you are not aware, PI is half of a circle. Simply take the radius and multiply it by 3.14159 to find the distance around the half-circle. Add another half of the circle and you get the formula 2 times PI times radius. Incidentally, take the integral of 2PIr to give you the arc of the circle, which is PIr2.

Next are angle conversions from degrees to radians. The computer does all of its calculations in radians and we normally do all of our calculations in degrees. They are simply different measurement systems, sort of like miles and kilometers, but radian distance is 6.28318, which you will find below as PI2. The Deg45 is a handy reference when you need 45 degrees converted to radians. For angles not listed, simply multiply the angle by DEGtoRAD and you can work from there. The constants are chosen to avoid the multiply step which costs processor time.

Note: On the Pentium, or really any machine, never divide. In integer-based math you may not be able to avoid it, but with float values, it is simply too slow. Preprocess the reciprocal or 1/ value. To covert radians to degrees, you could use DEGtoRAD and simply divide your angle by that value. But the reciprocal, RADtoDEG, will multiply eight times faster. It is preprocessed and will speed things significantly.

```
// struct.h

#if _MSC_VER
#pragma once                            // include only once per build
#pragma pack (2)                        // pack all structures to 2 bytes
#endif


#ifndef __STRUCT_H_
#define __STRUCT_H_

#ifndef NULL
#define NULL 0L
#define DEFINENULL
#endif

#ifndef __M_macro
#define __M_macro

#define  PI          3.141592653589    // 180 degrees
#define  PI2         6.283185307178    // 360 degrees
#define  PIx2        PI2               // 360 degrees
#define  PItimes2    PI2               // 360 degrees
#define  PIdiv2      1.570796326795    // 90 degrees
#define  PIover2     PIdiv2            // 90 degrees
#define  DEG90       PIdiv2            // same
#define  DEG45       0.7853981633974   // 45 degrees
#define  DEG5        0.087266462599    // 5 degrees
#define  DEG10       0.174532925199    // 10 degrees
#define  DEG20       0.349065850398    // 20 degrees
#define  DEG30       0.523598775597    // 30 degrees
#define  DEG60       1.047197551194    // 60 degrees
#define  DEG120      2.094395102388    // 120 degrees
#define  DEG40       0.698131700796    // 40 degrees
#define  DEG80       1.396263401592    // 80 degrees
#define  DEG160      2.792526803191    // 160 degrees
#define  DEG140      2.443460952792    // 140 degrees
#define  SQRT2       1.4142135623731   // 45* hypotenuse
#define  SQRT_2      0.7071067811865   // 1/SQRT2
```

```
#define   SQRT3     1.73205080757            // 30,60,90 60 degree side
#define   logNE     2.71828182845904523536   // natural log
#define   logN2     0.69314718055994530942   // doubling rate
#define   logN10    2.30258509299404568402   // 10x rate

#define   RADtoDEG  57.2957795132
#define   DEGtoRAD  0.0174532925199
```

Now on to the macros. ODD and EVEN look at the low bit of any number and effectively return a TRUE or FALSE value. SGN gets a –1, 0, or 1, based on whether the number is less than, equal to, or greater than 0. This is helpful for determining quadrants for graphing. You remember those, right? See Figure 6.1. Some people also use SGN for line clipping.

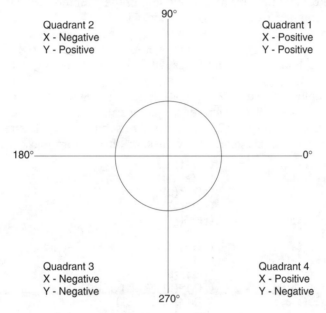

90°

Quadrant 2
X - Negative
Y - Positive

Quadrant 1
X - Positive
Y - Positive

180°　　　　　　　　　　　　　　　　0°

Figure 6.1
*Determining
quadrants for
graphing*

Quadrant 3
X - Negative
Y - Negative

Quadrant 4
X - Positive
Y - Negative

270°

6
Chapter

SQR is good if you have some complex argument that needs to be multiplied by itself. For example, (ScreenX+p->DistX) * (ScreenX+p->DistX) would be much better typed SQR (ScreenX+p->DistX). CUBE is similar. ABS returns the absolute value of a number. ROUND rounds a number off to the next integer number. TRUNC eliminates the fractional portion of a number.

MIN returns the smallest of two numbers. MAX returns the largest. MIN3 works for three numbers, as does MAX3. SWAP is a mighty cool number I found in *Graphics Gems Vol. 1*. This handy macro allows you to swap the values of two numbers without declaring another variable to store the intermediate value. SWAPPT does the same for the Windows POINT structure.

The next few may not be entirely useful but bear with me. RECIP gives the reciprocal, which you could easily do on your own. ASL is an Arithmetic Shift Left; it shifts the bits of the number left. ASL2 allows you to do more than 1 bit of shifting. BSL is the same.

LIMIT is good. It constrains a number to a range. Say that you are reading numbers from a database and they all need to be in the range of 1 to 30. You know that some of the numbers will be larger. Use limit like so: LIMIT (x, 1, 30); this is simply a macro but it's a good one.

TORAD and TODEG hide the math behind converting degrees to radians.

CSC gives the cosecant, SEC gives the secant, and COT gives the cotangent. These are simple reciprocals but I always forget which is the opposite of which. ARCSIN and ARCCOS are alternate ways of determining those values. AVG averages two numbers. perppos gives the perpendicular to an angle in the positive direction from your current angle. In Figure 6.1, that means an angle going in the counter-clockwise direction. perpneg goes in the negative direction, or clockwise.

SUM adds two numbers. LO_BTYE masks out the low byte from a value and HI_BYTE masks out the second byte which you may need to shift right. HI_LOSWAPshort swaps the high- and low-order bytes, while HI_LOSWAPlong swaps the high- and low-order words.

DIST is a simple distance formula. ANGLE gets an angle for you. It assumes that at least *x* or *y* is non-zero. The macro derive is for calculating simple derivatives. If you never took calculus, forget it. It's not terribly useful anyway. The rest of the macros are common conversions, geometric values, or physics formulas.

```
#define  ODD (a)          ((a)&1)
#define  EVEN (a)         (!((a)&1))
#define  SGN (a)          (((a)<(0) ) ? -1: ((a)>(0)) ? 1 : 0)
#define  SQR (a)          ((a)*(a))
#define  CUBE (a)         ((a)*(a)*(a))
#define  ABS (a)          (((a) < (0)) ? -(a) : (a))
#define  ROUND (a)        ((a)>0 ? (int) (a+.5) : -(int)(.5-a))
#define  TRUNC (a)        (int)(a)
#define  MIN (a,b)        (((a)<(b)) ? (a) : (b))
#define  MAX (a,b)        (((a)>(b)) ? (a) : (b))
#define  MIN3 (a,b,c)     (MIN(MIN(a,b),c))
#define  MAX3 (a,b,c)     (MAX(MAX(a,b),c))
#define  SWAP (a,b)       {(a)^=(b)^=(a)^=(b);}       // a xor b; b xor a;
                                                      // a xor b;
#define  SWAPPT (a,b)     (SWAP(a.y,b.y), SWAP(a.x,b.x)) // swap points
#define  RECIP (a)        ((1)/(a))      // a^-1
#define  NOT (a)          (~(a))         // exclusive or unary
#define  XOR (a,b)        ((a)^(b))      // exclusive or binary
#define  ASL (a)          ((a)<<1)       // bit shift left
#define  ASL2 (a,b)       ((a)<<(b))     // bit shift left by b positions
#define  ASR (a)          ((a)>>1)       // bit shift right
#define  ASR2 (a,b)       ((a)>>(b))     // bit shift right by b positions
#define  BSL (a)          ((a)<<1)       // bit shift left
#define  BSL2 (a,b)       ((a)<<(b))     // bit shift left by b positions
#define  BSR (a)          ((a)>>1)       // bit shift right
#define  BSR2 (a,b)       ((a)>>(b))     // bit shift right by b positions
#define  LIMIT (val,l,h)  ((val)<(l) ? (l) : (val) > (h) ? (h) : (val))
                                         // limit the range of a number
```

```
#define  TORAD (a)              ((a)* (DEGtoRAD))
                        // return the radian measure of the degrees passed
#define  TODEG (a)              ((a)* (RADtoDEG))
                        // convert to degrees from radians
#define  CSC (a)                (((a)==0) ? 0:(1/sin(a)))
#define  SEC (a)                (((a)==0) ? 0:(1/cos(a)))
#define  COT (a)                (((a)==0) ? 0:(1/tan(a)))//
#define  ARCSIN (a)             (atan((x)/sqrt(-(x)*(x)+1)))
#define  ARCCOS (a)             (-atan((x)/sqrt(-(x)*(x)+1))+PIdiv2)
#define  AVG (a,b)              (((a)+(b))/2)
#define  perppos (a)            ((a)+PIdiv2)
#define  perpneg (a)            ((a)-PIdiv2)
#define  SUM (a,b)              ((a)+(b))                   // add two numbers
#define  LO_BYTE (a)            ((a)&=255)
#define  HI_BYTE (a)            ((a)&=65280)
#define  HI_LOSWAPshort (a)     {a=((((a)&0xff)<<8) | (((a)&0xff00)>>8));}
#define  HI_LOSWAPlong (a)      {a=((((a)&0xffff)<<16) | (((a)&0xffff0000)<<16));}
#define  DIST (a,b)             (float)(sqrt(((a)*(a))+((b)*(b))))
                        // convert to polar distance
#define  ANGLE (x,y)            (float)((x!=0) ? (float)cos(x) : (float)sin(y))
                        // pass either the xdist or ydist and return angle
#define  TOCELSIUS (a)          (((a)-32)/5*9)
#define  TOFAREN (a)            (((a)*5/9)+32)
#define  TOCENT (a)             ((a)*2.54)
#define  TOINCH (a)             ((a)*.3937)
#define  derive (a,x,b,c)       (((a)*(b))*pow((x),(b)-1))   // take the
                        // derivative, in the form ax^b+c
#define  VOLCYLINDER (r,h)      ((h)*(PI*((r)*(r))))         // cylinder volume
#define  VOLCUBE (s)            ((s)*(s)*(s))                // cube
#define  VOLSPHERE (r)          (PI*((r)*(r)*(r)))           // sphere volume
#define  SURCYLINDER (r,h)      ((h)*2*(r)*PI)               // surface area
#define  SURCUBE (s)            ((x)*(x)*6)
#define  SURSPHERE (s)          (3*PI*(r)*(r))
#define  SURCONE (r,h)          (((PI*(r))*sqrt((r)*(r)+(h)*(h)))
#define  AREARECT (x,y)         ((x)*(y))
#define  AREACONE (r,h)         (((PI*(r)*(r))*h/3)
#define  AREACIRCLE (r)         ((PI*(r)*(r))
#define  AREATRIANGLE (b,h)     ((b)*(h)*0.5)
#define  GALTOLITRE (a)         ((a)*3.78541)
#define  LITRETOGAL (a)         ((a)*.264172)
#define  LB_toKG (a)            ((a)*.453592)
#define  KG_toLB (a)            ((a)*2.20462)
#define  GRAVITY (m1,m2,dist)   ((((m1)+(m2))*0.0000000000667)/((dist)*dist))
                        // attraction of two masses
#define  ACCELERATION (f,m)     ((f)/(m))
#define  VELOCITY (acc,time)    ((acc)/(time))
#define  WORK (m,v)             ((m)*(v)*(v))
#define  NEWTON (kg,meter)      ((kg)*(meter))

#endif
```

The next section defines a bunch of typedefs for simplifying code. U16 is the most common among the code in this book because it is used in the manipulation of screen data and the conversion of bitmaps into 16-bit. A U16ptr usually holds the data for a bitmap or a pointer to the screen used for blitting.

SCREEN_STRUCT is used for passing information about the blit screen pointer and such to other drawing routines. It used to be a struct, and the inertia of programming all these years has kept the name. It is the base class for a lot of drawing routines in my libraries, mostly because it is so simple and easy to use.

RGBVal is a very useful structure. It is used to convert 24-bit color values to 16-bit and vice versa. Microsoft decided to makes BMPs read BGR instead of RGB, which is the standard, so I made this structure in that form to simplify the reading of a BMP directly from a file.

There are a few others that need no explanation, but then there are the CREATURE_FLAGS and BITMAP_FLAGS that optimize space and hold information about AI stuff and bitmaps. We'll get to this stuff much later.

You may find some of these structures very useful, particularly the RGBVal struct.

```
// this library is intended for 16-bit graphics. All bitmaps will be
// converted from 4, 8, or 24-bit to a 16-bit compressed format called 11e.
// Ultimately, tiffs and some other formats will be supported.

typedef unsigned char  Uint8,  U8,  * U8ptr;
typedef unsigned short Uint16, U16, * U16ptr;
typedef unsigned int   Uint32, U32, * U32ptr;
typedef unsigned long  Ulong,  UL,  * ULptr;

typedef        char  Sint8,  S8,  * S8ptr;
typedef        short Sint16, S16, * S16ptr;
typedef        int   Sint32, S32, * S32ptr;
typedef        long  Slong,  SL,  * SLptr;

typedef              float FL, F32, *Fptr;
typedef              double DB, D80, *Dptr;

typedef unsigned int  BIT64[2], BIT128[4];

            //*******************************
            //*******************************

typedef
struct WPOINT
{
      short x, y, z;
      WPOINT () {Clear ();}
      inline void Clear () {x = 0, y = 0, z = 0;}
}WORLDPOINT, *WORLDPOINTPTR;

            //*******************************
            //*******************************
typedef
struct  DRAWSTRUCT
{
      int        x, y, w, h;
```

```
        U16ptr              Image;

} * DRAWSTRUCTptr;

                //********************************
                //********************************

typedef
struct RECTA
{
    int l, t, b, r;
}RECTA, *RECTAptr, **RECTAlist;

                //********************************
                //********************************

typedef
struct RECTANGLE
{
    int left, top, right, bottom;
}RECTANGLE, *RECTANGLEptr, **RECTANGLElist;

                //********************************
                //********************************
                //********************************
typedef
class SCREEN_STRUCT
{
public:
        U16ptr              Screen;
        int                 Width, Height, RealWidth;
public:
        SCREEN_STRUCT () {Screen = OL, Width = 0, Height = 0, RealWidth = 0;}
}SCREEN_STRUCT, *SCREEN_STRUCTptr, **SCREEN_STRUCTlist;

                //********************************
                //********************************

typedef
struct PARTICLE
{
        FL      x, y;            // screen position
        FL      Velocity;        // speed
        U32     Direction, Time; // integer based direction, time started in
                                 // millisecs
        U8      Counter, Brightness;

        PARTICLE () {Clear ();}
        void  Clear () {x = 0.0f, y = 0.0f, Velocity = 0.0f, Direction = 0,
                    Time = 0; Counter = 4; Brightness = 255;}
}PARTICLE, *PARTICLEptr, **PARTICLElist;
```

6

Chapter

```
//*********************************
//*********************************

typedef struct RGBVal
{
        enum  COLOR {RED, FUCHSIA, BLUE, CYAN, GREEN, YELLOW};
        U8  b, g, r;
        //*******************
        RGBVal () {r = g = b = 0;}
        RGBVal (U8 er, U8 eg, U8 eb) {r=er, g=eg, b=eb;}
        RGBVal (RGBVal& pal) {r=pal.r, g=pal.g, b=pal.b;} // copy constructor
        RGBVal (RGBVal* pal) {r=pal->r, g=pal->g, b=pal->b;}

        void SetVal (U8 er, U8 eg, U8 eb) {r = er, g = eg, b = eb;}

        //*************************
        RGBVal operator = (long val)     // in the form of 0x00ffffff
        {
            r = (U8) (val>>16);
            g = (U8) (val>>8);
            b = (U8) (val&0xff);
        return RGBVal (this);
        }

        //****************** conversion to and from 16-Bit
        U16 Convert15 () {return (U16) (((r&248)<<7) + ((g&248)<<2) + (b>>3)); }
        U16 Convert16 () {return (U16) (((r&248)<<8) + ((g&252)<<2) + (b>>3)); }
        RGBVal From15Bit (U16 bit)      // pattern 11111 11111 11111 for
                                        // red, green, and blue respectively
        {
            b=(U8) (((bit)<<3)&248);   // low portion of 16-bit value
            if (b) b|=7;               // fill in the low 3 bits in case this color
                                       // has a value. This is an effort to correct
                                       // the problem of lost color when converting to
                                       // 16-bit in the first place. Here we make
                                       // white really white instead of an off gray.
            g=(U8) ((bit>>2)&248); if (g) g|=7;
            r=(U8) ((bit>>7)&248); if (r) r|=7;
            return RGBVal (this);
        }
        RGBVal From16Bit (U16 bit) // pattern 11111 111111 11111 for
                                   // red, green, and blue respectively
                                   // notice the extra bit in the green bit
        {
            b=(U8) ((bit<<3)&248); if (b) b|=7;
            g=(U8) ((bit>>2)&252); if (g) g|=3;  // we are working with 6 bits
                                                 // so we only need the bottom 2
            r=(U8) ((bit>>8)&248); if (r) r|=7;  // red is one bit higher on
                                                 // the 16-bit group
            return RGBVal (this);
        }
        //****************** assignment
```

```
/*    RGBVal operator = (long val)      // in the form of 0xffffff
{
      r=(U8) (val>>16), g=(U8) (val>>8), b=(U8) (val);
      return RGBVal (this);
}*/
RGBVal operator = (RGBVal& pal)
{
      r=pal.r, g=pal.g, b=pal.b;
      return RGBVal (this);
}
//****************** equal test
bool operator == (long val)                // in the form of 0xffffff
{
      if (r==(U8) (val>>16) && g==(U8) (val>>8) && b==(U8) (val)) return
                true;
      return false;
}
bool operator == (RGBVal& pal)
{
      if (r==pal.r && g==pal.g && b==pal.b) return true;
      return false;
}
bool operator > (RGBVal& pal)             // based on an average value
{
      long dist = (r-pal.r) + (g-pal.g) + (b-pal.b);
      if (dist>0) return true;
      return false;
}
bool operator < (RGBVal& pal)
{
      long dist = (r-pal.r) + (g-pal.g) + (b-pal.b);
      if (dist<0) return true;
      return false;
}
//****************** addition
RGBVal operator += (RGBVal& pal)
{
      long er = pal.r, ir = r;         // store in a long for addition
                                       // below. remember that a
                                       // U8 wraps around at 255 so
                                       // any addition involving large
                                       // numbers ruins your day
      long eg = pal.g, ig = g;
      long eb = pal.b, ib = b;
      // limit is a macro defined above
      r=(U8) LIMIT (er+ir, 0, 255), g=(U8) LIMIT (eg+ig, 0, 255), b=(U8)
            LIMIT (eb+ib, 0, 255);
      return RGBVal (this);
}
RGBVal operator -= (RGBVal& pal)
{
      long er = pal.r, ir = r;         // store in a long for addition
```

```
                                         // below. remember that a
                                         // U8 wraps around at 255 so
                                         // any addition involving large
                                         // numbers ruins your day
        long eg = pal.g, ig = g;
        long eb = pal.b, ib = b;
        // limit is a macro defined above
        r=(U8) LIMIT (ir-er, 0, 255), g=(U8) LIMIT (ig-eg, 0, 255), b=(U8)
            LIMIT (ib-eb, 0, 255);
        return RGBVal (this);
}
RGBVal operator += (int amount) // range 1-15 is best,
                                         // this is RGB so more is possible
{
        long ir = r, ig = g, ib = b;
        // limit is a macro defined above
        r=(U8) LIMIT (ir+amount, 0, 255), g=(U8) LIMIT (ig+amount, 0, 255),
            b=(U8) LIMIT (ib+amount, 0, 255);
        return RGBVal (this);
}
RGBVal operator -= (int amount) // range 1-15 is best,
                                         // this is RGB so more is possible
{
        long ir = r, ig = g, ib = b;
        // limit is a macro defined above
        r=(U8) LIMIT (ir-amount, 0, 255), g=(U8) LIMIT (ig-amount, 0, 255),
            b=(U8) LIMIT (ib-amount, 0, 255);
        return RGBVal (this);
}
RGBVal operator + (RGBVal& pal) // used for col = c1 + c2;
{
        long er = pal.r, ir = r;   // store in a long for addition
                                   // below. remember that a
                                   // U8 wraps around at 255 so
                                   // any addition involving large
                                   // numbers ruins your day
        long eg = pal.g, ig = g;
        long eb = pal.b, ib = b;
                                   // limit is a macro defined above
        U8 tr=(U8) LIMIT (er+ir, 0, 255), tg=(U8) LIMIT (eg+ig, 0, 255),
            tb=(U8) LIMIT (eb+ib, 0, 255);
        return RGBVal (tr, tg, tb);
}
RGBVal operator - (RGBVal& pal) // used for col = c1 - c2;
{
        long er = pal.r, ir = r;   // store in a long for addition
                                   // below. remember that a
                                   // U8 wraps around at 255 so
                                   // any addition involving large
                                   // numbers ruins your day
        long eg = pal.g, ig = g;
        long eb = pal.b, ib = b;
```

```
                                        // limit is a macro defined above
        U8 tr=(U8) LIMIT (ir-er, 0, 255), tg=(U8) LIMIT (ig-eg, 0, 255),
            tb=(U8) LIMIT (ib-eb, 0, 255);
        return RGBVal (tr, tg, tb);
    }
    RGBVal operator ++ ()
    {
        long ir = r, ig = g, ib = b;
                                        // limit is a macro defined above
        r=(U8) LIMIT (ir+1, 0, 255), g=(U8) LIMIT (ig+1, 0, 255), b=(U8)
            LIMIT (ib+1, 0, 255);
        return RGBVal (this);
    }
    RGBVal operator -- ()              // used for col = c1 - c2;
    {
        long ir = r, ig = g, ib = b;
                                        // limit is a macro defined above
        r=(U8) LIMIT (ir-1, 0, 255), g=(U8) LIMIT (ig-1, 0, 255), b=(U8)
            LIMIT (ib-1, 0, 255);
        return RGBVal (this);
    }
    //*******************
void    SetVal ( COLOR c)
{
    switch ( c )
    {
        case RED:
            r = 255, g = 0, b = 0;
        break;

        case FUCHSIA:
            r = 255, g = 0, b = 255;
        break;

        case BLUE:
            r = 0, g = 0, b = 255;
        break;

        case CYAN:
            r = 0, g = 255, b = 255;
        break;

        case GREEN:
            r = 0, g = 255, b = 0;
        break;

        case YELLOW:
            r = 255, g = 255, b = 0;
        break;
    }
}
}RGBVal, *RGBptr;
```

6

Chapter

```
                    //********************************
                    //********************************

struct RGBfloat
{
    float r, g, b;
    RGBfloat () {r = 0.0F, g = 0.0F, b = 0.0F;}
    RGBfloat (RGBptr ptr)
    {
        r = (float) (ptr->r)/255;
        g = (float) (ptr->g)/255;
        b = (float) (ptr->b)/255;
    }
    void ConvertToRGB (RGBptr ptr)
    {
        ptr->r = (U8) (r*255);
        ptr->g = (U8) (g*255);
        ptr->b = (U8) (b*255);
    }
};

struct HSVfloat
{
    float h, s, v;
    HSVfloat () {h = 0.0F, s = 1.0F, v = 1.0F;}
    HSVfloat (float th, float ts, float tv)
    {
        h = th, s = ts, v = tv;
    }
};

                    //********************************
                    //********************************

                    //********************************
                    //********************************

typedef
struct FLAGS_FOR_BITMAP
{
        U16   ACTIVE:1;          // 0, 0-no response to any selection,
                                 // movement, and will not display
        U16   LOADED:1;          // 1, 1-file has been loaded
        U16   TRANSLUCENT:1;     // 2, 1-drawing will be with
                                 // translucent routines where avail
        U16   COMPRESSED:3;      // 3-5, 0-no compression, 1 is lle,
                                 // 2 is rle, 3 is lzw
        U16   IMAGE_TYPE:2;      // 6-7, 0-none, 1-lle, 2-BMP, 3-TARGA
        //***8
        U16   BIT_DEPTH:3;       // 8-10, 0 :2, 1:4, 2:8, 3:16 (5,5,5),
                                 // 4:16 (5,6,5), 5:24,
                                 // 6:32 regular, 7:32(24 regular, 8 alpha)
```

```
    U16   DRAW_ENABLED:1;          // 11, 0-will not draw but all
                                   // other activity is normal
    U16   WRITE_ENABLED:1;         // 12, 1-writing is possible, certain
                                   // sharing methods require
                                   // locking and unlocking of write ability
    U16   READ_ENABLED:1;          // 13, 1-reading is possible, see
                                   // write above
    U16   SELECTED:1;              // 14, 1-this object is selected
    U16   LINKED:1;                // 15, 1-this object belongs to a list

    //***16
    U16   CONTROLLED:1;            // 16, 1-this object is managed by
                                   // a managing class or tool
    U16   CLIP:1;                  // 17, use clipping rect-1, or not 0
    U16   ATTACHED_SHADOW:1;       // 18, beyond the end of the lle
                                   // compressed image is the shadow
                                   // for the image, which should be
                                   // drawn (bottom up) starting at the
                                   // height of the image (down)
    U16   ATTACHED_BITMAP:2;       // 19-20, this tells us how many
                                   // attached bitmaps there are
    U16   SPECIAL_BACKGROUND_COLOR:1;   // 21 is there a special
                                   // color like magenta for the
                                   // background
    U16   NO_SCRATCH_PAD:1;        // 22 0 means a scratch pad is
                                   // already loaded, 1 means that
                                   // one will need to be created.

    U16   PAD1: 2;                 // spacer only
    //U16  SPECIAL_DRAWING:2;      // 22-23, any special drawing rules
    //***24
    //U16  COLOR_TRANSFORMATION:5; // 24-28, 0 is no transform, otherwise
                                   //color number

    U16   BIT_PATTERN:1;           //_5x5x5_ or _5x6x5_
    U16   PAD:6;                   //25-32
}* FLAGS_FOR_BITMAPptr:


        //********************************
        //********************************

typedef union  BITMAP_FLAGS
{
    U32              Value;
    FLAGS_FOR_BITMAP Flag;
        //----------------------------
    BITMAP_FLAGS () {Clear ();}
    void Clear () {Value = 0;}
}* BITMAP_FLAGSptr;


        //********************************
```

```
                //*********************************

typedef struct FLAGS_FOR_CREATURES
{
      U32 ARTIFICIAL_INT:6;       // 0-5, which intelligence type; 0 is none

      U32 ALIVE:1;                // 6, 1-creature is alive and can function
      U32 DYING:3;                // 7-9, 0-creature is healthy and 7 stages of
                                  // dying; if a creature is already dead, this
                                  // is the level of decay starting with
                                  // 7 and decaying to 0
      U32 PRIORITY_SETTING:5;     // 10-14, how much processing time does this
                                  // object need
      U32 WRITE_ENABLED:1;        // 15, 1-writing is possible,
                                  // certain sharing methods require
                                  // locking and unlocking of write ability
      U32 READ_ENABLED:1;         // 16, 1-reading is possible, see write above
      U32 ADAPTABLE:4;            // 17-20, varying states of adaptability, 0 is
                                  // unadaptive
      U32 AGGRESSION:4;           // 21-24, aggression where 0 is docile and 15
                                  // is hostile
      U32 FULL_PATH_FOUND:1;      // 25, during the last pathing, was the full
                                  // path found
      U32 CURRENT_STATE:6;        // 26-31, 32 different states
                                  // may be replaced

      U32 BLOCKING:2;             // can walk over or through, 0-no, 1-slowly,
                                  // 2-moderate, 3-full speed
      U32 SELECTED:1;             // draw selection box
      U32 GROUP_ID:4;             // support for up to 15 group
      U32 TIME_SINCE_BIRTH:16;    // how long have I been alive, over 30 minutes
                                  // at 30 fps, every time this rolls over, add
                                  // one experience point

      U32  EXPERIENCE:9;          // experience points. adds to chance for
                                  // hitting, damage, or intelligence
}* FLAGS_FOR_CREATURESptr;        // 64 bits

                //*********************************
                //*********************************

typedef union  CREATURE_FLAGS
{
      BIT64                Value;
      FLAGS_FOR_CREATURES Flag;

         //---------------------------
      CREATURE_FLAGS () {Clear ();}
      void Clear ()
      {
           Value[0] = 0, Value[1] = 0;
      }
```

```
        CREATURE_FLAGS& operator = (CREATURE_FLAGS& c)
        {
              Value[0] = c.Value[0], Value[1] = c.Value[1];
              return *this;
        }
}* CREATURE_FLAGSptr;

              //*******************************
              //*******************************

typedef
 void (* FUNC_DRAW) (U16ptr, int, int, int, int, BITMAP_FLAGSptr);
typedef void (* FUNC_VOID) (void);
typedef void (* FUNC_CHARptr) (char*);
typedef void (* FUNC_WORDptr) (short*);
typedef void (* FUNC_INTptr) (int*);

              //*******************************
              //*******************************

#ifdef DEFINENULL // corrects for null definition
#undef NULL
#endif

#endif
```

Below you'll find another short library of common data types I use for 3-D games. Have fun with it.

```
//struct3d.h


#ifndef __STRUCT3D_H_
#define __STRUCT3D_H_

#ifndef NULL
#define NULL OL
#define DEFINENULL
#endif

              //*******************************
              //*******************************

typedef struct TEXTURE
{
      U16*      Index;
      U16       Width, Height;
}TEXTURE, *TEXTUREptr, ** TEXTURElist;

              //*******************************
              //*******************************
typedef struct VERT2D
{
```

```
        FL          x, y;
        S16         tx, ty;
        S16         sx, sy;
}VERT2D, *VERT2Dptr, ** VERT2Dlist;

typedef struct VERT2D_GROUP
{
        VERT2Dlist       Vert;
int     NumVert;

        VERT2D_GROUP () {Vert = NULL;}
        VERT2D_GROUP (int x)
        {
Vert = new VERT2Dptr[x];
NumVert = x;
for (int i=0; i<NumVert; i++)
Vert[i] = new VERT2D;
}
        ~VERT2D_GROUP ()
{
if (Vert) for (int i=0; i<NumVert; i++)
delete Vert[i];
delete Vert;
}
}VERT2D_GROUP, *VERT2D_GROUPptr, ** VERT2D_GROUPlist;

        //*******************************
        //*******************************

typedef struct VERT3D
{
        FL          lx, ly, lz;
        FL          wx, wy, wz;
        FL          cx, cy, cz;
        S32         sx, sy;
        S16         DrawFlag;
}VERT3D, *VERT3Dptr, **VERT3Dlist, POINT3D, *POINT3Dptr, **POINT3Dlist;

        //*******************************
        //*******************************
typedef struct POLY3D
{
        //FL         lx, ly, lz, wz; // used for clipping the entire POLY3D only
U8      NumVert;
U8      r, g, b;                     // a simple colored poly
        U16         DrawFlag;
        VERT3Dlist       Vert;

    POLY3D () {Vert=NULL;}
    ~POLY3D ()
{
if (Vert!=NULL)
```

```
{
for (int i=0; i<NumVert; i++)
delete Vert[i];
delete Vert;
}
}
}POLY3D, *POLY3Dptr, **POLY3Dlist;

                //********************************
                //********************************

typedef struct POLY3D_GROUP
{

        FL    lx, ly, lz;                    // used for clipping the group of polys
        FL    wx, wy, wz;
        FL    cx, cy, cz;
        S32   sx, sy;
        S32   DrawFlag, NumPoly, MinWidth;   // after rotation, is
                                             // this group drawn
    S32     Dist;
    POLY3Dlist  Poly;

    POLY3D_GROUP () {Poly=NULL;}
    ~POLY3D_GROUP ()
        {
if (Poly)
for (int i=0; i<NumPoly; i++)
delete Poly[i];
delete Poly;
}
}POLY3D_GROUP, *POLY3D_GROUPptr, ** POLY3D_GROUPlist;

                //********************************
                //********************************

typedef struct VECTOR // holds 3-d points and converts to vector values
{
        union {double x1, vx;};
        union {double y1, vy;};
        union {double z1, vz;};
        double  x2, y2, z2;

        VECTOR () {Clear();}
        VECTOR (VECTOR& v)
{x1=v.x1, x2=v.x2, y1=v.y1, y2=v.y2, z1=v.z1, z2=v.z2;}
        VECTOR (VECTOR* v)
{x1=v->x1, x2=v->x2, y1=v->y1, y2=v->y2, z1=v->z1, z2=v->z2;}
        VECTOR (double x, double y, double z) {vx=x, vy=y, vz=z; x2=y2=z2=0.0;}

        void  Clear () {x1=x2=y1=y2=z1=z2=0.0;}
```

6

Chapter

```
        VECTOR& operator = (VECTOR& v)
{
x1=v.x1, x2=v.x2, y1=v.y1, y2=v.y2, z1=v.z1, z2=v.z2;
return VECTOR (*this);
}
        VECTOR& operator = (VECTOR* v)
{
x1=v->x1, x2=v->x2, y1=v->y1, y2=v->y2, z1=v->z1, z2=v->z2;
return VECTOR (*this);
}

        //***************

        VECTOR CalculateNormal (VECTOR& v)
        {
            double  dx1=x2-x1, dy1=y2-y1, dz1=z2-z1;
            double  dx2=v.x2-v.x1, dy2=v.y2-v.y1, dz2=v.z2-v.z1;
            double  tx=dy1*dz2 - dz1*dy2;
            double  ty=dz1*dx2 - dx1*dz2;
            double  tz=dx1*dy2 - dy1*dx2;

            return VECTOR (tx, ty, tz);
        }

        VECTOR& CalculateNormal (VECTOR& v1, VECTOR& v2)
        {
            double  dx1=v1.x2-v1.x1, dy1=v1.y2-v1.y1, dz1=v1.z2-v1.z1;
            double  dx2=v2.x2-v2.x1, dy2=v2.y2-v2.y1, dz2=v2.z2-v2.z1;
            double  tx=dy1*dz2 - dz1*dy2;
            double  ty=dz1*dx2 - dx1*dz2;
            double  tz=dx1*dy2 - dy1*dx2;

            Clear ();

            vx=tx, vy=ty, vz=tz;
            return VECTOR (*this);
        }

        VECTOR GetVector ()
        {
            return VECTOR (x2-x1, y2-y1, z2-z1);
        }

        //***************

        void  Set1st      (double x, double y, double z) {x1=x, y1=y, z1=z;}
        void  Set1stPoint (double x, double y, double z) {x1=x, y1=y, z1=z;}
        void  Set2nd      (double x, double y, double z) {x2=x, y2=y, z2=z;}
        void  Set2ndPoint (double x, double y, double z) {x2=x, y2=y, z2=z;}
```

```
}VECTOR, *VECTORptr, **VECTORlist;

            //********************************
            //********************************
#ifdef  DEFINENULL                  // corrects for null definition
#undef  NULL
#endif

#endif
```

Chapter 7

Background

Visual C++ is the easiest programming tool to use when it comes to developing games. The debugger is part of the IDE; you can easily put in breakpoints and see all local variable values, except in MFC. The text editor is nice and works consistently, unlike the Windows editor for Watcom. It is easy to manage projects with multiple folders for different files and it has a pretty good interface in general.

Visual C++ has the worst profiler I have seen and it tells you very little. Watcom has a good profiler and I recommend using it. (*Profiling* is for seeing how fast certain sections of your code are.) Visual C++ takes a huge amount of hard drive space and any project you compile has huge temporary files. When you finish with a project, these temporary files can easily take over 20 MB; they serve no purpose once the project is complete, so delete them.

MFC, which is part of Visual C++, is not very good. It serves the purpose for which it was designed but the design is inherently flawed. Compare it to Builder C++ by Borland, which creates true drag and drop objects and works by setting parameters. The programming is kept to a minimum, allowing you to do windows editors, level editors, animation editors, and anything Windows-based in one-third the time that it would take you in MFC. In addition, Builder C++ has numerous drag and drop components, something like 150. I think MFC has 26.

Installation and Good Directory Setup

If you have already installed Visual C++, skip this section. First, select Custom Install. Unless you need them, never include ODBC or MFC in your install. They take a lot of extra space. (I think it's about twice as much as Visual C++ itself.) You really only need the basics, which include Windows development and the basic tools.

Choosing a directory is important. I recommend an alternate drive, if you have one, in the root. If you have a large enough hard drive, I recommend putting all of your programming on one of the partitions. This allows you to create other directories that will help you later. If you can, install the DirectX SDK in the root directory also (in a separate folder, of course) and name it DirectX. You'll need to obtain a copy of DirectX 6.0 from the Microsoft site:

**http://www.microsoft.com/windows/downloads/contents/updates/
DirectXfoundation/DL-core/coresites.asp**

This only gives you the end user version.

The development version will cost you $8.95. Then Microsoft will ship you a full version including help files. It is a total pain getting through all of the order information at the following address. It's one of the worst sites I have seen.

http://www.microsoft.com/directx/sdkcdorder.asp

Now create a folder for all of your Windows code in the root of that drive. Name it something like WinDevel or just Devel. Then create a folder for your basic DOS projects. Whenever you have a basic premise or concept you want to test, create a quickie DOS test and figure out the answer. You don't have to fool with Windows or large files. Lastly, you'll need to create a folder for all of your common library functions or common code. I call mine Library, but you can name yours whatever you like. All of the recurrent references (#include this and that) use this directory as a reference. You will need to change all of these files or simply create a folder on the root of your C drive and use them from there. This will be the repository of generic code, templates, assembly files, DirectDraw Windows code, AI management, etc. Anything that is generic enough to use in multiple projects should go in this directory.

Install with the Help Files

There is nothing more annoying than having your help files left on the CD. Make sure that you install them, but only the ones that apply. Then after installing DirectX, go into the DirectX folder and move the help files into your Visual C++ help file directory. This makes help come up quickly and will help you flip between subjects nearly instantly. This is a big time saver, especially when you are listening to your favorite CD in your CD player with your fancy Altec speaker system, and you have to eject your music just so you can look up "sprintf" and how to put a string into another string (%s, by the way).

Getting Used to Hot Keys

Hot keys are great in Visual C++. F7 does a compile. F5 compiles, then runs (provided that you need to recompile). It seems to offer to recompile even if you don't need it—a minor annoyance. F10 is the standard "step" that goes line by line through the code. F11 steps into a function. F9 sets a breakpoint. Hit it again to remove that breakpoint; of course, the cursor must be on the line of the breakpoint.

For editing you'll find some great hot keys. Ctrl-Tab is the most useful editing hot key. It flips between open text files. If you have three or more text files open, its behavior is a bit erratic, but you'll acclimate. Ctrl-] is used to find a matching parenthesis. Just place your cursor on a bracket, brace, or parenthesis and hit Ctrl-] to find its match. This helps you make sure they pair up like they should. F3 is used to find the next item. First hit Ctrl-F to find a word or phrase. Then F3 finds the next instance of it and Shift-F3 goes to the previous instance of it. Another keen feature of F3 is copying and pasting. Select a bit of code, copy it (Ctrl-c), and then hit Ctrl-f. Now paste (Ctrl-v) and the string you are looking for pops into the window. It saves a lot of typing.

Ctrl-F2 sets a "bookmark." This is like a jump point—when you hit F2, no matter where you are in the file, you will go back to that point. This bookmark is not permanent and when you exit the program, it disappears. For permanent bookmarks, use Alt-F2. It's kind of a pain (try it) but useful. Why should I have to name my bookmark? Just associate it with that file permanently.

Other commonly used hot keys include: Ctrl-s for save, Alt-Fl to save all, Ctrl-x for cut, Ctrl-c for copy, Ctrl-v for paste, and Ctrl-z for undo. You should learn all of these. They are great and some are only available from the keyboard (that I know of).

Rearranging the Desktop

I like the desktop setup shown in Figure 7.1. The help toolbar is on the left side. Right-click on the toolbars to see a menu of the possible toolbars available and select the help toolbar. One icon jumps to the last help item you looked at, another goes to a previous item, and one button sets a bookmark on a particular help subject for easy future access.

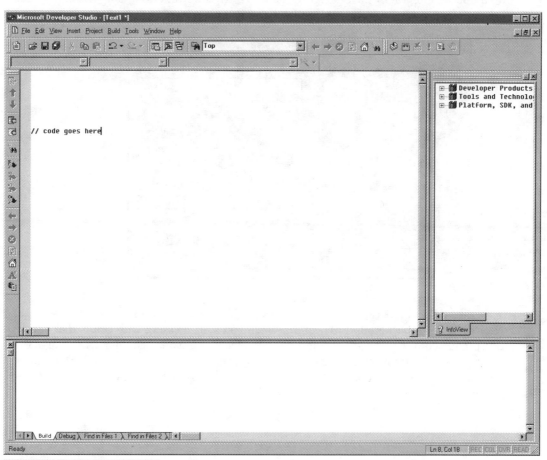

Figure 7.1 *Example desktop setup*

7

Chapter

I moved the project window to the right side of the IDE. This is helpful. It is out of the way and yet visible constantly. Try this setup for a few hours and you won't go back (unless you are a lefty—it makes a difference). This setup works well if you have at least 1024x768 resolution.

For those of you who can afford two monitors and two video cards, run them side by side and use both on your one computer. What a difference: You can run the debugger in one monitor and the program in the other. It is a programmer's dream come true. (It seems that no matter how organized I am, I am always minimizing the main IDE or exiting the game program because it was so much more difficult any other way to manage all of my windows.)

When debugging or when figuring out any math, the Windows calculator is helpful. See Figure 7.2. You'll find it in the Start menu under Accessories. I keep it on my desktop for easy access. Put a shortcut to it everywhere. It is a great little program. You can easily convert hex to integer to binary. I still have no use for octal, but maybe you do. All of the most important trig and algebra functions are there. Don't expect to do a double integral or have it figure the derivative of a function using the chain rule, but for most common programming issues, it is invaluable.

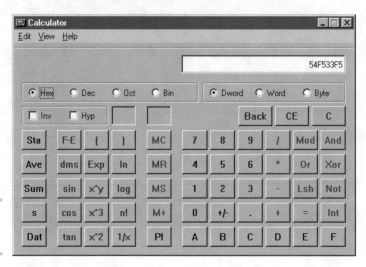

Figure 7.2
The Windows calculator

Editing the colors can be fun. Some people like the color setup I have in Figure 7.3. Notice the black background. Be careful when you start messing with colors that you don't make both the background and the text black; you won't see much. To change the colors, go to the Tools menu and then down to Options. Then click on the Format tab way to the right (use the spin edit control in the upper right), as shown in Figure 7.4.

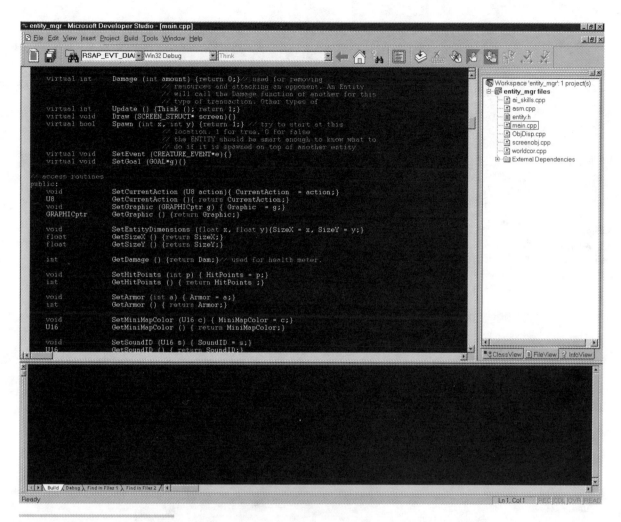

Figure 7.3 *Color setup*

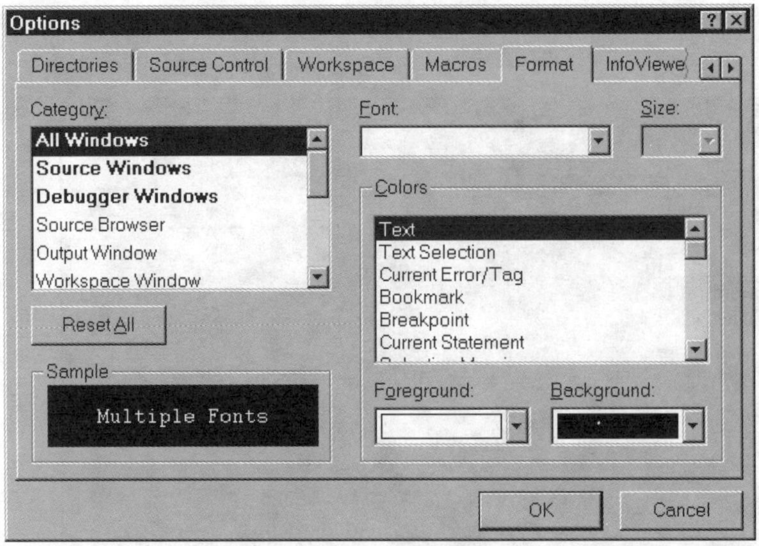

Figure 7.4
*The Options
dialog box
Format tab*

Notice that something is keeping track of the last few files that you have opened. Visual C++ does that magically for you. Go to the File menu and at the bottom, you'll find Recent Files and Recent Workspaces. It keeps track of the last four files that you opened and the last four projects. We can increase that number by going to Tools|Options again. Click on the Workspace tab and then modify the values in the bottom two text boxes, as shown in Figure 7.5. I like to use the number 12 for these boxes.

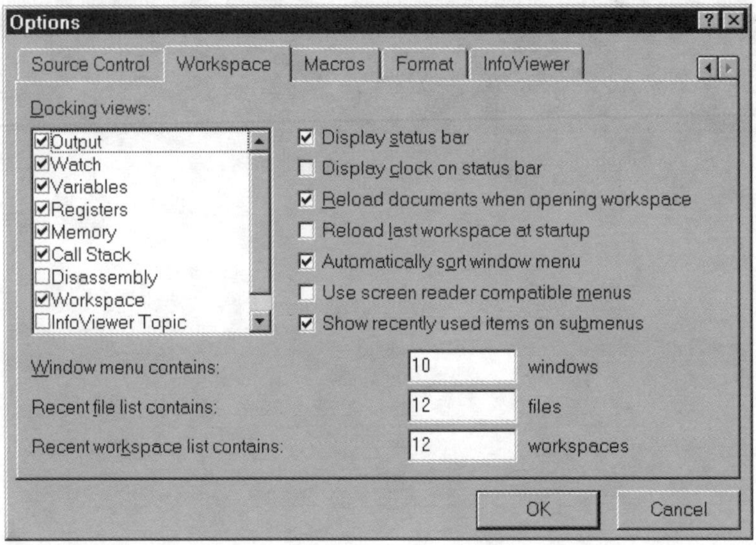

Figure 7.5
*The Options
dialog box
Workspace tab*

The last thing that you'll need to do is set up your environment to work in full screen. Go to Tools|Customize, and choose the Keyboard tab, as shown in Figure 7.6. From the pull-down Category edit box, select View and find ToggleFullScreen in the selection window. Now go to the box in the lower right of the dialog labeled Press New Shortcut Key. Click in the edit box and a few things change. I like the key combo Crtl-F6 but you can set whatever makes you comfortable. After hitting the key combo, click the Assign button. Then click Close. If you click Close before Assign, the box closes without assigning the key, which is rather annoying and has happened to me too many times. I understand why they did it that way—I just don't like it.

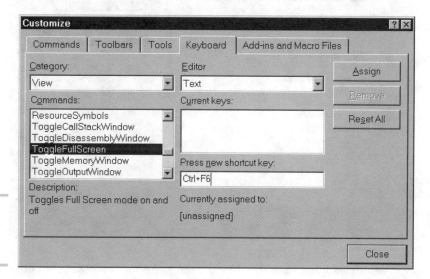

Figure 7.6
The Customize
dialog box
Keyboard tab

Before you get started, make sure that you have the latest drivers for your video card, sound card, ZIP drive, JAZ drive, Joystick, and any other devices attached to your PC. This will prevent (hopefully) lots of unintelligible errors and strange bugs.

Starting a New Project

This is about as easy as it gets. Launch the program and go to File|New. Now you have a lot of choices, most of which you can ignore. In fact, if you click around on the tabs, you'll see that you can even create Excel files (if you have Excel installed), which seems useless to me. If I want an Excel spreadsheet, I'll launch Excel. Anyway, the only two tabs you are likely to use are Projects and Files.

The only files you are likely to create are new text files. You also have the option of a C/C++ header file and a C++ source file. I have never used them, but they generate text files with the name you enter (there is a box for the filename on the right) with the proper extension. The bitmap, resource file, and other information is helpful in MFC and you may find a use for it. I haven't.

7

Chapter

Anyway, this section is about starting a new project, so let's do that. Select the Projects tab, illustrated in Figure 7.7, and select one of the following:

➤ Win32 Application—Windows project
➤ Win32 Console Application—Console project
➤ Win32 Dynamic-Link Library—DLL

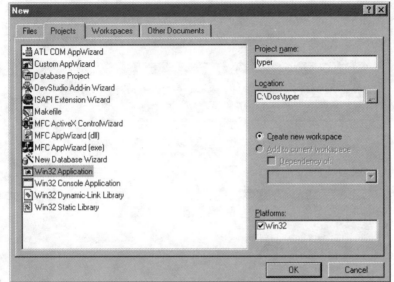

Figure 7.7
Selecting Win32 Application from the New dialog's Projects tab

When developing Windows-based games like for DirectX, you'll only need Win32 Application, but the other two can come in handy.

Win32 Application is the basis for every Windows application. This application, when compiled, will generate code for a Windows application and nothing else. Don't expect DOS or UNIX. This type of program expects a WinMain and a MessageHandler (or MessageLoop), which we'll discuss in a few chapters. This is the selection you will always choose when creating a new game.

Win32 Console Application is great for tests. I use it constantly. It generates code fast, it makes a small executable, and it is great for testing almost anything, except for graphics. It is great for when you need to see the output and you want to control all of the various inputs. Scientists call it a controlled environment. It only generates text-based information; calling interrupts to flip into a DOS-based mode 13h or something similar never seems to work. Stick to simple stuff and it will never disappoint.

Win32 Dynamic-Link Library is something you may never want to use, but it can be useful. A DLL is a different kind of library but you can link core sections of your code into your project as a DLL. This really helps reinforce the object model. You can think of a DLL as an object that you can use at run time but compile separately. It can cut compile times to one-third or less, depending on the size of your project and how many different DLLs you are willing to use. You should read up on how to use them; they aren't hard. You'll need to include the *.obj file generated by compiling the DLL in the game project to successfully use a DLL in a C++ project. In addition, your main code will need the header and the DLL file generated.

Project Settings

The settings that you'll need to modify before you compile your project are shown in Figure 7.8. Go to Project|Settings to get to this window, which is also Alt-F7 (like it says in the menu). Click on the various tabs and become familiar with what is available. Most of what you need is in the C/C++ tab, shown in Figure 7.9, and the Link tab, shown in Figure 7.10.

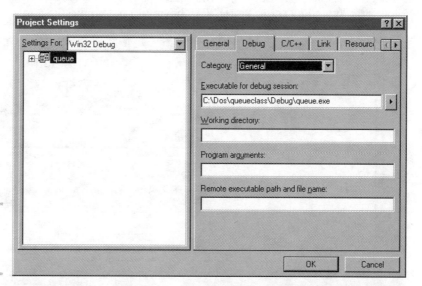

Figure 7.8
The Project Settings dialog box

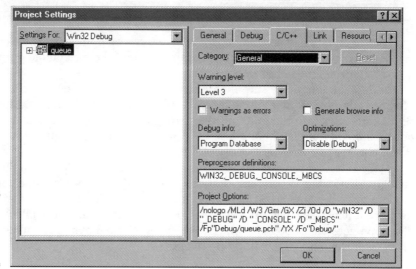

Figure 7.9
The Project Settings dialog's C/C++ tab

7

Chapter

On the C/C++ tab, look in the pull-down list under Category. There are eight items; you need to be familiar with General, Optimizations, and Preprocessor. In the Code Generation selection you can control the padding to a structure; the default is 8 bytes, but 4 or 2 is probably better. Other than that, the rest of the selections are not very helpful.

The General selection on the C/C++ tab has a bunch of helpful items. First, change Warning Level to 3; 4 is just plain annoying. Optimizations should be set to the default, or Disable (Debug) when compiling for debug. When doing a final build, change Optimizations to Maximum Speed. You can also change this in the Optimizations selection of the tab under Category. The Preprocessor selection and the preprocessor section of the General tab are the same. This is where you can put #define's without modifying any code. Better than having to recompile the entire project.

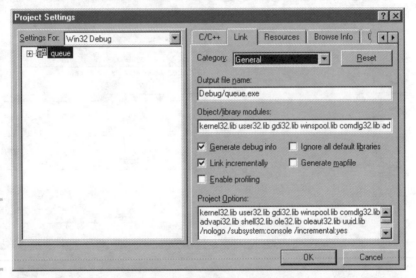

Figure 7.10
The Project Settings dialog's Link tab

On the Link tab, everything of significance can be done from the General selection of the pull-down menu. You can change the name of the executable output, add other lib's, or change a few other minor settings.

In the Link tab, make sure that you add the following files to the Object/Library Modules edit box: Winmm.lib, ddraw.lib, dxguid.lib, and dsound.lib. There are other DirectX files that you can add, but these are usually enough. On that same line, delete odbc32.lib and odbccp32.lib. These lib's are for database stuff and you won't need them, plus they slow compile times a little.

Make sure that you are in debug mode, which you can select from Build|Set Active configurations when developing. You should only go into release mode before a major test run or before a release. Debug does a lot of cool things for you. When you allocate memory, it allocates a few extra bytes before and after the memory allocated in case the allocation goes out of bounds, which keeps your PC from dying. It initializes most pointers to 0, preventing NULL pointer problems.

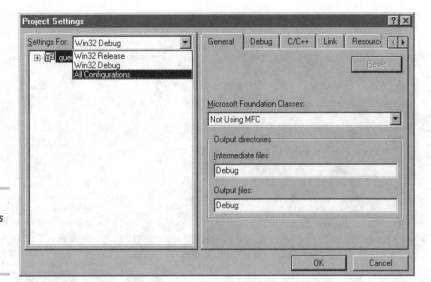

Figure 7.11
*Project Settings
dialog Win32
Application
Debug mode*

Make sure your settings are the same as your active configuration. When you go into release mode, you will run into problems. None of these nice things happen and you can't run the debugger right. Wrong. The debugger will work if you change your settings to still output debugging info. When in release mode (you don't need to do this in debug mode), go to Project|Settings. Select the C/C++ tab and midway down the dialog box, find the pull-down labeled Debug Info. Now select Program Database. Next, go to the Link tab. Select the check box labeled Generate Debug Info. Now you can run your release application just like in debug mode and you can find out where you went wrong. You can set breakpoints like before and fully debug. Remember to turn off these settings before the final release.

Creating Your Project

First, make sure that you have a new project Just name it test1 or something similar in a good directory on the hard drive. When you select New and then select the Projects tab, make sure that you define a base directory in the Location edit box. The name for the project goes in the Project Name edit box. (It does make a difference.) After entering the proper name and so on, select OK.

You can create new text files at any time, but when you do so, you must save them and then add them to the project. First, look at the box on the left (unless you moved it to the right). It should say something like workspace 'test1': 1 project (mine says Workspace 'Entity_mgr') and below that it says test1 files. The best way of adding files to the project is right-clicking on the project name, which is Entity_mgr. A selection pops up, as shown in Figure 7.12. Left-click on Add Files to Project. Now a dialog pops up. Select your files one by one by holding down the Ctrl key. See Figure 7.13. Then click OK. Wow, lookie there.

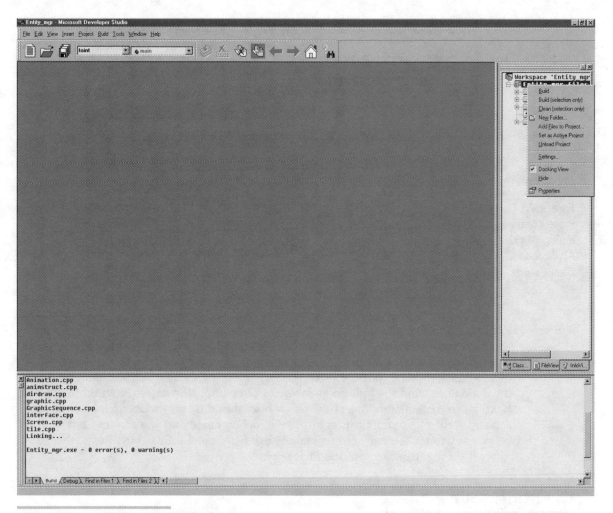

Figure 7.12 *Adding files to a project*

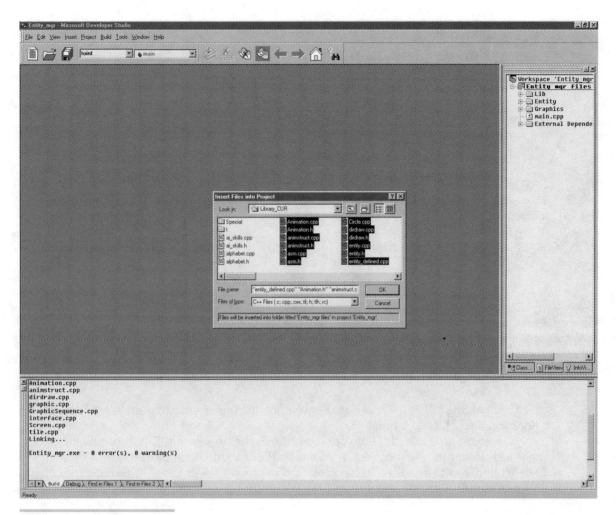

Figure 7.13 *Inserting files in a project*

Figure 7.14 shows multiple folders under the project name. You can add folders by right-clicking on the project name and selecting New Folder. A small dialog box pops up, asking for the name of the new folder, which you can name anything, and the extensions. Extensions does not help you or limit what you can put in the folder, so ignore it. Hit OK, then right-click on the folder to add files to it. This is a great way to keep the project organized.

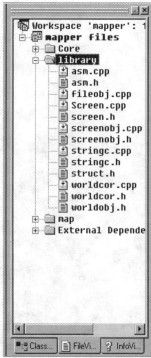

Figure 7.14
Folders under the project name

Figure 7.15
Files in a folder under the project name

You can see in Figure 7.15 how I have only one folder open and that way I can focus on a few files at a time.

Once you have added all of your .cpp files to the project, hit F7 and compile. Do not add header files to a project. If your .cpp files include these .h files, the .h files will automatically be added to the project in their own folder called External Dependencies.

Building a Test Bed

DOS is great for testing simple stuff and you should rely on it heavily. You can create a quickie project to test a theory and save yourself the headache of creating a window to test it and then output the results. I do this constantly and it saves so much time since it is so much easier to limit the unknowns.

The primary #include's for a basic DOS-based test bed will always be:

```
#include <string.h>
#include <iostream.h>
#include <conio.h>
#include <stdlib.h>
```

These should be included in every test bed. Sometimes, you may want to include:

```
#include <WINDOWS.h>
```

```
#include <mmsystem.h>
```

for testing time. You do not have to be developing a Windows app to use windows.h. Make sure to add winmm.lib to the link files for time testing.

When developing these test beds, you will always need:

```
void main ()
{
}
```

The rest is just like you learned in your beginning C++ class in college or that you can find in any C++ programming book. Just type in what you need.

Here is an example of code that is perfect for a test bed:

```
// main.cpp
#include <string.h>
#include <iostream.h>
#include <conio.h>
#include <stdlib.h>

//*******************

float  GetRand ()
{
        int x = rand ();            // 0-32767
        float y = (float) x;
        return y / 32767.0F;        // 0.0 to 1.0
}

//*******************

void main ()
{
        for (int i=0; i<100; i++)
            cout<<GetRand ()<<" ";

        cout<<endl;
        getch ();
}

//*******************
```

It just generates a bunch of random numbers between 0.0 and 1.0, but it lets you look at the results to make sure that it's what you want. Not exactly rocket science, but it gives you the idea.

A Long Word about How to Set Up Headers for Efficiency

Don't put a header inside a header if you can avoid it. There are ways to avoid this that will save you the dreaded one-hour compiles. Let's look at a bad header that will kill compile times and then the way to improve it:

```
//*************************
// unit.h

#include <unitdef.h>        // contains the UNIT class, let's say
#include <map.h>            // contains the TILE class


class UNIT_MGR
{
        UNIT unit[100];

        public:

        ...

        void AssignUnitToTile (TILE* tile, int WhichUnit);
};
//*************************
```

I guarantee that if you have this situation and you start including unit.h in a few other files, compiles will slow down significantly.

By replacing the UNIT allotment in the UNIT_MGR class with a pointer and then allocating it dynamically, you can use forward declarations. A forward declaration sets up the compiler, letting it know that the class in question will be defined later.

```
//*************************
class UNIT;        // forward declaration
class TILE;        // forward declaration


class UNIT_MGR
{
        UNIT*      unit;

        public:

        UNIT_MGR ();
        ...

        void AssignUnitToTile (TILE* tile, int WhichUnit);
};
//*************************
```

The trick is defining it before you get into the .cpp file. Below is how the .cpp file would look. You might think that this is a lot more work, but it really is just a different way of looking at things. By doing this, you can easily cut your compile times in half, and often a whole lot more.

```
//*************************
#include <unitdef.h>            // contains the UNIT class, let's say
#include <map.h>                // contains the TILE class
UNIT_MGR :: UNIT_MGR ()
{
        unit = new UNIT[100];
```

```
      }

      UNIT_MGR :: ~UNIT_MGR ()
      {
            delete UNIT;
      }
      //***************************
```

Another thing to help with compiles is to have a Struct.h file. This allows a single file to represent all of the #includes for classes. Any new file that you add that needs a bunch of different header files can simply include this one file. The big disadvantage is that this file is included by a bunch of different files, and one change to any of the headers it includes can cause most of the project to rebuild, taking a long time.

A file for variables is Global.h. This file can hold a lot of variables in the form:

```
      extern int NumCreatures;
```

Do not put actual declarations in here; leave that up to the .cpp files. You might want to include this file in all files requiring global variables, but be wary. This can also significantly increase compile times to intolerable levels.

Make sure that every header file you create has a compiler directive at the top and bottom of the file like so:

```
      #ifndef _HEADER_H_
      #define _HEADER_H_

      //header definitions ...

      #endif
```

What often happens is that a .cpp file will include a header twice or a header will include another header. When a .cpp file includes a header, say "struct.h," and then includes another header, say "animation.h," that also includes "struct.h," you get weird errors. This #include format can be found in my headers, so look at some of my code for reference; my solutions are typical. It really is quite helpful. The #define keyword can be anything unique but I recommend the filename, in caps, with some underlines thrown in.

Files to Delete

When you compile a bunch of files in Visual C++, or any compiler for that matter, it interprets the text you entered. When you compile, it generates an .obj, or object, file for every text file. These are roughly twice the size of the original text file, but it varies so much as to be almost unpredictable. Then it creates an .sbr file for every file you have. These contain "browser" information, which allows the class list to display. Now all of the files are generated from compiling and here comes the link. (*Linking* is when the compiler takes all of the .obj files and puts them together to create the final executable file.) All of the header info is put into one big file called a .pch, or precompiled header file. This file significantly reduces compile times. It will also be huge, probably on the order of 5 or 6 MB. Then an .ilk file is generated that contains the link information before the final program is built. Continuing with the link, a .pdb file (program database file) containing debugging info and an .idb file, which is the same thing for incremental builds, are generated. Now the program is finished. Your program will run, but now you have about 20 MB of useless (to you) stuff on your hard drive.

Periodically, especially when you finish a project, you should clean up huge sections of your hard drive by deleting these files. Say that all of your projects are on the C drive. Open up the Explorer by clicking on the Start menu, then going to Programs. (You can also right-click on the Start menu or hit the Windows-e key combo.) Once you see the directory tree, right-click on the C drive icon and select Find.

In the edit window with the cursor, type:

   .pch;.obj;*.sbr;*.pdb;*.idb;*.ilk;*.bak;*.000;*.001;*.002

and hit Enter. The *.bak files are old files and they are almost always useless. They usually are created when you reinstall Windows or install over an existing version of the same software. The same is true of .000, .001, and .002 files. Now that you are done finding all of these files, go to the Edit menu of the Find dialog and hit Select All. (You can also hit Ctrl-a.) Now hit the Delete key on your keyboard. Every one of these files was probably temporary or completely useless. You might also want to get rid of *.tmp files on your hard drive.

Now go back to the Explorer, right-click on the C drive icon, select Properties, and when the dialog pops up, select the Tools tab. Now click on Optimize and select the C drive. This may take a while, but it is good to optimize once a month or so anyway. It will definitely affect computer performance.

If you are running NT and you do not have a disk defragmenter, check out:

http://www.execsoft.com/dklite/download.htm

Now let's get back to work.

Chapter 8

Great Ideas

This chapter presents some of the greatest real-time strategy and real-time tactical games. There are many notable exceptions that I did not include in the screen shots but are perfectly good games nonetheless. I just didn't want to include 300 screen shots. These great games include Gettysburg, Myth, Command and Conquer (Version 1, Red Alert, and Tiberian Sun), Populous the Beginning, and Dungeon Keeper, which is marginally RTS. I picked a few great games to present interface issues, fog of war, battles, graphics, and other things that demonstrate the qualities of a great game.

Note: Of the games listed, three were designed by Sid Meier. The man has some great designs and I hope he keeps them coming. I remember the first ads for Dungeon Keeper back in 1995, and about three years later we saw the game. Great things take time to build. By the way, the rendering engine used in Magic Carpet seems to be the same rendering engine used in Dungeon Keeper. It is good to develop an engine that can be used in multiple games in multiple genres.

There has been a recent trend in RTS games to include a first-person view like in Battlezone and Dominant Species. The player is immersed in the action and he can control the movements of a few different units from a first-person perspective. I think these games lose the look and feel of controlling vast armies and marching them off to war. There is something truly satisfying about watching the catapult in Age of Empires tear down the ranks of oncoming archers. The "epic" nature of these games takes me back to the movie *Braveheart* or *Lawrence of Arabia*. This feeling just can't be captured by Battlezone; while it is a cool game, I wouldn't include it in RTS. It is real time and it is strategic, but it doesn't share many of the qualities of the games included here.

Figure 8.1
*The interface in
Seven Kingdoms*

Although Seven Kingdoms is not a great RTS game, it has some of the best elements in any RTS game. Here we see a great interface. The city is selected and we know its popul*tion, tax system (indicated by the number 90), and people in training (none). The city is linked to other structures that provide it support. When you click on the buildings, they in turn display their support for other buildings. You have the main resources at the top—food and money (bread and coin). A map off to the right shows the world in high relief, and the bottom of the screen displays messages that have significance to the kingdom. There are eight scrolls at the upper left that allow the player to click and display various statistics on the kingdom. This is a sweet interface, one of the best that I've seen. It gives you all the info you need, and yet it is really simple to use and understand.

Figure 8.2
The interface in
Seven Kingdoms

This screen shot shows another building in Seven Kingdoms that has trade support for the mine and two cities. The interface data on the right has changed to show the market trade status and the amount of tax revenue that it generates. The map to the upper right is now a high-color map. This minimap is easily changed with the three buttons above it.

Figure 8.3
The interface in
Seven Kingdoms

Here, I have clicked on the Villages scroll in the upper left part of the interface. Notice how nice the statistics are. You can still see what's happening behind them, faintly, but it is clear and generally concise. All of the info you need about your villages is right here. You don't see a lot of useless statistics, just what you need. One more thing of note is the number 54 in the top middle of the interface. This tells me my status or how I'm doing in general. The thumbs up could just as easily be a thumbs down telling me that I'm doing poorly. This gives a general flavor to how well a player is doing and is kinda cool.

Figure 8.4 *The interface in Age of Empires*

Age of Empires has the cleanest and simplest interface of the games discussed in this chapter. All of the resource quantities are at the upper left—these are wood, food, gold, and stone, from left to right. The icons could be a bit larger and are somewhat difficult to see, but they are clear enough for most people. The top middle displays the phrase "Iron Age" which tells us that our civilization has advanced from the Stone Age. This advancement in "ages" is an interesting concept. Just like Warcraft, the player advances by paying for a new level of technology. Then there are new weapons, units, and upgrades available with a higher level of technology. This gives the game a feeling of stages or levels of completion. When players finish a game of Age of Empires, they often talk about how fast they got to the Bronze Age or the Iron Age. It's a level of achievement for some players and a fun element in the game. The ages in order are Stone, Tool, Bronze, and Iron.

The lower right displays the diamond minimap showing the entire world. Normally, this map would be mostly black, obscuring all the areas that have not been visited. I have exposed the entire map using a setting at the beginning of the game called Reveal Map. The resources on the map appear here with piles of gold in yellow, stone in gray, and forest in dark green. The little white square shows us where the screen display is in relation to the entire world. All RTS/RTT games have this feature. All of our units appear as dark blue dots on the minimap. Next to the minimap are two icons. The question mark is Help. Clicking on it and then clicking on any icon or creature in the game brings up Microsoft Help. If you click on the S, a small display of everyone's score is brought up in the bottom right. Kinda cool for a relative status on how you are doing. It also gives the status of the other players.

When the building in the middle is selected, the icons on the bottom pop up. First, the bottom left displays an icon of the building and a green bar shows the relative health of the building—420 points remaining out of 420. This bar changes if a building's or a unit's health declines, like being hit by an enemy. The name of the building is here also—storage pit. It is a building where the resource gathering workers can store wood, gold, or stone. This adds to your grand total of resources.

The middle icons are all upgrades that only this type of building can provide, which, in this case, are various armor upgrades for various units. Each building has upgrades available from it. If you forget to build a government center, you will never have fire arrows; if you forget the granary, you will never have farms. There is a giant hierarchy chart showing the relationships between what you build and what you can do.

You can also see workers near the gold pile. Although you can't tell from the screen shot, the art is superb. Lastly, notice the fog of war. It is the grayish stuff around the areas where there are no units, around the outside of the screen in this figure. This is an area you can't see. Any unit can see far enough to cut through the fog so the areas around them are exposed. But an enemy unit can hide in the fog and your units will not be able to see it.

Figure 8.5
Age of Empires

Notice how the icons on the bottom of the screen are different when the army is selected. All of the units have health bars above their heads, and you can see that a few are hurt or damaged. The minimap indicates you are in a different location from the previous screen. The bottom left icon is now a Roman chariot archer. The icons there represent damage, armor, and chance to hit from top to bottom. These are great icons. The icon of the chariot archer looks great as well. This is a great interface.

One really cool thing about this interface is the emphasis on the game. Most of the screen is the game screen. The interface is out of the way, which makes the game more playable. Another nice thing is the high resolution. This game plays well in 640x480, 800x600, and 1024x768.

Figure 8.6
Age of Empires—
fog of war.

Notice the dead enemy lying down in the circled area. Most RTS games simply have the dead enemy disappear. This is a nice addition. If you look closely at the building, you can see there is a sword pointing to it. The mouse cursor changes to a sword when over enemy units to emphasize the current attack command when I click on that building. Notice how the fog of war—the grayed section in the left part of the screen—follows the units, exposing only the areas where they can see. Overall, this is a great interface. The game looks real nice too.

Look at the quality of the trees. There is even an elephant to provide food and kill peons. We even see a small pond here. One last detail is the flaming building. My units have been attacking it a bit and it is on fire. The fire doesn't hurt the building, but it lets the players know that the building is damaged. There is a nice accompanying fireside crackle from the speakers as the buildings burn too.

Figure 8.7
Age of Empires

Destroyed buildings are charred to the ground here. In the circled area, we see a peon in the first stages of dying who is falling to the ground. There are dead enemies everywhere, giving a battlefield feel to this game. The mouse cursor has reverted to its former state. All of these things add a lot of realism to the game.

Figure 8.8
*Age of Empires
—grouping*

Most RTS/RTT games offer grouping. The units here all have a selection box around them with a little 1 in the corner. This tells us that these units belong to group 1. It's a clever way to tell the player which group a particular unit belongs to. Here we see a tower. Most RTT/RTS games have some sort of tower or stationary long-range artillery unit. Also, notice the little boat at the bottom right of the screen. It has cast a net and is reeling in fish. Pretty neat subtlety. It does need to return to the dock to bring its fish in.

Figure 8.9
Age of Empires

This figure shows a farm being destroyed. The units here have different jersey colors. These colors are the only way to tell units apart since all players can have the same types of units. All of my units have dark blue as a jersey color while all of the opposition has red. (In the circled area, the standing figure is wearing blue and the fallen figure is wearing red.)

You may have noticed that as we go from one figure to the next, the resource numbers continue to increase. That is because the peons back at the home base are still working while I continue to destroy the opponent. The Roman axeman is the selected unit in the bottom left corner. Most RTS games have only three resources, but Age of Empires has four, presumably to make management a bit tougher and to help balance the game a little better.

Figure 8.10
Age of Empires

This figure shows how the player is told of a unit's directive. The four arrows in the circled area are animated and bright. In fact, you can't miss them. When you click on the screen to send units to a particular map spot, these bright arrows inform the player exactly where they are headed.

Look at the elevation here. The hills look rounded and it is very hard to tell where the tiles are. This is a good-looking game. Also, you can see the cliffs off the top of the screen. Another subtlety is all of the extra items on the map. There are rocks, cracks, and small plants, all of which combine to create a mood for the game.

Figure 8.11
Age of Empires

When you finally win, Age of Empires tells you in a very big way, with a triumphant drum. This becomes a thing of honor.

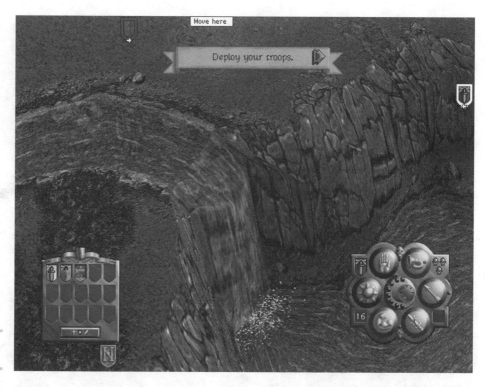

Figure 8.12
Dark Omen

Of all the 3-D landscape engines that I've seen, this is probably the best. Dark Omen has a great engine. Its interface is mostly exceptional, although there are a few quirks. This waterfall flows in real time. There is real height in the game and the units need to move up and down hills. The game itself is somewhat limited, even for an RTT game. There is virtually no resource management and no construction. New units are purchased at the end of a level with money earned from the spoils.

This is very much like traditional strategy games where you move squads or platoons of units, not individuals. Controlling squads is easy and can even be done off screen. Notice the little shield at the top right edge of the screen. This tells you the relative direction of one of your off-screen squads. You can click on that shield and give orders even though you can't see your units.

The floating interface is cool. The buttons turn gray when a particular function is not available or when a unit may not be able to perform it. Some of the functionality takes a bit of getting used to, but overall the interface is simple. I just wish that you could move the floating interface control.

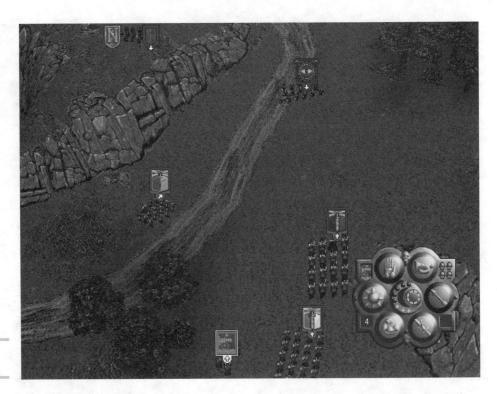

Figure 8.13
Dark Omen

Notice how clear the screen is. No extra garbage—only what you need. The hills off to the upper left are 3-D hills that have height. The cannons cannot fire over this embankment and neither can the crossbowmen. Another good interface choice is the color of the shields. As you can see, each combat unit has a shield associated with it. The dark red shields with the purple centers (at the top of the screen) represent the opposition. This clearly tells the player whose units are whose. The opposition has goblins, who have a shield with an eye, and orcs, who have a shield with a mushroom.

These units are about to engage in combat. From the left are my crossbowmen, a cannon unit, an infantry unit, and a cavalry unit. Each combat unit consists of all like types of combatants. There are no mixed groups of archers and cavalry. This is an interesting paradigm that not many games use, but it is a common theme among most Games Workshop games, the company that makes this game. (Games Workshop makes a bunch of really fun tabletop games too, like BloodBowl and 40,000. If you ever tire of computer games, you might try these.)

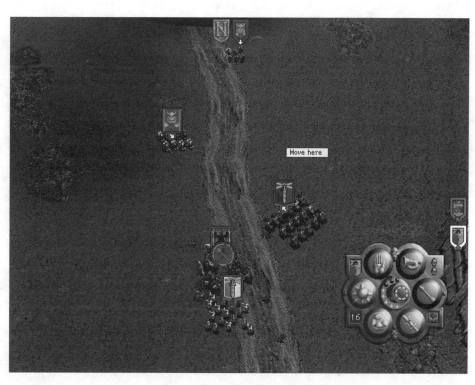

Figure 8.14
Dark Omen

Here we see, just barely, combatants in the center of the screen. This was a great battle. Off to the right on the hill, I set a cannon that fired at oncoming units while I fought hand to hand with any that got through. There is also a group of crossbow-men, indicated by the shield on the right side of the screen. This is how you can command units that are off the screen. Pretty nifty, eh?

That is real strategy and this game easily allows that. The game is also simple to command. And in many ways, it is too simplistic because the only thing to do is combat other units. Still, this single-mindedness has its appeal and makes for an entertaining game.

One thing of note here are the trees. This game has the best trees I have ever seen (aside from real ones). They are 3-D; as you rotate around the screen, you can see through different parts of the trees. You have to see it to believe how gorgeous they really are.

Note the text on the screen. This is an acknowledgement for a command I just gave. This lets you be sure that a unit received your command. These kinds of helpful information make the game a lot easier to play.

One nice thing about a 3-D game is the viewpoint. I can zoom in, zoom out, rotate around the battlefield, and see the action from just about any vantage point. This is a great benefit and makes the game a lot more enjoyable. It also makes mouse controls somewhat tricky. They are difficult and unintuitive to handle, but it's still worth the effort.

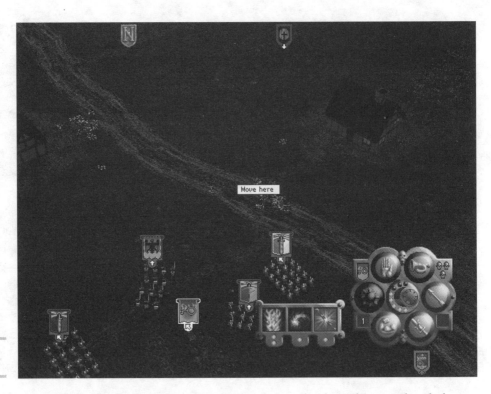

Figure 8.15
Dark Omen

The shield at the top of this screen tells me that undead zombies are headed my way. (This shield represents zombies and the enemies always head your way.) The scenery has changed to nighttime and it has an eerie lighting to it. There are eerie houses that look like the ones in Diablo and light-colored dead bodies everywhere. I have a new unit, a wizard, who has a key for a shield at the middle bottom. He is selected, and the new interface item shows me that he can cast three spells.

I have rotated the scene slightly so you can see how the camera angle can vary widely. It is quite fun to rotate around the battlefield. Notice there is no fog of war in any of these examples from Dark Omen. Dark Omen doesn't have fog of war and doesn't need it. It is a great game anyway.

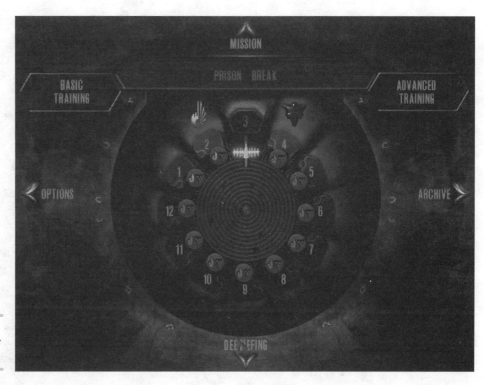

Figure 8.16
The interface of Dark Reign

Here we have a good startup interface from Dark Reign. The circle represents all of the levels available and 3 is the currently selected level. At any time, you can select either basic or advanced training to remind you how things work. There are two symbols to either side of the number 3. These represent the two sides in the "conflict"; you can play either army at any time. At top in red is the phrase "Prison Break," which is the name of this level. These cool startup features make this a solid interface and a cool game. If only the path finding code were better....

Figure 8.17
Dark Reign

Here we have an obvious case of fog of war. The top of the screen is completely obscured in black, making it your job to explore these areas to find hidden enemies. The grayed areas are areas that I have explored but that none of my guys can see right now. This is typical of fog of war.

The lush vegetation serves to block my path and look pretty but not much else. My units are selected; they have rectangular selection boxes around them with health meters on top. This is pretty standard but not too pretty. Age of Empires' selection boxes look nicer, as do the selection boxes in StarCraft.

At the top of the screen is the number 10000. This is my money, but you'd never know it by just looking at the interface. Everything in the game is based on money and since construction is so easy, this is definitely an RTT game.

Off to the right of the screen is the control interface. Like many RTT games before this one, you can control building units off screen. In Age of Empires or Warcraft, you have to click on a specific building to build a particular unit. Not here—if a unit is buildable, it is highlighted on the upper right side of the screen. I should point out here that the Build menu is selected. If other menus are selected, this list of buildable units disappears. This is a great interface feature. Almost all game control can happen from these six menus. Centralizing them like this makes the game a lot easier to control.

The bottom part of the control interface has three sections. The big black box is the minimap and it looks really empty. The white box shows where the screen on the left fits into the world. The meter with a lightning bolt over it represents energy or power available; you can see that I have no generators producing any power. The last meter is the water supply. The game emphasizes a world where water is valuable because most of it is poisonous, so you sell clean water for money.

The interface is simple with many functions at the top of the screen for instant access. These have functionality as follows: Sell building, power toggle, repair, attack, attack without moving, and stop. At all times during the game, these buttons are visible. This emphasizes control to the player and keeps the player focused on war, not on resources or what other things he can do at any particular moment.

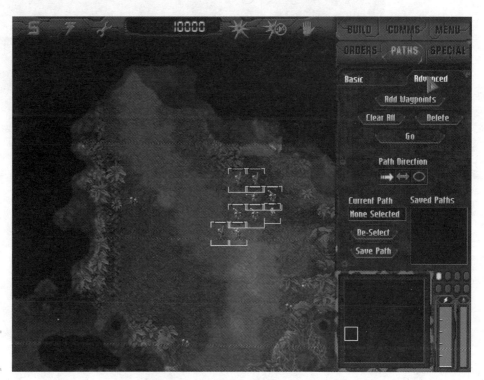

Figure 8.18
Dark Reign

Here, two of my units (the two nearest the top of the screen) are almost dead, as you can tell by their health meters. One nice thing about this game is pathing control, accessed in the Paths menu. The pathing itself is okay, but the control that the player has is exceptional. You have waypoint control; you can save a path and then load it up into another unit; and you can control how a path is followed: from beginning to end, from beginning to end and then back to the beginning, or in a circular fashion. This control panel is one of the best elements of this game.

Figure 8.19
Dark Reign

And the level of control gets better. You can give your units very specific orders in the Orders menu and control the way they react to enemies. This level of control beats any game I have seen so far.

8

Chapter

Figure 8.20
Dark Reign

The green circle is my mouse cursor moving over a target. I have selected all of my units and then selected an enemy unit, which tells all of my units to attack. You can see the bullets fly and this battle is over as fast as it began. That is a major downside to this game: The battles are short and the explosions are weak. It makes the fighting not as much fun as in Total Annihilation or Age of Empires.

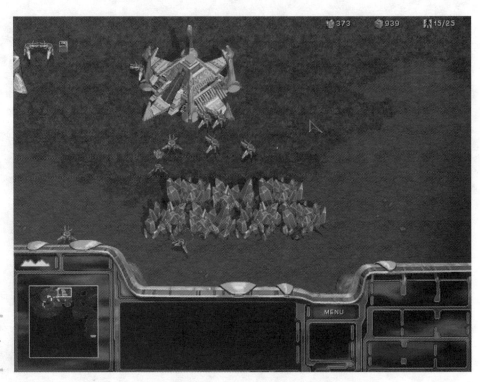

Figure 8.21
The interface of StarCraft

Most people would agree that StarCraft is good because it has character. There is nothing spectacular about it, but it has so many little cool things that it has become one of the best games around. StarCraft has three races, each with a completely unique history, interface, units, fighting tactics, defensive tactics, and gameplay. This game has long-term gameplay just because it takes a while to get good at each of the three races. Most "race-based" RTS/RTT games are essentially two sides of a conflict with almost the same units. The sides in StarCraft are so totally different, it's like three games in one.

This screen shot has the Protoss as our race. This insect-like race of perfectionists has force fields for all of the units. The town center is the pyramid-shaped building near the top of the screen. The peons are the golden fly-like objects. Notice that one is carrying a crystal. The crystals supply the main resource in the game. Crystals are used for building everything and all races use them liberally. In the upper left corner is another peon carrying a green box. This represents the other resource in the game, a special gas needed to build certain units. I have set a few units to the task of collecting this gas. The upper right corner tells me my resources and the number of units I have. Like most RTS/RTT games, I have a limit on the population at any time based on the number of support structures. Like Age of Empires, the number of houses you build affects the maximum number of units you can have at any given time.

The minimap at the bottom left shows the general lay of the land. The bright blue dots show supplies of crystals. I have explored this map a bit and that is why the fog of war doesn't cover it entirely.

The interface is great. The resources are clear and totally out of the way. They don't even obscure the terrain behind. The main interface on the bottom looks great and the clickable areas to the right on the bottom look clickable. The fog looks like real fog, although you can't tell really well from this screen shot. Even though a lot of the screen real estate is given up to the bottom interface section, it still works just fine. The colors work well too. This is a slick-looking game and the feel of the interface is good.

Figure 8.22
StarCraft

The fog is a lot more obvious here. Look at how well the fog is done; it looks like real fog. I am playing a different race here, the Zerg. The interface is different, of course, to match the organic nature of everything that the Zerg do. Here we have selected a creature and its description fills the middle part of the interface section. It's called a Zerg Egg and the way that it's displayed in the middle bottom showcases the object. The meter shows how far along this egg's mutation has come. The 200/200 indicates the health of the egg. In the center of this showcase is an icon used to represent the creature into which this egg will mutate. This center showcase is a perfect type of interface, giving the player everything he might want to know about a selected creature. Of course, you get to see the beautifully rendered organic creatures that make up the Zerg toward the top of the screen.

Figure 8.23
StarCraft

There's no fog here; all of my creatures can see too far and so the fog is off the edge of the screen. Remember, the fog reflects visibility; since my creatures can see far enough, there is no fog. This is generally true of all RTS/RTT games. Look at the selection cursor in the circle. It animates circularly and you can see that the spawning pool is morphing. The circle inside the spawning pool is StarCraft's great selection cursor. Most RTS/RTT games use some cheesy rectangle, but this looks marvelous.

The meter below the creature shows how far along its mutation is, further emphasizing its state. Putting information on the screen and in the info bar (interface element) helps the player quickly spot information that he needs to know.

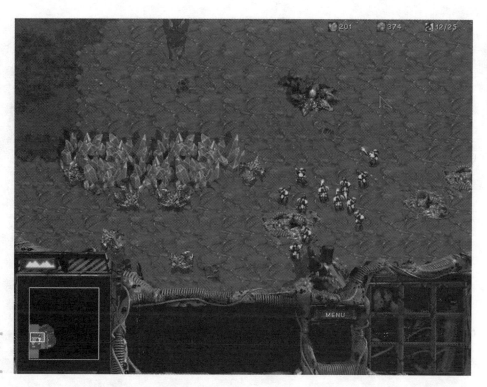

Figure 8.24
StarCraft

Here come human marines from the bottom of the screen. As they shoot my Zerg unit toward the middle, it spurts blood. Cool graphics and sound effects make the splattering blood realistic. Down in the minimap, the green lines are an alert telling me that my unit is being hit. If these units were offscreen, I could easily tell where they were and respond quickly.

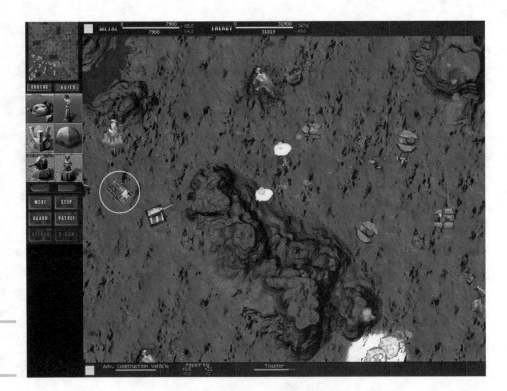

Figure 8.25
Total
Annihilation

What a great action scene! Total Annihilation has some of the coolest explosions and best combat situations I have seen in an RTS/RTT game yet. The terrain looks pretty realistic but a little drab since it only uses a few colors. Still, the hills look great and the acid water (upper left) looks good. It has 2-D bitmaps with a height map to make the land act like hills. The top-down perspective eases the programming by simply avoiding a lot of problems. There is no problem with objects in back blocking objects in front, and there are virtually no overdraw problems where you accidentally draw the same pixel with different graphics. There are only a few things affecting performance in this game—the number of entities in the world and the size of the display. I always play 1024x768; this makes it a much better game to play.

Total Annihilation emphasizes war, and battles are nearly incessant. The minimap in the upper left of the screen shows a bunch of differently colored dots that represent different units in the game. Mine are in the bottom left corner. I was playing against three computer opponents, and winning. You can see a bunch of buttons on the left side of the interface. These buttons are here because the unit I have selected is a construction unit and these are the things that it can build. That construction unit in the circle, has a small selection rectangle around it, which may be difficult to see in this image. The three units on the left part of the screen are my units, which are being attacked by the units on the right. One of the enemy units has fired a rocket, and the smoke trail behind the rocket remains on the screen. There are several explosions visible, which are truly something to behold. Pieces fly everywhere and they are accompanied by a great white bitmap emphasizing the hit. They seem like real explosions. With the great sound this game has, you'd think you were watching *Saving Private Ryan* or *Armageddon* all over again.

Unfortunately for the invaders, they don't have much hope. The two artillery units on the left will easily wipe them out. But the computer opponents are consistent and if you don't repair the units regularly, the computer will slowly wear you down until it destroys these units and invades your domain. This game requires nearly constant attention, which makes it quite fun actually. The AI is decent but the waves of invaders do come in single file, which makes them easy pickings to some degree. The computer opponent will come after you, even after you beat it down to one construction unit. It simply rebuilds. No other RTS/RTT game does that, to my knowledge, making the most innocuous opponent deadly.

The interface is superior in many ways to the others in our survey here. The amount of resources is displayed clearly along the top. The meters basically display the percentage of the total remaining. There are some numbers next to Metal. The 0 tells us when we are out of metal and the 7900 tells us when we are full; think of it like a fuel gauge on your car. The +85.5 is the amount of metal I am producing or mining per second and the –54.5 is the amount I am using per second. These are similar for the energy. This system allows you to use more metal or energy than you produce for a time and then things slow down. I have a huge stockpile here. Total Annihilation starts you out with 1000 of each resource. You need to build storage facilities to hold more. Also, some game units store extra so they become storage facilities.

The bottom part of the interface shows us which unit is selected and its health meter. The Adv. Construction Vehicle is shown here. The next section reads Repairing, which tells us what the construction unit is about to do. The +0.5 is the amount of metal that it refines per second and the +21 is the amount of energy that it generates per second. The last section is its target. It is going after the Toaster to repair it and the meter shows the Toaster's health.

One not-so-great feature of this interface is how to end the game or exit. There is no button or way to see a menu. You need to know that F2 brings up the menu system. Kind of lame, if you ask me.

Resources are simple here. At the top of the game screen, right below the number 31819, is a bright spot. That is a metal resource supply. Put a mining facility on top of it and you produce an endless supply of the metal resource. Energy is even easier to come by. You can build a solar panel or a nuclear power plant. Also, most units in the game generate a little energy that all adds to your pool of energy. Because these resources are so easy to manage, this lets the focus of the game be combat, and it is generally very fun combat.

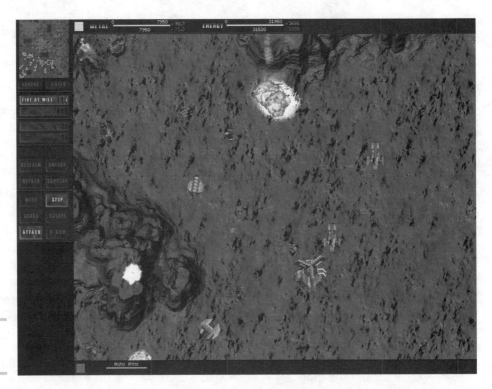

Figure 8.26
Total
Annihilation

The mouse pointer is pointing to a unit on the minimap. This unit is in the center of the screen right now but it is convenient to find a unit on the minimap and instantly find out its status. The unit is a Moho Mine that mines metal ore and it is in perfect health. It happens to belong to my enemy. The interface on the left has changed to follow the capabilities of an offscreen unit. This unit is clearly a military unit because its only control is Attack. It also has a Stop button, but that's not much of a command, is it? There is also an attitude adjustment. The three possibilities are Fire At Will, which makes a unit fire at any enemy within range, Hold Fire, which means the unit will not fire ever, and Return Fire, which means that a unit will only fire if fired upon. I wish it had a few more controls like only fire at flying enemies or only shoot factories. In the heat of combat, units can be hard to control.

Figure 8.27
*Total
Annihilation*

Total Annihilation has about 10 different types of terrain. Most of those are different types of rock, but this figure shows lush green land with a little forest.

The ability to assign a unit to do 100 things is quite cool. This is the best feature of the game perhaps. The commander here has a series of waypoints. He will chop down the trees and extract their energy. He has a path of nodes so he knows where to go. The interface has changed to reflect the things that he can build. On the middle left of the game screen are some of those solar panels I mentioned. Right next to them is a metal extractor. Near the water is another construction unit. The blue rectangles tell us that a unit has been assigned to build there and will get to it as soon as possible. The queuing feature of this game means that you can assign a unit to do 40 different things and then concentrate on something else, knowing that the unit will complete the task if able.

This minimap is quite different. It shows an ocean down the diagonal of the map and highlights the fact that this world has very little landmass. This is a pretty good map for playing.

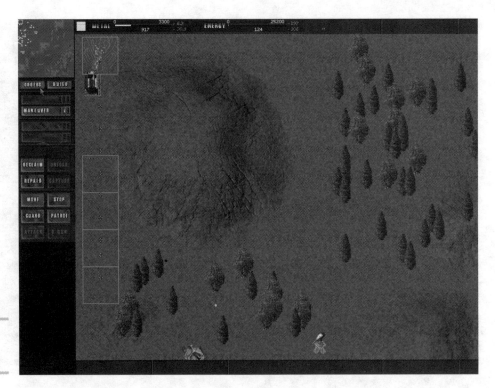

Figure 8.28
Total
Annihilation

Here we show another construction unit with a queue of items to build. These are all reactor cores that will generate energy. The construction units in this game all have at least three different interfaces. By selecting a construction unit and hitting 1, 2, or 3, you can see the different interfaces. Most of these interfaces are for constructing different units, but the one we see here allows for a few other instructions. The Repair option is obvious. Reclaim extracts metal from wreckage such as that seen in Figure 8.25.

Notice the spray that the construction unit at the top left is emitting. This spray is the way they construct units. The idea is that these are tiny robots that attach them-selves to the skeleton of the metal structure to form the final machine. Then they melt themselves and become the machine. Very different, and kinda weird, but the visual effect is nice. It's sort of a spray paint feel.

8
Chapter

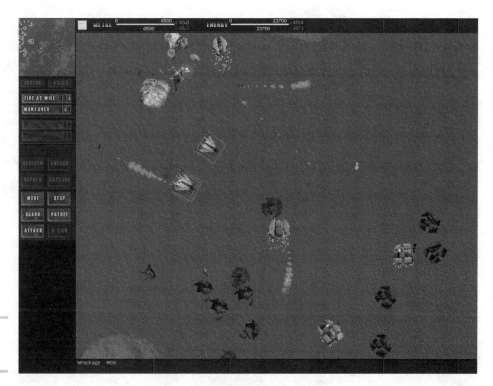

Figure 8.29
Total
Annihilation

Here we have a water battle. Getting just the right screen shot here was difficult since everything is always moving on the water. The darkened wreckage in the middle bottom is what's left of my opponent after my warplanes have fired missiles on them. These aircraft are fun and quite destructive. They almost make the game, just by themselves. Again, you see smoke trails behind one of the aircraft. You have to look closely, but in the middle just below center, is a missile that also has a smoke trail. All of the aircraft are grouped (Ctrl-1) and they have green selection boxes. The interface at left has changed to reflect what these units can do. The Maneuver button is another attitude adjuster. There are three settings: Maneuver, allowing the units to stray a little from their assigned path, Roam, which lets them chase another unit almost to the ends of the world, and Hold Position, making the unit do exactly what you tell it and nothing more.

One last thing is the mouse cursor. The mouse cursor hovering over a unit on screen or on the minimap controls the text that appears on the bottom of the screen. Which unit is selected has nothing to do with it. Here the mouse is hovering over wreckage under water and the bottom of the screen reads "wreckage." A strange quirk about water is that objects below the water are offset. The designers made it where a unit below the water has depth, so your mouse cursor has to be slightly higher on the screen (or negative y) to point at it. That is why my mouse cursor here is offset –y a little from the wreckage.

Overall, this is a well-designed game and I would put it in the drawing for the best RTT game of all time. It is so much fun to play, even if the ground doesn't look all that great.

Now on to programming. First, let's look at how to use DirectDraw.

Working with DirectDraw

About a year ago, some representatives from Intel came to Ion Storm and told us that Intel had been the company that actually implemented DirectDraw. I have not been able to confirm this, but let's assume it's true. I happen to know that Direct3D was written by a British company named Render Morphics. (I read this tidbit in the Direct3D professional reference by Michael Stein, Eric Bowman, and Gregory Pierce.) I'm not sure which portions Microsoft wrote, but of all the APIs in the DirectX system, DirectDraw and DirectSound are the easiest to use. So as you go through this section on creating a game from scratch and looking at the DirectDraw subsystem, try to remember not to blame me for its complexity. "But wait," you say, "isn't this one of the easiest sections?" Why, yes, and it is painfully convoluted. It is good to keep in mind that DirectDraw, the part that allows you to draw quickly in video memory, is the second easiest part of DirectX behind DirectSound. I will try hard to explain it in its easiest terms.

In this chapter, we'll create a black screen and ultimately a black window. The black screen is a full-screen drawing area and the black window is a smaller window without borders. I realize that this is not exciting. Should take only a few pages to explain, right? I wish. This code will be unbelievably complex to a beginner, so bear with me. For you experienced developers who don't already understand DirectDraw, this is a big hump. Once you understand this, you will gain a new respect for those who program games for a living.

What we really want to do here is create a system. We want page flipping, text for getting feedback, a screen to draw graphics, a windowed mode for debugging, a way to test for performance, and a way to get a pointer to a chunk of memory that we can use to draw. Once we create this system, we don't want to have to muck around with it again. Let's make it robust and easy to use. Let's design it for speedy compile times and long-term use.

Each of the things in the list above we will do, but it will take time and effort. The next few chapters will complete the entire drawing sequence, which includes bitmap loading, bitmap compression, bitmap drawing, bitmap sizing, and texture handling. But for now we get to do the grueling part of creating a game. Good luck "and may the force be with you."

One thing you may have noticed about DirectX is that new versions are constantly available. Microsoft has changed its numbering system to jump a full number for all changes. The software industry tends to follow this same premise (to my chagrin). Even a small change in DirectX, say version 2 to 3, takes a full number change even though version 3 should have been 2.1 or maybe 2.5. But since DirectX came out in January of 1996 or so (actually a bit later but I had an inside source), there have been six versions. Hence the name DirectX 6. I guarantee that within a few more years, we will have a DirectX 12 or so. I do appreciate the updates and minor changes from version to version, but the only major revisions have been 2 and 5. Incidentally, does anybody know what happened to DirectX 4?

Introducing DirectDraw

DirectDraw is a layer. Like all layers, it takes memory, processor time, and computer resources. Luckily, it is a good layer and it is thin. It makes drawing to your video card much faster than in the old DOS days (about 2½ years ago). This layer resides on top of your hardware. That means that all hardware will have the same interface if you use DirectDraw. If you make a function call to DirectDraw, say page flipping, you call that function the same way with every video card. ATI and VooDoo cards all work the same. Not internally, of course, but as far as you are concerned, they are the same. In terms of speed, DirectDraw can't be beat. It is reliable and fast. Implementation may be a bit lacking, but it's not too bad.

You've probably seen the layer diagram before, but here it is again in Figure 9.1. This is overly simplified but it correctly illustrates the layered system that DirectDraw is.

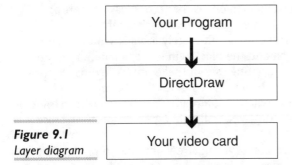

Figure 9.1
Layer diagram

DirectDraw does a lot, and emulates some things when the video card does not support it. Because DirectDraw is becoming the de facto standard for card manufacturers, you can expect that most everything will be handled by the video hardware. All of the function calls you make will go directly to hardware.

Direct3D has also upped the ante for 3-D standardization, which increases our expectations of 3-D support. Unfortunately, Direct3D is not as good as DirectDraw as an API, and VooDoo has established a new standard called GLIDE. The GLIDE API produces much faster draw times and is much easier to program than Direct3D. Many games use the GLIDE API for enhanced performance and since VooDoo produces the chipset and manufacturers are free to design the cards (or not so free because of VooDoo standards), they can focus on design and good coding and not worry about marketing. It may sound odd, but just this once, too much marketing may actually be hurting Microsoft in this area. Then again, I dabble in areas of expertise where I do not belong.

Note: Performance is driven by quite a few factors in Figure 9.1 that are hidden. The lowest layer in the layers diagram is the system hardware; this refers to the PCI bridge as well as the video card itself. If you have AGP, all the better. This is still a bottleneck when it comes to performance. Memory on the video card is a factor, but now with most retail cards having at least 8 MB, with 16 MB becoming the standard, the memory considerations are giving way to bus speed, cache size, and memory access time. Forget how fast your CPU is. Nowadays, it hardly matters. Memory cannot be retrieved fast enough. With a 400 MHz CPU and a 100 MHz bus, the CPU is processing data four times faster than it can retrieve it. Pipeline burst caches help by ramming memory into the cache for a faster access but even the cache bus is being outstripped by the performance of the CPU. How does this affect your video card, you ask? Well, the video card may need to access real memory, not just video memory. Across the PCI (or bridge, if you prefer) this is too slow, but across AGP this is possible. It just slows down computer performance as it blocks the computer's bus while it accesses memory. Since everything seems to rely on the bus speed, video card performance is not really a factor anymore, at least as far as DirectDraw is concerned.

The video card layer has a bunch of hidden interrupt calls, memory accesses, and so on. All of this would take so long for you to figure out that your game would never go to market. Most of these interrupt calls are pretty standard, but this might mean that you spend an extra month on a video game that might otherwise have been saved when you could have just written it using a standard API. Microsoft has standardized the way video cards are accessed by creating the layer above the video card called DirectDraw. Actually, it doesn't directly draw at all because it is a layer above directly drawing, but who wants to quibble. You could call DirectDraw an easy access to your video card.

How does the layer work? Where is DirectDraw? Is it a DLL or something? Direct-Draw is part of Microsoft's COM system. Basically, a bunch of functions are put into a file, like a DLL, and that file is then treated like a C++ object. There is an instantiation routine (a constructor), a cleanup routine (a destructor), and a lot of other functions in between. This is called COM. It is easier to use than a DLL, except in C. You'll have to look in the header files to see why, but the function calls get rather hairy and verbose in C. In any case, the COM system could also be thought of as a global object. It has an ID number that is unique to it and you can basically instantiate it from within any program by knowing that ID number. This ID number is kept in your Windows Registry and so is available to you at any time; think of it as your phone number. In the olden days (2½ years ago), you would have had to find the file by searching through directories for a DLL. No more searching through directories for the DLL; DirectDraw is just a function call away.

COM can be slow. Hence, DirectX can be slow. When you need data from COM, you need to pass a pointer to a structure to a function that will then be filled with that data. The contents of that structure are then duplicated. The COM system goes to work on the new structure, and then copies the new data onto the data in the pointer that you passed. This can use hundreds of extra clock cycles. A DLL can use a pointer directly, costing no extra time. Give and take. Luckily, most of these types of routines are called at startup time and so they generally don't affect speed at run time.

The DirectDraw File Structure

I have mentioned it before but in case you missed it: Do not include header files in your headers. Here is an example of what I mean:

```
//Header.h
#include <windows.h>
#include <ddraw.h>
#include "struct.h"

class DirectDrawHandler
{
    HWND                    WindowHandle;
    LPDIRECTDRAW            DDObject;
    LPDIRECTDRAWSURFACE     Primary;
    LPDIRECTDRAWSURFACE     BackBuffer
    ...
};
```

Now every file that could possibly need to access the DirectDrawHandler must first include windows.h, which itself includes about 30 other headers. If you don't include it, ddraw.h will not compile. Just compiling your headers can slow compile times by 400 percent. Case in point: While working on Age of Empires for Ensemble Studios, the code base had reached nearly 200 files. Our headers all included other headers, which slowed down the compile process. A full rebuild cost us close to an hour and everyone working on the project also had to do the rebuild. That cost us five to six man-hours. Mark Terrano spent about a week and a half pulling headers out of headers, after which our full rebuild time dropped to less than 20 minutes. That's still quite a while but much more tolerable. How you structure your code can affect the effectiveness of your program and your work environment as a whole. Do the extra work and rip the headers out of headers. Your savings will astound you.

The code below is a better example. I have done my homework and found that a HWND is really an unsigned long. That saves me needing to include windows.h. I won't include DirectDraw in the header but I will include it in the .cpp file and simply make the variables global to the file.

```
//***************************** header
//Header.h
#include "struct.h"

class DirectDrawHandler
{
    unsigned long WindowHandle;
    ...
};
```

```
//***************************** cpp file

//header.cpp
#include <windows.h>
#include <ddraw.h>

static LPDIRECTDRAW          DDObject;
static LPDIRECTDRAWSURFACE   Primary;
static LPDIRECTDRAWSURFACE   BackBuffer
```

This will effectively halve your compile times, especially when you don't include windows.h in every file that might need to access this class definition. Sure, you now have a few global variables, which destroys the perfect object model. So what! I'll take performance and easier compiles over perfect design every time. Besides, no design is ever perfect and accepting this fact makes you just one little bit more wise (Confucius says...).

In case you don't know the structure of how to define pointers in headers without including the respective header, simply create a marker for the compiler. Below is an example. The compiler sees the definition and adds it to the list of things it needs to find during link. This only works when you later define a pointer to an item. You cannot put the full object inside another without it being defined, but a pointer works nicely. This is called a forward declaration.

```
struct POINT;

class POINT_CONTAINER
{
      POINT* pt;
};
```

POINT isn't actually declared and the compiler does not know its size or anything about it. The compiler assumes that the .cpp file will define the structure. Then in the .cpp file, you can include the appropriate header, in this case, windows.h.

Data Types

We can't continue without a little more knowledge. This will not be an all-inclusive list, but here are quite a few Microsoft defined data types that will help you as you read further. These definitions can all be found in the online help of Visual C++ once DirectX is installed. You may have to copy the help files from the install directory into your Visual C++ help directory along with your lib files and your header files.

These definitions also include the newer variations of DirectDraw for DirectX 6. They are numbered the same, but they usually have some added functionality and a few modifications of older methods.

DIRECTDRAWSURFACE: A surface refers to a block of memory provided by DirectDraw for the purpose of maintaining or drawing graphics. When you request a surface, DirectDraw hands you a pointer that you can then draw on. This is mostly used for drawing to the screen or to an offscreen buffer. The names of the actual structures are IDirectDrawSurface and IDirectDrawSurface4. IDirectDrawSurface2 and IDirectDrawSurface3 both exist but belong to iterations of DirectX long since past (like the last version, DirectX 5; it was not so long ago, was it?). For our purposes, we only need the first two.

These buffers are usually allocated on the video card and are actually part of the video memory. You may remember the days of writing directly to 0xA000. Things have changed. This is a linear frame buffer. Surprise—no memory segmentation. That means speed and easier access. You don't need to allocate memory and then try to blit it to the screen. These surfaces are *cool beans*.

LP means long pointer. It is simply a 32-bit pointer. LP is a prefix to many Direct-Draw data types. If you are looking in the help files, you will not find the data types with this prefix; you must remove the prefix. For example, LPDIRECTDRAW is a pointer to DirectDraw, and LPDIRECTDRAWSURFACE is a pointer to a surface.

DIRECTDRAW is a class, or so it seems. It is actually a COM object and when you instantiate it, you gain access to the video hardware almost directly. After instantiation, almost everything you do related to drawing is a member function of this class. It handles surfaces and memory management. It is the encapsulation of the entire video driver process and provides an information service. The name of the structure that defines all of the raw data is IDirectDraw. Its DirectX 6 update is IDirectDraw4.

DDSURFACEDESC is a structure that you will find most useful. The following definition can be found in the DirectX 2 help files:

```
typedef struct _DDSURFACEDESC{
    DWORD   dwSize;
    DWORD   dwFlags;
    DWORD   dwHeight;
    DWORD   dwWidth;
    LONG    lPitch,
    DWORD   dwBackBufferCount,
    union
    {
        DWORD   dwMipMapCount,
        DWORD   dwZBufferBitDepth,
        DWORD   dwRefreshRate,
    };

    DWORD           dwAlphaBitDepth;
    DWORD           dwReserved;
    LPVOID          lpSurface;
    DDCOLORKEY      ddckCKDestOverlay;
    DDCOLORKEY      ddckCKDestBlt;

    DDCOLORKEY      ddckCKSrcOverlay;
    DDCOLORKEY      ddckCKSrcBlt;
    DDPIXELFORMAT   ddpfPixelFormat;
    DDSCAPS         ddsCaps;
} DDSURFACEDESC,  FAR* LPDDSURFACEDESC;
```

Only a few of the variables in the above definition will be used in the engine created in this book. dwHeight is the height of the screen/surface in pixels. dwWidth is the width of the screen/surface in pixels. lPitch is important; it defines the number of pixels until the start of the next line. On my Matrox Millenium card (that I used to have), 800x600 mode had an lPitch of 960. That meant that I could only see 800 pixels wide on the screen but internally the card was storing 960. I don't know why, but you need to take this into account to be backward compatible. I don't think that any cards still do this, but it's better to be safe than sorry. ddpfPixelFormat tells you how the pixels are defined. This is how you find out whether a 16-bit screen is 5x5x5 or 5x6x5. We'll discuss different 16-bit color models in a little while. lpSurface is a pointer to the currently selected screen/surface and may come in handy from time to time.

DirectX 6 introduced a slight variation of this, which will help us below. If you only need basic DirectDraw functionality, stick with the above. Since I've modified everything to work with DirectX 6, you might as well take advantage of it. This structure can also be found in the newest version of ddraw.h. Like its previous definition, we are only interested in a few variables, but we have more if we need them.

```
typedef struct _DDSURFACEDESC2
{
    DWORD         dwSize;              // size of the DDSURFACEDESC structure
    DWORD         dwFlags;             // determines what fields are valid
    DWORD         dwHeight;            // height of surface to be created
    DWORD         dwWidth;             // width of input surface
    union
    {
        LONG      lPitch;    // distance to start of next line (return value only)
        DWORD     dwLinearSize;        // Formless late-allocated optimized
                                       // surface size
    } DUMMYUNIONNAMEN (1);
    DWORD         dwBackBufferCount;   // number of back buffers requested
    union
    {
        DWORD     dwMipMapCount;       // number of mip-map levels requested
                                       // dwZBufferBitDepth removed, use
                                       // ddpfPixelFormat one instead
        DWORD     dwRefreshRate;       // refresh rate (used when display mode
                                       // is described)
    } DUMMYUNIONNAMEN (2);
    DWORD         dwAlphaBitDepth;     // depth of alpha buffer requested
    DWORD         dwReserved;          // reserved
    LPVOID        lpSurface;           // pointer to the associated surface
                                       // memory
    DDCOLORKEY    ddckCKDestOverlay;   // color key for destination
                                       // overlay use
    DDCOLORKEY    ddckCKDestBlt;       // color key for destination blt use
    DDCOLORKEY    ddckCKSrcOverlay;    // color key for source overlay use
    DDCOLORKEY    ddckCKSrcBlt;        // color key for source blt use
    DDPIXELFORMAT ddpfPixelFormat;     // pixel format description of the surface
```

```
    DDSCAPS2        ddsCaps;              // direct draw surface capabilities
    DWORD           dwTextureStage;       // stage in multitexture cascade
} DDSURFACEDESC2;
```

The purpose of the DDSURFACEDESC and the DDSURFACEDESC2 structures is to get information to and from the DIRECTDRAW object. These structures can also be used for information to and from surfaces or just about anything in DirectDraw. (You might find it amusing to note that I fixed a typo in Microsoft's comments. I'm sure I have plenty of my own, but I find it amusing—even funny. Compare this to the structure in ddraw.h and see if you can find it.)

DDSCAPS is used to describe what kinds of DirectDraw surfaces can be created and is part of the surface creation process. This is a parameter passed at screen/surface creation time. The newer version is DDSCAPS2. Both definitions are below. They are basically just for passing simple flags to DirectDraw. The dwCaps member variable is simply filled with a lot of #defines OR'd together (i.e., dwCaps = FLAG1 | FLAG2 | FLAG27;).

```
typedef struct _DDSCAPS
{
    DWORD           dwCaps;               // capabilities of surface wanted
} DDSCAPS;

typedef struct _DDSCAPS2
{
    DWORD           dwCaps;               // capabilities of surface wanted
    DWORD           dwCaps2;
    DWORD           dwCaps3;
    DWORD           dwCaps4;
} DDSCAPS2;
```

DIRECTDRAWCLIPPER allows you to run in windowed mode. The clipper is created as follows:

```
DDObject->CreateClipper (0, &DDClipper, NULL);
DDClipper->SetHWnd (0, WindowHandle);
PrimarySurface->SetClipper (DDClipper);
```

It automatically clips any drawing to the dimensions of the WindowHandle, which happens to be the main program window. Without a clipper, drawing can do some strange things. Rely on it, but if you want to see what happens, you can comment out those three lines of code and run the program later. The results are usually harmless but really strange.

Broad Concepts

So far, we have briefly talked about a host of different things without bringing you up to speed on some terminology and broad concepts. Hopefully, after this brief description, you'll be up and flying.

Double Buffering

Double buffering is the way you draw and display. It has to do with screen composition and seamless animation. In true animated films, screen composition problems do not exist, but in computers, this is an ever-present problem. If you draw directly on the screen, even very fast computers show item by item being placed and drawn on the screen. This destroys the illusion that games try to create. People won't have the "suspension of disbelief" that they get while watching a movie. It's sort of like watching a "B" movie where all of the special effects are cheesy and it's easy to figure out how everything is done.

So what you do is compose a scene out of view. You draw to another part of memory or another memory slot on the video card and then flip it into view. DirectDraw is designed for this very common event (in the game world) and has functionality to support it. See Figure 9.2.

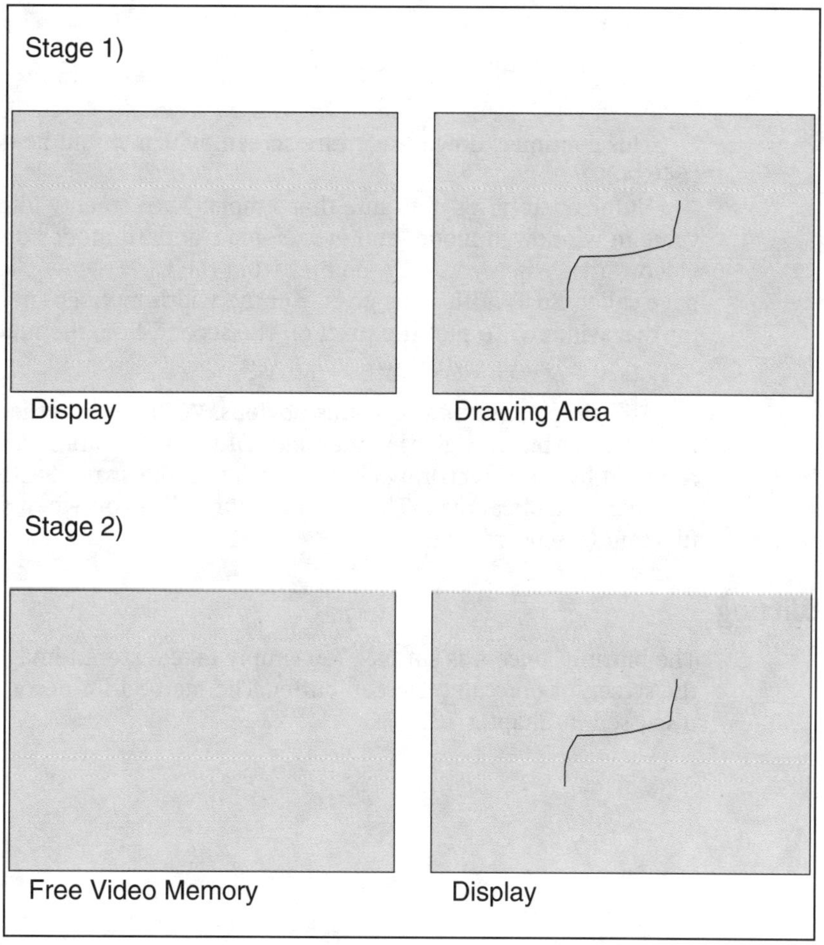

Figure 9.2
Example of double buffering. In Stage 1, ask the system for a pointer to an area for drawing. This happens every frame. A pointer to the Drawing Area is handed back to the program. The Display Area hasn't changed.

In Stage 2, you have finished drawing and now you are ready to draw the next frame. Call the Flip function which changes the Display Area to the former Drawing Area and releases the former display. This will become your new drawing area the next time you request a pointer to a drawing area.

Stage 1)

Display | Drawing Area

Stage 2)

Free Video Memory | Display

Offscreen Buffer or Back Buffer

The offscreen, or back, buffer is the real drawing area. It is also called a frame buffer. You will blit graphics and text into this memory region on the video card. Then when the flip happens, that drawing region becomes the display and you need a new offscreen buffer. This is simply memory. What you have is a pointer to some memory handed to you from DirectDraw. Treat this as a linear chunk of memory. To place a pixel value, say in the upper left corner, set the pointer value to 65535, which is white in 16-bit. Because it is linear, the pixel to its right is the pointer plus 1.

```
*(ptr+1) = 65535;
```

Easy math. The next pixel is the same pointer plus 1 and so on. Now what happens once you get to the end of the next line? That depends. Usually, the next pixel is the first pixel on the next line. Let's say that the width of your screen is 640. The first pixel is:

```
*ptr;
```

The start of the next line is:

```
*(ptr+640);
```

This continues down the entire screen, which would be 480 lines in this case (640x480).

Unfortunately, it's not quite that simple. The screen width can be any arbitrary value in windowed mode, and even some standard modes don't evenly align on some video cards. When you get a pointer from the DirectDraw class, it returns a value I have called RealWidth. This gives you the width in video memory that was allocated for that window. To plot the pixel on the second line, the math is like so:

```
*(ptr + Screen->RealWidth) = 65535;
```

Still simple, but maybe not as obvious. We'll get into the actual drawing in the next chapter but this gives you an idea of where we are headed. The actual pointer returned by the DirectDraw class is hidden in the struct SCREEN_STRUCT as the member variable Screen. This will be returned to you when you call the appropriate function (discussed later.)

Blitting

The blitting concept is simple. You simply take a stored image and put it quickly onto the screen or onto an offscreen buffer. The method for accomplishing this feat will be discussed in Chapter 13.

Flipping the Screen

Flipping works in a relatively simple manner. Your video card is always using part of its video memory to display the screen. It looks at its internal pointer 75 times a second to know where in its video RAM the image of the screen is displayed and then displays that on your monitor. Flipping works by changing the pointer. The video hardware points to one location in video memory while you draw to another. Then, when you flip, it really just makes the hardware point to a different location so you can draw to the first area, formerly the display area of the video RAM.

Graphics Device Interface (GDI)

The GDI is the standard method that Windows uses to display bitmaps, lines, scroll bars, etc. You can and should use it to display text, which is not a very difficult task. The unfortunate side effect is that GDI is a slow system. Eventually, we will replace the text drawing with a system or two of our own. You won't need GDI in this chapter.

Color Modes

There are six accepted color modes today, although 16-color mode, sometimes called 4-bit mode (remember EGA?), is no longer in common use so we will only examine five. The modes are 256-color or 8-bit, 15-bit, 16-bit, 24-bit, and 32-bit.

8-bit

8-bit uses an index table. A palette of 24-bit colors (typically) is defined for the video hardware. That palette is limited to 256 colors. Each pixel of the display can then hold one of the 256 entries; hence it is called 256-color. 256-color, which contains 24-bit colors, can be enough to make a good-looking game if the colors are chosen carefully. These days, however, players expect more, and since machines are so much faster we will be upping the ante. See the 8-bit color model diagram in Figure 9.3. 8-bit is compact, fast, and easy to use. Color matching is the hardest part, but this mode is still simple. Its only drawback is the limited number of colors.

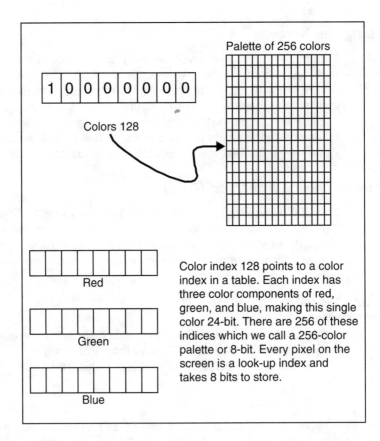

Color index 128 points to a color index in a table. Each index has three color components of red, green, and blue, making this single color 24-bit. There are 256 of these indices which we call a 256-color palette or 8-bit. Every pixel on the screen is a look-up index and takes 8 bits to store.

Figure 9.3
8-bit color mode.

15-bit

15-bit is a 16-bit graphics mode without the high bit. See Figure 9.4. Most video cards say 16-bit when they really mean 15-bit. This is fine, although I prefer 15-bit to actual 16-bit. 15-bit means that each pixel on your display is composed of 5 bits of red, 5 bits of green, and 5 bits of blue. The high bit is not used, so almost every pixel can be a different color. RGB is the color model, and each pixel requires color composition, which generally makes 15-bit a little faster than 8-bit because there is no lookup table and color matching is not required. When you factor in the fact that 15- and 16-bit take 2 bytes for each pixel, they become slower than 8-bit and may be as much as twice as slow. Still, the awe generated by good color composition in 16-bit is overwhelming. Pictures look real and graphics look true to life. It can be stunning.

Chapter 9

Figure 9.4 *15-bit color mode. 15-bit does not use the high bit. Masks are used to fill in the correct color data. All of the colors use the 5 high bits, or Most Significant Bits. The colors are then shifted into position. The code for assembling the colors is shown. You can modify this to suit your needs.*

	R	R	R	R	R	G	G		G	G	G	B	B	B	B	B

```
int r, g, b;   // you need the extra bits in these, otherwise too large
               // variables
int Color;

b>>=3;         // shift the color right and keep the 5 MSBs
g&=248;        // mask out the low 3 bits
g<<=2;         // shift it into position
r&=248;        // mask outh the low 3 bits
r<<=7;         // shift it into position
```

16-bit

16-bit is less common than 15-bit but produces almost the same quality. The bit pattern, as shown in Figure 9.5, is 5 bits for red, 6 bits for green, and 5 bits for blue. All 16 bits are used, but the enhancement is only in the green and it is usually not a visible difference. This mode is only slightly harder to work with than 15-bit but is still just as fast and well worth the effort. Still, the 15-bit model has symmetry and makes more sense. Since the video card may be either 15-bit or 16-bit, we'll need to write our graphics routines to support both.

Figure 9.5 *16-bit color mode. 16-bit is done much the same as 15-bit. It does use the high bit. Masks are used to fill in the correct color data. Red and blue use the 5 high bits, or Most Significant Bits, while green gets 6. The colors are then shifted into position. The code is only slightly modified from 15-bit color manipulation. The extra green bit is usually not perceptible.*

R	R	R	R	R	G	G	G		G	G	G	B	B	B	B	B

```
int r, g, b;   // you need the extra bits in these, otherwise too large
               // variables
int Color;

b>>=3;         // shift the color right and keep the 5 MSBs
g&=252;        // mask out the low 2 bits
g<<=2;         // shift it into position
r&=248;        // mask outh the low 3 bits
```

24-bit

24-bit is probably the hardest to work with. This has to do with byte alignment, as using 3 bytes per pixel creates some interesting problems. Still, for photographic quality and smooth gradients, this is the way to go. There are a full 8 bits of intensity for each composition color, as shown in Figure 9.6. It creates very smooth colors and a nice look. Since the graphic quality is about 10 percent better visually than 16-bit but about 50 percent slower because you are moving data at 3 bytes per pixel, the gain in the quality improvement isn't worth the performance degradation. Incidentally, with this level of quality, you can begin to notice lighting thresholds. The difference, visually, between a 32 red value to 64 red and 64 red to 96 red is not the same. There seems to be a much bigger difference going between 32 and 64 than 64 and 96. All this means is that the color intensity does not scale evenly.

Figure 9.6
24-bit color mode

24-bit data is unique among the color modes. It has the extra byte, meaning that moving from pixel to pixel cannot happen in even steps. memcpy becomes difficult and optimizations often disappear. But it has photographic quality offering 16.7 million colors, most of which you can't see the differences between anyway.

24-bit simplifies color modification and masking by making each color independent and hence quickly modified. It provides a full 256 shades for each color component, making it ideal for photographs.

32-bit

32-bit holds 4 bytes for every pixel. This is 8 bits for red, 8 bits for green, 8 bits for blue, and 8 bits for an alpha channel. See Figure 9.7. You may not ever need an alpha channel, but here is how it works. The higher the alpha channel value, the more opaque the pixel that you are drawing. This is really useful for translucency. Transparency is easy. To prevent pixels from drawing, hence the term transparency, make the alpha channel 0 for all pixels that you don't want drawn. Until computers double in speed, about 2½ years from now, this is out of the question. There is simply too much processing per pixel required to bother trying to use alpha blending, and there is not enough bandwidth to begin considering this alternative. Wait for the 800 MHz computer with a 200 MHz bus, a 32 MB video card, and 256 MB of RAM, and then you can do it. Again, about 2½ years from now. The first 32 MB card is now available from ATI, but wait until they become standard. I hear that 200 MHz bus motherboards will be available in the spring of 1999, so we are getting closer.

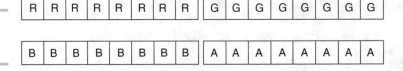

Figure 9.7
32-bit color mode

One pixel just got really complicated. Each pixel is now composed of a full range of color, easy access to each color element, 4-byte alignment for speed, and now we have an alpha channel. The alpha acts like a filter telling the video hardware how much of the color to put over the background. This means that the RGB color this pixel value has can be combined with the pixel already there to give a translucent resultant color. Since there are 4 bytes per pixel, not many video cards support this video mode in any reasonable screen resolution, say 1280x1024. Even if you could, computers are still too slow to be processing that much data. But we can dream of a big, bright future for graphics when 32-bit is supported.

Color Models

No description of color models in this book could ever be adequate. This is simply a brief overview to broaden your perspectives in case you've never heard of any of these. The RGB model is the one we're stuck with for now and for the foreseeable future. It's not bad or anything like that, but other models do exist and having choices is what I prefer.

RGB

Of all the color models, RGB is the most common in programming. It is also the most difficult for artists to use and not easy for many special effects. Look at your monitor very closely (put your nose on the screen or at least close; you may need a magnifying glass); you will find red, green, and blue dots. The screen is composed of three "additive" colors. Each color adds a part of the spectrum to the whole to create a color. In additive color, such as with two flashlights shining on the same wall, red, green, and blue combine to make a near-perfect white. Technically, they do form perfect white but you will never see that on your monitor.

RGB combines different values of red, green, and blue to compose a color. From a math standpoint, RGB is easy to program and games will continue to be RGB for years to come. There are 256 values for each color in a composition in 256-color, 24-bit, and 32-bit. That is, 256 values of red, green, and blue. 16-bit limits the values to only 5 bits for each component, meaning that each color has only 32 possible color values. Still, 16-bit almost always yields better results than 256-color.

CMYK

Used strictly in printing, CMYK is subtractive. The colors are cyan, magenta, yellow, and black. (K? This is because B is typically used for blue.) When you combine the colors of CMY, you get a near black because each element removes part of the color spectrum. Black is added to get pure black. No game has ever used CMYK and I doubt that they ever will.

YUV

Television uses this method for broadcasting. It emphasizes light and dark and then adds a little color on top. This method takes a lot less data per pixel and is the model behind JPEG and MPEG. It is tricky to use and requires encoding, which is a sort of compression that takes time. Because it is so computationally intensive, it may never be used in any kind of action game other than for cinemats.

HSV

This is a great model. It uses hue, saturation, and value. Here's how it works: You pick a color, say blue, decide on the intensity of the color, which means how much or little gray is in it, then you say how bright you want it. This model is much more intuitive to humans and much easier to work with as an artist, but it is not easy to program, and I don't know of any video card that supports it yet. If I had my choice of color models to program for, this would be it.

15-bit vs. 16-bit

These are both 16-bit. They both use 2 bytes per pixel but the bit pattern is different. The following is pasted from the DirectDraw help files. These are the color masks used to extract color values from a pixel:

```
15

R: 0x0000F800
G: 0x000007E0
B: 0x0000001F
A: 0x00000000

16

R: 0x00007C00
G: 0x000003E0
B: 0x0000001F
A: 0x00000000
```

After using these masks, the values need to be shifted into proper bit locations. This may not make a lot of sense but let me illustrate. Let's take the first "B" value of 0x1f. In 16-bit that is fine, but for a truer 256-color extraction (or its facsimile), we need to shift it left so that it becomes the higher bits in a byte. In other words, this mask gives us values between 0 and 31. Standard 256-color manipulation means that higher values are much more visible than lower values: The 1 bit turned on looks almost exactly the same as when off but the 128 bit turned on looks completely different. Well, any standard color manipulation requires all 256 colors or 8 bits, not just 5, and we really don't need the lower few bits of the 8 bits anyway since they normally don't change the color enough to make a visible difference. (See Figure 9.8.) So we shift the 5 bits (from our 16-bit masked value) into the most significant bits (MSB) position. This achieves the same visible color difference that we achieve with just 5 bits in 16-bit mode because these 5 bits are the MSBs in 16-bit mode.

8-bit Color to 5-bit Color

Here we have an 8-bit color element, say 8 bits of blue, as part of a 24-bit RGB color (8 bits of red, green, and blue). Since we are designing a 16-bit engine, the 8 bits must fit into the 5 bits allocated in 16-bit graphics mode.

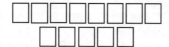

16-bit mode only needs significant bits. Subtle color differences are not possible because we need to cut off the low 3 bits. We just mask out the low 3 bits and right shift the blue color so that all 5 bits of significant color remain. Notice that, instead of color values of 0-255 we now have 0-31.

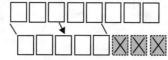

Lastly, we take the individual color elements, red, green, and blue, that have been masked and shifted into position and we ask them to create a composite 16-bit color. The high bit is not used in 15-bit. This method is almost identical for 16-bit but we keep 6 bits for green.

R	R	R	R	R		G	G	G	G	G		B	B	B	B	B

X	R	R	R	R	R	G	G	G	G	G	G	B	B	B	B	B

Figure 9.8
8-bit to 5-bit conversion.

DirectDraw Class

Below is the header file for the management of DirectDraw. You will find a class, and thus an encapsulation, of DirectDraw in the DIRECT_DRAW_MANAGER. This encapsulates everything needed for a 16-bit (or 15-bit) video. We will include this header only in two other files: dirdraw.cpp and the drawing routines manager covered in the next chapter. Including this file only in a few places is important to compile times and ultimately the development time.

The included headers are the common header struct.h, windows.h, and ddraw.h, which is what the header needs to access the DirectDraw routines in the API, standard Windows definitions, and our generic code used throughout the program. Also, notice the compiler directives #ifndef, #define, and #endif at the end of the file. These should be in every header file with different defined values following. This prevents strange compile errors in case you accidentally include the same header twice and often reduces compile times. They are useful and I recommend always using them. You'll also find them in struct.h.

Of note are a few of the beginning declarations, especially:

```
#if _MSC_VER >= 1000
#pragma once
#endif // _MSC_VER >= 1000
```

It helps us dictate that this header will be precompiled and compiled only once regardless of how many files include this. I use this a lot in the files. First, I need to determine if Visual C++ is loaded to make use of #pragma. There are equivalencies in Borland and Watcom, but this is good enough for right here.

We also have:

```
#define FC __fastcall
```

This is a way of cleaning up the code. __fastcall is a great way to make the compiler use register-based calling instead of stack-based function calls. It can speed up things significantly, but the keyword looks bad in the files, so I define it to be FC and the code looks a lot cleaner.

Note: Other compilers use the __fastcall notation with only one underscore, as in _fastcall. It is not a standard C++ keyword or anything like that; it is simply a compiler directive that has become common. I have yet to see it in any C++ manual.

The last thing of note is the comment:

```
//#define DIRECTDRAW_VERSION    0x0600
```

This can control which version of DirectDraw you compile in case you want to use an earlier version of the API.

The enums take the place of #defines. They are encapsulated and prevent dirtying the namespace. You can access them anytime by using DIRECT_DRAW_ MANAGER :: COLOR_TYPE or something similar. The values of COLOR_TYPE tell us whether we are drawing in 5 bits per color component for each pixel or whether green has 6. The value for MAXOFFSURFACES is arbitrary and could very well be set to 0 if you don't plan to use offscreen surfaces. (These are discussed later.)

Below is dirdraw.h, with explanations following the listing:

```
// dirdraw.h


#if _MSC_VER >= 1000
#pragma once
#endif // _MSC_VER >= 1000


#ifndef __DIRDRAW_H_
#define __DIRDRAW_H_
#define FC __fastcall
```

```
//#define DIRECTDRAW_VERSION      0x0600

#ifndef __STRUCT_H_
#include "c:/library_cur/struct.h"
#endif


#include <ddraw.h>
#include <windows.h>

//**************************************
//**************************************

//**************************************
//**************************************

class DIRECT_DRAW_MANAGER            // 16 bit only
{
public:
        enum COLOR_TYPE { _5x5x5_, _5x6x5_};
        enum {MAXOFFSURFACES = 200};

private:
        bool                NotInitializedFlag, FullScreenFlag;
        HWND                WindowHandle;
        int                 Width, Height, ColorType;
        int                 WindowX, WindowY;
        SCREEN_STRUCT       Screen;
        DWORD               TotalVideoMemory, AvailableVideoMemory;

        LPDIRECTDRAW        DDObject;
        LPDIRECTDRAW4       DDObjectNew;
        LPDIRECTDRAWSURFACE4 Primary;
        LPDIRECTDRAWSURFACE4 BackBuffer;
        DDSURFACEDESC2      Description;
        DDSCAPS2            ddsCaps;

        //********* offscreen buffers for faster drawing, in video mem
        int                 NumOffSurfaces;
        LPDIRECTDRAWSURFACE4 OffSurface[MAXOFFSURFACES];
        DDSURFACEDESC2      OffSurfaceDescription;
        int                 OffWidth[MAXOFFSURFACES],
                            OffHeight[MAXOFFSURFACES];

        //********* clipping in a window
        LPDIRECTDRAWCLIPPER  DDClipper;

        int  FC    CreateDirectDraw ();
        void FC    ErrorMessage (char* str);
        void FC    CreateOffSurface (int which, int w, int h);
                   // prep for bitmap loading
```

```
        int   FC    LoadOffSurface (int whichsurface, char* filename);


public:

        DIRECT_DRAW_MANAGER ();
        ~ DIRECT_DRAW_MANAGER ();
        void FC   Clear () {}
        int  GetColorType () {return ColorType;}

        //*************** this should be a fairly simple interface
        // call CreateMainWindow to create the HWND and start the program.
        // This should be called from within WinMain. Pass a DIRECT_DRAW_MANAGER
        // pointer to SCREEN_MANAGER and you are off and running.

        // 16-bit bit depth is assumed
        // note: fastcall won't help here
        HWND CreateMainWindow (int w, int h, char* ClassName,
            void* MessageLoop, void* hInst, bool FullScreen = true);

        void FC   ClearBackBuffer ();
        //***************

        SCREEN_STRUCT* FC PrepFrame ();
        SCREEN_STRUCT* FC GetScreen () {return & Screen;}
        void FC   InterruptFrame ();    // to stop for GDI or something else
        int  FC   DrawFrame ();         // returns 0 for OK and anything else for
                                        // try again later


        //***************

        void FC   DrawOffSurface (int x, int y, int which);

        // the GetOffSurface call must be followed by a call to ReleaseOffSurface
        // or the program will lock up
        SCREEN_STRUCT* FC GetOffSurface (int which);    // must exist first
        void FC   ReleaseOffSurface (int which );
        int  FC   CreateBlankOffSurface (int w, int h);

        //***************
        void FC   PaintText (int x, int y, char* string);

};


//**************************************
//**************************************
#undef FC
#endif
```

Let's look at the class members and see what they are and what they are used for.

NotInitializedFlag is a variable to determine whether or not everything in the class initialized correctly. If this class is used correctly, you will not need it, but in case you run into inexplicable errors, leave the line if (NotInitializedFlag == true) return; in nearly all of the member functions. You'll see it in the .cpp file. Otherwise, if you write good code and don't make silly mistakes, you won't ever use this flag.

FullScreenFlag tells us which way to go when moving the back buffer onto the screen. A full-screen window should use the DirectDraw function Flip, while a window should use BitBlt. We'll cover this later but this flag is important. It is set by one of the variables passed to this class when initializing DirectDraw. This function is CreateMainWindow.

WindowHandle is a void pointer returned by Windows to the program once the initial window is created. We'll use WindowHandle throughout the program. It is returned from the function CreateMainWindow to the calling function, which is the WinMain in this case. Everything affecting your program will be based on this void pointer and Windows is really the only entity capable of deciphering the WindowHandle's inner workings.

Width is the window width. Height is the window height. You determine this. If the size is odd, Windows will fail to create the window or it can fail when creating the DirectDraw screen. Full-screen modes are generally limited to 320x240, 512x384, 640x480, 800x600, 1024x768, and 1280x1024. Better video cards now support 1600x1200. Windowed mode limits size in a few ways. You cannot have a window of higher resolution than the current screen resolution. Windowed mode also limits you to the current color depth.

ColorType has either of two values: _5x5x5_ or _5x6x5_. This value is set with a simple mask test right after the screen mode is changed. We'll see this code later.

Screen is a local variable so that you can return this value to the main program. There are C++ methods for handing back data to the host of a class, but this is more convenient for maintaining the values for repeated access.

TotalVideoMemory and AvailableVideoMemory are provided here only for the programmer's reference. This class will initialize them, but no access routines have been provided. If you actually need these values, I'm sure that you can handle putting in your own.

DDObject is the DirectDraw object that we will initialize using DirectDraw calls. This holds the framework for the entire DirectDraw functionality and must be initialized before you can start drawing or creating surfaces. It polls the hardware, maintains lists of video capabilities, and allocates surfaces for you. All function calls pertaining to DirectDraw will ultimately be routed through this object. This is a COM object by the way, but why worry about details.

DDObjectNew is the secondary DirectDraw object, which simply adds a little meat to the standard DirectDraw object. As far as I understand it, it simply holds methods for video memory determination, simplification of surface restoration, hardware support for overlays, gamma control (fairly useful), and better hardware determination. The overlay support is not real common among hardware vendors yet, so this functionality may never be viable. The better hardware determination may be useful for some older machines, but video cards these days all have a minimum set of functionality, so this functionality will soon go the way of the dinosaur. DDObjectNew does change a few function call interfaces, but, for the most part, it is exactly the same as

DirectDraw proper. I have included it for the programmer to utilize but I don't find it much more helpful than a straight DIRECTDRAW. To initialize it, you must first initialize the DDObject and then "attach" DDObject to it. Kind of strange, but it fits within the COM protocol.

Primary is the visible frame buffer. It is like the back buffer, except you can see it. It will hold a pointer to BackBuffer and maintain other data, but you don't need to know about most of that and neither do I. The requirements of DirectX 6 mean that it should be a DIRECTDRAWSURFACE4. This new surface interface has quite a few new abilities. I find most of them not too useful for either 2-D or 3-D, but at least Microsoft is trying. The overlay stuff is, again, not real useful as yet. But you can now get back a lot more information about the surface than before, which can be helpful.

BackBuffer is the back frame buffer. It will never be visible. BackBuffer is the drawing buffer, the linear frame buffer we discussed earlier in this chapter. All drawing should happen here even though DirectX 6 allows drawing to the primary buffer now.

Description is a structure defined by DirectX that holds information about surfaces including color depth, size, current state, etc. This is a very useful structure and it will be used often within this class for information. You may be wondering why it is a DDSURFACEDESC2. DDSURFACEDESC4 doesn't exist yet because only certain parts of DirectX are changed between iterations. This version of DirectX has changed quite a few numbers but not all of them match. DDSURFACEDESC didn't have all of the information that DirectX 6 requires, so here is DDSURFACEDESC2.

ddsCaps is another structure that can be used to obtain information about the video hardware capabilities. It is defined in ddraw.h like Description and also has the new type: DDSCAPS2.

The next five variables are all related to offscreen buffers. These buffers can be filled with drawing information at startup time and blitted to the screen much faster than we could possibly draw them into the buffer. Their use will be covered in detail in a few chapters, but for now, let's just accept that they are here. These variables are NumOffSurfaces, OffSurface, OffSurfaceDescription, OffWidth, and OffHeight.

DDClipper is definitely an important variable. Defined in ddraw.h, it confines all drawing to the surface and doesn't let you draw outside the confines of the window. In full-screen mode, no problem, but in windowed mode, you can have serious problems and the drawing can come out pretty strange without it. You need this.

Now let's look at the function prototypes. You have probably noticed FC (_fastcall) used before a lot of the functions. This makes the compiler create register-based function calls (when possible) rather than stack based. This can make function calls significantly faster. Generally, none of these functions will be called more than once per frame, but they might be and speed always helps.

The interface is really quite simple. There is the constructor and destructor section, which contains GetColorType for lack of a better place to put it. The CreateMain-Window function resides by itself and is meant to create the main window and initialize DirectDraw all in one shot. The next section is filled with functions that lock down the frame buffer for drawing, unlock it, draw it onto the primary buffer, and grab the info for the screen. The next section is meant for offscreen surfaces but we won't detail those right now, and the last draws text on the screen using GDI calls.

Pretty simple stuff. At least, I've tried to keep it simple. Any complaints... tell my wife. Anyway, this is a really transparent layer I've put on top of DirectDraw and this simplifies its use more than you can imagine. The code follows.

By the way, a good book on DirectDraw is *DirectDraw Programming* by Bret Timmons (M&T Books). A little dry but a good programmers reference, especially if you plan to do 8-bit color.

The includes are simple. We include the header, which includes windows.h, struct.h, and ddraw.h, so we're set. We also include asm.h, a file I wrote. It looks like this:

```
// asm.h


#if _MSC_VER >= 1000
#pragma once
#endif // _MSC_VER >= 1000

#define FC __fastcall


void FC  Memset16Bit ( U16ptr dst, U16 fill, int num );
void FC  Memcpy16Bit ( U16ptr dst, U16ptr src, int num );

void FC  Memcpy16BitLightened ( U16ptr dst, U16ptr src, int num );
void FC  Memcpy16BitDarkened  ( U16ptr dst, U16ptr src, int num );
void FC  Memcpy15Bit50Percent ( U16ptr dest, U16ptr source, int num );
void FC  Memcpy15Bit25Percent ( U16ptr dest, U16ptr source, int num );
void FC  Memcpy15Bit75Percent ( U16ptr dest, U16ptr source, int num );

#undef FC
```

It is designed for fast memcpy's and fast memset's as well as a few other functions. They will generally outperform the standard memcpy by about 15 percent and memset by about 8 percent. Your mileage may vary, but these are useful. We'll detail the assembly code much later.

Below is the entire listing for dirdraw.cpp. A detailed explanation of each section follows:

```
// dirdraw.cpp

#include "c:/library/dirdraw.h"
#include "c:/library/asm.h"

    //****************************
    //****************************

DIRECT_DRAW_MANAGER :: DIRECT_DRAW_MANAGER ()
{
    // let's set all values to 0. This is a simple constructor that
    // simply initializes all of the member variables.
    WindowHandle = NULL;            // pointers
```

```
                DDObject     = NULL;
                DDObjectNew  = NULL;
                Primary      = NULL;
                BackBuffer   = NULL;

                AvailableVideoMemory = 0;        // numbers
                TotalVideoMemory = 0;

                Width    = 0;
                Height   = 0;
                WindowX  = 0;
                WindowY  = 0;

                FullScreenFlag = 0;
                NotInitializedFlag = true;


                //********* offscreen buffers for faster drawing, in video mem
                // we may use these later, but for now, let's just allocate them and
                // leave them alone

                NumOffSurfaces = 0;
                for (int i=0; i<MAXOFFSURFACES; i++)
                {
                    OffSurface[i] = NULL;
                    OffWidth[MAXOFFSURFACES] = 0, OffHeight[MAXOFFSURFACES] = 0;
                }
        }


        //***************************

DIRECT_DRAW_MANAGER :: ~ DIRECT_DRAW_MANAGER ()
{
        if (DDObjectNew != NULL)
        {
                DDObjectNew->Release ();   // takes care of all underlying objects

                if (DDClipper != NULL) DDClipper->Release ();
                if (Primary   != NULL) Primary->Release (); // kills all associated
                                                            // surfaces
                if (BackBuffer  != NULL) BackBuffer->Release ();
        }
}


        //***************************
        //***************************
HWND DIRECT_DRAW_MANAGER :: CreateMainWindow (int w, int h,
            char* ClassName, void* MessageLoop, void* hInst,
            bool FullScreen)
{
        if (NotInitializedFlag == false) return NULL;   // already initialized
        WNDCLASS    wc;
```

```
      FullScreenFlag = FullScreen;                    // store this value

      wc.style=           CS_HREDRAW | CS_VREDRAW;
      wc.lpfnWndProc =    (long (__stdcall *)(void *, unsigned int, unsigned
                           int, long)) MessageLoop;
      wc.cbClsExtra =     0;
      wc.cbWndExtra =     0;
      wc.hInstance =      hInst;
      wc.hIcon =          LoadIcon (hInst, IDI_APPLICATION);
      wc.hCursor =        LoadCursor (NULL, IDC_ARROW);
      wc.hbrBackground =  NULL;
      wc.lpszMenuName =   ClassName;                   // NULL;
      wc.lpszClassName =  ClassName;

      RegisterClass (&wc);

      if (FullScreen)     // there are some slight differences between
                          // fullscreen and not
{
      WindowX = 0, WindowY = 0;
      WindowHandle = CreateWindowEx (
            WS_EX_TOPMOST,
            ClassName,
            ClassName,
            WS_POPUP,
            WindowX,
            WindowY,
            640, // GetSystemMetrics (SM_CXSCREEN), // full screen
                                                    // dimensions
            480, // GetSystemMetrics (SM_CYSCREEN),
            NULL,
            NULL,
            hInst,
            NULL);
}
      else
{
      WindowX = GetSystemMetrics (SM_CXSCREEN)/2-w/2, // center window
      WindowY = GetSystemMetrics (SM_CYSCREEN)/2-h/2;
      WindowHandle = CreateWindowEx (
            0,
            ClassName,
            ClassName,
            WS_POPUP,
            WindowX,
            WindowY,
            w,
            h,
            NULL,
            NULL,
            hInst,
            NULL);
```

```
            }

            // there is a problem creating the window
            if (WindowHandle ==  NULL) return NULL;

            // we now have a real window and we are ready to proceed
            Width    = w;
            Height   = h;


            ShowWindow   ( WindowHandle, 1 );
            UpdateWindow ( WindowHandle );
            SetFocus     ( WindowHandle );
            ShowCursor   ( FALSE );

            int err = CreateDirectDraw ();
            if (err == 0) return NULL;

            NotInitializedFlag = false;
            return WindowHandle;
      }


      //***************************

void  DIRECT_DRAW_MANAGER :: ErrorMessage (char* str)
{
      MessageBox (WindowHandle, str, "Error", MB_OK);
      DestroyWindow (WindowHandle);
}


      //***************************

int  DIRECT_DRAW_MANAGER :: CreateDirectDraw ()
{
      HRESULT ddret = DirectDrawCreate (NULL, &DDObject, NULL);

      if (ddret != DD_OK) {DestroyWindow (WindowHandle);
      return 0;}

        //**************

      ddret = DDObject->SetCooperativeLevel (WindowHandle,
      (FullScreenFlag) ? (DDSCL_FULLSCREEN | DDSCL_EXCLUSIVE |
            DDSCL_ALLOWREBOOT) : (DDSCL_NORMAL));
      if (ddret != DD_OK) {ErrorMessage ("Cooperative level not set");
      return 0;}

      ddret = DDObject->QueryInterface (IID_IDirectDraw4, (LPVOID *)
                                    &DDObjectNew);
      if (ddret != DD_OK)
      {
          ErrorMessage ("Problem initializing IID_IDirectDraw");
```

```
        return 0;
}

        //***************

if (FullScreenFlag)
{
        // 16bit bit depth

        ddret = DDObjectNew->SetDisplayMode (Width, Height, 16, 0, 0 );
        if (ddret != DD_OK) {ErrorMessage ("Display not set");
        return 0;}
}
        //***************Get primary surface

ZeroMemory (&Description, sizeof (Description));
ZeroMemory (&Description.ddpfPixelFormat, sizeof (DDPIXELFORMAT));

Description.dwSize = sizeof (Description);
Description.dwFlags = DDSD_CAPS;
Description.ddsCaps.dwCaps = DDSCAPS_PRIMARYSURFACE;

if (FullScreenFlag)
{
        Description.ddsCaps.dwCaps |= DDSCAPS_FLIP | DDSCAPS_COMPLEX;
        Description.dwFlags |= DDSD_BACKBUFFERCOUNT;
}

// we can specify more than one back buffer
Description.dwBackBufferCount = 1;

ddret = DDObjectNew->CreateSurface (&Description, &Primary, NULL);
if (ddret != DD_OK) {ErrorMessage ("Surface not created");
return 0;}

        //***************Get pixel format

Description.dwSize = sizeof (Description);
Description.dwFlags = DDSD_PIXELFORMAT;
ddret = Primary->GetSurfaceDesc (&Description);
if (ddret != DD_OK)
{
        ErrorMessage ("pixel format not available");
        return 0;
}

        //************* get our color type

int g = Description.ddpfPixelFormat.dwGBitMask>>5;    // assumes 5 for red
if (g == 0x1F) ColorType = _5x5x5_;
else if (g == 0x3F) ColorType = _5x6x5_;
else {ErrorMessage ("color mode not supported");
```

```
                return 0;}

        //*************** create clipper

    if (FullScreenFlag == false)
    {
        ddret = DDObjectNew->CreateClipper (0, &DDClipper, NULL);
        if (ddret != DD_OK) {ErrorMessage ("clipper not created");
        return 0;}

        ddret = DDClipper->SetHWnd (0, WindowHandle);
        if (ddret != DD_OK)
        {
            ErrorMessage ("Surface not assigned to hwnd");
            return 0;
        }

        ddret = Primary->SetClipper (DDClipper);
        if (ddret != DD_OK)
        {
            ErrorMessage ("clipper not set on primary surface");
            return 0;
        }
    }


        //*************** Get BackBuffer surface

    if (FullScreenFlag)
    {
        ddsCaps.dwCaps = DDSCAPS_BACKBUFFER;
        ddret = Primary->GetAttachedSurface (&ddsCaps, &BackBuffer);
        if (ddret != DD_OK)
        {
            ErrorMessage ("primary surface not attached");
            return 0;
        }
    }
    else
    {
        Description.dwFlags = DDSD_CAPS | DDSD_HEIGHT | DDSD_WIDTH;
        Description.ddsCaps.dwCaps = DDSCAPS_OFFSCREENPLAIN;
        Description.dwWidth = Width;
        Description.dwHeight = Height;
        ddret = DDObjectNew->CreateSurface (&Description, &BackBuffer, NULL);
        if (ddret != DD_OK) {ErrorMessage ("back buffer not made");
        return 0;}
    }

    ZeroMemory (&ddsCaps, sizeof (DDSCAPS2));

    ddsCaps.dwCaps = DDSCAPS_OFFSCREENPLAIN;
    ddret = DDObjectNew->GetAvailableVidMem (&ddsCaps, &TotalVideoMemory,
```

```
                                            &AvailableVideoMemory);
        if (ddret != DD_OK) return 0;
        return 1;
}


        //****************************
        //****************************

int  DIRECT_DRAW_MANAGER :: CreateBlankOffSurface (int w, int h)
{
        if (NotInitializedFlag == true) return -1;
        if (NumOffSurfaces >= MAXOFFSURFACES) return -1;
        int which = NumOffSurfaces;
        CreateOffSurface (which, w, h);
        OffWidth[which] = w; OffHeight[which] = h;

        U16ptr ptr = (U16ptr) GetOffSurface (which);
        if (ptr != NULL) Memset16Bit (ptr, 0, w*h);
        ReleaseOffSurface (which);

        NumOffSurfaces++;                   // increment our count
        return which;
}


        //****************************

void DIRECT_DRAW_MANAGER :: CreateOffSurface (int which, int w, int h)
{
        if (NotInitializedFlag == true) return;
        ZeroMemory (&OffSurfaceDescription, sizeof (DDSURFACEDESC));
        OffSurfaceDescription.dwSize = sizeof (DDSURFACEDESC);
        OffSurfaceDescription.dwFlags = DDSD_CAPS | DDSD_HEIGHT | DDSD_WIDTH;
        OffSurfaceDescription.ddsCaps.dwCaps = DDSCAPS_OFFSCREENPLAIN;
        OffSurfaceDescription.dwHeight = h;
        OffSurfaceDescription.dwWidth = w;
        DDObjectNew->CreateSurface (&OffSurfaceDescription, &OffSurface[which],
                                NULL);
}


        //****************************

void DIRECT_DRAW_MANAGER :: DrawOffSurface (int x, int y, int which)
{
        if (NotInitializedFlag == true) return;
        if (Screen.Screen == NULL) return;

        BackBuffer->Unlock (NULL);          // first unlock the back buffer

        RECT rect = {0, 0, OffWidth[which], OffHeight[which]}; // draw
        BackBuffer -> BltFast (x, y, OffSurface[which], &rect,
                        DDBLTFAST_NOCOLORKEY | DDBLTFAST_WAIT);
```

```
            if (Screen.Screen != NULL)              // then, restore the lock
            {
                int ret;
                                                    // keep going until it get it right
                do{
                ret = BackBuffer->Lock (NULL, &Description, DDLOCK_SURFACEMEMORYPTR,
                                        NULL);
                }while (ret!=DD_OK);
            }
            Screen.Width = Width, Screen.Height = Height;
            Screen.Screen = (U16ptr) Description.lpSurface;
            Screen.RealWidth = Description.lPitch/2;
}


        //****************************
        //****************************


// this function call must be followed by a call to "ReleasePointerToOffSurface"
SCREEN_STRUCT*
        DIRECT_DRAW_MANAGER :: GetOffSurface (int which)      // must exist first
{
        if (NotInitializedFlag == true) return NULL;
        if (which >= NumOffSurfaces || which<0 || NumOffSurfaces<1) return NULL;

        ZeroMemory (&OffSurfaceDescription, sizeof (DDSURFACEDESC));
        OffSurfaceDescription.dwSize = sizeof (DDSURFACEDESC);
        if (OffSurface[which]->IsLost ()) OffSurface[which]->Restore ();

        HRESULT rval = OffSurface[which]->Lock (NULL, &OffSurfaceDescription,
                                                0, NULL);
        if (rval != DD_OK) return NULL;

        Screen.Width = OffWidth[which], Screen.Height = OffHeight[which],
            Screen.Screen = (U16ptr) OffSurfaceDescription.lpSurface;
        Screen.RealWidth = OffSurfaceDescription.lPitch/2;
        return &Screen;
}


        //****************************

void DIRECT_DRAW_MANAGER :: ReleaseOffSurface (int which)
{
        if (NotInitializedFlag == true) return;
        if (which >= NumOffSurfaces || which<0 || NumOffSurfaces<1) return;
        OffSurface[which]->Unlock (NULL);
}


        //****************************
        //****************************

void __fastcall DIRECT_DRAW_MANAGER :: ClearBackBuffer ()
{
```

```
        if (NotInitializedFlag == true) return;
        PrepFrame ();
        Memset16Bit (Screen.Screen, 0, Screen.Width*Screen.Height);
}


        //***************************

SCREEN_STRUCT*
        DIRECT_DRAW_MANAGER :: PrepFrame ()
{
        if (NotInitializedFlag == true) return NULL;
        ZeroMemory (&Description, sizeof (DDSURFACEDESC));
        Description.dwSize = sizeof (Description);
        int ret;
        do{
                ret = BackBuffer->Lock (NULL, &Description, DDLOCK_SURFACEMEMORYPTR,
                                        NULL);
        }while (ret!=DD_OK);

        BackBuffer->Unlock (NULL);
        Screen.Width = Width;
        Screen.Height = Height;
        Screen.Screen = (U16ptr) Description.lpSurface;
        Screen.RealWidth = Description.lPitch/2;
        return &Screen;
}


        //***************************

void DIRECT_DRAW_MANAGER :: InterruptFrame ()
{
        if (NotInitializedFlag == true) return;
        BackBuffer->Unlock (NULL);
        Screen.Screen = NULL;
}


        //***************************

int DIRECT_DRAW_MANAGER :: DrawFrame ()            // swap
{
        if (NotInitializedFlag == true) return 0;
        POINT pt = {0, 0};
        ClientToScreen (WindowHandle, &pt);

        RECT BuffRect = {pt.x, pt.y, pt.x+Width, pt.y+Height};
        RECT DRect = {0, 0, Width, Height};

        int pass = 0;                                  // DDFLIP_WAIT;

        if (FullScreenFlag)
        {
```

```
                        int ret = BackBuffer->GetFlipStatus (DDGFS_ISFLIPDONE);
                        if (ret == DDERR_WASSTILLDRAWING) return 1;

                        ret = Primary->Flip (NULL, pass);      // too slow

                        // int ret = Primary->Blt (&BuffRect, BackBuffer, &DRect, pass,
                                              NULL);

                        if (ret == DDERR_SURFACELOST)
                        {
                            ret = DDObjectNew->RestoreAllSurfaces ();
                            if (ret != DD_OK) {ErrorMessage ("Surfaces lost");
                            return 1;}
                        }
                    }
                    else
                    {
                        int ret = Primary->Blt (&BuffRect, BackBuffer, &DRect, pass, NULL);
                        if (ret == DDERR_SURFACELOST)
                        {
                            ret = DDObjectNew->RestoreAllSurfaces ();
                            if (ret != DD_OK) {ErrorMessage ("Surfaces lost");
                            return 1;}
                        }
                    }
                    Screen.Screen = NULL;
                    // DDObjectNew->WaitForVerticalBlank (DDWAITVB_BLOCKEND, NULL);
                    return 0;

            }


            //****************************
            //****************************

    void DIRECT_DRAW_MANAGER :: PaintText (int x, int y, char* string)
    {
            if (NotInitializedFlag == true) return;
            HDC hdc;
            BackBuffer->Unlock (NULL);

            BackBuffer-> GetDC (&hdc);
            SetBkMode (hdc, TRANSPARENT);
            SetTextColor (hdc, RGB (255, 255, 255));
            TextOut (hdc, x, y, string, strlen (string));
            BackBuffer->ReleaseDC (hdc);
            int ret;
            do{
                ret = BackBuffer->Lock (NULL, &Description, DDLOCK_SURFACEMEMORYPTR,
                                    NULL);
            }while (ret!=DD_OK);

    /* an older way to accomplish the same thing
```

```
            if (lpDDSBack->GetDC (&hdc) == DD_OK)              // must be locked
    {

            SetBkColor (hdc, RGB (0, 0, 255));
            SetTextColor (hdc, RGB (255, 255, 0));
            TextOut (hdc, 0, 0, szBackMsg, lstrlen (szBackMsg));
            lpDDSBack->ReleaseDC (hdc);
    }
    */
    }


    //*****************************
    //*****************************
    //*****************************
```

Our first function is the constructor. All of my .cpp files start with the constructor and destructor, so they're easy to find. The constructor sets all values to 0 or NULL (0L), which makes it easy to read. The destructor follows and cleans up all of the data in the reverse order it will be created. It is important to remember the test for NULL attempting to clean up memory or buffers (i.e., if(BackBuffer != NULL)). This is important in case the DirectDraw manager did not initialize correctly. Always check this. Also notice the Release function. This is how DirectDraw works. Do not delete these objects, or you will be in a "heap of trouble." (I recently moved to Texas and I get a kick out of using local vernacular.) This may lock your system. Use the function Release for all DirectX objects when cleaning up. Notice how the destructor does it.

That is the easy part. The constructor and destructor usually are. Now on to the hardest part:

```
HWND DIRECT_DRAW_MANAGER :: CreateMainWindow (int w, int h,
          char* ClassName, void* MessageLoop, void* hInst, bool FullScreen)
    {
          if (NotInitializedFlag == false) return NULL;   // already initialized
          WNDCLASS    wc;
          FullScreenFlag = FullScreen;                     // store this value

          wc.style=             CS_HREDRAW | CS_VREDRAW;
          wc.lpfnWndProc = (long (__stdcall *) (void *, unsigned int, unsigned
                                              int, long)) MessageLoop;
          wc.cbClsExtra =       0;
          wc.cbWndExtra =       0;
          wc.hInstance =        hInst;
          wc.hIcon =            LoadIcon (hInst, IDI_APPLICATION);
          wc.hCursor =          LoadCursor (NULL, IDC_ARROW);
          wc.hbrBackground =    NULL;
          wc.lpszMenuName =     NULL;
          wc.lpszClassName =    ClassName;

          RegisterClass (&wc);


          if (FullScreen) // there are some slight differences between fullscreen
                          // and not
          {
```

```
          WindowX = 0, WindowY = 0;
          WindowHandle = CreateWindowEx (
                WS_EX_TOPMOST,
                ClassName,
                ClassName,
                WS_POPUP,
                WindowX,
                WindowY,
                GetSystemMetrics (SM_CXSCREEN),
                GetSystemMetrics (SM_CYSCREEN),
                NULL,
                NULL,
                hInst,
                NULL);
    }
    else
    {
          WindowX = GetSystemMetrics (SM_CXSCREEN)/2-w/2, // center window
          WindowY = GetSystemMetrics (SM_CYSCREEN)/2-h/2;
          WindowHandle = CreateWindowEx (
                0,
                ClassName,
                ClassName,
                WS_POPUP,
                WindowX,
                WindowY,
                w,
                h,
                NULL,
                NULL,
                hInst,
                NULL);
    }

    if (WindowHandle ==  NULL) return NULL; // there is a problem creating
                                            // the window
    // we now have a real window and we are ready to proceed
    Width     = w;
    Height    = h;

    ShowWindow   (WindowHandle, 1);
    UpdateWindow (WindowHandle);
    SetFocus     (WindowHandle);
    ShowCursor   (FALSE);

    int err = CreateDirectDraw ();
    if (err == 0) return NULL;

    NotInitializedFlag = false;
    return WindowHandle;
}

//***************************
```

CreateMainWindow takes a lot of parameters. We could have simplified it and maybe made a bunch of functions like SetWidth, SetHeight, and so on. But that creates havoc—especially when you forget to initialize a variable—so here is a huge parameter list (actually only six). The first two are height and width, easy enough. The next is rather arbitrary and allows you to name the running program in terms of the windows naming. This string will show up (in windowed mode only) in the taskbar with that name and when you hit Ctrl-Alt-Del. The next is a pointer to a function. For simplicity in passing this pointer, I made it a void pointer; it is cast at the line wc.lpfnWndProc = (long (__stdcall *)(void *,unsigned int,unsigned int,long)) MessageLoop;. hInst is the instance variable that is handed to WinMain when it is instantiated; that value must be used to create the window. The last parameter simply tells us to make the window full screen or not.

You may have noticed that the first thing this function does is create the main window. Why not do that in WinMain where it belongs? Good observation. A few variables will need to be initialized and the window position will need to be controlled. This should probably not be in the WinMain. This is a hard issue, but I decided on this approach because of the DirectDraw clipper that needs the window dimensions and the upper left corner, the clutter of putting all of this in the WinMain, and how much easier it is to maintain here. WinMain could stand to be cleaned up anyway. DirectDraw needs the HWND, and so much more. If you like, you can always move it back and pass all of the parameters to DirectDraw. It's your call, but I like this paradigm.

The first thing we test is if DirectDraw has already been initialized in this class; we fail out if so. Then we declare a new structure of WNDCLASS, the Windows structure used to initialize the window. It is then formatted by Windows using RegisterClass. So far, so good. Now we prepare to declare values for some other variables based on the FullScreen flag.

If FullScreen is TRUE, then we make the window fill the screen by setting the upper left of the window to 0,0 and the lower right to GetSystemMetrics (SM_CXSCREEN), GetSystemMetrics (SM_CYSCREEN). Those are Windows calls to get the real width of the screen or the current resolution, depending on how you look at it. Then we are ready to proceed.

If FullScreen is FALSE, we take the desired dimensions for our window, divide them in half, and subtract those values from the center of the screen, which is GetSystemMetrics (SM_CXSCREEN) / 2, GetSystemMetrics (SM_CYSCREEN) / 2. Now your resultant window will be centered on the screen unless it is bigger than the current resolution, which usually causes it to fail in creating the window. The upper left location, WindowX and WindowY, is saved and will be used later when we initialize the DDClipper.

Now we have finished creating a window. If Windows liked what we did, then WindowHandle will have a value. If it is NULL, we need to quit the program. We'll deal with error messages next, but we need to return a NULL to the WinMain and then the program must quit.

Now we store the window dimensions locally, call a few Windows functions to display the window, and call our member function CreateDirectDraw. If it returns a 0, then an error occurred and we fail out, eventually exiting the program. Lastly, once everything is secure, we set the NotInitializedFlag and return the WindowHandle, which signals the rest of the program to continue.

Let's take a look at the Error Message function:

```
//****************************

void  DIRECT_DRAW_MANAGER :: ErrorMessage (char* str)
{
        MessageBox (WindowHandle, str, "Error", MB_OK);
        DestroyWindow (WindowHandle);
}


//****************************
```

This function simply displays a window with text telling us when an error occurs and where. Figuring out what went wrong is for you to discover, but at least you know where it failed. This dialog box will only work in windowed mode, but otherwise it works fine. This window simply has a single OK button. The last flag passed to the function MessageBox, MB_OK, determines this. You can find the function Message-Box in the Windows API. We will be using this function extensively to let users know when something goes wrong. Good error messages are a good practice anyway and the information you receive from them will cut debugging in half. I recommend using this function frequently.

Now comes the complicated part. Don't blow a fuse, just relax, take a deep breath, and pretend that this all makes sense:

```
//****************************
int  DIRECT_DRAW_MANAGER :: CreateDirectDraw ()
{
        HRESULT ddret = DirectDrawCreate (NULL, &DDObject, NULL);

        if (ddret != DD_OK) {DestroyWindow (WindowHandle);
        return 0;}

                //**************

        ddret = DDObject->SetCooperativeLevel (WindowHandle,
        (FullScreenFlag) ? (DDSCL_FULLSCREEN | DDSCL_EXCLUSIVE |
                DDSCL_ALLOWREBOOT) : (DDSCL_NORMAL));
        if (ddret != DD_OK) {ErrorMessage ("Cooperative level not set");
                return 0;}

        ddret = DDObject->QueryInterface (IID_IDirectDraw4, (LPVOID *)
                                          &DDObjectNew);
        if (ddret != DD_OK)
        {
                ErrorMessage ("Problem initializing IID_IDirectDraw");
                return 0;
        }
                //**************

        if (FullScreenFlag)
```

```
        {
            // 16-bit bit depth

            ddret = DDObjectNew->SetDisplayMode (Width, Height, 16, 0, 0 );
            if (ddret != DD_OK) {ErrorMessage ("Display not set");
            return 0;}
        }

                //***************Get primary surface

    ZeroMemory (&Description, sizeof (Description));
    ZeroMemory (&Description.ddpfPixelFormat, sizeof (DDPIXELFORMAT));

    Description.dwSize = sizeof (Description);
    Description.dwFlags = DDSD_CAPS;
    Description.ddsCaps.dwCaps = DDSCAPS_PRIMARYSURFACE;

    if (FullScreenFlag)
    {
        Description.ddsCaps.dwCaps |= DDSCAPS_FLIP | DDSCAPS_COMPLEX;
        Description.dwFlags |= DDSD_BACKBUFFERCOUNT;
    }

    // we can specify more than one back buffer
    Description.dwBackBufferCount = 1;

    ddret = DDObjectNew->CreateSurface (&Description, &Primary, NULL);
    if (ddret != DD_OK) {ErrorMessage ("Surface not created");
    return 0;}

            //***************Get pixel format

    Description.dwSize = sizeof (Description);
    Description.dwFlags = DDSD_PIXELFORMAT;
    ddret = Primary->GetSurfaceDesc (&Description);
    if (ddret != DD_OK)
    {
        ErrorMessage ("pixel format not available");
        return 0;
    }
        //************* get our color type

    int g = Description.ddpfPixelFormat.dwGBitMask>>5;    // assumes 5 for red
    if (g == 0x1F) ColorType = _5x5x5_;
    else if (g == 0x3F) ColorType = _5x6x5_;
    else {ErrorMessage ("color mode not supported");
    return 0;}.

        //*************** create clipper

    if (FullScreenFlag == false)
    {
        ddret = DDObjectNew->CreateClipper (0, &DDClipper, NULL);
```

```
                    if (ddret != DD_OK) {ErrorMessage ("clipper not created");
                    return 0;}

                    ddret = DDClipper->SetHWnd (0, WindowHandle);
                    if (ddret != DD_OK)
                    {
                        ErrorMessage ("Surface not assigned to hwnd");
                        return 0;
                    }

                    ddret = Primary->SetClipper (DDClipper);
                    if (ddret != DD_OK)
                    {
                        ErrorMessage ("clipper not set on primary surface");
                        return 0;
                    }
                }


                //************** Get BackBuffer surface

            if (FullScreenFlag)
            {
                ddsCaps.dwCaps = DDSCAPS_BACKBUFFER;
                ddret = Primary->GetAttachedSurface (&ddsCaps, &BackBuffer);
                if (ddret != DD_OK)
                {
                    ErrorMessage ("primary surface not attached");
                    return 0;
                }
            }
            else
            {
                Description.dwFlags = DDSD_CAPS | DDSD_HEIGHT | DDSD_WIDTH;
                Description.ddsCaps.dwCaps = DDSCAPS_OFFSCREENPLAIN;
                Description.dwWidth = Width;
                Description.dwHeight = Height;
                ddret = DDObjectNew->CreateSurface (&Description, &BackBuffer, NULL);
                if (ddret != DD_OK) {ErrorMessage ("back buffer not made");
                return 0;}
            }
            ZeroMemory (&ddsCaps, sizeof (DDCAPS2));

            ddsCaps.dwCaps = DDSCAPS_OFFSCREENPLAIN;
            ddret = DDObjectNew->GetAvailableVidMem (&ddsCaps, &TotalVideoMemory,
                                                &AvailableVideoMemory);

            if (ddret != DD_OK) return 0;

        return 1;
    }
    //***************************
```

First, CreateDirectDraw takes no parameters. The first thing it does is initialize DirectDraw by calling DirectDrawCreate. Any return value other than DD_OK is bad news and the program must fail out. The parameter passed is the LPDIRECTDRAW variable, a pointer to DIRECTDRAW.

After we finish this call, DDObject will point to a DirectDraw object. The NULL parameters are of no consequence. The first is the address of the video driver selected. Since we don't have this (called a GUID), we pass NULL and DirectDraw figures out the rest. The second allows for future versions of DirectDraw to pass other parameters and is not used now. Ignore it.

The next function call, SetCooperativeLevel, is a member function of our new DirectDraw class and requires only two parameters, a HWND and a set of flags telling DirectDraw how to set up this WindowHandle for DirectDraw. Based on the FullScreen-Flag, we have a choice. We can pass either three flags or just one: the conditional operator (i.e., (val)? 1:0). This is a conditional-expression and is common. Look it up if you're not familiar with it.

QueryInterface sets up DDObjectNew. Now we can request the amount of video memory available, among other things. Again, DDObjectNew, an LPDIRECTDRAW4 or pointer to DIRECTDRAW4, is almost exactly the same as regular DirectDraw; with some minor changes to this code, you can use regular DirectDraw instead. QueryInterface is a standard COM interface function call used to take an existing object (in this case, DDObject) and try to find an upgraded object to replace it. It is fairly complicated, but it allows you to always expect the base object and try for a better or improved one. This is really not too important, but you might want to understand it better. Otherwise, just follow my lead. If you have the time and inclination, read *Understanding ActiveX and OLE: A Guide for Developers and Managers* by David Chappell (Microsoft Press).

Now you can change your screen resolution if you are in full-screen mode. The DDObjectNew and the DDObject have a member function called SetDisplayMode. The parameters are simple: screen Width, screen Height, and screen color depth (16 in this case); the rest can be 0. These variables are primarily set based on the values passed to this class. You are in control—kind of nice in this hectic world.

Now we clear the structure Description. ZeroMemory is a Windows function that works exactly like memset. There are a few other similar Windows functions called CopyMemory, FillMemory, and MoveMemory. You can look these up in the help files. (Like I said before, they took all of the good function names.)

The dwSize parameter of Description allows Microsoft to change the structures at any time, and by looking at the size determine which version of the variable type you are using. They have changed this dynamic with the new structure type DDSURFACEDESC2, and thus defeated the purpose of having this variable in the first place, but fill it you must. So this structure's first parameter holds the size of the structure. It has a dwFlags member variable. You fill this variable with flags that tell the function to which you are passing this structure that you want a particular member variable looked up and set. These flags simply tell DirectDraw to fill the structure with whichever variables you tell it to fill. This is great for getting information about a device, driver, video capabilities, etc. Just set a few flags, call the function, and whichever flags you set will make DirectDraw change those variables.

The flags we'll be using are fairly straightforward. First, we clear the memory and set the dwFlags to DDSD_CAPS. This tells DirectDraw to fill in the DDSD_CAPS information when we try to set information about DirectDraw. Next, we set the ddsCaps member variable dwCaps to DDSCAPS_PRIMARYSURFACE. This means that we are trying to create the primary surface, i.e., the visible one. So, ddsCaps has a member variable called dwCaps. Got it? I didn't think so. Kind of confusing, but Microsoft sets the standards. dwCaps passes information to DirectDraw telling it what kind of surface to create. I hope that helps.

Now comes the confusing part. If the game is to be full screen (like most games are), we need to add a little information to the flags that we pass to DirectDraw. We OR the existing value of dwCaps, which is DDSCAPS_PRIMARYSURFACE, with some other flags. How this works is DDSCAPS_PRIMARYSURFACE is just a #define in ddraw.h that turns on a single bit. It happens to have a value of 0x200, which is the 10th bit. DDSCAPS_FLIP has a value of 0x10. When you OR them, you get a value of 0x210. The Microsoft libraries have code something like:

```
if (Description.ddsCaps.dwCaps & DDSCAPS_PRIMARYSURFACE) …
```

This is a fast test and allows you to put many parameters into a single variable. This is common in Windows, so get used to it. It is a good idea.

So we add a few flags to dwCaps, namely DDSCAPS_FLIP and DDSCAPS_COMPLEX. DDSCAPS_COMPLEX tells the initializing function that the surface you are creating will have other surfaces attached to it such as a back buffer. You can create surfaces without this but in full-screen mode, you must do it this way. These additional surfaces are attached to Primary and when you delete Primary, the rest are deleted as well. To delete, you must use the function call Release. DDSCAPS_FLIP tells DirectDraw that you will be using the function Flip to move DirectDraw surfaces from BackBuffer to the primary, or visible, buffer. This cannot be done in windowed mode.

Next we tell DirectDraw how many back buffers to attach to the primary surface by setting the value Description.dwBackBufferCount = 1;. Normally this will always be 1, but if you care to try triple buffering, set it to 2.

CreateSurface is a member function of DDObjectNew (which you can easily tell) that passes the information we just put together to DirectDraw and a pointer to our future Primary surface. You may note that we are passing a pointer to a pointer, or more precisely, we are passing the address of a pointer. That is so that DirectDraw can hand us a valid pointer. It could have been returned in a return statement, but if an error occurred, you might never know what caused it.

We have half the battle completed. The next few areas are information gathering and do not get us too much closer to getting the basic DirectDraw stuff operational, but in the long run, it may be better to just get it out of the way now.

We discussed 15-bit vs. 16-bit earlier in this chapter. Here is where we find out how your video card works. About 60 percent use 15-bit, but that means 40 percent use 16-bit. Better to be safe than sorry. We set the flag in Description to DDSD_PIXELFORMAT, telling DirectDraw that we want the pixel format information. Then we call the primary surface member function GetSurfaceDesc passing the variable Description. The structure has a few member variables changed and now we know what is happening.

Now let's look at it. Description has a member variable called ddpfPixelFormat that will hold our resultant data. The data is all about the individual pixels themselves. In 16-bit graphics, the only member variable that we care about is the green mask called dwGBitMask. Since green is the only color that changes between 15-bit and 16-bit, all we need to know is its maximum value. Since all colors need to be shifted into correct position, so does the mask. We will shift it right by five, eliminating any 0's and giving us a simple value. In 15-bit mode the color can be 0 to 31, so we test to see if the mask value is 31 or 0x1f. If so, we know that we are in 15-bit mode and we set the value ColorType to the enumerated value _5x5x5_. If that doesn't work, try 16-bit, which is 63 or 0x3f. If that works, set ColorType to _5x6x5_. If not, I don't know what it is, and we create an error message.

The clipper for our drawing is set next, but only in windowed mode. The clipper does not allow you to draw outside the window. Just create it (DDObjectNew->CreateClipper (0, &DDClipper, NULL);), make it aware of the main window (DDClipper->SetHWnd (0, WindowHandle);), and then attach it to the primary surface (Primary->SetClipper (DDClipper);). This is real easy. You provide all of the information it needs through a few function calls. You can create it in full-screen mode without visible effect.

Now we create BackBuffer. (We are almost done with this portion, hold on.) This is done differently if in windowed mode or full-screen mode. We'll cover full-screen mode first.

Set the ddsCaps member variable dwCaps (not that again) to DDSCAPS_ BACKBUFFER. This tells DirectDraw that we want a video buffer on the video card that will alternately be used as a display and then a back buffer. We'll pass this structure to the primary surface that will then create an offscreen buffer for our drawing pleasure and store a pointer in the BackBuffer address. Fairly straightforward.

Note: This kind of back buffer is seen half the time. Every time you call the Flip function, Primary and BackBuffer change places. The BackBuffer becomes visible and Primary becomes the BackBuffer. The pointers to video memory will now be opposite, that is. When you lock the surface, BackBuffer will give you a pointer to the memory where the primary buffer address used to be. Triple buffering makes this slightly more confusing. You can draw to one surface, finish, start drawing the second, and then flip the primary, making the one visible and letting the second finish its business. Now the formerly visible surface can be drawn to.

The windowed mode also allocates video memory for drawing, but you need to tell the system what size to allocate, send Description instead of ddsCaps, and set a different flag, namely DDSCAPS_OFFSCREENPLAIN. Now what you are doing is creating an offscreen buffer that must be blitted to the main screen. This surface will never be visible. The function you will use to transfer the data to the screen is Blt. We'll see it later in this discussion.

> **Note**: DirectDraw may not have enough video memory for the back buffer, and so it may allocate memory from your system memory. This can be notably slower, but it works. It's not very common these days with 8 MB video cards the minimum you can buy, but just in case....

All of the important steps of initialization are complete. Lastly, I used the function GetAvailableVidMem to find out how much memory is still available on the video card once all of the allocation is finished. The structure passing is much like before. You can look up the flags in the help files.

Now on to the next function, PrepFrame:

```
//****************************

SCREEN_STRUCT*
 DIRECT_DRAW_MANAGER :: PrepFrame ()
{
      if (NotInitializedFlag == true) return NULL;
      ZeroMemory (&Description, sizeof (DDSURFACEDESC));
      Description.dwSize = sizeof (Description);
      int ret;
      do
      {
            ret = BackBuffer->Lock (NULL, &Description, DDLOCK_SURFACEMEMORYPTR,
                              NULL);
      }while (ret!=DD_OK);
      // now we unlock the surface in case of a crash
      BackBuffer->Unlock (NULL);
      // *********************

      Screen.Width = Width;
      Screen.Height = Height;
      Screen.Screen = (U16ptr) Description.lpSurface;
      Screen.RealWidth = Description.lPitch/2;
      return &Screen;

}

      //****************************
```

PrepFrame is the function we will use to begin the drawing process. We will call this function every time we need to draw a new frame. It hands back to us a structure filled with all of the data that we will need.

The first thing we do is check to see if the DirectDraw object properly initialized. We clear out the structure Description, so that we can have DirectDraw fill it with good data. When we call the BackBuffer->Lock function, the Description structure will give us all of the data that we need to use the buffer for drawing.

> **Note**: You may have noticed that during the function CreateDirectDraw, the primary surface seemed like it was involved in all of the creation. Here we see for the first time that BackBuffer has a little control over its own functionality. Notice

9

also that DirectDraw objects, like DDObjectNew, aren't mentioned much after this point.

So the steps of PrepFrame are: clear structure, lock down BackBuffer, then retrieve needed information from the structure. There is one more step I've added. Notice the comment line with the asterisks. I immediately unlock the buffer. Microsoft doesn't recommend this. However, I do. While BackBuffer is locked, no other background functions can operate. You cannot hit Ctrl-Alt-Delete. A bug will lock the system because the debugger cannot operate. The system becomes completely out of control when this is locked. Unlocking it restores enough control to track down bugs. This is enormously important. Leave the line in there if possible. I have tried this on dozens of systems with no ill effects, but that does not guarantee good results on your machine. This is a debugging tool and you should remove it for the final build. If you run into a bunch of unexplained crashes (make sure that your program doesn't cause them), comment out the line of code and that may fix it. Again, I have tried this dozens of times with no side effects but who knows what you may encounter.

Otherwise, PrepFrame is a relatively simple function. We will show you how to use it later.

InterruptFrame is a helpful function that stops you from accessing the video buffer:

```
//****************************

void DIRECT_DRAW_MANAGER :: InterruptFrame ()
{
        if (NotInitializedFlag == true) return;
        BackBuffer->Unlock (NULL);
        Screen.Screen = NULL;
}


//****************************
```

InterruptFrame unlocks the surface. That's it. Once you call this, no more drawing can occur. You must call PrepFrame again to restore the buffer and the pointer. Don't worry, it is perfectly legal to do so. We will be using this function once we have completed drawing and are waiting to blit the drawing to the visible screen/surface.

The DrawFrame function takes the offscreen buffer that you have prepared and blits it to the screen. This can be fairly confusing, so I'll explain it thoroughly:

```
//****************************

int DIRECT_DRAW_MANAGER :: DrawFrame ()      // swap
{
        if (NotInitializedFlag == true) return 0;

        if (FullScreenFlag)
        {

                int ret = BackBuffer->GetFlipStatus (DDGFS_ISFLIPDONE);
                if (ret == DDERR_WASSTILLDRAWING) return 1;
```

```
                    ret = Primary->Flip (NULL, OL);

                    if (ret == DDERR_SURFACELOST)
                    {
                            ret = DDObjectNew->RestoreAllSurfaces ();
                            if (ret != DD_OK) {ErrorMessage ("Surfaces lost");
                            return 1;}
                    }
            }
            else
            {
            POINT pt = {0, 0};
                    ClientToScreen (WindowHandle, &pt);

                    RECT BuffRect = {pt.x, pt.y, pt.x+Width, pt.y+Height};
                    RECT DRect = {0, 0, Width, Height};

                    int ret = Primary->Blt (&BuffRect, BackBuffer, &DRect, pass, NULL);
                    if (ret == DDERR_SURFACELOST)
                    {
                            ret = DDObjectNew->RestoreAllSurfaces ();
                            if (ret != DD_OK) {ErrorMessage ("Surfaces lost");
                            return 1; }
                    }
            }
            Screen.Screen = NULL;
            //DDObjectNew->WaitForVerticalBlank (DDWAITVB_BLOCKEND, NULL);
            return 0;
    }


            //***************************
```

First, we test if everything is initialized properly, just like the other member functions in this class. If you are sure about your coding style, you could take these out; they really are unnecessary, just a precaution.

If we are in full-screen mode, this is not too difficult. First we get the status of the last buffer flip. What can happen is that BackBuffer may still be flipping from the last time that we told it to flip; after all, this does take a while if your video memory is low. Why? If video memory is unavailable, DirectX allocates a BackBuffer in RAM and when you call Flip, this memory is memcpy'ed to Primary. Nowadays, this is very rare because video cards are much better than they were before, but it can happen. What normally happens in this situation is that the video pointer is simply changed. The primary buffer video pointer (say 0xa0000) is swapped with the back buffer video pointer (say 0xc00000). The first time you request a pointer to the back buffer you get 0xc0000; the next time, 0xc0000 is visible and DirectX gives you a pointer to 0xa0000. (Those memory addresses were arbitrarily chosen and are not real addresses that will be returned.)

Anyway, if BackBuffer is still flipping, we return a 1 indicating that there was an error. This means that the main loop can do something else for a little while and try again later. We will design it so that this is exactly what happens. Every clock cycle counts.

Once we get past that point on our next time through, we call the Flip function, which normally switches the video pointers like I mentioned above. This is almost instantaneous.

Now what about the next little tidbit? What does DDERR_SURFACELOST mean? If a video mode changes, some program interrupts DirectX, or some other unforeseen error prevents the video card from behaving normally, this error may occur. The video driver data is now wrong or the pointers to the video buffers are no longer valid. We correct this by using the function RestoreAllSurfaces. DirectX 5 and previous versions made you restore each surface independently, but this single function call works great. It can also return an error and if it does, the time has come to exit the program. For now, let's just return a simple error.

If we don't have a full screen, we declare a Windows-defined POINT (see windef.h) that has two members—*x* and *y*. We initialize them to 0 and 0. Next we call the Windows function ClientToScreen that converts the 0,0 pixel location on the primary drawing surface to screen coordinates. This gives us screen coordinates for the upper-left corner of the window. In full-screen mode, you know that 0,0 is the same; in windowed mode you will need to get the upper-left coordinate. We already have this information, by the way. Two member variables, WindowX and WindowY, were set when we set up DirectDraw. I chose to show you how to do this in case you want to make a window that can be moved.

Using this x,y position, we can now declare a few Windows-defined RECTs to use for our blit. Flip requires pointers to two video buffers and the ability to exchange them. GDI prevents this and so a windowed application must memcpy BackBuffer to the screen. The RECTs help the blit function determine clipping area, etc.

Like before, if we lose our surfaces, they must be restored. Our last two steps are to clear our pointer since it is probably not valid anymore, and to return a 0 indicating that the Flip/Blt was successful.

The second to the last line is a commented-out WaitForVerticalBlink. This will make sure that the entire screen is flipped or blitted before the application continues. If the screen is in windowed mode, the screen will be blitted, and if full screen, it will be flipped. If you find your application is not drawing correctly or encounter some other drawing problems, uncomment this line of code and see what happens. You might also want to make it the second line of code in the function after the NotInitializedFlag.

Like PrepFrame, ClearBackBuffer gets the screen ready to draw on:

```
//****************************

void __fastcall DIRECT_DRAW_MANAGER :: ClearBackBuffer ()
{
        if (NotInitializedFlag == true) return;
        PrepFrame ();
        Memset16Bit (Screen.Screen, 0, Screen.Width*Screen.Height);
}


//****************************
```

ClearBackBuffer actually makes the BackBuffer black, which you won't need if you plan to fill the entire screen. But for the beginning, this is the function to use when you are about to draw. Once we build the rest of the engine, including the drawing engine, we'll use PrepFrame and save the time it takes it clear the buffer. By the way, on a PII300, clearing the BackBuffer takes just over 2 milliseconds, which is about the time it takes to give AI instructions to 100 or so creatures in the world.

Note: Only use the ClearBackBuffer function while you are building your engine. Once you are always filling the screen every frame, replace it with PrepFrame. This will have a good effect on engine performance. Make sure you look for drawing anomalies before you stay with PrepFrame. You may need ClearBackBuffer to clear all or part of the screen because a lot of the screen can be black.

Now onto the mysterious OffSurfaces. They really aren't very mysterious. They are simply pointers to small (usually) video buffers that you can quickly blit to the Back-Buffer much faster than you could ever do yourself.

```
//****************************

int  DIRECT_DRAW_MANAGER :: CreateBlankOffSurface (int w, int h)
{
        if (NotInitializedFlag == true) return -1;
        if (NumOffSurfaces >= MAXOFFSURFACES) return -1;
        int which = NumOffSurfaces;
        CreateOffSurface (which, w, h);
        OffWidth[which] = w; OffHeight[which] = h;

        U16ptr ptr = (U16ptr) GetOffSurface (which);
        if (ptr != NULL) Memset16Bit (ptr, 0, w*h);
        ReleaseOffSurface (which);

        NumOffSurfaces++;              // increment our count
        return which;
}


void DIRECT_DRAW_MANAGER :: CreateOffSurface (int which, int w, int h)
{
        if (NotInitializedFlag == true) return;
        ZeroMemory (&OffSurfaceDescription, sizeof (DDSURFACEDESC));

        OffSurfaceDescription.dwSize = sizeof (DDSURFACEDESC);
        OffSurfaceDescription.dwFlags = DDSD_CAPS | DDSD_HEIGHT | DDSD_WIDTH;
        OffSurfaceDescription.ddsCaps.dwCaps = DDSCAPS_OFFSCREENPLAIN;
        OffSurfaceDescription.dwHeight = h;
        OffSurfaceDescription.dwWidth = w;
        DDObjectNew->CreateSurface (&OffSurfaceDescription, &OffSurface[which],
                                NULL);
```

```
      }

      void DIRECT_DRAW_MANAGER :: DrawOffSurface (int x, int y, int which)
      {
            if (NotInitializedFlag == true) return;
            if (Screen.Screen == NULL) return;

            BackBuffer->Unlock(NULL);          // first unlock the back buffer

            RECT rect = {0, 0, OffWidth[which], OffHeight[which]};          // draw
            BackBuffer -> BltFast (x, y, OffSurface[which], &rect,
                                    DDBLTFAST_NOCOLORKEY | DDBLTFAST_WAIT);

            if (Screen.Screen != NULL)          // then, restore the lock
            {
                  int ret;
                  do{
                        ret = BackBuffer->Lock (NULL, &Description,
                                          DDLOCK_SURFACEMEMORYPTR, NULL);
                  }while (ret!=DD_OK);
            }
            Screen.Width = Width, Screen.Height = Height;
            Screen.Screen = (U16ptr) Description.lpSurface;
            Screen.RealWidth = Description.lPitch/2;
      }



            //****************************
            //****************************

      // this function call must be followed by a call to "ReleasePointerToOffSurface"
      SCREEN_STRUCT*
            DIRECT_DRAW_MANAGER :: GetOffSurface (int which)     // must exist first
      {
            if (NotInitializedFlag == true) return NULL;
            if (which >= NumOffSurfaces || which<0 || NumOffSurfaces<1) return NULL;

            ZeroMemory (&OffSurfaceDescription, 0, sizeof (DDSURFACEDESC));
            OffSurfaceDescription.dwSize = sizeof (DDSURFACEDESC);
            if (OffSurface[which]->IsLost ()) OffSurface[which]->Restore ();

            HRESULT rval = OffSurface[which]->Lock (NULL, &OffSurfaceDescription,
                                                0, NULL);
            if (rval != DD_OK) return NULL;

            Screen.Width = OffWidth[which], Screen.Height = OffHeight[which],
            Screen.Screen = (U16ptr) OffSurfaceDescription.lpSurface;
            Screen.RealWidth = OffSurfaceDescription.lPitch/2;
            return &Screen;

      }
```

```
//****************************
void DIRECT_DRAW_MANAGER :: ReleaseOffSurface (int which)
{
      if (NotInitializedFlag == true) return;
      if (which >= NumOffSurfaces || which<0 || NumOffSurfaces<1) return;
      OffSurface[which]->Unlock (NULL);
}

//****************************
```

I've created a small system so that you specify dimensions, and the system hands you an ID number that you can use to access that particular OffSurface buffer through a few different methods. You can get a pointer to it, draw it, or release it by that ID number. The pointer can be used to draw to it. Be careful to always use RealWidth for these buffers. They typically are allocated on 32-byte boundaries, so if you need a buffer 10x10, you will get a buffer 32x10 with only 10 pixels width visible. Video memory is rather limited, but if you feel the need, MAXOFFSURFACES can always be increased and you can have a lot more. You can always query for more video memory.

AGP allows for virtual video memory. You can use system memory for video memory, which is nearly as fast as real video memory in AGPII. AGPI is still way too slow. This means that you can have as many surfaces as you want. Unfortunately, AGP partially interferes with regular bus speed and so too many buffers could significantly slow your game down. Stick to a few buffers for commonly drawn elements that need to be drawn often (interface elements, mouse pointer, etc.) and these will speed the performance of your game significantly.

This system is easy to use so I won't detail it. Try it. Call CreateBlankOffSurface and use that number to call GetOffSurface. GetOffSurface returns a SCREEN_STRUCT* that you can use to draw some stuff on that video buffer. Then during the drawing update each frame, simply call DrawOffSurface, passing the x,y location and that ID number. It is really very fast and you cannot draw any faster.

___

Note: Don't bother calling ReleaseOffSurface unless you need to. These OffSurfaces are automatically cleaned up in the destructor of DIRECT_DRAW_MANAGER.

___

The PaintText function is simple:

```
//****************************

void DIRECT_DRAW_MANAGER :: PaintText (int x, int y, char* string)
{
      if (NotInitializedFlag == true) return;
      HDC hdc;
//    BackBuffer->Unlock (NULL);

      BackBuffer-> GetDC (&hdc);
      SetBkMode (hdc, TRANSPARENT);
      SetTextColor (hdc, RGB (255, 255, 255));
      TextOut (hdc, x, y, string, strlen (string));
```

```
BackBuffer->ReleaseDC (hdc);
/*  int ret; //
do{
      ret = BackBuffer->Lock (NULL, &Description, DDLOCK_SURFACEMEMORYPTR,
                              NULL);
}while (ret!=DD_OK);*/
}


//****************************
//****************************
//****************************
```

Paint uses standard Windows calls to draw. Because DirDraw can give you hell, you need to unlock the surface to which you are drawing first. Now, I already unlocked the surface when I called PrepFrame, as you may recall. If you decide to ignore my advice and immediately unlock the surface after obtaining a pointer to it, then uncomment the code that I've commented out above. Otherwise, just delete that code. You will not see it any more in this book. (It really does pay to read cover to cover, doesn't it?) Then you get a handle to a device context (HDC) and use that to draw like in regular Windows apps. You can set the text color and the background color. TextOut is the Windows call that draws the text on the window. TextOut is slow. We will be replacing it in the next chapter.

Integrating the DIRECT_DRAW_MANAGER

Now we come to the integration portion of our program. We need to make this new DIRECT_DRAW_MANAGER class work. Let's delve into a WinMain that will provide us with a little insight into how to use DirectDraw in the real world. A lot of things are different here. We've allowed DIRECT_DRAW_MANAGER to create the main window for us and we get an HWND back from that initialization. The new class will handle all of our DirectDraw worries, but until we get to a better design in a few chapters, we'll simply include dirdraw.h in all of our files. From here until the end of the chapter are just four more files. This is in an effort to illustrate the use of DIRECT_DRAW_MANAGER.

All you have to do is make a new project and add the four code files that follow along with the DIRECT_DRAW_MANAGER class defined previously in this chapter. I suggest that you create a new folder in your personal development directory (not the default one) and call it something like ddraw1. Copy the dirdraw.h and dirdraw.cpp files into it. Now create a new workspace and add dirdraw.cpp to it. Create a new document, name it winshell.h, and save it. Then type in the code below. Do the same thing for the other files that follow and then compile.

```
// winshell.h
#define WIN32_LEAN_AND_MEAN
#define NODEFAULTLIB
#include <windows.h>
#include <windowsx.h>
```

```
#ifndef _GLOBALS_
#define _GLOBALS_
extern BOOL ActiveApp;        // is the program active?
#define EVENT_DRAW_NEXT_FRAME   10000
#define EVENT_REPEAT_LAST_FRAME 10001
#endif
extern int  FullScreenFlag;

long CALLBACK MessageLoop (HWND hwnd, UINT message, WPARAM wParam, LPARAM
lParam);

void* GetWindowHandle (void);
void  ErrorMessage (char* str);
```

This is the header for WinMain and the message loop. It doesn't have much, but it is important. We define EVENT_DRAW_NEXT_FRAME, which we can use for frame-to-frame data management. We simply add this event to the message loop as if it were a regular Windows message. Our window's #include files are here. Since this file should be included only by winshell.cpp and message.cpp, this won't matter.

We define WIN32_LEAN_AND_MEAN and NODEFAULTLIB, both of which are defined by Windows to keep compile times short and not include a lot of extra unnecessary Windows stuff. It makes a big difference. We make a few variables semi-global and then we prototype our message loop for the winshell.cpp:

```
while(1)
{
      int t = PeekMessage (&msg, NULL, OU, OU, PM_NOREMOVE);
      if (t)
      {
      if (!GetMessage (& msg, NULL, 0, 0))
      return msg.wParam;
      TranslateMessage (&msg);
      DispatchMessage (&msg);
      }
      else if (ActiveApp)              // this is important here
      {
            RedrawScreen ((LPVOID) DDraw);
      }
      else if (!ActiveApp)
            WaitMessage ();
}
```

Two other prototypes exist but will only be used occasionally. You will find the functions at the end of winshell.cpp.

Now we'll look at the WinMain in detail. First, the #includes that are listed are expected in a small application like this one. We will move dirdraw.h out and replace it with a proper drawing class once we define a better structure for this program. We also include the header that we were perusing a few moments ago. We then prototype a few functions for later use. RedrawScreen is the only one we will use in this app.

```
//winshell.cpp
#include "dirdraw.h"
```

```
#include "winshell.h"

DWORD WINAPI RedrawScreen (LPVOID lpvParm);
DWORD WINAPI UpdateProc (LPVOID lpvParm);
DWORD WINAPI HandleEvents (LPVOID lpvParm);


BOOL ActiveApp;                          // is the program active?
static HWND WindowHandle;

int WINAPI WinMain (HINSTANCE hInstance, HINSTANCE hPrevInstance,
                    LPSTR lpCmdLine, int nCmdShow)
{
     MSG        msg;
     HWND       hwnd;

     DIRECT_DRAW_MANAGER* DDraw;

     bool FullScreenFlag = true;
     int SCREEN_WIDTH = 640, SCREEN_HEIGHT = 480;

     hPrevInstance = hPrevInstance;  // avoid C++ warning

     // here we instantiate the direct draw object
     DDraw = new DIRECT_DRAW_MANAGER;
     hwnd = DDraw->CreateMainWindow (SCREEN_WIDTH, SCREEN_HEIGHT, "Generic
          Name", MessageLoop, hInstance, FullScreenFlag);

     if (!hwnd) {delete DDraw; return FALSE;}
     while(1)
     {
          int t = PeekMessage (&msg, NULL, OU, OU, PM_NOREMOVE);
          if (t)
          {
          if (!GetMessage (& msg, NULL, 0, 0))
          return msg.wParam;
          TranslateMessage (&msg);
          DispatchMessage (&msg);
          }
          else if (ActiveApp)          // this is important here
          {
               RedrawScreen ((LPVOID) DDraw);
          }
          else if (!ActiveApp)
               WaitMessage ();
     }
     delete DDraw;                          // at the end of the program
     return 1;
}

void* GetWindowHandle (void)
{
```

```
        return (void*) WindowHandle;
}

void   ErrorMessage (char* str)
{
        MessageBox (WindowHandle, str, "Error", MB_OK);
        DestroyWindow (WindowHandle);
}
```

The global that we defined in our header now appears for other files to manipulate and access. Then we have WinMain, some initialization, and a little fooling around. Then we initialize DirectDraw and receive an HWND back. Ultimately, we will replace these locally defined variables by variables passed in from the command line. I will show you how it's done, but for now let's stick with simple. You can play with it if you like—go to your Visual C++ IDE menu Project|Settings (or Build|Settings for version 4.0 or so) and find the Debug tab on the tab sheet. Under Program Arguments, enter whatever text you want passed to your app at initialization; the char* (LPSTR) argument passed to WinMain will contain that text. This method is actually quite helpful. You can easily change program resolution, file to load, or just about anything without any recompile. This type of text can also be passed in to your app from a shortcut, so this is a realistic answer.

If the initialization process fails and the HWND returned from the DIRECT_DRAW_MANAGER calls is not valid, we return from the program, assuming that an error message has already been presented. If the HWND is not NULL, we assume that everything went OK and we continue in the application.

Now we enter the abyss—while(1). This is a continual loop, no escape. Notice there is no break, no return. How do you get out? This loop will be exited when Windows forces it to end by receiving a WM_QUIT message and processing it. There is a hidden return (not so cleverly disguised, I'm afraid).

The last thing we do is delete DDraw and return from our application.

Now we come to the message loop:

```
//message.cpp
#include "winshell.h"

LRESULT CALLBACK MessageLoop (HWND hwnd, UINT message, WPARAM wParam,
                                LPARAM lParam)
{
        int mousex, mousey;
        static DragMouse;

        switch (message)
        {
        case WM_ACTIVATEAPP:
            ActiveApp = wParam;
        break;

        case WM_CREATE:
        break;
```

```
case EVENT_DRAW_NEXT_FRAME:
/*    Flip ();
      HandleEvents ();
      RedrawScreen ();   */
break;

case WM_TIMER:
      PostMessage (hwnd, EVENT_DRAW_NEXT_FRAME, 0, 0);
break;

case WM_KEYDOWN:
switch (wParam)
{
      case VK_ESCAPE:
            DestroyWindow (hwnd);
      break;
      case VK_SPACE:
      break;

      case VK_END:
      case VK_DOWN:
      break;

      case VK_HOME:
      case VK_UP:
      break;

      case VK_LEFT:
      break;

      case VK_RIGHT:
      break;
      }
      break;
      case WM_MOUSEMOVE:
      mousex = lParam&0xffff;                // LOWORD (lParam);
      mousey = (lParam&0xffff0000)>>16;       // HIWORD (lParam);
/* if (wParam & MK_LBUTTON)                  // make sure that the left
                                             // button is pressed

      DragMouse (mousex, mousey);*/
      break;

      case WM_LBUTTONDOWN:
            {
                  int x = LOWORD (lParam);
                  int y = HIWORD (lParam);
            }
      break;
      case WM_RBUTTONDOWN:
            {
                  int x = LOWORD (lParam);
                  int y = HIWORD (lParam);
```

```
                    }
            break;

            case WM_DESTROY:
                ShowCursor (TRUE);
                PostQuitMessage (0);
            break;

            default:
                return DefWindowProc (hwnd, message, wParam, lParam);
        }
        return 0L;
}
```

There is a placeholder for the event we created—EVENT_DRAW_ NEXT_FRAME—but it is commented out. In the WinMain, where the function RedrawScreen is called, simply replace it with PostMessage (WindowHandle, EVENT_DRAW_NEXT_FRAME, 0, 0);. This will go through the message loop and you can manage it there if you like. Some of the other messages are here as placeholders as well. You can uncomment them and add functions that do something in the RedrawScreen function discussed earlier. Maybe you want to show a number when the Up arrow is pressed. Anyway, I encourage you to play with the different messages, maybe moving the frame number around the screen. See RedrawScreen in the help files for details.

The #include takes care of all of the basic include data but does not include ddraw.h. We will eventually eliminate its inclusion from all files but two, but for now, live with it.

Below is the main loop that should be called at least 30 times per second.

```
// loops.cpp
#include "dirdraw.h"

int frame = 0;
int time = 0, timelast = 0;
int count = 0;


DWORD WINAPI RedrawScreen (LPVOID Parm)
{
        DIRECT_DRAW_MANAGER* DDraw = (DIRECT_DRAW_MANAGER*) Parm;
        if (DDraw == NULL) return 1;

        time = timeGetTime ();              // get the current millisec
        count++;
        if (time-timelast>=1000)
        {
            frame = count;
            timelast = time;                // update time
            count = 0;
        }
        char buff[40];
        itoa (frame, buff, 10);
```

```
//*****************************

while (DDraw->DrawFrame ());

DDraw->ClearBackBuffer ();
// DDraw->PrepFrame ();

DDraw->PaintText (20, 20, buff);

DDraw->InterruptFrame ();

return 0;
}
```

The focus here is to show a blank screen and then track the number of frames per second. Later, this will be used to draw everything on the screen. You may be wondering why we pass a void pointer variable to this function. Well, look up Windows threads; this is the standard format used to manage a thread-friendly application. We'll examine threads much, much later. For now, just look at it and enjoy it.

The order of function calls within this function are a little strange and may not be intuitive. The function call order may be out of order to most people, but I'll explain and you'll begin to appreciate the beauty of it. First, let's review the part that calculates the frame rate.

We are including the dreaded header that will slow your compiles terribly. (We will eliminate it in the next chapter. For now, ignore this snafu.) We declare a few global variables for time-keeping purposes. The frame variable is how many frames have occurred since we've kept track. We'll update this number every 1000 milliseconds or so (that's 1000 1/1000ths of a second, or every second). The time variable is used to get the current millisecond count. Intel added to its x86 architecture (or so I understand) a counter to get the number of milliseconds that have passed since the computer was turned on. This number rolls over every 49 days or so, and considering the stability of Win95, it may never roll over on your machine. The Windows function to call is time-GetTime (); there is an interrupt you can use but I forget which one. After 1000 milliseconds has passed, we update the other variables. Our next variable, timelast, holds the last time recorded. count counts frame to frame. When we update our numbers, count is the number of frames that have passed in the last second.

By subtracting timelast from the recently updated time, we can easily determine if 1000 milliseconds has passed. We then store the current time in timelast, store the frame count, and reset count to 0. Pretty easy, huh?

We're going to print out the frame count in the upper-left corner of our black screen. We do some minor conversions (itoa) and prepare to mess with DirectDraw frame management.

Remember how we discussed earlier how DIRECT_DRAW_MANAGER has a member function DrawFrame? That function returns a 0 for OK when the drawing is actually done. If anything else is returned, it means that the drawing was not done. We can take advantage of that here. Speed can be critical in our engine and we may be able to do 3 to 5 milliseconds of extra work here and keep trying to use DrawFrame until it returns 0. For the time being, let's keep it simple and put it in a while loop.

You may have realized here that we are calling DrawFrame when we put nothing on BackBuffer. Won't garbage show up? It absolutely will, my dear Watson. The initialization process takes some time, however, and no one will ever be able to tell. Once the first frame has passed, we will be drawing to BackBuffer. This keeps the paradigm simple and lets us easily capture the extra few clock cycles at the beginning of the redraw cycle, rather than at the end when a lot of network messages may still be pending. Better to try blitting at the beginning of the frame; it will be faster than the other way and smoother—I promise.

The next thing we do is obtain a pointer to BackBuffer and then clear it. Notice the line I commented out. If you plan to clear the surface another way, or if you plan to fill the entire screen and you don't need to clear anything, then comment out the line that reads:

```
DDraw->ClearBackBuffer ();
```

And uncomment the line that reads:

```
DDraw->PrepFrame ();
```

There will be a significant performance difference if you can avoid clearing the buffer. That involves wiping a huge amount of memory clean and costs about 1 clock cycle per pixel. Multiply that times 30 frames per second, and your CPU dies and your frame rate bites the dust. On a screen that has sections of black on it, this is completely unavoidable.

Now we print our text on BackBuffer (which will always be one frame behind us, as if we'd ever notice) and then say that we're done drawing by calling InterruptFrame.

That is the basics of a game loop. Many people may like the traditional view of calling PrepFrame, doing the drawing, and then calling DrawFrame. You may even get better results. Tell you what, that is your homework assignment—figure out which way you prefer. This paradigm just seems to give me more time to do other things. This loop area is very important. We will use it to develop almost everything in the next chapter. This is also where all of your drawing will take place.

See you in the next chapter.

Chapter 10

How to Draw as Easy as 1, 2, 3

This is where we begin examining how to put pixels on the black screen we created in the last chapter. Drawing pixels isn't nearly as easy as Plot (1,0) but we'll make it that easy in this chapter. We have to contend with 15-bit vs. 16-bit as well as where to put everything. Below you will find the updated version of the RedrawScreen function set up to handle our new way of dealing with drawing. This is temporary and is used simply to instruct. The methods we develop here will be used to build a class in the next three chapters that will handle all of our drawing.

Our first order of business is by way of introduction only. We have added a prototype and a function as well as pointing out where the new code will go. There's not much else in the section of code that follows. You will notice in the main loop here (RedrawScreen) that we make the call to Draw and pass the DDraw parameter. This will be our drawing routine for now. Simple enough. Now that you have a functioning loop, from the last chapter, let's add to it.

Create a new folder named something like ddraw2 and copy all of the files from the last chapter into it. Now make the changes listed here to loops.cpp. It is worth noting that loops.cpp will eventually contain a lot of other code that will be managed here. Hence the name. I'll introduce you to some of it but most of the management of your game could find a nice home here. You'll need to create that yourself.

```
// loops.cpp
#include "dirdraw.h"

//*******************************

int frame = 0;
int time = 0, timelast = 0;
int count = 0;

//***************************** prototype

void  Draw (DIRECT_DRAW_MANAGER* ddraw);

//*****************************

DWORD WINAPI RedrawScreen (LPVOID Parm)
{
        DIRECT_DRAW_MANAGER* DDraw = (DIRECT_DRAW_MANAGER*) Parm;
```

```
        if (DDraw == NULL) return 1;

        time = timeGetTime ();              // get the current millisec
        count++;
        if (time-timelast>=1000)
        {
            frame = count;
            timelast=time;          // update time
            count=0;
        }
        char buff[40];
        itoa (frame, buff, 10);

        //*****************************

        while (DDraw->DrawFrame ());
        DDraw->ClearBackBuffer ();

        Draw (DDraw);               // here is the new call

        DDraw->PaintText (20, 20, buff);
        DDraw->InterruptFrame ();
        return 0;
    }

    //*****************************

    //This is where we will be putting all of our new functions. In case I don't
    //show you the entire file, this is where you put the new code.


    //*****************************
    void  Draw (DIRECT_DRAW_MANAGER* ddraw)
    {
        SCREEN_STRUCT* screen = ddraw->GetScreen ();
    }
    //*****************************
```

Run it just to be sure that everything still works. Once everything compiles OK, we can move on. If there are compile problems, make sure that you created a new project, added the proper .lib files to Project|Settings, added all of the proper .cpp files to the project, and included all #include files in the proper directory.

The Screen Layout and Pixels

First we need to examine the layout of the pixels a little closer. Every video card usually treats the video screen as a linear chunk of memory. Assuming a video mode of 640x480, the upper-left corner of the screen is location 0 and the upper right is location 639. The memory locations move from left to right across the screen, one after the other, moving slowly down the screen. To move to the next line, start over at location

640 and end at 1279. Although we (humans) see this as an x,y grid on the screen, the video card simply sees a bunch of numbers lined up—an array essentially. It displays 640 pixels across, moves down to the next line, and displays another 640. It continues until the next time to draw comes up and it resets its pointer to the upper left. Of course, these same rules apply in other video modes, for example in 800x600, the screen is 800 across, and is plotted downward in 800-pixel blocks at a time 600 times.

Since we normally think of position on the screen in terms of x,y, we need to make a function that figures x,y coordinates and translates it into the linear method of accessing pixels that your video card uses. Luckily, this is trivial. Take the y position, positive going down the screen, starting at the upper left, and multiply it by Width. So to access 100 *x* and 1 *y*, take *y**640 and add *x*.

```
y*640+x = 740;
```

This means that the screen memory location +740 is the 100,1 location on the screen. Now to plot 0,100, the 100th pixel down from the top and against the left edge, we simply multiply 640*100 and add x, which is 0. The result is 64000. In code, it would look like this:

```
void Plot (int x, int y, SCREEN_STRUCT* screen)
{
        int pos = y*screen->RealWidth + x;
        screen->Screen[pos] = 65535;        // white
}
```

All code we will be adding to this file must appear before the function RedrawScreen. This is our special code section. Add the Plot function to this section. Add the following code to the Draw function, and compile:

```
//*******************************
void  Draw (DIRECT_DRAW_MANAGER* ddraw)
{
        SCREEN_STRUCT* screen = ddraw->GetScreen ();
        for (int i=0; i<100; i++)
        Plot (rand () %screen->Width, rand () %screen->Height, screen);
}
//*******************************
```

It's not too fancy, but you do see lots of dots on the screen being changed every frame. For fun, you might try running it without ClearBackBuffer in the RedrawScreen function and replacing it with PrepFrame. See how long it takes to fill the screen. Remember, without ClearBackBuffer, BackBuffer never gets erased, so you will be continually redrawing the same sections over and over.

This is a simple implementation but illustrates the basics. We do, after all, need to draw pixels on the screen and this is how we do it. Let's play a little with color and then we'll move on to line drawing.

Color, Anyone?

We've talked about color before. Chapter 9 highlighted the difficulties in managing 16-bit vs. 15-bit. Also, bitshifting and masking were briefly covered. Let's modify the code we just created to make differently colored pixels. Let's use the RGBVal class in struct.h. This class contains all of the color manipulation routines you need. You can just make a few C routines if you don't want to use RGBVal, but I prefer its robust services and its simplicity.

First, let's modify the Plot function. We add an unsigned short variable to pass color so that we can dictate the color of the pixel that we'll be drawing. You can see that this is a minor change. The 65535 value has been replaced by the parameter we pass in.

```
//******************************

void Plot (int x, int y, U16 color, SCREEN_STRUCT* screen)
{
        int pos = y*screen->RealWidth + x;
        screen->Screen[pos] = color;
}


//******************************
```

Note: We have changed this Plot routine from three to four parameters. Normally this wouldn't matter, but if you are trying to optimize your code by using __fastcall, you will not obtain any better results. The PC has only a few registers and __fastcall attempts to use register-based calling. Not enough registers means that once you pass three parameters, register-based calling runs out of space to place the parameters, and therefore the compiler reverts to stack-based calling, which is usually slower.

This is the reason I created SCREEN_STRUCT in the first place. You usually need four variables to draw anyway, which surpasses this rather arbitrary limit. I put them all into one structure, which helps most of the time, just not here. A rule of thumb is to always limit your common functions to three parameters, at all costs. If it's not a very common function, don't worry about it.

Next, let's add color manipulation to our Draw function:

```
//******************************

void  Draw (DIRECT_DRAW_MANAGER* ddraw)
{
        SCREEN_STRUCT* screen = ddraw->GetScreen ();
RGBVal rgb;
U16    color;
        for (int i=0; i<100; i++)
        {
```

```
            rgb.SetVal (rand () %256, rand () %256, rand () %256);
(ddraw->GetColorType () == DIRECT_DRAW_MANAGER::_5x5x5_)
color = rgb.Convert15 ();
else color = rgb.Convert16 ();
Plot (rand () %screen->Width, rand () %screen->Height,
color, screen);
}
}


//******************************
```

Unlike the previous function, we've changed quite a few things here. First, we declare an instance of RGBVal and add a color variable that we can pass to our new Plot function. During our loop to draw 100 pixels, we create a random color by passing random red, green, and blue values to the RGBVal member function SetVal. Then we convert the RGB value to a number we can pass to the Plot function. Since we don't how your video card works—it could be 5x5x5 or 5x6x5—we do the conversion. You could set a breakpoint and find out what your video card does, just for fun, but remember that the numbers are 60-40 leaning toward 5x5x5, and you want to keep it open to the entire market.

The conversion code is discussed in Chapter 6, but here it is again:

```
//******************************
U16 Convert15 ()
{
return (U16) (((r&248)<<7) + ((g&248)<<2) + (b>>3));
}
U16 Convert16 ()
{
        return (U16) (((r&248)<<8) + ((g&252)<<3) + (b>>3));
}
//******************************
```

It's pretty straightforward. I found on my machine that this was entirely too fast and the 75 frames per second made things impossible for me to see. You might try a delay but that isn't exactly right. Let's drop the frame rate to make the code run one-third as fast so that we can at least tell what's happening.

```
DWORD WINAPI RedrawScreen (LPVOID Parm)
{
        DIRECT_DRAW_MANAGER* DDraw = (DIRECT_DRAW_MANAGER*) Parm;
        if (DDraw == NULL) return 1;

        time = timeGetTime ();              // get the current millisec
        count++;
        if (time-timelast>=1000)
        {
            frame = count;
            timelast = time;                // update time
            count = 0;
        }
        char buff[40];
        itoa (frame, buff, 10);
```

10

Chapter

```
//****************************

while (DDraw->DrawFrame ());

if (count%3) return 0;      // add this line here

DDraw->ClearBackBuffer ();

Draw (DDraw);               // here is the new call

DDraw->PaintText (20, 20, buff);
DDraw->InterruptFrame ();
return 0;
}
//****************************
```

Notice the code six lines from the bottom where we test count%3. We're testing to make sure that count divided by 3 has no remainder. This returns two out of three times. Now I tried one-third the speed and that was still way too fast. It is still drawing every frame, but it's not doing any of the other maintenance per frame. The apparent frame rate went way up but that was because of a math error involving the frame count calculation. You can correct it if you see fit. Anyway, one-third wasn't enough and I ended up using one-tenth the frame time, which is still very fast. Your results will vary but playing with this number may yield a better picture so you can see the color variation. Also, you may care to play with the number of pixels you draw. This can also be fun. Change the number to 1000 and see how it looks.

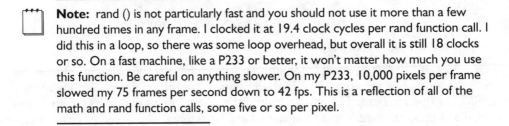

Note: rand () is not particularly fast and you should not use it more than a few hundred times in any frame. I clocked it at 19.4 clock cycles per rand function call. I did this in a loop, so there was some loop overhead, but overall it is still 18 clocks or so. On a fast machine, like a P233 or better, it won't matter how much you use this function. Be careful on anything slower. On my P233, 10,000 pixels per frame slowed my 75 frames per second down to 42 fps. This is a reflection of all of the math and rand function calls, some five or so per pixel.

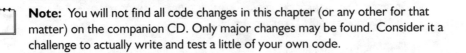

Note: You will not find all code changes in this chapter (or any other for that matter) on the companion CD. Only major changes may be found. Consider it a challenge to actually write and test a little of your own code.

Horizontal Line Drawing

How do I draw a line? you ask. Simple, it is just a bunch of lit pixels end to end. Let's start with a simple line drawing function and then we'll modify it. Horizontal lines are the easiest because they are simply a string of pixels. Creating a for loop from one end to the next is all it takes. Let's make sure that you understand the concept of a linear frame buffer before we go any further. I think I've explained it well enough, but you still may not get it.

First, the screen is always broken into a positive coordinate system. No, by positive, I do not mean friendly. I mean positive as opposed to negative (i.e., 1 vs. –1). x will go from 0 to 639 (except in other video modes in which it could be 0 to 799 or the like) and y will go from 0 to 479, assuming a screen of 640x480. The reason that the rightmost point is not 640 is because we start at 0, not 1. The upper right is considered to be 639 because we move across the top row of pixels from 0 until we reach the edge of the screen. The upper-left corner is considered 0,0 and the bottom right is considered 639,479. When we look at the memory locations, the upper left is considered 0 and the bottom right is considered to be 307199 (640*480-1). The bottom left is 306560.

The video card, internally, represents the screen as a string of memory locations. The video card, and hence the screen, does not have a coordinate system that uses x and y. You have to create this system. The computer just draws the pixels across the screen as it counts from 0 to 307199. We think of pixels in terms of x and y. How do we convert between the computer's system and our Euclidean system of plotting?

We pretend that x and y exist, to coincide with the way our minds work. When we want to plot a pixel, we do the multiplication and addition to convert this x,y coordinate into the computer's system. If we start in the upper corner at 0 and move right one, that is memory location 1 (moving to location 1,0). If we move again, that is memory location 2. Each pixel across is one more than the previous. What happens when we get to 639, the end of a line? Adding 1 moves us down to the beginning of the next line. Another way to look at this is: Every time we pass 640, we move down to the next line.

So in order to move from the topmost line to the next line down, add 640. If we're at screen location 320,0—the middle of the top line which is memory location 329—we simply add 640 to move to the middle of the next line. 969 is the middle of the next line but in our minds it is 320,1. Hey, a coordinate system. This is best calculated as $640*y + x$. So go ahead and work in coordinates and when you want to plot, simply multiply y by 640 and add x.

I hope that it's more clear now.

Below is our introductory HorizontalLine function. Starting at the leftmost point, $x1$, we plot a series of points until we arrive at the rightmost point, $x2$. The y never changes. You can see how simple the code is:

```
//*******************************

void Plot (int x, int y, U16 color, SCREEN_STRUCT* screen)
{
        int pos = y*screen->RealWidth + x;
        screen->Screen[pos] = color;
}


//*******************************
//*******************************
```

```
void HorizontalLine (int x1, int x2, int y, U16 color, SCREEN_STRUCT* screen)
{
        for (int i=x1; i<=x2; i++)
        Plot (i, y, color, screen);
}
//*****************************
//*****************************

void Draw (DIRECT_DRAW_MANAGER* ddraw)
{
        SCREEN_STRUCT* screen = ddraw->GetScreen ();
        RGBVal rgb;
        U16    color;
        rgb.SetVal (rand () %256, rand () %256, rand () %256);
        if (ddraw->GetColorType () == DIRECT_DRAW_MANAGER::_5x5x5_)
             color = rgb.Convert15 ();
        else color = rgb.Convert16 ();


        HorizontalLine (40, 600, 100, color);
}
//*****************************
```

What the above code does is create a flashing horizontal line across the screen. We are getting into the realm of too many parameters and we may want to use global variables or simply abstract all of this functionality to a class.

The pixels are drawn from left to right across the screen. The loop starts small and gets larger, meaning that a left-to-right pixel drawing is ideal. This is generally considered a standard and we will be using it throughout this text. Incidentally, you can go from right to left just as fast using the following chunk of code. It's just different. Most people are not used to going backward, so stick to the other method unless you have good reason.

```
//*****************************
void HorizontalLine (int x1, int x2, int y, U16 color, SCREEN_STRUCT* screen)
{
        for (int i=x2; i>=x1; i--)
        Plot (i, y, color, screen);
}
//*****************************
```

Some obvious assumptions are made here: $x1$ and $x2$ both have to be in the range of 0 to 639; y has to be in the range of 0 to 479; $x2$ must be larger than $x1$; the screen variable must be valid; and color should be non-zero. If any of these conditions are not met, disaster can strike. For now let's stick to this simple model, but we will account for most of these contingencies later in this chapter.

I've kept this system as simple as possible. It is notably (pitifully) slow but we will optimize the hell out of it and it will be very fast. For now, let's move on to other types of line drawing.

Vertical Line Drawing

Vertical line drawing is almost as easy as horizontal line drawing. You may have noticed that all we really needed was a Plot function and a loop. Same thing here but now we add the screen width each time we want to move down one scan line. That will be in our optimization a little later; for now let's stick to the model we used in HorizontalLine. You should always move down the screen as opposed to up the screen. It is more intuitive and is a generally accepted standard.

By simply copying and pasting the HorizontalLine function we developed earlier and making a few modifications, we now have the VerticalLine function:

```
//******************************
void  VerticalLine (int y1, int y2, int x, U16 color, SCREEN_STRUCT* screen)
{
        for (int i=y1; i<=y2; i++)
        Plot (x, i, color, screen);
}
//******************************
```

Ta da! Notice how similar it is to our previous function. But look closely at the parameters passed in the Plot function—they are slightly different. Range issues pervade. $y2$ must be larger than $y1$ and both must be in the range of 0 to 479, while x must be in the range of 0 to 639. The screen variable must be valid and color must not be 0.

Here is the code in context. HorizontalLine and Plot have been omitted for brevity:

```
//******************************
void  VerticalLine (int y1, int y2, int x, U16 color, SCREEN_STRUCT* screen)
{
        for (int i=y1; i<=y2; i++)
        Plot (x, i, color, screen);
}
//******************************
//******************************

void  Draw (DIRECT_DRAW_MANAGER* ddraw)
{
        SCREEN_STRUCT* screen = ddraw->GetScreen ();
        RGBVal rgb;
        U16    color;
        rgb.SetVal (rand () %256, rand () %256, rand () %256);
        if (ddraw->GetColorType () == DIRECT_DRAW_MANAGER::_5x5x5_)
             color = rgb.Convert15 ();
        else color = rgb.Convert16 ();

        HorizontalLine (40, 600, 100, color, screen);

        VerticalLine (10, 470, 10, color, screen);
}

//******************************
```

By making minor changes to Draw, we can draw a box. Give it a shot. Below is a simple modification and we've added a few variables to make it even easier. Look how I organized the variables, making it easy to understand. This function creates a box that almost frames the entire window.

```
//*******************************

void  Draw (DIRECT_DRAW_MANAGER* ddraw)
{
        SCREEN_STRUCT* screen = ddraw->GetScreen ();
        RGBVal rgb;
        U16     color;
        rgb.SetVal (rand () %256, rand () %256, rand () %256);
        if (ddraw->GetColorType () == DIRECT_DRAW_MANAGER::_5x5x5_)
                color = rgb.Convert15 ();
        else color = rgb.Convert16 ();
        // notice how the following variables all fall
        // within specified ranges.
        int left=10, right=630, top=10, bottom=470;

        HorizontalLine (left, right, top, color, screen);    // top line
        HorizontalLine (left, right, bottom, color, screen); // bottom line

        VerticalLine (top, bottom, left, color, screen);     // left line
        VerticalLine (top, bottom, right, color, screen);    // right line
}

//*******************************
```

Taking our function one step further, we'll make a bunch of rectangles inside each other (concentric-like), as shown in Figure 10.1. The rectangles are all different colors and this creates a colorful picture.

Figure 10.1
Concentric rectangles created with the Draw function

This code is worth trying and certainly worth the effort to try to understand what I've done. We have really simple math, but it makes a cool effect. Like before, the code is easy to understand and is simply a minor modification of what has come before. Make sure that you have created the HorizontalLine and VerticalLine functions before you use this function. Reading is nice, but actually typing it in is helpful.

```
//*******************************

void  Draw (DIRECT_DRAW_MANAGER* ddraw)
{
      SCREEN_STRUCT* screen = ddraw->GetScreen ();
      RGBVal rgb;
      U16  color;
      // notice how the following variables all fall
      // within specified ranges.
      int left=10, right=630, top=10, bottom=470;

      for (int i=0; i<15; i++)
      {
          int add = i*10;
          rgb.SetVal (rand () %256, rand () %256, rand () %256);
          if (ddraw->GetColorType () == DIRECT_DRAW_MANAGER::_5x5x5_)
              color = rgb.Convert15 ();
          else color = rgb.Convert16 ();
              // top line
          HorizontalLine (left+add, right-add, top+add, color, screen);
              // bottom line
          HorizontalLine (left+add, right-add, bottom-add, color, screen);
```

```
                                   // left line
                   VerticalLine (top+add, bottom-add, left+add, color, screen);
                                   // right line
     VerticalLine (top+add, bottom-add, right-add, color, screen);
     }
     }
```

```
//*******************************
```
That does it for vertical line drawing. Hope you enjoyed it as much as I did.

Introducing Bresenham's Line Drawing

In the 1950s, I believe, Bresenham came up with a nifty little line drawing algorithm. It draws between any two points on the screen by approximating where the line should be. For us to display a true line, we would need infinite resolution, but Bresenham's algorithm is close enough to look like a real line, especially at higher resolutions.

This algorithm is much too complex to explain in this text. But there are dozens of books that do explain it, including *Flights of Fantasy* and *Gardens of Imagination*, both by Christopher Lampton (The Waite Group).

The idea is to draw from any point on the screen to any other point on the screen. No clipping is done here (this is covered later in the chapter), and the values must be valid. The screen pointer is used by the Plot function and thus this function is made unnecessarily slow. Bresenham's line drawing is fast, but it is not as fast as HorizontalLine and VerticalLine are. There is simply too much math for it to be the same speed. When drawing horizontal lines and vertical lines, use those functions.

```
//*******************************
void  Line (int px1, int py1, int px2, int py2, SCREEN_STRUCT* screen, U16 color)
{
        if (screen == NULL) return;
    int SC_WIDTH = screen->RealWidth, SC_HEIGHT = screen->Height;

        //1) setup stage

        int y_unit,x_unit;         // Variables for amount of change in x and y
        int ydiff=py2-py1;         // Calculate difference between y coordinates

        if (ydiff<0)               // If the line moves in the negative direction
        {
            ydiff=-ydiff;          // ...get absolute value of difference
            y_unit=-1;             // ...and set negative unit in y dimension
        }
        else y_unit=1;             // Else set positive unit in y dimension

        int xdiff=px2-px1;         // Calculate difference between x coordinates
        if (xdiff<0)               // If the line moves in the negative direction
        {
            xdiff=-xdiff;          // ...get absolute value of difference
```

```
        x_unit=-1;                  // ...and set negative unit in x dimension
    }
    else x_unit=1;                  // Else set positive unit in y dimension
    int error_term=0;               // Initialize error term

    //2) drawing stage
    if (xdiff>ydiff)                // If difference is bigger in x dimension
    {
        int length=xdiff+1;         // ...prepare to count off in x direction
        for (int i=0; i<length; i++) // Loop through points in x direction
        {
                                    // Set the next pixel in the line to COLOR
            Plot (px1, py1, color, screen);
            px1+=x_unit;            // Move offset to next pixel in x direction
            error_term+=ydiff;      // Check to see if move required in y dir
            if (error_term>xdiff)
            {                       // If so...
                error_term-=xdiff;  // ...reset error term
                py1+=y_unit;        // ...and move offset to next pixel in y dir.
            }
        }
    }
    else                            // If difference is bigger in y dimension
    {
        int length=ydiff+1;         // ...prepare to count off in y direction
        for (int i=0; i<length; i++) // Loop through points in y direction
        {
                                    // Set the next pixel in the line to COLOR
            Plot (px1, py1, color, screen);
            py1+=y_unit;            // Move offset to next pixel in y dir
            error_term+=xdiff;
            if (error_term>0)       // Check to see if move required in x dir
            {                       // If so...
                error_term-=ydiff;  // ...reset error term
                px1+=x_unit;        // ...and move offset to next pixel in x dir.
            }
        }
    }
}

//****************************
```

Using the function is as easy as cake, a piece of pie (the clichés are a little dull, so I swapped them). Below is the same function as before with some minor modifications. (I get 14 fps on my machine, for comparison's sake.)

```
//*******************************

void  Draw (DIRECT_DRAW_MANAGER* ddraw)
{
    SCREEN_STRUCT* screen = ddraw->GetScreen ();
    RGBVal rgb;
    U16    color;
```

```
         // notice how the following variables all fall
         // within specified ranges.

         for (int i=0; i<1000; i++)
         {
              rgb.SetVal (rand () %256, rand () %256, rand () %256);
              if (ddraw->GetColorType () == DIRECT_DRAW_MANAGER::_5x5x5_)
                  color = rgb.Convert15 ();
              else color = rgb.Convert16 ();
         Line (rand () %640, rand () %480, rand () %640, rand () %480, screen, color);
         }
}

//*******************************
```

Clipping

Clipping horizontal and vertical lines is relatively easy. All other types of lines are trickier and take a bit of algebra. We'll show the two easy types here and get to the trickier part a little later in the chapter.

First, look at Figures 10.2, 10.3, 10.4, and 10.5. They all illustrate how clipping situations arise and the basics in code.

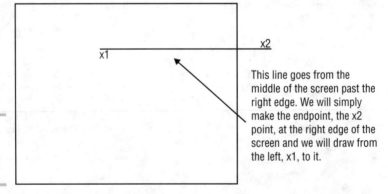

Figure 10.2
Horizontal clipping on the right

Here's the code for Figure 10.2:

```
//*******************************
void HorizontalLine (int x1, int x2, int y, U16 color, SCREEN_STRUCT* screen)
{
if (x2 >= screen->Width) x2=screen->Width-1; // right
       for (int i=x1; i<=x2; i++)
       Plot (i, y, color, screen);
}
//*******************************
```

Notice that we are using the Width variable. This is because the Width variable is the edge of the visible screen. Also, Width is a number between 1 and 1280, but the right edge is actually position 639, even if there are 640 pixels across. This is because the first position is 0.

Now let's clip on the left, as shown in Figure 10.3:

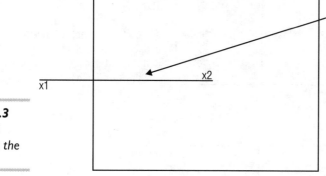

This line goes from past the left edge of the screen to about the middle.

We will simply move the endpoint, the x1 point, to the left edge of the screen and draw from the left, x1, to the middle of the screen at x2. Set x1 to 0.

Figure 10.3
Horizontal clipping on the left

```
//*****************************
void  HorizontalLine (int x1, int x2, int y, U16 color, SCREEN_STRUCT* screen)
{
         if (x1 < 0) x1=0;                         // left
    if (x2 >= screen->Width) x2=screen->Width-1;   // right
         for (int i=x1; i<=x2; i++)
         Plot (i, y, color, screen);
}
//*****************************
```

Now that wasn't so hard, was it? You can't draw anything that has a position below 0 anyway. In all cases where it starts below 0, simply make it 0. This clipping is like a branch outside your window: When you look at it, you assume that the entire tree is there even though only a small part is visible. Clipping is necessary; otherwise you draw into weird regions of memory which often makes your software very unstable.

Clipping from either the top or the bottom, as shown in Figures 10.4 and 10.5, is nearly identical, so I put it all into one routine.

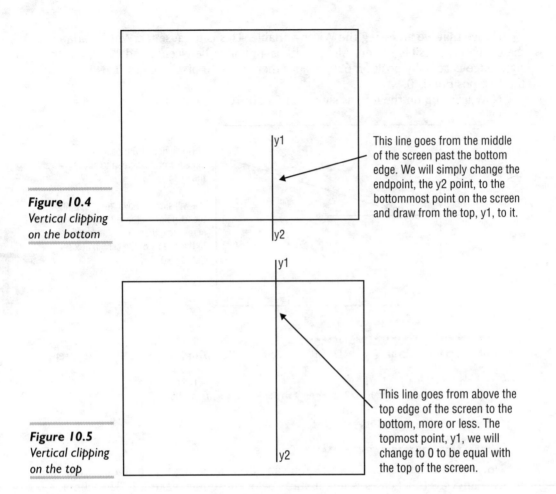

Figure 10.4
Vertical clipping on the bottom

This line goes from the middle of the screen past the bottom edge. We will simply change the endpoint, the y2 point, to the bottommost point on the screen and draw from the top, y1, to it.

Figure 10.5
Vertical clipping on the top

This line goes from above the top edge of the screen to the bottom, more or less. The topmost point, y1, we will change to 0 to be equal with the top of the screen.

Here is the code:

```
//******************************
void  VerticalLine (int y1, int y2, int x, U16 color, SCREEN_STRUCT* screen)
{
if (y1 < 0) y1=0;                              // top
if (y2 >= screen->Height) y2=screen->Height-1;  // bottom
        for (int i=y1; i<=y2; i++)
        Plot (x, i, color, screen);
}
//******************************
```

Now all of this drawing is slow, don't you think? Let's change that. The VerticalLine and HorizontalLine functions are about to be completely revamped.

Optimizing Line Drawing

Memset is one of the optimization keys that we use to make our line drawing faster. What is memset, you wonder? You should know that by now. Go look up memcpy and memset and then come back to this book. You'll find them in any beginning C programming manual or in the help files of your compiler.

The problem with memset is that it does a byte-by-byte memory fill which does not work in 16-bit where you need to fill 2 bytes at a time (8 bits per byte, 16 bits divided by 8 bits is 2 bytes). What happens is that each byte of a block of memory is filled with an 8-bit value, and in 16-bit this produces unpredictable color results. We are going to replace the existing memset with our own version.

Below you'll find our C/C++ version of the new memset. We will replace it with a simple assembly version a little later. In case you're wondering where we are going with this, a string of 16-bit values can be filled very quickly using an optimized routine. Since a horizontal line is simply a string of 16-bit values, we will now increase our horizontal line drawing speed by a factor of 20 or so. Watch the frame rate go way up after just this one simple optimization.

I have typedef'd U16ptr in struct.h to be an unsigned short *(pointer). The results are pretty amazing. The concentric rectangles program jumped from 28 fps to 32 fps or so. That's with the simple C version—and we are drawing vertical lines along with it, unoptimized. A closer look at our new HorizontalLine function will reveal some necessary changes.

Our new function—Memset16Bit—takes a pointer to a 16-bit memory location and slowly sets it to the fill value as it advances the pointer. Having almost no error checking here contributes to this function's speed. The memory at the address of dest (*dest) is set to fill, and once that happens the dest pointer advances to the next memory location. This is very fast pointer math and inherently makes this code very fast.

```
//**************************************************
void __fastcall Memset16Bit (U16ptr dest, U16 fill, int num)
{
if (num<1) return;
    while (num--)
    {
        *dest++=fill;
    }
}
//**************************************************


//**************************************************
void  HorizontalLine (int x1, int x2, int y, U16 color, SCREEN_STRUCT* screen)
{
    if (x1 < 0) x1=0;                // left
    if (x2 >= screen->Width) x2=screen->Width-1; // right

    int num = x2-x1;                 // how many pixels across
    U16ptr sc = screen->Screen;
    sc += y*screen->RealWidth;       // move the screen pointer down
```

```
                                       // to the proper scan line
        sc += x1;                      // move the pointer to the left
                                       // point on the line

        Memset16Bit (sc, color, num);

}
//****************************************************
```

HorizontalLine now has to advance the screen pointer to the exact point on the screen where our line begins. The math for it is supplied and we can simplify it into one line:

```
// move the screen pointer down to the proper place
U16ptr sc = (screen->Screen) + (y * screen->RealWidth) + (x1);
```

It also needs to know how many 16-bit pixels will need to be set:

```
int num = x2-x1;                       // how many pixels across
```

This math could simply be passed as a parameter to Memset16Bit, but it makes more sense to make it a variable. Your call. This simple optimization saves a lot of drawing time. But how much time? How do we find out how much we saved?

This brings up a good point; there is no point in optimizing if you do not test your results—before and after. You still have the last HorizontalLine function somewhere in loops.cpp commented out, don't you? (Rule of thumb—don't delete old code until you know that you don't need it, at least one day later. That rule is flexible.)

So now let's see what we need to do to properly test our code. Take the Draw function and comment out its contents so that you can play with it more later. Now add the following contents:

```
//******************************

void  Draw (DIRECT_DRAW_MANAGER* ddraw)
{
        SCREEN_STRUCT* screen = ddraw->GetScreen ();
        RGBVal rgb;
        U16    color;
        int left=10, right=630, top=10, bottom=470;

        long time1 = timeGetTime ();
        for (int i=0; i<10000; i++)
            HorizontalLine (left, right, top, color, screen); // top line

        long time2 = timeGetTime ();
        long result = time2-time1;

        char buff[40];
        itoa (result, buff, 10);
        ddraw->PaintText (20, 50, buff);


}

//******************************
```

We've left some of it the same. The only thing we will be doing is drawing 10,000 lines and timing it. Let's look at the numbers with the old HorizontalLine function:

```
//*******************************
// do not use this slow routine
void  HorizontalLine (int x1, int x2, int y, U16 color, SCREEN_STRUCT* screen)
{
        if (x1 < 0) x1=0; // left
if (x2 >= screen->Width) x2=screen->Width-1;          // right
        for (int i=x1; i<=x2; i++)
        Plot (i, y, color, screen);
}
//*******************************
```

The reason we draw so many times is that we want it to take a while. Drawing a single line takes so little time that we'd never be able to measure it. Even if it were slow enough, the only answer we would get is 1 or 2 milliseconds, which is too small a number. If we make an improvement on the speed, the number goes to 0, but that doesn't tell us how much faster. Drawing thousands of times gives us numbers like 800 to 1000, and if we make an improvement the number may go down to 200. That gives us a much better idea of how much faster our routine is.

Well, drawing 10,000 lines on my machine takes approximately 1065 milliseconds, or over 1 second. (The timing marks are in milliseconds, in case you've forgotten.) Now let's use the new HorizontalLine function that looks like this:

```
//*******************************
void  HorizontalLine (int x1, int x2, int y, U16 color, SCREEN_STRUCT* screen)
{
        if (x1 < 0) x1=0;                  // left
        if (x2 >= screen->Width) x2=screen->Width-1;     // right

        int num = x2-x1;                   // how many pixels across

        // move the screen pointer down to the proper place
        U16ptr sc = (screen->Screen) + (y*screen->RealWidth) + (x1);
        Memset16Bit (sc, color, num);
}
//*******************************
```

The timing is about 535 milliseconds. We have nearly chopped the amount of time it takes to draw a line in half. This is about the best that we can expect in C. It really won't get much faster. Let's try doing a simple assembly routine. If you don't understand what is happening after my very brief explanation, read *Pentium Processor Optimization Tools* by Michael L. Schmit (AP Professional).

```
//***************************************************
void __fastcall Memset16Bit (U16ptr dest, U16 fill, int num)
{
        if (num < 1) return;

        _asm
        {
        mov     ax, fill                   // store value
```

```
        mov    ecx, num              // how many copies
        mov    edi, dest             // to where


        rep    stosw
        }

}
//**************************************************
```

First, if we are asked to copy anything less than 1, we return. Next, we launch into assembly. The Pentium has a built-in memory "set" routine that works for single bytes, double bytes (word), or 4 bytes at a time (double word). That means that it will set memory in groups of 1 byte, 2 bytes, or 4 bytes.

You can use that copy routine along with a repeat operator ("rep") to make it repeat a number of times. The number of times it repeats is stored in the ECX register. The number you want stored goes into EAX, and the destination address goes into EDI. Then you call the repeat copy function—rep stosw. It copies a word (2 bytes) at a time. For single bytes, use stosb. For 4 bytes at a time, use stosd. That about explains it. This assembly code further reduces the line drawing code to about 383 milliseconds. Now we are down to nearly one-third of where we started, time-wise. But one further optimization should take us to about the fastest it gets.

Our limitation is that we are setting only 2 bytes at a time. We can speed it a little by setting 4 bytes at a time. A problem exists, however: What if we need to set only 2 bytes or 6 bytes? If we are trying to set four at a time, we run into an overage. We could just not use the last 2 bytes but then we miss pixel info. We will simply start out copying those two first in the case that the 4-byte alignment is not possible.

I have purposefully staggered these assembly operands to account for Pentium pipelining. This times out to be about 196 milliseconds, or over five times faster than we started with. Significant, if you ask me.

```
//**************************************************
void __fastcall Memset16Bit (U16ptr dst, U16 fill, int num)
{
        if (num <= 0) return;
        if (num&1) *dst++ = fill;       // one too many for stosd
        if (num <2) return;
        int f = fill;


        _asm
        {
        mov    eax, f                 // store value
        mov    ecx, num               // how many copies
        shl    eax, 16                // shift it into high order
        mov    edi, dst               // to where
        add    eax, f                 // do two pixels at a time
        shr    ecx, 1                 // divide by 2


        rep    stosd
        }

}
//**************************************************
```

Now on to the vertical line. So far we have this:

```
//*******************************
void  VerticalLine (int y1, int y2, int x, U16 color, SCREEN_STRUCT* screen)
{
      if (y1 < 0) y1=0;                              // top
      if (y2 >= screen->Height) y2=screen->Height-1; // bottom
      for (int i=y1; i<=y2; i++)
      Plot (x, i, color, screen);
}
//*******************************
```

The real problem is that we call Plot for every pixel. Let's make a local pointer and see what we get. First, let's change the main Draw function so that we set up our testing. Change it to be this:

```
//*******************************
void  Draw (DIRECT_DRAW_MANAGER* ddraw)
{
      SCREEN_STRUCT* screen = ddraw->GetScreen ();
      RGBVal rgb;
      U16    color;
      // notice how the following variables all fall
      // within specified ranges.
      int left=10, right=630, top=10, bottom=470;

      long time1 = timeGetTime ();
      for (int i=0; i<10000; i++)
            VerticalLine (top, bottom, left, color, screen);

      long time2 = timeGetTime ();
      long result = time2-time1;

      char buff[40];
      itoa (result, buff, 10);
      ddraw->PaintText (20, 50, buff);
}
//*******************************
```

Note: A word about testing and timing: Make code that works before you ever get started trying to do what we are doing. Make your code stable and relatively unbreakable, then go on to optimization.

Now we can time it. I come up with 981 milliseconds. Why is it faster than the initial HorizontalLine test? Fewer pixels are drawn from top to bottom than from side to side. Going across the screen, we drew 620 pixels, but vertically we are only drawing 460. The less you do, the faster the computer goes. Got it?

Let's make the Plot function local and remove some garbage. We have used the pointer advance system that we introduced in the Memset16Bit function listed at the beginning of this section. Otherwise, this is a simple modification of the previous code. Unfortunately, there is no magic bullet in assembly like before, and any assembly optimization will have dubious results. Just stick with C and this function will be about as fast as it gets. This times out to 476 milliseconds for 10,000 vertical lines, making it more than twice as fast.

```
//*******************************
void VerticalLine (int y1, int y2, int x, U16 color, SCREEN_STRUCT* screen)
{
        if (y1 < 0) y1=0;                          // top
        if (y2 >= screen->Height) y2=screen->Height-1; // bottom

        int num = y2-y1;                           // how many pixels down

        // move the screen pointer down to the proper place
        U16ptr sc = (screen->Screen) + (y1*screen->RealWidth) + (x);

        while (num--)
        {
                *sc = color;
                sc += screen->RealWidth;
        }
}
//*******************************
```

The while loop can be replaced with a for loop and the num declaration removed with exactly the same timing results. That about does it for optimization. We'll be using HorizontalLine-type drawing extensively for the next few sections throughout this chapter. But vertical line drawing can never be as fast, so we won't use it except here.

Rectangle Filling

We're going to start with simple rectangles. Let's avoid the clipping issue until later and just fill a rectangle with a color. The first thing to know about a rectangle is that you only need two x,y coordinates to draw it: the upper-left corner and the bottom-right corner. So the parameters we need are as follows:

```
int x1
int y1
int x1
int y2
U16 color
SCREEN_STRUCT* screen
```

Now you are ready to draw a rectangle, right? Maybe. The fastest way to fill a rectangle on the screen is to treat it like a series of horizontal lines. We will draw a bunch of parallel lines equal in number to the height. We use horizontal lines because that drawing routine is faster than vertical lines.

In terms of filling, there are other methods available: We could make a bunch of tightly packed concentric rectangles or we could pick a spot in the middle of the area and do a flood fill outwards. These ways of filling rectangular areas are a lot slower, so stick to the lines-across method described here.

Drawing a series of parallel lines is the best route because of speed, and since rectangles are equal on opposite sides, the math is simple. But why do we need filled rectangles? They are good for interface elements. More importantly, the routines we develop here and in later sections will be used to develop good bitmap drawing routines later. This simple concept of rectangle drawing will make our bitmap drawing scream.

First, let's take our existing code and add to it. Then we'll rip the guts out and make it local to our new RectangleFill function:

```
//***************************************************
void  HorizontalLine (int x1, int x2, int y, U16 color, SCREEN_STRUCT* screen)
{
        if (x1 < 0) x1=0;                               // left
        if (x2 >= screen->Width) x2=screen->Width-1;    // right
        int num = x2-x1;                // how many pixels across
        U16ptr sc = screen->Screen;
        sc += y*screen->RealWidth;      // move the screen pointer down
                                        // to the proper scan line
        sc += x1;                       // move the pointer to the left
                                        // point on the line

        Memset16Bit (sc, color, num);

}
//***************************************************
```

This routine is stable and does exactly what we need it to do for rectangle filling. Now we add the RectangleFill routine:

```
//******************************
void  RectangleFill (int left, int top, int right, int bottom, U16 color,
SCREEN_STRUCT* screen)
{
        for (int i=top; i<bottom; i++)
        HorizontalLine (left, right, i, color, screen);
}
//******************************
```

As you can see, this is relatively easy now that we have the HorizontalLine drawing function. We simply step down from the top of the rectangle to the bottom, all the while drawing one horizontal line at a time. Timing should be different since we are drawing so much more.

The Draw function has been slightly modified to accommodate our new routine. Here, we have reduced the number of iterations by a factor of 10 (see for loop). Of course, we are drawing ten times as many lines, so the amount of time should be roughly the same. Notice the new value for bottom. Filling the whole screen can take a long time so we'll just do 10 scan lines. My timing is 192 milliseconds, or roughly the same time as before.

10

Chapter

```
//*******************************

void  Draw (DIRECT_DRAW_MANAGER* ddraw)
{
      SCREEN_STRUCT* screen = ddraw->GetScreen ();
      RGBVal rgb;
      U16    color;
      // notice how the following variables all fall
      // within specified ranges.
      int left=10, right=630, top=10, bottom=20;      // new bottom

      long time1 = timeGetTime ();
      for (int i=0; i<1000; i++)
      RectangleFill (left, top, right, bottom, color, screen);

      long time2 = timeGetTime ();
      long result = time2-time1;
      char buff[40];
      itoa (result, buff, 10);
      ddraw->PaintText (20, 50, buff);
}

//*******************************
```

Rectangle Outlining

We have already done this, so let's put it into a function and then move on. You may remember the concentric rectangles we did earlier. Well, we use the same type of code and the same parameters here as in the RectangleFill function in the last section. The only thing we change is what we do with the parameters. You may want to name this function differently.

```
//*******************************
void  RectangleFrame (int left, int top, int right, int bottom, U16 color,
SCREEN_STRUCT* screen)
{
      HorizontalLine (left, right, top, color, screen);
      HorizontalLine (left, right, bottom, color, screen);

      VerticalLine (top, bottom, left, color, screen);
      VerticalLine (top, bottom, right, color, screen);
}
//*******************************
```

There is a little pixel overlap at the corners where a single pixel is drawn once by HorizontalLine and then drawn over by VerticalLine. All four corners have this problem but doing the extra tiny bit of math is not worth the effort. It gains us nothing, or practically nothing. The speed difference is not measurable.

Drawing 1,000 times is not enough to properly measure the time, so back to 10,000 we go. My numbers come out to 403 milliseconds. That's fairly fast to draw 10,000 rectangles.

```
//******************************

void  Draw (DIRECT_DRAW_MANAGER* ddraw)
{
        SCREEN_STRUCT* screen = ddraw->GetScreen ();
        RGBVal rgb;
        U16    color;
        // notice how the following variables all fall
        // within specified ranges.
        int left=10, right=630, top=10, bottom=20;      // new bottom

        long time1 = timeGetTime ();
        for (int i=0; i<10000; i++)
        RectangleFrame (left, top, right, bottom, color, screen);

        long time2 = timeGetTime ();
        long result = time2-time1;

        char buff[40];
        itoa (result, buff, 10);
        ddraw->PaintText (20, 50, buff);
}


//******************************
```

The last thing we are going to do is remove the function calls from within both rectangle routines. Speed is the key, and we can speed these puppies up a little by not calling the HorizontalLine function so much. The speed difference is about 2 percent, so it may not be worth your effort. However, this does illustrate an optimization we will elaborate on in Chapter 11.

First, we precalculate a few values that we will use frequently: num, the number of pixels across, height, the height of the rectangle, and width, the width of the draw area. Width is provided so that we can add it to our pointer to move down exactly one scan line each time we finish one line.

```
//******************************
void  RectangleFill (int left, int top, int right, int bottom, U16 color,
SCREEN_STRUCT* screen)
{
        int num = right-left;           // how many pixels across
        int height = bottom-top;        // make our math easier
        int width = screen->RealWidth;  // make the variable local
                                        // to speed memory access

        // move the screen pointer down to the proper place
        U16ptr sc = (screen->Screen) + (top*width) + (left);
```

```
        while (height--)
        {
              Memset16Bit (sc, color, num);
              sc+=width;
        }
}
//******************************
```

The RectangleFrame function should not be done this way. Leave it as it is.

Better Line Clipping, Rectangle Clipping, and Safety Measures

What are safety measures? These are things that keep your system from locking up. Say that you call HorizontalLine with $x2$ smaller than $x1$. Uh oh! The memset can go on forever overwriting all kinds of memory. Bad news. It's like an elephant walking through your computer's memory. Stomp, stomp; bye, bye, memory. Also, if you don't clip the rectangle and you happen to go above the topmost scan line or go below the bottommost, memory is stomped on and may also lock your computer. Most of the time, you will write software that will never require clipping, and for speed purposes, all of the checking can slow you down considerably. It is better to have two HorizontalLine functions, one when you are sure that everything will be OK and one for when you need the error checking.

Here is our HorizontalLineSafe function that clips. If the second point is smaller than the first point, then it uses the macro SWAP to exchange the two values. Basically, this is the same as our previous HorizontalLine function except we've added SWAP. SWAP can be found in the struct.h file.

```
//******************************
void HorizontalLineSafe (int x1, int x2, int y, U16 color, SCREEN_STRUCT*
screen)
{
if (y<0 || y>= screen->Height) return;
        if (x2<x1) SWAP (x1, x2);
if (x1>=screen->Width) return;
if (x2<0) return;

// regular clipping
        if (x1 < 0) x1=0;                          // left
        if (x2 >= screen->Width) x2=screen->Width-1;    // right

        int num = x2-x1;                           // how many pixels across

        // move the screen pointer down to the proper place
        U16ptr sc = (screen->Screen) + (y*screen->RealWidth) + (x1);
        Memset16Bit (sc, color, num);
}
//******************************
```

One thing to note is the order of tests. First we test to see if the line will be beyond the bounds of the screen. If so, there is no sense in drawing the line and we return. We SWAP before we test the borders. SWAP ensures that the lowest value is stored in *x*1 and the highest value is stored in *x*2. If the smallest *x* position (*x*1) is beyond the right edge of the screen, then we return because we know that nothing needs to be drawn. If the largest *x* value (*x*2) is less than the left edge, then we return because none of the line is visible. Then we test the borders and clip when necessary.

Now that we have clipping isolated into this function, why not pull it out of the other function? We can add a little speed to HorizontalLine by removing the error checking since we will use HorizontalLineSafe when we actually need error checking. This will only make it slightly faster and you may choose to make all line drawing HorizontalLineSafe because of the small speed difference. There is about a 0.8 percent difference in speed, which is almost not measurable. Notice that I've eliminated the num variable for a minor speed increase.

```
//*******************************
void  HorizontalLine (int x1, int x2, int y, U16 color, SCREEN_STRUCT* screen)
{
      // move the screen pointer down to the proper place
      U16ptr sc = (screen->Screen) + (y*screen->RealWidth) + (x1);
      Memset16Bit (sc, color, x2-x1);
}
//*******************************
```

Below, you'll find the two modified VerticalLine functions. The modifications are identical so they need no explanation.

```
//*******************************
void  VerticalLine (int y1, int y2, int x, U16 color, SCREEN_STRUCT* screen)
{
      int num = y2-y1;                  // how many pixels across

      // move the screen pointer down to the proper place
      U16ptr sc = (screen->Screen) + (y1*screen->RealWidth) + (x);

      while (num--)
      {
          *sc = color;
          sc += screen->RealWidth;
      }
}
//*******************************


//*******************************
void  VerticalLineSafe (int y1, int y2, int x, U16 color, SCREEN_STRUCT*
                        screen)
{
      if (x<0 || x>=screen->Width) return;
      if (y2<y1) SWAP (y1, y2);
      if (y1 < 0) y1=0;                                 // top
      if (y2 >= screen->Height) y2=screen->Height-1;  // bottom

      int num = y2-y1;                                  // how many pixels across
```

```
        // move the screen pointer down to the proper place
        U16ptr sc = (screen->Screen) + (y1*screen->RealWidth) + (x);

        while (num--)
        {
            *sc = color;
            sc += screen->RealWidth;
        }
}
//*******************************
```

The speed difference between VerticalLineSafe and VerticalLine is so minimal, I cannot measure it. Maybe you can.

Since the speed gains are minimal whether or not you do the clipping and checking math, we will simply add this new functionality to our rectangle routines. The rectangles spend so much time drawing that clipping code hardly slows it at all. This may be an advantage to you since you may often need clipping. Since you can't always know when a rectangle needs to be clipped, if the clipping code is fast enough you can just use it for every rectangle and not worry about which ones need to be clipped and which don't. I find that it is better to rely on code than to worry about speed differences of less than 2 percent. Use the clipping code and you will probably have a much easier time at it.

Here is the RectangleFill function without clipping. It basically has both types of clipping that we put into VerticalLineSafe and HorizontalLineSafe. Other than that it is the same. See how easy this is?

```
//*******************************
void  RectangleFill (int left, int top, int right, int bottom, U16 color,
SCREEN_STRUCT* screen)
{
        if (right<left) SWAP (left, right);
if (left < 0) left=0;                                        // left
        if (right >= screen->Width) right=screen->Width-1;   // right
if (left>=screen->Width) return;
if (right<0) return;

if (bottom<top) SWAP (top, bottom);
if (top>=screen->Height) return;
        if (bottom<0) return;
        if (top < 0) top=0;                                  // top
        if (bottom >= screen->Height) bottom=screen->Height-1;  // bottom

        int num = right-left;        // how many pixels across
        int height = bottom-top;     // make our math easier
        int width = screen->RealWidth;  // make the variable local
                                        // to speed memory access

        // move the screen pointer down to the proper place
        U16ptr sc = (screen->Screen) + (top*width) + (left);
```

```
      while (height--)
      {
            Memset16Bit (sc, color, num);
            sc+=width;
      }
}
//******************************
```

Boy, is this now a big chunk of code. Keep in mind that most of the testing and clipping is never performed. Normal drawing just falls through all of this with almost no slowing. In other words, very little of this code is actually executed.

Tough Clipping

Real line clipping is tough. This involves calculating the ratio of a line along one axis and multiplying the other axis by that ratio and then finding a point of intersection with the edge of the screen. Then after a divide and a multiply or two, you have the new clip point. This code is inherently slow because of the intensity of the math. There is very little you can do to speed it up. I have optimized it quite a bit and I have seen "better" clippers that were harder to read and marginally faster. This routine is "fast enough" and does all that we. want. You could play with it a while and see what you come up with.

It is worth noting that not much line drawing takes place in today's games and so you might want to clip every line anyway.

```
//******************************
int Clipper (int px1, int py1, int px2, int py2, RECTANGLE& ClipRect)
// returns 1 if no line is drawn
{
      if (py1==py2)                    // line off the screen test
      {
            if (py1<=ClipRect.top) return 1;
            if (py1>=ClipRect.bottom) return 1;
      }
      if (px1==px2)
      {
            if (px1<=ClipRect.left) return 1;
            if (px1>=ClipRect.right) return 1;
      }
      // ----------------------------- clip on the right and bottom
      if (px1>=ClipRect.right)
      {
            if (py2>=ClipRect.bottom || py2<ClipRect.top) return 1;
            int edge=ClipRect.right-1;
            int ratio=(((edge-px2)<<16) / (px1-px2)); // r= new / old
            px1=edge;                     // clipped to width of screen
            py1=py2 + ((((py1-py2)*ratio)>>16));      // new= old* r
      }
      if (py1>=ClipRect.bottom)
      {
```

```
             if (px2>=ClipRect.right || px2<0) return 1;
             int edge=ClipRect.bottom-1;
             int ratio=(((edge-py2)<<16) / (py1-py2));        // r= new / old
             py1=edge;                             // clipped to height of screen
             px1=px2 + ((((px1-px2) * ratio)>>16));
    }
    if (px2>=ClipRect.right)
    {
             if (py1>=ClipRect.bottom || py1<0) return 1;
             int edge=ClipRect.right-1;
             int ratio=(((edge-px1)<<16)/((px2-px1)));  // r= new / old
             px2=edge;                             // clipped to width of screen
             py2=py1 + (((py2-py1) * ratio)>>16);            // new= old* r

    }
    if (py2>=ClipRect.bottom)
    {
             if (px1>=ClipRect.right || px1<0)return 1;
             int edge=ClipRect.bottom-1;
             int ratio=(((edge-py1)<<16) / (py2-py1));        // r= new / old
             py2=edge; // clipped to height of screen
             px2=px1 + ((((px2-px1) * ratio)>>16));
    }
    //-------------------------------clip on the top and left
    if (px1<ClipRect.left)
    {if (py2>ClipRect.bottom || py2<0) return 1;
         int edge=ClipRect.left;
         int ratio=(((edge-px2)<<16) / (px1-px2)); // r= new / old
         px1=edge;                                    // clipped to left
         py1=py2 + ((((py1-py2) * ratio)>>16));          // new= old* r
    }
    if (py1<ClipRect.top)
    {if (px2>ClipRect.right || px2<0) return 1;
         int edge=ClipRect.top;
         int ratio=(((edge-py2)<<16) / (py1-py2));        // r= new / old
         py1=edge;                                  // clipped to top
         px1=px2 + ((((px1-px2) * ratio)>>16));
    }
    if (px2<ClipRect.left)
    {if (py1>ClipRect.bottom || py1<0) return 1;
         int edge=ClipRect.left;
         int ratio=(((edge-px1)<<16) / (px2-px1)); // r= new / old
         px2=edge;                                    // clipped to left
         py2=py1 + ((((py2-py1) * ratio)>>16));          // new= old* r
    }
    if (py2<ClipRect.top)
    {if (px1>ClipRect.right || px1<0) return 1;
         int edge=ClipRect.top;
         int ratio=(((edge-py1)<<16) / (py2-py1));        // r= new / old
         py2=edge;                                  // clipped to top
         px2=px1 + ((((px2-px1) * ratio)>>16));
    }
```

```
        return 0;
}
//*******************************
```

We've started using another item from struct.h. RECTANGLE is a type I defined that is exactly like the Windows RECT except that now I don't need to include the huge windows.h header. This allows us to define areas of clipping that do not necessarily equal the full window. What normally happens in a real-time strategy game is that you have the game screen area and then you have the interface areas. You definitely want to define these areas such that stray lines do not draw over them.

Another thing about clipped lines: A clipped line has less to draw. That means that it will draw faster. That also means that chopping 1 pixel from any line makes up for the time spent in the clipping math. This clipper is actually very fast. You can run every line you draw through this function and the speed difference will hardly be noticed. This clipper will clip all lines handed to it. It also tests for lines not visible. Anywhere in this function where a value of 1 is returned, the line is completely outside of the drawing area and should not be drawn.

The first section tests for horizontal and vertical lines that need to be eliminated and returns 1 in those cases. These test cases are fairly easy and are just like the VerticalLine and HorizontalLine tests we did earlier.

The next section begins the actual clipping. We test if one of the points in the x direction passes the right side of the clipping rectangle:

```
if (px1>=ClipRect.right)
```

If so, we proceed to test if the other end of the line is not visible; if it is not, we clip the entire line:

```
if (py2>=ClipRect.bottom || py2<ClipRect.top) return 1;
```

We set a local variable for faster access. This could probably be made faster by pulling the value out into the entire routine, but the difference would be trivial. In 640x480, edge now equals 639, the rightmost value on a scale of 0 to 639.

```
int edge=ClipRect.right-1;
```

Now we prepare another variable. The ratio gives us a slope. This value can be negative so we make sure that our variable is not unsigned. We calculate a ratio of what the new length will be by the old x length. This will always yield a result smaller than 1.0. We can do that because we know that the new x position has to be the edge of the screen. We know that $x1$ will be 639 when we are done. Based on that little bit of knowledge, we calculate the ratio, set $x1$ to the edge of the screen, multiply the old length by the ratio to get the new y distance, and then add the endpoint ($y2$) to set it to the correct location.

```
int ratio=(((edge-px2)<<16) / (px1-px2));
px1=edge;
py1=py2 + ((((py1-py2)*ratio)>>16));
```

We are doing the math in integer because it is faster. In order to maintain digits of precision, we shift it left by 16 before we divide, giving us the equivalent of 16 extra binary digits of precision. This is the effect of multiplying a number by 100,000 before dividing so you don't have to deal with decimal points.

10

Chapter

Math example for bit shifting:

10/85 = *x*;

Multiply the 10 by 100,000, which gives us 1,000,000.

Now we calculate 1,000,000/85 = 11764

Divide the result (11764) by 100,000 to get 0.11764

Some people insist that doing this clipping math in floating-point is faster, but I tried replacing the next section with floating-point math and the result was nearly twice as long. No joke—you try it. Here is the code:

```
float ratio=((float) (edge-px2)
px1=edge;
py1=py2 + (int) (((float) (py1-py2)*ratio));
```

That about does it. Clipping isn't too bad. Other clipping calculations can be a lot slower. This is the best method I've found. Actually I wrote it myself without any help. But I am sure that somebody has written the exact same clipping routine before or something very similar, so my original code is guaranteed to be not so original.

There are different drawing routines in the next chapter. The last thing we do in this chapter is revisit our line algorithm.

A Faster Bresenham's Line Algorithm

The last tidbit in this chapter is some optimizations on Bresenham's line algorithm. Let's talk about how this is different. We've eliminated the call to the Plot function, saving a lot of time and we've made the math simpler by reducing it to adds in the main loops. Whenever the line happens to be vertical or horizontal, the function takes care of it. Now we can make one function call unless we're sure that the line we are drawing doesn't need to be clipped. We even make Width local for faster access.

This is a pretty hefty speed improvement, but we had to cover all of the material before you could see the finished product. After this code is the new Draw function that tests the Line function.

```
//*******************************
void Line (int px1, int py1, int px2, int py2, SCREEN_STRUCT* screen, U16 color)
{
        if (screen == NULL) return;
        if (py1==py2) {HorizontalLine (px1, px2, py1, color, screen); return;}
        if (px1==px2) {VerticalLine (py1, py2, px1, color, screen); return;}
        int width = screen->RealWidth;

        //1)setup stage

        int y_unit, x_unit;        // Variables for amount of change in x and y

        U16* offset = screen->Screen;
        offset += py1*width + px1;
        int ydiff=py2-py1;        // Calculate difference between y coordinates
```

```
    if (ydiff<0)              // If the line moves in the negative direction
    {
        ydiff=-ydiff;         // ...get absolute value of difference
        y_unit=-width;        // ...and set negative unit in y dimension
    }
    else y_unit=width;        // Else set positive unit in y dimension

    int xdiff=px2-px1;        // Calculate difference between x coordinates
    if (xdiff<0)              // If the line moves in the negative direction
    {
        xdiff=-xdiff;         // ...get absolute value of difference
        x_unit=-1;            // ...and set negative unit in x dimension
    }
    else x_unit=1;            // Else set positive unit in y dimension
    int error_term=0;         // Initialize error term

    //2) drawing stage
    if (xdiff>ydiff)          // If difference is bigger in x dimension
    {
        int length=xdiff+1;   // ...prepare to count off in x direction
        for (int i=0; i<length; i++)    // Loop through points in x direction
        {
            *offset=color;  // Set the next pixel in the line to COLOR
            offset+=x_unit; // Move offset to next pixel in x direction
            error_term+=ydiff;        // Check to see if move required in y
                                      // direction
            if (error_term>xdiff)
            {                 // If so...
                error_term-=xdiff;  // ...reset error term
                offset+=y_unit;     // ...and move offset to next pixel
                                    // in y dir.
            }
        }
    }
    else
    {                         // If difference is bigger in y dimension
        int length=ydiff+1;   // ...prepare to count off in y direction
        for (int i=0; i<length; i++)    // Loop through points in y direction
        {
            *offset=color;  // Set the next pixel in the line to COLOR
            offset+=y_unit; // Move offset to next pixel  in y direction
            error_term+=xdiff;
            if (error_term>0) // Check to see if move required in x direction
            {                 // If so...
                error_term-=ydiff;  // ...reset error term
                offset+=x_unit;     // ...and move offset to next
                                    // pixel in x dir.
            }
        }
    }
}

//****************************
```

The following Draw function was used to test the old and new Draw functions. Testing the old function that used Plot for each point yielded a timing result of 609 milliseconds.

```
//*******************************

void  Draw (DIRECT_DRAW_MANAGER* ddraw)
{
        SCREEN_STRUCT* screen = ddraw->GetScreen ();
        RGBVal rgb;
        U16    color;

        // notice how the following variables all fall
        // within specified ranges.

        int left=10, right=630, top=10, bottom=20;
        int x1=300, y1=200, x2=200, y2=220;

        RECTANGLE ClipRect = {0, 0, 640, 480};

        long time1 = timeGetTime ();
        for (int i=0; i<30000; i++)
        {
              Line (x1, y1, x2, y2, screen, color);
        }

        long time2 = timeGetTime ();
        long result = time2-time1;

        char buff[40];
        itoa (result, buff, 10);
        ddraw->PaintText (20, 50, buff);
}

//*******************************
```

The new Draw function speeds us up to 391 milliseconds, which is about a 36 percent speed increase. Not bad and certainly worth the effort. You might try playing with optimizing it yourself, but also realize that there isn't much line drawing in games these days. If we were making Asteroids or some other vector game, okay, but there's not too much call for it in RTS/RTT games.

Chapter 11

How to Do Your ABC's

A is for apple, B is for banana, C is for Chuckie,
the doll who will stalk you....

Managing alphabets can be important. Terminology wise, an *alphabet* is a group of letters representing an established character set. We are not concerned with language here, only the letters. All games need at least one alphabet and most have three or four for different letter sizes. Why I do not call this collection of characters a font is for a good reason. *Fonts* refer to a character set that can be used anywhere, such as system fonts. Fonts have a general nature and most have been established since long before we were born. Fonts have specific properties like kerning, tracking, baseline, ascent, descent, em units, and so forth. Fonts have qualities like serif, point size, italic, bold, superscript, and so on. We won't have any of those things. Ours is simply an alphabet.

We have already seen how to use GDI calls to let Windows draw on the screen for us. It works fine for most things, except that it is slow. We will be able to more than double the speed. Also, we will have the capabilities of having multicolor alphabets, even pictures as alphabets. All this with a speed advantage. Nice, huh? We'll even introduce clipping. How sweet. Now try the following code and see what your timings are:

```
//*******************************

void  Draw (DIRECT_DRAW_MANAGER* ddraw)
{
        SCREEN_STRUCT* screen = ddraw->GetScreen ();
        long time1 = timeGetTime ();
        char buff[80];
        strcpy (buff, "This is a speed test for GDI drawing");
        for (int i=0; i<100; i++)
        ddraw->PaintText (90, 50, buff);

        long time2 = timeGetTime ();
        long result = time2-time1;

        itoa (result, buff, 10);
        ddraw->PaintText (20, 50, buff);

}

//*******************************
```

I came up with 35 milliseconds or so. We're not drawing thousands of things, just a few characters—36 to be exact. Now creating an alphabet may not be your idea of fun and quite frankly, it's not mine either. But it's not too hard to do, and it's worth the speed and functionality. If you do not see the benefit, move on to the next chapter. One other nice thing about creating your own alphabet is that you'll know how wide each character is, so you can center the text over a button or align it however you want. It takes quite a bit more time to do the same in GDI.

So, let's dive in.

Here is how I've defined the letter "A":

```
//----------A--65--0x41
1, 1, 1, 1, 1, 1, 1, 1,
1, 1, 0, 0, 0, 0, 1, 1,
1, 0, 0, 1, 1, 0, 0, 1,
1, 0, 0, 1, 1, 0, 0, 1,
1, 0, 0, 1, 1, 0, 0, 1,
1, 0, 0, 0, 0, 0, 0, 1,
1, 0, 0, 1, 1, 0, 0, 1,
1, 0, 0, 1, 1, 0, 0, 1,
1, 0, 0, 1, 1, 0, 0, 1,
1, 1, 1, 1, 1, 1, 1, 1,
1, 1, 1, 1, 1, 1, 1, 1,
1, 1, 1, 1, 1, 1, 1, 1,
```

I copied and pasted it from the alphabet.cpp file that you'll find on the companion CD. The entire usable alphabet is there, all represented by1's and 0's. You can edit it and change any of them at any time. Simple to use but not the greatest to work with, although it is reliable and fast. You may like the idea of having 1's be on and 0's be off but I think that the 0's are more readable, and thus easier to edit. You decide.

Notice that the "A" is 12 pixels high. This allows for a dangling "g" and a tall "T." All of the characters in the alphabet have a fixed width, making it easy to calculate total pixel width. This also simplifies clipping. I chose this 8x12 scheme a long time ago and it has served me well. Alphabets can be represented by other dimension schemes, with the smallest possible being 5x7. Remember that some letters are down-right impossible to make with any clarity.

Color is another issue. You can color these pixels or even have multicolor letters if you are willing to put in the art time. I prefer to leave the alphabet in alphabet.cpp alone and simply display it in black and white.

Characteristics of Characters

All characters are really just numbers to the computer. The letter "A" is 65, for example. When we get the number 65 to draw, we display an "A." When someone hands us a string such as "Hello world," we need to move along that string one character at a time and display each letter. All visible characters start above 32. The first 31 characters are reserved for control codes and things like the Enter key. The value 32 corresponds to the space bar and is not technically visible, but without spaces readingmightbeveryhardtodo. This means that our character set will begin with the first visible character available, which is "!". To our way of thinking, this is character 0 and we simply take whichever character is passed to our alphabet drawing routine and subtract 33 for the conversion.

Part of each letter is invisible. There is a hole in the letter "O" that should be transparent. We should be able to see through it to the pixels behind so that we can place text on buttons and have the background show through. Transparency really does make an alphabet look better.

Things can go awry if you put white letters on a creamy white background—the letters are nearly invisible. We could read the pixel color surrounding the pixel we are about to draw and make it black or some other color when appropriate. That begins to slow us down to about the same speed as GDI text drawing. Whenever you read from the video card, expect speed problems. Shadows are a better solution. Every time we draw a white pixel, we make its neighbor below and to the right of it black, as in Figure 11.1. Now the character always shows up. Good idea; glad I thought of it. Actually, this is an old technique I used on the Atari 800 when I used to do character animation. I'm sure you'll come up with better ideas on how you might solve this problem.

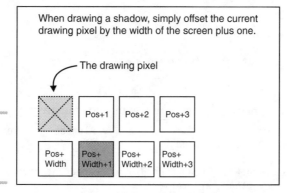

Figure 11.1
Using shadows to help letters stand out

An alternative to this is to make sure that text never appears on a white background. You also might try making the text a pink or a fuchsia color that will not conflict very often. Text in those colors is hard to read though, so this is probably not a good choice. The best option for solving this problem is to use shadows.

Each character has a width. This width can exceed the limits of the screen so we may need to clip. Generally, I leave clipping off to speed up the code, and so I have made clipping and non-clipping code. When you can be sure that text fits within specified boundaries, it is speedier to use non-clipping code.

Building an Alphabet Manager

Let's look at the code. On the CD you'll find a folder named smallprog3. This has two files named alphabet.cpp and alphabet.h. These files contain all of the information about a new class I'm introducing named ALPHABET_MANAGER. An interesting thing about any kind of alphabet manager is that it has a lot of the same characteristics as

SCREEN_STRUCT. It needs Height, Width, RealWidth, and Screen parameters to draw properly. This will be helpful in allowing us to reuse code and definitions.

We're going to build this class and create the functional code at the same time. It makes a lot more sense to treat it like an object. Explaining it as a bunch of C functions and conglomerating those into a class will take too many pages, so I decided to dive right in.

Note: Accessing an integer is three times faster than accessing a short. This normally doesn't matter and the way I handle 16-bit graphics pointers works out to roughly the same speed. But variables such as Height, Width, LoadedFontFlag, and others should be int's whenever possible. If you are concerned about space more than speed, then use U16's and reduce the code and data size. If speed is important and you will only have a few instances of a class in the entire program, use int's.

```
// alphabet.h
#include " struct.h"

class STRINGC;
//**************************************

typedef class ALPHABET_MANAGER : public SCREEN_STRUCT
{
protected:
        U8ptr       Alphabet;                       // Alphabet pointer
        int         PosX, PosY, ShadowAdd;
        U16ptr      ScreenPos;
        int         LoadedFontFlag, LoadedFontWidth, LoadedFontHeight,
                    LoadedFontNumCharacters;
        int         ClipFlag;

        void        DrawLetter (U8ptr alpha);       // normal character drawing
        void        DrawClippedLetter (U8ptr alpha);
        void        DrawLetter (U16ptr alpha);      // from a loaded font.
        void        DrawClippedLetter (U16ptr alpha);

        void        PrintASCIIchr (char text);
        U8ptr       RetrieveLetterArray ();

public:

        ALPHABET_MANAGER ();
        virtual ~ALPHABET_MANAGER ();

        void PrintText (int x, int y, SCREEN_STRUCT* screen, char* text);
        void PrintNumber (int x, int y, SCREEN_STRUCT* screen, int num);

        void PrintText (int x, int y, char* text); // assume local values are
```

```
                                                   // good from passed values
   void PrintNumber (int x, int y, int num);

       //*************************** information

int  GetWidth () const {return Width;}
int  GetHeight () const {return Height;}

       //*************************** external data

bool LoadFont (STRINGC& File);
       void SetScreenValues (SCREEN_STRUCT* screen)
       {
              Width = screen->Width;
              Height = screen->Height;
              Screen = screen->Screen;
              RealWidth = screen->RealWidth; ShadowAdd = RealWidth+1;
       }
}ALPHABET_MANAGER, *ALPHABETptr, **ALPHABETlist;

//*****************************************
```

This is the ALPHABET_MANAGER class in its glory. It is a child class of SCREEN_
STRUCT and it needs all of the member variables of its parent for drawing. The Alphabet variable points to an array of characters that always starts with "!" and ends with
"z." The array is filled with data of 1's and 0's telling us when to plot a pixel. You'll find
it after this explanation of ALPHABET_MANAGER. The array named Letters is global to
the program and all instantiations of ALPHABET_ MANAGER use it by default.

All letters in the Letters array have some common characteristics. They are all 8
pixels wide by 12 pixels high. I put a comment before each to help you find the letter
you're looking for.

The next member variables are PosX and PosY. This is the current screen position
for the drawing of text. This position is passed to the PrintText functions. Based on the
PosX position, we will move from left to right across the screen by 8 pixels for each
character. That is how we draw the letters in position. Numbers are drawn the same
way, but from right to left. We also need to convert them to ASCII format in order to
use the same drawing routines.

ShadowAdd is a simple optimization for drawing the shadow pixel. It should be
one pixel down to the right of the current drawing pixel. This is equal to Real-
Width+1. So when we calculate which pixel to "blacken," the math is simplified and
is therefore faster.

ScreenPos is the current screen position based on the pointer to the buffer
(Screen), plus whatever offset is obtained by the math of PosY*RealWidth + PosX. It
is a pointer into the frame buffer for the pixel location. Better put, it is simply a
pointer to memory.

The variables LoadedFontFlag, LoadedFontWidth, LoadedFontHeight, and Loaded-
FontNumCharacters are all used later in this chapter when we discuss the alphabet
tool and loading a font. Even the code in ALPHABET_MANAGER has been commented
out for now.

11

Chapter

ClipFlag is set when a character that is to be drawn needs to be clipped. We will use this flag to reroute our drawing to the proper function.

The bool type is a simple variable type; it is either TRUE or FALSE. You'll find it as a return type from one of the member functions. In Visual C++ 5.0 and later, this is predefined and no #include files are necessary. It has become part of the C++ language effectively and you can find it in any standard text on Standard C++. The values true and false must be lowercase in version 5.0 and higher. In previous versions of Visual C++, BOOL was defined in windows.h, and TRUE and FALSE had to be uppercase. This variable type is used to get an answer to a question: Did everything initialize correctly? Is a value non-zero? These questions are commonly answered with bools.

Note: TRUE has a value of 1 and FALSE has a value of 0. This is a common standard.

Now, let's examine the functions.

➤ DrawLetter takes a pointer to the character array. This is an offset to the proper character in that array so that DrawLetter does no math to figure out which character to draw. It is called from PrintASCIIchr like all of the following DrawLetter functions. The second one listed takes a U16ptr for a Loaded Alphabet.

➤ DrawClippedLetter does the same as DrawLetter but it does all the math to clip. It is significantly slower. The second one listed takes a U16ptr for a Loaded Alphabet.

➤ PrintASCIIchr is a dispatcher. Based on a few flags, it does the math and calls the appropriate function when given a single character to draw.

➤ RetrieveLetterArray simply sets Alphabet to the Letters array.

➤ The constructor and destructor take care of all initialization. If Alphabet was loaded, then the destructor deletes it. This is based on the LoadedFontFlag.

➤ The first PrintText function named takes a pointer to the screen data (SCREEN_STRUCT), an *x,y* position, and a pointer to a string. The string will be parsed and each character in the array displayed, one at a time, from left to right. This will start at screen position *x,y,* which is the upper left corner where the string begins. All drawing will take place on the Screen member variable of the SCREEN_STRUCT. This means that you can put text into any buffer. Pretty nice, huh?

➤ The second PrintText does not need the SCREEN_STRUCT variable, as it assumes that the current variables Width, Height, RealWidth, and Screen are valid values. Make sure to call SetScreenValues before calling this function or problems can occur.

➤ PrintNumber functions like PrintText but constructs a string from an integer. There is no parsing for floats or doubles. The second PrintNumber operates exactly like the second PrintText.

➤ SetScreenValues copies a SCREEN_STRUCT variable into local variables.

The rest of the functions will be covered later. You may notice how simple this class is. There isn't a whole lot to it and its focus is narrow, making it easy to debug and test. I strongly encourage you to look over the code on the CD to get a better idea of what I've put together. I simply do not have enough space to put all of the alphabet stuff in this book.

Now that we've looked at the class declaration, let's look at Letters.

```
#include "alphabet.h"
#include <string.h>
#include <stdlib.h>
#ifndef NULL
#define NULL 0L
#endif

U8 Letters[]={
//-----------!--33--0x21
1, 1, 1, 1, 1, 1, 1, 1,
1, 1, 1, 0, 0, 1, 1, 1,
1, 1, 1, 0, 0, 1, 1, 1,
1, 1, 1, 0, 0, 1, 1, 1,
1, 1, 1, 0, 0, 1, 1, 1,
1, 1, 1, 0, 0, 1, 1, 1,
1, 1, 1, 1, 1, 1, 1, 1,
1, 1, 1, 0, 0, 1, 1, 1,
1, 1, 1, 0, 0, 1, 1, 1,
1, 1, 1, 1, 1, 1, 1, 1,
1, 1, 1, 1, 1, 1, 1, 1,
1, 1, 1, 1, 1, 1, 1, 1,
//-----------"--34--0x22
1, 1, 1, 1, 1, 1, 1, 1,
1, 1, 0, 0, 1, 0, 0, 1,
1, 1, 0, 0, 1, 0, 0, 1,
1, 1, 0, 0, 1, 0, 0, 1,
1, 1, 0, 0, 1, 0, 0, 1,
1, 1, 1, 1, 1, 1, 1, 1,
1, 1, 1, 1, 1, 1, 1, 1,
1, 1, 1, 1, 1, 1, 1, 1,
1, 1, 1, 1, 1, 1, 1, 1,
1, 1, 1, 1, 1, 1, 1, 1,
1, 1, 1, 1, 1, 1, 1, 1,
1, 1, 1, 1, 1, 1, 1, 1,
//-----------#--35--0x23
1, 1, 1, 1, 1, 1, 1, 1,
1, 1, 1, 1, 1, 1, 1, 1,
1, 1, 0, 0, 1, 0, 0, 1,
1, 0, 0, 0, 0, 0, 0, 0,
1, 1, 0, 0, 1, 0, 0, 1,
1, 0, 0, 0, 0, 0, 0, 0,
1, 1, 0, 0, 1, 0, 0, 1,
1, 1, 1, 1, 1, 1, 1, 1,
```

```
1, 1, 1, 1, 1, 1, 1, 1,
1, 1, 1, 1, 1, 1, 1, 1,
1, 1, 1, 1, 1, 1, 1, 1,
1, 1, 1, 1, 1, 1, 1, 1,

etc.........
};
```

This is the beginning of the alphabet.cpp file. Since no file with NULL has been included, we define it here for simplicity's sake. We include the obvious header alphabet.h and a few others for string functions. The Letters array is declared next; it is nothing but a continuous array of 1's and 0's. The 1's represent empty space and 0's represent a plotted pixel. Again, this is because when you want to edit or change a pixel, the 0's are much easier to see than the 1's. The 0's actually hide the 1's, making it very difficult to edit if you reverse them and put 1's where there are 0's and 0's where there are 1's. Since it makes no practical difference, you might as well go with whatever makes your life easier.

Each letter has exactly the same dimensions. 12x8 equals 96, meaning that to find the xth letter, simply multiply it by 96. This simple math adds to the speed of the drawing routines. It is worth noting that I do not return to the beginning of a line when I encounter a 13 or \n.

Note: You could go through each letter and change some of the 0's to 2's and modify the code so that every time you see a 2, you draw a shadow pixel. That requires one more test in the main loop and significantly slows down the letter drawing. Remember to keep the main loop simple. In this case, there is only one test and a few variable increments.

In the following section, I'll break down the code to make the explanation easier.

First, we have our simple constructor. It initializes all of the characters by setting the Alphabet variable to the address of the array. All other variables are zeroed because they apply to loaded alphabets or don't need clipping, so we set the ClipFlag to 0:

```
//****************************

ALPHABET_MANAGER :: ALPHABET_MANAGER ()
{
        LoadedFontFlag = 0,
        LoadedFontWidth = 0,
        LoadedFontHeight = 0,
        LoadedFontNumCharacters = 0,
        Alphabet = Letters,        // see the above array
        ClipFlag = 0;
}
//****************************
```

Since our ALPHABET_MANAGER will actually do the loading for the loaded alphabet, we need to clean up its memory in the case when it is loaded. That is handled here in the destructor:

```
//****************************
ALPHABET_MANAGER :: ~ALPHABET_MANAGER ()
{
        if (LoadedFontFlag && Alphabet!=NULL) delete Alphabet;
}
//****************************
```

We'll cover the following LoadFont routine later. It contains the STRINGC class and a few other unmentioned classes, so I'll leave the framework but delete the contents.

```
//****************************

bool ALPHABET_MANAGER :: LoadFont (STRINGC& File) // we'll define this later
{
        return false;
}


//****************************
```

Here's where we start getting to the meat. Because numbers and letters are handled differently, I have two different routines. You can consolidate them if you like.

```
//****************************

void  ALPHABET_MANAGER :: PrintText (int x, int y, char* text)
        // assume local values are good
{
        if (Screen == NULL) return;
        int len = strlen (text);

            PosX = x; PosY = y;
        if (PosY+12<0 || PosY>Height) return;       // clipped entirely

        ScreenPos = Screen + PosY*RealWidth + PosX;

        for (int i=0; i<len; i++, PosX+=8)
        {
            PrintASCIIchr (text[i]);
            ScreenPos += 8;              // moving on to the next character space
        }
}
//****************************

//****************************
void  ALPHABET_MANAGER :: PrintNumber (int x, int y, int num)
{
        char text[20];
            if (Screen == NULL) return;
```

```
            itoa (num, text, 10);
            int len=strlen (text);

            PosX = x; PosY = y;
            if (PosY+12<0 || PosY>Height) return;      // clipped entirely
            ScreenPos = Screen + PosY*RealWidth + PosX;

            for (int i=len; i>=0; i--, PosX-=8)
            {
                  PrintASCIIchr (text[i]);
                  ScreenPos -= 8;                      // moving on to the next character
            }
      }
//****************************
//****************************
void  ALPHABET_MANAGER :: PrintText (int x, int y, SCREEN_STRUCT* screen,
                                          char* text)
{
            int len = strlen (text);

            SetScreenValues (screen);                  // member function
            if (Screen == NULL) return;

            PosX = x; PosY = y;
            if (PosY+12<0 || PosY>Height) return;      // clipped entirely
            ScreenPos = Screen + PosY*RealWidth + PosX;

            for (int i=0; i<len; i++, PosX+=8)
            {
                  PrintASCIIchr (text[i]);
                  ScreenPos+=8;
            }
      }
//****************************
//****************************
void  ALPHABET_MANAGER :: PrintNumber (int x, int y, SCREEN_STRUCT* screen,
                                          int num)
{
            char text[20];

            SetScreenValues (screen);                  // member function
            if (Screen == NULL) return;

            itoa (num, text, 10);
            int len=strlen (text);

            PosX = x; PosY = y;
            if (PosY+12<0 || PosY>Height) return;      // clipped entirely
            ScreenPos = Screen + PosY*RealWidth + PosX;

            for (int i=len; i>=0; i--, PosX-=8)
            {
```

```
                PrintASCIIchr (text[i]);
                ScreenPos -= 8;                    // moving on to the next character
        }

}
//****************************
```

The simple PrintText takes three parameters: x,y location information and a pointer to a string. We make sure that the Screen value has been initialized properly and return if it is not valid. Actually, we will eventually be clearing this value every frame, so it makes sense.

No testing is done on the string; it is assumed to be good. If it is NULL, the strlen function will return 0 and the routine will fall out, eventually returning anyway, without harm. We get the length of the string. We'll use that number in a loop below. We make our position information local, and clip in the y direction if the text is completely off the screen. Then we set our pixel plotting location.

Incidentally, we could use the plot routine from the last chapter. However, it does entirely too much math to plot a single pixel, and is therefore too slow. We'll do most of the math up front, like in this example where we precalculate ScreenPos, and simply add 8 each time we move to the next letter. Since the math is simple, this routine will be very fast.

Once we have our basic information, we move on to the loop that calls the appropriate pixel plotting routine. The for loop advances from the 0th element of the text array to the last item. This assumes that the text array is a reasonable length, of course. We'll do real clipping later. Each time we execute one loop, we advance PosX and we advance ScreenPos by 8. This is because we are assuming a width of 8. When we get to loaded alphabets, this must change and be dynamic.

That's all there is to it—for now at least. Let's move on to the dispatch routine. The rest of the PrintText and PrintNumber routines function in almost the same way as I just described. I'm sure that you can figure out the minor differences. Remember that PrintNumber moves from right to left.

Note: Generally referring to a member of an array costs you nothing. $x[i]$ is the fastest way to access the ith element of the x array. The Pentium is designed such that an index plus an offset costs no extra time, so often the fastest way to plot a pixel is to simply use pixel[y*RealWidth +x] = 1;. In the text array below, referring to the ith element is simply the fastest way. However, it is not always the fastest way, so you should test it on time-critical sections of code.

PrintASCIIchr is very straightforward:
```
//****************************

void ALPHABET_MANAGER :: PrintASCIIchr (char text)
{
        if (text<33 || text>122)  return; // this is the range for ascii values
        if (LoadedFontFlag==0)
        {
```

```
            // set a pointer to the global array
        U8ptr pixels= Alphabet+ (text-33) *96+8;

            DrawLetter (pixels);    // draw the character
    }
    else
    {
        int size = LoadedFontHeight*LoadedFontWidth;

            // set a pointer to the global array
        U16ptr pixels= (U16ptr) (Alphabet)+ (text-32) *size;

            DrawLetter (pixels);    // draw the character
    }
}
//***************************
```

It has one parameter, a letter of the alphabet or some other character. Since we don't care about any characters that we have not predefined, we test the range 33 to 122. That is all of the data that I prepared, being in the range of "!" to "z." If it doesn't fit, we return.

The LoadedFontFlag is our next test. For now, we will avoid discussing what happens if it is TRUE. When FALSE, we do a quick calculation into the array of 1's and 0's to a start point at the beginning of a letter. Since the first character I prepared is at location 0 in the Letters array and the first character is the ASCII equivalent of 33, we simply subtract 33 from that value. A space is character 32, and since we return automatically this makes a space since the PrintNumber function advances ScreenPos anyway.

The multiply by 96 is to offset it into the array properly. Each character is 8x12, or 96 U8's long. This is really simple math. The +8 is an offset that I add to draw in a specific way. You may have noticed that each character has a row of 1's on the top row, meaning that the first row is blank pixels anyway. Why not skip it? You may not want to, so simply eliminate the +8. Your call.

Then we call the DrawLetter routine that accepts a U8ptr as its parameter. Just a note: We have prepared all of the values up to here. The screen position is calculated, the character offset is done, and ShadowAdd has been prepared. Almost all of the math used in drawing our letter has already been calculated and should make our character drawing routine much faster.

Now we are up to the DrawLetter routine. This is where it is either fast or slow. All determinations as to the outcome are in this routine. Most of the complex math has been done for us and the rest should be simple addition. I'll show you how similar it is to our RectangleFill function that we did earlier.

```
//***************************
void ALPHABET_MANAGER :: DrawLetter (U8ptr alpha)
{
        // used for letters... drawing black only.. pixel by pixel
        int        h=12, CharWid=8; // to make sure we are on an 8-byte boundry
        U8ptr      LocalLetter = alpha;
        // major speed improvement by making local variables
```

```
        int     LocalWidth = RealWidth;
        int     LocalShadow = ShadowAdd;

        U16ptr LocalScreen = ScreenPos;
        // we could add another pointer for the shadow
        // but then we'd need to update that pointer every cycle which
        // takes too much time.

        while (h--)
        {
            for (register x=0; x<CharWid; x++, LocalLetter ++)
            {
                if (*LocalLetter == 0)
                {
                    *(LocalScreen + x) = 65535;
                    *(LocalScreen + LocalShadow) = 0; // add shadows
                }
            }
            LocalScreen += LocalWidth;                 // on to the next line
        }
}


    //***************************

void ALPHABET_MANAGER ::  DrawLetter (U16ptr alpha)
{
        if (Screen == NULL) return;
        // used for letters... drawing black only.. pixel by pixel
        int h=LoadedFontHeight, CharWid=LoadedFontWidth;
        int newwid = RealWidth-CharWid;

        U16ptr ptr2 = alpha;
        U16* ptr1 = ScreenPos;

        while (h--)
        {
            for (int x=0; x<CharWid; x++, ptr1++, ptr2++)
            {
                if (*ptr2 == 0) *ptr1 = *ptr2;
            }
            ptr1 += newwid;
        }
}
//***************************

U8ptr ALPHABET_MANAGER :: RetrieveLetterArray (void)
{
        return Letters;
}


    //***************************
```

The key here to speed is making most of the values local. We'll improve the speed in our optimization section coming up. For now, I want things to be clearer about how to use our Letters array.

First, we accept a pointer into the Letters array and assume that the offset is correct. We then set two variables to the fixed values that we know they are. We create a local pointer to the Letters array. Copy RealWidth into a local variable LocalWidth, and the shadow offset ShadowAdd into LocalShadow. We even copy the ScreenPos value into our local value LocalScreen. Making all of these variables local will mean a faster time frame. Also, our one-time assignment of these values locally costs us almost nothing.

Now on to the main loop. We can use a for loop here, but instead I've gone for a method that relies on the initial value being prepared. I like while (h--) because it often optimizes to a slightly faster loop.

Note: I occasionally have a problem with Visual C++ where turning on optimization will cause this type of loop to continue forever. That is, when h makes it down to 0, the loop keeps going. I'll warn you about other Visual C++ bugs later.

Next, we declare x, and since it will be in a tight loop, we tell the compiler to try to keep it in a register. This can speed it up and often does. That way, registers do not always have to be loaded and then stored after every value change. This saves at least 2 clock cycles per loop.

Our for loop goes from 0 to 8. Later we will put in the constant because it is slightly faster, but for now this simple comparison better illustrates what we are trying to accomplish and how other letter drawing routines must work. The loop is meant to work from left to right, pixel by pixel, reading each value and plotting appropriate pixels on the screen. Then after 8 pixels, we move down one scan line (down 1 in the y direction) and continue through the pixels until we have read 12 rows from the Letters array.

Every iteration through the x loop adds 1 to our position in the Letters array. The Letters array is sequential in the same way that the screen is, only it is 8 pixels wide instead. To move down one line in a letter, add 8 to your position, or step through each pixel and when you pass 8, you are on the next line—magically.

As we advance through the array, we continually test the values. This is the slowest part. Each time we encounter a 0, we drop into a section that does the plotting. Otherwise, we simply advance our pointer to the next letter's pixel and test it. Once we have gone through eight loops, we are ready to move down to the next scan line on the screen. You'll find this single line of code just below the for loop: LocalScreen += LocalWidth;. This advances our screen pointer down one full scan line. It just adds the width.

Now back to our test condition. If if (*LocalLetter == 0) is a true case, then we take the address of our current screen position plus an offset, and set it to white. In 15-bit and 16-bit, 65535 is white. We could say LocalScreen[x] = 65535; and achieve the same results, but the method I used in the example times out to be slightly faster. Then we add LocalShadow to our current screen position and place a black pixel, which gives us a shadow. You might play with different colors for a better shadow color.

That about does it for plotting alphabet characters. The last function in this class simply places the Alphabet pointer equal to the Letters array. The same code is used for drawing a loaded font. We'll be talking about that next.

The Alphabet Editor

The alphabet editor was completed using Borland Builder 1.0. This is a great tool (both are great tools), and spitting out a new alphabet is a breeze. See Figure 11.2. (Be sure to spell Alphabet Creator correctly. : -))

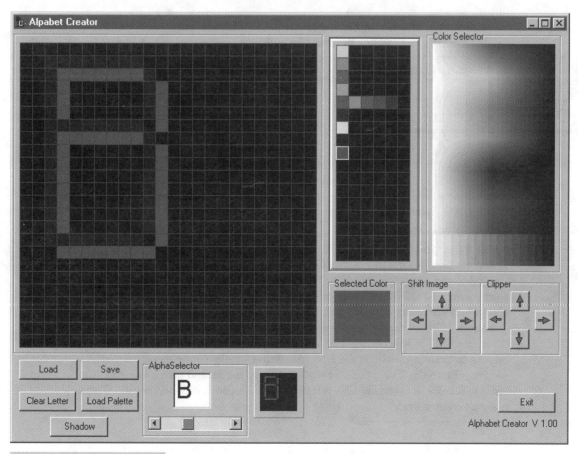

Figure 11.2 Using the Alphabet Creator built in Borland Builder 1.0

The best part is that it is well integrated with the alphabet.cpp code. Simply call the function LoadFont and pass it a string. The rest is hidden. Simply make PrintText function calls as normal, and the ALPHABET_MANAGER does the rest. The code for the font editor is included on the CD, so happy hunting.

It is limited, however. You must be in 15-bit graphics mode. Recompile it for 16-bit (it is only a change of a few numbers) if you must, but 256-color or 24-bit is simply not supported. Like all tools in the game world, pick a paradigm and stick with it. It doesn't make much sense to make a tool that works in all graphics modes. If it is meant to create graphics for only a 16-bit game, then require the artists to work in that mode. They will whine and complain, but they will accurately see the colors and you won't have to spend months getting a tool to work in every graphics mode. Keep your job simple. I could have spent a month making it work for all graphics modes, and for what purpose? My time is more valuable and so is yours. Make the tool suit the job. But remember the first rule of programming: Leave the code open-ended for future expandability.

There's not much else here. Play with the tool. It's fun.

By the way, the clipper defines the width of the letters in the file. Make it exactly the right size. Also, add a shadow if you want one because the ALPHABET_MANAGER does not place one for Loaded Alphabet.

Optimized Letter Drawing

The following is the fastest code I could come up with in C. Much of this is Pentium reliant and the optimizations depend on the way it works. This is the fastest non-clipping code in C that I can come up with. You may have a few ideas of your own, but this is really fast. The entire line "This is a speed test for GDI drawing" can be printed 100 times in 201 milliseconds. You can get better results in release mode.

Note: When you have 5 minutes, try going to the menu Build|Set Active Configuration and set it to Release. Go to the project settings and in the Link tab add "ddraw.lib winmm.lib dxguid.lib" to the Object/Library models. Eliminate anything marked ODBC which is for databases. Now compile and run your program. Breakpoints will not work. My very fastest time for the following code was about 197 milliseconds until I built a release version, and then my time dropped to 122 milliseconds—over a 30 percent increase in speed. Remember to set it back to Debug mode in the Build|Set Active Configuration menu item. Always get it to the fastest possible while in Debug mode, and then it will go a little faster in Release. Incidentally, GDI tests at 354 milliseconds in Release mode. There really is no comparison.

Note: Visual C++ can lose code, especially in Release mode with optimizations turned on. Optimizations can lose blocks of code. Also, surprising new bugs always appear in Release mode. Many of these are uninitialized variables, and many are Microsoft Visual C++ bugs. I suggest a targeted approach. Simply recompile your project periodically in release mode and test all the changes that you've made. This will never catch all of the bugs, but it really helps to find bugs later. Good hunting.

Now let's dissect this function:

```
//****************************
void  ALPHABET_MANAGER ::  DrawLetter (U8ptr alpha)
{
        // used for letters... drawing black only.. pixel by pixel

        // major speed improvement by making local variables
        int   LocalWidth = RealWidth;
        int   LocalShadow = ShadowAdd;

        U16ptr LocalScreen  = ScreenPos;        // we could add a pointer for the
        // shadow but then we'd need to update the pointer every cycle which
        // takes too much time.


        for (int height=0; height<10; height++) // the last line is never used
        {
                int width = 0;
                // speed up by testing for the 4 important test bits on in this
                // array of 8 bytes so that we can test 4 pixels at a time...
                // it's faster
                // we're testing to see if we have anything on a line and if not
                // we simply advance to the next line
                if ((*((int*) alpha)) == 0x01010101)
                {
                        alpha+=4; width=4;
                        if ((*((int*) alpha)) == 0x01010101) {alpha+=4; goto END;}

                }

                for (; width<8; width++)
                {
                        if (*alpha++ == 0)
                        {
                                *(LocalScreen + width) = 65535;
                                *(LocalScreen + LocalShadow) = 0; // add shadows
                        }

                }
        END:
                LocalScreen += LocalWidth;       // on to the next line
        }
```

```
}
//****************************
```

The first thing we do is copy a lot of variables locally. This keeps us from accessing members of "this" which means avoiding the index and offset required on the Pentium; this requires about 3 clock cycles total. We make it local and it drops to 1 clock cycle. This is for every time you access that variable. It could be slower—a lot slower—if you access it about 96 times for each letter of the alphabet you draw.

We now are drawing only 10 of the 12 lines of text available to us. The top line is always empty and the way I made the letters, the bottom is as well. You can change the alphabet, but make sure to change this number. Changing this number to 10 speeds draw time by about 10 percent. Next we declare a new variable, which I called Width; you can call it *j* or whatever. It is inside the height loop, meaning that it will be redeclared and reinitialized to 0 each time the loop repeats.

Now comes the hardest part of this loop. We want a quick way to test if a line of pixels to be drawn has any pixels to draw. In other words, is the alpha array good on this scan line, or is it simply 1's and we should go on to the next line? Four 1's in byte format is simply 1, 1, 1, 1, but that takes four tests to determine if we should skip it. So we cast the array to an int*, meaning that we can access 4 bytes as a single value. Pretty handy—we can test four Letters pixels at a time. Fast and convenient. It turns out that 4 bytes stuck together, each with a value of 1, is equal to 16843009 decimal, or 0x01010101 in hex. Hex looks better, so I put it in the code. How does this optimization work?

If the first four Letters bytes do not have any pixel information, the entire line may not, so we enter the open braces. We advance our pointer by 4, moving it past the four we just tested so we can test the next four. We also advance our Width variable, which is really just a counter for the number of pixels to draw and a screen offset (see below that). If the next 4 bytes are not useful, we advance that pointer by 4 bytes and we go to the label END which advances the screen position and then loops back to the height for loop.

> **Note:** I realize that this only tests the first four bytes in the case where the first four are good but the last four are not good. Still, this optimization yields better results most of the time, because this usually either eliminates a whole line or keeps it, almost never just half.

Basic Graphics Blitting

But wait you say? What about clipping letters? You haven't finished the alphabet stuff yet! You're right. We'll return to the clipping element once we cover some other graphics stuff. The clipping math for graphics blitting is almost identical to alphabets but easier to explain in the context of graphics blitting.

Graphics blitting has a long and glorious history. Well, not so glorious. It does, however, have a long history. People have been trying to draw images on their video displays as quickly as possible for a long time. Today, we have faster microprocessors available to us than ever before and so now we can do it faster. There are bad blit routines and good blit routines. A bad blit occasionally produces errors, doesn't clip correctly, or is slow. Good ones are the opposite.

Before I go much further, I should describe a graphic. A *graphic* is a 2-D representation that can be drawn on the screen. There are dozens of ways to draw a rectangular graphic like this, but the most common is simply to copy it to the screen. Graphics can be represented by a single-dimensional array drawn in passes, a two-dimensional array with pointers to the beginning of each scan line, or a compressed stream. All have their uses, but the most common is the first one with a continuous stream of data to be copied to the screen.

We divide the stream up by copying the width of the graphic to the screen, and then we move down to the next scan line and continue drawing the graphic where we left off. This is pretty straightforward and happens to be fast. We'll be emphasizing this method. See Figure 11.3 as an example.

The DIRECT_DRAW_MANAGER class handles blitting to the video card from video memory (better known as a hardware blit), but how do you get graphics into video memory in the first place? You need to blit it there using what is known as a software blit, so let's write some blitting code.

Other limitations on video cards, mostly memory concerns, prevent us from using hardware blits most of the time anyway. Most of your animation frames and graphics will need to reside in RAM. Intel promised that AGP used for hardware blits would be our savior, but AGP can't move more than a few hundred kilobytes per frame... and so we're back to software blitting. (See page 419) Also, the level of control we have over things like data compression means that video memory is rarely suitable for storing lots of images. This rather severe limitation really only applies to 2-D games that require huge repositories of animation graphics, interface graphics, scene graphics, tile graphics, buildings, trees, animals, cursors, etc. Most 3-D games need only about 4 MB and some may want upwards of 12 MB. A lot of 2-D games don't need all that much either.

RTT and RTS games both use way too much memory. Age of Empires had over 24 MB of graphics in the game and that was with compression. Once video cards come with 32 MB or more, we can accept hardware blitting as an option, but for now forget it, especially in 16-bit which requires twice as much memory.

11

Chapter

Here we have a stream of characters handed to us. I have represented each block as a single array element. You will find these in alphabet.cpp. I have broken it into blocks of eight for better visualization. The for-loop effectively does the same thing.

We take the stream and divide it into sections of eight.

```
for (width = 0; width<8; width++)
```

| 1 | 1 | 1 | 1 | 1 | 1 | 1 | 1 |

We test each array element in turn to see if it is 0 and plot a pixel when it is.

| 1 | 1 | 1 | 1 | 1 | 1 | 1 | 1 | 1 | 1 | 0 | 0 | 1 | 1 | 0 | 1 | 0 | 0 | 1 |

| 1 |

```
if (*alpha++ == 0)
{
        *(LocalScreen + width) = 65535;
        *(LocalScreen + LocalShadow) = 0;
}
```

We are always advancing the pointer (alpha++) and after we finish the eight, our width loop falls out and we advance our screen pointer one scan line.

```
LocalScreen += LocalWidth;
```

Lastly, we do the next line. This line will actually draw a few pixels.

```
for (width = 0; width<8; width++)
```

| 1 | 1 | 0 | 0 | 1 | 1 | 0 | 1 |

Figure 11.3
Plotting pixels

Creating a Fake Graphic

I can't very well show you how to blit without any graphics to blit. So let's create a simple graphic that we can begin blitting to the screen (offscreen frame buffer). The CreateGraphic function creates a SCREEN_STRUCT and fills it with black (sets all of the pixels to a value of 0). It then draws a star across the middle in fuchsia. Quite simple, but this gives us something to work with when writing blit code. Since this function allocates memory, we must make sure that we clean up after ourselves and delete that memory in the main function.

```
//*******************************
SCREEN_STRUCT*   CreateGraphic (int w, int h)
{
      SCREEN_STRUCT* screen = new SCREEN_STRUCT;
      Screen->Width = w, screen->Height = h;
      screen->Screen = new U16ptr [w*h];            // allocate the memory
      Memset16Bit (screen->Screen, 0, w*h);          // make the background black
      RGBval color (255, 0, 255);                     // fuchsia

      Line (0, 0, w-1, h-1, screen, &color);         // diagonal from upper-left
                                                      // to bottom-right
      Line (w-1, 0, 0, h-1, screen, &color);         // diagonal from upper-right
                                                      // to bottom-left
      Line (0, h/2, w-1, h/2, screen, &color);       // across the middle
      Line (w/2, 0, w/2, h-1, screen, &color);       // down the middle

      return screen;
}
//*******************************
```

Was that easy or what? Now with a bit of graphics on our side, we can create our first blit function.

Blitting a Simple Graphic

Here is a really basic blit function that is about the slowest I can create without putting in a delay. There is no clipping here, just a straight blit. Still, we do make a minor optimization of copying all variables to local variables. There will usually be problems if you modify the incoming variables anyway.

```
//*******************************
void   BlitGraphic (int x, int y, SCREEN_STRUCT* graphic, SCREEN_STRUCT* screen)
{
      int  SWidth = screen-> RealWidth, SHeight = screen->Height;
      U16ptr SPtr = screen->Screen + x +y* SWidth;
            // move to the starting pixel

      int  GWidth = graphic->Width, GHeight = graphic->Height;
      U16ptr GPtr = graphic->Screen;          // move to the starting pixel

      for (int i=0; i<GHeight; i++)
      {
            for (int j=0; j<GWidth; j++)
            {
                  GPtr[i*GWidth+j] = SPtr[i*SWidth+j];
            }
      }
}
//*******************************
```

We accept four parameters. The first two tell us where the upper-left corner of the graphic will be drawn on the screen. You can also view this as the translation value, which aligns the graphic with the screen. The next two parameters hold all of the values for the screen and the graphic. These values will contain all of the information needed to calculate the position, clip to the boundaries, and blit the graphic to the screen.

This is effective code—but like I mentioned, it is slow. The primary reason it is slow is because there is too much math in the main loop. I'll let you ponder that while we rewrite the Draw function for our new blit code. The loops.cpp file and the winshell.cpp file need some modifications before we even get to that. Here we see the winshell.cpp modifications. Keep the rest of the code the same.

```
//winshell.cpp
#include "dirdraw.h"
#include "winshell.h"

DWORD WINAPI RedrawScreen (LPVOID lpvParm);
DWORD WINAPI UpdateProc (LPVOID lpvParm);
DWORD WINAPI HandleEvents (LPVOID lpvParm);

void  InitLoops ();                  // new
void  CleanupLoops ();               // new


BOOL ActiveApp;                      // is the program active?
static HWND WindowHandle;


//************************
int WINAPI WinMain (HINSTANCE hInstance, HINSTANCE hPrevInstance,
        LPSTR lpCmdLine, int nCmdShow)
{
    MSG        msg;
    HWND       hwnd;

        DIRECT_DRAW_MANAGER* DDraw;

        bool FullScreenFlag = false;    // true;
        int SCREEN_WIDTH = 640, SCREEN_HEIGHT = 480;
        InitLoops ();                   // new
            … keep it the same

        delete DDraw;
        CleanupLoops ();                // new
        return 1;
}
//************************
```

The modifications are simple; they include an initialization function call and a cleanup call. These are basically the equivalent of a constructor and a destructor. We've also added prototypes. No biggie here.

Next we make some rather significant changes to the beginning of loops.cpp. These changes account for the initialization of the graphics and the cleanup.

```
// loops.cpp
#include "dirdraw.h"
#include "alphabet.h"

//******************************

int frame = 0;
int time = 0, timelast=0;
int count = 0;
ALPHABET_MANAGER alpha;

SCREEN_STRUCT* graphic = NULL;

//****************************** prototype

void  Draw (DIRECT_DRAW_MANAGER* ddraw);
SCREEN_STRUCT*   CreateGraphic (int w, int h);

//******************************
//******************************
void  InitLoops ()
{
      graphic = CreateGraphic (64, 64);
}
//******************************
void  CleanupLoops ()
{
      if (graphic)
      {
            if (graphic->Screen)
                  delete graphic->Screen;
            delete graphic;
      }
}
//******************************
.................
```

Notice the init routine and the cleanup routine. We also added a global SCREEN_STRUCT pointer named graphic to hold our future SCREEN_STRUCT*. The rest takes care of itself. We have a real simple Draw function that draws 1,200 times. Even this slow code draws so fast that we need to do 1,200 to get an accurate measurement. Otherwise, this is the same as you've seen before.

Below is our new BlitGraphic routine:

```
//******************************

void  Draw (DIRECT_DRAW_MANAGER* ddraw)
{
      SCREEN_STRUCT* screen = ddraw->GetScreen ();

      char buff[100];
      long time1 = timeGetTime ();
```

```
        for (int i=0; i<1200; i++)
                BlitGraphic (100, 100, graphic, screen);


        long time2 = timeGetTime ();
        long result = time2-time1;

        itoa (result, buff, 10);
        ddraw->PaintText (20, 50, buff);
}

//*****************************
```

Now we can see the results and get a good timing. I get 601 milliseconds and a pretty purple star on the screen. When we are done, we will be drawing almost four times faster.

Optimizing Blit Routines

This code is a faster version running at 541 milliseconds. We've kept all of the local variables. Our biggest change is in the main loop where we eliminate the multiplication. Multiplication is rather slow in integer-based math, and although Intel claims that the Pentium II multiplies in 1 clock cycle, there still is a slowdown when moving variables into registers. Better to avoid all math possible in any tight loop.

We also added another variable to hold the address of the screen offset at any given point. Once we get to the end of the graphics stream for a given scan line (draw a row of pixels), we offset by the width of the screen (we add 640 to move to the next y position).

```
//*****************************
void  BlitGraphic (int x, int y, SCREEN_STRUCT* graphic, SCREEN_STRUCT* screen)
{
        int  SWidth = screen->RealWidth, SHeight = screen->Height;
        U16ptr SPtr = screen->Screen + x +y* SWidth; // move to the starting pixel

        int  GWidth = graphic->Width, GHeight = graphic->Height;
        U16ptr GPtr = graphic->Screen;                // move to the starting pixel


        for (int i=0; i<GHeight; i++)
        {
            U16ptr TPtr = SPtr;
            for (int j=0; j<GWidth; j++)
            {
                    *TPtr++ = *GPtr++;
            }
            SPtr += SWidth;
        }
}
//*****************************
```

We can do this a different way. If we store SWidth minus the length of the single graphics scan line (int tempwidth = SWidth–Gwidth), we can add the result to SPtr. It makes the code harder to read and provides no apparent speed benefit. However, this approach is as valid as any other. Here is what that code in the main loop would look like:

```
//******** main loop only
int tempwidth = SWidth-Gwidth;

for (int i=0; i<GHeight; i++)
{
      for (int j=0; j<GWidth; j++)
      {
            *TPtr++ = *GPtr++;
      }
      SPtr += tempwidth;
}
//********
```

This full optimization only gives us a small speed increase of about 10 percent, or 541 milliseconds like I mentioned a little earlier. Not a great deal but many people would love to make their programs only 10 percent faster, especially when their games run at 28 frames per second. Still, we can do better. There is the old mainstay called memcpy that will save the day.

A Better Optimization

Notice that we've added memcpy to the code below. It moves memory as fast as the Pentium can. A simple Pentium assembly instruction called movsd paired with rep will make the microprocessor copy 4 bytes per clock cycle (almost) from one memory location to another. This is about 12 times faster than our previous example, yet the overhead involved rounds this function out to be 161 clock cycles, which is about 71 percent faster than our last example and about 74 percent faster than our first example. This is world-class speed. We can fill the entire screen with 64x64 bitmaps 3½ times per frame at 30 frames per second. Hopefully, we will never need to do that, because that takes nearly all of our bandwidth. That will change as technology pushes us to faster speeds, but for now we want enough space to fill it about two times per second. That means that we can do a lot of different stuff and still get everything in. The hard part is still having enough bandwidth to do all of the event-driven stuff, the networking, the sound, AI, and so on. It would be better if we could fill the screen six or seven times. Remember that we are only in 640x480. Once we go to 1024x768, we are moving 60 percent more data and things begin to bog down.

Here is the fast code:

```
//******************************
void    BlitGraphic (int x, int y, SCREEN_STRUCT* graphic, SCREEN_STRUCT* screen)
{
      int   SWidth = screen->RealWidth, SHeight = screen->Height;
      U16ptr SPtr = screen->Screen + x +y* SWidth; // move to the starting pixel
```

```
    int  GWidth = graphic->Width, GHeight = graphic->Height;
    U16ptr GPtr = graphic->Screen;          // move to the starting pixel

    int TWidth=GWidth<<1;                    // bitshift is faster than multiply

    while (GHeight--)
    {
        memcpy (SPtr, GPtr, TWidth);
        GPtr += GWidth;
        SPtr += SWidth;
    }
}
//*******************************
```

We added another variable to make sure that we copy 2 bytes for every one pixel (hence 16-bit) named TWidth for "temporary width." Since memcpy is designed to copy one byte at a time, we need to tell it 2 bytes for every pixel, so we use our new variable TWidth to tell it how much memory to copy.

Note: Rename variables as you see fit. This helps you and me by making the code more readable to both of us.

The for loop has been replaced by a while loop, which is slightly faster. Once inside the loop, we immediately call memcpy. It copies from one memory location to another as fast as possible. Then we add offsets to both the graphic pointer GPtr and the screen pointer SPtr. We loop until GHeight is 0. Simple and fast. The entire function has only one multiply and a few adds. No math means speed. The biggest killer here is the memcpy itself.

Compiling this code in Release mode yields only 153 milliseconds, making it barely faster than we already have but still notable. We have optimized this about as far as it will go. Now let's clip it.

Something to note is that 64x64 bitmaps are not very realistic. Most RTS/RTT games use creatures and buildings of differing sizes but rarely that big. Luckily, tiles are about that size and so we are justified using that size to test. Another limitation with this type of graphics routine is that all graphics drawn by it are rectangular. Well, I've never seen a square orc or a square catapult. The only square objects in the game should be tiles (unless you are using diamond tiles) and interface objects like buttons. This code is somewhat helpful because of what it teaches us about optimizations. We'll be doing sprite drawing later, and many of the principals are the same. We'll cover clipping next, which will also help us with alphabets and sprite drawing.

Clipping Graphics

Clipping is the hardest part of drawing a graphic. The math is kind of unusual and you may not have seen this type of clipping before. In addition, it slows us down. It is best to avoid clipping for objects that will never need clipping, like interface objects.

Tiles and anything else on the screen may need clipping, but avoid the overhead whenever possible.

Clipping the bottom and right are the easiest, so let's do that first. The right side is easy because all we do is shorten the width. The bottom is easy because all we do is shorten the height. This assumes that the graphic does not appear completely off the edge of the screen. We'll perform that clipping later. For now, let's do the bottom clipping:

```
//*******************************
void   BlitGraphicClipped (int x, int y, SCREEN_STRUCT* graphic, SCREEN_STRUCT*
screen)
{
       int   SWidth = screen->RealWidth, SHeight = screen->Height;
       U16ptr SPtr = screen->Screen + x +y* SWidth; // move to the starting pixel

       int   GWidth = graphic->Width, GHeight = graphic->Height;
       U16ptr GPtr = graphic->Screen;        // move to the starting pixel

       int TWidth=GWidth<<1;                  // bitshift is faster than multiply

       //******** clip against the bottom
       if (y+GHeight >= SHeight) GHeight = SHeight-y;

       while (GHeight--)
       {
              memcpy (SPtr, GPtr, TWidth);
              GPtr += GWidth;
              SPtr += SWidth;
       }
}
//*******************************
//*******************************

void   Draw (DIRECT_DRAW_MANAGER* ddraw)
{
       SCREEN_STRUCT* screen = ddraw->GetScreen ();

       char buff[100];
       long time1 = timeGetTime ();

       for (int i=0; i<1200; i++)
              BlitGraphicClipped (100, 440, graphic, screen);

       long time2 = timeGetTime ();
       long result = time2-time1;
       itoa (result, buff, 10);
       ddraw->PaintText (20, 50, buff);
}

//*******************************
```

11

Chapter

We have renamed the function because we want to keep the original function in order to draw the fastest possible in situations where we know that we do not need clipping. For testing, I've also included the minor modifications to Draw that will help us determine the speed differences and make sure that the clipping works. Make sure that you save all of your changes to loops.cpp before running the program. If you mistype something, chances are the program will lock up.

Notice our screen location in the function call in Draw. This allows us to test clipping on the bottom of the screen. We clip off 24 lines at the bottom of the screen. Now the program runs 101 milliseconds on my machine. It is faster, of course, because we aren't drawing as much.

The bottom clipping is a simple test. We see if the position plus the length is greater than 480 (bottom of the screen). If so, we figure out how much room is left between our position and the bottom of the screen. That result is the new height we will use. This kind of simple math will be used to clip against all sides, although the top and left take a bit more work.

Clipping on the right is exactly the same. A problem exists, however. We need to add the same offset to move to the next line in a graphic, but we need to copy less. So we simply declare a temporary variable to hold the value of the width before we do any math. We will perform any math on that variable and then assign it to TWidth. Still, you can see how easy all this math is.

```cpp
//*****************************
void  BlitGraphicClipped (int x, int y, SCREEN_STRUCT* graphic, SCREEN_STRUCT*
screen)
{
       int  SWidth = screen->RealWidth, SHeight = screen->Height;
       U16ptr SPtr = screen->Screen + x +y* SWidth; // move to the starting pixel

       int  GWidth = graphic->Width, GHeight = graphic->Height;
       U16ptr GPtr = graphic->Screen;        // move to the starting pixel

       int  tempwidth = GWidth;

       //********* clip against the bottom
       if (y+GHeight >= SHeight) GHeight = SHeight-y;
       if (x+tempwidth >= SWidth) tempwidth = SWidth-x;

       int Twidth = tempwidth<<1;              // bitshift is faster than multiply

       while (GHeight--)
       {
            memcpy (SPtr, GPtr, TWidth);
            GPtr += GWidth;
            SPtr += SWidth;

       }
}
//*****************************
```

In the Draw function, change the function call to:

```
BlitGraphicClipped (600, 100, graphic, screen);
```

When I run the program, my test speed runs at 103 milliseconds—faster still. If you can predict the clipping ahead of time and avoid the function BlitGraphicClipped except when necessary, you can actually speed up your program.

Now comes the trickier part—clipping on the top and left. I will put both the top and left clipping in one iteration of this function:

```
//*******************************
void  BlitGraphicClipped (int x, int y, SCREEN_STRUCT* graphic, SCREEN_STRUCT*
screen)
{
        int  SWidth = screen->RealWidth, SHeight = screen->Height;
        int  GWidth = graphic->Width, GHeight = graphic->Height;
        U16ptr GPtr = graphic->Screen;        // move to the starting pixel

        int  tempwidth = GWidth;

        //********* clip against the bottom
        if (y+GHeight >= SHeight) GHeight = SHeight-y;
        if (x+tempwidth >= SWidth) tempwidth = SWidth-x;

            // remember that the values are negative so adding
            // is actually subtracting and vice versa

        if (y<0) {GPtr-=y*GWidth; GHeight+=y; y=0;}
            if (x<0) {GPtr-=x; tempwidth+=x; x=0;}
            //************* get ready to draw

        U16ptr SPtr = screen->Screen + x +y* SWidth; // move to the starting pixel
        // we move this function because of the adjustments to the x and y
        // positions
        int TWidth = tempwidth<<1;                // bitshift is faster than multiply

        while (GHeight--)
        {
            memcpy (SPtr, GPtr, TWidth);
            GPtr += GWidth;
            SPtr += SWidth;
        }
}
//*******************************
```

We've moved the declaration of SPtr so that we can account for our changes to *x* and *y* due to clipping. We may have a new position once the clipping is performed and putting it after we change those values is the easiest way.

Here's a little more detail about the new code. We've added the following lines:

```
if (y<0) {GPtr-=y*GWidth; GHeight+=y; y=0;}
if (x<0) {GPtr-=x; tempwidth+=x; x=0;}
```

Here is how it works: If our position is above the top edge of the screen (y is less than 0), we need to shorten our bitmap. We also need to move our start location down a number of lines. The last thing we need to do is make sure that we do not start at less than 0 or crashes will occur.

We know that if y is negative, then math must be backwards. If we would normally subtract y to obtain a shorter height, here we must add y. So, multiplying y and the width of the graphic, we offset the start point of our graphic to somewhere in the middle of it. We need to subtract because y is negative. Now we add y to the height; since y is negative, it is the same as shortening the height. Lastly, we set y to 0. This step must be performed last, obviously. If you set it to 0 first, the math would do nothing.

The same math applies for the x direction. For testing, change our new position in Draw to:

```
BlitGraphicClipped (-10, -10, graphic, screen);
```

You will notice that clipping occurs nicely in the upper-left corner. You might try all four corners for fun. This clipping shortens our graphic, but most importantly it is clipping completely. Our last look at clipping finishes this job nicely. I'll leave it to you to examine; the math is trivial, after all.

```
//*******************************
void  BlitGraphicClipped (int x, int y, SCREEN_STRUCT* graphic, SCREEN_STRUCT*
screen)
{
        int  SWidth = screen->RealWidth, SHeight = screen->Height;
        int  GWidth = graphic->Width, GHeight = graphic->Height;
        U16ptr GPtr = graphic->Screen;  // move to the starting pixel

        if (x+SWidth<0) {return;}        // clipped completely on the left
        if (y+SHeight<0) {return;}       // clipped completely on the top
        if (x >= SWidth) {return;}       // clipped completely on the right
        if (y >= SHeight) {return;}      // clipped completely on the bottom

        int  tempwidth = GWidth;

        //********* clip against the bottom
        if (y+GHeight >= SHeight) GHeight = SHeight-y;
        if (x+tempwidth >= SWidth) tempwidth = SWidth-x;

        // remember that the values are negative so adding
        // is actually subtracting and vice versa

        if (y<0) {GPtr -= y*GWidth; Gheight += y; y = 0;}
        if (x<0) {GPtr -= x; tempwidth += x; x = 0;}
```

```
U16ptr SPtr = screen->Screen + x +y* SWidth; // move to the starting pixel
// we move this function because of the adjustments to the x and y
// positions
int TWidth = tempwidth<<1;        // bitshift is faster than multiply

while (GHeight--)
{
     memcpy (SPtr, GPtr, TWidth);
     GPtr += GWidth;
     SPtr += SWidth;
}
}
//*****************************
```

Note: We are assuming 0 for the top edge and 0 for the left edge. In reality, we will clip to a region because you never use the entire screen when drawing in a game. There are usually other things like interface objects, frames, text, etc., that aren't redrawn. Clipping is usually handled through a clipping rectangle.

Clipping Text

Now that we've clipped graphics, we're ready to start clipping text. Not surprisingly, the same clipping code will be used. Some of the optimizations become impossible because a lot of assumptions are thrown out the window. Still, it is pretty fast and it does the job. Here is the code that clips letters. Note how similar it is to the previous clipping we have performed.

```
//****************************

void ALPHABET_MANAGER ::  DrawClippedLetter (U8ptr alpha)
{
     int x = PosX, y = PosY;        // store locally
     int  LocalWidth = RealWidth;   // major speed improvement by making
                                    // local variables
     int LocalShadow = ShadowAdd;

     int SWidth = RealWidth, SHeight = Height;
     int LetterWidth = 8, LetterHeight = 12;

     if (x+LetterWidth<0) {return;}  // clipped completely on the left
     if (y+LetterHeight<0) {return;} // clipped completely on the top
     if (x >= SWidth) {return;}      // clipped completely on the right
     if (y >= SHeight) {return;}     // clipped completely on the bottom


     //********* clipping
     if (y+LetterHeight >= SHeight) LetterHeight = SHeight-y;
```

```
        if (x+LetterWidth >= SWidth) LetterWidth = SWidth-x;

        // remember that the values are negative so adding
        // is actually subtracting and vice versa

        if (y<0) {alpha-=y*LetterWidth; LetterHeight+=y; y=0;}
        if (x<0) {alpha-=x; LetterWidth+=x; x=0;}

        U16ptr LocalScreen  = Screen+x+y*SWidth;;
        //***************

        for (int height=0; height<LetterHeight; height++)
        {
            U8ptr tempalpha = alpha;

            for (int width = 0; width<LetterWidth; width++)
            {
                if (*tempalpha++ == 0)
                {
                    *(LocalScreen + width) = 65535;
                    *(LocalScreen + LocalShadow) = 0;    // add shadows
                }
            }
            alpha += 8;                     // move to the next letter scan line
            LocalScreen += LocalWidth;      // on to the next line
        }
    }

    //****************************
```

The only thing left is to make sure that clipping is performed on a line of text.

Chapter 12

The Drawing Manager

This chapter puts the entire thing together. We don't want to have to supply drawing routines all the time so we need to put them somewhere. I have encapsulated all of the drawing routines into a class called DRAWING_MANAGER. The project file is on the CD under Chapter 11, section .2. For the first time, you can see a neat little Direct-Draw package. We do not include windows.h or ddraw.h and our compile times drop to nearly nothing. This encapsulation holds all of the same behavior as the DIRECT_DRAW_MANAGER as far as page flipping or swapping, waiting for redraw in DrawFrame, clearing the BackBuffer, setting up drawing, and so on. But now we've added drawing to the package including text so now all drawing (excluding compressed images) can be handled through the DRAWING_MANAGER interface.

The DRAWING_MANAGER can be found in a new file called screen.h and screen.cpp. You do not need to see or touch dirdraw.h anymore, but you will need to include ddraw.cpp in the project file; the project on the CD includes it for you. Let's tear apart the header and then we'll pour over some other code. The actual implementation is not important but you can check out screen.cpp if you have the time. We are only interested in familiarizing you with how to use this code. We have already covered various drawing routines throughout the previous three chapters, so there's no need to rehash them here.

```
//screen.h

#if _MSC_VER >= 1000
#pragma once
#endif                    // _MSC_VER >= 1000


#ifndef __SCREEN_H_
#define __SCREEN_H_

#define FC __fastcall

#ifndef __ALPHABET_H_
#include "alphabet.h"
#endif

#ifndef __STRUCT_H_
#include "C:/library/struct.h"
```

```
        #endif


        //****************************************
        //****************************************

        class  SPRITE;
        struct RECT2;
        class  POLY_F;
        class  STRINGC;
        class  DIRECT_DRAW_MANAGER;


        //****************************************
        //****************************************

        typedef class DRAWING_MANAGER : public ALPHABET_MANAGER
        {
        public:
                enum STATUS {BAD, GOOD};
                enum {WHITE=255, BLACK=0, RED=249, BLUE=252, YELLOW=251, GREEN=250,
                      ORANGE=194};
                enum {NONE, _8BIT, _16BIT_5X5X5_, _16BIT_5X6X5_};

        protected:

                int        FullScreenFlag;
                int        ColorType;

                U8ptr      MousePointer;
                U16        Color, ColorDest;
                RECTANGLE  ClipRect;
                void*      WindowHandle;

                int        px1, py1, px2, py2;      // points used for lines and clipping
                //U8*      Alphabet;                // Alphabet pointer inherited from
                                                    // ALPHABET_MANAGER
                //int      PosX, PosY, ShadowAdd;
                //U16ptr   ScreenPos;
                //int      LoadedFontFlag, LoadedFontWidth, LoadedFontHeight,
                //         LoadedFontNumCharacters;
                //int      ClipFlag;
                int        NUM_PIXEL;               // the number of pixels on the screen
                                                    // stored for speed only

                //U16ptr   Screen;                  // inherited from SCREEN_STRUCT
                //int      Width, Height, RealWidth;

                DIRECT_DRAW_MANAGER* DirDraw;
                //***************************

                void SetClipRect (int x, int y, int w, int h);  // used by 3 different
                                                                // clipping set routines below
```

```
        void CreateOffSurface (int which, int w, int h);
        int  Clipper ();

        void HorizontalLine ();
        void VerticalLine ();
        void ErrorMessage (char* str);

public:

        //****************************

        DRAWING_MANAGER (const int w, const int h, void* MessageLoop, void* hInst,
                         const bool fullscreen = true);

        ~DRAWING_MANAGER ();

        void*GetWindowHandle () const {return WindowHandle;}

        //*************************** before and after the drawing process

        void PrepareDrawing ();     // prep and end drawing
                                    // call these before and
                                    // at the end of any drawing cycle
        void EndDrawing ();

        //*************************** page flipping

        void ClearScreen ();
        int  Swap () const;         // moves offscreen into screen, returns 0 if
                                    // OK and any other value for "try again later"
        //*************************** direct draw stuff

        SCREEN_STRUCT* ObtainBackBuffer () const;
        SCREEN_STRUCT* GetScreen () const;

        //*************************** off surface stuff

        void DrawOffSurface (const int x, const int y, const int which) const;
        int  CreateBlankOffSurface (const int w, const int h) const;
        SCREEN_STRUCT* GetOffSurface (const int which) const;       // lock
        void ReleaseOffSurface (const int which) const;            // unlock

        //*************************** draw external data

        // this is a straight image without any compression
        void DrawBitmap (SCREEN_STRUCT* image, int x, int y);
        void DrawBitmap (U16ptr image, int x, int y, int w, int h);

        //*************************** lines

        void Line (const int x1, const int y1, const int x2, const int y2);
```

12

Chapter

```
//*************************** special lines

void FastLine (const int x1, const int y1, const int x2, const int y2);
void InterpretedLine (const int x1, const int y1, const int x2,
                           const int y2);
void HorizontalLine (int y, int x1, int x2) const;
void VerticalLine (int x, int y1, int y2) const;
// must set Color and DestColor first
void BlendedLine (const int x1, const int y1, const int x2, const int y2);


//*************************** mouse

void LoadMousePointer (const STRINGC& file);
void MousePointerPrepare ();
void DrawMousePointer (const int x1, const int y1);


//*************************** pixels

void Plot (const int pos);
void Plot (const int x1, const int y1);


//*************************** rectangles

void FrameRect (const RECTA& rect) const;
void FrameRect (const RECTANGLE& rect) const;
void FrameRect (int x1, int y1, int x2, int y2) const;
void FillRect (const RECTA& rect) const;
void FillRect (const RECTANGLE& rect) const;
void FillRect (int x1, int y1, int x2, int y2) const;
void FillDiamond (const int x1, const int y1, const int x2, const int y2);
// must set Color and DestColor first
void BlendedRectVertical (int x1, int y1, int x2, int y2);
void BlendedRectHorizontal (int x1, int y1, int x2, int y2);


//*************************** circles

void Circle (const int x, const int y, const int radius);
void FilledCircle (const int x, const int y, const int radius);


//*************************** set params

void AddColor (const int c);    // allows negative colors
void SetColor (const U16 c) {Color = c;}
void SetDestColor (const U16 c) {ColorDest = c;}
void SetColor (const U32 r, const U32 g, const U32 b);
void SetDestColor (const U32 r, const U32 g, const U32 b);
// return colors
void DisassembleColor (const U16 color, int& r, int& g, int& b);
void AssembleColor (const int r, const int g, const int b, U16& color);
void SetClippingRect (const RECTANGLE* r);
void SetClippingRect (const RECT2* r);
void SetClippingRect (const int x1, const int y1, const int x2,
```

```
                                const int y2);
        void RestoreClippingRect ();

        //*************************** text

        void PassAlphabet (const U8* ar) {Alphabet = (U8*) ar;}
        void RestoreAlphabet ();

        // the following functions are inherited from the ALPHABET_MANAGER
        /*
        void SetPosition (int x, int y) {PosX=x; PosY=y;}
        void DrawLetter (char which);
        void DrawText (char* text);
        void DrawNumber (int num);
        void DrawLetter (U8* stuff);
        void PrintText (int x, int y, char* text);
        void PrintNumber (int x, int y, int num);
        */

        //*************************** GDI text

        void PaintText (const int x, const int y, const char* string);
        void PaintText (const int x, const int y, STRINGC& string);

}DRAWING_MANAGER, *DRAWING_MANAGERptr, **DRAWING_MANAGERlist;

//**************************************
//**************************************
//**************************************

#undef FC
```

Our first section, as usual, ensures that this header is only compiled once and put into a precompiled header. Then, we make sure that this header has not already been included or is not circularly included by our test of the definition of __SCREEN_H_. If it is not defined, then we define it and the header is read (parsed). If it is defined, then everything between the #ifndef and the #endif at the end of the file is ignored. We define FC as __fastcall for clarity in the text of the class, which allows us to take advantage of performance gains where function calls are concerned. We'll be deriving a lot of behavior from the ALPHABET_MANAGER, so we must include the header file, and to ensure that all of our standard #defines are used, we include struct.h.

We then make a few forward declarations to prevent us from needing to include a bunch more header files, and then proceed with the official class definition. As you may have noticed, all of the header files in this book and the library on the CD have this same format. This format makes good sense and decreases compile times, so you may want to adopt it.

Now we inherit all of the functionality of the ALPHABET_MANAGER in our new DRAWING_MANAGER class, which in turn inherits from SCREEN_STRUCT. This means that all of the behavior that we've discussed regarding text still applies. You can draw text directly in this class just like you would in the ALPHABET_MANAGER.

12

Chapter

This also means that the DRAWING_MANAGER class has member variables of Screen, Width, Height, and RealWidth from the SCREEN_STRUCT. I've put them into the header commented out.

Although I no longer use the first enumeration with BAD and GOOD, I left them here for you in case you might want to use them. If there was a problem initializing DirectDraw, then I would make sure that all functions returned BAD, but since the Windows initialization is handled through this interface, the program will simply not run if there is a problem, so we no longer need it. You can re-establish its usage at your convenience. Using the standard Windows palette in 256-color, the next enumerations hold true. Converting this class to 256-color is almost trivial, so I left these here. During initialization, we need to know how the bits line up. Since we are dealing mostly with 16-bit, our bit patterns, as you may recall from Chapter 9, are 5x5x5 and 5x6x5. When I call the SetColor function, we need to know which bit pattern is used so we can apply the appropriate color manipulation. Also, our GRAPHIC class in the next chapter relies on this information when loading a graphic to convert it to the proper format so that the loaded graphic looks right.

I have stored the FullScreenFlag here for quick reference. The ColorType variable stores the enums _16BIT_5X5X5_ or _16BIT_5X6X5_. Our next variable, Mouse-Pointer, stores an array of chars used to look like a mouse pointer. You can call an internal routine MousePointerPrepare to use the predefined mouse pointer code in screen.cpp or LoadMousePointer to load a pointer from an 8-bit prepared file. You'll need to write the code for LoadMousePointer, but I provided the wrapper. You could simply use the load code from the GRAPHIC class in the next chapter if you like. Then you can call DrawMousePointer every frame to draw the mouse pointer from this array. That code is included.

The member variable Color stores the current color for drawing, while ColorDest stores colors for blended lines, that is, lines that start with one color and end with another. Some rectangles can be filled this way too. These colors will always be 16-bit color in this class. The ClipRect variable holds the region for drawing. Any line or graphic drawn will be clipped against this rectangle. We have quite a few functions for modifying this rectangle. An HWND is really a void*, so rather than including windows.h, I simply declare a WindowHandle variable of type void pointer. The initialization of the program and the Windows handle are handled in dirdraw.h by the DIRECT_DRAW_MANAGER class, but a local copy of the WindowHandle is maintained.

Our next four variables are local variables used for lines and clipping. These values are set when you call Line and then clipping routines are called to prevent the passing of a lot of variables. This speeds up function calls significantly. Speed is the key, and I do what I can to help.

NUM_PIXEL is an old variable and holds the number of pixels on the screen. I don't use this variable, but you might find it useful. Our last member variable is Dir-Draw, which is a DIRECT_DRAW_MANAGER*. This is our key to using DirectDraw. All of these variables bring the grand total for the size of this class to 112 bytes. Pretty small considering that it will be the only instance of this class in the entire project and it does so much.

Next we come to member functions. All of these functions are private and cannot be accessed externally. SetClipRect is used to centralize the setting of the ClipRect referred to earlier. CreateOffSurface is an internal function to create an offscreen surface for quick blitting to the screen. We discussed this when we talked about offsurfaces in Chapter 11. The function Clipper takes the local variables px1, py1, px2, and py2 and clips them to the ClipRect. This function is called when you try to draw a line. If you are sure that all lines will not need clipping, then you should comment out this code. Since we are rarely ever sure about this, you might want to leave well enough alone. I do a quick test during all line drawing for vertical or horizontal lines in case a Line call has x1 and x2 the same or y1 and y2. This speeds line drawing considerably, as discussed in Chapter 11. These two functions rely on variables px1, py1, px2, and py2 for the line end points.

Our last private member function is ErrorMessage. Any DirectDraw error that occurs will display a dialog box with text and this function handles that. Then the program should end.

Now on to the interface to this class. This class interface, the part that should concern you, is fairly self-explanatory. There are a few questionable function names, but for the most part, the functions do exactly what their names imply.

The constructor takes the place of the function CreateMainWindow in the DIRECT_DRAW_MANAGER class that we created earlier. It is a slightly simplified interface, but it is mostly a wrapper for the function DirDraw->CreateMainWindow which will be called during the initialization of the class. The variables it takes are Width, Height, a pointer to the MessageLoop (see message.cpp in the project file), an HINSTANCE, and a flag to tell it to make the application full screen or not. The destructor cleans up everything. In case you need an HWND for anything, you can always call the function GetWindowHandle. You should think of this as the main place to get Windows properties or any other variables related to the window.

The next four functions are all wrappers for DIRECT_DRAW_MANAGER functions. PrepareDrawing encapsulates DirDraw->PrepFrame and stores the SCREEN_STRUCT values in this class. EndDrawing calls DirDraw->InterruptFrame which interrupts the drawing cycle and waits for you to call Swap, which is the same as DirDraw->DrawFrame. Now that we've started drawing, finished drawing, and then blitted that to the screen, we need to call ClearScreen which makes the screen black. In order to allow this class to work with stuff other than DirectDraw, I always use Width*Height pixels to fill. I do fill the background with the currently set color, not black, so be sure to use SetColor before calling Swap.

Anytime you need a SCREEN_STRUCT for drawing directly on the surface, use the functions GetScreen or ObtainBackBuffer, which both do the same thing. The next four functions are only wrappers; they do nothing else. They are exactly like the DIRECT_ DRAW_MANAGER functions of the same name. CreateBlankOffSurface creates an offscreen blitting surface for using hardware blitting. It returns an index number. Next, you'll want a SCREEN_STRUCT for drawing on that surface, so use GetOffSurface with the proper index number. DrawOffSurface blits the off surface to the screen. Lastly, ReleaseOffSurface releases the memory associated with the OffSurface.

Remember the BlitGraphic function from Chapter 11? Well, here it is again, only now it's called DrawBitmap. Prepare a SCREEN_STRUCT and tell it the x,y coordinates where to draw the graphic, and this function works. If you don't want to maintain a SCREEN_STRUCT, then call DrawBitmap (U16ptr image, int x, int y, int w, int h). The image variable is the same as the SCREEN_STRUCT member variable Screen and the w and h are the dimensions. The variables *x* and *y* are the screen position.

Pretty easy so far, I hope. You should examine the code in screen.cpp. Some of it is really very insightful. Now for line drawing.

A simple line should call the Line function, which always produces perfect lines. I've included a FastLine, which is faster than the Line function but somewhat inaccurate. The line looks "fuzzy" or unclear. We'll see more of this later. The function InterpretedLine produces lines that are not always the proper length, sometimes a pixel or two too long (rarely). HorizontalLine makes very fast lines horizontally, while VerticalLine makes very fast vertical lines. These are remarkably faster than Line. BlendedLine is very slow but allows your line to start with one color and slowly blend to another color. Make sure to always call SetColor and SetDestColor before calling BlendedLine.

Using MousePointerPrepare, you end up with a default and sort of cheesy mouse pointer, but it works well enough. I put a placeholder function for LoadMousePointer but no code. I wasn't sure what you, or anyone else, would use. I suggest that you look at the load code for GRAPHIC.h and GRAPHIC.cpp to load a Targa or BMP file to use for your mouse pointer. Lastly, I included a function to draw the mouse called DrawMousePointer, which takes x,y coordinates for the upper left corner of the mouse.

The next two functions plot a single pixel on the screen in whatever color you like. If you want to do the plotting math yourself, you can call Plot with a single parameter. Most of the time, you'll probably call Plot (const int x1, const int y1) which takes x,y coordinates. The next three FrameRect functions all outline a rectangle, in the current color, that has an upper left corner and lower right. If the order is mixed up, it'll be sorted. The next three FillRect functions fill a rectangle, with the current color, that has an upper left and a lower right.

FillDiamond makes an evenly shaped diamond to fit inside the rectangle defined by the passed-in coordinates with the current color. Now we're back to blended stuff. Going from Color to DestColor, the function BlendedRectVertical fills a rectangle from top to bottom. BlendedRectHorizontal moves from left to right doing the same thing. See how complete this library is?

The next two functions draw circles. In order to use this functionality, you need to include Trig.cpp and Circle.cpp in your project. We won't examine these here, but you're welcome to play with them.

Now on to drawing environment settings. AddColor takes the current value of Color and adds a little to it. This functionality isn't very common so I haven't done much with this. It does work. SetColor sets the color for drawing lines or filling rectangles. On blended rectangles or lines, SetDestColor sets the end color for the color blend and Color is the other end or start color. There are two variations of these color setting functions based on what the user wants to do. By passing a 16-bit value to this function, the RGB values are extracted and returned. AssembleColor takes an RGB color and returns a 16-bit value based on the current bit selection: _16BIT_5X5X5_ or _16BIT_5X6X5_. The next three SetClippingRect functions take various parameters for setting the clipping area on the screen. The function RestoreClippingRect restores the ClipRect to full screen again.

On occasion, I have needed to load and save an alphabet, and the function PassAlphabet allows me to set the current alphabet to something different. It must be a char array like in the ALPHABET_MANAGER. Then we can easily restore the old alphabet by calling RestoreAlphabet.

Our last two functions put text on the screen using GDI calls. This is the same way that Windows puts text on the screen. It is slow but it allows all of the standard text handling capabilities. If you want to use this to any large extent, I suggest that you add functions for font manipulation.

That explains it. But you can't just be expected to use it without seeing how it works. The WinMain must change and most of the loops.cpp file must also change. Let's start with WinMain.

```
//***************************
int WINAPI WinMain (HINSTANCE hInstance, HINSTANCE hPrevInstance,
                    LPSTR lpCmdLine, int nCmdShow)
{
        MSG         msg;
        HWND        hwnd;

        DRAWING_MANAGERptr Draw;

        bool FullScreenFlag = false;
        //bool FullScreenFlag = true;
        int SCREEN_WIDTH = 640, SCREEN_HEIGHT = 480;
        InitLoops ();

        hPrevInstance = hPrevInstance;          // avoid C++ warning

        // here we instantiate the direct draw object
        Draw = new DRAWING_MANAGER (SCREEN_WIDTH, SCREEN_HEIGHT, MessageLoop,
                                 hInstance, FullScreenFlag);
        hwnd = Draw->GetWindowHandle ();
        Draw->MousePointerPrepare ();

        if (!hwnd) {delete Draw; return FALSE;}

        while (1)
        {
              int t = PeekMessage (&msg, NULL, OU, OU, PM_NOREMOVE);
              if (t)
              {
                   if (!GetMessage (& msg, NULL, 0, 0))
                   return msg.wParam;
                   TranslateMessage (&msg);
                   DispatchMessage (&msg);
              }
```

```
                    else if (ActiveApp)        // this is important here
                    {
                            RedrawScreen ((LPVOID) Draw);
                    }
                    else if (!ActiveApp)
                    WaitMessage ();
            }
            delete Draw;
            CleanupLoops ();
            return 1;
}
//*************************
```

First, it is more similar than different. We have simply replaced usage of the DIRECT_DRAW_MANAGER with the new DRAWING_MANAGER class. Everything else is the same. The first change is the line:

```
DRAWING_MANAGERptr Draw;
```

This declares a pointer to the DRAWING_MANAGER and allows us to use new to create an instance of it. The next line of code we'll ignore. Then the following three lines create the window, get an HWND or WindowHandle, and then start up the mouse pointer. That's it for the WinMain. All other calls and lines of code are about the same. See how great this new class is?

Now in loops.cpp, we have major changes:

```
// loops.cpp
#include <windows.h>
#include "screen.h"

//******************************

int frame = 0;
int time = 0, timelast = 0;
int count = 0;
SCREEN_STRUCT* graphic = NULL;

//******************************
//******************************

SCREEN_STRUCT*   CreateGraphic (int w, int h, DRAWING_MANAGERptr ptr);

//******************************
//****************************** prototype

void  Draw (DRAWING_MANAGERptr ddraw);

//******************************
//******************************

void  InitLoops ()
{
        graphic = NULL;
```

```
}
//******************************
void  CleanupLoops ()
{
     if (graphic)
     {
          delete graphic->Screen;
          delete graphic;
     }
}


//******************************
```

We only need to include windows.h and our new screen.h file. All other #includes are hidden by what screen.h includes. We have the standard global variables like before, and then a new function called CreateGraphic that functions much like Chapter 11's version of this same function. We don't have any line drawing functions, so we use these capabilities in the DRAWING_MANAGER. Then we have InitLoops and CleanupLoops that are nearly identical to these functions like we had before. Init-Loops does not initialize the graphic because the DRAWING_MANAGER is not yet available (see the WinMain).

Our RedrawScreen will now be receiving a DRAWING_MANAGERptr instead of the DIRECT_DRAW_MANAGERptr, but other than that and a few updated function names, this is largely the same as before. The biggest difference here is the appearance of the function CreateGraphic which creates the graphic that we'll be using to blit to the screen:

```
//******************************
DWORD WINAPI RedrawScreen (LPVOID Parm)
{
     DRAWING_MANAGERptr DDraw = (DRAWING_MANAGERptr) Parm;
     if (DDraw == NULL) return 1;
     if (graphic == NULL)
          {graphic = CreateGraphic (64, 64, DDraw);}

     time = timeGetTime ();           // get the current millisec
     count++;
     if (time-timelast>=1000)
     {
          frame = count;
          timelast = time;            // update time
          count = 0;
     }
     char buff[40];
     itoa (frame, buff, 10);

     //******************************

     while (DDraw->Swap ());          // keep trying to swap
     // returns 0 when done

     DDraw->PrepareDrawing ();
```

12

Chapter

```
        DDraw->SetColor (0, 0, 0);
        DDraw->ClearScreen ();

        Draw (DDraw);                        // here is the new call

        DDraw->PaintText (20, 20, buff);
        // finish the drawing cycle
        DDraw->EndDrawing ();
        return 0;
}
```

`//*******************************`

I had a little fun with the Draw function. I wanted to show off a few new capabilities of the DRAWING_MANAGER class, so I drew lines, a mouse pointer, blended lines, blended rectangles, and so on. Look it over. It's really straightforward, so I won't bore you with mundane details. It almost reads like a book, so good luck. By the way, the mouse pointer drawing should be the last thing you draw in any frame. You don't want anything hiding the mouse by drawing over it. See Figure 12.1 for an example of what you'll see.

```
        //*******************************

        void  Draw (DRAWING_MANAGERptr Draw)
        {
            char buff[100];
            long time1 = timeGetTime ();

            //*************** timed section ****************

            Draw->SetColor (192, 192, 32);
            Draw->Line (10, 10, 110, 100);

            Draw->FastLine (20, 10, 120, 100);
            Draw->SetColor (0); Draw->SetDestColor (255, 255, 255);
            Draw->BlendedLine (30, 10, 130, 100);        // black to white
            Draw->InterpretedLine (40, 10, 140, 100);

            Draw->SetColor (255, 0, 0); Draw->SetDestColor (0, 0, 255);
            Draw->BlendedLine (10, 110, 110, 200);       // red to blue
            Draw->SetColor (0, 0, 255); Draw->SetDestColor (0, 255, 0);
            Draw->BlendedLine (30, 110, 130, 200);       // blue to green
            Draw->SetColor (0, 255, 0); Draw->SetDestColor (255, 0, 0);
            Draw->BlendedLine (50, 110, 150, 200);       // green to red

            Draw->DrawBitmap (graphic, 288, 208);        // centered on 640x480

            Draw->SetColor (0, 255, 0); Draw->SetDestColor (255, 0, 255);
            Draw->BlendedRectVertical (200, 50, 300, 190);
            Draw->SetColor (0, 255, 0); Draw->SetDestColor (255, 0, 255);
            Draw->BlendedRectHorizontal (310, 50, 410, 190);
```

```
        Draw->DrawMousePointer (100, 12);

        long time2 = timeGetTime ();
        long result = time2-time1;

        itoa (result, buff, 10);
        Draw->PrintText (60, 460, buff);
}

//*******************************
```

Figure 12.1
Screen shot of drawing using the DRAWING_ MANAGER class

Our last change simply sets temporary dimensions for the DRAWING_MANAGER and then uses the drawing functions to draw onto this new surface. After doing something like this, make sure to call the function DDraw->Swap to restore the real screen dimensions and a pointer to the real screen for drawing.

```
//*******************************

SCREEN_STRUCT*    CreateGraphic (int w, int h, DRAWING_MANAGERptr DDraw)
{
        SCREEN_STRUCT* screen = new SCREEN_STRUCT;
        screen->Width = w, screen->Height = h,
        screen->RealWidth = w;
        screen->Screen = new U16 [w*h];        // allocate the memory
```

```
        DDraw->SetScreenValues (screen);

        DDraw->SetColor (0);                    // black
        DDraw->ClearScreen ();                  // make the background black
        DDraw->SetColor (255, 0, 255);          // fuchsia

        DDraw->Line (0, 0, w-1, h-1);           // diagonal from upper-left to
                                                // bottom-right
        DDraw->Line (w-1, 0, 0, h-1);           // diagonal from upper-right to
                                                // bottom-left

        DDraw->Line (0, h/2, w-1, h/2);         // across the middle
        DDraw->Line (w/2, 0, w/2, h-1);         // down the middle

        return screen;
    }


//*******************************
```

As you can see, even with all of the changes, the code looks and feels much the same. Now it is more efficient, compiles better, is encapsulated well, and has a superb interface for handling all of the standard drawing needs. I hope you enjoy this class. You really should look over the code in screen.cpp to learn how each function works.

Chapter 13

Loading Graphics

In fileobj.h and fileobj.cpp on the companion CD, you will find a class named FILE_MASTER that encapsulates file opening and closing as well as writing.

A while back when I worked at Ion Storm, I had decided to use ReadFile/ReadFileEx and WriteFile/WriteFileEx on a level editing tool that I had created. These functions were the new standard Windows load and save functions and since Microsoft was setting all of the standards...

What a big mistake. After using it successfully for months, suddenly I tried saving an unsigned short and it blew up, saving a long instead. We were using a huge save file and those extra 2 bytes screwed everything up. It took Mike Maynard and me three hours to find the bug. We, of course, assumed that we were doing something wrong, but after repeated and successive tests, we found the bug was Microsoft's. I had to replace the function WriteFileEx everywhere in the code. I GREP'd for it and found over 300 instances. We tried for about half an hour to discover why the bug was happening, under which circumstances, if there was a workaround, etc. It was especially strange because the function appeared hundreds of times throughout the code of my tool, but only one instance of the function call caused the error.

That was good enough for me. I decided to create a class to encapsulate file writing and reading so that if I ever had to make a major change again, I could simply change my class. Here is the header file description:

```
//****************************************************
typedef int FILE_PTR;

typedef class FILE_MASTER
{
public:
        enum READWRITE_FLAGS {NO_IO, READ, WRITE};
        enum ERR {NONE, NOT_READABLE, NOT_WRITABLE, PROBLEM};

protected:
        READWRITE_FLAGS        rwflag;
        FILE_PTR               file;

public:

        FILE_MASTER (char* str, READWRITE_FLAGS);
        FILE_MASTER (STRINGC* str, READWRITE_FLAGS);
```

```
            ~ FILE_MASTER ();

                //*************************

        ERR  Status ();              // gets the file status, should be NONE
        ERR  Write (void* data, long size);
        ERR  Read  (void* data, long size);

                //*************************

        int  Seek (long where);
        int  Advance (long howmuch);
        int  SeekFromEnd (long where);
    }
    FILE_MASTER, FILEM, *FILE_MASTERptr, **FILE_MASTERlist;

        //****************************************************
```

This is how you might use it in code. You can see that it is easy to use, just like I designed it to be. The Read and Write functions return a non-zero number if any kind of problem arises. If these functions tell us that a problem occurred, we must return an error code. I didn't bother with extensive error checking. Most of the time, errors don't occur, but when they do, either you misspelled the filename or something much more serious happened that is completely beyond your control.

The destructor closes the file, so declaring FILE_MASTER locally is the preferred way to use it. Once the enclosing function falls out of scope, FILE_MASTER automatically closes the file. Magic.

Look at my implementation if you have the inclination. It is simple and somewhat clever:

```
    int x, y;

    FILE_MASTER     file (str, FILE_MASTER :: READ);
    if (file.Status () != FILE_MASTER::NONE) return false;

    if (file.Read (&x, sizeof (int))) {return false;}
    if (file.Read (&y, sizeof (int))) {return false;}
```

You'll also see some other classes in fileobj.cpp like FILE_DIRECTORY and FILEOBJECT. FILE_DIRECTORY loads an entire directory and stores it in a linked list of strings. FILEOBJECT encapsulates all of the good stuff like file verification, path information, file size information, etc. You may find both helpful.

How to Load a Targa

Targa is an old graphics format. It is easy to read and not too bad to use. Much like a bitmap, it contains a stream of data that we'll use to blit to the screen. It comes in a few different bit depths but unlike its BMP equivalent, it is easy and intuitive to use. Later in this chapter and in Chapter 14, we'll discuss eliminating black space in a loaded bitmap.

A Targa is not a BMP. A Targa, or TGA, has a small header and reads from bottom up like a BMP. The header simplicity is reason enough to support it over BMP. Targa is widely supported and very easy to read. It supports 8-bit graphics but I have never used that mode. Artists almost always insist on 24-bit when saving Targas. When they don't care about image quality, they will save in 16-bit color. I have yet to see an artist save an 8-bit Targa. Also, Photoshop won't even save in the old 8-bit format anyway, so getting hold of an 8-bit Targa may be difficult. Even Paint Shop Pro requires 24-bit, so good luck.

In any event, the header of a Targa is tiny, especially compared to a BMP, which has 56 bytes just for basic info. All things considered, it is a great little format that is widely supported. The Targa header looks like this:

```
//*******************************************

struct TARGA_HEADER
{
        U8      IDLength;
        U8      ColorMapType;
        U8      ImageType;
        U16     CMapStart;
        U8      CMapDepth;
        U16     XOffset;
        U16     YOffset;
        U16     Width;
        U16     Height;
        U8      PixelDepth;
        U8      ImageDescriptor;
};

//*******************************************
```

Wow! It's only 16 bytes. Even some of that is wasted. We need only a few members of the header: Width, Height, and PixelDepth.

Stringy Strings

Here is where I need to talk about my string class a bit.

The loading process for a Targa is rather complex and will take a lot of describing. But before we get started, I'll need to introduce the STRINGC class. You'll find it in stringc.h and stringc.cpp.

There are only two member variables to STRINGC. The char array has a fixed size. Some people might see this as a weakness or they simply don't like it, but dynamic char arrays lead to too much memory fragmentation, especially when parsing filenames, copying strings, and so on. Also, ensuring that memory cleanup is handled properly is a complete pain; just try using the MFC class CSTRING for any length of time. Overall, this is the best string class I have seen and you are welcome to it. I developed it, so you can blame any problems on me.

The class definition for it looks like this:

```
// stringc.h

//*****************************************

#if _MSC_VER >= 1000
#pragma once
#endif                                          // _MSC_VER >= 1000


#ifndef  __STRINGC_H_
#define  __STRINGC_H_

//typedef  int Bool;

#ifndef false
#define false 0
#define true 1
#endif

//*********************************************
//*********************************************
//*********************************************
// this class maintains strings, rips apart filenames, and has a linked list
// for storing lists of strings.
typedef class  STRINGC
{
        enum        {TEXTLEN = 120};
        char        str[TEXTLEN];
        STRINGC*  next;

              //***********************

        char*       PointToLastCharacter (char* str, char search);
        char*       PointToNextCharacter (char* str, char search);

        // returns string
        char*       ConvertFloatStringToRealString (char* temp, int decimal, int
                                                    sign);

        char*       GetPositionFromEnd (int pos);
        char*       GotoEnd ();                  // points to last character
public:
              //***********************

        STRINGC ();
        STRINGC (const STRINGC* s);
        STRINGC (const STRINGC & s);
        STRINGC (const char* s, STRINGC* ptr);   // for a sequence
        STRINGC (const char* s);
        STRINGC (const int   s);
```

```
STRINGC (const unsigned long s);
STRINGC (const float s);
STRINGC (const STRINGC* s, const int num); // number of characters to copy
STRINGC (const STRINGC & s, const int num);
// STRINGC (STRINGC s, int num);
STRINGC (const char* s, const int num);


~STRINGC ();

void      Clear ();
void      Zero ();                                  // sets full string to 0
char*     GetString () {return str;}
int       GetStringLength () const;
int       Len () const;
bool      IsValid () const { if (str[0] == 0)return false;
return true; }

    //***********************

STRINGC operator =  (const int x);              // assignment
STRINGC operator =  (const unsigned long s);
STRINGC operator =  (const char * x);
STRINGC operator =  (const float x);
STRINGC operator =  (const STRINGC * x);
STRINGC operator =  (const STRINGC & x);

bool operator == (const char * x);              // comparison
bool operator != (const char * x);
bool operator <  (const char * x);
bool operator >  (const char * x);

bool operator == (const STRINGC * x);           // comparison
bool operator != (const STRINGC * x);
bool operator <  (const STRINGC * x);
bool operator >  (const STRINGC * x);
bool operator == (const STRINGC & x);
bool operator != (const STRINGC & x);
bool operator <  (const STRINGC & x);
bool operator >  (const STRINGC & x);

STRINGC& operator += (const int x);             // concatenate
STRINGC& operator += (const unsigned long x);
STRINGC& operator += (const char * x);
STRINGC& operator += (const float x);
STRINGC& operator += (const STRINGC * x);
STRINGC& operator += (const STRINGC & x);

STRINGC operator +  (const int x) const;
STRINGC operator +  (const unsigned long x) const;
STRINGC operator +  (const char* x) const;
STRINGC operator +  (const float x) const;
```

```
STRINGC operator +  (const STRINGC * x) const;
STRINGC operator +  (const STRINGC & x) const;
STRINGC operator << (const int x); // move the front 'x' characters off
STRINGC operator >> (const int x); // add 'x' number of blank spaces

char       operator [] (const int x) const;

void       Set (const char c, const int which);       // set a value

     // returning a converted value
operator char* ();
operator int ();
operator float ();

STRINGC& ToDec ();                 // conversion to and from decimal and hex
STRINGC& ToHex ();

     //*********************** file functions

STRINGC ExtractFileName ();      // these change the internal value
STRINGC ExtractName () {return ExtractFileName ();}
STRINGC ExtractExtension ();
STRINGC ExtractPath ();          // path without the last forward slash
STRINGC ExtractFilePath () {return ExtractPath ();}
void    EliminateExtension ();
void    EliminateFilename ();
bool    HasExtension ();

     //***********************

void    Lower ();
void    ConvertToLowerCase ();                    // case changes
void    Upper ();
void    ConvertToUpperCase ();

// complex
void    ConvertAllType1ToType2 (char* str, char type1, char type2);
void    ConvertAllBackslashesToForwardslashes ( ); // simplified
void    ConvertBackslash ();

     //***********************

void    AlignLeft ();
void    AlignRight (int BufferSize);
void    AlignCenter (int BufferSize);

     //***********************

STRINGC LeftStr (int num);
STRINGC RightStr (int num);
STRINGC MidStr (int left, int right);
```

```
                    //************************

        STRINGC*    GetNext () {return next;}
        STRINGC*    PlaceInList (STRINGC* list);
        STRINGC*    GetNthItem (int which);
        STRINGC*    AppendList (STRINGC* list);                    // not implemented
        void        AppendToList (STRINGC* item);
        void        AppendToList (STRINGC item);

                    //***********************

    }
    STR, *STRptr, **STRlist;

    //*******************************************
    //*******************************************
    //*******************************************
    #endif
```

There are a bunch of sections to this rather complex string class. First, we have the private members. The enum is simply for internal use; you can change it to accommodate smaller file paths. Almost all paths are under 40 characters anyway. Then we have our actual string, named str. This is where we hold all of our string data. The next pointer is used for a linked list of strings. It is tricky to use, and I'll leave it to you to read about its use. You'll find it used in code in fileobj.cpp of FILE_DIRECTORY for holding entire directories.

The next section deals with parsing the string once we have it filled with something. PointToLastCharacter returns a pointer to the last character of type "search" in the array. PointToNextCharacter is meant to start at the beginning of the array and find the "search" character repeatedly as if you were searching for spaces in a sentence. It is used mostly for finding "/" in a file path. ConvertFloatStringToRealString uses a few different methods to parse the data returned from fcvt, which is a standard C function. You'll need stdlib.h to use this function. I've converted all of the fcvt's to gcvt's, but I've kept this code for reference and "just in case." GetPositionFromEnd tells us how many more characters are in the string before we get to a 0. GotoEnd returns a pointer to the last character in the string.

The next section has to do with instantiation and cleanup. We can instantiate this class in seven different ways. The most common is without any parameters. But you can pass most anything to this class and it will accept it and set the string correctly. The only tricky constructor is STRINGC (char* s, STRINGC* ptr);. What we are doing is storing the string and saving the linked list that follows.

The last three constructors accept parameters that allow us to copy only part of a string. This can be very useful when parsing strings or reading data from a text file. I'm sure that you can come up with other uses for it.

The destructor is easy. It deletes the "next" item, so a single destructor call deletes the entire linked list. Mostly, it does nothing special. The Clear function sets the first item in the array to 0, effectively clearing the string, and clears the "next" pointer. GetString returns a char pointer to the array, a simple access routine. GetStringLength is the same as strlen, and this function in fact calls that standard function. IsValid

13

Chapter

simply tells us if something is stored in the array. This is a great function to use in arrays or after attempting a file directory.

The next section is operator overloading. This always seems useless to a beginning programmer, but it is as useful as pointers. You use these like this:

```
STRINGC string = FilePath + "/" + FileName + ".tga";
```

The trickiest part of these overloaded operators is the operators << and >>. These shift the text left or right, adding space or chopping off characters where appropriate. Simply pass the number of shifts you need.

The next section involves files and filename extraction. These functions allow you to manipulate filename info better. All of the functions rely on forward slashes for filenames because backslashes perform rather strangely in strings. Backslash has a special meaning in strings, and since you can use the forward slash as easily as backslashes, why not use it instead? Whenever you have a file path from some standard C function, make sure you use the STRINGC function ConvertBackslash in the next section. This goes through the string and does the conversion from "\" to "/". None of the extraction functions work without performing this simple step first.

ExtractName and ExtractFileName are two functions that do the same thing. Over the years I've found myself typing both, but I only had the ExtractFileName function, so I've decided to add the other. You can eliminate one if you prefer. ExtractFileName rips off the file path info and the extension and simply returns the filename. The original value also changes, so make a copy of the string before you call this function. ExtractExtension rips out all of the guts of the string, leaving only the extension. ExtractPath and ExtractFilePath both eliminate the filename in the path, leaving only the path without the last forward slash. EliminateExtension stores a 0 on the last "." in the string, effectively eliminating the extension if there is indeed one. EliminateFilename essentially does the same as ExtractFilePath but leaves the last slash. HasExtension just tells us if the string has an extension or not, a simple true/false situation. All of these functions help a lot with DOS/Windows file manipulation.

Error checking is not extensive in the class, as I didn't want to bog it down with error checking. I assume that you know what you are doing and also that you can track your own bugs. You might want to verify that shifts are less than 128 characters and that you don't store beyond 128 characters. You may need these tests or you may not. I don't.

Next is a section that deals with standard string functionality that you have come to expect from C/C++. Lower converts the string to lowercase. ConvertToLowerCase does the same. Upper and ConvertToUpperCase both convert the string to uppercase. ConvertAllType1ToType2 is special. It looks through the string for a type of character and when it finds an instance of that character, it replaces it with "t2." ConvertAllBackslashesToForwardslashes and ConvertBackslash converts each "\" in the string to "/," just like we discussed above.

The next section helps with string alignment. Often, you'll have an input box like the kind you might see in Windows. Sometimes the text will need extra spaces to be right aligned and centered in a field. To left align a string, we need to eliminate all of the spaces preceding the string. These functions do all of that. Just pass an integer telling the function how many total characters there can be in the text box.

Back in the BASIC programming language, we could copy a part of a string. This included the left part, anywhere in the middle, and the right part. The following example illustrates this:

```
print left$ ( "hello", 4)
```

The output from this is "hell," literally. Below is something similar that achieves the same results:

```
STRINGC str = "hello";
STRINGC temp = str.LeftStr (4);
```

It is as easy as that. The LeftSrt, RightStr, and MidStr functions are the few that don't modify the original string. These are good for limiting string length to a certain size since text takes up a large amount of space.

The last six functions will not be described in this text but you can look in fileobj.cpp for how to use them. They mainly allow you to create a linked list of strings for such things as a directory or a pull-down menu.

This class hides all of the implementation details from you. This is not to say that you won't understand how it works. It only means that it can simplify your life. If nothing else, it saves typing and is a lot more intuitive. Take the following example. Using the class yields:

```
int which = 10;
float x = 20.001F;
STRINGC str = "testcase " + which + " has a value of " + x;
```

This string can then be printed, copied, etc. Here is what you have to do to get the same results without the string class:

```
int which = 10;
double x = 20.001;
char str[128], tempstr[20];

strcpy ( str, "testcase " );

itoa        ( x, tempstr, 10 );
strcat ( str, tempstr );

strcat ( str, " has a value of" );

gcvt        ( x, 15, tempstr );
strcat ( str, tempstr );
```

Now be honest, which is easier to read? Which would you rather type 100 times a day? Which is easier to debug? The string class saves a lot of needless effort and reduces code size, making your program significantly smaller. You write all of the functions one time, and everything after that is simply a function call with a lot less overhead. One caveat: It isn't any faster. In fact, it is slower. How much? About 8 to12 percent, depending on what you are doing. Still, it simplifies your life enough to make it worthwhile. You can also inline a lot of your functions for speed increases, but then your code becomes the same size as if you didn't use the class in the first place.

13

Chapter

Remember that inline places a copy of the original code in the space where you made the function call.

Your other option is to make all of the functions __fastcall, which will make them about the same speed as if you performed all of your string functions without the class. I'll leave that up to you. Remember, don't bother optimizing areas of your code that don't truly affect performance.

That does it for the STRINGC class. It really is useful and it hides all of the implementation details, allowing it to be defined one time and used forever like that. Just think about having to write code to parse every filename throughout your code; that might change your mind if you have any doubts. This class will save you a lot of headaches, and I'll be using it from here on out.

The Load Targa Function

The following code is part of a class that we haven't created yet. This is one of the few preview times in my book, so enjoy it. This is ultimately what we're shooting for. I won't go into any detail, but this will help you down the line. Examine it closely and try to understand it.

```
//********************************
bool  GRAPHIC :: LoadTGA ()
{
        STRINGC string = FilePath + "/" + FileName + ".tga";
        TARGA_HEADER header;

        FILE_MASTER        file (string, FILE_MASTER :: READ);
        if (file.Status () != FILE_MASTER::NONE) return false;
        if (file.Read (&header, sizeof (TARGA_HEADER))) return false;

        Width = header.Width;
        Height = header.Height;

        // scratchpad is a variable used to temporarily load in data,
        // this allows us compression/encoding
        // we can declare this globally and set the flag
        // "flags.Flag.NO_SCRATCH_PAD"
        // when we pass the memory pointer to this class
        // so that we don't allocate and then deallocate memory, hopefully
        // preventing memory fragmentation
        if (flags.Flag.NO_SCRATCH_PAD && ScratchPad) delete ScratchPad;
        if (flags.Flag.NO_SCRATCH_PAD) ScratchPad = new U16 [Height*Width*2];

        if (header.PixelDepth == 8) return false; // no support for 8 bit
        if (header.PixelDepth == 16)
        {
            for (int i=Height-1; i>-1; i--)
            {
                U16ptr ptr = ScratchPad+i*Width;
                if (file.Read (ptr, Width<<1)) return false; // 16 bit
```

```
                }
                Image = LLECompression16Bit (ScratchPad, Width, Height);
        }
        if (header.PixelDepth == 24)
        {
                int readlen = 3*Width;
                RGBVal* read = new RGBVal[Width+1];  // an array for temp storage
                                                     // and conversion

                for (int i=Height-1; i>=0; i--)
                {
                U16ptr ptr = ScratchPad+i*Width;          // offset pointer
                    if (file.Read (read, readlen)) return false;

                    ConvertTo16Bit (ptr, read, Width );  // stores the 16 bit
                                                         // data in ptr
                }
                delete read;
        }
        flags.Flag.LOADED = true;

        if (flags.Flag.NO_SCRATCH_PAD && ScratchPad)    // clean up temporary
                                                        // memory if necessary
        {
                delete ScratchPad;
                ScratchPad = NULL;
        }

        return true;
}
//*******************************
```

Typical Graphic Storage

Almost all simple graphics formats use the same basic structure. There is usually a small header, followed by a palette when necessary, followed by a stream of graphic information. The stream is much like the Letters array that we encountered earlier. JPEG is considerably different and TIFF has quite a lot of variation. In fact, most graphics file formats do not qualify as simple graphics file formats. Even so, you can expect to find this basic structure in many of these file formats:

```
//*******************************
bool  LoadTGA (SCREEN_STRUCT* screen, char* filename)
{
        TARGA_HEADER header;
        STRINGC string = filename;

        FILE_MASTER     file (string, FILE_MASTER :: READ);
        if (file.Status () != FILE_MASTER::NONE) return false;
```

13

Chapter

```
        if (file.Read (&header, sizeof (TARGA_HEADER))) return false;

        int Width = header.Width, Height = header.Height;
        screen->Width = Width;      Screen->Height = Height;
        int CopyWidth = Width<<1;                        // easier copying

        screen->Screen = new U16 [Height* CopyWidth];   // 2 bytes for each pixel

        if (header.PixelDepth == 8) return false;        // no support for 8 bit
        if (header.PixelDepth == 24) return false;
        if (header.PixelDepth == 32) return false;

        if (header.PixelDepth == 16)
        {
            for (int i=Height-1; i>-1; i--)
            {
                U16ptr ptr = screen->Screen + i*Width;

                if (file.Read (ptr, CopyWidth)) return false; // 16 bit
                                                     // 2 bytes for each pixel
            }
        }
        return true;
}
//********************************
```

We've see the header information in a Targa file, and since the data you read in is a straightforward data stream, the stripped-down LoadTGA function is quite basic.

We declare a local TARGA_HEADER structure so that we can simply read it in as a chunk; you can see that once we open the file, we read in the header info first. Next, we make all of the necessary variables local. The new variable CopyWidth is included to simplify our memcpy, which should copy 2 bytes for every pixel, so CopyWidth is two times the length. All other main local variables will be returned in the SCREEN_STRUCT that was passed to the LoadTGA function. Now we need to allocate memory for a buffer large enough to hold our entire bit stream. We allocate 2 bytes for every pixel times the height, using our new CopyWidth variable. We copy from the file into the memory from the bottom up. Like BMPs, Targas are upside down. This memory chunk is the memory that we use for drawing later.

For simplicity, I have made 8-bit, 24-bit, and 32-bit not loadable in this function. Later, we will support 24-bit, but the other two are rare enough that we do not need to bother with them. Since a 16-bit Targa is always a 15-bit image, we will need to make modifications on occasion. That is, we will need to change 15-bit to 16-bit. For now, let's leave it as it is.

This function leaves us with all of the info we need to begin drawing. Remember CreateGraphic from Chapter 11? We can now avoid using that and have DrawGraphic draw our new loaded picture. Pretty cool.

Now let's add 24-bit.

Converting 24-bit to 16-bit

This implementation makes the process of converting 24-bit images to 16-bit trivial. Because we already have code for converting from 24-bit to 16-bit hidden in struct.h, we can simply use this to our advantage and create a very simple routine. The LoadTGA function can add to its repertoire of functionality by simply using the existing RGBval structure defined in struct.h. There are a lot of little gems in struct.h that I've collected over 12 years or so. I hope you can find something you like.

```
//*********************************
void  ConvertTo16Bit (U16ptr buff, RGBVal* read, int num, int BitPattern)
{
      if (BitPattern == DIRECT_DRAW_MANAGER :: _5x5x5_)
      while (num--)
      {
           *buff = read->Convert15 ();
           buff++, read++;
      }
      else
           while (num--)
      {
           *buff = read->Convert16 ();
           buff++, read++;
      }
}
//*********************************
bool  LoadTGA (SCREEN_STRUCT* screen, char* filename)
{
      TARGA_HEADER header;
      STRINGC string = filename;

      FILE_MASTER     file (string, FILE_MASTER :: READ);
      if (file.Status () != FILE_MASTER::NONE) return false;
      if (file.Read (&header, sizeof (TARGA_HEADER))) return false;

      int Width = header.Width, Height = header.Height;
      screen->Width = Width;     Screen->Height = Height;
      int CopyWidth = Width<<1;                      // easier copying

      screen->Screen = new U16 [Height* CopyWidth];   // 2 bytes for each pixel

      if (header.PixelDepth == 8) return false;       // no support for 8 bit
      if (header.PixelDepth == 16)
      {
           for (int i=Height-1; i>-1; i--)
           {
                U16ptr ptr = screen->Screen + i*Width;

                if (file.Read (ptr, CopyWidth)) return false;  // 16 bit
                                                    // 2 bytes for each pixel
           }
```

```
        }
        if (header.PixelDepth == 24)                    // here is is
        {
            int readlen = 3*Width;
            RGBVal* read = new RGBVal[Width+1];

            for (int i=Height-1; i>=0; i--)
            {
                U16ptr ptr = ScratchPad+i*Width;
                if (file.Read (read, readlen)) return false;

                ConvertTo16Bit (ptr, read, Width, Ddraw->GetColorType ());
                                            // stores the 16 bit data in ptr
            }
            delete read;
        }
        if (header.PixelDepth == 32) return false;

        return true;

}
//********************************
```

That's it. Notice that we read in the 24-bit data as a gestalt (all at once) and then essentially "parse" the data. The ConvertTo16Bit function is new to our code base and it converts the group of data as an array. Pretty nifty, huh? It does require the BitPattern to tell it how the conversion will proceed. This function should always be used for loading graphics because it works no matter how the 16 bits are arranged. As far as loading a Targa, that's it.

One more important thing: If we load our data in 15-bit and our display is 16-bit, we'll need to make the conversion. The following function will do nicely:

```
//********************************
void ConvertTo_5x6x5 (U16ptr ptr, int num)
{
        U16 RMask = 31<<10;
        U16 GMask = 31<<5;
        U16 BMask = 31;
        while (num--)
        {
            U32 r = *ptr & RMask;
            U32 g = *ptr & GMask;
            U32 b = *ptr & BMask;
            *ptr++ = (U16)((r<<1) + (g<<1) + b);
        }

}
//********************************
```

inside the LoadTGA function ....

```
//********************************
        if (header.PixelDepth == 16)
        {
            for (int i=Height-1; i>-1; i--)
```

```
                    {
                        U16ptr ptr = ScratchPad+i*Width;

                        if (file.Read (ptr, Width<<1)) return false; // 16 bit
                    }
                    if (flags.Flag.BIT_PATTERN == GRAPHIC_MGR::_5x6x5_)
                        ConvertTo_5x6x5 (ScratchPad, Width*Height);
        }
//*******************************
```

You'll notice a little tidbit, the GRAPHIC_MGR. We'll cover it in depth in Chapter 15.

How to Draw

Drawing these newly loaded graphics is now our goal. Drawing is now trivial. We defined a graphic drawing function in Chapter 11 called BlitGraphic. This is the answer to our prayers. Simple enough. Let's go back to loops.cpp:

```
// loops.cpp
#include "dirdraw.h"
#include "alphabet.h"

//*****************************

int frame = 0;
int time = 0, timelast = 0;
int count = 0;
ALPHABET_MANAGER alpha;

SCREEN_STRUCT* graphic = NULL;
//***************************** prototype

void  Draw (DIRECT_DRAW_MANAGER* ddraw);

bool LoadTGA (SCREEN_STRUCT* screen, char* filename);

//*****************************
//*****************************
void  InitLoops ()
{
        graphic = new SCREEN_STRUCT;
        LoadTGA (&graphic, "generic.tga");
}
//*****************************
void  CleanupLoops ()
{
        if (graphic)
        {
            if (graphic->Screen)
                delete graphic->Screen;
            delete graphic;
        }
```

```
}
//*******************************
```

We change the InitLoops internals and the rest takes care of itself. The problem may be getting a Targa to begin with. There is a wonderful program called Paint Shop Pro available in shareware version (the professional version is around $100). It spits out Targa files. Photoshop also can spit out Targa files.

Notice the "generic.tga" filename I used. You need to change it to something else in order to get this section of code to work. The Draw function should take care of the rest. Replace the code as listed, create a Targa file to match, and run the program. You will need to add the LoadTGA function if you haven't done so already.

That's it. We've built up to this point but all the work we did before made this part a cinch. We'll make a class out of our graphics management beginning in the next section, but it'll take a while to put the entire thing together. Don't worry—we'll be done by the end of the chapter, with almost everything anyway.

One more thing: How do you create a Targa? The Paint program that comes with Windows spits out BMPs, but how do you get a Targa? Paint Shop Pro is your best bet; it's something I like and use. You can get a free trial version at **http://www.jasc.com/pspdl.html**, although you might want to buy a copy. I think it's under $85. (And if you're lucky, you might find it for around $50 after rebate. What a great deal!) If you work for a production studio, you might want to use PhotoShop. I think it normally sells for about $450.

Storage and Reindexing

Keeping the data together and making sure it all works together is key. So now here comes the class. *Classes*, as you probably know, contain all data relating to a single subject. We need to find all of the common types of data associated with a class dedicated to storing graphic data. Once we have the basic class explained, you will have a huge chunk of code. The class needs a few goals, so let's talk about those.

It needs:

➤ Position information—where it is on the screen

➤ Width, height, etc.

➤ Filename information—this information can also be used for identifying a particular graphic. When loading a graphic, we can use this name, which functions like the name of a person, instead of an index number. We'll discuss this more later, but this is the system that Quake uses to identify a texture associated with a surface. (Go, John Carmak.)

➤ A pointer to 16-bit data.

➤ A pointer to a temporary buffer. We can make this pointer one time to reduce memory usage.

➤ A bunch of flags to define behavior.

➤ Code to support compression. We'll discuss this in a little while so that you will understand why.

Now that we have the primary goals defined, let's examine the implementation in the following sections.

The SCREENOBJECT Portion of a Graphic

The position information is generic, and this code should be a separate class from which we can derive our soon-to-be graphic class. The reason is simple: Many items other than simply a loaded graphic will have this information and we don't want to write the same code 20 different times for different classes or situations. Some of the many objects that need this information are mouse pointers, interface buttons and menus, clickable areas, or just about anything that you will draw on the game screen.

Here is my class definition. You may want to change some of the names to suit your taste, but the names scx and scy were chosen carefully. Later on, when we discuss maps and world locations, we will introduce another set of x,y coordinates, so this can get really confusing. Any object on the screen will have a screen x,y and maybe a world x,y as part of its definition. Also, world objects will have their own Get and Set routines, which make a simple Get or Set difficult to use. It is up to you, but I prefer being wordy for two reasons: clarity and because I can type.

```
//*********************************************
typedef class SCREENOBJECT
{
protected:
      S16        scx, scy;      // screen position
      S16        Width, Height;

public:

      SCREENOBJECT ();
      ~SCREENOBJECT ();
         //---------------------------
      inline void  Clear ();
         //---------------------------

      //*************************
      // the following code segments are all inline code
      //*************************

      void  SetPosition ( int x, int y, int w, int h )
         {scx = (S16)x, scy = (S16)y; Width = (S16)w, Height = (S16)h;}
         //---------------------------
      void  SetScreenPosition ( int x, int y ) {scx = (S16)x, scy = (S16)y;}
      void  SetScreenX ( int x ) {scx = (S16)x;}
      void  SetScreenY ( int y ) {scy = (S16)y;}
         //---------------------------
      void  GetScreenPosition ( int& x, int& y ) {x = (S16)scx, y = (S16)scy;}
      int   GetScreenX () const {return scx;}
      int   GetScreenY () const {return scy;}
         //---------------------------
      void  SetDimensions ( int w, int h ) {Width = (S16)w, Height = (S16)h;}
```

```
    void   SetWidth  ( int w ) {Width = (S16)w;}
    void   SetHeight ( int h ) {Height = (S16)h;}
        //---------------------------
    void   GetDimensions ( int& w, int& h ) {w = (S16)Width, h = (S16)Height;}
    int    GetWidth () const {return Width;}
    int    GetHeight () const {return Height;}
        //---------------------------
    void   AddPosition ( int x, int y ) {scx += (S16)x, scy += (S16)y;}
    // offset
    void   AddX ( int x ) {scx += (S16)x;}
    void   AddY ( int y ) {scy += (S16)y;}
        //---------------------------
    bool   IsInside (int x, int y)
    {if (x>=scx && x<scx+Width && y>=scy && y<scy+Height) return 1;
    return 0;}
        //---------------------------
        //---------------------------
}SCREENOBJECT, * SCREENOBJECTptr, ** SCREENOBJECTlist;
//*********************************************
```

This class has very little information and is simple. By "simple," I mean it defines a basic component. This is a great way to define a base class. It doesn't do a lot or have a lot, but it provides functionality basic and necessary to all of its "children." (Kinda sounds like me and my kids.)

I don't think I need to explain much since this is really basic. The Get functions, when getting multiple variables, pass by reference. This is typical in my code and you might use it like the following:

```
//*********************************************
void main ()
{
    SCREENOBJECT obj;
    obj.SetScreenPosition (100, 100);
    int x, y;
    obj.GetScreenPosition (x, y);
}
//*********************************************
```

IsInside is used to tell if a point is inside the rectangle defining this SCREENOBJECT. Again, this is all very basic.

Hey, what is that SCREENOBJECTptr stuff at the end of the class? I like to define a pointer variable type to the class or structure I am defining. This prevents the use of too many asterisks, which some people like. I happen to prefer code I can read and ptr is easier (at least slightly) for me to read. Plus, having a special data type is cool.

Let's move on to the next section.

Filenames

We need our new graphic class to have a file-naming convention. You can pick anything you like. I prefer to waste about 220 bytes in an effort to simplify my life. You can reduce this significantly by changing the array size in string.h to something more like 64 bytes and it will almost always still work. The array size is just Mickey being paranoid, and I'm not talking about Mickey Mouse.

You may remember the file management system of the class FILEOBJECT. This class has three member variables that are essentially three filenames stored in the form of STRINGC, a string class I created. Actually, there is only one filename, but we break up the filename into its components. FileName is just the name of the file without an extension. The variable EXTENSIONS holds an enum of that value. FilePath is probably not too useful anymore, and I suggest that you try to eliminate it. However, I like it there. The last variable is FullName, which is great for fast loading but may not be terribly useful in this case. You may try to eliminate the FilePath and FullName variables, and with a little effort, you'll be just fine. For those who think that I'm wasting space… you're right. However, the smallest graphic that you are likely to encounter is 32x32, meaning at 16-bit its memory footprint is 2048 bytes. A few extra bytes in the name portion won't hurt anything. By the way, a 64x64 image takes 8K.

I suggest reducing the size if you are so inclined. It probably won't affect anything, but it may. I'll leave it as an exercise for you. It is useful to store the entire name in some instances. You will probably need the FilePath at least. When you save a level, you will want to know on the hard drive where you can find the original graphic.

Now that our GRAPHIC class has its necessary components, let's make it usable.

The GRAPHIC Class Definition

Here is the pinnacle of achievement. Well… maybe not. This is a good class for the encapsulation of drawing and loading graphics from BMPs and TGAs. The last few variables that we discussed earlier are in this code. We have a pointer to 16-bit graphics (U16ptr Image), a pointer to a temporary buffer (U16ptr ScratchPad), and a bunch of flags to define behavior at the end of the class definition (BITMAP_FLAGS flags).

We also now have code to support compression. These functions will be discussed at length, but you can get an idea by looking them over here.

```
// graphic.h

#ifndef _GRAPHIC_H_
#define _GRAPHIC_H_


#include "c:/library_cur/struct.h"
#include "c:/library_cur/fileobj.h"
#include "c:/library_cur/screenobj.h"


//*************************************************
//*************************************************
//*************************************************
class FILE_MASTER;
struct VERT2D_GROUP;


//*************************************************
```

```
//***************************************************
//***************************************************
// an encapsulation of loading, saving, bitmap conversion, and drawing

typedef class GRAPHIC : public FILEOBJECT, public SCREENOBJECT
{
        enum {MAXWIDTH=128, MAXHEIGHT=128};
protected:
        U16ptr      Image;
        U32         NumPixels;

        // a global bit of memory used by each GRAPHIC during the
        // load process to temporarily store data for processing static
        U16ptr      ScratchPad;

        static U16 SearchColor;
        static RECTANGLE  ClipRegion;                   // used for clipping

    //***************************
        U16ptr      CopyScratchPadIntoImage ();         // once we have data in the
                                                        // ScratchPad, we'll make it
                                                        // local

        // draw at the x,y location
        void        NormalBlit (SCREEN_STRUCT* screen, int x, int y);
                                                // draw clipped
        void        NormalBlitClipped (SCREEN_STRUCT* screen, int x, int y);
    //***************************

        // special compression that is a form of RLE, compressing only the
        // empty area around the actual data. The color eliminated is stored
        // in the gloabl class variable "SearchColor" above. Black can be used
        // in a graphic, so the most often used color is fuschia, red 31,
        // green 0, blue 31.
        // this color will never occur naturally.

        U16ptr      LLECompression16Bit (U16ptr Image, int wid, int hgt, U32ptr
                        NumPixels) const;               // compress this chunk
                                                        // of data, return a pointer
                                                        // to the compressed data.
        int         CountOsInAnArray16Bit (U16ptr a, int num) const;
        int         CountNonOsInAnArray16Bit (U16ptr a, int num) const;
        int         CountRuns16Bit (U16ptr Index, int num) const;
        void        LLECompressSingleLine16Bit (U16ptr Compress,
                        U16ptr Index, int width, int* BytesInLine) const;

    // ***************************
        // drawing routine for the special compression

        void        DrawLLECompressed16Bit (SCREEN_STRUCT* sc, int x, int y);
        void        DrawLLECompressed_Clipped16Bit (SCREEN_STRUCT* sc, int x,
                        int y);
```

```
       void        DrawLLECompressed16Bit (SCREEN_STRUCT* sc);
       void        DrawLLECompressed_Clipped16Bit (SCREEN_STRUCT* sc);

       // ***************************
       // various loading routine for BMP

       bool        Load24Bit (FILE_MASTER* file); // bitmap loading
       bool        Load8Bit (FILE_MASTER* file, int numcolor);
       bool        Load4Bit (FILE_MASTER* file, int numcolor);
       void        ConvertTo16Bit (U16ptr buff, RGBVal* read, int num);
       void        ConvertTo_5x6x5 (U16ptr ptr, int num);

           // the void* below is the windows defined PALETTEENTRY, but I
           // don't want to include windows.h in this header, it will be
           // cast on the far end
       void        ConvertIndexToRGB (RGBVal* rgb, U8* index, void* pe, int len);
       void        Convert4BitIndexToRGB (RGBVal* rgb, U8* index, void* palent,
                                           int len);

       // ***************************
       // other loading routines

       bool        LoadLLE ();
       bool        LoadTGA ();

       void        ConvertTo_5x5x5 ();
       void        ConvertTo_5x6x5 ();

       // ***************************

public:
       GRAPHIC ( int IndependantFlag = 0 );
       ~GRAPHIC ();
       void        SetScratchPad (U16ptr ptr) {ScratchPad = ptr;}
       void        PassScratchPad (U16ptr ptr) {ScratchPad = ptr;}
       void        SetClipRectangle (RECTANGLE& r) {ClipRegion = r;}
       void        GetClipRectangle (RECTANGLE& r) {r = ClipRegion;}
       void        Clear ();
       void        SetIndependant (int flag = 1);

       bool        IsValid () {if (Image && NumPixels) return true; return false;}

       void        operator = (GRAPHIC& gr);        // assignment operators
       void        operator = (GRAPHIC* gr);        // duplicates image, new memory
       // FileName and FilePath are copied

       //***************************

       // load by filename and convert to 16 bit compressed
       bool        Load (STRINGC* str) {SetPath (str); return Load ();}
       // derived from the parent class
       bool        Load () {return true;}
```

```
bool        Load (STRINGC* , int CompressFlag = 1);
bool        Load (FILE_MASTER* file); // load as part of a save file


//***************************

bool        Save () ;
bool        Save (STRINGC*);       // save the compressed data to a new file
bool        Save (FILE_MASTER* file);


//***************************

void        DrawAt (SCREEN_STRUCT* screen, int x, int y);
void        Draw (SCREEN_STRUCT* screen);   // draws at 0, 0
void        DrawSkewedSprite (SCREEN_STRUCT* screen, VERT2D_GROUP* sp, int
                            SplitFlag = 0);
// not split/ 1 top half fills area /2 bottom half fills area
void        DrawAtCorner (SCREEN_STRUCT* screen, int x, int y);


//***************************

inline int    GetWidth () const {return Width;}
inline int    GetHeight () const {return Height;}
inline int    GetNumPixels () const {return NumPixels;}
inline U16ptr GetImage () const {return Image;}


//***************************
//***************************

BITMAP_FLAGS    flags;              // public flags available to all for
                                    // the bitmap
}*GRAPHICptr, MGRAPHIC;


//**************************************************
//**************************************************
//**************************************************
```

The GRAPHIC.CPP Listing

Look over the following code. Take a day or so to thoroughly understand it. Parts of it are really complex. This code loads BMPs and TGAs, compresses data when told to do so into my own format (LLE, or Line Length Encoding), clips data, and even draws images centered on a frame buffer. It even supports 4-bit and 24-bit BMPs, compressing them when called for. All read data is converted to 16-bit and any loaded are converted to 15-bit and 16-bit when appropriate. This is a robust class that will provide the foundation for all the 2-D graphics. Inspect it carefully.

```
#include <windows.h>
#include "graphic.h"
#include " asm.h"
#include " fileobj.h"
```

```
#ifndef NULL
#define NULL OL

#endif

//*******************************************
U16 GRAPHIC :: SearchColor = (248<<7)+ (248>>3);
RECTANGLE GRAPHIC :: ClipRegion = {0, 0, 640, 480};

//*******************************************
//*******************************************

GRAPHIC :: GRAPHIC (int IndependantFlag)
{
     Clear ();
     flags.Flag.NO_SCRATCH_PAD = (U16) IndependantFlag;
}


               //********************************

U16ptr GRAPHIC :: ScratchPad = NULL;   // init the scratchpad

               //********************************
               //********************************

GRAPHIC :: ~GRAPHIC ()
{
     if (Image) delete Image;
}


               //********************************
               //********************************
inline
void  GRAPHIC :: Clear ()
{
     Image = NULL;
     NumPixels = 0;
     // ScratchPad = NULL;
     flags.Flag.COMPRESSED = true;
}


               //********************************

void  GRAPHIC :: SetIndependant (int flag)
{
     flags.Flag.NO_SCRATCH_PAD = flag;
}


               //********************************

void  GRAPHIC :: operator = (GRAPHIC& gr)
{
```

```
          Width = gr.Width;
          Height = gr.Height;
          scx = gr.scx;
          scy = gr.scy;
          FileName = gr.FileName;
          FilePath = gr.FilePath;
          FileType = gr.FileType;
          NumPixels = gr.NumPixels;
          Image = new U16 [NumPixels];
          Memcpy16Bit (Image, gr.Image, NumPixels);
}


          //*******************************

void  GRAPHIC :: operator = (GRAPHIC* gr)
{
          Width = gr->Width;
          Height = gr->Height;
          scx = gr->scx;
          scy = gr->scy;
          FileName = gr->FileName;
          FilePath = gr->FilePath;
          FileType = gr->FileType;
          NumPixels = gr->NumPixels;
          Image = new U16 [NumPixels];
          Memcpy16Bit (Image, gr->Image, NumPixels);
}
          //*******************************

          //*******************************
          //*******************************

void  GRAPHIC :: DrawAt (SCREEN_STRUCT* screen, int x, int y) // centered
{
        // x = 100, y = 100;
        if (flags.Flag.COMPRESSED == false) NormalBlit (screen, x-(Width>>1),
           y-(Height>>1));
        else DrawLLECompressed16Bit (screen, x-(Width>>1), y-(Height>>1));
}


          //*******************************

void  GRAPHIC :: Draw (SCREEN_STRUCT* screen)           // draws at 0, 0
{
        int cx = (screen->Width/2)-(Width/2);
        int cy = (screen->Height/2)-(Height/2);
        if (flags.Flag.COMPRESSED == false) NormalBlit (screen, cx, cy);
        else DrawLLECompressed16Bit (screen, cx, cy);
}

void  GRAPHIC :: DrawAtCorner (SCREEN_STRUCT* screen, int x, int y)
{
```

```
            if (flags.Flag.COMPRESSED == false) NormalBlit (screen, x, y);
            else DrawLLECompressed16Bit (screen, x, y);
}

                //********************************

void  GRAPHIC :: NormalBlit (SCREEN_STRUCT* screen, int x, int y)
{
        if ((y<ClipRegion.top) || (x<ClipRegion.left)
            || (y+Height > ClipRegion.bottom) || (x+Width > ClipRegion.right))
            { NormalBlitClipped (screen, x, y); return;}
        U16ptr  image = Image, sc = screen->Screen;
        int  scwid = screen->Width;
        int h = Height, w = Width;

        sc += y*scwid+x;
        while (h--)
        {
            Memcpy16Bit (sc, image, w);
            sc+=scwid, image+=w;
        }
}

                //********************************

void  GRAPHIC :: NormalBlitClipped (SCREEN_STRUCT* screen, int x, int y)
{
        if (screen == NULL) return;
        int  SC_WIDTH = screen->Width, SC_HEIGHT = screen->Height;
        int wid = Width, w = wid, h = Height;
        U16ptr mp = Image;

        if (x+w<ClipRegion.left)    {return;}
        if (y+h<ClipRegion.top)     {return;}
        if (x>=ClipRegion.right)    {return;}
        if (y>=ClipRegion.bottom)   {return;}


        if (x >= ClipRegion.right-w)  w = ClipRegion.right-x;
        if (y >= ClipRegion.bottom-h) h = ClipRegion.bottom-y;
        if (x < ClipRegion.left) {mp += ClipRegion.left-x; w -=
            ClipRegion.left-x; x = ClipRegion.left;}
        if (y < ClipRegion.top) {mp += (ClipRegion.top-y)*wid; h -=
            ClipRegion.top-y; y = ClipRegion.top;}

        U16ptr ptr= screen->Screen + x+ y*SC_WIDTH;

        while (h-- > 0)
        {
            Memcpy16Bit (ptr, mp, w);
            ptr+=SC_WIDTH, mp+=wid;
        }
}
```

```
//*******************************
//*******************************

//*******************************
//*******************************

bool  GRAPHIC :: Load (STRINGC* str, int CompressFlag)
// load by filename and convert to 16 bit compressed
{
      flags.Flag.COMPRESSED = (U16) CompressFlag;
      // make sure we have this flag

      if (!flags.Flag.NO_SCRATCH_PAD && ScratchPad == NULL) return false;
      if (Image != NULL) {delete Image; Image = NULL;}
      SetPath ( str );

      if (FileType == LLE) return LoadLLE ();
      if (FileType == TGA) return LoadTGA ();
      if (FileType != BMP) return false;

      // bmp by default
      BITMAPFILEHEADER Header;
      BITMAPINFOHEADER Info;

//*************** assumes a BMP for now ***********************
      FILE_MASTER      file (str, FILE_MASTER :: READ);
      if (file.Status () != FILE_MASTER::NONE) return false;

      if (file.Read (&Header, sizeof (BITMAPFILEHEADER))) {return false;}
      if (file.Read (&Info, sizeof (BITMAPINFOHEADER))) {return false; }

      Height = (U16) Info.biHeight, Width = (U16) Info.biWidth;
      if (Info.biBitCount == 16) return false;
      // we do not support 16 bit bitmaps

      if (flags.Flag.NO_SCRATCH_PAD && ScratchPad) delete ScratchPad;

      if (flags.Flag.NO_SCRATCH_PAD) ScratchPad = new U16 [2*Height*Width];

      if (Info.biBitCount == 24) if (Load24Bit (&file)==false) return false;
      if (Info.biBitCount == 8) if (Load8Bit (&file, Info.biClrUsed)==false)
         return false;
      if (Info.biBitCount == 4) if (Load4Bit (&file, Info.biClrUsed)==false)
         return false;
      if (Info.biBitCount != 1)
      {
           if (CompressFlag) Image = LLECompression16Bit (ScratchPad,
              Width, Height, &NumPixels);
           else
           {
                Image = CopyScratchPadIntoImage ();
                NumPixels = Width*Height;
```

```
            }
        }

        //***************
        flags.Flag.LOADED = true;
        if (flags.Flag.NO_SCRATCH_PAD && ScratchPad)
        {
            delete ScratchPad;
            ScratchPad = NULL;
        }

        return true;
}

            //********************************
bool   GRAPHIC :: Load (FILE_MASTER* file) // load as part of a save file
{
        if (Image) delete Image;
        int temp = flags.Flag.BIT_PATTERN ;

        if (file->Status () != FILE_MASTER::NONE) return false;

        if (file->Read (&flags, sizeof (int))) return false;
        if (file->Read (&Width, sizeof (int))) return false;
        if (file->Read (&Height, sizeof (int))) return false;
        if (file->Read (&NumPixels, sizeof (int))) return false;

        Image = new U16 [NumPixels];
        if (file->Read (Image, NumPixels*sizeof (U16))) return false;
        if (flags.Flag.BIT_PATTERN != temp)
        // if the saved file is a different pattern than the current display
        {
            if (flags.Flag.BIT_PATTERN == GRAPHIC_MGR::_5x5x5_)
            {
                ConvertTo_5x6x5 ();
            }
            else
            {
                ConvertTo_5x5x5 ();
            }
        }
        flags.Flag.LOADED = true;
        return true;
}

            //********************************
bool   GRAPHIC :: LoadLLE ()                // only called if passed name was an lle
{
        STRINGC string = FilePath + "/" + FileName + ".lle";
        int temp = flags.Flag.BIT_PATTERN ;
```

13

Chapter

```
            FILE_MASTER        file (string, FILE_MASTER :: READ);
            if (file.Status () != FILE_MASTER::NONE) return false;

            if (file.Read (&flags, sizeof (int))) return false;
            if (file.Read (&Width, sizeof (int))) return false;
            if (file.Read (&Height, sizeof (int))) return false;

            if (file.Read (&NumPixels, sizeof (int))) return false;
            if (file.Read (Image, NumPixels*sizeof (U16))) return false;

                if (flags.Flag.BIT_PATTERN != temp)
            // if the saved file is a different pattern than the current display
            {
                if (flags.Flag.BIT_PATTERN == GRAPHIC_MGR::_5x5x5_)
                {
                    ConvertTo_5x6x5 ();
                }
                else
                {
                    ConvertTo_5x5x5 ();
                }
            }
            flags.Flag.LOADED = true;
            return true;
    }

    void  GRAPHIC :: ConvertTo_5x6x5 ()
    {
            int num = NumPixels;
            U16ptr ptr = Image;
            U16 RMask = 31<<10;
            U16 GMask = 31<<5;
            U16 BMask = 31;
            while (num--)
            {
                U32 r = *ptr & RMask;
                U32 g = *ptr & GMask;
                U32 b = *ptr & BMask;
                *ptr++ = (U16)((r<<1) + (g<<1) + b);
            }
    }

    void  GRAPHIC :: ConvertTo_5x5x5 ()
    {
            int num = NumPixels;
            U16ptr ptr = Image;
            U16 RMask = 31<<11;
            U16 GMask = 31<<6;
            U16 BMask = 31;
            while (num--)
            {
                U32 r = *ptr & RMask;
```

```
                    U32 g = *ptr & GMask;
                    U32 b = *ptr & BMask;
                    *ptr++ = (U16) ((r>>1) + (g>>1) + b);
            }
    }


void  GRAPHIC :: ConvertTo_5x6x5 (U16ptr ptr, int num)
{
        U16 RMask = 31<<10;
        U16 GMask = 31<<5;
        U16 BMask = 31;
        while (num--)
        {
                U32 r = *ptr & RMask;
                U32 g = *ptr & GMask;
                U32 b = *ptr & BMask;
                *ptr++ = (U16) ((r<<1) + (g<<1) + b);
        }
}


                //*********************************
                //*********************************

bool  GRAPHIC :: LoadTGA ()
{
        STRINGC string = FilePath + "/" + FileName;
        string += ".tga";
        TARGA_HEADER header;

        FILE_MASTER        file (string, FILE_MASTER :: READ);
        if (file.Status () != FILE_MASTER::NONE) return false;
        if (file.Read (&header, sizeof (TARGA_HEADER))) return false;

        Width = header.Width;
        Height = header.Height;

        // scratchpad is a variable used to temporarily load in data,
        // this allows us compression/encoding
        // we can declare this globally and set the flag
        // "flags.Flag.NO_SCRATCH_PAD"
        // when we pass the memory pointer to this class
        // so that we don't allocate and then deallocate memory, hopefully
        // preventing memory fragmentation
        if (flags.Flag.NO_SCRATCH_PAD && ScratchPad) delete ScratchPad;
        if (flags.Flag.NO_SCRATCH_PAD) ScratchPad = new U16 [Height*Width*2];

        if (header.PixelDepth == 8) return false; // no support for 8 bit
        if (header.PixelDepth == 16)
        {
                for (int i=Height-1; i>-1; i--)
                {
```

13

Chapter

```
                        U16ptr ptr = ScratchPad+i*Width;

                            if (file.Read (ptr, Width<<1)) return false; // 16 bit
        }
                if (flags.Flag.BIT_PATTERN == GRAPHIC_MGR::_5x6x5_)
                    ConvertTo_5x6x5 (ScratchPad, Width*Height);
                if (flags.Flag.COMPRESSED == false) Image =
                    CopyScratchPadIntoImage ();
                else Image = LLECompression16Bit (ScratchPad, Width, Height,
                    &NumPixels);
        }
        if (header.PixelDepth == 24)
        {
        int readlen = 3*Width;
        RGBVal* read = new RGBVal[Width+1];             // an array for temp storage
                                                        // and conversion
                for (int i=Height-1; i>=0; i--)
                {
                U16ptr ptr = ScratchPad+i*Width; // offset pointer
                    if (file.Read (read, readlen)) return false;

                    ConvertTo16Bit (ptr, read, Width);
                    // stores the 16 bit data in ptr
                }
                delete read;
                if (flags.Flag.COMPRESSED == false) Image =
                    CopyScratchPadIntoImage ();
                else Image = LLECompression16Bit (ScratchPad, Width, Height,
                                            &NumPixels);
        }
        flags.Flag.LOADED = true;

        if (flags.Flag.NO_SCRATCH_PAD && ScratchPad) // clean up temporary
                                                     // memory if necessary
        {
                delete ScratchPad;
                ScratchPad = NULL;
        }

        return true;
}


                //*******************************

                //*******************************
                //*******************************

bool  GRAPHIC :: Save ()            // save the compressed data to a new file
{
        // if (flags.Flag.COMPRESSED == false) return false;
        STRINGC string = FilePath + "/" + FileName + ".lle";
```

```
        FILE_MASTER            file (string, FILE_MASTER :: WRITE);
        if (file.Status () != FILE_MASTER::NONE) return false;

        if (file.Write (&flags, sizeof (int))) return FALSE;
        if (file.Write (&Width, sizeof (int))) return FALSE;
        if (file.Write (&Height, sizeof (int))) return FALSE;

        if (file.Write (&NumPixels, sizeof (int))) return FALSE;
        if (file.Write (Image, NumPixels*sizeof (U16))) return FALSE;

        return true;
}


        //********************************

bool  GRAPHIC :: Save (STRINGC* str)
{
        SetPath (str);
        return Save ();
}


        //********************************

bool  GRAPHIC :: Save (FILE_MASTER* file)
{
        // if (flags.Flag.COMPRESSED == false) return false;
        if (file->Status () != FILE_MASTER::NONE) return false;

        if (file->Write (&flags, sizeof (int))) return FALSE;
        if (file->Write (&Width, sizeof (int))) return FALSE;
        if (file->Write (&Height, sizeof (int))) return FALSE;

        if (file->Write (&NumPixels, sizeof (int))) return FALSE;
        if (file->Write (Image, NumPixels*sizeof (U16))) return FALSE;
        return true;
}


        //********************************
        //********************************
        //********************************
        //********************************

bool  GRAPHIC :: Load24Bit (FILE_MASTER* file)
{
        // int LoadWidth = (Width&3) ? (Width+(4-(Width&3))):(Width);
        int readlen = sizeof (RGBVal)*Width+(Width&3);
        RGBVal* read = new RGBVal[Width+1];

        for (int i=Height-1; i>=0; i--)
        {
            U16ptr ptr = ScratchPad+i*Width;
```

```
                        if (file->Read (read, readlen)) return false;

                        ConvertTo16Bit (ptr, read, Width);
                            // stores the 16 bit data in ptr
                }
                delete read;
                return true;
        }


                    //*******************************

bool   GRAPHIC :: Load4Bit (FILE_MASTER* file, int numcolor)
{
        if (numcolor == 0) numcolor = 16;
        int LoadWidth = (Width&7) ? (Width+(8-(Width&7))):(Width);

        PALETTEENTRY* pe = new PALETTEENTRY[numcolor];
        RGBVal* rgb = new RGBVal[Width];
        U8ptr   index = new U8[Width];

        if (file->Read (pe, sizeof (PALETTEENTRY)*numcolor)) return false;

        // read indexes
        for (int i=Height-1; i>=0; i--)
        {
            U16ptr ptr = ScratchPad+i*Width;

            if (file->Read (index, LoadWidth>>1)) return false;

            Convert4BitIndexToRGB (rgb, index, pe, Width);
                    // now we have the colors in 'rgb'
            ConvertTo16Bit (ptr, rgb, Width);
                    // stores the 16 bit data in ptr
        }

        delete index, rgb, pe;
        return true;
}

                    //*******************************

bool   GRAPHIC :: Load8Bit (FILE_MASTER* file, int numcolor)
{
        if (numcolor == 0) numcolor = 256;
        int LoadWidth = (Width&3) ? (Width+(4-(Width&3))):(Width);

        PALETTEENTRY* pe = new PALETTEENTRY[numcolor];
        RGBVal* rgb = new RGBVal[LoadWidth];
        U8ptr   index = new U8[LoadWidth];

        // read palette
        if (file->Read (pe, sizeof (PALETTEENTRY)*numcolor)) return false;
```

```
            // read indexes
            for (int i=Height-1; i>=0; i--)
            {
                  U16ptr ptr = ScratchPad+i*Width;

                  if (file->Read (index, LoadWidth)) return false;

                  ConvertIndexToRGB (rgb, index, pe, Width);
                              // now we have the colors in 'rgb'
                  ConvertTo16Bit (ptr, rgb, Width);
                              // stores the 16 bit data in ptr
            }

            delete index, rgb, pe;
            return true;
      }


                  //********************************
                  //********************************
      inline
      void  GRAPHIC :: ConvertTo16Bit (U16ptr buff, RGBVal* read, int num)
      {
            if (flags.Flag.BIT_PATTERN == GRAPHIC_MGR::_5x5x5_)
            while (num--)
            {
                  *buff = read->Convert15 ();
                  buff++, read++;
            }
            else
                  while (num--)
            {
                  *buff = read->Convert16 ();
                  buff++, read++;
            }
      }


                  //********************************
      inline
      void  GRAPHIC :: ConvertIndexToRGB (RGBVal* rgb, U8* index, void* palent, int len)
      {
            if (len < 1) return;
            PALETTEENTRY* pe = (PALETTEENTRY*) palent;
            while (len--)
            {
                  PALETTEENTRY* p = &pe[*index];

                  rgb->b = p->peRed;
                  rgb->g = p->peGreen;
                  rgb->r = p->peBlue;
                  rgb++; index++;
            }
      }
```

```
                    //*******************************
inline
void  GRAPHIC :: Convert4BitIndexToRGB (RGBVal* rgb, U8* index, void* palent,
                                        int len)
{
      if (len < 1) return;
      PALETTEENTRY* pe = (PALETTEENTRY*) palent;
      int l = len;
      l>>=1;
      while (l--)
      {
            int x = *index++;
            PALETTEENTRY* p = &pe[x>>4];    // high 16

            rgb->b = p->peRed;                  // colors are backwards in 4 bit
            rgb->g = p->peGreen;
            rgb->r = p->peBlue;
            rgb++;

            p = &pe[x&15];                      // low 16
            rgb->b = p->peRed;
            rgb->g = p->peGreen;
            rgb->r = p->peBlue;
            rgb++;
      }
      if (len&1)
      {
            int x = *index++;
            PALETTEENTRY* p = &pe[x>>4];    // high 16

            rgb->b = p->peRed;                  // colors are backwards in 4 bit
            rgb->g = p->peGreen;
            rgb->r = p->peBlue;
            rgb++;
      }
}
                    //*******************************
                    //*******************************


U16ptr
GRAPHIC :: CopyScratchPadIntoImage ()
{
      U16ptr ptr = new U16[Width*Height];
      Memcpy16Bit (ptr, ScratchPad, Width*Height);
      return ptr;
}

//***********************************

U16ptr GRAPHIC :: LLECompression16Bit (U16ptr Image, int wid, int hgt,
                                       U32ptr NumPixels) const
{
```

```
        int w = wid, h = hgt, size;
        int BytesInLine = 0;

        U16ptr TempCompress, CompressPtr, RetCompress;
        U16ptr ImagePtr = Image;               // used for the bitmap; we'll be using
                                               // this for the actual compression

        TempCompress = new U16[w*(h<<2)];    // we don't know how big this
        // compressed data will be so we make it really big just in case.
        CompressPtr = TempCompress;            // a pointer to the temporary buffer
        if (TempCompress == NULL)              // memory not available
        {
            if (TempCompress != NULL) delete TempCompress;
            *NumPixels = 0;
            return NULL;
        }

        //********************

        while (h--)
        {
            // ****** get all of the necessary data for this scan line ******
            LLECompressSingleLine16Bit (CompressPtr, ImagePtr, w, &BytesInLine);

            CompressPtr += BytesInLine;        // offset pointer
            ImagePtr += w;                     // move to the next scan line
        }

        size = CompressPtr-TempCompress;       // memory handling

        RetCompress = new U16[size];           // 2 bytes for every one
        if (RetCompress == NULL)               // no memory
        {
            if (TempCompress != NULL) delete TempCompress;
            return NULL;
        }

        Memcpy16Bit (RetCompress, TempCompress, size);

        *NumPixels = size;                     // global

        delete TempCompress;                   // clear up our temporary memory
        return RetCompress;
}

        //*******************************
inline
int GRAPHIC ::  CountOsInAnArray16Bit (U16ptr a, int num) const
{
        int count=0;
        while ((*a == SearchColor) && (count<num))
```

```
                {count++; a++;}

        return count;
}

                //********************************
inline
int GRAPHIC ::  CountNonOsInAnArray16Bit (U16ptr a, int num) const
{
        int count=0;
        while ((*a != SearchColor) && (count<num))
        {a++; count++;}

        return count;
}

                //********************************

int GRAPHIC ::  CountRuns16Bit (U16ptr Index, int num) const
{
        int w = 0, count = 0;
        while (w<num)
        {
            int r=CountOsInAnArray16Bit (Index, num-w);
            w+=r;
            if (w==num) break;                  // in case we finish the full line
            Index+=r;

            int g=CountNonOsInAnArray16Bit (Index, num-w);
            w+=g;
            Index+=g;

            if (count == 0)
            {
                count=1;                        // at least one block of real data
                if (w==num && !r) break;   // for a full single line of data
            }
            count++;                            // a split line
            if (w==num) break;                  // in case we finish the full line
        }
        return count;
}

                //********************************

void GRAPHIC :: LLECompressSingleLine16Bit (U16ptr Compress, U16ptr Image, int
                                    width, int* BytesInLine) const
{
        U16ptr  ptr=Compress+1;      // skip the first 2 bytes to store the count
        int NumBytes = 1;            // we will have at least one "byte" to
                                     // return, this will be the count at the
                                     // beginning of the scan line
```

```
        int count = CountRuns16Bit (Image, width);
        *Compress = (U16)count;        // store that value

        if (count==0)                  // nothing in this line
        {
            *BytesInLine = 1;          // minimum
            return;
        }
        if (count==1)                  // this is a solid line, no block section
        {
            Memcpy16Bit (ptr, Image, width);
            *BytesInLine = width +1;
            return;
        }


            //*******************
    // now we know that we have at least one block section
    while (--count>0)
    // this assumes that we start with 0s and end with 0s
    // subtract one to start
    // ---we do 2 sections at a time... the last 0's section will not
    // count in the end
    {
            int c=CountOsInAnArray16Bit (Image, width);
        *ptr++=(U16)c;              // we store how many 0's and advance pointer
            width -=c;              // we update our distance left
            Image += c;             // advance the pointer to the picture data
            NumBytes++;             // one more byte for the count

            int l=CountNonOsInAnArray16Bit (Image, width);
            *ptr++=(U16)l;          // we store the number of non 0 colors
            NumBytes++;             // one more byte
        Memcpy16Bit (ptr, Image, l);
                                    // now we store the colors and then offset both
            ptr+=(U16)l;            // offset the destination pointer
            NumBytes+=l;            // a few more bytes
            Image += l;             // offset the pointer for the next section of 0's
            width -=l;              // we update our distance left
    }
        *BytesInLine = NumBytes;   // minimum
    // all of the data has been stored and compressed so now we return
}

//***********************************
//*******************************


void GRAPHIC :: DrawLLECompressed16Bit (SCREEN_STRUCT* sc, int x, int y)
{
        if (Image == NULL) return;
        if (sc->Screen == NULL) return;

        int  w = Width, h = Height;    // local variables
```

```
        // handle clipping here, testing for partially clipped.
        // DrawLLECompressed_Clipped16Bit may end up clipping the entire image

        if ((y<ClipRegion.top) || (x<ClipRegion.left)
            || (y+h > ClipRegion.bottom) || (x+w > ClipRegion.right))
        {
            DrawLLECompressed_Clipped16Bit (sc, x, y);
            return;
        }


        //**************** regular drawing

        U16ptr pointr = sc->Screen+ x+ (y*sc->Width);        // starting location
        U16ptr scptr;
        U16ptr index  = Image;
        int  len, wid = sc->Width;
        int  runs;


        //**************** loop

        while (h-- > 0)                 // once for each scan line
        {
            scptr = pointr;             // temp screen pointer
            runs = *index++;            // get the number of runs for the
                                        // line and advance the pointer
            if (runs == 1)              // copy entire scan line.
            {
                Memcpy16Bit (scptr, index, w);
                index += w;
            }
            else                        // 0 will fall out automatically, we
                                        // don't need to test for it
            {
                while (--runs>0)
                {
                    scptr += *index++;  // move the screen pointer over
                                        // to its new destination 0's
                    len = *index++;     // get run length and advance

                    Memcpy16Bit (scptr, index, len);    // grab data
                    scptr += len;       // advance temp pointer
                    index += len;       // advance image pointer
                }
            }
            pointr += wid;              // advance screen position in y direction
        }
    }


            //*******************************ClipRegion

void GRAPHIC :: DrawLLECompressed_Clipped16Bit (SCREEN_STRUCT* sc, int x, int y)
{
```

```
U16ptr  pointr = sc->Screen + x + (y*sc->Width);     // starting location
U16ptr  scptr;
U16ptr  index  = Image;
int  len, bytes, clipleft = 0, clipright = 0, newlen, newdist;
int  runs;
int  top = ClipRegion.top, left = ClipRegion.left, bottom =
     ClipRegion.bottom, right = ClipRegion.right,
     height = sc->Height, width = sc->Width;
int  w = Width, h = Height;

if (y < top-h) return;              // totally clipped, do not draw
if (y >= bottom) return;
if (x < left-w) return;
if (x >= right) return;

if (y+h > bottom)                   // clip bottom
{
    h = bottom-y;                   // shorten height...simple
}

// run through normal drawing to get to the desired line advance
// index pointer. We are pretending to draw here so that we can clip
// properly in the y direction.
while (y<top)
{
    y++; pointr += width; h--;      // move toward our goal
    int runs = *index++;            // get the number of runs for the
                                    // line and advance the pointer

    if (runs == 1) {index += w;}    // a full scan line of data to skip
    else                            // 0 will fall out automatically, we
                                    // don't need to test for it
    {
        while (--runs>0)
        {
            index++;                // move the screen pointer over to
                                    // its new destination 0's
            len = *index++;         // get run length and advance
            index += len;
        }
    }
}
if (x < left) {clipleft = left-x;}  // set the relative distance,
                                    // this will give us a distval
if (x+w > right) {clipright = right-x;}

while (h-- > 0)                     // once for each scan line
{
    scptr = pointr;                 // temporary screen pointer

    runs = *index++;                // get the number of runs for the
                                    // line and advance the pointer

    if (runs == 1)
```

```
        {
                if (clipleft)               // clipping on the left.. complicated
                {
                        len = w-clipleft;
                        scptr += clipleft;
                        index += clipleft;
                        Memcpy16Bit (scptr, index, len);     // grab data
                        index -= clipleft;
                }
                else if (clipright)         // clipping on the right, easy
                {
                        len = clipright;
                        Memcpy16Bit (scptr, index, len);     // grab data
                }
                else Memcpy16Bit (scptr, index, w);
                index+=w;
        }
        else                                // 0 will fall out automatically,
                                            // we don't need to test for it
        {
                bytes = 0;
                while (--runs>0)
                {
                        bytes += *index;        // for a count
                        scptr += *index++;      // move the screen pointer over
                                                // to its new destination 0's

                        len = *index++;         // get run length and advance
                        if (clipleft)
                        {
                                if (bytes >= clipleft)          // no clip
                                {
                                        Memcpy16Bit (scptr, index, len);
                                                // grab data
                                }
                                else if (bytes+len >= clipleft)
                                                // we need to clip it
                                {
                                        newdist = clipleft-bytes;
                                        newlen = len-newdist;
                                        scptr += newdist;
                                                // move to the 0 location
                                        index += newdist;
                                        Memcpy16Bit (scptr, index, newlen);
                                                // store data
                                        scptr -= newdist;
                                                // complete adds
                                        index -= newdist;
                                                // this will be updated below
                                }
                                                // dont draw
```

```
                                    // else
                    }
                    else if (clipright)
                    {
                         if (bytes >= clipright) {}        // do nothing
                         else if (bytes+len < clipright)
                         {
                              Memcpy16Bit (scptr, index, len);
                                        // grab data
                         }
                         else              // clip
                         {
                              int newdist = clipright-bytes;
                              Memcpy16Bit (scptr, index, newdist);
                                        // store data
                         }
                    }
                    else Memcpy16Bit (scptr, index, len); // grab data
                    bytes += len;        // update count
                    scptr += len;
                    index += len;
               }
          }
          pointr += width;
     }
}


//*******************************
//*******************************


//**************************************
//**************************************
```

Using Our New LLE

Here are a few changes to our LoadTGA function. This is the same code given at the beginning of this chapter. The main change is the LLECompression16Bit call, which is where we now compress this data. Notice this line of code:

```
if (flags.Flag.COMPRESSED == false)…
```

This flag is set by you. You have to tell the GRAPHIC, before you load the image data, if you want the data compressed. It may seem like an extra step, but flags.Flag.COMPRESSED is set to TRUE by default so you must turn it off. Almost all images you will load into your game will probably need the compressed image anyway.

And now that we have this code completed, we'll pop the class into our loop after we load it:

```
//********************************

bool  GRAPHIC :: LoadTGA ()
{
     STRINGC string = FilePath + "/";
     String += FileName;
     string += ".tga";
     TARGA_HEADER header;

     FILE_MASTER      file (string, FILE_MASTER :: READ);
     if (file.Status () != FILE_MASTER :: NONE) return false;
     if (file.Read (&header, sizeof (TARGA_HEADER))) return false;

     Width = header.Width;
     Height = header.Height;

     // scratchpad is a variable used to temporarily load in data,
     // this allows us compression/encoding
     // we can declare this globally and set the flag
     // "flags.Flag.NO_SCRATCH_PAD"
     // when we pass the memory pointer to this class
     // so that we don't allocate and then deallocate memory, hopefully
     // preventing memory fragmentation
     if (flags.Flag.NO_SCRATCH_PAD && ScratchPad) delete ScratchPad;
     if (flags.Flag.NO_SCRATCH_PAD) ScratchPad = new U16 [Height*Width*2];

     if (header.PixelDepth == 8) return false; // no support for 8 bit
     if (header.PixelDepth == 16)
     {
          for (int i=Height-1; i>-1; i--)
     {
          U16ptr ptr = ScratchPad+i*Width;

               if (file.Read (ptr, Width<<1)) return false; // 16 bit
     }
          if (flags.Flag.BIT_PATTERN == GRAPHIC_MGR :: _5x6x5_)
               ConvertTo_5x6x5 (ScratchPad, Width*Height);
          if (flags.Flag.COMPRESSED == false) Image =
               CopyScratchPadIntoImage ();
          else Image = LLECompression16Bit (ScratchPad, Width, Height,
                                             &NumPixels);
     }
     if (header.PixelDepth == 24)
     {
     int readlen = 3*Width;
     RGBVal* read = new RGBVal[Width+1];           // an array for temp storage
                                                   // and conversion
          for (int i=Height-1; i>=0; i--)
          {
          U16ptr ptr = ScratchPad+i*Width;        // offset pointer
               if (file.Read (read, readlen)) return false;
```

```
                         ConvertTo16Bit (ptr, read, Width);    // stores the 16 bit
                                                               // data in ptr
                    }
               delete read;
               if (flags.Flag.COMPRESSED == false) Image =
                    CopyScratchPadIntoImage ();
               else Image = LLECompression16Bit (ScratchPad, Width, Height,
                                                  &NumPixels);
          }
          flags.Flag.LOADED = true;

          if (flags.Flag.NO_SCRATCH_PAD && ScratchPad)
          // clean up temporary memory if necessary
          {
               delete ScratchPad;
               ScratchPad = NULL;
          }

          return true;
     }


//*******************************
```

Remember the code in loops.cpp? I've made some minor modifications here. The init is modified to accommodate the GRAPHIC class and the compression does take place. This means that all you will see is the red X. You will need to change the directory to whatever your CD-ROM drive is.

```
//*******************************
GRAPHIC* Graphic = NULL;

//*******************************
void   InitLoops ()
{
     int NoExternalScratchPad = 1;
     int compress = 1;
     Graphic = new GRAPHIC (NoExternalScratchPad);
     STRINGC str = "e:/pictures/test2.tga";
     Graphic->Load (&str, compress);
}
//*******************************
void   CleanupLoops ()
{
     if (Graphic)
     {
          if (Graphic)
               delete Graphic;
     }
}
//*******************************
//*******************************
void   Draw (DIRECT_DRAW_MANAGER* ddraw)
{
```

```
        SCREEN_STRUCT* screen = ddraw->GetScreen ();


        char buff[100];
        long time1 = timeGetTime ();

// 300 time for a regular screen fill
        for (int i=0; i<450; i++)
        Graphic->DrawAt (screen, rand () %630+5, rand () %470+5);


        long time2 = timeGetTime ();
        long result = time2-time1;

        itoa (result, buff, 10);

        alpha.PrintText (60, 60, screen, buff);
    }


    //*****************************
```

The number of draws for the image is carefully chosen. Each image is 32x32. Allow me to do a little math:

640 / 32 = 20
480 / 32 = 15
20 * 15 = 300
50 percent overdraw is 450.

This gives us an idea of how fast our drawing is with 50 percent overdraw. We fill the entire screen 1½ times. Obviously this is not a great example, but it gives us an idea. The screen can hold 300 of the images, so play with the numbers if you like. You might also consider that part of the screen will be given up to interface elements.

That does it for using this compression in reality.

Span Lists

What can happen in a game is "overdraw." *Overdraw* is simply drawing the same pixel twice. "Now why would I ever do that?" you ask. You wouldn't intentionally. This is something that happens as a result of layering. We'll discuss layering in detail in Chapter 16, but basically we draw a tile layer, then a building and tree layer, and then flying objects, then the mouse, etc. On a busy screen, 50 percent overdraw is fairly common. That means that 50 percent of the pixels on the game screen are being drawn twice. So if your frame rate resides around 20 fps (frames per second), then going to span lists may bring you back up around 30 fps, not counting CPU time spent doing AI, networking, update cycles, movement, animation, sounds, and so on.

Another major concern is special effects, such as fog of war, explosions, blending, color transformation for friendly units and unfriendly units, shadows, etc. In order for these effects to work, you need to do a final pass on the frame buffer before you blit it to the screen. That means that you may need to read pixels from video memory, and boy, is that slow. The minimum time necessary to read a single byte from video memory is 4 clock cycles. This number can go higher than 12 clock cycles depending on what else is happening on your computer. If you have 30 fps now, try reading from video memory and watch it drop to 2 fps or 3 fps. This is a fact, not an exaggeration.

Span lists are a useful tool to help decrease drawing time. The technique is simply to avoid drawing any pixels into the frame buffer. We wait until all pixels that will appear in the frame buffer have been determined, and then blit them all at once. This is especially helpful if you are doing special effects like translucency that require you to know the color of the pixel underneath. If you already blitted that to the video buffer, then that means you need to read from video memory, which is horribly slow.

There are about half a dozen different ways to implement a span list. Matt Pritchard at Ensemble Studios seems to have the best idea. He creates a span list for each frame buffer scan line. Basically, there is one span list maintained for every *y* on the screen. This means that a group of span structures "belongs" to a single screen scan line. When that line goes to draw, all of its spans fit into the memory cache. We then just go through the list from left to right, drawing one span after another. If everything was inserted into the list correctly, there will be no overdraw and special effects can be drawn with almost no extra time. Accolades to Matt.

Areas for interface do not need span lists since there is rarely any overdraw and what little there is comes from the mouse. Span lists are not a new idea. They are in such games as Quake, Age of Empires, and Monster Truck Madness. I just like Matt's implementation best. The reason is its lack of cache-thrashing.

The full description of a good span list would require a full chapter of at least 50 pages. I will, however, cover the basics here on creating a span list using the method described above. By the way, the text we created in Chapter 11 should not make it into a span list but should be drawn last. Letters are usually drawn pixel by pixel and span lists are better with groups of pixels.

Every blit routine in your code (Memcpy16bit) is changed to call a span list routine (something like SetSpan (U16ptr, int x, int y, int len)) that puts the pixels to be blitted into a list that will be referenced when the actual drawing takes place. As you may imagine, a few steps are added to make this technique work:

1. Create a span list structure.
2. Create a way of inserting this structure into a linked list.
3. Create a new container class for holding thousands of spans.
4. Create a way to quickly find an available span among thousands.
5. Create the SetSpan routine.

The term "span" refers to a group of pixels. The list (as in "span list") is simply a list of these spans. The span structure can look like a lot of different things but most often it looks like this:

```
//**************************************************

typedef struct SPAN          // 12 bytes
{
```

```
U16ptr      Data;
U16         XPosition;
U16         Length;
U16         ID;
U16         Next;

        void Clear () {Data = OL, XPosition = 0, Length = 0, Next = OL;}
}*SPANptr, ** SPANlist;
```

//**

This satisfies our first requirement: creating a span list structure. Other data may need to be included such as special effects, possibly a text structure for text starting at that position, and maybe some flags. But for the most part, that completes it. The most likely addition is a z-buffer, or depth value. This can help you determine if the pixels that you are about to draw go on top of existing pixels or behind, in which case you don't draw them. I'll leave that code to you.

Let's move on to a simple container class used to keep track of items. All you do is initialize it with the number of items you want to keep track of, and it creates a list of bits so you can easily track which items have been used. We'll use this in conjunction with a list of spans so we can quickly track which spans are in use and find available ones quickly. By the way, this class will be used by a few more container classes in this book, so get familiar with it.

```
#if _MSC_VER >= 1000
#pragma once
#endif                                    // _MSC_VER >= 1000


#ifndef __TAG_LIST__
#define __TAG_LIST__

#include <string.h>
#ifndef __STRING_H_
#include "struct.h"
#endif

#define FC __fastcall

//****************************************************
//****************************************************
//****************************************************

typedef class  TAG_LIST
{

private:

        enum {MAX_LIST = 64, BIT_SHIFT = 3, DIVIDE = 8, WHICH_BIT = 7, FULL =
                (1<<DIVIDE)-1};

        int          ListLength;      // number of items in list
```

```
        int             Current;        // the current byte we are using
        int             Last;           // stores last find position
        int             CountOn;
        U8ptr           Tag;
        U8ptr           BitMask;

        //**********************
        void IncCountOn () {CountOn ++;}
        void DecCountOn () {CountOn --;}

public:

        //**********************

        TAG_LIST (int num = MAX_LIST)
        {
            // init the BitMask list
                BitMask = new U8[8];
        //   U8    bits[8] = {1,2,4,8,16,32,64,128};
            for (int i=0; i<8; i++)
                BitMask [i] = 1<<i;

            if (num == 0) ListLength = MAX_LIST;
            else ListLength = num;
            Tag = new U8 [(ListLength>>BIT_SHIFT)+1];       // 8 bits
            Clear ();
        }
        //**********************
        TAG_LIST (TAG_LIST & TL)
        {
            // init the BitMask list
                BitMask = new U8[8];
            for (int i=0; i<8; i++)
                BitMask [i] = 1<<i;

            ListLength = TL.ListLength;

            Tag = new U8 [(ListLength>>BIT_SHIFT)+1];       // 8 bits
            Clear ();
            Current = TL.Current;
            CountOn = TL.CountOn;
            memcpy (Tag, TL.Tag, (ListLength>>BIT_SHIFT)+1);
        }
        //**********************
        ~TAG_LIST ()
        {
            delete Tag;
            if (BitMask) delete BitMask;
            BitMask = OL;
        }
        //**********************
        void FC  Copy (TAG_LIST& copy)
```

```
    {
        // make sure that we have the space for copying
        if (ListLength > copy.ListLength)
        {
            if (copy.Tag) delete copy.Tag;
            copy.Tag = new U8 [(ListLength>>BIT_SHIFT)+1];
            copy.ListLength = ListLength;
            //Clear ();
        }
        copy.Current = Current;
        copy.CountOn = CountOn;
        memcpy (copy.Tag, Tag, (ListLength>>BIT_SHIFT)+1);
}
//***********************
void FC  Clear ()
{
    memset (Tag, 0, (ListLength>>BIT_SHIFT) + 1);
    Current = 0, Last = 0, CountOn = 0;
}

//***********************
//***********************
int  FC  GetTag (int i)
{
    if (i>=0 && i<ListLength)
    return  Tag[i / DIVIDE] & BitMask[i & WHICH_BIT];

    return 0;
}
//***********************
void FC  SetTag (int i)
{
    if (i>=0 && i<ListLength)
    {   // set on
        if (! (Tag[i / DIVIDE] & BitMask[i & WHICH_BIT])) IncCountOn ();
        Tag[i / DIVIDE] |= BitMask[i & WHICH_BIT];
    }
}
//***********************
void FC  ClearTag (int i)
{
    if (i>=0 && i<ListLength)
    {   // set off
        if (Tag[i / DIVIDE] & BitMask[i & WHICH_BIT]) DecCountOn ();
        Tag[i / DIVIDE] &= ~ (BitMask[i & WHICH_BIT]);
        Current = i>>BIT_SHIFT;
    }
}
//***********************
int  FC  OnOffTag (int i)                // simple test
{
    return (Tag[i / DIVIDE] & BitMask[i & WHICH_BIT]);
```

```
}
//**********************
int  FC  FlipTag (int i)
{
    if (OnOffTag (i))
        ClearTag (i);
    else SetTag (i);
    return Tag[i / DIVIDE] & BitMask[i & WHICH_BIT];
}
//**********************
//**********************
int  FC  Get (int i)
{
    return GetTag (i);
}
//**********************
void FC  Set (int i)
{
    SetTag (i);
}
//**********************
void FC  Clear (int i)
{
    ClearTag (i);
}
//**********************
int  FC  Test (int i)
{
    return OnOffTag (i);
}
//**********************
int  FC  Flip (int i)
{
    return FlipTag (i);
}
//**********************
//**********************
int  FC  FindOpenTag () // uses the Current pointer to start; remember to
// call FindOpenTag in continuous succession if you need this functionality.
{
    int NumBytes = (ListLength>>BIT_SHIFT)+1;
    int StartByte = Current;
    while (Tag[Current] == FULL && Current < NumBytes)        // full
        {Current++;}
    if (Current >= NumBytes)
    {
        Current = 0;                              // none available
        while (Tag[Current] == FULL && Current < StartByte)  // full
            {Current++;}
        if (Current >= StartByte) return -1; // none available
    }
```

```
        // go bit by bit to find an available one
        int WhichBit = Current<<BIT_SHIFT;
        for (int i=0; i<DIVIDE; i++, WhichBit++)
        {
                if (GetTag (WhichBit) == 0) return WhichBit;
        }

        return -1;                      // nothing available
}
//**********************
int  FC  FindFirstSet ()
{
        Last = 0;
        while (Last<ListLength)
        {
                if (GetTag (Last)) break;
        }

        if (Last >= ListLength) return -1;
        return Last++;
}
//**********************
int  FC  FindNextSet ()
{
        while (Last<ListLength)
        {
                if (GetTag (Last)) break;
        }

        if (Last >= ListLength) return -1;
        return Last++;
}
//**********************
//**********************
int  FC  CountSet ()
{
        return CountOn;
}
//**********************
//**********************
TAG_LIST& FC  operator = (const TAG_LIST& TL)
{
        if (TL.ListLength != ListLength)
        {
                if (Tag) delete Tag;
                ListLength = TL.ListLength;
                Tag = new U8 [(ListLength>>BIT_SHIFT)+1]; // 8 bits
        }
        Clear ();
        Current = TL.Current;
        CountOn = TL.CountOn;
        memcpy (Tag, TL.Tag, (ListLength>>BIT_SHIFT)+1);
```

```
        return *this;
    }
//***********************
    bool  FC  operator == (const TAG_LIST& TL) const
    {
        if (ListLength != TL.ListLength) return false;
        int t = (ListLength>>BIT_SHIFT)+1;
        for (int i=0; i<t; i++)
        {
            if (Tag[i] == TL.Tag[i]) return false;
        }
        return true;
    }
//***********************
bool    FC  operator != (const TAG_LIST& TL) const
    {
        return (! (*this == TL));
    }
//***********************
    int   FC  operator [] (int which)
    {
        if (which<0 || which>=ListLength) return 0;
        int val = GetTag (which);
        return val;
    }
//***********************
//***********************
    TAG_LIST& FC  operator <<= (int num)      // num must be less than DIVIDE
    {
        if (num<0) return (*this >>= num);

        int n = ListLength;

        while (n--)
        {
            if (GetTag (n-num)) SetTag (n);
            else ClearTag (n);
        }
        return *this;
    }
//******
    TAG_LIST  FC  operator << (int num)
    {
        return (TAG_LIST (*this) <<= num);
    }
//***********************
    TAG_LIST& FC  operator >>= (int num)      // must be less than DIVIDE
    {
        if (num<0) return (*this <<= num);

        int n = ListLength;
```

```
            for (int i=0; i<n; i++)
            {
                    if (GetTag (i+num)) SetTag (i);
                    else ClearTag (i);
            }
            return *this;
}
//******
TAG_LIST  FC  operator >> (int num)
{
            return (TAG_LIST (*this) >>= num);
}
//**********************
TAG_LIST& FC  operator |= (TAG_LIST& TL)
{
        int len = (ListLength>>BIT_SHIFT)+1;
        int testlen = (TL.ListLength>>BIT_SHIFT)+1;
        if (testlen < len) len = testlen;    // take the shorter of the 2

        for (int i=0; i<len; i++)
        {
                Tag[i] |= TL.Tag[i];
        }
        return *this;
}
//******
TAG_LIST FC  operator | (TAG_LIST& TL)
{
        return (TAG_LIST (*this) |= TL);
}
//**********************
TAG_LIST& FC  operator &= (TAG_LIST& TL)
{
        int len = (ListLength>>BIT_SHIFT)+1;
        int testlen = (TL.ListLength>>BIT_SHIFT)+1;
        if (testlen < len) len = testlen;    // take the shorter of the 2

        for (int i=0; i<len; i++)
        {
                Tag[i] &= TL.Tag[i];
        }
        return *this;
}
//******
TAG_LIST& FC  operator & (TAG_LIST& TL)
{
        return (TAG_LIST (*this) &= TL);
}
//**********************
TAG_LIST& FC  operator ^= (TAG_LIST& TL)
{
        int len = (ListLength>>BIT_SHIFT)+1;
```

```
            int testlen = (TL.ListLength>>BIT_SHIFT)+1;
            if (testlen < len) len = testlen;    // take the shorter of the 2

            for (int i=0; i<len; i++)
            {
                Tag[i] ^= TL.Tag[i];
            }
            return *this;
    }
    //*****
    TAG_LIST FC  operator ^ (TAG_LIST& TL)
    {
            return (TAG_LIST (*this) ^= TL);
    }
    //*********************
    //*********************
    TAG_LIST  FC  operator ~ ()
    {
            TAG_LIST t (*this);
            int len = (ListLength>>BIT_SHIFT) +1;

            for (int i=0; i<len; i++)
            {
                t.Tag[i] = ~t.Tag[i];
            }
            return t;
    }

    //*********************
}*TAGptr, **TAGlist;

//****************************************************
//****************************************************
//****************************************************

#endif
```

This class's sole purpose is to track which items in a list are being used and which are not. After every frame, we call its member function Clear. Then we build our spans, continually calling FindOpenTag as we go along. This code is fast but could be a bit faster by adding the member variable CurrentBit to give a launching point for finding the next available. We do track through the list anyway, in case you set another bit. This helps other situations but may not help the span list. Anyway, there are a few minor optimizations that may gain you a little speed, and I encourage you to spend a little time trying out some of those.

The TAG_LIST class uses bits for storage, and so we store single bits by breaking up bytes into pieces. This requires a little math but is still super fast. The TAG_LIST is only interested if a bit is on or off. This class satisfies one of our requirements: creating a way of quickly finding an available span among thousands. We'll define its use in a little while. This class can be used when you need to keep track of dozens or even hundreds of on/off or true/false situations.

13

Chapter

Insertion is a bit trickier. We can't do that without at least defining a few more things. We need a stronger framework, so let's define a new class:

```
//*****************************************************
typedef class SPAN_GROUP
// this is just a container class for spans, it does no
// calculations or other management
{
        enum {SPAN_COUNT = 100, MAX = 65536};

        SPANptr         Span;
        TAGptr          Tags;
        int             NumSpans;
        int             CurrentSpan;

        //**********************

        void FindSpan ()            // looks through spans to find one unused
        {
            int CurrentSpan = Tags->FindOpenTag ();
            // set a pointer to the currently available span
            if (CurrentSpan == -1) Realloc ();    // we need more spans
        }
        void Realloc ()             // sometimes, you just need a few more spans
        {
            CurrentSpan = NumSpans;    // point beyond the last item
            NumSpans += 10;            // now we add 10 items, we may
                                       // need to raise or lower this number
            SPANptr    TempSpan = new SPAN[NumSpans];
                                       // allocate new memory
            TAGptr     TempTags = new TAG_LIST (NumSpans);
            memcpy (TempSpan, Span, sizeof (SPAN) * (NumSpans-10));
            Tags->Copy (*TempTags);

            CleanUp ();                // delete the old memory
            Span = TempSpan;           // reset our pointers
            Tags = TempTags;

        }

public:

        //**********************

        SPAN_GROUP (int num = SPAN_COUNT)
        {
            if (num >MAX) num = MAX;   // never more that 65536
            NumSpans = num;
            Span = new SPAN[NumSpans];
            for (int i=0; i<NumSpans; i++)
            {
                Span[i].ID = i;        // each span must know its own place
                                       // in the list
```

```
        }
        Tags = new TAG_LIST (NumSpans);
        Clear ();
}
~SPAN_GROUP ()
{
        CleanUp ();
}
void  CleanUp ()
{
        delete Span;
        delete Tags;
}

//*********************

void Clear ()
{
        CurrentSpan = 0;
        Tags->Clear ();
}
SPAN* GetSpan ()                    // finds an vailable span and returns it.
{
        if (CurrentSpan >= NumSpans) FindSpan ();
                                    // search a little harder

        Tags->Set (CurrentSpan);   // set the tag list for when we may
                                    // need it
        Span[CurrentSpan].Next = 65535; // no next item
        return &Span[CurrentSpan++];
}
SPAN* GetSpan (int ID)              // find an item by ID
{
        if (ID >= NumSpans) return 0L;
        return &Span[ID];
}
void ReleaseSpan (int ID)
{
        if (ID >= NumSpans) return;
        Tags->ClearTag (ID);
}

//*********************

}*SPAN_GROUPptr, **SPAN_GROUPlist;

//****************************************************
```

This container class, SPAN_GROUP, simply allocates memory and maintains a list of spans along with a TAG_LIST. You may be wondering why I have an integer "pointing" to the next item to return when requested from SPAN* GetSpan (). Well, it is common for a span to completely overwrite another span. Sometimes a long span is drawn in a position where another span is. It has the effect of freeing up that second span to be used again. TAG_LIST keeps real tabs on what is available while CurrentSpan is a quick optimization to get spans a lot quicker. It's the best of both worlds.

There's not a lot to this class. It allocates spans based on the value you pass to the constructor. The number you need is a rough guideline, because if you don't have enough and a request is made for more, it reallocates more spans and a new TAG_LIST.

When you need a new span, such as when you are getting ready to draw a stream of pixels, call the function GetSpan (). It finds a span for you, come hell or high water, and returns it to you. Never delete a span. If you no longer need it, call the member function ReleaseSpan (span->ID), and that span will be released and made available again. When you are creating your linked list, the links are made by ID number. If you have an ID number and you need the span itself, call the function GetSpan (ID), which returns a pointer to the specific span you need.

Looking at this, you might think that there is a lot of unnecessary work here and things might be slower than just drawing the stinking pixels. It may seem like that. You'll have to weigh your overdraw versus span lists. If you are certain that your overdraw is minimal, I recommend avoiding span lists altogether. They are not easy and too many problems exist. However, if you don't know how much overdraw you'll have, and if you need to read from video memory for such things as shadows, span lists are the way to go. They will improve your performance.

Now that we have that class defined, we come to one of the most complex classes you are ever likely to see. Essentially, it is a linked list with position and length as requirements for insertion. Because new items overwrite part of the previous ones, the math and length matching can be hairy. I could easily spend 30 pages explaining this code to you, but we have *way* too many other subjects to cover. I leave the code here for you with best wishes:

```
//****************************************************

// one of these classes should be declared for each y position/scan line
// this class manages the insertion of data into the spans

typedef class SPAN_LIST
{
        SPAN_GROUPptr   Spans;
        SPANptr         FirstSpan;
private:
        //***********************
        // go from FirstSpan forward and find out which
        SPANptr         FindSpan (int x)      // span contains this x position
        {
              if (FirstSpan == OL) return OL; // the span list is empty now
              SPANptr   Temp = FirstSpan;
              while (Temp->Next != 65535)
              {
                    SPANptr Next = Spans->GetSpan (Temp->Next) ;
                    if (Next->XPosition >= x) return Temp;
                                              // if next X is greater
```

```
                    if (Next->Next == 65535) return Next;
                                    // then the previous pointer must be the one
               Temp = Next;
      }
      return Temp;                        // must be the last one
}
SPANptr          FindPrev (int ID)      // looking for the link in the
                                        // list pointing to this item
{
      SPANptr ptr = FirstSpan;
      if (ptr->ID == ID) return ptr;   // this is the one
      if (ptr == OL) return OL;
      while (ptr->Next != 65535)
      {
            SPANptr Next = Spans->GetSpan (ptr->Next) ;
            if (Next->ID == ID) return ptr;
            ptr = Next;
      }
      return OL;
}
//***********************
void      InsertBefore (SPANptr item, SPANptr newitem)
{
      SPANptr prev = FindPrev (item->ID);
      if (prev == item || prev == OL) // the first span is this item
      {
            newitem->Next = item->ID;
            FirstSpan = newitem;
      }
      else                            // normal insertion
      {
            prev->Next = newitem->ID;
            newitem->Next = item->ID;
      }
}
void      InsertAfter (SPANptr item, SPANptr newitem)
{
      newitem->Next = item->Next;
      item->Next = newitem->ID;
}
void      InsertReplace (SPANptr item, SPANptr newitem)
{
      SPANptr prev = FindPrev (item->ID);
      if (prev == item || prev == OL)      // the first span is this item
      {
            FirstSpan = newitem;
            newitem->Next = item->Next;
            Spans->ReleaseSpan (item->ID);
      }
      else                                 // normal replacement
      {
            prev->Next = newitem->ID;
```

13

Chapter

```
                    newitem->Next = item->Next;
                    Spans->ReleaseSpan (item->ID);
          }
}
//***********************
void        CorrectOverDrawPrevious (SPANptr prev, SPANptr newitem,
                                         int& length)
{
     int prevoverwrite = 0;
     if (prev == newitem) return;              // oops

     // do the prev section first
     int position = newitem->XPosition - prev->XPosition;
     if (prev->XPosition+prev->Length < newitem->XPosition)
     {
          prev->Next = newitem->ID;
          return;
     }

     if (position>0)                            // normal distribution
     {
          int overlap = prev->XPosition + prev->Length -
               newitem->XPosition;
          if (overlap <= newitem->Length) // normal
          {
               prev->Length -= overlap;
               length -= overlap;
               prevoverwrite = overlap;
               InsertAfter (prev, newitem);
          }
          else            // the length of the new item puts it fully
                          // inside the "prev"
          {
                          // this will hold the extra bit
                          // beyond the end of our newitem

                    SPANptr NewSpan = Spans->GetSpan ();
                    int offset = position + newitem->Length;
                    NewSpan->XPosition = prev->XPosition + offset;
                    NewSpan->Data = (prev->Data + offset);
                    NewSpan->Length = prev->XPosition + prev->Length –
                                        NewSpan->XPosition;

                    // the difference between the start positions
                    prev->Length = position;
                    if (prev->Next != 65535)
                        NewSpan->Next = Spans->GetSpan (prev->Next)->ID;
                    newitem->Next = NewSpan->ID;
                    prev->Next = newitem->ID;
                    return;   // no need to continue
          }
     }
```

```
            // they are equal position, the newitem->XPosition can
            // never be less unless they don't touch, and then we don't care
            else if (position == 0)
            {
                  int overlap = prev->Length - newitem->Length;
                  if (overlap <= 0)     // completely write over
                  {
                        length -= newitem->Length;
                                            // to continue onto the next item
                        InsertReplace (prev, newitem);
                  }
                  else                  // partial write over
                  {
                        InsertBefore (prev, newitem);
                        prev->XPosition += length;
                        prev->Data += length;
                        prev->Length -= length;
                        return;         // no need to continue
                  }
            }
      }
}
// this potentially recursive function takes the newitem and writes
// over part or all of the "next" item that will follow. The return
// value lets the calling routine know that the next item was
// completely covered
int      CorrectOverDrawFollowing (SPANptr newitem, SPANptr next,
                                        int& length)
{
      // now the variable length is equal to the remaining length to
      // draw on top of "next", since this is overlap, both positions
      // are assumed to start at the same place

      if (next == newitem) return 0;  // oops
      if (next == OL) return 0;       // this was the last time
      if (length < next->Length)      // this will most often be the case
      {
            next->XPosition += length;
            next->Data += length;
            next->Length -= length;
      }
      else if (length == next->Length)     // complete replacement
      {
            InsertReplace (next, newitem);
            return 1;
      }
      else
// very complicated recursion. "next" appears completely inside of
// "newitem" and others spans following may also be wiped out by this.
      {
            length -= next->Length;
            InsertReplace (next, newitem);
```

```
                    // that was the last item in the list
                    if (newitem->Next == 65535) return 1;

                    SPANptr temp = Spans->GetSpan (newitem->Next);
                    if (CorrectOverDrawFollowing (newitem, temp, length))
                    return 1;
            }
        return 0;
    }

public:

//***********************
SPAN_LIST (int numspans = 100)
{
    Spans = new SPAN_GROUP (numspans);
    Clear ();
}
~SPAN_LIST ()
{
    delete Spans;
}
void Clear ()
{
    Spans->Clear ();
    FirstSpan = 0L;
}
//***********************
void SetSpan (U16ptr ptr, U16 position, U16 length)
{
    SPANptr NewSpan = Spans->GetSpan ();
    NewSpan->Data = ptr;
    NewSpan->XPosition = position;
    NewSpan->Length = length;
    // length will now determine how much draw area we have left
    // as we slowly draw over existing spans.
    // now we have the span that will point to this one
    SPANptr temp = FindSpan (position);
    if (temp == 0l) // put our new item in the list as the first item
    {
        FirstSpan = NewSpan;
        return;
    }

    int len = length;

    // insert before first item
    if (temp->XPosition>NewSpan->XPosition)
    {
        int dist = temp->XPosition - NewSpan->XPosition;
        int ElimFlag = 0;
        if (dist>NewSpan->Length)  // they do not overlap
```

```
                    {
                        InsertBefore (temp, NewSpan);
                        return;
                    }
                    len = NewSpan->XPosition + NewSpan->Length -
                        temp->XPosition;
                    // the previous item is completely covered
                    if (NewSpan->XPosition < temp->XPosition &&
                            (NewSpan->XPosition + NewSpan->Length) >=
                            (temp->XPosition + temp->Length))
                    {
                        len = NewSpan->Length;
                        ElimFlag = 1;
                    }

                    CorrectOverDrawFollowing (NewSpan, temp, len);
                    if (!ElimFlag)
                    NewSpan->Next = temp->ID;
                    FirstSpan = NewSpan;
                    return;
            }

        SPANptr next = Spans->GetSpan(temp->Next); // leave this here
        // the next function call may change the Next value
        CorrectOverDrawPrevious (temp, NewSpan, len);


        if (next)
        {
            CorrectOverDrawFollowing (NewSpan, next, len);
            NewSpan->ID = next->ID;
        }
}
//**********************
void DrawSpans (U16ptr image)
{
        SPANptr span = FirstSpan;

        while (span)
        {
            // set copy position
            U16ptr ptr = image + span->XPosition;

            // copy data into frame buffer
            Memcpy16Bit (ptr, span->Data, span->Length);

            // advance to next span
            span = Spans->GetSpan (span->Next);
        }
}
//**********************
```

13

Chapter

```
}SPAN_LIST, *SPAN_LISTptr;
```

```
//****************************************************
```

Its usage couldn't be a whole lot easier. Each scan line on the frame buffer gets one instance of SPAN_LIST. Every time you want to draw an item, figure which SPAN_LIST of the 480 scan lines gets the draw (assuming 640x480). Now, just like when you memcpy, call the member function SetSpan (U16ptr ptr, U16 position, U16 length). It does all of the storage for you, but for a good exercise you could try tracing into the code. It is tough to follow but educational. After you finish building the frame buffer, you go from the top to bottom telling each SPAN_LIST to DrawSpans (U16ptr image) and hand it a pointer to the current frame buffer scan line. It takes care of all of the drawing for you. You can see that this loop is unbelievably fast.

Another cool thing about this method is SPAN_LIST slowly accumulates pointers, which cost almost nothing in terms of time. When you go to draw, the frame buffer scan line and the SPAN_LIST classes will both easily fit into the instruction and data caches of your PC, making drawing much faster. Since the frame buffer pointer will remain in the cache, no cache loading will occur and this will speed things. If you have overdraw exceeding 8 to12 percent, using a span list will probably be faster in general.

The SPAN_LIST class is not perfect; it does need work. It works fine for me, but it does not have any legacy and until it does, I'm not completely confident in it. E-mail me with any corrections at Mkawick@sprintmail.com.

Full Offscreen Buffer

Some people like using offscreen buffers. You simply allocate a bunch of memory, draw into it, and blit it into video memory. Almost every PC game in history (so far) has done this. Only recently would anyone have considered drawing directly to video memory. DirectDraw gave us this freedom and we are no longer limited to drawing to an offscreen buffer. In fact, the last three years have brought amazing changes like VESA 2, caches, direct blits, AGP, and DirectDraw. All of these things in some small way work to speed up graphics and reduce the amount of work that it takes (except DirectDraw, which takes more work).

Reading from memory is fast, so video effects are fast and easy. The only real problem comes when you want to move all of that memory onto the screen. A 640x480 blit in 256 colors amounts to about 340,000 clock cycles. At 30 fps, that is about 10 million cycles per second. Remember, you aren't drawing, and you aren't moving characters in the world; all you are doing is displaying the graphics. When you jump up to 1024x768, the time jumps up to 27 million cycles per second. That is a huge percentage of your overall time just to display the pixels that you've drawn, especially when you double the memory requirement for 16-bit.

DirectDraw allows you to freely draw directly into video memory. Once you are ready to display the image, a pointer in video memory is moved where the screen gets its image information. That means that the video blit is nearly instantaneous, which frees up a fair percentage of CPU time.

Many games like Dungeon Keeper and Warcraft still use this method of drawing directly to an offscreen buffer (or so I'm told), and that means it is still a valid method to use. There are only a few things you still need to do:

➤ Obtain a pointer to the screen for blitting.

➤ Wait for vertical refresh, the time between the drawing of the screen.

➤ Obtain a pointer to memory into which you will be drawing, an offscreen buffer.

➤ Blit that memory to the screen pointer.

That's it. Check out *Flights of Fantasy* by Chris Lampton (The Waite Group). This is the classic way to handle drawing in 320x200; it's been done with an offscreen buffer since the dawn of graphics.

An Alternative to Span Lists

There is an alternative to span lists—update regions. The screen is treated like a bunch of small rectangles and everything that intrudes on those regions triggers a flag that redraws that section. The rest of the screen is static. So once you draw the screen, the only thing that changes every frame is the stuff moving on the screen. Everything else is not redrawn.

Most games simply redraw the entire screen every frame. While this is easy to implement, it can be very slow. Using update regions is a good alternative and gives you a huge amount of CPU time back.

Scrolling can be extra slow, however. Everything is drawn by small blocks, and that can take a lot of time in itself. Take Warcraft II, for example. It uses update regions of 8x8, which may be too small. The game runs super-smooth until you scroll with a lot of stuff on the screen, at which point things slow down a lot. You'll need an older machine to notice, so you may not see it. Luckily, the screen is stationary 80 to 90 percent of the time in real-time strategy games.

Update regions are much easier to implement than span lists, and my little description here should have you off and running in no time.

Particle Systems

They say that the little things in life are what make it worthwhile. I'm not so sure that I agree with that assessment, but particle systems fit the bill. A former coworker of mine, Matt Bogue, suggested that I should at least include a discussion about particle systems in this book.

Particles can be anything. In Total Annihilation, there are two types of particles. The CaveDog developers created a pixel system that emulates bubbles for boats and repair/building energy. I haven't seen the code or talked to the guys at CaveDog, but the system looks like a 2-D one where the particles are simply groups of pixels that move in a 2-D plane. They are a great touch and add uniqueness to the game. They create "atmosphere."

The other particle system that CaveDog created was 3-D. You see it best when a vehicle explodes. Polygons go flying, smoking parts zip up in the air, and rolling parts bounce off the ground. It's quite cool, especially since the explosions are coupled with a "white flash" animated bitmap appearing beneath the explosion. The look is well worth the effort it took to get it perfect.

The PARTICLE structure in struct.h is a decent example of a particle for a 2-D world. It is initialized with a position, direction, velocity, etc. Once you start it in motion, you continue to update it until the counter runs out; then it simply dies. This 2-D system is obviously much easier than a 3-D system, but it illustrates the basics:

```
typedef
struct PARTICLE
{
        FL          x, y;                   // screen position
        FL          Velocity;               // speed
        U32         Direction, Time;        // integer based direction, time started
                                            // in millisecs
        U8          Counter, Brightness;

        PARTICLE () {Clear ();}
        void  Clear () {x = 0.0f, y = 0.0f, Velocity = 0.0f, Direction = 0,
            Time = 0; Counter = 4; Brightness = 255;}
}PARTICLE, *PARTICLEptr, **PARTICLElist;
```

Chapter 14

The Black Space and the Wild Void of Life

Almost no animated graphics on the screen are rectangular. After all, square dinosaurs marching across the screen look terrible. A graphic usually shows just the character that fits into an area, but not the rest, not the black area around the creature. You want to eliminate this "black space." If you were to draw the full rectangular graphic, it might look like Figure 14.1.

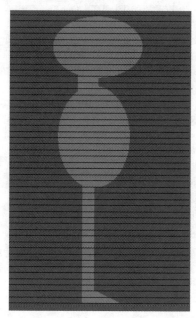

Figure 14.1
The full graphic

I put the lines in to represent the boundaries between rows of pixels. What happens in RLE (run-length encoding, commonly used in bitmaps) is that a count is kept of repeating pixels. Our 64-pixel-wide graphic, shown in Figure 14.2, has a complete row across the top that is black or near black (just think of it as black.) The next row is mostly black—they all are—and about one-third of the way across, the color section begins. Just for grins, let's assume that the first pixel begins at the 24th pixel across, meaning that 0 through 23 are black. We assume that 0 is black. In a bitmap, we would have a bunch of 0's all in a row— 64+24, or 88, 0's in a row. In a file you might see this, and although you wouldn't want to count them, all of them would be there. In 16-bit, there would be 2 bytes for every pixel, bringing our total bytes to 172.

RLE would compress this, kind of. RLE stores 1 byte, which is a count telling us how many repeats to expect. Then it tells us the color. The above example would read like this: 88 00. This is in hexadecimal, of course. For long runs of the same pixel color, this works great. Decompression takes a bit of work, because you must do 64 pixels (the width) at a time, making a bit of extra math and slowing the drawing process if

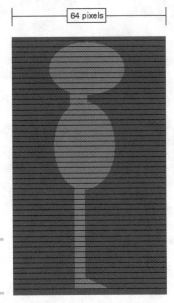

├─── 64 pixels ───┤

Figure 14.2
*64-pixel-wide
graphic*

you are drawing on the fly. Most people want to go directly from compression to drawing, so expect slowdowns.

RLE has another big drawback. In realistic images, not very many pixels repeat. A bunch of pixels in a row are very likely to be completely different from one another. RLE stores one byte that tells us the length and another byte that stores the color. What if we have just one pixel—such as 01 00, meaning that single pixels take up twice the memory. This is especially evident in 16-bit where subtle differences occur between any two pixels side by side. Still, I have never seen an image grow in size. Many people complain about RLE making an image larger, and I'm sure that it happens, but I haven't seen it yet in any game.

So space considerations aside, how do we eliminate that black space? A straight blit will draw them in over any background you have. We can rely on the hardware. Video hardware can be set up to have transparent colors set and then you can blit faster by using the hardware instead of your own code. You dictate the transparent colors, which makes it easy. When the hardware goes to draw the image that you tell it to draw, it compares each pixel to the colors you told it not to draw and blits that way. That sounds slow until you realize that the hardware is doing it in the background, with instant access to video memory, and not using any CPU time.

Given the number of frames of animation, however, you would constantly be putting stuff into video memory and setting up no-draw colors, meaning that performance would become an issue. However, video cards are getting better with more and more video memory. Once 64 MB becomes standard, this problem will disappear for the most part, but even with a 32 MB video card, there would be a pretty big limit on the amount of animation that you could have in video memory. But it is becoming an alternative.

Note: I've said it before in this book, but I cannot overemphasize it: Writing to video memory is fast, almost as fast as writing to regular memory in AGP, but reading is still really slow. Never read from video memory if you can avoid it. If you plan to support non-AGP machines, then writing to video memory is slow too, so only write pixels when you have to. Overdraw will cost you a lot.

This also presents another problem. When allocating video "surfaces," if the surface you are allocating exceeds video memory, DirectDraw will allocate it using system memory. Not a bad thing, but when the supposed hardware blit occurs, DirectDraw will manhandle the image to remove colors. Each pixel will be compared to the list that you provided, using CPU time, and really slow down the machine.

Note: Your transparent color should always be fuchsia/magenta. Forget black. The color fuchsia is 5 bits of red and 5 bits of blue. No green. Fuchsia is not a naturally occurring color, which makes it ideal for game graphics. Black is a color you may need to use to accent a shadow or for some other effect. You will probably never need fuchsia, or magenta, as some people call it. (This note is more about art asset delivery than about programming.)

So what other options do we have? Not too many. We can use RLE for taking out the black, but the way it was designed it does not decompress quickly enough. That brings us to a little trick of the trade. This kind of encoding, which we will describe shortly, produces the fastest drawing code, makes your graphic smaller—about a 46 percent compression rate on average—and is not too difficult to implement. The old types are gone, so I will describe my own style of encoding, which is much faster than what most programmers use.

LLE Compression

I used to call this method extra space compression, or ESC, and all of my files had that extension. I have long since changed it to LLE, or line length encoding. The original idea, for me, came from a good friend, Geoff Audy, a French-Canadian programmer who worked with me at Konami. If you have been doing this a long time, move on to the next section. If not, this may sound very confusing at first. Just hang in there. This is the fastest method I've found (well... invented really).

The nice thing about this type of compression is its speed. Compared to a straight blit, it is most often faster. There is significantly less data to transfer to the screen, making this 20 to 30 percent faster even with all the extra math. Also, a regular image that is rectangular and has no black space still draws almost as fast using this method even though no compression of the original image is created.

Note: So you think you've created some cool new way of doing things in code. Think again. As original as my code is, and I did not get it from anyone else, I'm sure that someone else has coded it before. There are very few new ideas under the sun, and you and I are never as smart as we like to think.

The concept is this:

1. We use RLE-like compression on all of the no-draw areas, now colored fuchsia.

2. We take draw areas and leave them the same so that we can use a straight memcpy to blit them to the screen.

3. We put a counter at the beginning of each scan line telling us how many sections of draw and no-draw areas to expect. This may sound confusing, but we simply count how many sections of fuchsia and then how many sections to blit. In Figure

14.1 earlier in this chapter, the scan lines that have information would have a count of 1 because there is one no-draw area followed by one draw area. If you have an area with legs, then the area between the legs counts and the count will be 2. The last no-draw area to the right of the image is always ignored. We don't need to account for something that isn't there and doesn't affect anything.

4. As we go to draw, we will look at this number to help us determine what to do, especially during clipping.

Now that we have the basic concepts, let's create some tools to help us in trivial ways. If you don't get it yet, just be patient. Figure 14.3 describes fairly well the concept of how this code works. The count of 2 may be confusing in the figure. We will reserve the number 0 for a line of pixels that will never be drawn like the first line of pixels in Figure 14.2. When a full line of pixels exists without spaces before or after, we can simply blit the entire line of pixels to the screen without any extra math, so we store the count as 1 and then a full line of pixels follows. All others possibilities start at the number 2.

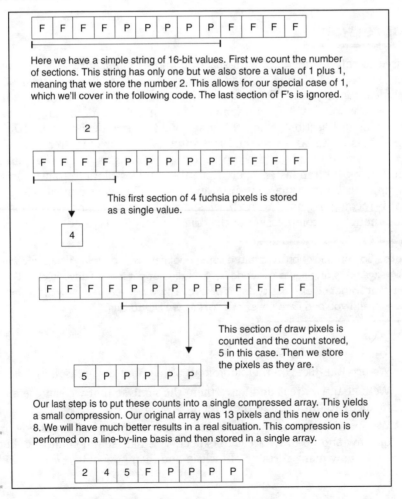

Figure 14.3
Example of line length encoding

```
//********************************
inline
int GRAPHIC :: CountOsInAnArray16Bit (U16ptr a, int num)
{
      int count=0;
      while ((*a == SearchColor) && (count<num))
      {count++; a++;}

      return count;
}

//********************************
inline
int GRAPHIC :: CountNonOsInAnArray16Bit (U16ptr a, int num)
{
      int count=0;
      while ((*a != SearchColor) && (count<num))
      {count++; a++;}

      return count;
}

//********************************

int GRAPHIC :: CountRuns16Bit (U16ptr Index, int num) const
{
      int w = 0, count = 0;
      while (w<num)
      {
            int r=CountOsInAnArray16Bit (Index, num-w);
            w+=r;
            if (w==num) break;    // in case we finish the full line
            Index+=r;

            int g=CountNonOsInAnArray16Bit (Index, num-w);
            w+=g;
            Index+=g;

            if (count == 0)
            {
                 count=1;         // at least one block of real data
                 if (w==num && !r) break; // for a full single line of data
            }
            count++;              // a split line
            if (w==num) break;    // in case we finish the full line
      }
      return count;
}

//********************************
```

The first function, CountOsInAnArray16Bit, does not use any private members or anything that would qualify it for being in this class. Since this code will probably not be used elsewhere, better to keep it here, although you can make it a global function if you like. The next two functions have this characteristic as well.

Notice the inline keyword that will increase the performance a trifle for this potential loading bottleneck. The point of the first two functions is to count and nothing more. The first function looks through an array and counts the number of fuchsia pixels. You can change SearchColor to anything, preferably a color that you won't use in your game. The function falls out after you reach the end of the array or when it discovers a non-fuchsia color. SearchColor is a 16-bit value. You will need to modify SearchColor in the case where your display is in 16-bit and not 15-bit.

You may have noticed that the only difference between these two functions is the equals versus the not-equals sign. That is true; this method of handling this situation is probably the fastest. You might be able to improve these functions, but hey... why? All of this will be performed at load time and no perceivable wait will exist. Later, we will discuss ways of saving LLE files, and then this compression will only be performed at one time—when you load it—and the LLEs will always be loaded, cutting load time to almost nothing.

The last function here counts items in a scan line. CountRuns16Bit simply goes through a string of 16-bit values and alternates between counting the number of fuchsia sections and then the non-fuchsia sections in that 16-bit array. If the entire string of 16-bit values is fuchsia, it returns a 0.

If a scan line does not have any black space, it returns a 1. The 1 is a special marker telling us that the entire scan line is pure data and that we simply blit a widths-worth of pixels to the frame buffer. Or else it returns a number corresponding to a pair of sections. Since every fuchsia section that does not take up a whole scan line will be accompanied by a group of useful colored pixels, we count the two and return the number 2 unless we have more sections. When we have a "normal" image, this number will always be greater than 1. The only other possibility is 1 for a full scan line of actual data as shown in Figure 14.4. In the figure, I've reserved 1 for the special case where a full scan line is used. All other counts are the draw section plus 1. I could have made the special case –1 or some other oddity, but it's easier to just make it 1 and then add 1 to all counts per scan line.

You may wonder why we need to worry about multiple sections. If a graphic of a man has his arms held above his head, we need to count three sections—one for each arm and one for the head. This would entail three no-draws and three draws. Again, the last fuchsia section is ignored. Three sections would be stored as four because of the special case.

The legs of any bipedal creature also have two draw/no-draw sections. Something to consider. Anyway, this means that we need to count the number of sections in a scan line and then store that as part of our compressed data at the beginning of the scan line. This would be stored as the number 3. We'll outline the format for the final data in a minute.

So, all that CountRuns16Bit does is count runs, exactly as the name implies. Knowing this helps us to prepare for the next section where we discuss the compression format.

The LLE Compression Format

Compression and encoding are terms that I do not think are precisely defined. RLE is encoding, but Huffman encoding should be called compression—at least I think so. The common vernacular is not so clear. Professors will tell you that *encoding* keeps the original form of the data squished while *compression* actually modifies the original data to produce a special form of data that is especially difficult to decipher.

That's hogwash. To me, compression is when you reduce the file size and encoding is when you change the data. But even that is inadequate. The book *Graphics File Formats* has a chapter on data compression which says "compression algorithms are used to re-encode data into a different, more compact representation conveying the same information." The only reason I bring this up is that everyone seems to have an opinion about what compression and encoding are. I use the word "compression." You may call it "encoding" if you prefer. They are generally synonymous.

We are going to look at the compression of a single line of data first and then simply extend that to a series of rows to make this form of compression easier to digest.

The compression format for LLE is as follows:

1. If a scan line has no pixel data, we store a 0 and move on to the next scan line.

2. If a scan line has only pixel data and no space, we store a 1 which is a special marker telling us to blit the entire scan line following. We don't need a count because it will be the full width.

3. When we have data, we store the number of "runs" (discussed previously).

4. Following the number of runs, we store a single count of the number of fuchsia pixels or no-draw pixels. This number allows us to offset our screen position to account for the position where our draw pixels go.

5. Following that count number is a count of the number of pixels to draw. We will use this number in a memcpy to blit the next few pixels to the screen.

6. Following that count is an array of colored pixels which we simply memcpy into the frame buffer, assuming we offset our frame position correctly...

That is it. This is illustrated in Figure 14.4.

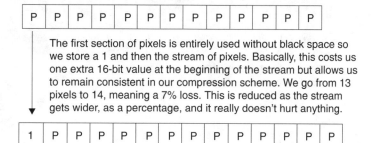

The first section of pixels is entirely used without black space so we store a 1 and then the stream of pixels. Basically, this costs us one extra 16-bit value at the beginning of the stream but allows us to remain consistent in our compression scheme. We go from 13 pixels to 14, meaning a 7% loss. This is reduced as the stream gets wider, as a percentage, and it really doesn't hurt anything.

Figure 14.4
Example of LLE compression

The F's represent fuchsia pixels while the P's represent the colored pixels that we will be blitting. This is not a really good representation since I have only put in a few pixels. The real width would probably be 24 or 32. Some games use really wide graphics, but usually 24 and 32 are good sizes. Anyway, the compression for these larger sizes is much higher.

One thing that is almost always true about this drawing is the fact that we have only a single section. Almost all drawings you will see are mostly single sections. These single sections can be across the body or head, along a tank or building, a tree trunk, or even a mouse pointer. There is usually only one strip of data per line. But in the few cases where there is more than one draw section, we need the data ahead of time to know how much to put on a single scan line in our frame buffer. I'm sure there is an optimization in here somewhere, but I'm not sure where.

When you go through the code we're about to cover, you will notice that all numbers are stored in 16-bit, even the counts. Since it is unlikely that a graphic's scan line will ever have more than 255 sections, this may seem wasteful, and it is. The difficulty that I see is when you memcpy from a non-2-byte aligned source to any destination, you take a major cache hit and the memcpy is slowed significantly. I'd prefer to keep everything WORD aligned and pay the price of an extra byte or two per image scan line. It also makes writing the code and reading it in easier.

Now that you have a pretty good idea of how the compression works, you'll find its analysis much easier to understand.

```
//***********************************

void GRAPHIC :: LLECompressSingleLine16Bit (U16ptr Compress,
             U16ptr Image, int width, int* BytesInLine) const
{
        U16ptr  ptr=Compress+1;   // skip the first 2 bytes to store the count
        int NumBytes = 1;         // we will have at least one "byte" to
                                  // return, this will be the count at the
                                  // beginning of the scan line

        int count = CountRuns16Bit (Image, width);
        *Compress = (U16)count;   // store that value

        if (count==0)             // nothing in this line
        {
            *BytesInLine = 1;     // minimum
            return;
        }
        if (count==1)             // this is a solid line, no block section
        {
            Memcpy16Bit (ptr, Image, width);
            *BytesInLine = width +1;
            return;
        }

        //******************

// now we know that we have at least one block section

while (--count>0)
// this assumes that we start with 0s and end with 0s
```

```
        // subtract one to start
        // ---we do 2 sections at a time... the last 0's section will not
        //    count in the end
        {

                int c=CountOsInAnArray16Bit (Image, width);
        *ptr++ = (U16)c;             // we store how many 0's and advance pointer
                Image += c;          // advance the pointer to the picture data
                width -= c;          // we update our distance left
                NumBytes++;          // one more byte for the count

                int l=CountNonOsInAnArray16Bit (Image, width);
                *ptr++ = (U16)l;     // we store the number of non 0 colors
                NumBytes++;          // one more byte
        Memcpy16Bit (ptr, Image, l);
                                     // now we store the colors and then offset both
                ptr += (U16)l;       // offset the destination pointer
                NumBytes += l;       // a few more bytes
                Image += l;    // offset the pointer for the next section of 0's
                width -= l;          // we update our distance left
        }
            *BytesInLine = NumBytes;  // minimum
        // all of the data has been stored and compressed so now we return
        }
        //***********************************
```

We start with a function used to compress a single line of data. The function name is LLECompressSingleLine16Bit and it takes a few distinct parameters. First, it takes a pointer to a buffer large enough to hold our soon-to-be compressed data (hopefully). This is almost always easy since in nearly every case the compressed data will be smaller than the original data. Even if you try to draw a series of single pixel vertical lines, the image data amount is only about 50 percent longer; in many other compression schemes (like RLE) the data will be 100 percent longer. The second parameter is a pointer to the line of original data. We then need to know how many pixels we will be compressing so we pass in the width. A pointer to the variable BytesInLine will tell the calling function how many pixels are in the newly compressed section.

Our function could simply return a value rather than accepting a pointer to return the value we need. That is a change you may want to make. It does not modify any variables belonging to the class so we use the const operator to optimize performance.

Note: The const operator can eliminate the this pointer most often passed as a "hidden" parameter to a function. The this pointer is used to point to the current instance of the class (GRAPHIC in this case), allowing you access to the members of this class/struct. const gets rid of this necessity, and because one less parameter is passed to your function, things are speeded up slightly. You really notice the difference in load time when you have thousands of files to load and compress. The const operator does nothing for performance when you access members of the class within a function, and within a function it becomes impossible to modify class variables, so use const sparingly and only in cases where performance may become an issue.

First, we declare a few local variables. ptr points to our compression area, the allocated memory where we will store the soon-to-be-made data. We offset by one because the final count will be stored in this first position. This count is the number of draw sections we discussed earlier. The next variable, NumBytes, is the number of bytes of compressed data. If nothing is on the image scan line, then we will store a 0, meaning that NumBytes will always have a minimum value of 1 byte (16-bit).

Next we count our sections. Recall the tool that we created a little while ago, CountRuns16Bit; we will now count and store this value. Immediately after the count we do some testing. We immediately store that count value at the beginning of the compression data: *Compress = (U16) count;.

If count is 0, we know that the entire line is clear (black space), and so we store the minimum amount of data possible, a 0 at the beginning of the compressed line of data that we stored above. We then let the calling function know that we wrote just one 16-bit value and then we return.

The case for count being 1 is very similar. We know that there is no compressible data on this scan line of image data. We copy the uncompressed data after Compress and store the count equal to the number of 16-bit values that we wrote. Then we return.

Now that we have the rather rare exceptions out of the way, we can move on to the actual compression part. We just got the count, so we can use that number to work through the sections. The count will always be greater than 1 because we always add 1 for our special case, so first we begin by subtracting 1: while (--count>0). This loop will go through section by section storing a number for blank spaces, a number for the count of valid pixels, and then a run of stored pixels.

The very next line of code counts the number of 0's (blanks or fuchsia) between our current pointer position and the first section of valid pixels. We store this value in a temporary variable called c. Now we need to offset our Image pointer because we have already counted these pixels, so we are advancing to the next section of real pixels when we count again. We reduce width so that we do not read beyond the end of the image scan line. Lastly, we add to our counter so that we know the total number of pixels in our compressed array. This value will be returned via the passed-in integer BytesInLine.

Now we move on to storing real data, which is really the whole point of this exercise anyway. The function CountNon0sInAnArray16Bit counts our pixels and we store this value in l. This value is then stored in our pointer to the compressed data. We increment the value of NumBytes to account for our newly stored 16-bit value. Then we simply copy the run of valid pixels into our compressed data pointer. We offset the pointer, add the run length to our Image pointer and the NumBytes for returning, and then subtract that value from the width to help track our progress across this single scan line.

The loop continues in this manner, counting spaces, storing its values, incrementing counts and pointers, counting non-spaces, memcpy-ing those pixels into our compressed pointer, and advancing the counters and pointers. When the last section is finished, we fall out of the loop.

The last thing we do before we return is store the number of 16-bit values in the passed-in variable BytesInLine so that the calling function knows how much data to expect.

You might wonder what happens if the row starts with valid pixels. The function Count0sInAnArray16Bit will simply return a 0 and the next part of counting valid pixels begins. If the row ends in valid pixels we might have to worry about reading beyond the end of the line, so we reduce width as we move through the row of data, and the function CountNon0sInAnArray16Bit will fall out once the end of the line is reached. See how it all fits together nicely?

The only remotely kludge-like thing about this code is the special case for 1. You might try coming up with your own solution to account for a complete row of pixels. You'll need to change a small amount of my code, but I encourage you to find better solutions to my algorithms.

Now that we've completed a single line and all of our counting routines, we are ready to compress a full image. In the next section of this chapter, we'll examine the practical use of this technique but for now we'll simply break down the last part of this compression technique.

The following code shows how to compress a full pixel image:

```
//************************************
U16ptr GRAPHIC :: LLECompression16Bit (U16ptr Image, int wid, int hgt, U32ptr
NumPixels) const
{
        int w = wid, h = hgt, size;
        int BytesInLine = 0;

        U16ptr TempCompress, CompressPtr, RetCompress;
        U16ptr ImagePtr = Image;             // used for the bitmap we'll be using
                                             // this for the actual compression

        TempCompress = new U16[w*(h<<2)];
        // we don't know how big this compressed data will be so we make it
        // really big just in case.
        CompressPtr = TempCompress;          // a pointer to the temporary buffer
        if (TempCompress == NULL)            // memory not available
        {
                if (TempCompress != NULL) delete TempCompress;
                *NumPixels = 0;
                return NULL;
        }

        //********************

        while (h--)
        {
                // ****** get all of the necessary data for this scan line ******
```

```
            LLECompressSingleLine16Bit (CompressPtr, ImagePtr, w,
                                        &BytesInLine);

            CompressPtr += BytesInLine;        // offset pointer
            ImagePtr += w;                     // move to the next scan line
    }

        size = CompressPtr-TempCompress;       // memory handling

        RetCompress = new U16[size];           // 2 bytes for every one
        if (RetCompress == NULL)               // no memory
        {
            if (TempCompress != NULL) delete TempCompress;
            return NULL;
        }

        Memcpy16Bit (RetCompress, TempCompress, size);

        *NumPixels = size;                     // global

        delete TempCompress;                   // clear up our temporary memory
        return RetCompress;
}

//***********************************
```

At this stage we assume that SearchColor has been set correctly to account for either 15-bit or 16-bit fuchsia. We assume that the image data is valid and that the pointers are valid. We assume that the width and height are valid numbers.

This is legacy code and could probably be written a little cleaner, but it works and it is reasonably fast. I used to have an LLECompression8Bit, so I use the name LLE-Compression16Bit to be more specific. You may wish to rename it. It accepts four parameters. The first is the raw image data named Image (go figure). The second and third are width and height. The last parameter is a count for the number of pixels in the compressed array that will be the result of calling this function. This value is only useful for saving the compressed image data in a separate file.

While working on Doppelganger at Ion Storm, I would load thousands of tiles and then save them immediately back out to a *.lle file. The next time I loaded the level, I just loaded the *.lle files when they were available instead of the *.tga files; load time dropped to one-twelfth of the original load time. In addition, when we made the level file, which consisted of thousands of tiles put into a single file, we just stored the compressed data and load times dropped even more. In each case, we used the NumPixels parameter to know how many pixels to write to a file. Again, this parameter has no meaning while playing the game, only during the saving and loading of the pixels. You will notice in the class description the function LoadLLE, which loads the stored data. The Save functions then only save LLE data.

There are a lot of local variables, so bear with me. We make the width and height local in w and h. size is the final size of our compressed data before we return.

BytesInLine tells us how many pixels we get in each scan line as we compress line by line. This will just be used to offset pointers.

TempCompress is a pointer to a 16-bit buffer that will hold the entire image data before we actually know how big it really needs to be. This variable must point to a really large 16-bit buffer in case the image data produces a large compressed data. This pointer is permanent in the sense that we will not offset the pointer as data is added to this buffer. CompressPtr is what we will use to offset our position in Temp-Compress as we slowly create compressed data and store it in TempCompress. Basically, CompressPtr is just a pointer to track where to write in the TempCompress array. RetCompress is a pointer to the final data to be returned to the calling function. We could return TempCompress, but then we would have allocated three to eight times the necessary memory in most cases, and I think that it's better to get a compact compressed image. Now we declare a local pointer, ImagePtr, to our original image data. That does it for local variables.

Next we create a huge buffer for storing our compression data since we have no idea how big our compression data will finally be. You might think that this is excessive in size and I would tend to agree. However, in a few rare cases, this code has broken because I did not allocate a large enough buffer here. The buffer needs to be slightly bigger than the original image anyway since the compressed data can be 50 percent larger. For example, if you have a Targa only 1 pixel wide and 64 pixels high, the final image will be 2 pixels per scan line, or 128 bytes, as shown in Figure 14.5.

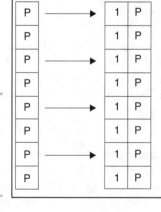

The only time an image will be larger using LLE is when a full line of pixels is involved. This example here is very rare when a single vertical line of pixels doubles in size since each line needs a count, and here we add the number 1 to tell us how many pixels to draw. More common is a graphic like a button which is completely square. It picks up one extra pixel, making the image just slightly larger, as in Figure 14.4.

Figure 14.5
Compressed data enlarges amount of memory required

It is a lot bigger, and although I wouldn't recommend using compression on an image 1 pixel wide, you might want to use LLE for all of your loading and saving, so I have to make sure that it never breaks. At this huge size, I have never broken this code. If you are careful about not using LLE everywhere, you should be able to reduce the size of this buffer to two times the width*height. You might want to also consider making this buffer really large and global. This would prevent any issues arising from allocation and deallocation of memory.

Note: Memory allocation is slow, in some cases very slow. If you are considering speeding up your code, one of the first things you should avoid during gameplay is memory allocation. Allocate all of the blocks of memory you will need before the game begins; this will dramatically increase performance. For argument's sake, malloc is about 0.5 percent faster than new but because new is so much easier to use, I always use it.

We set our pointer to the beginning of the buffer; we won't touch the buffer again until we memcpy it into a secondary and final buffer. Then we will deallocate it. We test to make sure that our allocated memory is valid and then start on the main compression loop. Testing to see if the memory is valid may seem like an unnecessary precaution, especially with computers shipping with 128 MB these days, but Windows 95 sometimes has problems handling memory over 64 MB and other apps may still be running and hogging resources. Still, you could probably eliminate the test and be just fine.

The main loop begins by testing if the remaining height left to traverse is not equal to 0. If not, it reduces the height value and enters/continues into the loop. Then once inside the loop, we call LLECompressSingleLine16Bit, which we declared earlier. It takes a few parameters and then returns a counter telling how many bytes were put into the buffer pointer. CompressPtr is offset by the number of 16-bit values put into the array based on the returned value BytesInLine. Then we offset our ImagePtr by the width of our image, effectively moving us to the next image scan line. The loop repeats until (h == 0).

Note: In Visual C++ 5.0, I once had a bug in a while loop that read while (h--) {}, where the loop continued forever no matter what the value of h. This obviously should have stopped once h was equal to 0 but something odd happened during compile. No matter what I did, the bug persisted. You might want to change the loop to while (h-- > 0) just to be safe.

Moving on, we calculate the difference between the TempCompress pointer and the CompressPtr pointer, which will tell us how many total bytes we wrote. You can keep tabs as you step through line by line, but this method is easier. One thing to note here is that the pointer subtraction yields the number of 16-bit values, not the number of bytes, which would be twice as much. Since we know how many 16-bit values have been written, we can allocate memory for our destination buffer, RetCompress. Then we memcpy the compressed data into its new home, set the return value of NumPixels, deallocate our local memory, and return the new buffer.

As you can see from this code, this process is pretty straightforward and easy to understand. We just compress each image scan line in turn. This code would have been much more complex if I hadn't broken it down into multiple functions. When you have a really complex problem, build simple routines to solve easy parts of it and the rest kind of falls into place.

This code has been thoroughly tested throughout the years and minor improvements have made it bullet-proof to my knowledge. However, knowing that many more people will now use this code, I am sure that someone will break it. Still, it is mostly reliable and I wish you many hours of fun using it.

Drawing with LLE

When you first read through this you may wonder just how fast all of this code is. There are a lot of little optimizations in here that make it very fast. For an image that is 25 to 70 percent black space, this code is much faster than a straight blit. That may not impress you, but this code is about as fast as this kind of thing gets outside of hardware.

The next section will cover the actual clipping, but here we have the call to clip when it seems necessary. The intent of this function is to take a compressed image and only draw the non-black (non-fuchsia) areas. Since the compression is done, which is the hard part, this decompression onto the screen should be easy. The difficulty is moderate to hard.

```
//***********************************
void GRAPHIC :: DrawLLECompressed16Bit (SCREEN_STRUCT* sc, int x, int y)
{
      if (Image == NULL) return;
      if (sc->Screen == NULL) return;

      int      w = Width, h = Height;               // local variables

      // handle clipping here, testing for partially clipped.
      // DrawLLECompressed_Clipped16Bit may end up clipping the entire image

      if ((y<0) || (x<0)                            // clip top left
          || (y+h > sc->Height) || (x+w > sc->Width))   // clip bottom right
      {
            DrawLLECompressed_Clipped16Bit (sc, x, y);
            return;
      }

      //*************** regular drawing

      U16ptr pointr = sc->Screen+ x+ (y*sc->Width);        // starting location
      U16ptr scptr;
      U16ptr index  = Image;
      int    len, wid = sc->Width;
      int    runs;
      //*************** loop

      while (h-- > 0)                      // once for each scan line
      {
            scptr = pointr;                // temp screen pointer
            runs = *index++;               // get the number of runs for the line and
```

```
                                        // advance the pointer
            if (runs == 1)              // copy entire scan line.
            {
                Memcpy16Bit (scptr, index, w);
                index += w;
            }
            else                        // 0 will fall out automatically, we don't
                                        // need to test for it
            {
                while (--runs>0)
                {
                    scptr += *index++;    // move the screen pointer
                                          // over to its new  destination 0's
              len = *index++;             // get run length and advance

                    Memcpy16Bit (scptr, index, len); // grab data
                    scptr += len;   // advance temp pointer
                    index += len;   // advance image pointer
                }
            }
            pointr += wid;              // advance screen position in y direction
        }
}
//**********************************
```

DrawLLECompressed16Bit take three parameters and returns nothing. The sc pointer holds all of the frame buffer data, and x and y hold the screen position where we will be drawing the image.

Since this is part of a class, we will be relying on some data in the class for drawing, namely Image, Width, and Height. The first thing we do is some preliminary testing to make sure that all is well. This is a good idea but you may wish to eliminate this code. We make Width and Height local and then test for clipping. If the position for *x* or *y* is beyond the edges of the screen, we send control on to the clipping routine and return immediately afterward.

If clipping is not necessary, we prepare for regular drawing using LLE data. We declare pointr, which is the leftmost *x* position of our screen position and will change only at the end of drawing each scan line. We then declare scptr, which will be set equal to pointr at the beginning of each scan line of drawing, and then advance from left to right while drawing pixels. You might think of pointr as your *y* position and scptr as your *x* position during the drawing cycle, although that would not be entirely accurate. We then declare a local pointer to the image data and declare wid, len, and runs. wid holds the width of the screen and is declared local for speed. len is a value we read from each section moving across a scan line telling us how many pixels to draw or not draw. runs tells us how many runs or sections are in a scan line of drawing.

The main loop is quite simple, which makes it fast. Here you will find my loop correction to fix the Visual C++ bug. This fix has remained in this legacy code. The loop moves down the screen h scan lines, one at a time.

Once inside the loop, we set our scptr to our current screen position; all drawing and manipulation will be performed on this pointer. We then read the first byte of our image data, which is the number of sections per scan line. At the same time, we advance our image data pointer index since we no longer need that piece of data.

When runs equals 1, we just memcpy the data following it to the screen. We know that the number of pixels to copy is equal to the width of our image, so we simply copy w number of pixels and advance our index (image data) the same number. This completes the case of 1, so we fall down to the end of the loop where we advance our screen position by the screen width value we stored earlier in wid.

That was the super easy part. In any case but 1, things get a little hairy. 0 is easiest, so let's start with that. When the value of runs is equal to 0, the while loop will fall out immediately and never execute:

```
while (--runs>0)
```

What this does is subtract 1 from runs and tests to make sure that it is still larger than 0. Since we have a 0, the loop falls out and we automatically advance to the next frame buffer scan line. You might think that we need a special case for testing for 0, but that test actually slows things down. What happens is that not very many lines are completely clipped (with a value of 0). This means that we are adding a test for every scan line even though this instance rarely occurs. We are testing for nothing and slowing things down. Plus, not testing simplifies things, making the code faster on top of that. The smaller the code, generally, the faster the execution, since the instruction cache is limited, meaning that large functions will flush other calling functions. This slows down everything.

Let's step through the execution of this small inner loop, assuming that runs is equal to 3. That means that we actually have two runs, plus one for the encoding. That equates to two times through our loop. The while loop first subtracts 1 from runs, meaning that the very first test is when runs equals 2, so the loop will only execute twice, just like it should.

The first line in the loop advances the screen pointer to the first place where we will begin drawing. This effectively skips over the fuchsia data so we can copy the image data onto the screen. Then we advance the index pointer:

```
scptr += *index++;
```

We know that this data appears in pairs, with no-draw areas followed by draw areas. The next 16-bit data piece in index is a count for the number of pixels to copy onto the screen. We grab that number and advance the index pointer:

```
len = *index++;
```

Then we copy the pixel data onto the screen and advance the index pointer and the screen pointer past the copied data. The last thing that happens is the loop continues and then falls out to where the screen pointer, pointr, advances and we move down to the next scan line:

```
Memcpy16Bit (scptr, index, len);
scptr += len;
index += len;
```

372 ■ Chapter 14

That about does it. Not the easiest thing in the world to follow but not too bad, eh? Clipping is much harder and much slower. We'll discuss that next.

Clipping with LLE

As difficult as it is to perform—and this is rather tough, especially on the left—clipping is a necessary evil. You have to make the drawing happen anywhere on the screen and when you happen to be on an edge, things can get messy. You may remember regular clipping as described in Chapter 11. That was easy enough because no decoding was necessary. You better put on your thinking cap, because this is not easy to explain. Incidentally, this code works great and seems to be pretty fast, especially considering how much simple math is in here.

You may notice right off the bat that there are a lot more local variables to contain various clipping data. The parameter list is the same as in DrawLLECompressed16Bit (discussed above), making this function very similar, and most of the local variables are the same as well. I will forego the explanation of the same variables.

```
//**********************************
void GRAPHIC :: DrawLLECompressed_Clipped16Bit (SCREEN_STRUCT* sc, int x, int y)
{
    U16ptr  pointr = sc->Screen + x + (y*sc->Width); // starting location
    U16ptr  scptr;
    U16ptr  index  = Image;
    int  len, bytes, clipleft = 0, clipright = 0, newlen, newdist;
    int  runs, wid = sc->Width, hgt = sc->Height;
    int  w = Width, h = Height;
    if (y < -h) return;              // totally clipped, do not draw
    if (y >= hgt) return;
    if (x < -w) return;
    if (x >= wid) return;

    if (y+h > hgt)                   // clip bottom
    {
        h = hgt-y;                   // shorten height...simple
    }

    // run through normal drawing to get to the desired line
    // advance index pointer. We are pretending to draw here so that we
    // can clip properly in the y direction.
    while (y<0)
    {
        y++; pointr += wid; h--;     // move toward our goal
        int runs = *index++;         // get the number of runs for the
                                     // line and advance the pointer
        if (runs == 1) {index += w;} // a full scan line of data to skip
        else                         // 0 will fall out automatically, we
                                     // don't need to test for it
        {
            while (--runs>0)
            {
```

```
                    index++;            // move the screen pointer over to its new
                                        // destination 0's

                    len = *index++; // get run length and advance
                    index += len;
                }
            }
        }
        if (x < 0) {clipleft = -x;}     // set the relative distance, this will
                                        // give us a distval
        if (x+w > wid) {clipright = wid-x;}

        while (h-- > 0)                 // once for each scan line
        {
            scptr = pointr;             // temporary screen pointer

            runs = *index++;            // get the number of runs for the
                                        // line and advance the pointer
            if (runs == 1)
            {
                if (clipleft)           // clipping on the left.. complicated
                {
                    len = w-clipleft;
                    scptr += clipleft;
                    index += clipleft;
                    Memcpy16Bit (scptr, index, len);            // grab data
                    index -= clipleft;
                }
                else if (clipright)  // clipping on the right, easy
                {
                    Memcpy16Bit (scptr, index, clipright);      // grab data
                }
                else Memcpy16Bit (scptr, index, w);
                index+=w;
            }
            else                                // 0 will fall out automatically,
                                                // we don't need to test for it

            {
                bytes = 0;
                while (--runs>0)
                {
                    bytes += *index;    // for a count
                    scptr += *index++;  // move the screen pointer over
                                        // to its new destination 0's

                    len = *index++;     // get run length and advance
                    if (clipleft)
                    {
                        if (bytes >= clipleft)                  // no clip
                        {
                            Memcpy16Bit (scptr, index, len); // grab data
                        }
```

14

Chapter

```
                                else if (bytes+len >= clipleft)
                                // we need to clip it
                                {
                                        newdist = clipleft-bytes;
                                        newlen = len-newdist;
                                        scptr += newdist;
                                        // move to the 0 location
                                        index += newdist;
                                        Memcpy16Bit (scptr, index, newlen);
                                        // store data
                                        scptr -= newdist;
                                        // complete adds
                                        index -= newdist;
                                        // this will be updated below
                                }
                                // dont draw
                                // else
                        }
                        else if (clipright)
                        {
                                if (bytes >= clipright) {}              // do nothing
                                else if (bytes+len < clipright)
                                {
                                        Memcpy16Bit (scptr, index, len); // grab data
                                }
                                else // clip
                                {
                                        int newdist = clipright-bytes;
                                        Memcpy16Bit (scptr, index, newdist);
                                        // store data
                                }
                        }
                        else Memcpy16Bit (scptr, index, len);      // grab data
                        bytes += len;                              // update count
                        scptr += len;
                        index += len;
                }
        }
        pointr += wid;
        }
}
//**********************************
```

We do have a few new local variables. bytes is a temporary value holder for track-ing the number of bytes left before clipping can occur on the left or right side. clipleft and clipright tell us how many pixels to chop off on the left or right side of an image. newlen and newdist are used to temporarily store values while we change other val-ues in order to change the originals back. We'll discuss these later.

After our declarations, we try to clip the entire image if possible, saving consider-able processing time if nothing is to be drawn. This test becomes a simple intersection of rectangles test: Is one rectangle partially inside another? If not, return. We do need to test all four sides.

That part was quick and painless. Because it is so fast to completely clip a graphic, you could run every graphic in the game through the clip routine and most simply wouldn't make it on screen. Still, that is not a great method and it does waste a small amount of CPU time. It's better to only try and draw the items on screen. We'll get to that in Chapter 16 when we discuss tile systems.

Note: Looking at the screen, you need to realize that most clipping will happen along the top and bottom of the screen. In 640x480, most of the real estate is along the horizontal, meaning that images are more likely to clip on the top and bottom of the frame buffer. Since our clipping is designed to be fastest along these two sides, that means it will be fast in general. It is fast because we simply do not draw full scan lines along the top and bottom. Avoiding drawing a scan line or two will always be faster than drawing the full image.

Our first actual clipping is performed when our graphic goes beyond the bottom of the screen; this form of clipping is about the easiest possible. We simply don't go as far down the screen when drawing. This is set up by reducing the height to the maximum position in the y direction minus the current y position. Easy math and very fast. Another interesting thing about clipping on the bottom, and the top for that matter, is that drawing time is always reduced, meaning that this clipping will actually be faster than not clipping. Sorry to say, but clipping on the sides is not so good. Right-side clipping is slow and left-side clipping is dreadful.

Clipping on the top is a bit trickier. We need to advance in the y direction until y is 0. We go through the normal draw loop, pretending to draw each image scan line until we reach the point where y is 0 and pixels will actually start appearing on the screen. This drawing is exactly like drawing in DrawLLECompressed16Bit, only no blitting is happening, which makes this code very fast.

Note: This routine clips to 0,0 and the width and height of the screen. If you need clipping to occur at other places on the screen, which is very likely, you will want to use the global variables that you test against instead of 0,0 and width and height. I have left the clipping rectangle variables out of this code for simplicity. You will find them later in this chapter when we look at the final class. Look for clipleft, clipright, cliptop, and clipbottom.

The last thing to do before entering the main loop is to set the two variables for left-side clipping and right-side clipping. When x is a negative number, we want to chop off our image on the left side equal to x but not negative. Since x should always start at 0 or greater, we need to offset the start position in our image so that we can at least start at 0 on the screen. That means $-x$.

For right-side clipping, we cannot let a memcpy go beyond the rightmost edge of the screen. If it will go over, we need to calculate the maximum length that we can copy before running over. That happens to be wid–x.

14

Chapter

Now we come to our main loop. One important fact: At this stage, the top clipping and bottom clipping have been performed. This loop is dedicated to left and right clipping only. Clipping may only need to be done on the top or the bottom, so we also need to account for the fact that clipping on the left and right may not be necessary.

Glance over the structure of this main loop. You will notice that it looks identical in structure to the function DrawLLECompressed16Bit listed in the previous section of this chapter. This is by design. We want our code to be consistent and readable. We definitely do not want it to work one way in one routine and differently in a similar routine.

> **Note:** For this book, there was a lot of rewrite in order to make things more consistent and readable. I do not code this consistently or perfectly in real life. The amount of change I had to make was minimal, but the point remains.

We start with the while (h-- > 0), like we had before, which loops through each remaining image scan line. I say "remaining" because many scan lines may have been clipped off before we arrived at this point. We assign our screen position pointer scptr to pointr to begin at the leftmost edge of each frame buffer scan line. Next, we store the number of runs and advance our index pointer.

If the number of runs is 1, we have a full image scan line of image data to blit to the screen; this makes clipping on the sides very easy. For clipping on the right, we just don't blit as much data to the screen. For clipping on the left, we start later in the image to blit. For example, if x== –3 then we start blitting from the third pixel and only blit the width–3.

If we clip on the left, we calculate the number of pixels to blit, len. We take the entire length, *w*, minus our clipleft value which should be the absolute value of our *x* position. The scptr was set to some position off the left portion of the screen, so we add clipleft to make it 0 and add a little to our image scan line position, index, so that we start in the proper position. We blit the remaining pixels to the frame buffer and then subtract clipleft to restore the index to its original position. After we fall out of the if statement, the normal addition takes over: index += w.

This may be somewhat controversial. I've played with several ideas including temporary variables, doing all of the math locally, and using more variables for tracking changes. This makes things more complex and really does slow things down. The method I chose, as contrived as it is, seems to work the fastest and the best, so I'll stick with it.

Clipping on the right is simplicity itself. We know our clipright value, which is the image width minus any clipping. That math is already performed for you, so all we need to do is blit the number of pixels equal to clipright. Our index pointer advancement will happen naturally below that: index += w. Because all three possibilities use the same pointer advancement code, this helps keep the code smaller. Our three possibilities are clip left, clip right, and no side clipping, which is the most common.

The last possibility is handled quite nicely: Memcpy16Bit (scptr, index, w). This possibility occurs when only the top or bottom was clipped and the sides didn't need it. We advance our index pointer the same way as before: index += w.

Note: This clipping code, you may have noticed, does not handle clipping on opposite sides. It will clip on any single side and any two adjacent sides. If you have clipping regions that are intentionally small, then change the else if's in the code to if's where it tests for: if (clipleft) {} else if (clipright) {} else...

That completes our section on single section blitting with clipping. Now comes the hairy part. Most of the time, we will have a section count of 2 or greater, meaning that most of our clipping time will be spent in the next section.

Our friend is the variable named bytes. It will help us track our position and perform all testing before we do any blitting. Basically, all math will be performed on bytes to determine when we need to draw pixels on the screen.

The first thing we do when preparing to draw a multisection area is set the bytes count to 0 and start our while loop. Remember from the previous section that this loop falls out immediately if the number of runs is 0, which then advances to the next frame buffer scan line. Now that we have entered the loop with one or more runs, we begin the clipping.

Because this is a loop, it is designed to repeat. Our first line inside the loop adds to the existing value of bytes, which will start as 0 the first time but will be more if the loop repeats. We store the number of pixels for no-draw and offset our screen pointer the appropriate number of pixels. Then we set len to the number of draw pixels. Now we are ready for the clipping.

Clipping on the left has three possibilities: Draw the complete run of pixels, draw a partial line of pixels, or don't draw at all. We test first for a complete run where the bytes accumulation is equal to or has passed the clipleft value. A simple memcpy suffices and we then fall out of the test and offset bytes by len, scptr by len, and index by len. This moves us on to the next section.

The next possibility for clipping on the left is a partial draw. We need to calculate how much of the line needs to be drawn, so we need to know the difference between the clipleft value and the bytes accumulator. We store the difference in newdist and then subtract it from len, producing the actual number of pixels we will draw. Now we offset scptr to the position where we can copy directly into it. We offset our source pixels in index to where we need to copy from, and then we do a straight blit. Lastly, we reset the pointers to their original position and fall out of this if statement to offset our values to the appropriate amounts.

You may want to go over the code and my description several times to fully understand it.

One last possibility still remains: Don't draw at all. Well, that is pretty simple: Don't do anything. Then fall out to where the pointers are offset and repeat the loop.

14

Chapter

The last clipping section in the DrawLLECompressed_Clipped16Bit code is the right-side clipping. This is easy in comparison to the left but our same three possibilities exist: Draw the entire graphics scan line, draw part of the graphics scan line, or draw nothing at all. This time, the test is easy for drawing nothing at all and is actually performed first. If the accumulator, bytes, has accumulated more pixels than the right side, we fall out. Our next test is if the full line can fit. If so, we can do a straight blit of the pixels into the frame buffer. Our last test doesn't need to be performed since it is an else situation. This is the fastest way since the last test is somewhat more complex. Anyway, we recalculate the number of pixels to blit based on the difference of clipright and our bytes value. This section, as you can tell, is much simpler than clipping on the left.

The remaining else occurs if neither the clipleft nor clipright variables were used, meaning that no clipping on the left or right is needed. Here we perform a straight blit. That does it. The clipping is now complete. The last thing we do is advance our pointers, like we mentioned earlier, and complete the loop.

Of course, that was a single iteration through the height of the image. We need to go through all of this work again for the next scan line of graphics data after we advance the screen pointer using our final listing:

```
pointr += wid;
```

Just a few final thoughts: This code can be improved from a speed point of view. A few areas of consideration would be to have a separate loop for left-side clipping and right-side clipping, maybe in different functions. Making the top and bottom clipping a separate function when only those are necessary will speed things a lot. Conversion to assembly might be a good idea but is extensive work. I tried that and achieved about a 6 percent performance increase, hardly worth bothering about except on older machines.

This code is designed to work and it works well. However, it could be designed much better if you were to simply optimize it and not worry about how a reader might read it. My concern here was for readability and functionality. I hope that I achieved both.

Chapter 15

Animation

Animation has been around for a long time now. Walt Disney brought it to popular media with his first full-length feature *Snow White*. Animation is so common in games that we take it for granted. Creatures walk around the screen, buildings are slowly constructed, workers go between the mine and the home base, and even the cursor pulses.

Animation can be organized in so many different ways and with so many different structures that no one has established a clear "right" way of doing animation yet. I will provide many considerations in this chapter to help you decide how to do the animation in your game. There are many factors that go into the design and maintenance of good animation code, and all of these considerations may boggle your mind. I will try to provide a few different designs in this chapter, as well as all related design considerations.

Animation is simple, right? Basically you have a series of "frames" that need to play in a particular order to make the animation look smooth. Then there is the world position change. As a creature, tank, car, or spaceship animates, it usually moves somewhere. How much does it move? Is it a set distance or does it vary? In StarCraft, a number of ships move across the screen without any apparent motion (animation) like the Protoss workers. They don't animate but they move. What about animating special effects like lightning or magical spells? Consider that the thrust from a spaceship should be animated.

Something interesting has changed in the past few years. While playing some of the old arcade games, I began to notice how little animation they supported. Take a game like Mappy. He has an animation cycle of four frames for walking side to side, a falling animation (two frames), a bouncing animation (two frames), and a few frames when he dies, perhaps six. That's the main character. The other creatures in the game have even fewer. Not counting blowing up, Dig Dug seems to have three frames of animation for all of its creatures. Boy, have we come a long way, baby.

Animation is now a major part of any game, and some game companies have programmers dedicated solely to animation. This is an intractable problem that has a lot in common with state machines and AI. So you'll hear a lot of prelude about AI and different states in this chapter.

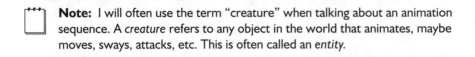

Note: I will often use the term "creature" when talking about an animation sequence. A *creature* refers to any object in the world that animates, maybe moves, sways, attacks, etc. This is often called an *entity*.

The Cycle and the Sequence

The concepts established early in the animation industry remain with us today. A frame of animation is a single image of something happening. It could take 30 frames of a person walking before the walking starts to look the same, or repeats.

The concept of a *cycle* is critical. A repeating sequence of frames makes up a cycle and that cycle is the basis of our first animation class. The animation that I typically use as an example is the walk cycle. There are hundreds of potential cycles and sequences such as an attack sequence, a run cycle, a transformation sequence, a fly cycle, a launch sequence, a spear throwing sequence, a digging cycle, ad infinitum. A walk "cycle" typically takes about eight frames but can be as few as four or as many as 32. I have never heard of anyone using more than 32 frames for any animation sequence, but somebody may someday, especially for really complex motion.

The last concept important here is the sequence. A *sequence* is a group of animation frames that do not repeat, like an attack or a jump. There is usually a starting frame that runs until it reaches an end frame that leads to a different animation sequence. "Sequence" is a more general term and applies to animation in general. You can always use it, while cycle is more specific.

How this is done from an art perspective requires a lot of work from the artists, but software is making it easier for artists to deliver the kind of art necessary in most of today's games. Typically, an artist will first compose a 3-D model of some creature, robot, or vehicle using one of today's 3-D modeling packages.

Most artists create a model, which usually takes from a few days to several weeks depending on its complexity. Then they animate the model, creating whichever sequences are required by the designer/producer.

Preparing the Art

If your game has 3-D models, the fun has just begun. You have an animated model. Now you need texture maps for it, you need a way to put the textures on the models that will go easily into the game, and you need to develop a good delivery system for all of this. None of the current 3-D modeling software packages offer a way to do this effectively (that I know of), so you will need to develop the tools for this.

There are quite a few benefits to developing 3-D animation, however. 3-D animation is delivered as a series of morph targets or vertex transformations. This has the effect of reducing memory requirements between frames since you only need to save between 200 and 500 bytes per frame of animation, and you don't need to worry about eight directions since you are doing real-time rotations.

You can also crunch textures. *Crunching* involves figuring out which parts of a texture map will actually be rendered, and fitting all of these pieces onto a single texture. This will also dramatically reduce the memory footprint. The 3-D animation can face any direction. Moving in the world becomes a series of simple offsets based on angles. This adds a lot to a game like Total Annihilation, but can be quite difficult to accomplish. Direct3D is not very easy to use, and in addition you need to do special calculations for different angles, for conservation of rotational momentum when turning, and for coefficient of friction when vehicles accelerate, etc. The physics needs to be realistic, and can be computationally intensive.

The hardest part of doing the game with 3-D is delivery. No 3-D package delivers the 3-D information well. You will need tools for texture mapping, transforming, and converting the data to a usable format. The worst thing about 3-D characters is that they require dozens of polygons to make a good-looking model, assuming a small guy on screen. They require more if your characters are going to be close up or large. If you have 80 guys on the screen, boy, will your game get slow. Things don't slow down too bad in 2-D, especially with span lists where every pixel is only drawn once.

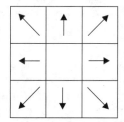

Figure 15.1
The eight directions commonly used for animation

2-D delivery is only slightly easier. You will need to decide the number of angles needed for your game. Most games use eight directions as shown in Figure 15.1. These are the four cardinal directions and the diagonals in between. That makes movement fairly easy to calculate and keeps the number of frames of animation fairly low.

You need to remember that there will be a sequence of animation for each direction. That means eight frames (more or less) of walk animation for each of the eight directions. So a simple walk cycle, as illustrated in Figure 15.2, in eight directions takes a total of 64 frames of animation. A 32x32 image in 16-bit using LLE compression (described in Chapter 14) will still take roughly 1,090 bytes. That means that a single walk cycle for one creature in the game takes about 70 K. When you figure in all of the different animation sequences and cycles and all of the different creatures, you are talking about a lot of memory. Newer games like StarCraft use 16 directions, which doubles that memory footprint.

Figure 15.2
An eight-frame walk cycle

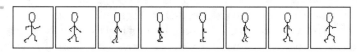

In terms of the rendering angle, tell the artists to render from 30° above the horizon (azimuth) when preparing 2-D art for your game. Also remember that you may want to play with this number but generally 30° is the best way to go. Then have them set the rendering angle on the horizon at 45° to achieve eight separate rendering angles. In case that is not clear, imagine the character in the middle of a room. Now keeping your distance, walk 45° clockwise around him, stop, render, and now walk another 45°. Once you set up the rendering angles, the animation sequences, and the different creatures that will follow those animations, you are ready to render. All current 3-D art packages offer 3-D rendering as a batch process, meaning that they can render all frames to a single directory or multiple directories.

3-D Art Packages

3-D packages most often are one of the following (listed in order of decreasing popularity): 3D Studio Max or V4, Alias, Soft Image, Lightwave, and Nichimen. There are others but their popularity is so low they are not worth mentioning.

In talking to artists who know more than one package, they seem to favor certain art packages depending on ease of use, quality of rendering, special effects, and the number of steps required to achieve desired results. It isn't fair to talk to an artist who only knows how to use one art package; after all, who could you find to be more biased than somebody who hasn't tried something else?

In terms of modeling, most of the artists I've talked to like Lightwave best. Animating is a toss-up between Alias and Lightwave. Quality of renders is generally given to Alias. The package that uses the most number of steps to achieve desired results is 3D Studio Max. These opinions are completely unscientific, but my experience tells me these artists are right. The best bang for the buck award definitely goes to Lightwave. It does almost everything that the others do straight out of the box for about $1,500 while Alias costs as much as $30,000 or more. I do not know all of the details, but 3D Studio costs $3,500 and you can't animate (creatures or anything using kinematics) in it. That requires an add-on called Character Studio that costs about another $1,200. Don't forget all of the other modules it requires until it finally is equal to Lightwave. 3D Studio does have a few sweet bells and whistles, but bang for the buck is definitely not in 3D Studio's favor. It can do more than some packages, but you end up paying close to $8,000.

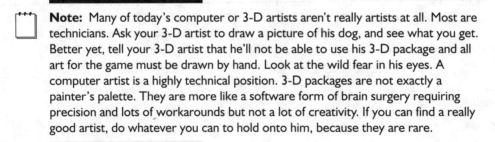

Note: Many of today's computer or 3-D artists aren't really artists at all. Most are technicians. Ask your 3-D artist to draw a picture of his dog, and see what you get. Better yet, tell your 3-D artist that he'll not be able to use his 3-D package and all art for the game must be drawn by hand. Look at the wild fear in his eyes. A computer artist is a highly technical position. 3-D packages are not exactly a painter's palette. They are more like a software form of brain surgery requiring precision and lots of workarounds but not a lot of creativity. If you can find a really good artist, do whatever you can to hold onto him, because they are rare.

Mirroring

One great memory utilization optimization that you can make is only rendering half the animation directions, maybe four of eight directions. Then you flip those directions horizontally during draw time to "reflect" and draw facing the other way. This would mean that a walk cycle moving to the right could be flipped to look as though the character is walking left. By doing this, the walking to the left graphics could be eliminated, saving a significant chunk of memory. You can also mirror position information so when a frame of animation is supposed to offset the creature world position, just take the negative value for reflecting. If you are new to this idea, I'll let you in on a little secret: Most 2-D games use "mirroring" or something very similar. It really cuts your memory footprint nearly in half.

> **Note:** You cannot mirror walking north, or toward the top of the screen. The creature is facing fully away and you can't see its face. When heading south, toward the bottom of the screen, he would be facing you completely. Still, mirroring on the sides reduces eight directions to five: upper-right (and mirrored), right (and mirrored), bottom right (and mirrored), top, and bottom. 16 directions are reduced to 9. The more directions you have, the bigger the savings as a percentage.

No game uses four directions for animation anymore. If you release a game with only four animated directions, I will track you down and beat you with an organic carrot. Also, mirroring wouldn't do you much good.

There is a problem with mirroring. If you have realistic shadows, they do not mirror at all since they are at an odd angle, maybe 45°. In Age of Empires, our solution was to have a frame of animation as a graphic and its shadow as a separate graphic. Then we stored five directions of animation and stored eight directions of shadows. What a pain, but even this wasn't enough to keep our complete graphics from taking less than about 25 MB. I did something very similar on Doppelganger. The artists would render a graphic as one image and a shadow as another. I made a tool that would combine the two as one graphic with a SHADOW flag set to TRUE. That way I knew that the shadow was attached, and I could mirror it.

> **Note:** When preparing graphics for your game, make sure that the artists turn off anti-aliasing. You will be rendering your creatures onto a fuchsia background (or black) and the edge pixels of that creature will be faded. LLE compression will not eliminate these pixels, so your graphics will have a fuchsia "halo." It looks bad.

Mirroring can be slow. You are copying memory backward, and unless you do the math right you are in for a huge slowdown. You'll need separate memcpy routines to copy backward. This code is simple but never as fast as a memcpy. You might think that there is a flag for making memcpy go backward, and you'd be right. There is an assembly instruction STD that tells memcpy to go backward. Another instruction, CLD, tells memcpy to go forward. The problem is, if you copy backward the pixels turn out the same. When you copy backward, both the source and destination pixels are copied backward and two negatives make a positive. In other words, you get the same result as if you copied forward. What we need to do is draw forward and read the pixels backward.

Here we have a little assembly to help you accomplish this mirroring feat. Simply pass in pointers to the beginning of the source line and the pixel where the beginning of backward drawing will start, the destination pixel. This is at the beginning of a line of pixels. That is to say, use it like any other memcpy routine. This code is fast but could be faster by taking advantage of Pentium pairing rules. I left it ordered like this for clarity.

```
//*********************
void memcpy16BitBackwards (U16ptr dest, U16ptr src, int num)
{
        __asm
        {
        mov        eax, [src]
        mov        ecx, [num]
        mov        edx, [dest]

LOOP1:

        sub        ecx,1
        test       ecx,ecx
        je         END1

        mov        bx, [eax+ecx*2]
        mov        [edx],bx
        add        edx,2
        jmp        LOOP1
END1:
        }

}
//*********************
```

I like little ovals beneath the characters, like StarCraft uses. Basically, there are three or four types of shadows in the game; I haven't counted. The size of the graphic determines the size of the shadow, but the shadow does not animate; it is simply an oval that appears beneath the creature. It is good enough. By the way, a game without shadows these days is completely unacceptable. If you release a game without shadows, I will track you down and beat you with a wet sock.

The artists will need to deliver these animation sequences to you in a digestible form. You'll have to decide what that is. I prefer a folder on the network with the name of the creature/model. Inside the folder is a Graphics folder that contains folders like Walk, Run, Eat, Die1, etc. Inside Walk, for example, will be a bunch of Targas named walk_a1.tga, walk_a2.tga, walk_a3.tga, etc. All of these will sort normally, or you can sort them at run time based on name. "walk_" is the name of the graphic. The "a" is the direction, and there should be a "b", "c", "d", etc. The number is the first, second, third, etc., frame in that particular animation sequence. I prefer this delivery method. You can choose your own, but decide what that is early on in the process and your artists will love you.

Another minor decision for you to make is which direction is which, at least in naming. Direction "a" or "1," depending on your preference, could be any direction. Is it up, left, or down to the right? I prefer the first direction to be up, or away from the screen. I understand that most people prefer the first direction to be facing right. You choose. After that you have to choose which is direction "b" or "2". Do you go clockwise or counter-clockwise? Most people go clockwise. Again, you choose.

The images that are delivered to you are generally referred to as *assets*. Assets include sound, AVI files (animated movies), and any type of graphics. Asset delivery and storage is not a trivial matter. Difficult-to-find directories or impossible-to-remember names can slow the game development cycle to a halt. Make sure that everyone understands the delivery process. Also, make sure that everyone has a say into how delivery of assets takes place; you'd be surprised how smart those artists can be.

Those images, the ones being delivered, are the topic of a minor issue. People are beginning to use BMPs more and more. My GRAPHIC class loads both BMPs and TGAs, so tell your artists to use whatever they like. Problem solved.

Establishing the Need for Animation

Now that we've established the basics about the animation process, we can move on to the meat of animation. This has a lot of parts to it so I'll break it down. A single frame of animation is actually quite complex. It has a lot more information than simply the graphic data associated with it:

1. Keep, change, and maintain the current frame number in a sequence.

2. Maintain a position in the world and have some means to translate that into screen coordinates.

3. A creature in the world should, somehow, be associated with an animation. The means can be a pointer, an index, a function call, etc.

4. All animations should be designed to work at 30 fps. Hopefully your game will run at that speed. Tell the artists to make it for that speed; you can always pause on a frame of animation for a few game frames.

5. A means must be devised to translate this animation into a final form for a large data file so that frames can be loaded directly from a single file. This greatly speeds load times and you should account for this programming early in the game development.

6. You need to devise a means of defining sound related to a frame of animation. For example, you need a way to say that a stepping sound should happen on the 13th and 24th frames of this animation.

7. You need to devise a way of skipping frames. (When editing, the artists might want to try leaving out a frame.) You also need to go back and forth through frames. A tree swaying in the wind might take 30 frames, but if you allow the animation sequence to go backward, you would only need 15 or 16. This becomes a continuous animation and can look pretty cool. Also, certain things in the world will repeat continuously, like a waterfall, so we need this availability.

8. You need timings. A frame of animation may need to wait or be used two times in a row before advancing to the next frame. This is particularly true for creatures that move slowly because the same frame of animation may need to be played three or four times before the creature takes a step. 30 fps will make all frames of animation need to wait for a game frame or two.

9. You need to plan on a full group of animation. Standard animations include: walk, wait, run, jump, attack, react (to being hit), build, return (with resources), and fire (projectile). Not all characters will have all of these animations. A character will need to have a way to transition between these various states. We'll discuss this in detail when we discuss AI.

10. You will need a way of designating when the main part of a sequence happens. Most animations are simple, but some have a point of action. The fire animation, for example, assuming the character has a bow, has the character pull out an arrow, draw the string, and then release. At the point of release, we need to make a new object, an arrow, fly across the screen until it hits something.

You also need an editor, a way of viewing the frames of animation in sequence with timings, so you can see how smooth the animation looks. It will need to show the creature moving so that the artists can set the x,y movement offsets between frames correctly. It must let the user modify timings. Be sure to try all of this in eight directions. It has to be able to step through the frames one by one and run from the first frame to the last and restart at the first so you can see if the last frame meets up well with the first frame when the sequence wraps around.

A First Look at Graphics Maintenance

Now you are ready to start loading graphics. I first want to build an understanding of a few different classes, so I will be presenting the header files to you for the next few pages. Then we'll discuss how to put all of this together. Before we go too much further, let's look at another container class. In graphic.h, you'll find the GRAPHIC_MGR class that will help us manage graphics. All it really does is manage a list of pointers to GRAPHIC. If you need a GRAPHIC, you ask for it by name and the GRAPHIC_MGR will return a pointer to it, whether it has to load it or if it already exists. Of course, if the file is not found, no harm done; a NULL value will be returned instead of a pointer to the GRAPHIC.

There are other ways to handle your graphic animation. I'm simply providing options. You may notice that this class does not use TAG_LIST (covered in Chapter 13) to help optimize search performance. It isn't designed to use that because when you request a GRAPHIC, you request it by name and the GRAPHIC_MGR looks it up for you. This is very helpful in case you need a GRAPHIC and you only want it loaded once during the game. Although there are dozens of ways to handle this functionality, I like how this is centrally located and how I can guarantee no memory leaks.

The purpose of this class is simply graphics maintenance. You'll find the code in graphic.cpp on the CD and in Chapter 13.

```
#ifndef  _GRAPHIC_MGR_H_
#define  _GRAPHIC_MGR_H_


#include "struct.h"
// this class is a container class specifically for graphics
// when using the GetGraphic method, the name checking is
// performed and the proper graphic is returned. It does dynamic
// allocation but it owns all of the pointers and it will do the final
// deallocation when it is deleted. Never delete any graphic returned
// from this class.
// The same filename passed in 2x will return the same pointer to a
// GRAPHIC. By default, the graphics handled herein are not compressed
// but calling SetCompressionFlag will change that.
// The tag list is a leftover and will be left in the class if I later
// decide to not make the list dynamic and make it static;



//*************************************************
//*************************************************
//*************************************************

class GRAPHIC_MGR
{

public:

        enum MAXTYPES {MAXIMUM = 2000};
        enum {_5x5x5_, _5x6x5_};

protected:
        // variables

        GRAPHIC**  Graphic;
        S16        Max, Last;
        U16ptr     ScratchPad;            // loading and compression
        U8         Bits, CompressionFlag;


        // functions
        void       Allocate ();
        void       Deallocate ();

                   //*******************************

        int        FindItem (GRAPHIC* item);
        int        FindFirstAvailable ();
        int        FindNextUnavailable (int which, int num);

                   // returns the beginning num of available
        int        FindRunOfAvailable (int num = 1);
```

```
        int        FindNextAvailable (int which);

                   //*******************************

    public:

                   //*******************************

        // functions
        GRAPHIC_MGR ();
        GRAPHIC_MGR (int num);
        ~GRAPHIC_MGR ();

        void       Clear ();

        void       SetCompressionFlag (int set = true) {CompressionFlag = (U8)
                                                         set;}
        void       SetBitPattern (int val = _5x5x5_) {Bits = (U8) val;}

                   //*******************************

        GRAPHIC*   New ();
        void       Delete (GRAPHIC*);

                   //*******************************
        // tries to find the existing graphic but if unable, declares a new
        // one, loads it and returns it without compression; NULL is returned
        // if the list is too long and the grapic is not already loaded
        GRAPHIC*   GetGraphic (STRINGC& str);

        // from an opened file, a graphic is loaded and maintained by this
        // manager; never delete the graphic returned
        GRAPHIC*   GetGraphic (FILE_MASTER* file);
    };


    //****************************************************
    //****************************************************
    //****************************************************

    #endif
```

The FRAME Structure

Looking back at our needs, the following structure would be needed:

```
struct FRAME
{
        short       Index;          // id number in the list
        U8      :4  Time;           // how long should I stay on this frame
        U8      :4  TimeCount;      // how long have I been on this frame
        U8          Next, Prev;     // frame of animation
```

```
char        addx, addy;     // since these are only offset values,
                            // they can be +/-127
GRAPHICptr  Graphic;
U8          :1 Direction;   // normally set to 0 for forward, can be 1
                            // for backward
U8          :1 SkipThisFrame;  // instantly move onto the next frame
U8          :1 LaunchFlag;     // something special happens on this frame
short       :12 Sound;  // index of sound to be played, allows 4096 sounds
U8          :1 Pad;     // we have a bit left over in our bit fields
};
```

Again, this is only one of many ways to organize the frame data. This structure takes 13 bytes. Other things could appear in this structure but this is about the minimum. You would use this FRAME structure in conjunction with the GRAPHIC_MGR we saw a little earlier. Each FRAME holds a pointer to a GRAPHIC, which the GRAPHIC_MGR maintains and will eventually delete.

Other games require a lot more information for a structure, such as branching. *Branching* allows you to immediately change from one frame to another animation altogether. Then you need the condition information (why does it change?) and, of course, the new graphic information. There is also start/stop animation. Before you walk, you need to start walking, then walk, then come to a stop. This may not seem important, but what about a hovercraft? It needs to leave the ground, move to its destination, and then settle back down onto the ground. This is a good example of start/stop. How do you handle that? One animation sequence needs the ability to move on to another for this to happen. This scheme works just fine, and many people use it or something very similar for animation in their games.

The Index variable tells the frame which frame it is. This allows us to simply pass the frame to functions and we instantly know which object it is in our massive array, assuming thousands of frames of animation.

Time tells us how many times to play the same frame of animation before advancing to the Next or Prev frame. TimeCount is a counter set to 0 the first time we use this frame and incremented until it is equal to Time. You'll need to be careful here: These numbers belong to the frame of animation; if more than one instance of the creature exists, these numbers will behave strangely because each instance of the creature will be counting time. Bad news. You need to also maintain TimeCount in the instance of the creature himself. This is here for convenience but will serve as a temporary holding space. Next is the Index ID of the frame immediately following this one, while Prev is the frame immediately before this frame. In case the frame you are initializing is the last in a cycle, make Next point back to the first frame. If the animation plays back and forth, the end frame has the responsibility of setting the direction flag of all of its predecessors and then moving onto Prev. The Prev value of the first frame in a cycle should point to the last frame in an animation.

The variables addx and addy are screen offset positions telling the character his new position. Ideally, these should be world offset positions to let the creature offset his position as he goes. You'll have to decide how to handle that. An important thing to note: In a slightly different setting, you would want to handle offsets through a simple calculation. You might handle it like this: Design your editor to calculate all frame offsets based on walking to the right only, store the offset information only based on the frame, then at run time a simple offset calculation is done. Say that the offset is 3 pixels when the animation is going to the right (east). When the character goes north, you'll need to offset worldy by 3 pixels. Another consideration is the viewing angle. If your tiles are half as tall as they are wide, then movement in the y direction will need to be in fractions, in which case you'll need to maintain a fractional position in the world. Generally, maintaining the world position using a float value is a good idea. That would extend the size to 19 bytes, but you could use bit-shifted integer values to represent the float values, and a couple of WORDs would only make this structure 15 bytes.

This method can be extended. If movement is treated as a constant, say 3 pixels per movement cycle, a simple computation will allow world movement. This has the benefit of reducing memory footprint, a little bit of data management, and the over-head of figuring out offsets. This has the detriment of not always allowing smooth animation because movement is almost never completely smooth.

Graphic is the actual image data. After all of this, doesn't it seem amazing how much work goes into displaying one simple graphic? This FRAME structure is simpli-fied too.

Direction is simply a way to determine whether to go to Next or Prev when we move to the next frame of animation. The variable SkipThisFrame may be set during the editing process to eliminate a frame from a sequence without getting rid of it. The LaunchFlag tells us that, depending on the type of animation, something special should happen on this frame. A missile might be launched, an explosion might occur, a tree might be cut down, etc.

The Sound variable holds an index number to a sound that would be played at that particular frame of animation. The sound manager holds a series of indices to dif-ferent sounds and the Sound member variable of FRAME simply stores that number. Using this format, we are limited to 4,096 sounds.

The Pad variable is the 1 leftover bit. Just in case you don't understand "bit fields," the colon with a number following tells the compiler to only use bits to repre-sent that variable. The compiler handles masking, bit shifting, and all of the other various sundries. The CPU time needed to perform these operations is usually negligi-ble, always less than 3 clock cycles and usually 0.

There are a few things about this method I don't like. It is too C-like. You have to write all kinds of code just for maintenance, setup, and cleanup. There is a lot of setup work, meaning that you need to set up Next and Prev every time you load the data. The frames could be numbered differently the next time because frames of ani-mation may have been added. Also, Sound will need to be set up since you may be adding sound to the game and the ID number is likely to change. The last thing I hate about this method is how large this structure is. I've reduced it to its minimum size, and it is still 13 bytes. If you need float offsets for world position, it could be 19 bytes. This also doesn't account for quite a few things, and getting it to work can be difficult. Still, most games use this structure or something very similar to it. It does have the advantage of having all animation data in one neat little package.

Incidentally, if you are doing 3-D animation, this same structure will work, or at least something very similar to it. The definition of GRAPHIC would be the key here. If you either changed the definition of a GRAPHIC or put a different pointer in this structure, you could easily accomplish the same result. Basically, you would store a vertex transformation in a structure that holds dozens of vertices. You can find a full vertex class in vector.h (and also vector.cpp) included on the CD, and there you will find the Frame3D class that will define one full frame of 3-D animation.

Since some companies are going to 3-D animation for games, it is worth noting that they are beginning to use bones. Bones are a lot like the bones that you and I have. Often, an animator will animate the bones only. The body around the bones is linked to them and the vertex position is calculated relative to the bone it is attached to. This takes extra math, but can save tons of memory. A bone has very little vertex information, while an arm may have 40 vertices. A vertex is typically an x, y, z, meaning 96 bits, or 12 bytes. It is good for byte alignment to use 128 bits, or 16 bytes, but for argument's sake, let's say 12 bytes. 40 vertices times 12 bytes is 480 bytes while the bone might take 36 or so. Multiply that by 200 frames and you can see the savings. Bones can be "spit out" by all of the major 3-D software packages.

Note: I'll do a little math for you. Let's use a worker as an example. He can stand, walk, carry wood, hunt, attack, and build. The stand/wait animation is three to five frames of animation in eight directions—let's just say 40 frames total. A simple eight-frame walk cycle in eight directions is 64 frames total. A carry wood cycle would be the same as a walk cycle but with wood in the worker's hands, meaning another 64 frames of animation. the hunt cycle would involve taking a spear, pulling it back, and then throwing, taking a minimum of six frames for eight directions for 48 more frames. Attacking others will cost you the same 48 frames or so. The last animation, build, assuming that it is real simple, is four frames of animation for a total, in eight directions, of 32 frames. So for simple animation of a simple worker guy, we need 296 frames of animation.

Note: A lot of memory would be used as well. A 32x32 graphic takes 2,048 bytes in 16-bit (32 * 32 *2 bytes). LLE compression reduces that to about half, meaning that each frame of animation takes about 1,024 bytes. When we multiply this by 296 in our previous example, we get 296 K for a single animated worker. Now, how many different units were you going to put in your game?

The Animation Data Structure

If we reduce the amount of information per frame, we may have a slightly better approach. First, let's define the minimum set of information needed for sequencing a set of frames of animation. Assuming that we have a group of frames fewer than 256 that are numbered from 0 on up, we can store sequences in the frame range of 0 to 255. You will find this structure in animstruct.h. It tells us if the animation goes forward or backward, which frame in the sequence is the first, last, and current frame, and what kind of animation it is supposed to be, say a walk cycle.

Because you may stick 35 frames in a single sequence and then order frames 0 to 8 to be the start walk, 9 to 28 to be the walk cycle, and 29 to 34 to be the walk stop animation, I have structured this class with just the right amount of info. I did exactly the same on Doppelganger. What you can do is have an array of animation pointers that define the entire walk cycle from start to finish. Then you would define three ANIMATION_DATA structs to hold the section for WALK, WALKBEGIN, and WALKEND. Each of them would have different StartFrame and EndFrame values but they are associated with the animation separately.

The way I set it up also allows you to put all frames of animation in a long sequence and simply index into the array of animation frames using a bunch of ANIMATION_DATA structs. The disadvantage of this is that you must always have fewer than 257 frames of animation total per creature. Luckily, this is rarely a problem. However, it is noteworthy that many characters in Doppelganger had over a thousand frames of animation.

You may be wondering where we will be storing the frames of animation. We could store them in this struct, but I've decided to put them in a class containing instances of ANIMATION_DATA. The reason for this is the tool mostly. When setting up animation, you may not have all frames of animation clearly defined in categories by directory, so you may just have 200 frames of animation numbered sequentially. These frames may include all possible animations for a creature, basically a stew pot with a lot of carrots, potatoes, and beef. Then you'll need to assign groups of frames to particular ANIMATION_DATA structs. If the ANIMATION_DATA struct contained the information, then moving frames from one structure would become a necessity. Then what happens if the animation of WALKBEGIN needs to repeat a few frames in WALK? It is just a whole lot easier for ANIMATION_DATA to contain index data and little more.

The following struct contains the type used to store ANIM_TYPES. You can change the variable type to match if you like, but a U8 is a lot smaller. The flag is strictly used for the back and forth flag. The struct does not advance the frame or change anything, but it does hold the information that its container class will use.

```
//*********************************************
typedef struct  ANIMATION_DATA
{

        U8      StartFrame, EndFrame, CurrentFrame;
        U8      Flag;
        U8      Type;

        //****************************
```

```
enum  ANIM_TYPES
{
        NONE,                            // 0
        WALK, WALKBEGIN, WALKEND,        // 1
        RUN, RUNBEGIN, RUNEND,           // 4
        JUMP, JUMPBEGIN, JUMPEND,        // 7
        SWIM, SWIMBEGIN, SWIMEND,        // 10
        CLIMB, CLIMBBEGIN, CLIMBEND,     // 13
        EATNORMAL, EATGRAZE, EATBROWSE,  // 16
        ATTACK1, ATTACK2,                // 19
        ATTACK3, ATTACK4,                // 21
        DOWNWARDATTACK, UPPERCUTATTACK,  // 23
        THROW1, THROW2,                  // 25
        TURN45LEFT, TURN45RIGHT,         // 27
        TURN90LEFT, TURN90RIGHT,         // 29
        AMBIENT, STAND,                  // 31
        REACT_TO_HIT, BLOCK, MAXTYPES    // 33
};
enum ANIM_FLAGS
{
        BACK_AND_FORTH = 1
};

//***************************

ANIMATION_DATA ();
~ANIMATION_DATA ();
void  Clear ();
bool  IsValid ();

//***************************

bool  Save (FILE_MASTER* file);
bool  Load (FILE_MASTER* file);

//***************************

void  SetBackAndForth (int val = 1);
int   GetBackAndForth ();

//***************************

STRINGC  GetTypeName (int x = 0); // get a string associated with the type
ANIM_TYPES  GetType  (STRINGC* str);
}ANIM_DATA, *ANIM_DATAptr, **ANIMlist;
//*********************************************
```

The names of the types of animation must be available for an editor and possibly for other reasons. I have included a brief excerpt from the animstruct.cpp file for obtaining the real names of the ANIM_TYPES. This can be done a completely different way.

```
//********************************************
STRINGC ANIMATION_DATA :: GetTypeName (int x)
{
        if (x == WALK)           return STRINGC ( "Walk" );
        if (x == WALKBEGIN)      return STRINGC ( "Walk Begin" );
        if (x == WALKEND)        return STRINGC ( "Walk End" );
        if (x == RUN)            return STRINGC ( "Run" );
        if (x == RUNBEGIN)       return STRINGC ( "Start run" );
        if (x == RUNEND)         return STRINGC ( "End run" );
        if (x == JUMP)           return STRINGC ( "Jump" );
        if (x == JUMPBEGIN)      return STRINGC ( "Start jump" );
        if (x == JUMPEND)        return STRINGC ( "End jump" );
        if (x == SWIM)           return STRINGC ( "Swim" );
        if (x == SWIMBEGIN)      return STRINGC ( "Start swim" );
        if (x == SWIMEND)        return STRINGC ( "End swim" );
        if (x == CLIMB)          return STRINGC ( "Climb" );
        if (x == CLIMBBEGIN)     return STRINGC ( "Start climb" );
        if (x == CLIMBEND)       return STRINGC ( "End climb" );
        if (x == EATNORMAL)      return STRINGC ( "Eat" );
        if (x == EATGRAZE)       return STRINGC ( "Graze" );
        if (x == EATBROWSE)      return STRINGC ( "Browse" );
        if (x == ATTACK1)        return STRINGC ( "Attack 1" );
        if (x == ATTACK2)        return STRINGC ( "Attack 2" );
        if (x == ATTACK3)        return STRINGC ( "Attack 3" );
        if (x == ATTACK4)        return STRINGC ( "Attack 4" );
        if (x == DOWNWARDATTACK) return STRINGC ( "Smash" );
        if (x == UPPERCUTATTACK) return STRINGC ( "Uppercut" );
        if (x == THROW1)         return STRINGC ( "Throw item" );
        if (x == THROW2)         return STRINGC ( "Throw creature" );
        if (x == TURN45LEFT)     return STRINGC ( "Rotate 45° left" );
        if (x == TURN45RIGHT)    return STRINGC ( "Rotate 45° right" );
        if (x == TURN90LEFT)     return STRINGC ( "Rotate 90° left" );
        if (x == TURN90RIGHT)    return STRINGC ( "Rotate 90° right" );
        if (x == AMBIENT)        return STRINGC ( "Ambient" );
        if (x == STAND)          return STRINGC ( "Stand" );
        if (x == REACT_TO_HIT)   return STRINGC ( "React" );
        if (x == BLOCK)          return STRINGC ( "Block" );
        return STRINGC ();
}
//********************************************
```

If we create a structure for holding the integer (enum) and the string, then an array of these can be initialized and handled a little easier. The problem is the memory.

```
//********************************************
struct ANIM_TYPE
{
        int      Val;
        char*    String;
};
//********************************************
```

```
//*******************************************
typedef struct  ANIMATION_DATA
{
        ...
        ANIM_TYPE[]     AnimType;
        ...

}
//*******************************************
```

Taking the approach of only storing frame offset information for a single direction, we have the following OFFSET_DATA structure. We will need to do the math for multiple directions, but this is the most efficient way. You don't want to store this information in a FRAME structure because of its size.

```
//*******************************************
typedef struct  OFFSET_DATA
{
        S8  OffX, OffY, OffZ, Delay;
        OFFSET_DATA (int offx, int offy, int offz, int delay)
        {
                OffX = (S8) offx, OffY = (S8) offy, OffZ = (S8) offz,
                        Delay = (S8) delay;
        }
        OFFSET_DATA ()
        {
                Clear ();
        }
        void  Clear ()
        {
        // OffX = 0, OffY = 0, OffZ = 0, Delay = 0;
        int* x = (int*) this;            // clear all 4 bytes in one pass
        *x = 0;
        }
}OFFDAT, *OFFSET_DATAptr, **OFFlist;
//*******************************************
```

There are two things of note that may need explaining. First is the Delay. This allows a character to stay on the same frame for a while before advancing to the next frame. Hence the name. It also has the effect of moving the character by fractional amounts. You could offset your character by float values and slowly accumulate fractional movement until finally the character offsets a full pixel, or you could offset one full pixel every loop when the delay has been used up.

Delay is an absolute must. Say you have a walk cycle and the character should repeat his walk cycle every second or so. Let's assume that you are using an eight-frame animation walk cycle. If your game is running at 30 fps, and it should, then the walk cycle would repeat almost four times a second. Putting a Delay of 3 in there (or 4) solves this issue and will seemingly make the game run more smoothly. An instance of this structure is used for every frame, so Delay will need to be set for the entire animation. While this may seem like a pain, you can set six of your eight frames to a Delay of 4, and the remaining two to a delay of 3, making a perfect 30 fps walk cycle that seems smooth.

Creating good tools is the key to this. Let your art team set the number of frames per second. Let them deliver the art and you focus on the game. So what if you spend two to three weeks programming a good tool for them to use? This will all be paid back to you when you don't have to manually store all of the data yourself. And then there is the tweaking of that data and game observation to make sure it's right. If you have a good animation tool, the artists can do the tweaking up front and the art then plops right into the game, like magic. There will still be some tweaking, but a good tool will cut thousands of man-hours out of a project.

The other thing of note is OffZ. For world position, I use OffX and OffZ for offsetting position relative to the map. Some characters will have a vertical animation, like a ship taking off or a rabbit hopping across the screen. These should also use OffY to give vertical motion without changing world position.

One thing blaring out to be added is Repeat. If you have a spaceship taking off, it needs to move vertically (OffY) but without an animation change in terms of having another frame or graphic. You want to continue to use the same frame of animation. Or maybe not—it may need to animate while taking off, but you may not need it and that's my point. Flying across the screen, it may also look exactly the same and you may need to repeat the frame of animation and the offsets of the animation. I suggest changing Delay to 4 bits and Adding Repeat at 4 bits (bit fields). No delay should ever be more than four or five frames anyway, let alone 15, and you should never repeat the same frame and offset more than 16 times in a row. That allows you to assign only 4 bits to each. After all, the size of the structure is 4 bytes, making it the perfect size. Why muck with that unless you need to?

You may ask why I don't have Repeat in this structure. This is legacy code and I haven't needed that yet. If I do a game like StarCraft with non-animating movement, then I will add it.

You will need to convert from world coordinates to screen position. How you do that is up to you, but you'll probably want to manage the conversion through a simple class interface like the following. The conversion process will be discussed in detail when we get to tile systems in the next chapter. For now, I'll leave this placeholder code here.

```
//*********************************************
typedef struct ANIMSCREEN_POS
{
        int  scx, scy;

        ANIMSCREEN_POS () {scx = -1, scy = -1;}
        ANIMSCREEN_POS (ANIMSCREEN_POS* ptr)  {scx = ptr->scx, scy = ptr->scy;}
        ANIMSCREEN_POS (int x, int y) {scx = x, scy = y;}

        //****************************

        void  SetScreenPosition (int x, int y) {scx = x, scy = y;}
        void  SetPosition (int x, int y) {scx = x, scy = y;}
        void  SetScreenX (int x) {scx = x;}
```

```
void  SetScreenY (int y) {scy = y;}

//***************************

void  GetScreenPosition (int* x, int* y) {*x = scx, *y = scy;}
void  GetPosition (int* x, int* y) {*x = scx, *y = scy;}
float GetScreenX () const {return scx;}
float GetScreenY () const {return scy;}

//***************************

void  ConvertWorldToScreenPosition (int* x, int* y)
{
     // conversion code
     // modify x and y
}
float ConvertWorldToScreenX (int x)
{
     // conversion code
}
float ConvertWorldToScreenY (int y)
{
     // conversion code
}

//***************************

void  AddPosition (int x, int y) {scx += x, scy += y;}
void  AddX (int x) {scx += x;}
void  AddY (int y) {scy += y;}

//***************************

ANIMSCREEN_POS operator += (ANIMSCREEN_POS* pos)
     {scx += pos->scx, scy += pos->scy; return ANIMSCREEN_POS (this);}
ANIMSCREEN_POS operator -= (ANIMSCREEN_POS* pos)
     {scx -= pos->scx, scy -= pos->scy; return ANIMSCREEN_POS (this);}
ANIMSCREEN_POS operator += (float val)
     {scx += val, scy += val; return ANIMSCREEN_POS (this);}
ANIMSCREEN_POS operator -= (float val)
     {scx -= val, scy -= val; return ANIMSCREEN_POS (this);}
bool operator == (ANIMSCREEN_POS* pos)
     {if (scx == pos->scx && scy == pos->scy) return true; return false;}

//***************************

ANIMSCREEN_POS operator + (ANIMSCREEN_POS* pos)
{
     return ANIMSCREEN_POS (scx+pos->scx, scy+pos->scy);
}
ANIMSCREEN_POS operator - (ANIMSCREEN_POS* pos)
{
```

```
                    return ANIMSCREEN_POS (scx-pos->scx, scy-pos->scy);
            }

        //****************************

    }ANIMSCREEN_POS, *ANIMSCREEN_POSptr, **ANIMSCREEN_POSlist;
    //********************************************
```

The Encapsulated Approach

We're starting to put all of the pieces in place. The class GRAPHICSEQUENCE is old code, but it works very well. The structure of the class is clean and easy. To fill it with a bunch of frames of animation, you need to create a linked list of filenames to load and then call its Load function. This class is available on the CD, but designing an animation sequencer is very individualized, so you'll probably want to create your own.

```
// GraphicSequence.h

#ifndef _GRAPHIC_SEQUENCE_H_
#define _GRAPHIC_SEQUENCE_H_


#include "graphic.h"

// this class will exist for each direction, that is 8 'GraphicSequence's
// will be declared for the walk cycle, 1 for each direction

// pass a list of STRINGC's to the load function and it loads whatever num
// is listed

// load with a file handle loads a num first and then initializes each
// GRAPHIC in turn calling each load function

typedef class GRAPHICSEQUENCE
{
        GRAPHICptr   Graphic;
        U8           Num;          // number of graphics
        U8           Selected;     // the current frame for display

        // screen position, remember to set in bitmap before drawing
        U16          PosX, PosY;

        //*****************

public:

        //*****************

        GRAPHICSEQUENCE ();
        ~GRAPHICSEQUENCE ();
        void  Clear ();
```

```
        void  Reset ();                              // resets the sequence to frame 0

        //*****************

        void  SetFrame (int frame);
        int   GetFrame ();

        //*****************
        void  SetPosition (int x, int y);
        void  DrawNext     (SCREEN_STRUCT* screen);
        void  DrawCurrent  (SCREEN_STRUCT* screen);
        void  DrawPrev     (SCREEN_STRUCT* screen);
        void  DrawFrame    (SCREEN_STRUCT* screen, int frame);

        //*****************

        void  SetNumberToLoad (int num);
        int   GetNum () const {return Num;}
        GRAPHICptr GetGraphic (int which) const;

        //*****************

        bool  Load (STRptr str, int num, U16ptr ScratchPad);
        bool  Save (STRINGC dest);                  // probably not used

        bool  Load (FILE_MASTER* file);             // this loads the number and the
                                                    // sequence
        bool  Save (FILE_MASTER* file);

        //*****************
}GraphicSequence, *GRAPHICSEQUENCEptr;

#endif
```

Some things that you might think should be in here I put in another class further on in this chapter. The choices I've made for what I put in this class were carefully thought out. I put in a GRAPHIC pointer to store a series of GRAPHICS. The group is allocated once the number of graphics is known and then each one is loaded. The Num variable tells us the total number of items allocated. This could belong to the parent, but I keep it here as a checksum so that I can verify the number of frames loaded. Plus, I've included two methods, DrawPrev and DrawNext, that will need this number.

The Selected member variable is a bit tricky. You need to understand a little about the overall structure to get this part. We have a class called CREATURE (defined a little later), which represents all semi-intelligent life in any RTS/RTT type game. Obviously, you'll need to tweak the structure to apply it to your game. Anyway, it has a pointer to an animation class which will have a series of GRAPHICSEQUENCEs. The animation class sets all variables pertinent in the proper GRAPHICSEQUENCE class based on what the CREATURE tells it. GRAPHICSEQUENCE has a SetFrame function, which is used by the animation class. The member function DrawNext can advance the current frame. There are also DrawCurrent and DrawPrev. Selected exists solely to facilitate these functions.

Then the CREATURE can use the function GetFrame to find out which frame it is on. This is a good encapsulation and it keeps the creature from needing to know anything about the animation other than which frame it was last on. This will be especially key as you make submissions to your publisher and they request animation changes. A CREATURE that needs to know about the animation makes this process especially difficult unless you have awesome tools. The GRAPHICSEQUENCE knows all and will advance the frame, wrap around to 0, and return the proper frame. By the way, the animation class has the world and screen position information.

The Load function, which takes a STRptr, is really a linked list containing all of the filenames for loading the graphic sequence. You only need to use this method early in development, but as assets are solidified, you can use the other Load function. num is good for allocation purposes, and ScratchPad is that globally allocated block of memory used to simplify the load process. After you load the graphics, a call to Save (FILE_MASTER* file) will put all of these graphics into the file handle you give it. The next time you run the program, simply use the Load (FILE_MASTER* file) and reload the graphics. Everything is transparent, making your life easy.

Putting All Eight Directions Together

Now that we have established all of the basics, we are ready to put the full eight directions of animation into one handler. You would have a GRAPHICSEQUENCE structure for each of the eight directions for each animation sequence but modify this paradigm to suit your needs. Remember, you may want to use mirroring.

```
//********************************************


typedef class  ANIMATION          // used for a single type of animation
// it groups 8 directions into a single class.
{
public:

        enum {NUMDIR = 8};
        enum DIR {EAST, SOUTHEAST, SOUTH, SOUTHWEST, WEST, NORTHWEST, NORTH,
                 NORTHEAST};


        //***************************


protected:

        OFFSET_DATAptr      Offset;
        ANIM_DATA :: ANIM_TYPES AnimType;
        GRAPHICSEQUENCEptr  Sequence [NUMDIR];  // limited to 8 directions
        STRINGC             FilePath, FileName;
```

```
        U8              CurrDirection;
        U8              NumFiles;           // this is the num per direction
        U8              CurrFrame;

        U16ptr          ScratchPad;

        FILEOBJECT :: EXTENSIONS Extension;
        //***************************

        int  CountTotalFiles ();
        STRINGC* GetAllFileNames ();
        void LoadSequences (STRINGC* str);  // loads all groups of animation
                                            // in one chunk

public:

        //***************************

        ANIMATION ();
        ANIMATION (STRINGC* path);          // init with path, calls Load
        // format directory like "c:/dir1/dir2/graphicdir/walk"
        ~ANIMATION ();
        void Clear ();

        //***************************

        void SetDirection (int which = 0) {CurrDirection = (U8) which;}
        int  GetDirection () {return CurrDirection;}
        int  GetNumFiles () {return NumFiles;}
        ANIM_DATA :: ANIM_TYPES
        GetAnimType () {return AnimType;}

//***************************

        // bool Save (STRINGC* path);       // create an anim file
        // bool Load (STRINGC* path);       // load from an anim file
        bool Save (FILE_MASTER* file);      // save to a larger file
        bool Load (FILE_MASTER* file);      // load from a larger file

        //***************************
        // path to a directory

        bool LoadFromGraphicDirectory (STRINGC* path, U16ptr ScratchPad);
        // containing the files to be counted, divided by 8, and loaded into
        // separate GRAPHICSEQUENCE's also, the name of the actual directory
        // will be parsed to discover the type of anim being loaded

        //***************************

        void SetFrame (int which) {CurrFrame = (U8) which;}
        int  GetFrame () const {return CurrFrame;}
```

```
//***************************

void  DrawAt (SCREEN_STRUCT* screen, int x, int y);

//*************************** editing functions

// based on currframe
void  SetOffsetData (int offx, int offy, int offz, int delay);
OFFSET_DATAptr GetOffsetData ();
void  GetOffsetData (int* offx, int* offy, int* offz, int* delay);
void  GetOffsetDataCalculated (float* offx, float* offy, float*
          offz, int* delay);          // based on direction
int   GetDelay (int whichframe);

//***************************
//***************************

}ANIMATION, *ANIMATIONptr, ** ANIMATIONlist;

//*********************************************
```

Tearing apart the class, first we establish the number of directions as eight and then we enumerate the names of the directions for convenience. We then declare a few variables. Offset will be an array of offsets used for moving the character around in the world for each frame, one for each frame of animation. This will be recalculated and reapplied to each frame regardless of direction. AnimType is a variable that gives us the type of animation. Look at the ANIMATION_DATA structure that I created a few pages ago and you will see the common possibilities for types of animation sequences. Feel free to add others.

Now we define eight GRAPHICSEQUENCEs. Each will be loaded and saved once the class is initialized. We now see FilePath and FileName. We will use the path for loading all of the graphics and as a directory source for the eight GRAPHICSEQUENCEs we will later load. FileName is used for the name of the animation but you can choose to eliminate this if you prefer. It exists mostly for the tool to get the string telling the filename loaded to match it up with the proper animation. Look at Figures 15.3, 15.4, and 15.5 for a better idea of how animation filenames might be handled. This art was prepared by one of the hardest-working artists in the industry, Jeff Mills. He prepared dozens of different art items for me, and I hope we can work together again real soon. He is also a decent programmer.

15
Chapter

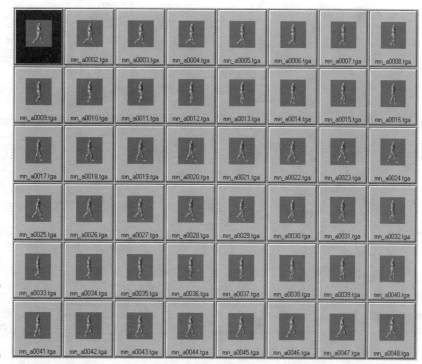

Figure 15.3
Animation of creature walking to the right

Figure 15.4
Animation of creature walking southeast

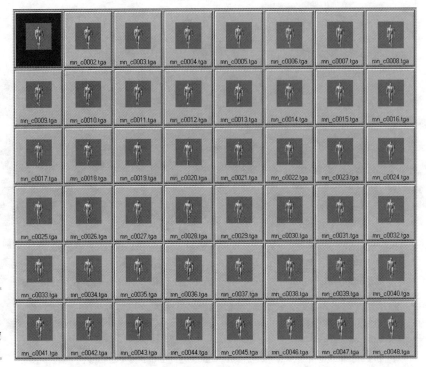

Figure 15.5
Animation of creature walking forward

CurrDirection is the direction of the animation that the class recognizes as the direction the creature will be moving in. There are eight directions, allowing this variable to hopefully contain numbers only from 0 to 7. These will be used to draw animation frames belonging to the Sequence[CurrDirection]. CurrFrame is a duplication of data higher in the class definitions; you can eliminate it by providing an access routine like the following:

```
int    ANIMATION :: GetCurrFrame ()
{
       return Sequence[CurrDirection].GetFrame ();
}
```

I prefer to leave the duplication since it costs only a byte, although the variable is renamed Selected in GRAPHICSEQUENCE. ScratchPad is the same pointer to a large 16-bit group of memory used for compression and loading. You may want to make it global but I want it everywhere, so I pass it as a parameter so no one forgets about it. This also ensures that its values are always valid but something like a critical section (or another synchronization object) would have the same effect, so call it a preference.

One of the responsibilities of this class is to take a base directory for a creature, say c:\art\goblin\walk, and load all of the graphics into a sequence based on what it finds in the directory. It takes the number of files and divides by 8 for each direction, yielding the number of frames in the sequence. It assumes that you render the same number of frames for each of the eight directions. NumFiles is the variable used to hold this value. The class then loads the names of all of the files into a linked list and alphabetizes them. It then divides the list into eight sections and tells the GRAPHICSEQUENCEs to load the files. It is assumed that files are named such that all animations can be easily grouped by name, first into animation direction and then by frame number. walka-1.tga precedes walk1-2.tga but is an entirely different direction from walkb-1.tga, which should be the next direction going clockwise.

As mentioned previously, delivery issues are always tricky, but make sure that your artists and you are "on the same page."

> **Note:** Notice how I commonly lay out my class definitions. I start the class with public, then declare protected, and then go back to public. The first section is for enumerations that other classes may need to "see" and utilize for return values or values passed. The second section marked by the protected keyword is for variables and functions that only this class can access. The last section is the common interface and all functions are public. You won't find variables here unless there are some flags that are used too often to avoid putting them here. This class structure is common throughout my code.

That does it for a single type of animation. It is fairly complete and it does everything you might expect. For the final release, you may wish to kill the editing functions since you probably don't need Offsets to change during the game. No need but you may like it better anyway. I put a few hooks (Load and Save) in for saving to special files if you like. Just a reminder in case you might want to manage your system this way. It does keep the data all together, which makes editing easier.

Each creature in the world may need a pointer to this animation. Each creature will need to maintain data like direction and frame so that another creature does not overwrite its info. Otherwise, each creature can tell this class directly to draw. The rest is simplicity itself.

Animated Backgrounds

Creating a living world is hard, or at least the illusion is. God made a living world easily. But creating the illusion is the responsibility of any good designer, and one good way to do that is to animate certain aspects of the background.

This is much tougher than it sounds, as there are only a few things you can do to animate the backgrounds. You can have flowing lava, moving trees, flowing water, shifting sands, twinkling stars, rain and weather, and splashing waves. Not to be uncreative, but there really aren't too many more until you create your own kinds of landscapes. Since there are special cases for animating all of these, let's discuss them individually. I do have to say that animating landscape is a little tough, so expect a little work here.

Flowing Lava and Water

Water and lava have a lot of the same characteristics, so I'll talk about them in the same category. A few unique things are: Lava should produce steam, water flows quickly and splashes more than lava, lava might burn objects so you'll need a special case, boats and other watercraft can travel on water, different creatures might tolerate the water or lava.

Animating water can be handled in a variety of ways but is usually handled as a special case, so you need to decide ahead of time and work toward it if that's what the design calls for. There aren't a lot of broad generalizations or any good ways of simplifying the code. Two ways to animate water are with color cycling and tile swapping.

With color cycling, the crest of the waves could appear to move by changing the color of the pixels. This is done in 8-bit by making a series of palettes, each with the blue colors slightly offset from the others, and changing which palette is used for rendering the water tiles each frame. What you do is keep the blues in order but rotate them in the palette, essentially "cycling" them. Most games create a series of palettes and simply swap out the palette for the entire game. This makes color cycling easy. Color cycling is a good way to give apparent motion and a lot of games use it. You can use a similar scheme but it requires the use of palettes in 16-bit, which sort of defeats the purpose.

Tile graphics are just that, graphics. By preparing 12 to 20 slightly different tiles, and then playing them in succession, you are animating them. It takes a bit of work but is worth the effort. Don't go overboard with the number of tiles used, as this begins to chew up a lot of memory quickly. On Doppelganger, we animated large groups of tiles (9x9 groups), with the entire group necessary for the animation. A single LLE compressed group took 300 K, and so a simple animation of eight frames took 2.4 MB. All that memory for animated water. Is it really worth it?

The difficult part of animating water is its intersection with the surrounding ground. For the waves to splash up on the shore, you need shore tiles, and then you need to swap them out. So now you need more graphics for water and for the landscape. Now your assets are growing.

Moving Trees

Wind blowing across the landscape can be captured. Trees moving in a slow flowing motion, one waving after another, can create life in your world. This effect, while unbelievable when you see it, is equally unbelievably difficult to do. You can set a tree in motion and all trees in the world respond to any trees next to them. But then you have to avoid the feedback, because once the trees start in motion, what makes them stop? They continue moving because other trees nearby are moving.

Another approach is to manage the waving by having the land tiles set motion. A tile would be able to call a method that would start the tree moving or do nothing for any other object on top of it. This allows a "wind" of tiles to sweep across the landscape and affect objects on top of them.

The simplest, and hence the lamest, way to manage the wind is to have the trees sway randomly, occasionally swaying for no apparent reason. To keep this in the realm of the reasonable, make sure to limit their motion. Keep the side-to-side motion to a minimum. Anything too great, and your trees begin to look wild and crazy. Also, make sure they sway only once every 60 seconds or so. This is to add realism; you don't want to create the tree discotheque.

Animating the trees is another issue. You'll need a casual sway as part of the tree's draw cycle. This can be four to eight frames of the leaves rustling and some other minor fluctuations. Then, for the wind, you'll need to create a secondary animation of the tree moving a lot more, a big sway of 8 to 16 frames. If you feel ambitious, you can make the trees sway in four or even eight directions. I bet your art team will love that idea (right).

Other things in your world can sway or shake in the wind. These can be a ribbon or flag hanging from a pole, the sheets on a clothesline, a ship's sails, the hair of a warrior (or maiden), bushes, the shake tiles on the roof of a small cottage, or tumbleweeds. These would all require that you have wind for animation.

Be careful. You don't want to animate too many world objects because they all take a little processing time and they all require graphics, which means memory. Stick to things that add realism and help with the mood/tone of the game.

Shifting Sands and Shifting Landscape

The sands may move in your world or the earth may slowly shift. You will need to decide how this motion occurs. You can make this really hard on yourself, so be careful. If the dunes move, you'll need to be able to bury cottages and even trees. If cracks open in the ground, people will need to fall into the cracks on occasion. These types of dynamic landscapes are also very difficult to animate and control. These work a little better in a 3-D landscape where you can raise the ground over a house or move a sine wave slowly over an area to create the illusion of shifting sands.

You can achieve the effect of moving sand by color cycling or animating with multiple tiles like in the lava example mentioned a few pages ago. The effect is minor, though; you'd get a better effect if you simply animated a small dust cloud or tornado.

Creating seasons, however, can easily be solved using either of these two methods. Usually, the best method is to have 12 different sets of tiles, one for each month, and simply replace the land tiles every five minutes or so of game time. Just load the new tiles over the existing ones, keeping the pointers and all. The biggest problem with seasons is not the land but all of the things that need to change: Units need to have snow on them, trees need to be bare in the winter and have bright orange leaves in the autumn, etc. Do your lakes drain and swell based on the rainfall? Is there famine and disease? Does a diseased character have a buzzard over his head at all times like in Populous? Seasons are tough, especially when you change them during the course of the game. Allowing the player to choose a starting weather/landscape type is easy. Just provide a few different tile sets and unit sets.

Twinkling Stars

Stars are easily handled with color animation. You could maintain a list of individual stars with an Update () that makes it change slightly in diameter and color. This is a lot of work and may take a little processor time but the effect is far superior to straight color cycling. This would be for a space game, of course. StarCraft has stars in some of its levels, but I don't remember them twinkling. In fact, you may realize that twinkling is an effect of our atmosphere where the swirling eddies of air pressure changes refract the light slightly, creating the twinkling effect we see. Once in space, this effect disappears completely. That is the major advantage of the Hubble telescope. While it is not big, it is clear, which is probably more important. But I digress.

Another easy possibility is color cycling. By limiting the stars to a certain color range, you can remap the colors during the star refresh. This cannot be performed easily in any true-color mode but must be done in 256 colors or something similar. A space-based RTS/RTT game is a great possibility, although no one has done one yet to my knowledge. If you go this route, a great many things will be simplified. Rather than drawing a whole list of tiles during refresh, and possibly animating them, you would simply draw the graphics of the stars, which are relatively small and very fast to draw. The planets and other celestial objects would scroll around the screen, presumably on different layers to give the illusion of parallax. Drawing times would be reduced, leaving more computation time for the ever-popular, and computationally intensive, AI.

This kind of game could lend itself to a fixed background (i.e., bitmap) with stars plastered on it. The background might scroll or it might not, but this is an old idea that has come and gone. It doesn't look particularly good and there are simply so many other better ideas, let this sad horse die.

Rain and Weather

Weather effects can add a lot to a game. The first RTT game that I remember with weather effects was PowerMonger. It's a rather weak game by today's standards, but what a great game it was when it was released. Anyway, the landscape changed when it rained and when it snowed. The creatures (humans mostly) slowed down when the snow and rain came. The weather was kind of a pain to deal with as a player, but it made you think and plan your fights around the seasons, and it made me a better strategist. More designers should consider putting weather into their games.

Having said that, boy, is weather difficult to manage. Snow has accumulation, so you need more graphics assets. Rain affects the speed of creatures in the world, so there is another case for AI and commanders. Showing the changing of the seasons in graphics takes a lot more assets and a lot more memory. The effects can be very difficult to make look right, which is why more games do not feature weather. If you are ambitious, and weather will add something to your game besides graphics, I say put it in. Expect an extra man-month or two of development. It really does take a lot of work to perfect.

Reacting to Action

Ever been to a baseball game? Did you know that when you get hit in the head with a baseball the legal reasoning is "assumed risk," and because you could have expected that this might happen, you will not win a lawsuit? Of course, that won't stop it from hurting any less.

Animating the ball flying through the air would not be enough to create realism in a game. (Not only that, baseball probably wouldn't make a very good RTS/RTT game.) Most of the realism comes from the reaction of the "victim." You will need to add a "react" animation to the ANIMATION_DATA structure (you may have noticed it there). The enum reads REACT_TO_HIT, but you can shorten it to REACT. You might even want two or three different REACTs so that you can show variation, such as responding to different types of blows or taking different amounts of damage from an attack. There are lots of reasons to have multiple REACTs, but remember that they will all take four to eight frames of animation to execute in eight directions for each of the 80 or so creatures in your world, so consider carefully the requirements of REACT.

REACT is not an option, by the way. Only in StarCraft would REACT be inappropriate, as the weapons are energy based. Even so, it should have had REACT animation sequences. It really does create a new level of realism and I think that it is an absolute must for any modern game.

BLOCK is another reaction that a player might take to being hit. Most hand-to-hand combat games should support this kind of animation. Hand-to-hand games are not Command and Conquer type games. Think Warcraft or Age of Empires, before anyone had real big long-range weapons.

Communicating between creatures is handled in Chapter 18, but you might want to think how you would communicate a hit from one creature to another and then how you would make the hit creature react. We'll discuss this more later.

Preparing Animation for Each State

Each creature in your game will have about 10 different things that he might be able to do that the player can visually see. You'll need to look at the things that the designer will want the creatures to do. All creatures should be defined by the same base class, with all possible actions enumerated. Only in the child classes for the creatures should there be any differences between creatures in your world. This allows you to focus on creating generic/reusable code. With a good design, you will save hundreds of programming hours recoding the same action for 20 different creatures with only slightly different parameters.

When preparing to assemble the assets for an animated creature, make sure that you have the creature defined and his actions outlined. The artists get rather upset when they render a skipping cycle (as in, lou, lou, skip to my lou) for every creature in the world to find that only one creature in the world will ultimately skip. Also, animation, for the artists, is a long and arduous task that is often thankless. They like doing it because it can be fun at times, not for any other reward.

So if you have a hand in the design of the game, help out your artists by preparing a list of all animations required for each creature. This will greatly assist you as a programmer and you can begin solving strange problems that occur when the monkey-riders need to have a climbing animation for trees, mountains, and the side of a tower. This type of analysis is key to surviving the animation development cycle. It doesn't just matter which animations are available but how the terrain affects it. Do you need to animate creatures with different armor or weapons like in Diablo (not an RTS/RTT game)? Can creatures get into vehicles?

Defining all possibilities helps define states that your creatures can be in which will help us later in AI and definitely help when defining animation sequences. You should also spend the time to define the result of an animation sequence. Does the character simply move across the screen, or does he move vertically up the side of a mountain? Do the mountains allow a better range of vision? What happens on the last frame of the throw spear animation? Where does the spear come from? How do you track the spear back to the creature that threw it and then back to the player for his statistics? Many of these details will be covered later, but it is good to remember all of these considerations while preparing the animation.

Independent Entities and Animation

Your game may be populated by a variety of "wild" animals and other living entities that have nothing to do with the game. They add character to the game, a sort of ambient reality. Games may have deer, lions, birds, or dragons. These will all have their own animation, independent of the players. The deer may be there to provide food for hunter-gatherers. The lions provide a deadly element to the game when the player isn't paying attention to his infantry or gatherers. Birds will fly over the game field and add "life" to your otherwise lifeless landscape. The dragons would be a deathtrap to anybody daring to venture close enough. They might be guarding a lot of gold and thus could be a main storage resource for the players in a game where you must kill dragons to obtain enough gold to build troops and attack the other players effectively.

Other things in your world might require animation as well including fire, trees, treasure chests, waterfalls, supernovae, wormholes, ad infinitum. The fire could be set by the creatures in the world or by a player's wizard. The trees could sway in the wind while the waterfall flows in the background. All of these add character, and you should consider adding them to your game.

In terms of animation, keep it simple. These creatures and world objects are eye-candy and do not add a lot to your game. Limit the types of animation to two to five and limit the number of frames per animation sequence to between three and eight. These numbers are rather arbitrary and you should feel free to express your creativity, or at least that of the art staff. However, no matter how little you add, memory will still be an issue, as well as performance.

This is not to say that these animated objects aren't important. They give life to an otherwise dead game. If your team has the time, inclination, and dedication (as well as funding) to make a great game, you should include at least a few creatures and/or vehicles that do not belong to either player, and maybe a whole lot more.

Note: Windows 95 does not use all of its memory effectively. I don't understand why, but Win95 only will use up to 64 MB and then it generates swap files (virtual memory) after that instead of using any more memory that you might put in the machine. 128 MB of RAM is, effectively, the same as 64. Win NT does not have this problem and neither does Win98.

Skipping Frames

During the assembly of the animation sequences and the accumulation of assets, the frame animators will want to edit the animation to death. That is, they will want to make one frame of animation last for two game frames, and increase the distance traveled between frames six and seven. Provided that your animation editor is robust enough, you ought to be able to add frames and eliminate them. What you do during the construction process and then for the final build should be two different things.

When editing and allowing the artists to edit, all frames of animation should be available, even if the time spent on a frame in a sequence is 0. This allows artists (or anyone else) to bring back a frame of animation that was lost. Most editors might simply require that the art be reloaded and the animation sequence be reanimated. What a pain. It can also produce undesirable results. When editing, the artists ought to be able to turn frames on and off. They are trying to reduce the memory requirement for a given animation sequence and (hopefully) add realism. Your tools should help them. Spend a few extra days helping the artists and the game will never have to wait on assets.

Note: I have never seen a game late because of assets. The programmers are always the ones holding up the game unless there is a producer who wants to make the game better (changes, changes, changes). Making a better editor is great and very helpful to the game by helping to create more realistic animation. However, the code you write for the animation editor must be transferable to the game. First of all, why reinvent the wheel when you already have the code working in a different environment? Secondly, you'll never have the time necessary to create two different versions of essentially the same code. Plan on reusability and design your code thusly.

When editing, the artist should have a toggle switch that allows him to turn off (hide) all animation frames that have their Delay set to 0. Remember that this is the number of game frames spent on this particular frame of animation. By doing this, if an artist 0's out a frame, he can go on to edit all of the other frames without having to edit that frame again, unless he wants to.

Another, rather difficult, thing that the artists may need to do is change the order of an animation sequence or repeat the same animation frame later in the sequence. Your editor needs to be robust enough to handle this, without allowing yourself to duplicate the graphics data. You should be expected to have 40 frames of animation and put them into any order, delete any, and repeat any.

When you save out the animation information, make sure that no frames are deleted or that you don't delete the assets based on the artist dictating 0 time given to a frame. The file should contain all of the animation information; this will allow artists to go back and edit frames, reintroducing deleted frames if it becomes necessary.

When you go for the final build of the game, about two weeks before you ship, you should have developed an automated process that goes back for a final edit on the animation and eliminates frames of animation (graphics and animation info) from the sequence information. Of course, you should back up the old stuff because you can count on two or three animation changes the day of the release. You won't want it to happen, but I guarantee that a frame will be out of place or there is a bad bit of data—which makes an animation sequence jump 24 pixels across the screen—that needs to be changed.

In any event, plan on last-minute changes, but get the artists started on the final build rehash of the animation sequences for the game in order to save memory/hard storage.

The Simple Act of Turning Around

When I was at Ion Storm, I distinctly remember Todd Porter telling Mike Maynard and me, along with the art staff, how good Dominion would be because of the turning animation given to each of the units. Apparently, a creature marching to the west (Direction 4) and turning to the northwest (Direction 5) would stop first, and then go through a turning animation sequence—take a few steps or whatever—and then proceed in the new direction. While this did sound reasonable and even kind of cool, it did not make the game more fun.

However, Todd was on to something. In the case of a game like Age of Empires, it simply isn't practical with hundreds of different units (including buildings, trees, etc.) to double the amount of walk animation required for walking units (turning takes about the same amount of animation as a regular walk cycle). Not only that, the units are small enough so that it doesn't make that much of a difference anyway. You can't see the effect on a very small graphic.

StarCraft, which has less than half as many units (I estimate) that walk and big units (or so they appear in 640x480 mode), could have used turning animation to add something to the game. Of course, it has 16 directions of movement, which probably does more for the game.

Another consideration is gameplay. The requirement to stop, turn, and then continue slows down the responsiveness of the creatures. While this adds realism, it slows down the game and makes your units more susceptible to attack. Still, I like the idea.

You'll need to decide how your game will work. Incidentally, this problem does not go away in 3-D animated units. Total Annihilation units need to turn around to escape being fired upon and they take a beating in the process. I think the designers pulled it off quite well. There was a turning problem that Cavedog solved in a sort of cheesy way. Units that are jammed into a corner and are having difficulty turning slide sideways as they turn which "pushes" them out of the corner. Clever solution, but seeing a large, slow-moving walking unit slide on the ground looks odd.

The Remains and the Resources

When a creature dies, it may leave behind more than just its body. Peons might be carrying wood, gold, or food. The wheelbarrow someone was using might be invaluable. What is the head of an ogre worth anyway? Can you strip a dead wizard of his bowels and create a special wand with the crushed dust of that body part? A smashed tank ought to be worth something. Depending on the nature of your game, leaving remains may be a cool feature. After the death sequence, the dead creature remains there until somebody picks his bones dry. If yours is a tank-based game, then metal husks might populate the landscape.

Regular resources are much the same. There is something visible (in the game) that provides resources. This goes for other things in the world like berry bushes, trees, dead cows (for food), dragons (for armor plates), and basilisks (for blood used in potions of death).

In terms of animation, nothing could be simpler. The idea is simple: You put a graphic on the screen when a dead creature's body is visible. It will have a resource (or two) associated with it that a player's units can extract. The creature's body essentially changes into a resource. I have yet to see a game where a resource or a dead creature's body was animated. You could have a banner flapping in the wind or show the slow disintegration of the body over time. There are many possibilities, but I have yet to see a game that incorporates this. This makes your job easier or gives you a new idea for depth.

The resource should look different as you extract its resources. As you take the tank's treads off, the tank will look different, and as you cut down the tree, it will look different. If the resource percentage remaining changes how the husk looks onscreen, then the RESOURCE_ENTITY will have multiple frames and it will interpret what it draws based on the remaining percentage of resources. You might limit this to 25 percent decrements, so that the final 25 percent would look like almost nothing is left.

We'll examine the ENTITY class when we get to Chapter 18. The RESOURCE_ ENTITY is slightly more involved than what you see here, but the animation portion is enough. This is a really basic class, so don't expect a lot.

```
//**********************************
//**********************************

class RESOURCE_ENTITY : public ENTITY
{
     int            Num;
```

```
        GRAPHICptr      Graphic;
        Int             ResourceValue;

public:
        HUSK_ENTITY (int num, GRAPHICptr graphic, int resource);
        Void    DecrementResource (int quantity);

        void    Draw (SCREEN_STRUCT* sc);
};
//************************************
//************************************
```

Animated Buildings

The world is not static; many things change. Your game may reflect the construction process of a building, showing it in various states of construction from the foundation on up. It can be quite cool to watch the construction of the buildings that will ultimately process your resources. I've seen some games that show the entire construction process, such as Constructor. You see the foundation being laid, beams and walls going up, and finally the walls bricked and the roof finished. There are at least 20 frames of animation for these buildings. Most RTS/RTT games show buildings in three or four stages of construction at different percentages of completion. Anything more is probably overkill, but if your game has fewer units, say 20 units per player, more frames may add a subtle depth to your game.

Most games feature animated lights bouncing around the building or some whirligig spinning as a unit is being created inside it. This is a good visual clue for the player that lets him know that his building is in the process of doing something. The more you can give quick, unobtrusive clues about what your units are doing, the more successful your game will be—within reason, of course.

Animating buildings include the case where a building is burned down. The flames should be associated with a particular building because flames coming out of a window from one building might look odd on another building, especially if that building does not have windows. You can use generic flames that might apply to any building, but most games have pushed the realm of realism to where you must have a building burning down with its own animated fire. This has become the industry standard with regard to 2-D animated games.

As a building burns down (from missile fire or fire arrows), it needs to be shown in various stages of decay. This means a few frames of a building as it burns down. This adds a little to the animation sequence needed for the building. In addition, as the building burns down, the flames should look different, maybe higher. Plan on three or four stages of dying and differently animating fire for each of about eight frames of animation. This may seem like a lot, but fire is usually bits and pieces. That is to say, fire is never a solid block of data. There are a few flames here and there, and a flame LLE graphic usually compresses down to about 30 percent of whatever the size of a single frame of the building is. It is really tiny: Eight frames of animation takes about the same memory as three building graphics.

In StarCraft, the human's buildings can move; they lift up and float to a new destination. Quite cool. They don't actually animate, but they do move across the screen. Since all of the human's buildings in StarCraft have flashing lights, they could be considered to animate. But that type of animation is better handled with overlays, like fire.

Effects

These are called special effects in the movies. These include the lightning that flies from the hand of your magician to kill a band of orcs, the bomb detonation that obscures everything on the screen, and the fog that scrolls slowly across the screen and covers everything. These effects can range from a simple animation sequence to complex graphics that modify the colors of the background pixels.

You can use the ANIMATED_ENTITY class in Chapter 18 for simple things like this. A player or creature in the game will "spawn" an overlay entity that kills itself after a specific amount of time but first plays an animation sequence. Basically, you create a new "creature" at the right moment which only lives for a few seconds and plays an animation. You have to remember that most players will not be able to interact with the overlay. These are quite simple, and we'll discuss ANIMATED_ENTITY's more in tile systems and entities. For now, just think of it as an animated sequence belonging to a temporary creature.

Animated Overlays

Overlays can be fire for a torch or a building. They can be the moving lights on a building or the circle under the feet of a selected creature. Overlays can be tricky. First of all, there is the animation. Second, they do not have their own position in world space; it is always relative to a creature, building, or screen location. Third, they have to be controlled by an external force—a creature, building, or computer opponent.

The animation component of the three listed above is easy, right? Yes, but overlays can be more than a simple animated flame. They can be the selection box for around a creature (like in Diablo) that may need to animate. In Diablo, there is an "aura" of one pixel around creatures in the shape of the creature's outline. It should look different based on the health of the creature. You can handle this using an overlay, which in this case would have to exactly match each frame of animation so that each frame of creature animation would exactly correspond to a frame of overlay animation that would exactly trace a line around the creature.

All overlays (well, almost all) have a host—like a creature, building, or whatever. The overlay could be smart enough to get the information it needs from its host. Or the host could control the overlay. This is a design issue, but a reciprocal relationship works best. When the creature is spawned (ENTITY), it needs to spawn an ANIMATED_OVERLAY and hand it a pointer to itself. This will allow the overlay to figure out the information it needs. ANIMATED_OVERLAYs should be smart. They need to know how to play a frame of animation:

➤ Do they need to know the frame of animation and direction to match for the halo effect described above?

➤ Or do they play an animation sequence over the top of a building?

➤ Is there only one frame of animation, like a circular shadow for a creature?

➤ Does the creature's shadow change color depending on the relative health of the creature, meaning that you have frames for animation but no actual animation?

ANIMATED_OVERLAYs need to know what behavior they will have. This generally falls into those four categories listed above.

Overlays do not need a world position. They only need a screen position for drawing. They do not appear in the world and are more of an interface issue than a world entity issue. They are eye-candy. As such, they rely on a graphic for the position information, so you can limit their involvement to simply screen x and y. Then depending on which of the four types the overlay is, it will get screen information from the host, frame information, direction information, etc. Then it simply matches its frames up. It's nothing more than a matching game.

There need to be a few limitations to the graphics when planning on overlays. The frames of animation all need to be the same dimensions. What happens often is artists simply render a creature and the 3-D renderer spits out differently sized frames, although the width is usually the only thing that changes. Overlays require that you put a graphic over the top of another and so it must be the same dimensions as the "target" cell (of animation). It sounds easy, but if the target cells are different sizes, you could be in trouble.

It is always a good idea to keep the base animation with frames that are all the same size, but it may be a little difficult to accomplish. Have the artists render all of the frames in a fixed size and then write a utility to transform those into the smallest possible while keeping them all the same size.

Animating Death

Sounds boring, doesn't it? This is one of those depth issues that you will have to work out with your development team, but death is an important part of the game. There are a few common possibilities when dealing with the question of death and some more unusual ones. Since death can be morbid, you may find some of these ideas a little unnerving:

➤ When a creature dies, it collapses and then slowly rots into the ground. (Age of Empires, Warcraft II)

➤ When a creature takes its final hit, it animates a simple blowup sequence and then disappears. (Command and Conquer, StarCraft)

➤ The creature takes its final hit and explodes, sending pieces everywhere and sometimes leaving resources behind. The explosion can be hard in 2-D but can be done. (Total Annihilation)

➤ The creature collapses, and its soul flies upward, sometimes going to heaven and sometimes wandering the landscape wreaking havoc on the player who killed it. (No game I've seen yet)

➤ The creature melts and his life force feeds back to the player, allowing the player to build another. The limit on creatures is based on time-to-build. (None seen yet)

➤ The creature explodes, taking all within a radius with him. (Total Annihilation)

➤ The dying creature releases a bunch of creatures hidden inside of it. (Defender)

➤ The creature dies, leaving his body on the ground. When the moon passes over (or some other game trigger), the undead come to life and can be a hazard to your armies. (None yet have added this cool feature)

➤ The dead creature's body attracts large insects that roam the landscape looking for more food, including live bodies. The more creatures dead at the same time, the more insects appear, making bloody wars difficult because of the insects. (Could make a great game)

This list could number in the dozens, but these are simply design ideas and have nothing to do with animation. Each of these ideas carries its own series of headaches with regard to the amount of animation work and how you manage the animation, the death itself, a dying creature, a dead and rotting creature, etc. There are a lot of aspects to the dying creature, so let's cover them individually.

While designing the game, the designer should consider the work that will go into the entire death sequence of the creatures. If it is somewhat complex, this can affect the game schedule and cause delays. Also, a full discussion with the programming staff on this and other issues can save hundreds of hours in retooling. Basically, look before you leap.

> *"The way we handle death is at least as important as the way we handle life – don't you think?" – Captain Kirk*

The death sequence can be exciting. Some of the animated sequences in Age of Empires are so beautiful, you may find yourself asking your opponent to kill one of your units just to watch the death sequence. A good death sequence is worth the effort and makes a game more fun. Take Total Annihilation. The creatures explode, sending pieces everywhere. The death sequence for this game is one of the best. Another thing is that the "dead" robots leave their twisted metal shells behind, thus contributing metal resources. Good idea.

The death sequence should be eight or fewer frames. There is no point spending lots of animation frames for something that only happens once during the course of a creature's life. The Age of Empires designers outdid themselves by animating eight frames for each of eight directions. The result is unbelievable with different deaths and twisted bodies lying on the ground based on the direction the creature was facing when killed. In some games, when 50 creatures of the same type die, the battlefield has a "dead body" pattern to it, sort of like a new kind of wallpaper. Age of Empires will never have that problem—bodies lie twisted and decaying, facing in up to eight different directions. No apparent pattern ever develops.

Some games let the bodies simply disintegrate, while others have complex death scenes. For the most part, you should treat death as another animation sequence, albeit a short one, that should be played once the creature dies.

Beyond death is the next animation sequence, the rotting. Many games leave the body on the ground after the creature dies and over time show it in various states of decay. The first RTS game that I know that did this was Warcraft, although I am told that Dune had something similar. This is a very slowly played animation of three or four frames lasting 60 seconds to 2 minutes. In Age of Empires, the bodies never completely disappear, but it is perfectly acceptable to have them disintegrate into nothing over a long period. Having decaying bodies is a cool effect and I think that it is worth the effort, but most RTS/RTT games do not feature this.

Also, the information for a living creature should be transferred to a dying entity. The following class is essentially a counter with a pointer to a list of graphics. The point is to save on update time and memory. This structure is smaller than a creature structure and is greatly simplified, making computation time minimal. We want dying creatures, but we don't want to spend any real time computing them. The biggest bang for the buck, you might say. Since the only purpose of this class is to play a sequence until that sequence ends, the class is highly simplified. You may want to add more detail as necessary, such as the resource value of the dead creature.

```
//***********************************
//***********************************

class DYING_ENTITY : public ENTITY
{
        int        NumFrames, Delay;
        int        CurrentFrame, CurrentDelay;
        GRAPHICptr Graphic;

        DYING_ENTITY (int num, GRAPHICptr graphic);

        bool       Update ();      // returns true if DYING_ENTITY continues,
                                   // false if it stops
        void       Draw (SCREEN_STRUCT* sc);
};
//***********************************
//***********************************


//***********************************
DYING_ENTITY :: DYING_ENTITY (int num, int delay, GRAPHICptr gr)
{
        NumFrames = num, Delay = delay;
        CurrentFrame = 0, CurrentDelay = 0;
        Graphic = gr;
}
//***********************************
int    DYING_ENTITY :: Update ()
{
        CurrentDelay ++;
        if (CurrentDelay > Delay) CurrentFrame ++;
```

```
        if (CurrentFrame > NumFrames) return false;

}
//***********************************
void   DYING_ENTITY :: Draw (SCREEN_STRUCT* sc)
{
        // assumes that scx and scy are valid conversions from wx and wy
        if (CurrentFrame > NumFrames) return;       // dead
        Graphic[CurrentFrame]->DrawAt (scx, scy, sc);
}


//***********************************
//***********************************
```

When a creature dies, credit should go to the player responsible for killing it. The creature doing the killing might even learn from the experience, making it a better warrior next time. We'll cover this aspect later but you'll need to consider this in your design.

Blending Color with Backgrounds for Cool Explosions

Our last discussion is about blending animation. Sometimes, a partially transparent explosion looks best. This is more often than not the case. But how do translucent overlays work? And what about partially translucent overlays that also have solid parts?

Blending foreground and background is a tricky thing. In order to mix two paint colors, you need to have both paints. So obtaining the two colors for these pixels and then mixing them might be somewhat tricky. Our objective is to take a foreground pixel and mix it at 50 percent with a background pixel at 50 percent. Most of the time, this looks great, but on occasion, both the foreground and background are dark and you get a muddled look. Percentages other than 50 percent may look better but are much slower per pixel. This is already 7 clock cycles per pixel. A palette-based graphics system is faster with a simple table lookup, but the colors are always wrong. Better to go with something that works and almost always looks great.

The biggest problem is the pixel read. Video memory is notoriously slow to read from and this can slow your system to 12 clock cycles per pixel. AGP can reduce this slowdown (Intel's Accelerated Graphics Port), but AGP doesn't seem to deliver nearly as much as Intel promised. That's why video cards still feature tons of their own memory, which is much faster to access than going across AGP.

After obtaining the foreground color, the one we are going to write, and the background color, the color already there, we mix them. We divide the RGB color values by 2 and then add the two RGB colors. You can tear apart the 16-bit color value into RGB components and do the math, but a little trick may help you and certainly speeds up the process.

First, we mask out the low bits of the RGB components. Assuming that we have a 15-bit color value, we run it through a binary 11110 11110 11110. See how the low bit is set to 0 in each 5-bit group. This number happens to be hex 0x7BDE, or decimal 31710. To AND a register with this number takes 1 clock cycle (or ½), costing us practically nothing. Now we shift the remaining color value right by 1. This divides the RGB values by 2. Now we've done in 2 clock cycles what could have taken 12 by dividing the 16-bit color value into its components. Our color value is now 50 percent as bright as it was.

The masking was to prevent a blue 1 bit on shifting right from becoming a green 32 bit on. It might have gone from very dim blue to very bright green. That would be bad. Now that we have one color at 50 percent, we'll do the same with the other color. When we have foreground and background at 50 percent, we can add them. This also has the effect of eliminating overflow. The colors can never increase and have bits added to create odd colors. After all, 50 percent foreground plus 50 percent background can never be more than 100 percent color.

The code looks like this:

```
//**************************************************
void __fastcall Memcpy15Bit50Percent (U16ptr dest, U16ptr source, int num)
{
        if (num <= 0) return;

        _asm
        {
        mov     ecx, num            // how many copies
        mov     edi, dest           // to where
        mov     esi, source         // set source
        nop

repeat:

        mov     edx, [edi]
        add     edi, 2

        mov     eax, [esi]
        add     esi, 2

        and     eax, 0x7BDE         // mask off low bits 111101111011110 // 31710
        and     edx, 0x7BDE         // mask off low bits 111101111011110 // 31710

        shr     eax, 1              // 50 % value
        dec     ecx                 // counter stores flag

        shr     edx, 1
        mov     [edi-2], ax

        add     [edi-2], dx

        cmp     ecx, 0
        jg      repeat
        }
}
//**************************************************
```

Chapter 16

The Landscape

The game's framework is defined by the landscape. Almost everyone focuses on the units or their destructiveness. Some people focus on the race, tribe, or "side" that you choose. Others often focus their games based on the resources to be gathered or the tech tree. However, the most important part of the game to spend time getting right is the landscape. This defines the entire framework of the game and if it is designed well, programming your game will be easy. If your landscape system is not well defined, you could face a lot of problems later.

Landscape is the ground, the hills, and the trees. How these all fit together is critical and is a very important part of your design. Do not skimp on the design of this part of the game. The code you write to go into the landscape engine should be flexible enough to fit into the level editor and yet be compact. It should be the one part of the code where you focus on ease and elegance. All code for putting things onto a tile and moving them off should be fully tested before it makes it into the engine. This must be completely and thoroughly tested before you really begin to focus on the game. First of all, you must be able to rely on this code. Secondly, any bugs in this code will be next to impossible to find around delivery time.

Landscape does more than provide a framework for the programming of the game. It provides a link to the story and can provide depth. You can put triggers on the ground, special resources, people to rescue, and graveyards. You can provide factories, warp field areas, mutation regions with high radiation, and areas filled with disease. The landscape is where the foundation of your game begins, creating a realism that keeps the player coming back.

We'll be examining 2-D landscape in this chapter, at least in the sense that the graphics are 2-D. If we add height to the 2-D landscape, do we now have 3-D? Yes and no. Total Annihilation does not really have 3-D landscape, at least in the true 3-D sense. But it does have height in the landscape that obscures views and blocks missiles. That still doesn't look 3-D, so we'll call it 2-D with height.

Looking at some of today's better RTS/RTT games, true 3-D landscape seems to be the wave of the future. Interpreting what is meant by 3-D is another issue altogether, but I like games where I can rotate around the battlefield. Unfortunately, until DirectX 5, 3-D games were very difficult to implement. (I tend to agree with John Carmak in that Direct3D could have been designed a lot better to begin with.) Still, some RTS/RTT game developers are taking the plunge and a few of these games are pretty cool. Take a look at Dark Omen by Bullfrog and Gettysburg by Sid Meier. Although it doesn't fall neatly into the RTS category, Dungeon Keeper—also by Sid—is a great game and also features 3-D landscape. In my humble opinion, 3-D landscape is where RTS/RTT is headed. For more on this sordid subject, check:

http://www.jpa.com/editorials/1997/microsoft_3d_api_7797.html

But, to address the complexity question, Direct3D is best explored in another text, although I haven't seen one worth a hill of beans yet. The help files that come with DirectX are minimally helpful, and the only source that seems to have anything worthwhile is the Web.

What Does the Landscape Look Like?

Setting a theme for the look of your tiles helps to define the mood of a game and should be considered carefully. If the colors are dark, the game takes on a space or mystery theme. If your colors are bright and cheerful, your game may have a cartoonish feel.

The brightness issue goes well beyond the simplicity of mood. The landscape should be somewhat subdued. Grayish colors (unsaturated or low saturated colors) are the best for the landscape. On Doppelganger, we had beautiful, lush light-green jungles and bright white snow landscapes, and when we put our animals and monsters in the world, they became difficult to see. The colors all seemed to blend together. Striking a balance of color is difficult, but starting with a relatively subdued landscape is the first step.

The question of how the landscape looks is largely a question of taste and design. But a good-looking game like Age of Empires does not happen by accident. You need to look at the game, go home for the night, come back the next day, and look again. Then you make choices like "that spaceship looks too bright against the background." You compare and contrast different types of landscape next to each other: "Does the desert tile set need border tiles where it touches rocky terrain?" The look of the terrain, and the world in general, is an iterative process. Don't expect to sit down for an afternoon and decide exactly what is going to look good.

Mostly, you should look at the landscape every day of the development cycle and ask the question: "Does it look right for what we are trying to achieve here?" This is a good rule of thumb that applies to most of the development cycle anyway, not just to the landscape. If there ever comes a day when you walk in and find that there is nothing you can improve upon, ship the game. Until then, continue to improve up until a few months before the ship date.

The Concept of a Tile

Tiles are usually the foundation for the landscape. Your game may not actually have tiles and may be 3-D (3-D games often don't use tiles), but the tile concept remains the same. A *tile* is a body of land that contains graphics, a list of objects that are on it at any given moment, its dimensions, and world coordinates. Your tiles may contain additions like VECTORs, rotational information, sounds, triggers, a pointer to a tile that might appear on top of it, etc. But for the most part, these tile objects are simply containers of a chunk of land or water. They provide the terra firma for the creatures to build and walk on.

Tiles don't do much. During the update cycle, a tile should not need to do anything. There are special cases like wind or flowing water where the tile could conceivably perform some action, but they are like a skeleton: They are rigid and the most critical part of your framework, but they don't do anything themselves.

Tile-based games are essentially a 2-D grid with pointers to graphics. Even a 3-D tile game has this 2-D index system, which is a simple top-down view of what the world looks like. For more detail, check out:

http://www2.msstate.edu/~gpb1/tilestructure.html.

The graphic that the tile points to (or the index) should be a common graphic. In other words, the tile should not own the graphic, just point to it. This allows you to have 50 of the same type of land with the same graphic, and not take up any more memory. As an added benefit, the tile doesn't need to load, store, or maintain the memory associated with the graphic. All it does is display the graphic. Easy, schmeasy.

Tiles can be either of three shapes, not counting 3-D, of course. These are illustrated on pages 437 and 438. Tiles can be isometric (see Figure 16.1), rectangular (see Figure 16.2), or hexagonal (Figure 16.3). Warcraft II uses rectangular tiles while Age of Empires uses isometric tiles. StarCraft uses rectangular tiles but makes them look isometric. The look of isometric tiles is often better than 3-D or rectangular tiles. Play with the StarCraft level editor that comes with the game or the scenario editor from Age of Empires for a while and you'll see what I mean.

Note: I worked on the scenario editor and it is largely the same as I programmed it to be, at least functionally.

One game, Fallout, uses isometric tiles that are not at 45° like most other tile games. It is pretty unique and I'm sure that managing the tile positions in the world was a fun task, albeit difficult. In terms of programming, rectangular tiles rate about 3 on a scale of 1 to 10, while isometric rates about 7. It is much harder to manage movement and world position. However, the look of a true isometric game is head and shoulders above rectangular.

Every tile has a world position, but it does not need to be maintained in the list of world objects, so it doesn't need the registration process in WORLDOBJECT. Tiles should be derived from WORLDCOORDINATE instead. You'll see these WORLDOBJECTs pop up in the next few chapters, but for now, just concentrate on the WORLDCOORDINATE. You'll see this structure again later, but you'll need to see it here as well:

```
//*****************************************
class WORLDCOORDINATE
{
protected:
      S16    wx, wy, wz;              // world map position
```

```
        S8      offx, offy, offz;       // object offset in world terms

        //*******************

public:

        //*******************

        WORLDCOORDINATE ();
        ~WORLDCOORDINATE ();
        inline void  Clear ();

        //*******************

        WORLDCOORDINATE operator =  (WORLDCOORDINATE* obj);
        WORLDCOORDINATE operator += (WORLDCOORDINATE* obj);
        WORLDCOORDINATE operator -= (WORLDCOORDINATE* obj);
        WORLDCOORDINATE operator += (WPOINT* pt);
        WORLDCOORDINATE operator -= (WPOINT* pt);

        //*******************

        int            operator == (WORLDCOORDINATE* obj); // a test

        //*******************
        //*******************

        void SetWorldCoordinates  (int x, int y, int z) {wx = (S16) x,
            wy = (S16) y, wz = (S16) z;}
        void GetWorldCoordinates  (int* x, int* y, int* z) const {*x = (S32)
            wx, *y = (S32) wy, *z = (S32) wz;}
        void SetOffsetCoordinates (int x, int y, int z) {offx = (S8) x,
            offy = (S8) y, offz = (S8) z;}
        void GetOffsetCoordinates (int* x, int* y, int* z) const {*x = (S32)
            offx, *y = (S32) offy, *z = (S32) offz;}

        //*******************

        void SetWorldX (int x) {wx = (S16) x;}
        void SetWorldY (int y) {wy = (S16) y;}
        void SetWorldZ (int z) {wz = (S16) z;}

        //*******************

        int  GetWorldX () const {return wx;}
        int  GetWorldY () const {return wy;}
        int  GetWorldZ () const {return wz;}

        //*******************

        void SetOffsetX (int x) {offx = (S8) x;}
        void SetOffsetY (int y) {offy = (S8) y;}
```

```
                void SetOffsetZ (int z) {offz = (S8) z;}

        //*****************

        int  GetOffsetX () const {return offx;}
        int  GetOffsetY () const {return offy;}
        int  GetOffsetZ () const {return offz;}

        //*****************

};
//*******************************************
```

Basically, we have world coordinates—wx, wy, and wz—with offsets. The tiles won't need the offsets, which are used to tell us where an object appears within a tile. Since we are dealing only with tiles, this is a bit silly. If your game will not have height, you could eliminate wz but that would prevent creatures, also derived from WORLDCOORDINATE, from being on top of a building or some other object. You should probably leave it. Chapter 18 discusses this structure in detail.

The tile class can contain just about anything, depending on your needs:

```
//*******************************************
struct TILEFLAGS
{
        U32 Passable : 1;            // can it be traversed
        U32 Buildable : 1;           // can it be built upon
        U32 HasHeight : 1;           // can this tile have elevation
        U32 PassableByShip : 1;      // water or any tile that can have a watercraft
        U32 DifficultToPass : 1;     // hard to traverse
        U32 CausesDamage : 1;        // normal creatures traversing receive damage
        U32 SpawnsLife : 1;          // new trees and plants
        U32 ProvidesEnergy : 1;      // energy supply
        U32 ProvidesMinerals : 1;    // contains minerals that can be mined
        U32 ProvidesWater : 1;       // contains water
        U32 ProvidesFood : 1;        // can provide food
        U32 ColorCycleStage : 3;     // this allows 8 levels of color cycling
        U32 TriggerPointID : 4;      // allows up to 15 triggers on the map,
                                     // this is an ID number
        U32 TransportPointID : 4;    // allows transport point on map
        U32 Fog : 2;                 // various strengths of fog, usually 0, 1,
                                     // and 2 only
                                     // 0 is no fog, 1 is border fog, and 2 is
                                     // full fog.
        U32 Pad : 32-24;             // remaining bits
};
//*******************************************
//*******************************************

typedef class  SINGLE_TILE : public WORLDCOORDINATE
{
        ENTITY*      Object;
        U16          MiniMapColor;
```

```
        GRAPHIC*        Graphic;

        //TILE_TYPE_DEFINED :: TILETYPE
        U8          TileType : 8;
        //TILE_TYPE_DEFINED :: RESOURCES
        U8          Resource1 : 8, Resource2 : 8;
            // a single tile can only have 2 resources max

public:

        SINGLE_TILE ();
        ~SINGLE_TILE ();

        void  Clear ();

            //***********************

        void      SetTileType (int type) {TileType = (U8) type;}
        int       GetTileType () {return TileType;}
        void      SetResources (int res1, int res2 = 255)
                  {Resource1 = (U8) res1, Resource2 = (U8) res2;}

        void      SetGraphic (GRAPHIC* g) {Graphic = g;}

            //***********************

        void      Draw (SCREEN_STRUCT* screen, int x, int y) ;
        void      DrawObjects (SCREEN_STRUCT* s, int x, int y);

            //***********************
        void      SetMiniMapColor (U16 c) {MiniMapColor  = c;}
        U16       GetMiniMapColor ();

            //***********************
            //***********************
        void      AddObject (ENTITY* o);
        void      RemoveObject (ENTITY* o); // find object in list and remove it
        ENTITY*
              GetObject ();              // returns list
        ENTITY*
            RemoveBottomObject ();         // removes object and returns it

        //***********************
        TILEFLAGS Flags;                   // flags for easy access

}TILE, SINGLE_TILE, *SINGLE_TILEptr, **SINGLE_TILElist;

//*******************************************
```

The basics are a Graphic and an Object. It already has world coordinates based on its derivation. The objects should be smart enough to add themselves to a list and remove themselves from a list, even if the list is NULL. You'll notice the TILEFLAGS structure, which makes your tile much more powerful. All of the flags are explained in the comments. The flags are generally set by the level designer, with triggers, transports, and passability being especially tweakable. The ProvidesWater flag is automatically set when you paint water terrain on the map but you may want to provide other functionality with it.

The flags, as usual, are made public to the TILE class. This only makes sense since making access routines to the members of this TILEFLAGS structure is a waste of time and is not worth the effort. It also breaks the encapsulation of normal C++ by making the TILE know too much about TILEFLAGS.

The graphic associated with a tile should not change during the course of a game, so this pointer is probably better than an index into a global array. Just remember that the graphic does not belong to this class. If you delete the graphic, you'll be in trouble, guaranteed. The member variable Object is a WORLDOBJECTptr list, a linked list of all of the items on the tile. MiniMapColor is a pixel color that will be used when creating the minimap.

There are possibilities for resources on any type of land, but to help with the distinction, you can limit the types available on certain sections of land. The Resource1 and Resource2 variables allow you to set limits on the types of resources available. TileType lets you set grass, desert, etc. See tile.h on the companion CD and the TILE_TYPE_DEFINED class.

As well defined as the class is, none of it defines much more than a few variables. The meat of the code is yet to come. One thing of note: The last variable in the class definition is the Flags variable. I put it last in the public section to make its access easier.

The constructor does nothing but clear the variables. Since the SINGLE_TILE class does not allocate any memory, the destructor does nothing. The Graphic member variable is meant to hold a graphic but not to allocate it. The allocation should be handled by some external class that will load and maintain all of the graphics.

The Draw function draws the tile. The DrawObjects function draws the linked list of objects on the tile, provided that a list is valid. The GetMiniMapColor function allows the minimap to access the tile and know what color to draw that would represent that tile. This could easily be replaced by an actual image, but simple blocks of color in the minimap usually suffice.

The rest of the functionality is used for moving objects around in the world. The last section of code gives some common definitions for tile types:

```
//*******************************************
SINGLE_TILE :: SINGLE_TILE () : WORLDCOORDINATE ()
{
        Clear ();
}

//***********************

SINGLE_TILE :: ~SINGLE_TILE () {}

//***********************
```

```
//***********************

void   SINGLE_TILE :: Clear ()
{
       Object = NULL;
       MiniMapColor = 0;
       Graphic = NULL;
       TileType = 255;                  // invalid
       Resource1 = 255;                 // invalid
       Resource2 = 255;                 // invalid
}


//************************

void   SINGLE_TILE :: Draw (SCREEN_STRUCT* screen, int x, int y)
{
       if (Graphic != NULL)
       {
           Graphic->SetScreenPosition (x, y);
           Graphic->DrawAt (screen, x, y);
       }
}


//************************

void   SINGLE_TILE :: DrawObjects (SCREEN_STRUCT* s, int x, int y)
{
       ENTITY* p = Object;
       while (p)
       {
           p->SetScreenPosition (x, y);     // needs some math here
           p->DrawAnimation (s);
           p = reinterpret_cast <ENTITYptr> (p->GetNext ());
       }
}


//************************

U16    SINGLE_TILE :: GetMiniMapColor ()
{
       if (Object) return Object->GetMiniMapColor ();
       return MiniMapColor;
}

//************************
//************************

void   SINGLE_TILE :: AddObject (ENTITYptr o)
{
       Object = reinterpret_cast <ENTITYptr> (o->AddObject (Object));
}
```

16

```
        //************************

void    SINGLE_TILE :: RemoveObject (ENTITYptr o)
{
        ENTITYptr p = Object;
        Object = reinterpret_cast <ENTITYptr> (Object->Remove (o));
}

        //************************

ENTITYptr  SINGLE_TILE :: GetObject ()              // returns list
{
        return Object;                              // Object
}

        //************************

ENTITYptr  SINGLE_TILE :: RemoveBottomObject ()  // removes object and
                                                 // returns it
{
        ENTITYptr p = reinterpret_cast <ENTITYptr> (Object);
        Object = reinterpret_cast <ENTITYptr> (Object->RemoveObject (p));
        return p;
}

//*******************************************

class TILE_TYPE_DEFINED
{
public:
        enum TILETYPE   {GRASS, DESERT, ROCK, FOREST, WATER, BEACH,
                        LAVA, SAND, SAVANA, SWAMP, MUD, NUMTYPES};

        enum LIFE_SUPPORT {NO_LIFE, ALGAE_LIFE, DESERT_PLANT_LIFE,
                        GRASSLAND_PLANT_LIFE, EVERGREEN_LIFE,
                        DECIDUOUS_LIFE, FRUIT_LIFE, ANIMAL_INSECT_LIFE,
                        ANIMAL_FISH_LIFE, ANIMAL_REPTILE_LIFE,
                        ANIMAL_MAMMAL_LIFE, ANIMAL_BIRD_LIFE,
                        ANIMAL_DOMESTICATED_LIFE, ANIMAL_HUNTER_MAMMAL_LIFE,
                        ANIMAL_HUNTER_REPTILE_LIFE, ANIMAL_OTHER_LIFE,
                        NUM_LIFE_SUPPORT};

        enum RESOURCES  {NO_MINERALS, COPPER, TIN, IRON, SILVER, GOLD,
                        RARE_EARTHS, HERBS, PEAT_MOSS, ADOBE, FLINT,
                        WATER_RES, COAL, COMMON_GEMS, SEMI_PRECIOUS_GEMS,
                        PRECIOUS_GEMS, FERTILE_SOIL, SILICON, PLANT_FOOD,
                        ROOTS};

        ...
};
//*******************************************
```

What Do You Put on the Landscape?

Creatures are the obvious things that you put on a tile. But what kinds of other things are acceptable? Conceivably, you could have a flat world in which the only thing appearing on the map is player creatures and battle tanks, which would simplify your game considerably. It would also make your game very boring, so forget it. We want to be able to put everyone and his mother on a tile to add that creative element to the game. We want a wide and varied landscape, and one of the easiest ways to accomplish that is to allow anything to go onto the tiles.

Things that you should consider are:

➤ Resources. These include metal, water, wood, food, money or gold, bricks, rocks, steel, various energy sources like plutonium or magic crystals, etc. Resources can change graphics when used up, stay the same, disappear, or be replaced by something else.

➤ Terrain features: trees, rivers, lakes, hills, mountains, abandoned cities, crevices, cliffs, lava flows, caves, etc. The nice thing about most terrain features is that they can be the tile itself. A water tile, for example, would actually be the tile or it could be an overlay.

➤ Different types of land: desert, grass, forest, beach, rock, obsidian, slate, flower bed, broken dirt, moss, jungle, thorn bed, etc. These are mostly different graphics or border overlays that reside between different types of terrain. The tile would normally own this as a graphic. Some of these, like forest, would also have a tree associated with it, meaning that the graphic would be different for the tile and would also need to have a tree object on top of it.

➤ Symbols: crosses, circles of power, and arrows. These symbols are usually just markers for triggers but they can appear anywhere. These are usually just a simple unanimated graphic.

➤ Landscape decorations: flowers, ground cracks, small flora, rubble, broken wheels, and discolored ground. These usually offer no benefit or distraction to the player. They are almost always aesthetic.

➤ Triggers: These are places on the landscape where players must send their troops or where a special item is hidden. A trigger can be an object or just about anything. Usually, assigning an entity as a trigger makes this easier.

➤ Buildings and vehicles: Since these are normally entities, this should be a no-brainer. They will have unique characteristics, but they are just entities.

➤ Creatures: orcs, demons, dragons, wizards, martians, aliens—entities with behavior is the best description of a creature. Most RTS/RTT games have plenty of these.

Lots of different things can appear on a tile as we have seen here. You might be able to come up with other categories, but this covers most of them.

Can the Landscape be Damaged?

Damaging landscape is a cool idea. Explosions should, after all, create a crater, right? Trees should burn down when struck by a Sidewinder missile. Tanks should be able to trample walls. There are dozens of possibilities and these can be managed in a few different ways. However, whichever form you choose to implement, you will probably pull out a little hair in the process.

Craters can be real or imagined. That is to say, you can deform the landscape or you can place a graphic overlay on the ground where the hole is supposed to be. Then you'd need to make the hole take up object space, meaning no object could walk on it. Deforming the landscape requires a stacking system where tiles can exist on top of one another. No game (that I know of) supports this paradigm, but stacking tiles allows the tiles to have height, and thus you can just as easily dig a hole.

Craters can be managed easily in a system like this, because a crater is a deformity in the ground and creatures cannot move between tiles that have a height difference greater than 1. As an example, say the ground has a default height of three tiles. A mortar shell blows a hole into the ground that is about three tiles deep. Around the edges of this hole, a few tiles were knocked out to give the effect of an inverted cone. Any tank could drive around the edges of the hole without any problem, but going from the edge through the middle of the hole would be impossible because the height difference from the edge to the center of the hole is greater than 1. You can decide what restrictions this might generate in your game, but putting height in tile games is a great idea that can be used to solve the crater issue.

The graphic overlay is a much simpler solution and a perfectly acceptable one. Basically, you place a blocking object that happens to look like a hole on the ground. The difficulty is having five or six different holes for different types of terrain. And how about when a hole is on the border of two types of terrain? Ouch, what a tough problem. The best solution is to make a generic hole that can look good on any type of terrain. This is hard for an artist, but much easier for the programmer. We'll talk about blocking objects in a few chapters and blocking terrain in a little while.

What about fire? If you burn down a building, what does it do to the surrounding terrain? How about forest fires? What do they do to the scorched earth? Can a player intentionally trap a second player's creatures by building a trench around that player's starting position? Is there a limit to the number of holes/ craters allowed at any given time? Are there different sizes of craters? Do you need different graphics for different holes or do you just choose one at random?

Damaged terrain adds a lot to a game but all of the above considerations come along with it. I suggest that for large explosions you use a small graphic overlay and do not block the terrain. This simplifies the problem domain significantly.

16

Chapter

3-D Texturing vs. 2-D Blit

It used to be a question of speed, but now that newer 3-D video cards are rocket speed, 3-D textured landscapes are a good possibility. So now, the decision becomes a question of look. Since most video cards support bilinear filtering, the look of low-resolution textures is astounding. The dynamic changes a lot, however. First of all, all buildings need to be 3-D. You can use 2-D creatures with simple animation over the 3-D landscape, but you must have 3-D buildings. Then there is the 3-D animation that you will probably want to support for animated buildings. You can, of course, animate everything in 3-D, and newer video cards won't even flinch at 5,000 polygons per frame at 30 fps. This makes an entire 3-D army possible, and gives you license to create a beautiful game.

3-D adds a whole new aspect to this game but will add three to six months to the development cycle. You'll need tools, great 3-D animators, and texturers for low polygon models. If you have the bucks/backing and the know-how, I highly recommend going to 3-D. The level of effort, however, can be prohibitive and 3-D introduces a whole new bunch of headaches.

In addition, 2-D buildings will almost always look better, depending on your artists. The look of 2-D can still be tailored to look better. If you want to focus on game content, go with 2-D. If you want to focus on cool interface and the ability to rotate around the battlefield, go with 3-D.

Resources

Resources are the cornerstone of any good RTS game and are also important in RTT games. There are different kinds of resources: permanent and declining. There are also other considerations such as type and availability. Planning the different types of resources that will be needed to, say, hire, train, and equip mercenaries is part of the fun of design.

Permanent or Declining

From a programming standpoint, permanent and declining resources are different to manage.

A permanent resource will give resources forever. This might be a fishing hole that provides fish forever or a gold mine that seems to go on forever. Nothing could be simpler to program. Once a creature's body space intersects the body space of a resource, the creature acts upon the resource. We'll discuss this in a few chapters, but this is very easy to manage. Without defining a full RESOURCE_ENTITY, the code might look like the following. The CONTROLLING_PLAYER is inherited, but I put it here for discussion purposes.

```
//**************************************
class RESOURCE_ENTITY
{
    enum RESOURCE_TYPE {FOOD, WATER, WOOD, METAL, IRON, COPPER,
```

```
                 TIN, GOLD, GEMS, SILVER, MANA, POWER, ELECTRICITY};
float                    Resource;
RESOURCE_TYPE            TypeResource;
CONTROLLING_PLAYER*  Controller;
......
float       GetResource (float force = 1)
{
      if (Resource <0.0) return 0.0;
      Resource -= force;
      If (Resource> 0.0) return force;
      ResourceMGR->SetToRemove (this);
      return force + Resource;   // resource is negative at this point
}
};
//***************************************
```

First, this class defines a few possibilities for resource type. We then store the resource value in a float value called Resource, the resource type, and the controlling player for resources that a player might own. Owned resources are good for certain types of games requiring a constant supply of mana or energy. This value would normally be NULL.

The GetResource function does all of the bookkeeping necessary; this illustrates how simple this all is. We'll talk about ResourceMGR later, but it simply keeps a total list of all resources, changes them appropriately, and creates them when necessary. We'll discuss tailoring this better to your game much later.

This poses the question whether you should use declining or permanent resources. A minor change to GetResource takes care of that, but you might want permanent resources to be restricted to gold or maybe food for the Cornucopia Temple in your game. This is a simple condition test. Just test for the specific type of resource before you return anything.

Generally, declining resources are more realistic and more prevalent in RTS/RTT games. Not only that, they create a sense of urgency to dominate resources early in the game. The metal worlds in Total Annihilation are too easy and provide abundant and infinite resources. I can set the game up to play by itself and it can play for days with no effort on my part. It kind of defeats the purpose. If resources are limited and non-permanent, however, it becomes too easy to dominate by simply placing a missile launcher near an important resource or two. This is a gameplay and balance issue, and I'll leave it to you to decide.

Types and Availability

Deciding how many types of resources and how much there should be of each type is probably the most important game balance issue that you will decide. This is easy: However much you decide to use, make sure that all players have access to the same amount. They do not all need it the same distance from their start point, nor do they need all of the resource concentrated in the same location. They just need access to the same amount. That balances the game in terms of fairness.

Now, how much of the resources should be available to each player? Use a simple formula. Take the cost of every unit available to a player and add those costs together. Now divide that cost by 2; that is the amount of resources that should be near the starting location for a player. This usually is enough to pay for modest increases in the tech tree, pay for a small army and small upgrades to those army units, pay for eight to ten peons/workers, and build a modest defense. Remember, these are the resources close to each player's start location, and thus these resources are easy to get and generally accepted as the "initial resources" for a player, even though he has to do a little work for them. The rest of the map should be littered with small enclaves of resources that are concentrated (have a high resource value) and they should be fairly distributed on the map. There should be enough extra resources on the map to allow each player to build three to five full-sized armies, even though a player will only build certain types of units and usually in small groups. There is also the cost of upgrades and traversing the tech tree to consider. These should be added when doing your calculations.

When deciding on the types, you'll need to decide if you are seeking RTS or RTT. If you want to focus more on fighting and not "micromanagement," stick to one to three types of resources. Although limiting the number of resources to less than three doesn't necessarily make the game more tactical, it does make the game less strategic. Strategy focuses a lot more energy on logistics, and part of that is having enough different resources to challenge the player's balancing skills. RTS games should also limit the quantity of the resources more to really give the players a challenge, or at least offer resource limiting as a startup option. Strategic games should begin with three types of resources and scale upwards. Five resource types begins to get unmanageable, so six and above is unreasonable. Plus, the interface begins to run out of real estate.

The real question is one of balance and game style. Not all resources need to be found. What about combining two resources to create gunpowder? What if you need iron and coal to make steel? Think about the character of your game and pick resources that seem to match.

Resource types depend on the game. If you are planning a space-type game, try using metal, energy, gas, and rubber/polymers (for suits, guns, tires, etc). For a western game, try horses, gold, silver, and guns. For an underwater city game, players can take advantage of the natural environment and use seaweed (food), whales (transport), sharks (attack creatures), eels (weapons), and coral (construction materials). For a game set in ancient Rome, use stone, bronze, food, water, and wood. For a medieval game, use iron, mana, wood, oil (for sieges), and gunpowder.

These are just suggestions. You should pick your own resources based on your own judgment.

Background and Ambience

The game world should, somehow, feel alive. This is the ambience. Not very many RTS/RTT games capture this elusive element, but a few do and it can be breathtaking.

Age of Empires is a great example. There are gazelles that run away from people as they approach, lions that eat the gazelles, birds that fly overhead, etc. After playing for 20 minutes or so, you begin to sympathize with the prehistoric humans and you almost feel a part of it all. Of course, that all becomes a farce as the game wears on and battles ensue. Ambience is, thus, an unimportant element that pushes a game up a percentage point or two when the ratings come out, but only if done well.

Note: Ratings for games are ubiquitous, but only a few game magazines seem to affect public opinion. *Computer Gaming World* is one that has a percentage rating system. It has rated games like BattleCruiser 3000 around 13 percent and StarCraft around 97 percent (I forget the exact percentages). If a game can hit 85 percent in *CGW*'s rating system, that is a sure hit. For each percentage point above 85, you can be guaranteed around 100,000 in units sold. You'll need to trace history to see what I mean, but games that have a 93 percent rating or higher easily sell over a million with only a few exceptions. Considering the widespread availability of PCs these days, this is getting easier to do, but even older games did very well. The point is, if you think you have an 85 percent game, fight for the extra time it takes to make it a 90 percent or 95 percent. The rewards will be in prestige and in your pocketbook.

If you don't understand ambience, move on to the next section. Ambience is hard. It is also important. As such, you should pick creatures, colors, background creatures, and sounds to create the mood. This should be reflected in your landscapes, which should be the types of worlds in which a creature could live.

When building your world, most people think about the creatures first—"I want three types of demons, two demon lords, a butcher, skeletons, blah, blah, blah." Where do these creatures live? What do they eat? They don't just sit around all day waiting to eat, do they? What do they do during their spare time? Think about how cool it would be to play an RTS game in which you are marching your army to the other side to kill your opponent and you run into a group of orcs playing rugby, who then engage you in combat. Or how about the sleeping dragon that hordes gold? If you are willing to risk your entire well-equipped army to get its treasure, then you can afford specialized equipment to use against your opponent's army. The issue, then, is whether you will have enough time to equip before your opponent attacks.

Beyond external creatures, what about the player's creatures? Why are they there? What does this world have to offer them and why haven't they moved to a more peaceful part of the planet? What do they eat? Do they simply live to serve the player's interests? If not, what do they do when not actively assigned to do something? In Red Alert, the soldiers get down and do pushups when they aren't marching. Great ideas lead to great games and hence great sales.

Passable and Impassable Terrain

Creating passable and impassable terrain is easy, you say. Every tile needs a flag indicating whether you can walk on it or not. What's so hard about that? I've heard people ask this question, and the answer is almost laughable.

Is a tile with height passable? If I were looking for the shortest path between two points, would I ignore the little hill along the way, or would I use it in my calculations? Can a creature walk inside a building? If so, how do I get him into the building if the building blocks him from ever getting there? What if a building only blocks part of a tile? Is the tile passable or not? How many creatures can I fit onto a tile before it becomes impassable?

Passable terrain is generally black and white: It is either passable or not. But I'm suggesting that there are other possibilities such as mostly blocked or difficult to get to. The simpler your paradigm, the faster the pathing code will go. *Pathing* is the wonderful art of finding a route between where you are and where you'd like to go. (There are dozens of Web sites dedicated to pathing or a-star (A*), and any decent search engine will point the way.) When finding a path, a creature is looking throughout the world for a way to point B. If a tile is blocked, it then looks at the tile's neighbors. But what if the tile is partially blocked? This is covered in detail in Chapter 19.

If you are planning on a flat world, or faking height in your landscape with graphic cliffs, then the black and white—passable or blocked—is suggested. If you plan to have real hills such as in Age of Empires or Total Annihilation, then plan on having another way to use path finding.

Landscape Elevation

Should you use real elevation or not? Most RTS/RTT games don't. Some of the new 3-D games do but Total Annihilation doesn't use it for pathing (or doesn't look like it does). Elevation looks great and can add a few new and cool strategic elements to your game. Maintaining the high ground could offer added damage or better chances to hit. Attacking someone on a hill lessens damage or odds of hitting (minuses on damage or chance to hit or both). Plus, the hills break up the landscape, giving it "texture" and more character. Elevation can also be a pain.

Elevation adds a new dimension and difficulty to your landscape. In a true 3-D tile system, you have difficulties with elevation. How much does a creature speed up or slow down when traversing a hill? You also have to determine whether a building can be built on uneven ground. If it can, how do you know how uneven it can be? Do the graphics for that building need to change? Are there any limits? How does elevation affect pathing? Can a creature path just as well up an incline or would he rather go around a small hill? The fact that the graphics in 3-D can look strange from certain angles is another consideration.

In a 2-D or a 3-D tile system simulated with 2-D graphics, you have all of the same difficulties as 3-D plus a whole lot more. First of all is the issue of needing about 25 new graphics per tile. Look at the graphics diagrams for details later in this chapter. That is, to represent all of the new angles and permutations of the tiles, about 25 more tiles are needed for every one we had before. Wow, that's a lot of data/memory/hard drive space. Matching graphics can be difficult. On flat ground where two types of terrain meet, assuming that you can have more than one type of terrain per map, you would want a natural-looking border tile. If you have a graphic that represents grass and borders rocky terrain and also runs down the middle of a hill, how do you do the border? These could have hard edges, but it looks awful. Better to have a border overlay, which means more graphics.

Actually, there are scores of problems that arise when raising or lowering land tiles. The base tiles seem to not align well with raised tiles, and you often get gaps or holes where tiles are supposed to meet. How should the graphics on the top of a raised section look? These art issues swiftly become programming problems because the artists can create the tiles but not manage the way they fit together in the program.

Start with a diagram of all the possible raised tiles. There are several diagrams here illustrating a lot of different concepts, so let's take them one by one. This is a good guide to help the artists get started. Look at the following tile diagrams closely. There are baseline diagrams to show you what the tiles look like when everything is flat, including full representations for rectangular tiles, diamond/orthogonal/isometric tiles, and a sampling of hexagonal tiles. Hexagonal tiles, although they are much more rare and very difficult to program, can look very good. Look these diagrams over. Now imagine them looking like grass, rocks, or whatever. Then put them together in any combo—now you have a mess.

First are the baseline diagrams, shown in Figures 16.1, 16.2, and 16.3:

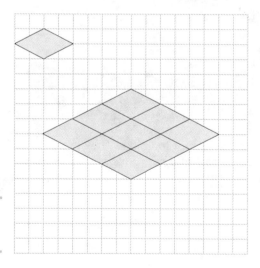

Figure 16.1
Baseline isometric tile

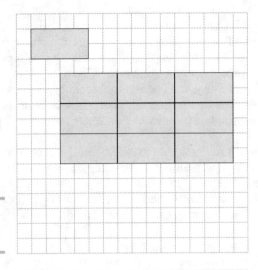

Figure 16.2
*Baseline
rectangular tile*

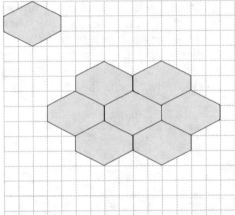

Figure 16.3
*Baseline
hexagonal tile*

These show you what these tile groups look like. They are on a background grid, which should serve as a guide in terms of dimensions and placement.

Next are diagrams in which a single tile is raised, as shown in Figures 16.4, 16.5, and 16.6:

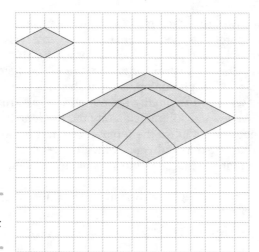

Figure 16.4
Raised isometric tile

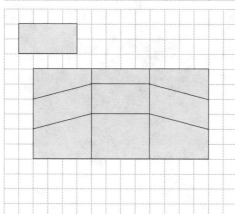

Figure 16.5
Raised rectangular tile

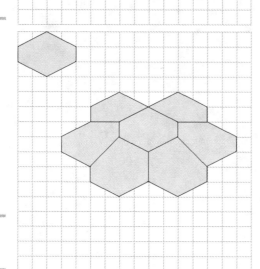

Figure 16.6
Raised hexagonal tile

We still have the base nine tiles (or seven for hex), and the raised or center tile has the exact same shape as before. The tiles surrounding the center have all changed shape, so you'll need more graphics to represent each of these new shapes. This is where 3-D tiles would be nice. Change a vertex or two and rerender. Remember, we're doing this for looks, not for ease of programming. Look at the tiles surrounding the center tile closely. Your artists will need to modify the output of grass, rocks, sand, and so on to fit within these shapes and still match along the borders. It is worth noting that the center tile does not extend above the topmost tile in the diagram. This makes your job easier when drawing the landscape, which we'll talk about in the next section. Also notice that the center tile has been moved up one grid square. That is, it is actually moved/raised.

Similarly, we have lowered tiles in Figures 16.7 and 16.8. (Since I'm not really interested in presenting hex tiles, I won't be showing any more hex diagrams. You can apply most of these concepts to hex tiles anyway.)

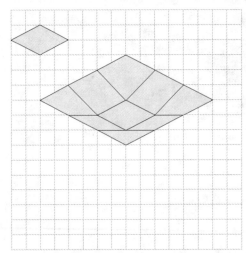

Figure 16.7
*Lowered
isometric tile*

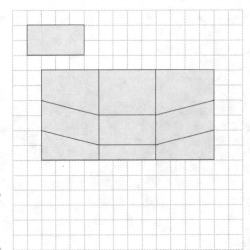

Figure 16.8
*Lowered
rectangular tile*

We lower the center tile and swap out the old tiles for new ones. So far, we have the center tile, plus its surrounded raised and lowered tiles. This count is 17 tiles so far, but we are still missing a few.

Figures 16.9, 16.10, 16.11, and 16.12 introduce a few unusual tiles. Two tiles are raised one tile apart, but now need a different tile between them diagonally. This was first pointed out to me by Matt Pritchard of Ensemble Studios. Smart guy. The diamond tiles have eaten a member.

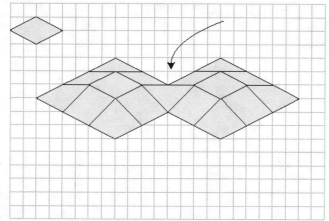

Figure 16.9
Raised isometric tiles

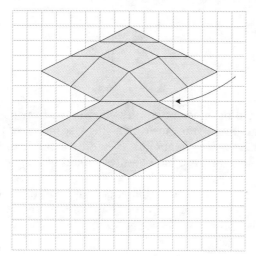

Figure 16.10
Raised isometric tiles

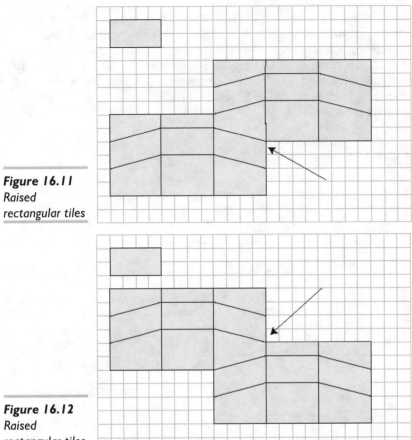

Figure 16.11
*Raised
rectangular tiles*

Figure 16.12
*Raised
rectangular tiles*

In Figure 16.9, there should have been two tiles where the arrow points, but the back one is covered up. For graphics, you can store a single scan line to remain consistent, or not draw the tile at all. Same rule applies in Figure 16.10. Figures 16.11 and 16.12 show us that with rectangular tiles, the two tiles should become one. Still, you can divide it into two tiles just as easily.

Next we have a lowered diagram showing the effect with two tiles lowered. Notice that Figures 16.13 and 16.12 have the same shape of tile. The same goes for Figures 16.14 and 16.11. This brings our tile count up to 20.

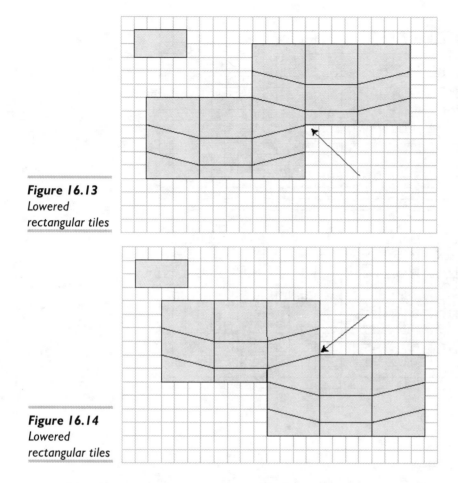

Figure 16.13
Lowered
rectangular tiles

Figure 16.14
Lowered
rectangular tiles

Instead of doing a dozen more diagrams, I created Figure 16.15. This is the top-down view of a tile diagram. This applies to both diamond tiles and rectangular tiles. You should prepare one of these to represent all of the types of tiles you hope to support in your game. In addition, Figures 16.16 and 16.17 show a raised and a lowered tile diagram so you can see how the tile diagram corresponds to graphics. Figure 16.15 shows that the very basic count for a raised set of tiles is 25, 24 including 0.

Height   **Tile**

raised   *raised*

1	1	1	1	1	1	1	1	1	1
1	1	1	1	1	1	1	1	1	1
1	1	2	1	1	1	2	1	1	1
1	1	1	1	1	1	1	1	1	1
1	1	1	1	2	1	1	1	1	1
			1	1	1	1	1		
			1	1	1	1	1		
1	1	1	1	1	1	1	1	1	
1	1	1	1	2	1	1	1	1	
1	1	2	2	2	2	1	1	1	
1	1	1	1	2	1	1	1	1	
1	1	1	1	2	1	1	1	1	
			1	1	1	1	1		
			1	1	1	1	1		

0	0	0	0	0	0	0	0	0	0
0	1	2	3	0	1	2	3	0	
0	8	0	4	0	8	0	4	0	
0	7	6	17	2	18	6	5	0	
0	0	0	8	0	4	0	0	0	
			0	7	6	5	0		
			0	0	0	0	0		
0	0	0	1	2	3	0	0		
0	1	2	21	0	22	3	0		
0	8	0	0	0	0	4	0		
0	7	6	24	0	23	5	0		
0	0	0	8	6	4	0	0		
			0	7	6	5	0		
			0	0	0	0	0		

lowered   *lowered*

1	1	1	1	1	1	1	1	1
1	1	1	1	1	1	1	1	1
1	1	0	1	1	1	0	1	1
1	1	1	1	1	1	1	1	1
1	1	1	1	0	1	1	1	1
			1	1	1	1	1	
			1	1	1	1	1	
1	1	1	1	1	1	1	1	
1	1	1	1	0	1	1	1	
1	1	0	0	0	0	1	1	
1	1	1	1	0	1	1	1	
1	1	1	1	0	1	1	1	
			1	1	1	1	1	
			1	1	1	1	1	

0	0	0	0	0	0	0	0	0
0	9	10	11	0	9	10	11	0
0	16	0	12	0	16	0	12	0
0	15	14	19	10	20	14	13	0
0	0	0	16	0	12	0	0	0
			0	15	14	13	0	
			0	0	0	0	0	
0	0	0	9	10	11	0	0	
0	9	10	23	0	24	11	0	
0	16	0	0	0	0	12	0	
0	15	14	22	0	21	13	0	
0	0	0	16	0	12	0	0	
			0	15	14	13	0	
			0	0	0	0	0	

Figure 16.15
Top-down view
of a tile diagram

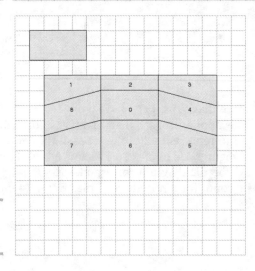

Figure 16.16
Raised tile
diagram

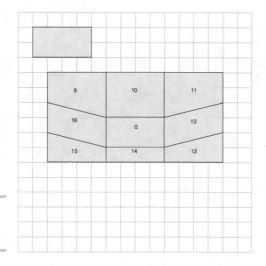

Figure 16.17
Lowered tile diagram

16
Chapter

Look again at Figure 16.15. This height and tile type of map helps you define exactly how many of each tile angle you need. All you have to do is set up a map like this and diagram every possibility you can think of. My diagram accounts for most possibilities excluding some rather rare ones, allowing the programmer to go hog wild. This pretty much opens up full map elevation functionality for any programmer and hence for any gamer. For purposes of programming, treat diamond tiles like rectangular tiles and rotate your square map. This may seem strange, but this is the easiest way to program this kind of map.

Note: Dominion and a few other true isometric (diamond) tile games have their world map rectangular. Each tile has a world coordinate that corresponds exactly to screen position. This system is easy for the general programmer, but the pathing programmer has a nightmare on his hands. Take a look at how complicated moving can be.

These matching diagrams, such as Figure 16.15, are easy to program, as long as you look at one tile at a time. Assuming that these diagrams match (Height and Tile), the code goes something like this next section of code. I have avoided the case where a tile might be bordered by both a raised and a lowered tile, but you'll be able to figure that out. One thing that you'll need to avoid is a single tile, either lowered or raised, surrounded by five or six tiles with different height. You can resolve it however you like, but it mostly doesn't work. I recommend not allowing users or artists to do this. It unnecessarily complicates matters and you don't want to spend three months perfecting something that could take only three days.

```cpp
//*********************************************
// main.cpp

#include <string.h>
#include <iostream.h>
```

```
#include <conio.h>

//********************************************
int    NumTiles = 49, MapWidth = 7, MapHeight = 7;
int    StandardHeight = 2;         // this is the baseline for the tile height
// all tiles in the world for land are this high. This allows dips in the
// terrain
int    Heightmap[] =
       {
              2,    2,   2,   2,   2,   2,   2,
              2,    2,   2,   2,   2,   2,   2,
              2,    2,   1,   2,   2,   2,   2,
              2,    2,   1,   1,   1,   2,   2,
              2,    2,   1,   2,   1,   2,   2,
              2,    2,   2,   2,   2,   2,   2,
              2,    2,   2,   2,   2,   2,   2
       };

// 8 directions starting with the upper left and going clockwise
int    Dir [][2] = {{-1,-1}, {0,-1}, {1,-1}, {1,0}, {1,1}, {0,1}, {-1,1}, {-1,0}};
int    NumDir = 8;
//********************************************
struct SIMPLETILE
{
       char Height;    // :3;
       char Tile;      // :5;
};

SIMPLETILE* tiles;

//********************************************
//********************************************
void   InitTiles ()     // empty pointer
{
       tiles = new SIMPLETILE [NumTiles];
       for (int i=0; i<NumTiles; i++)
       {
              tiles[i].Height = Heightmap[i];
       }
}
//*********************
// we pass the height for comparison. if I'm looking for a height value for
// a tile that is off the edge of the map, I want it to be the same height
// as the edge to which I am surely comparing.
int    GetTileHeight (int x, int y, int height)
{
       if (x<0) return height;
       if (y<0) return height;
       if (x>=MapWidth) return height;
       if (y>=MapHeight) return height;
       return tiles[x + (y*MapWidth)].Height;
}
```

```
//**********************
int     CountHighNeighbors (int x, int y)
{
        int num = 0;
        int Height = GetTileHeight (x, y, 0); // the height passed is unimportant
                                              // we know that this tile exists

        for (int i=0; i<NumDir; i++)
        {
                if (GetTileHeight (x+Dir[i][0], y+Dir[i][1], Height) > Height) num++;
        }

        return num;
}

//**********************
int     CountLowNeighbors (int x, int y)
{
        int num = 0;
        int Height = GetTileHeight (x, y, 0); // the height passed is unimportant
                                              // we know that this tile exists

        for (int i=0; i<NumDir; i++)
        {
                if (GetTileHeight (x+Dir[i][0], y+Dir[i][1], Height) < Height) num++;
        }

        return num;
}
//**********************
void    ModifyMaskAndCountWhenAppropriate (int& num, int& mask)
{
        if (num <2) return;
        int array[] = {mask&128, mask&64, mask&32, mask&16, mask&8, mask&4,
            mask&2, mask&1};

        for (int i=0; i<8; i++)
        {
                if (array[i]) break;
        }
        if (i==8) {num = 0, mask = 0; return;}

        int which = i;                          // where to start
        int count = num;                        // set the count
        while (count)
        {
                if (which>=8) which=0;          // fixing wraparound
                if (array[which++] == 0) break; // the end of the run
                count --;
        }
```

```
        if (count>0)          // we did not get a continuous run clockwise,
                              // try counter clockwise
        {
            which -=2;        // where to start, start where we left off,
                              // the decrement
            // is correct for where we left off and one less.
            // also, below we decrement to put the pointer 1 less
            count = num;                        // reset the count
            while (count)
            {
                if (which<0) which=7;           // fixing wraparound
                if (array[which--] == 0) break; // the end of the run
                count --;
            }
        }
        if (count>0)          // there is a problem. These may be opposites
                              // or unconnected flags
            return;

    // since corners do not affect the choice of a tile except in the
    // case of 1 border tile, we will make out the corners, count the
    // remaining mask items, and return those values.

    mask &= 85; num = 0;
    if (mask&64) num++;
    if (mask&16) num++;
    if (mask&4) num++;
    if (mask&1) num++;
    // the values are passed by reference so they are essentially pointers
}
//*******************************************
void    ResolveTile (int x, int y)
{
    SIMPLETILE* tile = &tiles[x + (y*MapWidth)];
    int numhigh = CountHighNeighbors (x, y);
    int numlow = CountLowNeighbors (x, y);
    int height = GetTileHeight (x, y, 0);

    tile->Tile = 0; // default flat tile, we need to assign at least
                    // this value to the tile no matter what our decision

    if ((numhigh == 0 && numlow == 0) || (numhigh == 8 || numlow == 8))
    {
        return;
    }

    // now we need specifics
    int upleft      = GetTileHeight (x+Dir[0][0], y+Dir[0][1], height);
    int up          = GetTileHeight (x+Dir[1][0], y+Dir[1][1], height);
    int upright     = GetTileHeight (x+Dir[2][0], y+Dir[2][1], height);
    int right       = GetTileHeight (x+Dir[3][0], y+Dir[3][1], height);
    int downright   = GetTileHeight (x+Dir[4][0], y+Dir[4][1], height);
```

```
int down       = GetTileHeight (x+Dir[5][0], y+Dir[5][1], height);
int downleft   = GetTileHeight (x+Dir[6][0], y+Dir[6][1], height);
int left       = GetTileHeight (x+Dir[7][0], y+Dir[7][1], height);
// we have to choose another tile.
if (numhigh && numlow)      // these can be tricky, most will be tile 0
{
    return;
}
else if (numhigh)
{
    int mask =
        ((upleft     >height) ? 128:0) + ((up    >height) ? 64:0) +
        ((upright    >height) ? 32:0)  + ((right >height) ? 16:0) +
        ((downright  >height) ? 8:0)   + ((down  >height) ? 4:0) +
        ((downleft   >height) ? 2:0)   + ((left  >height) ? 1:0);
    // if 3 sides are different height and they compose an
    // arc or are sequential going around the circle then we only
    // need to consider the number of non-diagonal sides. Diagonals
    // are only used for opposites or a single
    // differently than just the solid borders (up/down/left/right).
    // otherwise, this function modifies the mask and the number of
    // sides.

    ModifyMaskAndCountWhenAppropriate (numhigh, mask);

    switch (numhigh)
    {
    case 1:
        {
            // this will apply to 2 side by side tiles that may have
            // one masked out because it is a diagonal
            if (mask == 128) {tile->Tile = 5; return;}
            // slope down right
            if (mask ==  64) {tile->Tile = 6; return;} //slope down
            if (mask ==  32) {tile->Tile = 7; return;}
            //slope down left
            if (mask ==  16) {tile->Tile = 8; return;} // slope left
            if (mask ==   8) {tile->Tile = 1; return;}
            // slope up left
            if (mask ==   4) {tile->Tile = 2; return;} // slope up
            if (mask ==   2) {tile->Tile = 3; return;}
            // slope up right
            if (mask ==   1) {tile->Tile = 4; return;} // slope right
        }
        break;
    case 2:
        {
            // we'll test adjacent, up/right, down/left, these are
            // inverted corner pieces # 23, 24, 25, & 26
            if (mask&64)
            {
                if (mask&16) {tile->Tile = 24; return;} // slope up right
```

```
                    if (mask&1) {tile->Tile = 23; return;} // slope up left
                }
                if (mask&4)
                {
                if (mask&16) {tile->Tile = 21; return;}
                // slope down right
                if (mask&1) {tile->Tile = 22; return;} // slope down left
                }

                // now check for opposites. We won't allow up/down
                // or left/right since there is no tile for a dip.
                // We simply raise the tile we're working on.
                if (mask&64 && mask&4) {tile->Height = up;
                        tile->Tile = 0; return;}          // fix height
                if (mask&16 && mask&1) {tile->Height = left;
                        tile->Tile = 0; return;}          // fix height

                // diagonal upleft/downright
                if (mask&128 && mask&8) {tile->Tile = 17; return;}
                // diagonal downleft/upright
                if (mask&32 && mask&2) {tile->Tile = 18; return;)
            }
            break;
        case 3:    // these should all be treated the same unless we
                   // have a better scheme
        case 4:
        case 5:
        case 6:
        case 7:
            tile->Tile = 0;      // default flat tile
/*          // now we may need to raise to be equal to our neighbors
            if (mask&64) {tile->Height = up;    return;}
            if (mask&16) {tile->Height = right;return;}
            if (mask&4)  {tile->Height = down; return;}
            if (mask&1)  {tile->Height = left; return;}*/
            break;
        }
    }
    else                              // numlow
    {
// similar in most ways to the numlow above but we are testing lowering
        int mask =
            ((upleft    <height) ? 128:0) + ((up    <height) ? 64:0) +
            ((upright   <height) ? 32:0)  + ((right <height) ? 16:0) +
            ((downright <height) ? 8:0)   + ((down  <height) ?  4:0) +
            ((downleft  <height) ? 2:0)   + ((left  <height) ?  1:0);

        ModifyMaskAndCountWhenAppropriate (numlow, mask);

        switch (numlow)
        {
```

```
case 1:
    {
    // this will apply to 2 side by side tiles that may have
    // one masked out because it is a diagonal
    if (mask == 128) {tile->Tile = 13; return;} // slope up left
    if (mask ==  64) {tile->Tile = 14; return;} // slope up
    if (mask ==  32) {tile->Tile = 15; return;} // slope up right
    if (mask ==  16) {tile->Tile = 16; return;} // slope right
    if (mask ==   8) {tile->Tile =  9; return;} // slope down right
    if (mask ==   4) {tile->Tile = 10; return;} // slope down
    if (mask ==   2) {tile->Tile = 11; return;} // slope down left
    if (mask ==   1) {tile->Tile = 12; return;} // slope left
    }
    break;
case 2:
    {
    // we'll test adjacent, up/right, down/left, these are
    // inverted corner pieces # 23, 24, 25, & 26
    if (mask&64)
    {
        if (mask&16) {tile->Tile = 22; return;} // slope up right
        if (mask&1) {tile->Tile = 21; return;}  // slope up left
    }
    if (mask&4)
    {
        if (mask&16){tile->Tile = 23; return;}  // slope down right
        if (mask&1) {tile->Tile = 24; return;}  // slope down left
    }

    // now check for opposites. We won't allow up/down or
    // left/right since there is no tile for a dip. We simply
    // raise the tile we're working on.
    if (mask&64 && mask&4) {tile->Height = up; tile->Tile = 0;
                    return;}                 // fix height
    if (mask&16 && mask&1) {tile->Height = up; tile->Tile = 0;
                    return;}                 // fix height
    if (mask&128 && mask&8) {tile->Tile = 19; return;}
                        // diagonal//upleft/downright
    if (mask&32 && mask&2) {tile->Tile = 20; return;}
                        // diagonal//downleft/upright

    }
    break;
case 3:          // these should all be treated the same unless we
                 // have a better scheme
case 4:
case 5:
case 6:
case 7:
    tile->Tile = 0;        // default flat tile
    // now we need to raise to be equal to our neighbors
/*  if (mask&64) {tile->Height = up;    return;}
    if (mask&16) {tile->Height = right; return;}
```

```
                    if (mask&4)  {tile->Height = down;  return;}
                    if (mask&1)  {tile->Height = left;  return;}*/
                    break;
            }
        }
}
//*******************************************
//*******************************************
void main ()
{
        InitTiles ();

        // print the starting heights
        for (i=0; i<MapHeight; i++)
        {
            for (int j=0; j<MapWidth; j++)
            {
                int x = tiles[i*MapWidth+j].Height;
                if (x >9) cout << x<< " ";
                else cout << " "<< x << " ";
            }
            cout<<endl;
        }
        cout<<endl;

        // which tiles have been chosen
        for (i=0; i<MapHeight ; i++)
        {
            for (int j=0; j<MapWidth; j++)
            {
                ResolveTile (j, i);
                int x = tiles[i*MapWidth+j].Tile;
                if (x >9) cout << x<< " ";
                else cout << " "<< x << " ";
            }
            cout<<endl;
        }

        // look for any change to the map
        cout<<endl<<endl;
        for (i=0; i<MapHeight; i++)
        {
            for (int j=0; j<MapWidth; j++)
            {
                int x = tiles[i*MapWidth+j].Height;
                if (x >9) cout << x<< " ";
                else cout << " "<< x << " ";
            }
            cout<<endl;
        }
```

```
        getch ();


        delete (tiles);
}
//********************************************
```

This code is really easy, but you may not understand it at first glance. First, I recommend that you put it into a class when you have the chance; you can manage it however you like. For simplicity, this is a bunch of C-like functions, but you won't be able to compile this in C without moving a few variable declarations; remember that in C all variables must be declared at the top of the function.

Notice Heightmap declared toward the beginning of the file. This is an artificial map of heights from which this code generates matching tile numbers or indices. In order to modify this map, you'll need to change the variables above it: NumTiles, MapWidth, and MapHeight. The variable StandardHeight is simply to establish a baseline. It is perfectly acceptable to choose 0 for this value but allowing dips or the lowering of land from a baseline is a good idea. For our purposes, we'll need to lower and raise tiles during testing. This code works well, but you may want to optimize parts (I recommend it) and that means testing. The output in the main function will output text in a DOS window to allow you to verify your results.

It is important that you be sure you don't have more than one height level of difference between any two tiles. It is possible, if you're willing to quadruple the number of required tiles, to account for two levels of tile height change, but it is a lot harder. As level designers modify the height of a map, you'll need to do smoothing. This is best handled by never allowing the designer to raise or lower a single tile. By limiting raised sections to 2x2, you'll avoid a lot of strange tile possibilities in cases where a tile type cannot be resolved. There is a perfect example in the code.

If you look closely under HeightMap, you'll notice a series of 1's in the rough shape of an "h." In the hole of the h, notice the 2 all by itself. What would the graphic for this tile look like? Smoothing would never allow a single tile like this to exist. As the designer fills in the map by raising sections, the code would search around the newly raised section. Then it would raise (or lower) newly isolated tiles. Remember height smoothing when building your editor and your game will be helped enormously.

This code is not optimal, but it is plenty fast. The first optimization you'll want to add is in ResolveTile. You'll want to optimize the variables up, down, etc., into an array to allow you to set up the height analysis much easier. Look over the code and I'm sure you'll see what I mean. The reason that I used the separate variables is because I wanted the code to be clearer. Although this code is not perfect, it is actually quite fast and a few optimizations I added make it lightning fast. A 100x100 map can be completed in about 8 milliseconds. Not bad if you ask me.

By the way, this code would be used in the map creation process. Unless the map is dynamic, this code would not be needed at run time.

One more note: I created a SIMPLETILE structure for purposes of developing this code. This should be the minimum needed to define tile basics, without considering graphics or objects on the tile. The member variables can and should be replaced by

454 ■ *Chapter 16*

bit fields. There is no reason to have more than eight levels of elevation/height. Even if you decide on more, 16 is plenty. There's 3 or 4 bits, depending on your dis/pleasure. We have defined 25 possible variations of the single tile, which easily makes it into 5 bits. If you are willing to limit your elevation/height to eight levels or 3 bits, then we get a nice even 8 bits used for both the height and tile ID. Pretty smooth, eh?

One obvious deficiency that I mentioned earlier is the lack of code for both higher and lower tiles near a tile. Since this is implementation dependent, I'll leave it to you. It shouldn't be too hard to get right.

The code works, so if you have trouble running it, just copy it from the CD, and modify it from there.

Note: The map is global here. I recommend making the map in your game global. It simplifies a lot of things. You'll still want access routines for analysis like the CountLowNeighbors function for most interactions with the map. Those functions should be global, or at least part of a class declared globally. The map is one thing with which almost every part of your game will interact, so do yourself a favor and make it global.

Map access can be tricky, so I recommend a few functions that you make global for the handling of map access:

```
//********************************
float  GetMapPassability (int x, int y)      // returns an float 0.0 to 1.0
                          // the code here is overly simplistic and the
                          // number should reflect height considerations
                          // as well as other factors
{
        if (x<0 || y<0) return 0.0;                      // off of the map
        if (x>=MapWidth || y>=MapHeight) return 0.0;

        if (Map[x+y*MapWidth].GetObject ()) return 0.0; // impassable, has
                                                        // object on it

        return 1.0;                              // looks good
}


//********************************

int    Dir [][2] = {{-1,-1}, {0,-1}, {1,-1}, {1,0}, {1,1}, {0,1}, {-1,1}, {-1,0}};
void   FindNearestClearTile (int x, int y, int& posx, int& posy)
{
        if (GetMapPassability (x, y) == 1.0)
        {
            posx = x, posy = y;
            return;
        }
        int dist = 1;
```

```
        int found = 0;
        while (found == 0)
        {
            for (int i=0; i<8; i++)                 // 8 directions
            {
                int dx = x+Dir[i][0]*dist, dy = y+Dir[i][1]*dist;
                if (GetMapPassability (dx, dy) == 1.0)
                {
                    posx = dx, posy = dy;
                    found = 1;
                    break;
                }
            }
            dist++;
        }
    }
//********************************
```

This is a smattering of what you'll really need. These routines simply help with map access and give you functionality that you would have to redo dozens of times if you didn't centralize it into a few functions.

Rendering the Landscape and Overdraw

Rendering the world isn't too complicated to manage if you remember one simple rule—down the screen and layer by layer. Other methods have been tried by dozens of people with dismal failure. It would be nice to call the Draw function of a tile and have it draw all of the items on top of it, but it doesn't work that way. If you draw a tile and everything on it, then any neighbor tile you draw next will cut off a portion of the creature or unit that was on that tile.

When drawing, draw in layers. First draw all of the tiles, since they are behind and under everything. Then draw everything on the tiles from back to front. If you draw items from front to back, items in front will be overdrawn by items in back. This is easily handled using the tile function DrawObjects (SCREEN_ STRUCT* s); as part of the tile class. The top part of Figure 16.18 shows what happens when you draw front to back. The bottom part of the figure shows a properly drawn map.

Figure 16.18
If we place tiles from front to back, the later tiles and objects draw over the previously drawn items.

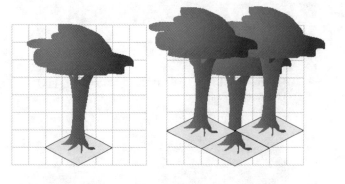

By starting at the top and drawing the items toward the bottom of the screen, everything works fine on land without elevation.

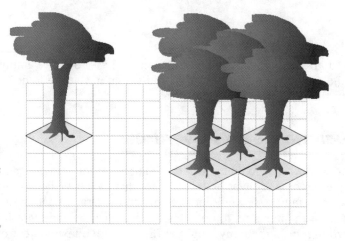

Elevation adds a lot more problems. Layers become the key, as in Figure 16.19. The top part of the diagram shows what happens when you simply draw front to back, while the bottom part of the diagram shows layering.

Figure 16.19
Drawing back to front is not enough when elevation is in the game. Here, we see drawing back to front and left to right. The house is eaten by layers in front of it.

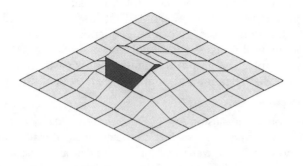

Here, we draw a layer at a time and then we draw the objects on top of that layer. The top layer has a house on it and the house would be the last thing drawn in this example.

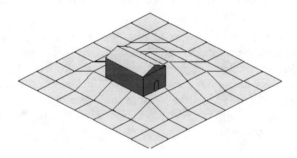

First you draw a layer of land, starting with elevation 0, and then you draw the items on it. Next you draw elevation 1 and the items on it. So tiles in your draw area are queried as to their elevation before you draw. It's not very difficult really, but it can be confusing. If you get it wrong, it will become immediately obvious.

Cliffs

While I was working on cliffs for Age of Empires, I found out one interesting thing: Cliffs are very complex. Just matching one cliff graphic with another is difficult. True cliffs are exceptionally difficult because you need a way to declare a tile impassable, but only when trying to move from one height to the next. Pathing around cliffs is hard, and managing the graphics for raised landscape is rough. Then there is height calculation for attackers who gain a height advantage over opponents below the cliff. Cliffs in a true height situation are a hair-pulling situation, so plan on quite a bit of development time when adding them.

Now here we have another good argument for real 3-D: A creature simply cannot move from a very high point to a very low point. That is to say, a creature cannot simply walk from a high elevation to a low elevation, which is what a cliff is. In 3-D, you simply connect the points in 3-D space with a polygon and texture it. 2-D drawing makes this task not so simple. The graphics management is easier in 3-D. Dark Omen does a sweet job with its 3-D terrain and it makes cliffs look beautiful.

Sidebar: The final decision about cliffs on Age of Empires was made by Rick Goodman to do overlays. We simply put graphics on the ground and made players and creatures walk around. There were 17 different cliff tiles as I recall, and Angelo Lauden controlled most of the aspects of the game. He gave a bonus to the creatures in the game that fired across one of these cliffs/overlays in a certain direction, simulating a bonus for being on the high ground. Angelo is the true engine architect of Age of Empires and a great programmer, as well as a great guy to work with.

I spent over two weeks on the overlay system because I didn't know what I was doing. I had the help of a fantastic artist, Duncan McKissick, who helped me to come up with the 17 tile number. The two weeks I spent developing the cliff editing would have been much longer if not for the help of Tim Deen, a skilled and insistent programmer with whom I've had the pleasure to work. I recommend that you buy Age of Empires and play with the Scenario Editor. Select Map|Cliffs and go to it.

True cliff height represents a major problem with regard to managing putting graphics over the hole you create when raising one tile much higher than its neighbors. First, you need graphics. Work with your artists to come up with these. You'll need at least 13 graphics for this. Then you need to think about individual tiles. You should add a set of 8 bits for passability so that the pathing can easily determine if it cannot pass a certain direction across a tile. Then when a designer raises a tile to create a cliff, turn the passability bit off in that direction. Next, you'll need to account for height. Since elevation is already part of the ENTITYs that you'll see in Chapter 18, you can rely on that. Store the elevation of a projectile as it is launched. When it hits its designated target, see what the target's elevation is and make any damage adjustments.

If cliffs are important for your game, you may want to consider a system like StarCraft's. It has the basic landscape with blocking graphics over the top, kind of like in Age of Empires. The scheme used by Blizzard is much simpler. I recommend that you buy StarCraft and play with the editor for a few hours. It is really a great tool.

Mountain Passes and Other Graphics Overlays

Some of the best-looking elements of an RTS/RTT game will be overlays. Buildings, cliffs, rivers, and other blocking landscape like mountain passes are good examples. These could be land tiles, but considering the variety and possibilities when done with tiles, this soon becomes unmanageable. These beautiful elements add character and dimension to a mostly flat world. This is especially true if you go with the flat-world paradigm with graphics for elevation simulation.

The diagrams of StarCraft in Chapter 8 show what's involved in adding 2-D graphics to a 3-D simulated world. First, we establish a bunch of small rectangular tiles. Next, we place a graphics element over the tiles, and then we have a passability map. This will be used during pathing. There is no height consideration in this paradigm, but it offers a great alternative to the actual map height adjustments we just talked about.

Setting up this system is trivial. You need fairly small tiles, perhaps 16x8, and graphics that work well on this small scale. Then you'll need a bunch of overlays. Lastly, you'll need to make an editor that allows the artists to make a passability map that will match the underlying 16x8 tile size. Basically, you need to make a painting program that paints over loaded graphics and stores the large blocks in an array along with the compressed graphics, or perhaps as a separate file. Now, when editing the map, these graphics with passability will affect the underlying tiles by changing the passability of the tiles, thereby restricting movement over them.

Mountain passes would simply be very large graphics with passability through the middle but blocked on the sides. This simplifies many things in your game and can significantly reduce time to market. However, the map with true elevation usually looks a lot better. You'll have to make that choice.

Elements of Pathing

There is a lot of terrain that affects pathing. Blocking terrain can be a cliff, river, mountain, forest, or lava. Another impassable element is large changes in elevation. You should limit your use of these, because they will slow down pathfinding considerably and hence the game will slow down. It is usually best to restrict use of items that potentially block a path to either clumping or making them sparse. Clumps make pathfinding around an object easy, while sparse placement hardly restricts movement.

Just about any item can be declared a blocking item. Buildings, trees, and rivers all qualify. It is always easiest if a blocking item blocks an entire tile, so making the tiles just the right size is a crucial point. Some buildings will be passable so that it becomes easy for a creature to walk through the town square or the market place.

Forests should be kept dense because pathing into them or trying to go through chews up tons of CPU time and rarely results in a nice path. Simplicity is the key here. A forest, by this definition, could be any collection of similar objects that have the potential to easily trap most pathfinding algorithms. If you must have forests that are not densely packed, make sure that there is always a path through them.

Should elevation affect pathing decisions? This is a tough one. In the Landscape Elevation section earlier in this chapter, there is a function called GetMapPassability that returns a float value. If a tile has a different height than the location of the creature looking for the path, perhaps this function could return a 0.5, which then could be used in the distance calculation and therefore influence which direction the pathfinding will choose.

Setting destinations should be easy for the player—a right-click away (or perhaps a left-click). We'll get to entities in Chapter 18, but they have two SetDestination functions: one that accepts a pointer to another entity and one that accepts x, y coordinates. This makes setting the destination quite easy.

The bigger the map, the longer it takes for units to find a path across it, even though players generally don't send units all the way across the map. Keep map sizes to less than 200x200; for gameplay reasons, 120x120 is as big as you probably want anyway.

Random vs. Fixed Maps

Random maps can be very cool. John Romero insists that random maps are the single feature about Age of Empires that makes him want to play it over and over. Other people agree that random maps are a great feature, but few would say that it is the best thing about a game. Anyway, random maps are cool for games against other players. However, the process for random map generation can be somewhat difficult. A few Web sites are dedicated to random map generation, but even this is little consolation when you consider the time involved in creating random maps.

First, you need a tile map that is fluid, meaning that all landscape types need to be able to meet with most others with a border tile. The concept of a "supertile" makes doing this sort of thing almost impossible. A *supertile* is a collection of smaller tiles and special associated graphics for this group. Red Alert and Dominion use supertiles, which look better than a bunch of small tiles but are practically impossible to use in creating random maps. If you are planning to use map overlays or supertiles, use a map editor and forget random maps. The map must be composed of nothing but small tiles if this is to work (most of the time) or voxels, which are too slow and beyond the scope of this discussion.

You must have a good map cleanup routine. After all of the tiles are placed, your routine must smooth out the rough edges and place border tiles, rivers, lakes, etc. The generator must then distribute player start locations an equal distance apart (not as easy as it sounds), and put resources around each player's start locations and randomly around the map.

The map editor will need to be built in any case. You will need to build training levels anyway (the beginning levels used in doing the levels behind the storyline). When a person buys your game, it is most likely that he will play the beginning levels that will help him familiarize himself with the game without referring to the manual. The last thing a player wants to do is read a manual, so you'd better plan on building a lot of beginning levels. These are known as startup levels, scenario levels, training levels, or beginning levels. Building these is tricky. Players need to be introduced to the game in the first level, with new units, buildings, terrain, resources, goals, and enemies introduced at each new level. You'll need talented level designers to manage this and, of course, great tools. The map editor is code you will have to write. If you make the level designers design over 40 generic levels that aren't related to the scenario level, there will be enough variety to create continued interest in the game, and random maps may not be necessary.

Let's say that you have a landscape filled with water and you want to fill it in mostly with land. Fractals use a mathematical model for generating shapes. They start with a point and branch out a few directions at a time. The tiles for land are filled in, and the process is repeated a set number of times to a certain predictable depth. This can be used from a series of starting points on the map where each player begins and branches outward, creating a completely random map without a lot of control. See Figure 16.20.

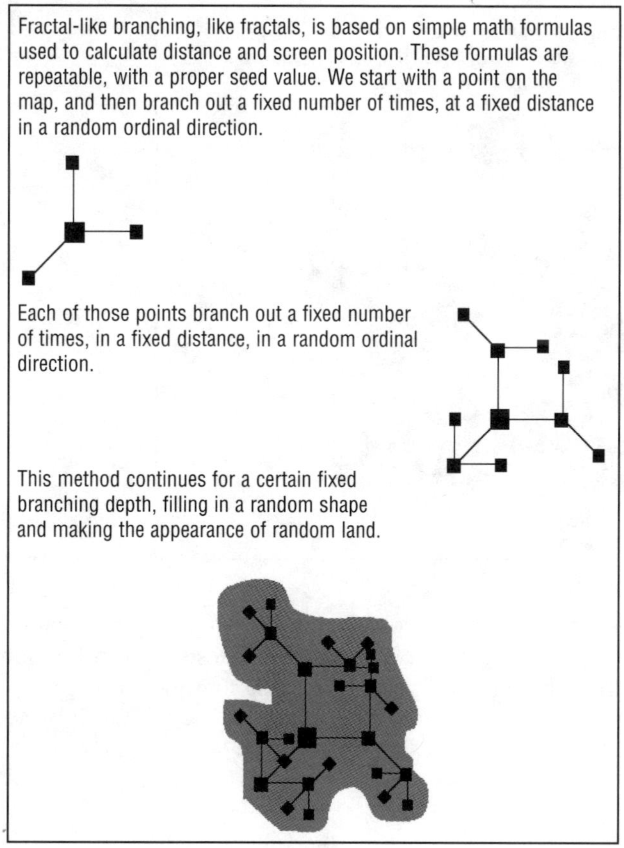

Fractal-like branching, like fractals, is based on simple math formulas used to calculate distance and screen position. These formulas are repeatable, with a proper seed value. We start with a point on the map, and then branch out a fixed number of times, at a fixed distance in a random ordinal direction.

Each of those points branch out a fixed number of times, in a fixed distance, in a random ordinal direction.

This method continues for a certain fixed branching depth, filling in a random shape and making the appearance of random land.

Figure 16.20
Using fractals to create a random map

Bitmap models take a bunch of predefined black and white images and "splat" them down on the world map to create land masses. This works pretty well, but you must have pretty decent bitmaps to begin with. See Figure 16.21.

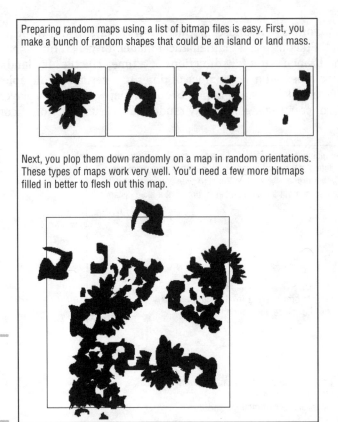

Preparing random maps using a list of bitmap files is easy. First, you make a bunch of random shapes that could be an island or land mass.

Next, you plop them down randomly on a map in random orientations. These types of maps work very well. You'd need a few more bitmaps filled in better to flesh out this map.

Figure 16.21
Creating a random map using random bitmaps

Creating a random map using Blobs is another easy way to create a map. Drawing circles and squares of varying sizes on the map creates very random landscape, but the shapes are a little obvious. Still, this is an easy method for creating random maps. See Figure 16.22.

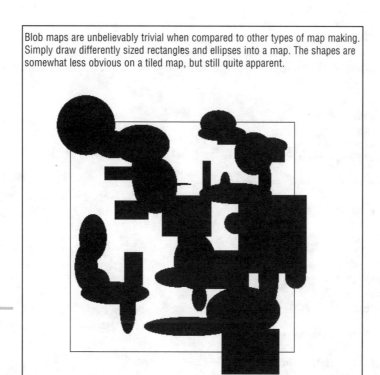

Blob maps are unbelievably trivial when compared to other types of map making. Simply draw differently sized rectangles and ellipses into a map. The shapes are somewhat less obvious on a tiled map, but still quite apparent.

16

Chapter

Figure 16.22
Creating a random map using Blobs

Crystalline growing is another method for creating random maps. Starting with seeds like in the fractal method, you move in a few random directions, checking parameters at each stage. These areas tend to grow outward, always building at the edges of existing land. The map can only grow at those points. This method offers a little more control since you are checking every tile before you place it, but you can check every tile in any of these methods before you place it. Basically, take the basics of Figure 16.20, and grow outward along the edges.

Doing a random map generator is fun. Search for fractals on the Internet, and you will find hundreds of discussions on random maps. They aren't terribly difficult to develop, just time consuming. Don't forget to add random resources, trees, water, mountains, creatures, etc. Expect developing a random map generator to take 8 to 16 weeks.

Random Starting Locations

Making the starting locations fair <u>and</u> random is about the toughest thing you can do, especially considering fairness. You want to push players away from each other as far as possible and still provide adequate land to build on. When creating a random map generator, use the random player start locations as seeds for your map generation, thereby guaranteeing that all players start on roughly equal land.

If you have a map with tile dimensions of 100x100 (for simplicity's sake), calculating random location distances becomes easier to track. For testing completely random locations on the map, here is a demo program that I encourage you to run:

```cpp
// main.cpp

#include <stdlib.h>
#include <string.h>
#include <conio.h>
#include <iostream.h>

//*********************************

struct POINT
{
      int x, y;
};

//*********************************

#define SQR (a) ((a) * (a))

//*********************************

int Width = 100, Height = 100;

//*********************************
int    Dist (POINT* p1, POINT* p2)
{
      int distx = p2->x - p1->x, disty = p2->y - p1->y;
      return SQR (distx) + SQR (disty);
}
//*********************************
void    GenerateListOfRandomLocations (POINT* list, int num)
{
      while (num--)
      {
            list[num].x = rand () %Width;
            list[num].y = rand () %Height;
      }
}
//*********************************
int    VerifyDistances (POINT* list, int num, int MinimumDist)
{
      int i, j;
      for (i=0; i<num-1; i++)
      {
            for (j=i+1; j<num; j++)
            if (Dist (&list[i], &list[j])< MinimumDist)
            return 0;                           // bad
      }
      return 1;
```

```
}
//*********************************
void   main ()

{
       POINT points[10];

       int count, num = 2, dist = 80;
       for (int i=num; i<10; i++)
       {
              cout<<endl<<"----------------------"<<"Num:"<<I;
              cout<<":"<<"----------------------"<<endl;

              for (int d=10; d<100; d++)
              {
                     cout<<"  D:"<<d<<" ";
                     count = 0;
                     for (int j=0; j<1000; j++)
              {
              GenerateListOfRandomLocations (points, i);
                     count += VerifyDistances (points, i, SQR (d));
                     // distance is based on the square
              }
                            cout<<"  C:"<<count<<"\t";
       }
       cout<<endl;
       getch ();
       }

}
//*********************************
```

A list of random locations is generated for *i* number of players. After the random locations are generated, we see if they are at least *j* distance apart. The idea here is that if players are at least such and such distances apart, the game will be fairer. It seems that as you increase the number of players on our 100x100 map, the less distance you can put between them. A very interesting thing happens once you get to five players: You can't put players in the corners and still have a lot of distance between them since you only have four corners. One player will have to be in the middle. Also consider that this test is designed for the entire map. In the real world (real game world, that is), you would never place a player on the edge of the map, so the area of free rein is somewhere inside the 100x100 range, maybe only 80x80 or 90x90.

The distance calculation here is testing for relativity, that is, one distance as compared with another. Since we don't need the actual distance, we can use the approximation, which is simply the square of the distance. This greatly reduces the overhead involved in the calculation and speeds the calculation by a factor of 3 or so.

Pointers to Graphics vs. Indexing

Whether to use pointers or indexing depends on what you are doing. Pointers are 2 bytes larger, but indexes are somewhat harder to work with. An entity with a pointer to a graphic is simpler to manage than an entity with an index number to a graphic that then needs to look that graphic up in a list in order to reference it. Indexing slows things, but it does provide a convenient way of telling which object is which when debugging. The pointer 0x083f543a means nothing to me, but index 1097 means that I need to look at the 1097th item in the list (it is really the 1098th, counting 0).

Accidental deletion of a graphic is avoided by using indices since creation and deletion of a graphic is centralized in a list manager. (See the ALLOCATOR class in Chapter 18.) This is a rare problem, but it is the kind of problem that can haunt a programmer for weeks when the occasional bad pointer creates the intermittent blue screen.

File management becomes a breeze with indexing. When a map is saved, a tile that has an object on it saves a number that it already has. Using pointers forces the tile to get the index from the graphic management class, save that, and then request the pointer from the graphic manager class when the class is reloaded.

You'll have to decide. Indexing is a little cleaner but requires more work at almost every point.

Pointers to Entities

All of the issues applying to graphic pointers also apply to entity pointers. Indexing provides:

➤ Easier memory management
➤ Slightly easier setup, especially when loading a file
➤ Cleaner use that is less likely to cause headaches

Pointers provide:

➤ A slight increase in speed
➤ Easy access to data
➤ Better linked list management

I designed a pointer management class called ALLOCATOR in Chapter 18 that manages a list of pointers and is used to handle ENTITYs mostly. The nice thing about using this paradigm is that crashes can be avoided. Say you have a creature assigned to go across the map and attack a building. In the meantime, that building is destroyed. If you are using a dynamic system, the creature will have an invalid pointer to a building that no longer exists. When the creature tries to reference the building, the bad pointer causes a crash.

Using a static list of pointers to creatures prevents this problem. When a creature or building is destroyed, its ALIVE flag is set to 0 and any other creature assigned to go to that location should see that during its update cycle. The dead creature stores the number of frames since death in the TIME_SINCE_BIRTH flag. The creature still gets updates, but since it is dead, it simply increments the TIME_SINCE_BIRTH flag and returns. The UNIVERSAL_ENTITY_MANAGER class then will know not to use that pointer for a few cycles (it examines the ALIVE flag before it says OK). This allows us to wait 10 frames or so to make sure that everyone else has caught up and figured out what to do about the destination entity's death before using that entity again.

Once a creature detects that its destination no longer exists, it can either stop or grab the location information from the dead creature and go to that location.

The Minimap

Every RTS/RTT game has a minimap. This is the miniature version of the level/map/world that shows you everything except unexplored areas.

If you remember back to the tile definition provided much earlier in this chapter, you'll recall the member variable MiniMapColor. Now you can create the minimap. You can use this variable to generate a pixel-by-pixel coloration that will represent all map tiles and ultimately all creatures that also have the same member variable.

A MINIMAP class should have a list of tile pointers, one for each tile in the world. This is very simple. The MINIMAP pointers are filled in with pointers to actual tiles on the map. Now when the MINIMAP is updated, about three or four times per second, it simply references the tile and requests the color using GetMiniMapColor. If this tile has an object on it, it returns the MiniMapColor of the object on top of it. Then the MINIMAP simply goes and draws a bunch of pixels on the screen. See how easy that was?

Although the program could tell each tile what its color is, the tile can also look at the graphic to which it points and extrapolate a rough color for the entire tile when the graphic is assigned to the tile.

This MiniMapColor variable can be replaced by a GRAPHIC pointer in case you want more info. Or it could be 4 pixels. In any case, think about how you want your minimap to look. Usually a single color is enough, even if the MINIMAP needs to draw four of them in a 2x2 configuration.

The MINIMAP does need to communicate with some global variables, like the screen position relative to the world. The mouse click on the map needs to move the screen around. That is probably the hardest part.

Making the map is like filling in an array. It should only take a millisecond or 2. This is a fast, easy class to develop and should take you less than two hours.... I'll leave it to you.

Map Size Considerations

The biggest consideration about map size is gameplay. A small map makes the game go quickly, with early clashes over resources inevitable. A large map takes a lot longer, while a huge map becomes unplayable; it just takes an army too long to move from one side of the map to the other. Really small maps have the players on top of each other, and these are so bloody in the early game that a player can win by not building peons and simply building warriors with the very few resources he has. That isn't strategy; it also pisses off the other players.

Memory can be a killer on really large maps. Each tile structure can be as large as 40 bytes, maybe bigger. On a 500x500 map, you'll have 250,000 tiles, or 10 MB of RAM for the map. Big maps mean more creatures and landscape features, and on a map that huge you're looking at about 26 MB for a four-player game, just for the world. Add sound, graphics, and the program, not to mention the bloated operating system, and you are well over 100 MB. Ouch. Limit the maps, at the extreme, to 200x200.

On large maps, the minimap gets difficult to use. Moving the mouse pointer a few pixels and clicking jumps to some faraway region on the map and the players end up scrolling the screen using the edges of the screen, which is a pain. The minimap will deliver more desired results on smaller maps.

Fog of War

Fog of war is the greatest invention ever to come to strategy games. I first remember seeing it in Sid Meier's and Bruce Shelly's game Civilization. A big part of the game became the exploration and unveiling the entire map, which was randomly generated every time. Fog of war probably existed before Civilization, but that is the first game I'm aware of that did.

Fog of war is the black cloud that hovers over the map, preventing players from seeing the entire map unless they have units in an area. There are a few varieties of fog of war. Some games feature fog that only exists until a player's unit passes through an area, then that area is revealed for the rest of the game. Some games feature permanent fog of war. Once a unit leaves an area, the black cloud descends once again. Some games have fog of war but allow radar to see units in darkened areas. Some games offer options for play for all of these. Fog of war can be a great balancing agent. It allows mediocre players to hide in a corner and build up their defenses to protect against an aggressive player. But sometimes it's better to play without it, especially for well-matched players or beginners.

Each tile needs a fog flag. You'll notice the Fog flag in TILEFLAGS in the next section. It has 2 bits for different fog. Most games feature fog of war with a haze around the edges. The fog of war is black and anything in it is invisible, but at the edge of sight for a unit usually you'll see a hazy area where you can see the units underneath. However, they are grayed, as is the landscape. The Fog flag allows both dense and hazy fog. You could even come up with a fourth setting, but I'm not sure what it could be.

Tile Grouping

Organization is the key to developing good software. But keeping everything organized can be a pain, and deciding about organizational methods is no trivial task either. Keeping tiles in a tile group is helpful. You will want to put all of the grass tiles in a group. The water tiles will also go nicely into a group that manages all of the standard characteristics for any particular land type. Let's look at a typical grouping. The following contains the code for a tile group. The group characteristics, pointers to graphics, possible border tiles, and so on are included in this class. This class definition is in tile.h and the code is in tile.cpp.

We are already familiar with the TILEFLAGS structure defined earlier in this chapter, but here it is again:

```
//******************************************
struct TILEFLAGS
{
        U32 Passable : 1;           // can it be traversed
        U32 Buildable : 1;          // can it be built upon
        U32 HasHeight : 1;          // can this tile have elevation
        U32 PassableByShip : 1;     // water or any tile that can have a
                                    // watercraft
        U32 DifficultToPass : 1;    // hard to traverse
        U32 CausesDamage : 1;       // normal creatures traversing receive damage
        U32 SpawnsLife : 1;         // new trees and plants
        U32 ProvidesEnergy : 1;     // energy supply
        U32 ProvidesMinerals : 1;   // contains minerals that can be mined
        U32 ProvidesWater : 1;      // contains water
        U32 ProvidesFood : 1;       // can provide food
        U32 ColorCycleStage : 3;    // this allows 8 levels of color cycling
        U32 TriggerPointID : 4;     // allows up to 15 triggers on the map,
                                    // this is an ID number
        U32 TransportPointID : 4;   // allows transport point on map
        U32 Fog : 2;     // various strengths of fog, usually 0, 1, and 2 only
                         // 0 is no fog, 1 is border fog, and 2 is full fog.
        U32 Pad : 32-24;            // remaining bits
};
//******************************************
//******************************************

typedef class TILE_TYPE_DEFINED
{
public:
    enum TILETYPE  {GRASS, DESERT, ROCK, FOREST,
                    WATER, BEACH, LAVA, SAND, SAVANA, SWAMP,
                    MUD, NUMTYPES};

    enum LIFE_SUPPORT {NO_LIFE, ALGAE_LIFE,
                    DESERT_PLANT_LIFE, GRASSLAND_PLANT_LIFE,
                    EVERGREEN_LIFE, DECIDUOUS_LIFE, FRUIT_LIFE,
                    ANIMAL_INSECT_LIFE, ANIMAL_FISH_LIFE,
```

```
                          ANIMAL_REPTILE_LIFE, ANIMAL_MAMMAL_LIFE,
                          ANIMAL_BIRD_LIFE, ANIMAL_DOMESTICATED_LIFE,
                          ANIMAL_HUNTER_MAMMAL_LIFE,
                          ANIMAL_HUNTER_REPTILE_LIFE,
                          ANIMAL_OTHER_LIFE,
                          NUM_LIFE_SUPPORT};

        enum RESOURCES {NO_MINERALS, COPPER, TIN, IRON, SILVER, GOLD,
                          RARE_EARTHS, HERBS, PEAT_MOSS, ADOBE, FLINT,
                          WATER_RES, COAL, COMMON_GEMS, SEMI_PRECIOUS_GEMS,
                          PRECIOUS_GEMS, FERTILE_SOIL, SILICON, PLANT_FOOD,
                          ROOTS};

        enum {MAXTILE = 24};


        //************************

        int  CountValidGraphics ();

protected:
        GRAPHIC**  Graphic;                         // a list of 24 graphics
        int        ThisType, BorderType;            // TILETYPE
        int        Support1, Support2, Support3;    // LIFE_SUPPORT
        int        Res1, Res2, Res3;                // RESOURCES
        U16ptr     ScratchPad;

static S32 Pattern [MAXTILE];                       // for pattern labeling

        //************************


public:
        TILE_TYPE_DEFINED ();
        ~TILE_TYPE_DEFINED ();
        void  Clear ();

            //************************
        bool  SetGraphic (int which, STRINGC *);
        bool  LoadTile (int which, STRINGC *);
        GRAPHIC* GetGraphic (S32ptr pat);           // a list of the surrounding
                                                    // tile types only
        GRAPHIC* GetGraphic (int which);            // {return Graphic;}


            //************************

        void  SetTileType (int Type = GRASS);
        int   GetTileType ();

        void  SetBorderType (int Type = DESERT);
        int   GetBorderType ();
```

```
void  SetLifeSupports (int s1, int s2, int s3);
void  SetResources (int r1, int r2, int r3);
void  GetLifeSupports (int* s1, int* s2, int* s3);
void  GetResources (int* r1, int* r2, int* r3);
      //***********************

STRINGC  GetTILETYPEText (int index);
STRINGC  GetLIFE_SUPPORTText (int index);
STRINGC  GetRESOURCESText (int index);

int  GetTILETYPEIndex (STRINGC& str);
int  GetLIFE_SUPPORTIndex (STRINGC& str);
int  GetRESOURCESIndex (STRINGC& str);

      //***********************

bool Save (FILE_MASTER*);
bool Load (FILE_MASTER*);

bool Save (STRINGC&);                 // pass the filename
bool Load (STRINGC&);

TILEFLAGS Flags;    // flags for easy access, these are important here

}TILE_TYPE_DEFINED, *TILE_TYPE_DEFINEDptr, **TILE_TYPE_DEFINEDlist;

//*********************************************
```

Notice that the tile group TILE_TYPE_DEFINED has its own TILEFLAGS structure. This will allow you to use this as a template for all tiles of this type in the world.

Now everything that defines a particular type of tile is contained in this tile grouping. You'll need to create your own and stylize it to fit your game. This particular one was designed to make tile groups match each other. The code in tile.cpp also helps with this. This class works on a flat world (no tile elevation) and you hand a tile to every instance of TILE_TYPE_DEFINED. Now the tile, with its tile type defined, can search around itself for different types of tiles and match using TILE_TYPE_DEFINED. This system works great, but you are likely to have a different paradigm. I recommend just identifying the class definition and making sure you don't forget anything in your definition.

Some important elements that you'll definitely need are the enums: TILETYPE defines standard landscape types, LIFE_SUPPORT defines the types of life that this landscape can support, and RESOURCES defines the types of resources that this land type can have.

All of these should be maintained in the tile type definitions and generated randomly at run time or during map creation, perhaps allowing for tweaking by level designers.

Tile Size—51x25 vs. 48x24

Deciding on a size for tiles is completely a matter of taste. How do you want your game to look? Assuming diagonal tiles, sizes can be odd or even. The strangest tile size that I've ever heard of is 51x25. There are a few problems with uneven tile sizes, and the math in figuring world position and screen position is a little tougher. We can easily calculate even numbers in our heads, while odd numbers are tougher. Getting alignment in odd sizes takes a little work. In addition, there is a speed issue. Even sizes offer the benefit of being faster in memcpy because of the assembly function rep movsd. This allows you to copy 4 bytes at a time; in 16-bit graphics mode, that is two pixels at a time. A single scan line (memcpy) being faster won't be obvious, but with 80 to 100 tiles on the screen and 20 to 50 scan lines drawn per frame, this can give you another frame or two per second.

The size also can be more even. Most RTS/RTT games use a 2 wide to 1 high ratio in determining tile dimensions. However, Total Annihilation uses square tiles. I'm not sure about the size but I would guess 64x64. Your choices are unlimited, but I suggest picking isometric tiles and keeping the size relatively small to allow you greater flexibility when placing individual tiles. Large tiles are unwieldy; it's difficult to match edges with other tiles, and the sheer size of the memory footprint required to store them limits the number of types of terrain in a level. Small tiles allow a lot of flexibility when matching, and allow four or five types of terrain. Also avoid tiles smaller than 32x16; these become a nightmare for the poor level designers. Even random map generators take a long time when faced with really small tiles. The best tile sizes seem to be 48x24 or 64x32. Anything larger is too big and anything smaller becomes difficult.

World Coordinate System

The world coordinate system can be somewhat tricky. I cannot talk about the world coordinate system without a few diagrams. Here you'll see different organizational methods for arranging the tiles in the world.

Figure 16.23 shows a basic diagram for isometric tiles.

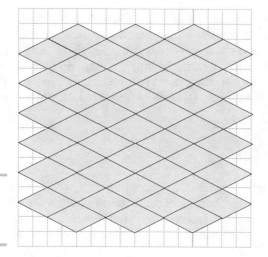

Figure 16.23
Basic diagram for isometric tiles

Imagine, for argument's sake, that all of these isometric tiles are 64x32 pixels. The *x* in the upper left is at 0,0 in world coordinates. The first thing to remember about isometric tiles is their location. Although we see a diamond shape on the screen, the tile actually fits inside of a rectangle. So a tile at 0,0 world coordinates looks as though it doesn't start there at all because it is missing all of its corners.

The topmost and leftmost tile has its start location at 32,0. How do I know? I look at edges: The leftmost point corresponds to the leftmost edge of the tile even though most of the edge is invisible. The left edge is moved over in the world half a tile. Since a tile is 64 pixels wide, its *x* location is 32. Now its topmost corner corresponds to the topmost edge and that is against the top of the map, which is a *y* location of 0.

The rectangle over the top of the map in Figure 16.24 represents how your computer screen might be a window into the world coordinates.

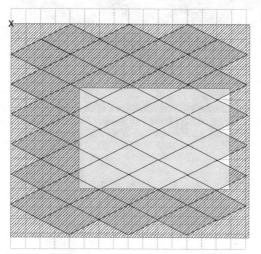

Figure 16.24
Viewing world coordinates on your computer screen

The grayed area is the world that the screen cannot see, while the open area is our view on the world. The screen in this small world has upper coordinates of about 70,85.

Clearly, this is not to scale, but it does provide you with a better idea of how the whole thing takes place. Even if you use a map-based coordinate system, you'll need world coordinates to represent the screen coordinates. Simply offsetting the rectangle represented here gives you a different window into the map. So essentially, you give the screen world coordinates as a starting point for rendering. Then everything within the boundaries of the rectangle coordinates will be rendered during any given game frame.

Map Coordinate Systems

Now, let's look at map coordinate systems. Map coordinate systems are much easier to work with than world coordinates. Pathing becomes somewhat easier, calculating distance is easier, and figuring out where a creature is in the world is easier. When dealing with a rectangular world, doing the math conversion between world coordinates and map coordinates is trivial. It isn't so trivial in isometric. You'll have to decide how your map will be laid out. Once you make that decision, then map coordinates will be a little more meaningful to you.

Figure 16.25 shows the easiest, by far, map coordinate system to work with:

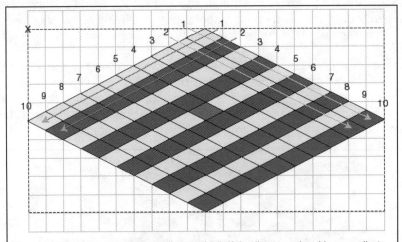

The marked tile in the center has coordinates of 5,5. If the tiles were placed in a coordinate placement system, then this tile would have world coordinates of 288,128. The best way to set this system up is to have a default position for position 1,1 of 288,0. Now, every change in the x direction adds 32 worldx and 16 worldy. This math is fast and trivial. Using this formula, tile 5,5 is found:

```
x = 4; y = 4;     // the real position relative to 1,1, we should
                  // start 0,0 instead these numbers represent offsets.
int newx = 288 + x *32, newy = x * 16;
newx += y * -32, newy += y * 16;
```

Figure 16.25
Map coordinate system using diamond tiles

Tile 1,1 is the topmost while 10,10 is the bottommost. The major disadvantage is the diamond shape of the map. Along the edges of the world, you see a big, black void. It looks a little odd (as in Age of Empires), and you begin to understand why early explorers feared falling off the edge of the world.

Probably a little harder but still pretty easy to work with is the coordinate system illustrated in Figure 16.26:

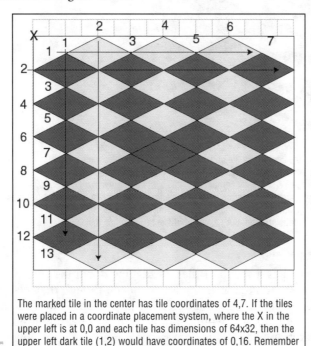

The marked tile in the center has tile coordinates of 4,7. If the tiles were placed in a coordinate placement system, where the X in the upper left is at 0,0 and each tile has dimensions of 64x32, then the upper left dark tile (1,2) would have coordinates of 0,16. Remember that a diamond tile is still within a square space like in the diagram below. The tile at 4,7 is world coordinates 96,96.

Figure 16.26
Map coordinate system using isometric tiles

These isometric tiles are lined up horizontally and vertically the best way you can. Looking at the darker tile at the center, we can see an interesting oddity. When a creature moves horizontally, say to the immediate right of the tile, you need to add 2 to its *x* position. If the creature's map position is 4,4, then moving to the right means its new position will be 6,4. All other directions are normal.

The most difficult of these examples to understand and work with is illustrated in Figure 16.27:

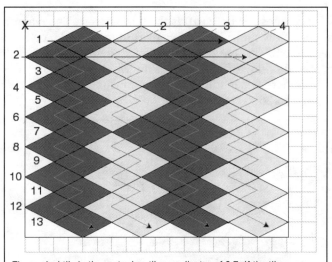

The marked tile in the center has tile coordinates of 2,7. If the tiles were placed in a coordinate placement system, then this would be the same as our previous example. What really complicates this system is movement between tiles. Say a creature is on the marked tile and wants to move straight up. His x position would remain the same, but his y position would be −2. It is a little strange, but I know of at least two games that use this method.

Figure 16.27
Map coordinate system using zigzagging tiles

A column is treated as a group of tiles zigzagging down the screen. All of the dark tiles on the left edge are treated as being aligned even though they clearly are not. This is an interesting setup and poses interesting movement issues. From the colored tile in the center of the map, you would subtract 2 to move straight up. Moving clockwise, the *x* and *y* addition is as follows: upper right, straight right, lower right, down, lower left, straight left, and upper left. Pretty strange, if you ask me. At least two games that I know of use this setup.

Movement in any isometric or rectangular tile system is a bit odd. All tiles are twice as wide as they are high, thus moving in the *x* direction would take twice as long, which doesn't make a whole lot of sense. If you were on a baseball field, and you move from one base to the next, it always takes the same amount of time (traveling at the same speed), no matter what angle above the field someone watches you. Assuming that tiles are supposed to be squares at an angle (even diamond tiles), the time it takes to travel from one tile to the next should always take the same amount of time. You will need to make creatures moving in the world move twice as fast in the *x* direction than in the *y* to fix this inconsistency.

Sidebar: Doppelganger never had a map coordinate system. It relied strictly on world coordinates for every object in the world. An object merely took its own world coordinates, did a little math, and figured out which tile it was on.

Graphic Storage for a Map System

Like the GRAPHIC_MGR in the last chapter, we should store graphics centrally in a large "depository" where we can manage it better. In addition, we'll need to index GRAPHICs and grab pointers to GRAPHICs. The best way to work this system is to have one giant list for all of the map graphics, separate from all of the graphics for animation, creatures, icons, interface elements, etc.

A flat tile world is obviously the easiest graphic system to manage, where you have one tile for each of three or four types of land and overlays for border tiles.

The Map Editor

The map editor is probably the single most important key to finishing your game. As the tool evolves, new ideas are thrust into the design and the game grows in depth; this is better known as feature creep. Spending the extra time to make tools that are intuitive and powerful takes a lot of work but can be rewarding.

Other Considerations

There are many features that can add a lot to your game that you need to be aware of. Among these are seasons, animated landscape, traps and mines, triggers, specialized equipment, kingdom and region boundaries, walls and trenches, and decaying bodies. Each of these is discussed below.

Seasons

Seasons add a lot to a game. It is even better if the snow, rain, fog, hail, etc., has an effect on movement. But nobody will ever tell you that doing seasons is easy.

For example, you'll need a complete new set of tiles with snow on them for winter, as well as new buildings, and possibly creatures and armies with coats on to keep warm. Fog is really tough. This means that every pixel on the screen will need to be color mixed with white at 25 percent or so. You can find assembly code in asm.cpp to do this, but it is slow, particularly if you are reading from video memory. Plus the code does it on a pixel-by-pixel basis. Ouch. You might want to redesign it so that it does the entire screen or at least a huge portion of it in rectangular regions.

You also need falling, drifting snowflakes, and driving rain. What many games do rather than creating snow that falls onto the world is create a foreground. They render the scene and then draw diagonal gray or blue lines over the screen image in a rather cheesy effect.

Most RTS/RTT games do not offer weather effects. Once the standard PC has 600 MHz or better (starting in the fall of '99) and 4x AGP port and 200 MHz bus (spring of '99), there will be enough processing speed to handle all of the extra work that goes into weather. Until then, you'll need to do cheesy effects like those in Seven Kingdoms.

There is an old, very cool game called Power Monger by Bullfrog. It had pretty good weather effects: When it snowed, the armies moved at half speed, and when it rained, they moved at three-quarters speed. The snow or rain fell on the ground, or at least I remember it so.

Animated Landscape

Land that moves—what a cool idea! But the only landscape that would ever move would be water—if you can call it landscape. No other land really moves except in geologic time. In order for moving landscape to work, you'll need supertiles, and lots of them.

Another approach is simply to color cycle.

Trap and Mine Management

"Ouch, oh that hurts"—I have said that more than once while treading across the terrain of Total Annihilation near an opponent's base. I don't use mines much but some players love them. Total Annihilation has done the best job of mine laying in a real-time tactical game. In fact, not many games support mines or traps. This is definitely over the top in terms of the basics in getting a good RTS/RTT game finished. This should be one of the last things you consider putting in.

Although this might seem like a landscape issue, it is more of an entity issue and probably belongs in Chapter 18. Mines should be treated as non-blocking buildings. Once a creature intersects with it, it does damage to all creatures in the area and then kills itself. Quite simple. It does require an animation sequence for an explosion.

Traps are a different story. They can do damage and can capture. Both types require special animation. Say you have a pit trap that a creature must walk on to fall into. A player will path around any pit he sees; in fact, any creature will path around any obstacle, unless it doesn't see the pit as an obstacle. Covering the pit is a good way to make creatures ignore it. When pathing, the tile that holds a trap looks at the ENTITY on it and asks if it is BLOCKING. An unexposed trap says no (returns 0), while a used or exposed trap says yes (returns 3).

Hot Points and Triggers

Most RTS/RTT games have training levels. These are the beginning levels used to teach the players how to play the game. These training levels are most often given victory conditions like kill the enemy, store 1,000 gold, or build four farms. These numbers are easy for you to test on a player-by-player basis.

But now you need to define how a player moves his special cavalry to the base of the mountain to the north. You need to define a region, a hot point, a trigger. You might think that the best way to handle this is to have the tiles hold a trigger flag. Probably not. If a tile holds a trigger flag, and you want multiple triggers, which trigger applies? Can a tile hold multiple triggers?

The best way to handle triggers is to have a trigger manager that periodically checks each player and sees if a victory condition has been met. For ideas on victory conditions, see the scenario editor for Age of Empires and StarCraft.

Triggers can do other things as well. How about a trigger that signals the computer to march an army south when the player sends a creature near the river? There needs to be signaling from the trigger manager to players, but the trigger manager needs to be more robust than just handling a few simple conditions. Set your trigger manager to query the map and the players, maybe resources too. That will give you enough flexibility to handle all situations.

Specialized Equipment

Having specialized equipment—such as flying devices, land devices, water devices, and swamp devices—means you need a specialized type of terrain. Perhaps the most common specialized devices are water items: boats, transports, warships, submarines, submersible tanks, etc. The problem isn't the device, although pathing becomes rather limited, but the landscape. You need a simple way to define which areas are passable to different devices and which aren't. Devices in this context can also mean creatures or objects that can only exist in that medium.

Creating an overlay map can help your game tremendously. An overlay map can be used by pathing and devices in managing passability much easier. We'll discuss pathing in some detail in Chapter 19, but one thing that will help performance in this area is an overlay map. The overlay map is a passability map that exists for each type of limiting terrain. You might want one for all different types of terrain, but a slightly more general one will help your ground troops walk across several types of land terrain including rocky, grass, desert, beach, etc.

Figure 16.28 shows an overlay map with different terrain.

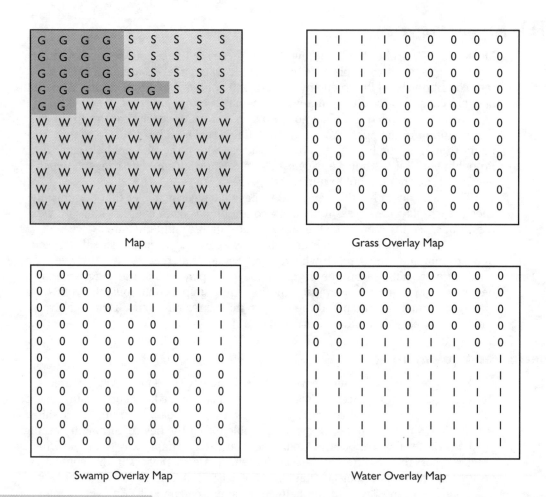

Figure 16.28 *Overlay maps representing grass, swamp, and water*

Say the G's on the map represent grass, W's represent water, and S's represent swamp. An overlay map of the terrain appears as a series of 1's and 0's. This should conserve space and memory by using the TAG_LIST class that we defined in Chapter 13. Whatever the case, this will greatly simplify pathing. You might be able to display some pretty cool stuff for the user as well.

Kingdoms and Region Definitions

A natural extension of overlay maps is defining regions. A great feature of large map games can be kingdom boundaries. This is not nearly as easy to manage as landscape region overlays because kingdom boundaries vary during the course of the game. Since region boundaries are primarily to boost the ego of the players (or crush their egos), you may opt to avoid them.

The problem domain is straightforward: How do you define the region owned by a player? Let me suggest three options: unit occupation, building occupation, and command of predefined regions. Let's start with the basics. All players need their own map overlays. These will be used for display on top of the minimap. We also need a map overlay for all players that will be a conglomeration of the other maps. This should also be available to all players.

Unit occupation is very easy. As a unit moves around the map, it carries a sphere of influence, an aura, that affects its player's map overlay. Basically, as the unit moves around the map, his sphere of influence moves with him. On the overlay map, the player sees a bunch of circles overlapping.

Building occupation is as easy as unit occupation, in fact easier. Updates to the overlay map are limited to when a building is finished or destroyed. This method is somewhat better than unit occupation since it makes a player take the extra effort to build a tower or station far from home in order to build up his region.

The last option is also cool. Say you have a map of 160x160 tiles divided into 16 even regions of 40x40. A player with the most number of units in a region is considered to own the entire region. This should be weighted so that a player can't just send 30 peons to a region and hide them behind a mountain and own the region. A player who moves 20 battle tanks into that region, however, should own the region because these are combat units. The regions could be divided geographically by the level designers. Also, you will need to be able to display the region outlines on the minimap somehow.

Updates should be infrequent, perhaps once every 2 seconds or so, unless units can move fast around the world, which may require more frequent updates. Also, no two players should have map overlay updates during the same frame of the game. This can be somewhat time consuming, and player overlay map updates should be staggered.

Walls and Trenches

Walls and trenches are blockers. They make the terrain beneath them impassable. For game purposes, these should be treated like buildings, which also block terrain. Since pathing should take into account the area around all creatures in the world, these are a simple task. Basically make a building that takes up a full tile width and center it on a tile to make a wall or trench. Lowering terrain for a trench is unreasonably difficult, so just use a graphic overlay.

Walls serve no purpose other than to block movement, so these are easy. If you decide to add the ability for units to mount the walls and fire arrows or whatever, you are looking at a big problem. First of all, walls are no longer just a blocking building. They are only blocking from certain angles; that is, you can climb them from different directions. Secondly, how does the unit get up on the wall, how long does it take to mount the wall, how does the enemy attack units on the wall, how will you represent ladders for enemy units besieging the walls, and which units cannot go on the walls? All of this information needs to be stored somewhere and it begins to make the game much more difficult.

Trenches are somewhat easier. However, they can be filled with spikes, water, or monsters, which can complicate matters. Also, enemies need to get across. How do you do this and maintain fairness in your game? All of these tough questions lead to one startling conclusion: Walls and trenches should act the same as blocking terrain. They should be able to be battered down or destroyed with a few good catapult hits.

Note: After reading this, you may come to the conclusion that all I want to program are easy things. Hardly. What I mean is that it takes much too long to program these things and the reward does not come close to matching the effort. Almost anything is possible in software if you have enough time, and that is the real point.

In futuristic games, walls wouldn't deter many people. The game Dominion allows players to play force field generators around the map, and as long as you provide power to the towers, you have a pretty secure wall. This makes wall building much simpler. Most people would agree that the game is simplistic, but I think it does have a few really good ideas in it. The force fields are easy to program and solve a lot of issues, like who can get up on top or who can walk through. Still, options like one-way force fields that allow units to leave but not enter create a cool dynamic. Also, force fields that allow physical objects like missiles to pass but block all energy weapons makes things interesting. How about force fields that destroy units touching them? Personally, I like force fields that absorb the energy of a weapon and increase their energy reserves.

Decaying Bodies

Decaying bodies require updates. Other things that also require updates are rivers, trees, buildings, and other background items that you don't need to update every frame. If you plan on having a global list of objects do all of the updates, I recommend having several global lists for these lower priority items that you can afford to update every few frames in order to conserve CPU time. You will need to modify the update routines of these low priority items to include a parameter that will tell the ENTITY how many frames have passed since the last update. This will allow a full update for buildings that are constructing units or producing resources.

The Update Cycle

As already mentioned, a game usually processes all info in two passes, although three or four passes are not unheard of. These are normally the draw cycle and the update cycle. Others might include the IO cycle, which handles all mouse and keyboard input, and the network cycle, which handles all new network traffic and checks for sync messages (messages that tell the computer to wait if all games are not on the same frame of animation). But who handles the update cycle?

The map can update items but this tends to take a little longer. The reason is simple: You have to go through each tile. But as you can see here, this is a relatively minor slowdown. You can add a timer and fall out after 8 or 9 milliseconds. To do this you have to start where you left off, so you'll need to store that value. The function timeGetTime takes a little while, so you might want to get the time every 5 to 10 tiles.

Note: Keep in mind that most RTS/RTT games never have more than one creature per three tiles and never more than one item per tile. Anything more, and the map gets too muddled and crowded with garbage. It becomes too difficult to tell what's happening and people won't play your game.

There are a few advantages to doing things on a tile-by-tile basis. First, you can control game speed by update area. Consider dividing your map into 36 rectangular regions that are all the same size and don't overlap in any way. Now your map is in 6x6 regions of tiles, and all regions where the screen isn't looking can be updated periodically. The screen region and all regions near the screen area are updated every frame. All other regions are updated in a round robin fashion, allowing only periodic updates. When a region "gets a turn," it will simulate running all creatures on its map section through 10 or 20 frames. When a creature leaves this region, it gets a frame/stamp for its neighbor region and the creature's sim stops until the new region takes over.

Managing sections of the map this way is tough. When you consider that many regions of the map will have no player creatures, this is perfectly acceptable. You might just want to manage updates on a per player basis. But whatever you decide, one thing is certain: On huge maps on the order of 1,000x1,000 tiles (that's 1,000,000), the update cycle would be about 3 to 4 seconds, depending on what you are doing. Now put that on a network, and oh, my, god—it becomes unmanageable. Update regions, which update buildings, water supplies, and other unimportant things, can be done periodically. Also, for things like that you can fake the update cycle. You can add functions that will fake a building doing four updates at a time to speed up Update calls.

I don't suggest that you make any of your first games on huge maps, but this is one way of managing the enormous time invested in the update cycle:

```
//*********************
int numtiles = NumTiles;
while (numtiles--)
{
        WORLDOBJECTptr p = Tile[numtiles].GetObject ();
        while (p)
        {
              p->Update ();
              p = p->GetNext ();
        }
}
//*********************
```

An alternative is to modify the TILE Update function and manage it internally, which protects the encapsulation better. It's your call.

```
//*********************
int numtiles = NumTiles;
while (numtiles--)
{
        Tile[numtiles].Update ();
}
//*********************
int        TILE :: Update ()
{
        WORLDOBJECTptr p = Object;
        while (p)
        {
             p->Update ();
             p = p->GetNext ();
        }
}
//*********************
```

The global list of objects is another way this can be done. You'll see in Chapter 18 when we begin talking about entities that a global list of all world objects will be maintained. If you are planning on a reasonably sized map (200x200 or smaller), then just run through the list of world objects every frame and call each one's Update function.

Chapter 17

The Interface

The interface is the great communicator—forget Ronald Reagan. The interface is also the means to an end. The end, or goal, is having the player share input with the computer and the computer share information with the player. The interface facilitates the sharing of information. It provides two things to a player: communication with his units and feedback on what he has accomplished. Without a good interface, a game will fail by any measure. Most importantly, a good interface helps and doesn't hinder; it stays out of the way and does its job.

One of the biggest mistakes you can make in developing a game is to think "We'll put in the interface last; it's easy to put in buttons and we'll just use hot keys for now." Your game will fail. After getting the basic engine working, and I mean basic, you should begin getting the interface elements working. There should not be corner cutting when it comes to an interface. Get it working correctly and robustly. The model provided here will help you with much of that but this part is highly individualized, so most of it will be left up to you.

Gameplay is the most important aspect in whether or not a game succeeds, but interface is the second most important. If your interface is kludgy and difficult to work with, even the best game will fail. The interface, and its seamless integration into the game, is part of the gameplay, after all. You need to build it and test it to make sure that the two purposes it serves are fulfilled.

The first purpose is communicating to the computer. How do I get units to move? How do I select a building? Which buttons pop up when I select a unit? Do buttons appear and disappear or do they just stay there and become grayed when I click on a certain unit that has nothing to do with those buttons? Where is a good spot on the screen for my buttons? Should the player be able to move groups of buttons around like in the Windows button bars? How do I connect a group of buttons to a creature so that when I click on it a particular button bar shows? We'll answer many of these but some you'll have to design; that's just part of the job of programming. Maybe your designer will help you.

The next issue is communicating with the player. How do you display which creature is selected? Do you put a selection box around it, or do you show a small icon of the creature off to the side like in Warcraft II? How do you tell the player how much of each resource he has? How do you tell the player how many kills he has, what his score is, how many army units he has, his overall strength, how he compares to his opponents, his current level of technology, and other game stats? What about bubble help, where the text pops up next to a button to give a better explanation of it?

We'll try to cover most of this.

Utility vs. Beauty

Regardless of what some people may think, in terms of interfaces, utility and beauty can coexist, and this is often what makes a game really work. Good games have good interfaces. The more complicated the interface, the less likely a player is to buy the game. And the players do know; all they have to do is look at screen shots on the back of the box. If the interface looks simple and the game seems to have depth, they'll probably want to buy your game.

As mystical as the art of designing an interface is, there are a few simple utility rules. For starters, don't let the interface get in the way of gameplay. Windows and buttons on top of the play field make playing the game a chore. If you must put something on the play field for giving information, limit it to non-selectable text. Icons work, as in the case of Dark Omen where they give battle clues. The designers of that game skillfully placed these icons in a nonobtrusive way. Whatever you do, do not put any clickable or dragable elements in the way of playing the game. A few RTS/RTT games have offered dragable windows in the game window to allow a player to see several areas at once. Unless a player has multiple monitors or some other similar setup, these windows tend to get in the way and become just one more thing to manage.

Don't give the player more information than he needs to manage the game. Don't give him less information than he needs to manage the game. This delicate balance can only be reached through hundreds of hours of gameplay and tweaking.

A player certainly needs:

➤ to see his current inventory of stockpiled resources

➤ a minimap showing the placement of all units in the world

➤ buttons that appear when he clicks on a unit to let him see what the unit can do

➤ a dialog box that he can check for game statistics and some way of seeing his current levels of technology

➤ keyboard means for assigning a unit to a group number and quickly selecting that unit

The buttons should look like buttons. One of the first things you'll need to do is create a basic interface. You'll soon notice that your buttons don't look like buttons, but your graphics will have to reflect the look and feel of buttons. Follow the Windows example on making buttons (Microsoft stole it from Apple, who stole it from Xerox...). The Windows interface is quite slick and you would do well for yourself to copy its design. Just don't copy it exactly or you'll be in trouble.

Make sure that interface elements do not look like game elements. You don't want a button that looks exactly like a unit in the game or players will mistake it during the heat of battle. Buttons should appear similar to each other or be the same with a differently colored backdrop.

Players, and computer users in general, have a peculiar interface preference. A study of computer users has found that users like the left and bottom of the screen for button placement. Microsoft took advantage of this with its placement of the Start menu and the tool bar. Information can be anywhere, preferably on the top or right side of the screen, but the left and bottom should be reserved for buttons or other clickable interface elements.

Make it Easy to Understand and Intuitive

An easy-to-use interface is almost as important as gameplay. When a new player takes your game home for the first time and installs it, he doesn't want to read a manual. Maybe after playing for a few hours he'll want to learn more tricks to have a better game. So plan on giving as much help as is possible to the beginning player. Pop-up text is good, and text on the buttons and windows is helpful. Or you could design a brief tutorial, highlighting buttons, etc.

Having both pictures and words on the buttons is helpful. A number on a button can mean how many items are in the queue of items to build. StarCraft shows little icons in the interface section that are associated with particular buildings. When you click on a building, there is a list of icons showing what will be built next and in what order.

Hide buttons that don't matter. When you click on a creature in the game, hide all buttons that do not pertain to him. You only want to show the player the options he has, not all of the others that he wishes he still had. This is quite helpful.

Avoid putting buttons on the main screen that are one way. Anytime I get into a situation without a Cancel button I get pissed. Many times I just want to click around on the interface to see what buttons do. When they lock me into a situation, I want to rip the designer's throat out.

Just make it simple. A complex game does not require jet engine controls. Stick to mouse-driven controls with hot keys for players who want to speed things up. Some of the best interfaces belong to Command and Conquer, Warcraft, StarCraft, Total Annihilation, and Age of Empires. Pick up a few of these games and you'll see why they are all huge sellers.

Feedback and Tracking Progress

The second most important part of the interface is feedback. The player needs information to help in the split-second decision making that comes with the management of a war machine.

Every unit needs a health meter. When I click on a unit, I want to instantly know its health status. Total Annihilation goes one better—all you have to do is point at the unit with the mouse pointer to see its health on the bottom of the screen. This is done by the mouse pointer having the ability to query the map and find a unit that is on a particular tile for a mouse hit. You could also do this by limiting the mouse hit checks to objects that made it onto the screen (were rendered). However, you cannot do a mouse hit check on every unit on the map 30 times a second. If each player has 200 units and there are four players, that's 800 checks, mostly for nothing since the mouse is rarely over a unit. This can start to slow your game, even on a P500.

Every unit has a set of buttons associated with it. When you click on that unit, most other buttons go away and the buttons associated with the unit appear. This can be accomplished in about a dozen ways. I like the method of creating standard button bars that become visible and force the others to disappear. Each creature type in the game has these button bars associated with it, and most units simply have movement icons. Another method is to give each unit type a list of buttons that are displayed when you click on it and have the interface clear all others before allowing the click.

Resource icons along the top of the screen seem to be the best. They need to be tied to the player so that the interface element can look up the player's stats.

Passing Messages via Windows

Windows has its own message queue that you can use to pass messages to the Message Loop and ultimately to a unit or interface element. The Windows function call PostMessage puts a message in the queue, while SendMessage calls the Message Loop directly and sends it the appropriate data.

If you have a message to pass from a button to a unit, something like REPAIR_BUILDING, this message must have an ID number that you can use to tell it apart from other messages. Standard Windows messages are things like WM_MOUSEMOVE, WM_KEYDOWN, and so on. Any message that you post cannot conflict with these, so Microsoft provides a convenient starting point: WM_USER. When you define your messages, make sure that you start at WM_USER. For example:

```
#define REPAIR_BUILDING    WM_USER +1
#define FIND_FOOD          WM_USER +2
#define FIND_PATH          WM_USER +3
...
```

These messages still need to be handled by the Message Loop, but this is a convenient mechanism for doing things like selecting a creature, giving a command, etc. Even scrolling around the map can be handled by the INTERFACE_MGR by posting SCROLL messages.

Getting messages to the interfaces is another story, and that happens because the INTERFACE_MGR should be a global class that a lot of different sections of the code can access. The Message Loop can directly call the INTERFACE_MGR for things like mouse clicks and keyboard hits.

Here we see the INTERFACE_MGR class:

```
//*******************************************
//*******************************************

class  INTERFACE_MGR : public ALLOCATOR <INTERFACE>
{
```

```
      enum {MAXWINDOWS = 20};
      INTERFACE* MainWindows[MAXWINDOWS];      // main dialog boxes that can be
                                               // turned on and off and respond to
                                               // commands, buttons on
                                               // these windows, do not count
      int      Selected;                       // which MainWindow is selected
      int      StartX, StartY;                 // the starting selected location
      int      EndX, EndY;                     // the ending selected location

      QUEUE<STORED_MESSAGE>* Messages;

      //*************

public:
      INTERFACE_MGR () : ALLOCATOR <INTERFACE> (100)
      {
           for (int i=0; i<MAXWINDOWS; i++)
           {
                MainWindows [i] = NULL;
           }
           Messages = new QUEUE <STORED_MESSAGE> (16);
           Selected = 0;
      }
      ~INTERFACE_MGR ()
      {
           for (int i=0; i<MAXWINDOWS; i++)
           {
                delete MainWindows[i];
           }
           delete Messages;
      }

      // just send the windows message through
      // and we'll handle it here. This puts a message in the queue
      // which we need to clear out using Update.
      // this only holds a maximum of 16 messages, so periodic updates
      // are possible like 1 in 3 frames or so.
      int  Message (int WindowsMSG, long WParam, long LParam);
      int  Update ();                          // post, use, and clear messages
      void Draw (SCREEN_STRUCT* screen);
      void ClearAllMessages () {Messages->Clear ();}
      //*************

      void SetInterfaceWindowOn (int which);          // change the currently
                                                      // displayed window to
                                                      // this window item
      void SetInterfaceWindowOn (INTERFACE* inter);

      void AddInterfaceToList (INTERFACE* inter);     // receives an interface
                                                      // description
      int  SetAsMainWindow (INTERFACE* inter);        // returns ID INTERFACE*
           Create ();      // create generic INTERFACE item and return a
```

```
                                              // pointer to it for initialization
      int   GetID (INTERFACE*);

      //************

      bool Load (FILE_MASTER* file);  // loads and saves all of the
                                      // interface elements in list
      bool Save (FILE_MASTER* file);
      bool Load (STRINGC& str);
      bool Save (STRINGC& str);

      //************
};
//******************************************
//******************************************
```

This class has all of the basic characteristics of the ALLOCATOR class (which you'll find in Chapter 18; see memmgr.h on the CD) and quite a bit more. This INTERFACE_MGR is hardly complete. It contains most of what you'll need but a lot of things like communicating with creatures, scrolling, etc., are just not handled.

It is designed to hold a few messages before you give it time to process those messages. This will allow you to control the amount of time that the processing takes. Normally this time will be nominal, but in some rare cases it could be significant. After storing its messages for a frame, call Update and it will take care of the rest, including clearing the queue.

The code for all of this is below. You'll find it interesting. The first function dissects the incoming Windows message and sends it on to the various interface elements. The only tricky thing to figure out here is the Windows function GetAsyncKeyState, which grabs the current state of the key that you specify.

The rest of this code is mostly self-explanatory.

```
//******************************************
//******************************************
int    INTERFACE_MGR :: Message (int WindowsMSG, long WParam, long LParam)
{
      STORED_MESSAGE msg (WindowsMSG, WParam, LParam);
      int SaveMessageFlag = 0;
      // for the mouse
      if (WindowsMSG == WM_LBUTTONDOWN || WindowsMSG == WM_RBUTTONDOWN ||
          WindowsMSG == WM_MBUTTONDOWN || WindowsMSG == WM_LBUTTONUP ||
          WindowsMSG == WM_RBUTTONUP || WindowsMSG == WM_MBUTTONUP)
      {
          int xPos = LOWORD (LParam), yPos = HIWORD (LParam);
          int shiftstate = WParam & MK_SHIFT, ctrlstate = WParam & MK_CONTROL;
          SaveMessageFlag = 1;
          msg.Message = 0x80000000 | ((xPos|0x7fff)<<16) | (yPos|0xffff);
          msg.WParam = (shiftstate) | (ctrlstate<<1);

          if (WindowsMSG == WM_LBUTTONDOWN)    msg.LParam = INTERFACE::
                          BUTTON_LEFT + (INTERFACE::CLICKDOWN<<2);
          if (WindowsMSG == WM_LBUTTONUP) msg.LParam = INTERFACE::
```

```
                                    BUTTON_LEFT + (INTERFACE::CLICKUP<<2);
              if (WindowsMSG == WM_RBUTTONDOWN)    msg.LParam = INTERFACE::
                                    BUTTON_RIGHT + (INTERFACE::CLICKDOWN<<2);
              if (WindowsMSG == WM_RBUTTONUP) msg.LParam = INTERFACE::
                                    BUTTON_RIGHT + (INTERFACE::CLICKUP<<2);
              if (WindowsMSG == WM_MBUTTONDOWN)    msg.LParam = INTERFACE::
                                    BUTTON_CENTER + (INTERFACE::CLICKDOWN<<2);
              if (WindowsMSG == WM_MBUTTONUP) msg.LParam = INTERFACE::
                                    BUTTON_CENTER + (INTERFACE::CLICKUP<<2);
       }

       // for click and drag only, moving windows around perhaps

       if (WindowsMSG == WM_MOUSEMOVE)
       {
              int lstate = WParam & MK_LBUTTON, rstate = WParam & MK_RBUTTON;
              if (!(lstate | rstate)) goto END;
              int xPos = LOWORD (LParam), yPos = HIWORD (LParam);
              int shiftstate = WParam & MK_SHIFT, ctrlstate = WParam & MK_CONTROL;
              SaveMessageFlag = 1;
              msg.Message = 0x80000000 | ((xPos|0x7fff)<<16) | (yPos|0xffff);
              msg.WParam = (shiftstate) | (ctrlstate<<1);
              msg.LParam = (INTERFACE::CLICKDOWN<<2);
              if (lstate) msg.LParam += INTERFACE::BUTTON_LEFT;
              if (rstate) msg.LParam += INTERFACE::BUTTON_RIGHT;

              msg.LParam |= 0x4;          // (data1 & 4) dragging
       }

       // for the keyboard

       if (WindowsMSG == WM_KEYDOWN)
       {
              int key = LParam;
              int  lshift = GetAsyncKeyState (VK_LSHIFT), rshift =
                             GetAsyncKeyState (VK_RSHIFT);
              int  lctrl = GetAsyncKeyState (VK_LCONTROL), rctrl =
                             GetAsyncKeyState (VK_RCONTROL);
              msg.Message = key, msg.WParam = lshift|rshift, msg.LParam =
                             lctrl|rctrl;
              SaveMessageFlag = 1;
       }

       // all other messages are ignored

END:
       if (SaveMessageFlag) Messages->Push (&msg);
       int x = Messages->Count ();
       return x;
}

//***************
```

17

Chapter

```
int     INTERFACE_MGR :: Update ()        // post, use, and clear messages
{
        // there will almost always be no messages but once every 200 frames,
        // or so, we will use this code.
        STORED_MESSAGE* msg;
        int ret = 0;
        while ((msg = Messages->Pop ()) != NULL)
        {
                ret = 1;
                Items[Selected]->Message (msg->Message, msg->WParam, msg->LParam);
        }
        return ret; // this is whether or not a message was sent down the line
}

//***************

void    INTERFACE_MGR :: Draw (DRAWING_MANAGER* DDraw)
{
        for (int i=0; i<MAXWINDOWS; i++)
        {
                Items[i]->Draw (DDraw);
        }
        if (SelectionBoxFlag)
        {
                //DDraw->SetColor16 (0, 255, 0);                    // green
                //DDraw->FrameRect (StartX, StartY, EndX, EndY);
        }
}


//***************

void    INTERFACE_MGR :: SetInterfaceWindowOn (int which)
        // change the currently displayed window to this window item
{
        if (which<0 || which>=NumberAllocated) return;
        Selected = which;
}

//***************

int     INTERFACE_MGR :: SetAsMainWindow (INTERFACE* inter)  // returns ID
{
        AddInterfaceToList (inter);
        for (int i=0; i<MAXWINDOWS; i++)
        {
                if (MainWindows[i] == NULL)
                {
                        MainWindows[i] = inter;
                        return i;
                }
        }
        return -1;
}
```

```
        //***************


void    INTERFACE_MGR :: SetInterfaceWindowOn (INTERFACE* inter)
{
        int which = GetID (inter);
        if (which<0) return;
        Selected = which;
}


        //***************

void    INTERFACE_MGR :: AddInterfaceToList (INTERFACE* inter)
        // receives an interface description
{
        for (int i=0; i<NumberAllocated; i++)
        {
            if (inter == Items[i]) return;        // already added
        }
        int which = Tag->FindOpenTag ();
        if (which >= 0 && which<NumberAllocated)
        {
            Tag->Set (which);
            if (Items[which] != NULL) delete Items[which];
                Items[which] = inter;
            NumberAllocated++;
            return;
        }
        if (NumberAllocated >= MaxItems)
        {
            ReallocateList ();
        }
        else
        {
            if (Items[NumberAllocated]) return;  // abnormal and strange
        }
        Tag->Set (NumberAllocated);
        if (Items[NumberAllocated] != NULL) delete Items[NumberAllocated];
            Items[NumberAllocated++] = inter;
        return;
}


        //***************


INTERFACE*
            INTERFACE_MGR :: Create ()      // create generic INTERFACE item and
                                            // return a pointer to it
                                            // for initialization
{
        return GetNewItem ();
}
```

17

Chapter

```
           //**************
int            INTERFACE_MGR :: GetID (INTERFACE* inter)
{
           return ALLOCATOR <INTERFACE> :: GetID (inter);
}


           //**************
           //**************

bool   INTERFACE_MGR :: Load (FILE_MASTER* file)
           // loads and saves all of the interface elements in list
{
           if (file->Status () != FILE_MASTER :: NONE) return false;
           int count = 0;
           if (file->Read (&count, sizeof (INTERFACE*))) {return false; }

           int which = Tag->FindOpenTag ();
           while (which != -1 && count--)
           {
               INTERFACE* i = GetItem (which);
               i->Load (file);
               Tag->Set (which);

               which = Tag->FindOpenTag ();
           }
           return true;
}


           //**************

bool   INTERFACE_MGR :: Save (FILE_MASTER* file)
{
           if (file->Status () != FILE_MASTER :: NONE) return false;

           int count = Tag->CountSet ();

           if (file->Write (&count, sizeof (INTERFACE*))) {return false; }

           int which = FindFirst ();
           while (which != -1)
           {
               Items[which]->Save (file);

               which = FindNext ();
           }
           return true;
}


           //**************

bool   INTERFACE_MGR :: Load (STRINGC& str)
{
```

```
            FILE_MASTER               file (str, FILE_MASTER :: READ);
            if (file.Status () != FILE_MASTER :: NONE) return false;

            int count = Tag->CountSet ();

            if (file.Read (&count, sizeof (INTERFACE*))) {return false; }

            int which = Tag->FindOpenTag ();
            while (which != -1)
            {
                  INTERFACE* i = GetItem (which);
                  i->Load (&file);
                  Tag->Set (which);

                  which = Tag->FindOpenTag ();
            }
            return true;
      }

      //***************
      // we assume that the interface items are sequential and that items
      // have not been deleted and added
      bool   INTERFACE_MGR :: Save (STRINGC& str)
      {
            FILE_MASTER               file (str, FILE_MASTER :: WRITE);
            if (file.Status () != FILE_MASTER::NONE) return false;

            int count = Tag->CountSet ();

            if (file.Write (&count, sizeof (INTERFACE*))) {return false; }

            int which = FindFirst ();
            while (which != -1)
            {
                  Items[which]->Save (&file);

                  which = FindNext ();
            }
            return true;
      }


//*****************************************
//*****************************************
```

Selections

When the interface manager receives a click on the map, it stores that location in
StartX, StartY. As you drag around, the drag box will follow you by storing your current mouse location using the Windows message WM_MOUSEMOVE. When you let go
of the mouse, each creature in the selected range will need to be informed that it is
selected. We'll talk about that in Chapter 18, but the concept is easy enough. Anyway,

the click and drag for selecting is very simple: When a user clicks the mouse, and it's not on a button but in the screen somewhere, you store a point as both StartX, StartY and EndX, EndY. As you move the mouse, EndX, EndY will change while the start position stays the same.

The Windows message passed to your application is WM_LBUTTONDOWN for placing the initial point. The code for decipherment of the Windows parameters is in INTERFACE_MGR :: Message. A flag is then set, letting the interface manager know that you are clicking and dragging. This sets up a rectangle for the drawing of the selection box during the drawing cycle.

The next message is WM_MOUSEMOVE, which allows you to update the position of EndX and EndY. Depending on the game, you might want to show creatures selected as you drag the mouse over them. It could be useful.

The last Windows message to handle is WM_LBUTTONUP. At this stage, you would dispatch a selection function call to all items in the map giving the coordinates of the selection box. Each item will tell you if it is in the selection area. Then you can choose to select it or not, based on its type or which player owns it. You don't want to allow players to select hundreds of trees or rocks on the ground (presumably).

Scrolling

When the mouse goes to the edge of the screen, the map should scroll by. All real-time strategy games support this. The interface manager should have knowledge of the global ScreenX and ScreenY locations and do the updates to these variables through some access routine that keeps these values within acceptable ranges.

Moving to the edge is not enough. A player moving his mouse very near the edge should have the screen scroll slowly, perhaps 4 or 5 pixels per frame. This number is rather arbitrary, and you can pick your own value better. This action should begin within 10 pixels or so; 6 or 7 is probably better. Once the mouse is on the edge of the screen, scrolling can begin in earnest. Perhaps half a tile per frame should scroll. Most RTS games have two or three speeds for scrolling, depending on the location of the mouse. You should do the same. The alternative, a single speed for scrolling, is inadequate and jumpy.

Cursors

There are two kinds of cursors: mouse cursors and text cursors. They are not related in any way but in name, but since they are both simple, I'll talk about them here.

Windows does a nice job with the flashing text cursor. The interface manager routes messages to whichever item is selected. The interface element should be able to handle text as it comes in. Much of that code is written in the INTERFACE class, but you'll have to update it for your game including things like backspace and the "home" key. If you want it to flash, add a FlashState variable and a timer. Once the time passes 5, reset it to 0 and change the FlashState; this draws a line or rectangle after the last text character. The timer should be based on the number of frames that have passed, and since you're testing for 5, make it a bit field with 3 bits (0-7) and the FlashState a bit field of 1. Four bits will accomplish your goal.

The mouse cursor is drawn in the DIR_DRAW_MANAGER class in screen.h. Use the function call during the interface drawing, which should be drawn after the landscape. Use the last known mouse position stored in EndX, EndY. Could that be any easier? I think not. The function call is DrawMousePointer.

> **Note:** The draw order is typically, from bottom to top, landscape, units, interface, interface elements (score, text, etc.), and lastly the mouse cursor.

Windows and Buttons

The interface elements rarely appear on the screen by themselves. They are usually on some sort of backdrop or dialog box.

> **Note:** Who came up with the name "dialog box"? It has nothing to do with a dialog and has very little to do with a box. How about "interrupt window" or "input window"? I like those names.

These buttons belong to the window, and in Windows terminology, they are the children. See Figure 17.1.

The INTERFACE class has the ability to have children, and you will see the Child variable, which is a pointer to another interface element. This element should be part of a group with circular linked pointers to other elements that the button has in common. This allows the button to give control to another button in the linked list when the player hits the Tab key or Shift key to go to prev.

This, of course, assumes that you want to be able to allow players to just hit Enter as the equivalent of clicking on the selected button. No game, other than Age of Empires, has offered this feature. Even in Age of Empires, this functionality was limited to dialog boxes where you could hit Tab or arrow keys to move between dialog box items. It is nice on occasion to simply hit Enter 40 times rather than clicking on the mouse button 40 times.

There is ownership here. A window controls the buttons to which it points by making them appear and disappear when the player clicks something else. These windows are controlled by the interface manager by declaring them MainWindows, and these pointers can readily be accessed. Also, having a data-driven model for moving between interface elements could be helpful. You might consider developing one. All interfaces are still part of the array declared as the interface manager initializes, so make sure you have fewer than 20 windows. The number of total window elements doesn't matter, since the allocator class reallocates on the fly. The default is 100 items, as you can see in the constructor, but feel free to make as many as you like. You can always have more than 20 windows if you need them.

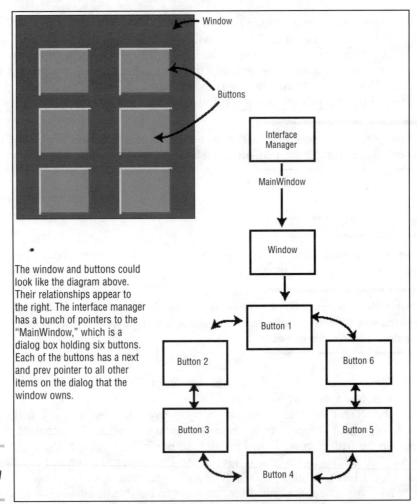

The window and buttons could look like the diagram above. Their relationships appear to the right. The interface manager has a bunch of pointers to the "MainWindow," which is a dialog box holding six buttons. Each of the buttons has a next and prev pointer to all other items on the dialog that the window owns.

Figure 17.1
Parent and child windows

You'll also need duplicate buttons, as the tractor will need the same goto button that the soldier has.

I have included a linked list class. A linked list can be very helpful. But do you really need them? Some would say no and that they are dangerous, especially when you are constantly allocating and deallocating memory. There is some truth to this. Managing memory and making sure that memory is free is a slow and painful process. You never know if a pointer is valid unless it is set to 0x00, and that can be a problem. Still, a linked list has its places.

An alternative to the link is an ID number. A link, rather than having a pointer to next, has an ID number that can be accessed to get the item in question. It is somewhat slower but prevents some of the possible mangling in untested (or under-tested) linked list code.

Anyway, the code for a doubly linked list is here. Here is an example of how you might add items to the list:

```
//*********************************************
CIRCULAR_LINK_OBJ obj[10], *ptr = NULL;


for (int i=0; i<10; i++)
{
        ptr = obj[i].AddLink (ptr);
}
//*********************************************
```

Or you can do it the other way:

```
//*********************************************
CIRCULAR_LINK_OBJ obj[10], *ptr = NULL;

for (int i=0; i<10; i++)
{
        ptr = ptr->AddLink (&obj[i]);
}
//*********************************************
```

The list starts empty and the variable ptr slowly fills up with pointers. As you can see, it's pretty flexible. If you want to remove the fourth item in the list, you can do either of the following:

```
ptr = obj[4].RemoveSelf (ptr);
ptr = ptr->RemoveLink (&obj[4]);
```

This works amazingly well. The ptr = reassigns the pointer when necessary, making your job, and my job, easier. Don't worry about the front of the list or any of that garbage; it cleans up after itself. Use the code in the prescribed methods and it works very well. The buttons that are peers need this list to allow the user to hit Tab and advance to the next button. Depending on what you decide in your interface design, tabbing can allow a selection cursor to move between the buttons.

The code is in link_obj.h. You'll find other link objects in there including a circular linked list and a simple linked list.

```
//*********************************************
//*********************************************

class CIRCULAR_LINK_OBJ
{
protected:
        CIRCULAR_LINK_OBJ* next;

        char        DeleteFlag;

        CIRCULAR_LINK_OBJ*
              FindLinkPointingTo (CIRCULAR_LINK_OBJ* obj)
        {
```

```
                    if (next == NULL) return NULL;
                    CIRCULAR_LINK_OBJ* n = next, *p = this;
                    while (n!=obj)
                    {
                         n = n->next;
                         p = p->next;
                         if (p == this) return NULL;
                    }
                    return p;
               }

          int FindInList (CIRCULAR_LINK_OBJ* list)
          {
                    if (list == NULL) return 0;
                    CIRCULAR_LINK_OBJ* n = list->next, *p = list;
                    while (n!=this)
                    {
                         n = n->next;
                         p = p->next;
                         if (p == list) return 0;         // not here
                    }
                    return 1;
          }

     public:

          //*********************

          CIRCULAR_LINK_OBJ () {Clear (); next = NULL;}
          ~CIRCULAR_LINK_OBJ ()
          {
                    if (DeleteFlag)
                    {
                    //    delete next;
                    }
          }

          virtual void    Clear () {DeleteFlag = 0;}

          //*********************

          void SetDelete (int onoff = 1) {DeleteFlag = onoff;}
          int  GetDelete () {return DeleteFlag;}

          CIRCULAR_LINK_OBJ* GetNext () {return next;}

          //*********************

          CIRCULAR_LINK_OBJ* AddLink (CIRCULAR_LINK_OBJ*1)
          // always adds onto the end
          {
```

```
        if (l == NULL) return this;

        if (next == NULL)                        // all must be NULL
        {
            if (l->next == NULL)
            {
                next = l, l->next = this;  // point back
                return this;
            }
            CIRCULAR_LINK_OBJ *p = l->FindLinkPointingTo (l);
            next = l, p->next = this;        // point back
            return this;
        }
        else                                     // insert before next
        {
            l->next = next;
            next = l;                            // now insert existing pointers
        }
        return l;
}

//********************

CIRCULAR_LINK_OBJ* RemoveSelf (CIRCULAR_LINK_OBJ*l)
// removes self (this) from list
{
        if (l == NULL) return NULL;
        if (l->next == NULL) return NULL;
        int x = FindInList (l);
        if (x == 0) return l;

        if (l == this)                           // this is the top of the list
        {
            if (next == NULL) return NULL;
            CIRCULAR_LINK_OBJ *p = l->FindLinkPointingTo (this);
            if (!p) return NULL;
            p->next = next;
            next = NULL;
            return p;
        }

        CIRCULAR_LINK_OBJ *p = l->FindLinkPointingTo (this);
        if (p == NULL) return l;

        p->next = next; // this has been removed from the list
        next = NULL;
        return l;
}

//********************

CIRCULAR_LINK_OBJ* RemoveLink (CIRCULAR_LINK_OBJ*l)
```

```
                    // removes the LINK_OBJ pointed to
                    // we return a pointer in case the removed item is the
                    // head of the list
        {
            if (l == NULL || l->next == NULL) return NULL; // not in this list
            if (next == NULL) return l;

            int x = FindInList (l);                 // are we in the list
            if (x == 0) return l;

            if (l == this)                          // remove self
            {
                return RemoveSelf (l);
            }

            // we reassign the pointers
            CIRCULAR_LINK_OBJ* p = FindLinkPointingTo (l);
            if (p == NULL) return this;

            p->next = l->next;                      // we are now out of the list
            next = NULL;
            return this;
        }
        //*********************
};


//*******************************************
//*******************************************
```

Here is the INTERFACE class. It is not complete but close to it. You'll find links to other members in the parent class DBL_LINK_OBJ, but you don't need to worry about the functionality because all of the linkages are handled by the parent. The code for drawing, as you'll see in the .cpp file, needs to be done. This is not complete because this section of code should be completed by you, the software designer. I suggest using the following code:

```
void    INTERFACE : Draw (DIR_DRAW_MANAGER* DirDraw)
{
    if (Graphic)
    {
        Graphic->SetScreenPosition (scx, scy);
        Graphic->Draw (DirDraw ->GetScreen ());
    }
    else
    {
        // draw the box that is the button or window
        if (Selected) DirDraw->SetColor16 (ColorSelected);
        else DirDraw->SetColor16 (Color);
        DirDraw->FillRect (&Rect);

        // draw upper left lines which should be lighter in most cases
        // except when selected
        if (Selected) DirDraw->SetColor16 (ColorShadow);
```

```
                else DirDraw->SetColor16 (ColorLight);
                DirDraw->Line (Rect.left, Rect.top, Rect.left, Rect.bottom); // left
                DirDraw->Line (Rect.left, Rect.top, Rect.right, Rect.top);    // top

                // now the bottom right
                if (Selected) DirDraw->SetColor16 (ColorLight);
                else DirDraw->SetColor16 (ColorShadow);
                DirDraw->Line (Rect.right, Rect.top, Rect.right, Rect.bottom);
                // right
                DirDraw->Line (Rect.left, Rect.bottom, Rect.right, Rect.bottom);
                // bottom
        }
}
```

You might want to have several lines to do the fancy outline. Also, be careful about the colors because the frame may overshadow the button too much. Here is the class:

```
struct RECTANGLE;
class DIR_DRAW_MANAGER;
class FILE_MASTER;
//********************************************
//********************************************

// Interface elements can take 2 different forms.
// A parent-child situation where all children receive
// messages from and are controlled by the parent.
// The second is a peer-to-peer relationship where
// the messages are passed from the parent to the list
// where the single child communicates with his peers
// telling the parent about who is in charge of the
// peer group.

class INTERFACE : public DBL_LINK_OBJ, public SCREENOBJECT
{
public:

        enum TEXT_POS {PLEFT=1, PCENTER=2, PRIGHT=4, PTOP=8, PBOTTOM=16};
        enum TYPE {WINDOW_BOX, EDIT_BOX, BUTTON_BOX, RADIO_BOX, SLIDER_BOX};
        enum MBUTTON {BUTTON_LEFT, BUTTON_RIGHT, BUTTON_CENTER};
        enum BUTTON_STATE {CLICKUP, CLICKDOWN};

protected:

        TYPE       Type;
        int        ID;                               // for loading and saving
        GRAPHIC*   Graphic;                          // writes over "Color"
        STRINGC*   Text;
        RECTANGLE  Rect;
        U16        Color, ColorSelected,
                   ColorLight, ColorShadow;          // for shading

        U32        Selected:1;                       // mouse push
```

```
        U32        Selectable:1;              // a few items can never be selected
        U32        RedrawFlag:1;              // the interface elements do not need
                                              // to be drawn every frame
        U32        Visible:1;                 // stops draw dead in its tracks
        U32        DeleteChildFlag:1;         // do we delete the children
        U32        LeftClickMessage:13;       // when clicked, what value do we
        U32        RightClickMessage:14;      // send to the system; this is like
                                       // an ID message that the message handler
                                       // can forward to the player or creature.
                                       // range 0-8192, make sure to add WM_USER
                                       // when messages post

        INTERFACE* Parent, *Child;
        bool       Read (FILE_MASTER&);
        bool       Write (FILE_MASTER&);
public:

        INTERFACE ();
        ~INTERFACE ();
        void       Clear ();
        void       Create (TYPE t,
                   RECTANGLE* dimensions,     // see struct.h for RECTANGLE
                   STRINGC& text,
                   U16 color = 16912,         // medium gray
                   INTERFACE* parent = NULL);

        // inherited
        // LINK_OBJ* AddLink (LINK_OBJ*e)
        // LINK_OBJ* RemoveSelf (LINK_OBJ*e)
        // LINK_OBJ* RemoveLink (LINK_OBJ*e)

            //**************            // access routines

        void       SetGraphic (GRAPHIC* g) {Graphic = g;}
        GRAPHIC*GetGraphic () {return Graphic;}
        void       SetText (STRINGC& s) ;
        STRINGC*GetText () {return Text;}
        void       SetPosition (RECTANGLE* r);
        RECTANGLE*
            GetPosition () {return &Rect;}
            //********
        void       SetAllColors (U16);
        void       SetColor (U16 c) {Color = c;}
        U16        GetColor () {return Color;}
        void       SetColorSelected (U16 c) {ColorSelected = c;}
        U16        GetColorSelected (U16 c) {return ColorSelected;}
        void       SetColorLight (U16 c) {ColorLight = c;}
        U16        GetColorLight (U16 c) {return ColorLight;}
        void       SetColorShadow (U16 c) {ColorShadow = c;}
        U16        GetColorShadow (U16 c) {return ColorShadow;}


        //********
```

```
    void        SetLeftClickMessage (int m) {LeftClickMessage = m;}
    int         GetLeftClickMessage () {return LeftClickMessage;}
    void        SetRightClickMessage (int m) {RightClickMessage = m;}
    int         GetRightClickMessage () {return RightClickMessage;}

        //********
    void        SetRedraw () {RedrawFlag = true;}
    int         GetRedraw () {return RedrawFlag;}
    void        SetSelectable () {Selectable = true;}
    int         GetSelectable () {return Selectable;}
    void        SetID (int id) {ID = id;}
    int         GetID () {return ID;}

        //**************
    bool        Load (FILE_MASTER*);
    bool        Save (FILE_MASTER*);
    bool        Load (STRINGC&);
    bool        Save (STRINGC&);
    void        Disconnect ();              // change all pointers into ID
                                            // numbers from the interface manager
    void        Connect ();         // change all ID numbers into pointers.
    void        DisconnectCircular ();   // disconnects all children
    void        ConnectCircular ();      // reconnects all children

public:                                     // parental control

    void        Move (int offx, int offy); // moves all associates as well.
    void        Hide () {Visible = 0;}
    void        Show () {Visible = 1;}
    void        Message (int type, int data1, int data2) ;
                        // respond to input
                        // keys are: type is the key 0-255
                        // data1-with shift key
                        // data2-with ctrl key
                        // if type high bit is set (0x80000000)
                        // mouse click
                        // messages only happen on left click up
                        // x = (type&0x7fff0000)>>16;
                        // y = (type&0xffff);
                        // (data1 & 1) is shift key held
                        // (data1 & 2) is ctrl key held
                        // (data2 & 3) is type MBUTTON
                        // (data2 & 4) BUTTON_STATE
                        // (data1 & 4) dragging
    void        Draw (DRAWING_MANAGER* DirDraw);     // depending on type

// useful only for generic buttons
    void        AddChild (TYPE t, RECTANGLE* dimensions,
// see struct.h for RECTANGLE
                STRINGC& text,
                U16 color =  16912);        // medium gray
    void        AddChild (INTERFACE* child);
```

```
        void       SetGraphicsForGroup (GRAPHIC**, int num);

public:                                              // peer control

        void       Deselect () {Selected = 0;}
        int        TestSelect (int x, int y);        // mouse position
        void       Select () {if (Selectable) {Selected = 1; RedrawFlag =
                        true;}}
        int        IsSelected () {return Selected;}
        void       DeselectCircular ();
        int        SelectCircular (int x, int y);  // mouse position

};
//*****************************************
//*****************************************

//*****************************************
//*****************************************

INTERFACE :: INTERFACE () : DBL_LINK_OBJ ()
{
        Clear ();
}


        //**************

INTERFACE :: ~INTERFACE ()
{
        if (DeleteFlag)
        {
            DBL_LINK_OBJ *item = next,* item2;
            while (item != this)                     // full circle delete
            {
                if (item == NULL) break;             // strange error.
                item2 = item->GetNext ();
                delete item;
                item = item2;
            }
        }
        if (DeleteChildFlag)
        {
            INTERFACE *item = Child,* item2 = NULL;
            while (Child != item2)
            {
                if (item == NULL) break;
                item2 = reinterpret_cast <INTERFACE*> (item->GetNext ());
                delete item;
                item = item2;
            }
        }
}
```

```
        //***************

void    INTERFACE :: Clear ()
{
        Graphic = NULL;
        Text = NULL;
        Color = 16912, ColorSelected = 16912,      // 16R, 16G, 16B in 5x5x5
        ColorLight = 21140,                          // 20R, 20G, 20B in 5x5x5
        ColorShadow =  12684;                        // 12R, 12G, 12B in 5x5x5

        Selected = false;
        RedrawFlag = true;
        Selectable = true;
        Visible = true;
        DeleteChildFlag = false;
        LeftClickMessage = 0;                        // when clicked, what value do
                                                     // we send to the system
        RightClickMessage = 0;

        Parent = NULL;
        Child = NULL;
        next = NULL;
        prev = NULL;
        Type = WINDOW_BOX;
}


        //***************

void    INTERFACE :: Create (TYPE t, RECTANGLE* dimensions, STRINGC& text,
                        U16 color, INTERFACE* parent)
{
        Type = t;
        Text = new STRINGC;
        *Text = text;
        Rect = *dimensions;
        Parent = parent;
        if (Parent)
        {
            RECTANGLE* r = Parent->GetPosition ();
            Rect.left += r->left, Rect.top += r->top,
            Rect.right += r->left, Rect.bottom += r->top;
        }
        Color = color, ColorSelected = color;
        RGBVal c1, c2;
        c1.From15Bit(color); c1 += 4;                // increase 4 light levels (if
                                                     // possible)
        c2.From15Bit(color); c2 -= 4;                // decrease 4 light levels

        ColorLight = c1.Convert15 (),
        ColorShadow =  c2.Convert15 ();
}
```

17

Chapter

```
//**************
//**************

void   INTERFACE :: SetAllColors (U16 color)
{
       Color = color, ColorSelected = color;
       RGBVal c1, c2;
       c1.From15Bit (color); c1 += 4;       // increase 4 light levels (if
                                            // possible)
       c2.From15Bit (color); c2 -= 4;       // decrease 4 light levels

       ColorLight = c1.Convert15 (),
       ColorShadow =  c2.Convert15 ();
       RedrawFlag = true;
}


//**************
//**************

void   INTERFACE :: SetText (STRINGC& s)
{
       if (!Text) Text = new STRINGC;
       *Text = s;
       RedrawFlag = true;
}


//**************

void   INTERFACE :: SetPosition (RECTANGLE* r)
{
       Rect = *r;
       RedrawFlag = true;
}


//**************
//**************

void   INTERFACE :: Move (int offx, int offy)
       // moves all associates as well.
{
       INTERFACE *item,* item2;
       item = reinterpret_cast <INTERFACE*> (next);

       while (item != this)             // full circle
       {
           if (item == NULL) break;  // strange error.
           item2 = reinterpret_cast <INTERFACE*> (item->GetNext ());
           item->Move (offx, offy);
           item = item2;
       }
       RedrawFlag = true;
```

```
        Rect.left += offx, Rect.right += offx, Rect.top += offy, Rect.bottom += offy;
}


//***************


void    INTERFACE :: Message (int type, int data1, int data2)
                    // respond to input
                    // keys are: type is the key 0-255
                    // data1-with shift key
                    // data2-with ctrl key
                    // if type high bit is set (0x80000000) mouse click
                    // messages only happen on left click up
                    // x = (type&0x7fff0000)>>16;
                    // y = (type&0xffff);
                    // (data1 & 1) is shift key held
                    // (data1 & 2) is ctrl key held
                    // (data2 & 3) is type MBUTTON
                    // (data2 & 4) BUTTON_STATE
{
    // MBUTTON {BUTTON_LEFT, BUTTON_RIGHT, BUTTON_CENTER};
    // CLICKUP, CLICKDOWN
    if (type & 0x80000000)          // handle mouse
    {
        if (data1 & 4) return;      // no click and drag.
        if ((data2 & 4) == CLICKDOWN) return; // respond only to mouse up
        int x = (type&0x7fff0000)>>16;
        int y = (type&0xffff);
        if (TestSelect (x, y))      // is this point inside
        {
            if (next && SelectCircular (x, y)) return;
            if (Child && Child->SelectCircular (x, y)) return;
            Select ();
        }
        return;
    }
    if (!Selected) return;                  // no message processing if not selected
    switch (type)                           // these are all Windows messages. I
                                            // copied the messages and you can find
                                            // them in "messages.h"
    {
        case VK_BACK:
            break;
        case VK_DELETE:
            break;
        case VK_RETURN:
            break;
        case VK_ESCAPE:
            break;
        case VK_END:
            break;
        case VK_HOME:
```

```
                        break;
              case VK_SPACE:
                        break;
              case VK_PRIOR:
                        break;
              case VK_NEXT:
                        break;
          }
      }


      //***************

int   INTERFACE :: TestSelect (int x, int y)     // mouse position
{
      if (x>=Rect.left && x<=Rect.right &&
          y>=Rect.top && y<=Rect.bottom)
      {
          return 1;
      }
      return 0;
}


      //***************

void  INTERFACE :: DeselectCircular ()
{
      Selected = 0;
      INTERFACE *item,* item2;
      item = reinterpret_cast <INTERFACE*> (next);

      while (item != this)                      // full circle
      {
          if (item == NULL) break;              // strange error.
          item2 = reinterpret_cast <INTERFACE*> (item->GetNext ());
          item->Deselect ();
          item->SetRedraw ();
          item = item2;
      }
}


      //***************

int       INTERFACE :: SelectCircular (int x, int y)      // mouse position
{
      int found = 0;
      INTERFACE *item,* item2;
      item = reinterpret_cast <INTERFACE*> (next);

      while (item != this)                              // full circle
      {
          if (item == NULL) break;                      // strange error.
          item2 = reinterpret_cast <INTERFACE*> (item->GetNext ());
```

```
                if (item->TestSelect (x, y)) {found = 1; break;}
                item->SetRedraw ();          // the mouse must be close, redraw anyway
                item = item2;
        }
        if (found)
        {
                DeselectCircular ();
                item->Select ();
                return 1;
        }
        return 0;
}


        //***************
        //***************
        //***************
void    INTERFACE :: Draw (DRAWING_MANAGER* DirDraw)              // depending on type
{
        if (RedrawFlag == true)
        {

                if (Graphic)
                {
                        Graphic->SetScreenPosition (scx, scy);
#ifndef TEMP_MIK
                        Graphic->Draw (DirDraw ->GetScreen ());
#endif
                }
                else
                {
                        // draw the box that is the button or window
                        if (Selected) DirDraw->SetColor (ColorSelected);
                        else DirDraw->SetColor (Color);
#ifndef TEMP_MIK
                        DirDraw->FillRect (Rect);
#endif
                        // draw upper left lines which should be lighter in most cases
                        // except when selected

                        if (Selected) DirDraw->SetColor (ColorShadow);
                        else DirDraw->SetColor (ColorLight);
#ifndef TEMP_MIK
                        DirDraw->Line (Rect.left, Rect.top, Rect.left, Rect.bottom);
                        // left
                        DirDraw->Line (Rect.left, Rect.top, Rect.right, Rect.top);
                        // top
#endif

                        // now the bottom right
                        if (Selected) DirDraw->SetColor (ColorLight);
                        else DirDraw->SetColor (ColorShadow);
#ifndef TEMP_MIK
```

17

Chapter

```
                        DirDraw->Line (Rect.right, Rect.top, Rect.right,
                                       Rect.bottom);           // right
                        DirDraw->Line (Rect.left, Rect.bottom, Rect.right,
                                       Rect.bottom);           // bottom
#endif
                }
        }
        INTERFACE *item,* item2;
        item = reinterpret_cast <INTERFACE*> (next);

        while (item != this)                               // full circle
        {
            if (item == NULL) break;                       // strange error.
            item2 = reinterpret_cast <INTERFACE*> (item->GetNext ());
            item->Draw (DirDraw);
            item = item2;
        }
        RedrawFlag = false;
}


        //**************
        //**************

void    INTERFACE :: AddChild (TYPE t, RECTANGLE* dimensions, STRINGC& text, U16
color)
{
        INTERFACE* child = new INTERFACE;
        child->Create (t, dimensions, text, color, this);
        DeleteChildFlag = true;

        Child = reinterpret_cast <INTERFACE*> (child->AddLink (Child));
}


        //**************

void    INTERFACE :: AddChild (INTERFACE* child)
{
        Child = reinterpret_cast <INTERFACE*> (child->AddLink (Child));
}


        //**************
        //**************

void    INTERFACE :: SetGraphicsForGroup (GRAPHIC**graphic, int num)
{
        int Count = 0;
        num--; // to start
        if (num<0) return;

        INTERFACE*item = Child,* item2;

        do
```

```
            {
                if (item == NULL) break;                  // strange error.
                item2 = reinterpret_cast <INTERFACE*> (item->GetNext ());
                item->SetGraphic (graphic[Count++]);
                item = item2;
            }
        while (num-- && item != Child);                   // full circle
    }


    //***************
    //***************

bool    INTERFACE :: Load (FILE_MASTER* file)
    {
        return Read (*file);
    }


    //***************

bool    INTERFACE :: Save (FILE_MASTER* file)
    {
        return Write (*file);;
    }


    //***************
    //***************

bool    INTERFACE :: Load (STRINGC& str)
    {
        FILE_MASTER             file (str, FILE_MASTER :: READ);
        if (file.Status () != FILE_MASTER :: NONE) return false;

        return Read (file);
    }


    //***************

bool    INTERFACE :: Save (STRINGC& str)
    {
        FILE_MASTER             file (str, FILE_MASTER :: WRITE);
        if (file.Status () != FILE_MASTER::NONE) return false;

        return Write (file);
    }


    //***************

bool    INTERFACE :: Read (FILE_MASTER& file)
    {
        int which;
        int len;
        U8    s1, s2, r, v, d;
```

```
        U16   l, rc;
        if (Text == NULL) Text = new STRINGC;

        if (file.Read (&next,   sizeof (INTERFACE*))) {return false;}
        if (file.Read (&prev,   sizeof (INTERFACE*))) {return false;}
        if (file.Read (&Child,  sizeof (INTERFACE*))) {return false;}
        if (file.Read (&Parent, sizeof (INTERFACE*))) {return false;}

        if (file.Read (&Type,  sizeof (TYPE))) {return false;}
        if (file.Read (&ID,    sizeof (int))) {return false;}
        if (file.Read (&which  sizeof (int))) {return false;}
        Graphic = GraphicManager.GetGraphic (which);
        if (file.Read (&len,   sizeof (int))) {return false;}
        if (file.Read (Text->GetString (), sizeof (len))) {return false;}

        if (file.Read (&Rect,          sizeof (RECTANGLE))) {return false;}
        if (file.Read (&Color,         sizeof (U16))) {return false;}
        if (file.Read (&ColorSelected, sizeof (U16))) {return false;}
        if (file.Read (&ColorLight,    sizeof (U16))) {return false;}
        if (file.Read (&ColorShadow,   sizeof (U16))) {return false;}

        if (file.Read (&s1, sizeof (U8))) {return false;}
        if (file.Read (&s2, sizeof (U8))) {return false;}
        if (file.Read (&r,  sizeof (U8))) {return false;}
        if (file.Read (&v,  sizeof (U8))) {return false;}
        if (file.Read (&d,  sizeof (U8))) {return false;}
        if (file.Read (&l,  sizeof (U16))) {return false;}
        if (file.Read (&rc, sizeof (U16))) {return false;}

        U8    Selected = s1, Selectable = s2, RedrawFlag = r, Visible = v,
              DeleteChildFlag = d;
        U16   LeftClickMessage = l, RightClickMessage = rc;
        return true;
    }


        //***************

bool    INTERFACE :: Write (FILE_MASTER& file)
    {
        if (file.Write (&next,   sizeof (INTERFACE*))) {return false;}
        if (file.Write (&prev,   sizeof (INTERFACE*))) {return false;}
        if (file.Write (&Child,  sizeof (INTERFACE*))) {return false;}
        if (file.Write (&Parent, sizeof (INTERFACE*))) {return false;}

        int len = (Text) ? Text->GetStringLength (): 0;
        int which = GraphicManager.GetID (Graphic);
        char* s = NULL; if (Text) s = Text->GetString ();

        if (file.Write (&Type,   sizeof (TYPE))) {return false;}
        if (file.Write (&ID,     sizeof (int))) {return false;}
        if (file.Write (&which,  sizeof (int))) {return false;}
        if (file.Write (&len,    sizeof (int))) {return false;}
```

```
              if (file.Write (s,              len)) {return false;}
              if (file.Write (&Rect,          sizeof (RECTANGLE))) {return false;}
              if (file.Write (&Color,         sizeof (U16))) {return false;}
              if (file.Write (&ColorSelected, sizeof (U16))) {return false;}
              if (file.Write (&ColorLight,    sizeof (U16))) {return false;}
              if (file.Write (&ColorShadow,   sizeof (U16))) {return false;}

              U8 s1 = Selected, s2 = Selectable, r =RedrawFlag, v = Visible, d =
                      DeleteChildFlag;
              U16  l = LeftClickMessage, rc = RightClickMessage;
              if (file.Write (&s1, sizeof (U8))) {return false;}
              if (file.Write (&s2, sizeof (U8))) {return false;}
              if (file.Write (&r,  sizeof (U8))) {return false;}
              if (file.Write (&v,  sizeof (U8))) {return false;}
              if (file.Write (&d,  sizeof (U8))) {return false;}
              if (file.Write (&l,  sizeof (U16))) {return false;}
              if (file.Write (&rc, sizeof (U16))) {return false;}
              return true;
        }


        //***************

void   INTERFACE :: Disconnect ()         // change all pointers into ID numbers
                                          // from the interface manager
        {
              if (next) next = reinterpret_cast <DBL_LINK_OBJ*>
                  (InterfaceManager.GetID (reinterpret_cast <INTERFACE*> (next)));
              if (prev) next = reinterpret_cast <DBL_LINK_OBJ*>
                  (InterfaceManager.GetID (reinterpret_cast <INTERFACE*> (prev)));
              if (Child) Child = reinterpret_cast <INTERFACE*> (InterfaceManager.GetID
                                                       (Child));
              if (Parent) Parent = reinterpret_cast <INTERFACE*> (InterfaceManager.GetID
                                                        (Parent));

              ID = InterfaceManager.GetID (this);
        }


        //***************

void   INTERFACE :: Connect ()            // change all ID numbers into pointers.
        {
              if ((int) next != -1) next = InterfaceManager.GetItem ((int) next);
              if ((int) prev != -1) prev = InterfaceManager.GetItem ((int) prev);
              if ((int) Child != -1) Child = InterfaceManager.GetItem ((int) Child);
              if ((int) Parent != -1) Parent = InterfaceManager.GetItem ((int) Parent);
              ID = InterfaceManager.GetID (this);
        }
//*******************************************
//*******************************************
```

The Mouse

You don't have to deal with the mouse too much; the operating system does a lot of the work for you. All of the mouse movement and button clicks are captured and sent to your program in the form of messages. Mouse position is readily available from parameters passed to the MessageLoop, so all of this is trivial. The hard part is the redraw.

Assuming that you use your own mouse pointer—a series of pixels turned on in the shape of a mouse pointer—then you need to worry about overdraw and redraw. This is never a problem if you redraw the entire screen every frame. Not a bad idea and with computers as fast as they are these days, you can probably get away with it. Still, why strain your CPU when those clock cycles can go into a better gaming experience?

Since the map will probably be redrawn every frame, you don't need to worry about it. But you do need to worry about the interface elements. This is relatively simple and you can handle it by redrawing only the interface elements over which the mouse rests. The interface function TestSelect will test a mouse point and return TRUE if the x,y coordinates are on the button. You can modify it for a region or simply test the four corners of the region surrounding the mouse. If so, tag it for redraw; otherwise move on. All interface elements can be tested this way with very little time overhead.

If you plan to do incremental updates of the screen, then you'll need small update regions and since you'll most likely be using span lists (discussed in Chapter 13) to manage this, just set multiple spans for redraw. Or you can simply update the screen with an update region surrounding the mouse. All of this usually takes a few hours of programming at the most.

Buttons

A button is a button, right? Not! There are tabs like on a tab sheet that could be considered buttons. Scroll bars are just a set of buttons. What about radio buttons? After all, the name implies buttons. You'll need to code for all of these, right? Not really, since they all have the same basic characteristics. They need mouse control and they need to know when they are selected, that is, when you click on them a message goes to the system for something in the game to change. The tab buttons only tell the interface manager to change to another interface and hide the displayed one. All of this falls under the button paradigm.

Drawing a button or window is generally trivial. It involves filling a rectangle or drawing an assigned graphic, drawing lines to make it look raised or lowered, and putting text on top of it when needed. The existing code in the draw function will manage the first two, but you'll have to decide how to handle the text portion (this was covered back in Chapter 12). Simply control the location of the text by dividing the number of characters in the text by the normal width of a single character. In my case, I made them all 8 pixels wide, but your alphabet may vary considerably. You'll have to code this yourself.

You can also have a sound associated with a button so that the player gets an audible acknowledgement from any button he clicks. The best way to handle this is to have a sound manager with a huge list of hundreds of sounds and an ID list. Then the INTERFACE can have a "short" ID number for the sound to play. When you click on the button, the button posts a Windows message, which makes its way back to the INTERFACE_MGR.

Note: Technically, this is not a Windows message. Windows messages are messages that Windows passes around. We will be passing our own kind of messages through the Windows messaging system.

The INTERFACE_MGR will need to be aware of the sound manager; when it receives the message from the INTERFACE to play a sound, the INTERFACE_MGR will pass it along to the sound manager, which will then add it to its play list.

Circular messages are how the buttons are designed. A simple call to INTERFACE :: SelectCircular will allow you to figure out which button is selectable from the current mouse position. A button that receives a tab message (the Tab key) should deselect itself, select next, and then tell the parent to select the next as its child. This makes the parent pass the messages to it quicker.

A button may have numbers associated with it. This comes under display properties and you should derive from the INTERFACE class. This allows you to account for all of the needed varieties of interface elements for displaying score, resources, health, etc., in the game. Counters are common for telling the player how many units a building plans on making. These mean a button or interface element needs additional variables for storing these values. The player, when his variables change for health or any vital statistic, can post a message that the proper interface element will eventually receive, provided you set all of the #defines for those messages in messages.h. You'll find it on the CD; all of the standard input messages from the keyboard are there as well.

You might set up interface elements to poll for values as well. This requires that you make them aware of the functions to call for getting the score and so on. I don't like this model because it makes the buttons too powerful and too difficult to set up in the setup phase when you start a game, but it's your decision.

A Selected Creature

The button you click will post a message to the INTERFACE_MGR that needs to be aware of the UNIVERSAL_ENTITY_MGR. Any messages that affect selected creatures will be passed on to the UNIVERSAL_ENTITY_MGR, which you'll find in Chapter 18.

The player should only be able to select his own units and possibly neutral units. This means making sure, when a player clicks on the map, that you grab the PlayerID values of all of the creatures before you select them. The UNIVERSAL_ ENTITY_MGR will test a certain area for the click when you tell it to, and return a pointer to the items that the player selected. You simply need to go through that list and select the proper items. The function GetPlayerID will be useful. Each player, at the start of the game, should have a unique ID number that a host computer can select. Objects in the world should have a PlayerID of 0 unless they belong to or are built by the player. Each computer on a networked game will know the number or PlayerID of the player on its end, and therefore this testing becomes trivial.

Getting messages to a selected creature can be somewhat tricky, but when a player clicks on the map for the creature to move, the INTERFACE_MGR simply passes that message down the line. Buttons that are clicked affect all creatures selected, which the UNIVERSAL_ENTITY_MGR manages. You'll see a lot more about this in the next chapter.

Networking and Making Sure All Players Get the Same Data

Passing around frame info is about all of the network traffic that you'll need. In a client-server situation, all I/O messages go to the server, which then distributes that message to all clients. That keeps the I/O in sync and keeps the game flowing. Just make sure that everything in the game is predictable and no creature information will need to be passed. Random numbers are always produced the same way; just make sure that a seed is passed to all the clients before the game starts. That way, all random numbers generated can happen on all sides without having to constantly pass data. Just imagine if you had to update the position information of every creature in the world once every frame. Even with a good Internet connection, the best you can expect is about 5 K per second. That's kilobytes, not megabytes. Some people have T1 connections, which can handle several hundred kilobytes per second, but very few people have those. The best that you can count on, until everyone gets cable modems, is about 5 K a second. Divide that by 30 frames per second and that is about 170 bytes per frame of traffic on a really stable connection. Not very likely, but possible.

Under TCP/IP, every packet of information passed carries a 24-byte overhead. The best paradigm seems to be a five-frame sync message. The host/server passes messages every five frames to tell everyone which frame the game is supposed to be on. Those who are behind will skip drawing until they catch up, processing only pending I/O messages and the Updates. If a computer stays out of sync more than three times in a row, he is dropped from the game—either his connection is bad or his computer is too slow. This five-frame wait can produce noticeable pauses and disrupt good gameplay, so dropping really slow players can be helpful.

In addition to the five-frame sync message, I/O messages are updated every frame. They go to the server, which relays them back to all machines. No machine ever acts until the server says so and if it drops messages, so be it. No one person's game will act without a signal from the server. This helps if a computer in the network misses a message. The server can send it again until everyone gets it, and then the server says go. By having the five-frame sync message and then only I/O, the network traffic can be kept to about 2 K per second, leaving a little room for other things. You might even send sync messages every three frames to improve game performance, since five frames ahead may be too much latency. If you feel real confident, you might even reduce it to two frames. Don't forget the occasional text messages players pass to each other.

Interface Color Choices

The look of your interface elements sets tone. I have designed INTERFACE to simply fill rectangles with color when being drawn, but actually every button or interface element should be a graphic prepared by the artists. You'll notice the load and save portions of the INTERFACE class. This will make it easy to pop these little devils into an interface editor, which you should build. That way, artists can pop graphics onto individual graphics elements, play with the interface as it will appear in the game, and then save it to a file which the game can load in. You can then set up a script-based language to tell you which files to load and where to place the individual elements on the screen, or you can simply make that part of the editor if you make it robust enough.

Have the artists prepare designs and mockups of the interface well before you write any code, however. You'll need to know how much more code to write before you begin working on the interface, and they may ask for some animated buttons, moving buttons, repeated buttons, or more. Make sure you take into account as much as possible before you begin writing code. This is a good rule of thumb anyway.

The mockups of the interface should carry a tone or feel to them. This is for the designer or producer to approve, but don't be afraid to speak up if it looks awful. This is very common, as designers look at so much art that they can become complacent after a time. Make sure that you wake them up now and again.

Too many colors become difficult to see. Artists seem to like bright colors. Actually dull—for interface and landscape—is better. The creatures in the world should be somewhat bright, but even they need to be subdued. Too bright hurts your eyes and playing for hours on end will be a strain. Tell your artists and designers to make it look natural and you'll be happy.

Bright colors should be reserved for a few items such as highlights, player colors for each unit, lights on buildings, explosions, and lasers. Remember that the explosions in your game will look very bright if the game is normally relatively dark and then you display a white circle. That circle, in contrast to the dark background, looks as bright as the sun. Take a look at the explosions in Total Annihilation and you can see that the designers knew a lot about contrast. The explosions aren't all that bright, but they appear so because of the contrast.

Different Player Colors

Each creature belonging to a player needs an identifying color. This allows the player to quickly identify which units are his and which belong to other players. This interface element is critical to good, fast-paced gameplay. These special colors need shading, so most RTS games offer three shades of the same color so that lighted, normal, and shadowed versions of the color look more natural. A creature in the world with a big black blob on his head looks awfully strange. But with two grays and a black for shading, he'll look good.

17

Chapter

Even with just eight players, you might run out of colors. The problem is creating colors for each player that are visually unique. Orange often is too close to red or yellow to be distinguished from them. The generally accepted colors that most games use for identification are red, green, yellow, blue, purple, and brown. Then games offer colors such as gray, black, orange, white, fuchsia, and baby blue. That's 12—and that's about it. Other subtleties include light green, light purple, pink, mauve, dark blue, brick, light orange, etc. However, these colors easily can be confused with other colors, making the game difficult. This is a design issue that should take some effort on your part, especially if your game is supposed to support 32 players.

Sidebar: A designer at Ion Storm had a novel idea. Make the player one color, say blue. Make all of his allies another color, say green. Then make all of his opponents yet another color, say red. This dramatically reduces the total number of colors required. Then to check whose unit you are attacking, put your mouse cursor over it, and the text of the player's name appears.

Chapter 18

Objects and Creatures in the World

Your game means very little without a solid definition of the "things" that you can put in it. We discussed this subject briefly in Chapter 16, but we'll continue that discussion here. We have already established what a "creature" is, but that description may not be enough. Most games define an object of any type in the world as an entity. Entities have certain characteristics, such as a position in the world, dimensions, graphics or animation, health status, and hit points/breaking points. In addition, they usually have armor, resource value, behaviors, and associations—groups to which they belong, including the player to which they belong.

These characteristics are what this chapter is about. We will talk about the world coordinate system a little and the entity description in detail. We'll talk about some of the possibilities of what you might do to add to these and a lot of considerations relating to how this ties into your game. Lastly, we'll discuss how this all relates to AI and behavior, and hopefully we'll redefine the term AI for you in new ways.

Defining an Entity

An *entity* is anything in the world that has characteristics and possibly a personality. Entities must be able to have an update cycle that allows them to communicate with the user or other entities. An entity may be able to move around in the world and search for things. It can attack and fire weapons. It can be a weapon. Basically, an entity is a thing in your game. It isn't a tile (normally) and it isn't an interface element. You might call an entity a world object.

What Does an Entity Do?

If you can do it, so can an entity. Since entities are essentially world objects, they can do almost anything. It is for you to decide on the scope of an entity's actions. For most RTS/RTT games, you should limit the actions to something like the following list. You'll find the complete code in the ai_skills.h file on the companion CD. The SK_ prefix is just a notation letting me know that this is defined as a skill. You can do whatever you want with it.

```
//*********************************************
typedef class SKILLS
{
```

```
public:
enum  SKILL_TYPE {
                // depending on intelligence, these skills may be used to build
                // one's home or save money. these skills scale based on
                // intelligence and creatures use these skills in problem
                // solving. in order to solve their motivational problems,
                // creatures resort to skills to solve these. When a creature
                // has solved all of his needs, he will resort to "frivolous"
                // or rarely used skills in order to pass the time. humans may
                // choose a profession that reflects one of their skills.

        SK_STORAGE,       // a chipmunk stores food for winter, lions do not
        SK_HUNTING,       // a tiger can hunt, a pigeon cannot
        SK_RESEARCH,      // a wizard can research a new spell, a snail cannot
                          // (this is learning and the desire to learn)
        SK_BUILDING,      // a bird builds a nest, a cat does not
        SK_TRACKING,      // a wolf can track prey by scent, buzzards cannot
        SK_WOODCUTTING,   // a beaver cuts down trees for a home, bears do not
        SK_CLIMBING,      // a leopard climbs trees, a badger does not
        SK_TOOLUSE,       // a chimpanzee uses a branch in an anthill to get
                          // ants for food, a duck does not
        SK_HIDING,        // a raccoon hides when threatened,
                          // a rhinoceros does not
        SK_JUMPING,       // a horse can jump a crevice or wall, a goose cannot
        SK_FISHING,       // bears can fish, dogs cannot
        SK_MINING,        // birds dig for worms, elephants do not
        SK_SWIMMING,      // dogs can swim, lemmings cannot
        SK_WEATHERSENSE,  // most animals know when it will rain,
                          // insects do not
        SK_SPELLCASTING,  // a wizard can cast a spell, a fly cannot
        SK_FARMING,       // a human puts seeds in the ground for food,
                          // dragons don't
        SK_STONECUTTING,  // masonry and marble cutting
        SK_GEMCUTTING,    // for purposes of refining objects
        SK_METALWORKING,  // making weapons and armor, i.e., blacksmithing
        SK_FLETCHING,     // making arrows and bows
        SK_COBBLING,      // making shoes
        SK_NEGOTIATION,   // used for haggling and discussion
        SK_DIPLOMACY,     // used for finding peaceful solutions
        SK_LEADERSHIP,    // used to motivate others to do your bidding
        SK_MUSIC,         // playing an instrument
        SK_LANGUAGE,      // ability to learn a language and communicate
        SK_FIREMASTERY,   // use and making of fire
        SK_TRAINING,      // this refers to training others of the
                          // same species, like a warrior opening a school
        SK_PAINTING,      // artistic and artisan painting
        SK_CARPENTRY,     // building of wooden things, tree houses, etc.
        SK_COOKING,       // the fixing of good food
        SK_DANCING,       // how to dance
        SK_RIDING,        // horseback or griffin
        SK_SEAMANSHIP,    // a sailor
```

```
        SK_TAILOR,       // a maker of clothes
        SK_JESTER,       // tightrope walking, juggling, jester stuff
        SK_ENGINEERING,  // knowledge of advanced construction
        SK_RELIGION,     // knowledge of all local gods
        SK_NAVIGATION,   // ability to guide a ship
        SK_DISGUISE,     // ability to look and act like someone else
        SK_TRAPSETTING,  // knowledge of how to make a trap
        SK_MOUNTAINEERING,   // climbing mountains
        SK_SURVIVAL,     // how to survive cold or unusual conditions
        SK_HERBALISM,    // identification of plants and knowledge of
                         // their uses
        SK_READING,      // ability to read
        SK_WRITING,      // ability to send letters or messages
        SK_SAGE,         // knowledge of research and lore
        SK_GROVEMASTER,  // ability to plant rows of fruit-bearing trees
        SK_REPAIR,       // basic knowledge on repairing everyday objects

        END_SKILLS
        };
    };
    //*******************************************
```

How Does an Entity Live?

This is a question that only the designer can answer. But it should be answered. Too often, RTS/RTT games define a life-and-death struggle between two or three races over a rock in space. Why do they want the chunk of dirt and how do they live off of the world? Personally, I would never fight for a piece of land unless it had valuable minerals that are difficult to find elsewhere or provided a great food source. Establishing how a creature or society survives on its own, without having to fight another race over territory (such as Palestinians and Israelis fighting over a chunk of the Holy Land), helps define the mood of the game.

What does the entity eat? This will define if the entity can survive in the new area he is attempting to conquer. Maybe he needs to bring food with him. Can the entity grow food or must he try to take over an area that belongs to the opponent where food grows naturally? This question is the most basic question that all humans have struggled with since the dawn of civilization. Most of the very early fighting that humans did was over hunting territory.

What type of environment is the entity used to seeing? Lush green forests or arid Martian landscape? Does he breathe oxygen, carbon dioxide, or nitric oxide (a precursor to nitric acid)? Would this race of entities attempt to alter the atmosphere and win a level by transforming all oxygen-based air into something like sulfur dioxide? Sounds like a deadly race and a great premise for a game. Maybe this race has emerged from post-modern Earth near a radioactive dumping ground. Also related to environment are construction considerations. Humans tend to build very square buildings. What type would an alien race build? How about orcs or goblins? What kinds of buildings do elves like—tree houses? Dwarves are known for liking underground dwellings where they can find metals and gems.

18

Chapter

How do these creatures live? Are they intelligent or do they live by brute force? How is their government structured? What kinds of beasts do they ride? Do they relax; if so, what do they do? What does an average citizen do in an average day? These questions are great for story line and, more importantly, lead to design decisions that affect gameplay and increase the interest in the game. Try playing the Zerg race in StarCraft. You'll love them because they are so different from any type of race you've played before. Their differences makes the game more interesting.

It is worth noting that not all entities are alive, per se. Some are rocks, some are rivers, and some are trees, which are alive but don't move. The above questions obviously do not apply to some types of entities… just animal or moving types.

Where Do Entities Fit into the Design?

This is a complex question with a not-so-easy answer. An entity is an empty shell. It has no personality and is of no value by itself. It has all of the basic characteristics necessary to be a creature, tree, or any other object in your game, but that is about all. It doesn't know what to do nor does it have any formal definition. Consider it an outline or template for all of the creatures in your world.

What you do with the outline is up to you. You can fill it in with tons of code for each type of creature and object in the world and have it figure out what it needs to do at run time based on a lot of different variables. You can derive classes from the basic ENTITY class and program each one with a different think action; after all, the think function is about all that will change from entity to entity. You can have each entity defined by a set of parameters in a database and load it in dynamically at run time, making the entities data driven, which is a great way to help the game in terms of game balancing. There are literally dozens of methods to use, but these three are the most common.

Once you've examined your choices and you have a course of action, work with the ENTITY class listed in this chapter and your job will get a lot easier. Break your creatures and buildings into groups of entities with similar properties. This will be your design outline. Pick out common characteristics that all within a group share. Now see what the ENTITY class has to offer and expand it to fulfill your needs. It will need expansion because I never intended to answer all of the questions or provide fat, bloated code.

The design comes when you start your grouping. The more you can group the entities into common functionality and variables, the easier it will be for the programmers, and the game will generally be done faster. Don't overgeneralize, because a building has very little in common with an X-Wing (remember *Star Wars*?). But limit the number of categories to 5 to 10. This keeps things generalized enough to help your programmers but distinct enough to make the code intelligible. Striking this balance is not easy and seasoned programmers have struggled with this, so if it takes you a while, relax. Breaking up components of a hierarchy can be a daunting task, especially when you are likely to have 30 to 40 classes (creatures) in the same hierarchy.

If your creatures will be code driven, I recommend having different classes for each creature in the game derived from the proper ENTITY class. There is a class hierarchy to the ENTITY class. If they are data driven, they will still need a hierarchy for base classes to be dynamically declared at run time. Remember the use of the virtual function? It helps a lot since you won't know exactly what type of creature you will be dealing with when the game is loaded or a random map is generated. For this reason, you'll notice that the base class has almost all possible function calls that any entity could ever use, even though most can't be used by the base class.

Basic Entity Characteristics

All entities have battle or combat characteristics. You do want to know how much missile damage a frigate or carrier can take before exploding, right? These characteristics include armor, hit points, current damage level, weapon damage, and combat experience.

All entities have a graphic associated with them for drawing the associated icon. They need to have a place in the world, so they have world coordinates. They all need to have a screen position for drawing their icon and setting screen position before drawing. For entities that are involved in the world, they'll need a queue for things that happen to them. That way, during the update cycle, they know how to react.

The exact characteristics vary considerably from game to game and entity to entity, but this begins to give you an idea.

What Kind of Group Behavior Does an Entity Exhibit?

When entities get together, all hell breaks loose. It's a big party where the limits of the code become painfully apparent. If you think getting entities to operate in groups is easy, boy, do you have another thing coming.

First, do you want them to communicate with each other? Maybe one of the units is in charge. Do they need pointers to each other, or is there a group structure that has 50 pointers just waiting for entities to fill it? Do they need to communicate with each other? Why not just have a top-down communication model? If you decide to do that, how does an entity let the system know that it is dead and that the group can go on without him?

Pathing raises other questions. How does a group of guys move across the map? Do they get into formation before departing and then march to their destination? How long does getting into formation take? Most groups performing a path move simply go from location to destination, and the entities often stumble over each other on the way there. Total Annihilation is the worst: Moving units just a little forces them all into single file. It is a lot easier to path for single file, but groups can be hard. Do the units try to maintain their position relative to each other when going to their destination, like in Age of Empires? Do they simply try to force their way past each other, like in StarCraft? We'll reserve this discussion for Chapter 19.

What Kinds of Actions are Available to the Average Entity?

Check the SKILLS class under "What Does an Entity Do?" earlier in this chapter to see what actions are available to entities. The problem is programming all the behavior. Also, the amount of code required to perform all of those actions makes your program large and unwieldy. With more and more people complaining about code bloat, this would give people another reason to complain, especially if they see no benefit from the extra code. After all, it is hard to tell if a unit is repairing a shoe or fixing armor. Better to just have a simple repair animation and not worry about the specifics.

It is not enough to say which actions are available to the average entity. The type of entity plays a critical role in making that decision. A building just sits there, while a combat unit can move. A resource gatherer can pick up crystals; a tank cannot. Once you define what an entity is in your game, you can begin thinking about which actions or states a creature may have.

The best list I have is in ai_skills.h. You'll see this in the GOAL structure, which is shown later in this chapter.

Who Owns an Entity?

I intentionally left the ownership issue up to the programmer. There are at least three different, suitable ways to handle this and I simply cannot recommend one over the others; it is all a matter of taste. Ultimately, the real owner of any entity is really the computer anyway.

Looking at the CREATURE_FLAGS structure in the worldobj.h file (see the "Creature Definition" section), we could add another 4 bits, or find room in the existing bit, for up to eight players. This could be a PlayerID associated with each player. Any object in the world not associated with a player would have an ID of 0. This way, an entity "knows" who owns him and can easily send reports back to that player through some mechanism. Reports would include things like: "I have died," "I have collected the gold," and "I have killed someone." The difficulty is determining quickly who owns what. If a player wants to click and drag over the battlefield to select creatures, every creature on that field needs to be tested and then have the SELECTED flag set.

Another option is to have a container class for each player that maintains pointers to all entity objects in the world that belong to someone. This gives quick access and is a great method for determining whether a player has selected a creature or not, since he can only select his own creatures. The problem arises from pointer maintenance and keeping player pointers in sync with the ENTITY_MANAGER, but this is a minor nuisance and not a reason to avoid this method. The memory overhead is completely trivial, being 1 K for 250 entity pointers.

The last method is a communication structure. A communication structure would hold a pointer to an ENTITY and a PlayerID number. The Player structure would have hundreds of these communication structures but never an entity. An ENTITY would hold a pointer to a communication structure. When an entity is "born," the player finds an available communication structure, fills in the necessary data, and then uses it to communicate to the entity. All communication is carried out through the communication structure. This structure is easily extensible for handling a group of entities, making this method even sweeter for a player to easily communicate with a group. Also, this is a great method for a group of entities to communicate with each other. The downside is the maintenance. There are four pointers—player to structure, structure to player, structure to entity, and entity to structure. That can be a headache.

How Do Entities Communicate?

There are many solutions to this problem, but I like this method. Entities need to talk to each other on occasion and so they'll have GOAL structures with a pointer to an entity. This means that they have direct access to another entity and post messages in the queue of the destination entity. The queue "mailroom" or "whiteboard" method gets too messy. This involves posting messages for each entity in the world in a giant mailroom, which is part of some global class. At the update cycle, each entity checks his mailbox to see what he got, and responds to any queries by returning mail to the entity that requested info. This does help with issues such as when the destination entity dies and you have a bad pointer to the destination entity. Under my scheme, a dead creature still lingers for a short time and can easily tell anyone requesting info that he is dead.

There are only a few things that entities need to communicate anyway like "I am causing damage to you" or "I am healing you." It seems like a short list, but not much other communication needs to take place. You can make resource gathering a little bit of communication, as well as queries like "How is your health?" or "What is your world position?" That about does it. These messages should be posted in the entity's queue and he'll respond when appropriate, that is, when his next update cycle comes up.

Entities should communicate through a third party, in any case. Communicating directly can be bad, especially if an entity dies and another has a pointer to it, which now becomes invalid or at least may produce odd program behavior. I suggest that you post messages through some global system like the OBJECT_ DISPATCHER. The WORLDOBJECT class (discussed shortly) has a function called MESSAGE, and all objects in the game can pass messages to other objects by calling the object dispatcher function MessageSend which will pass the message on to the creature or object if appropriate. Some other method similar to this is equally good, but the mechanisms are in the code, so you can check it out.

How Do Entities Think?

You can't program a computer to think, let alone some creature in a game. What you can do is set a series of states for an entity and allow it to move between them with relative ease based on environmental conditions. Or you build a goal-oriented system that allows the entity to set and achieve goals. These are more similar than different, but they do have differences.

First, let's define what things an entity must do of its own free will:

➤ If an enemy attacks, fight back, unless the player tells you otherwise.
➤ If the player clicks on the map when you are selected, you are to move to that location.

➤ Once assigned to farming, continue farming until attacked or until food runs out. Then start farming somewhere else nearby.

➤ When attacking a building, if an enemy retaliates, turn and fight unless you are set to follow directions precisely. (This is like the entity settings in Dark Reign under the Advanced tab.)

➤ When flying, attack all enemy units indiscriminately unless told to follow directions precisely. (Total Annihilation offers this.)

➤ After killing all units in a group, begin destroying buildings.

You can go on for hours defining these conditions, but you shouldn't have to. This is the designer's job. These are general questions, but they'll need to be answered for some units individually because some units are, and should be, much different from the rest of the units in the game.

Once you have a complete list of behaviors similar to this list, you are ready to start coding. Stick to placing all thinking code in the Think function of the entity class and the rest should be easy. In RTS/RTT games, the AI of the creatures (unit AI) is relatively easy, especially when compared to making a computer opponent that is difficult to play against. Also, each unit in the game can use tweaking that is hard-coded. This gives you enough leeway to code all of the unit AI fairly easily.

The interesting part of this chapter is that the AI will be defined by the structure we build. The ENTITY class has the structure for the AI and all you have to do is fill in a few blanks and your units will be smart enough. Making them smarter is your job, but the basic framework will all be set forth here.

How Do Entities Remember?

I do not provide a mechanism in this game book for entities remembering anything but what you tell them to do. These commands will be stored in their GOAL queue since a command is really just a goal to an entity. Real-time strategy games have units that are supposed to take orders, and maybe gain a little experience along the way. RTS games generally do not need units capable of remembering that Knor the Dwarf holds the key to the Room of the Silver Orb in the Dungeon under Skeleton Peak. They don't need to learn a trade or where the nearest food supply is. These things are not part of an RTS game. If your game needs them, I suggest adding an intelligence characteristic to the ENTITY class along with a queue for MEMORY.

You'll find enough space for experience in the CREATURE_FLAGS structure that is part of the base class WORLDOBJECT. The variable name is EXPERIENCE; it holds up to 511 experience points useful for making the entity a better combatant. This is the closest thing to memory I have put in here.

Creature Definition

We are about to embark on the wonderful discovery of ENTITY's that are essentially "things" in your game world. Before we do that, we'll need to rehash some old info introduced earlier. AI definitions are complex enough without being taken out of context.

All of the objects that might appear in the game "world" will be derived from WORLDCOORDINATE, which gives them a position. This class contains position information and is the foundation of any object appearing in world space.

```
//*******************************************

class WORLDCOORDINATE
{
protected:
     S16     wx, wy, wz;         // world map position
     S8      offx, offy, offz;   // object offset in world terms

     //******************

public:

     //******************

     WORLDCOORDINATE ();
     ~WORLDCOORDINATE ();
     inline void  Clear ();

     //******************

     WORLDCOORDINATE operator =  (WORLDCOORDINATE* obj);
     WORLDCOORDINATE operator += (WORLDCOORDINATE* obj);
     WORLDCOORDINATE operator -= (WORLDCOORDINATE* obj);
     WORLDCOORDINATE operator += (WPOINT* pt);
     WORLDCOORDINATE operator -= (WPOINT* pt);

     //******************

     bool  operator == (WORLDCOORDINATE* obj);

     //******************
     //******************

     void SetWorldCoordinates (int x, int y, int z)
         {wx = (S16) x, wy = (S16) y, wz = (S16) z;}
     void GetWorldCoordinates (int* x, int* y, int* z) const
         {*x = (S32) wx, *y = (S32) wy, *z = (S32) wz;}
     void SetOffsetCoordinates (int x, int y, int z)
         {offx = (S8) x, offy = (S8) y, offz = (S8) z;}
     void GetOffsetCoordinates (int* x, int* y, int* z) const
         {*x = (S32) offx, *y = (S32) offy, *z = (S32) offz;}

     //******************
```

```
    void SetWorldX (int x) {wx = (S16) x;}
    void SetWorldY (int y) {wy = (S16) y;}
    void SetWorldZ (int z) {wz = (S16) z;}


    //*****************

    int  GetWorldX () const {return wx;}
    int  GetWorldY () const {return wy;}
    int  GetWorldZ () const {return wz;}


    //*****************

    void SetOffsetX (int x) {offx = (S8) x;}
    void SetOffsetY (int y) {offy = (S8) y;}
    void SetOffsetZ (int z) {offz = (S8) z;}


    //*****************

    int  GetOffsetX () const {return offx;}
    int  GetOffsetY () const {return offy;}
    int  GetOffsetZ () const {return offz;}


    //*****************

};

//*********************************************
```

The position information will be stored in wx, wy, and wz. These three short int's give a world coordinate position possibility of 0 to 32,768, or if your world allows negative coordinates, –32,767 to 32,768. Perhaps your map will be centered at 0,0 with the world going left and up for negative and down and right for positive. In any event, this allows for amazingly large maps, certainly larger than any game currently available.

Depending on your particular coordinate system, and mine for that matter, you may want these numbers to represent tile numbers on a grid-like tile system. If so, I have included offx, offy, and offz to allow a creature to move around on the tile. Basically, a creature or anything else in the world would have a tile coordinate and then an offset. If your tile system has absolute coordinates and the tiles just fit in that system (the tiles have coordinates too), I encourage you to delete these extra offset variables and the access routines associated with them. You may wish to forego this altogether and use float values. At least one game I know of uses float values for position information in the map. The integer portion is used to tell which tile is used and the mantissa is used to approximate position within the tile. Any of these methods is fine, although float might be a little slower. Of course, this hardly matters since this will never be your bottleneck and you probably would not notice a speed difference from one to the other. Use whatever makes you comfortable.

Next, we examine the WORLDOBJECT class, which allows us to define a whole host of new ideas. This has been with us for some time and you will find a brief discussion of that information in Chapter 16, but this class encapsulates something much more important—registration.

```
//**************************************************

// worldobj.h




#ifndef  _WORLDOBJ_H_
#define  _WORLDOBJ_H_

#include "c:\library_cur\struct.h"
#include "c:\library_cur\objdisp.h"
#include "c:\library_cur\worldcor.h"
//**************************************************
//**************************************************
//**************************************************

#ifndef NULL
#define REMOVE_NULL
#define NULL 0L
#endif

typedef class WORLDOBJECT : public WORLDCOORDINATE
{
public:
     enum TYPE {WORLDOBJ = 1000, WORLDCOORD = 1001};

protected:
     U16          Type;
     S16          ID;
     WORLDOBJECT* next;
     U16          MiniMapColor;

public:

  //********************        variables

     CREATURE_FLAGS CreatureFlag;

  //********************        functions

     WORLDOBJECT () : WORLDCOORDINATE () {Clear ();}
     ~WORLDOBJECT () {ObjDisp.ClearID (ID);}

  //********************
```

```
        void  SetID (int x) {ID = (S16) x;}
        int   GetID () {return ID;}

        int   Test (WORLDOBJECT* w1, WORLDOBJECT*w2)
        {
            if ((w1->wz) < (w2->wz)) return -1;
            if ((w1->wz) ==(w2->wz)) return 0;
            return 1;
        }
        // for passing messages, it does nothing right now.
        // a -1 sender means a generic message has been passed
        virtual void Message (int type, int data1, int data2, int Sender = -1){}

        //********************

        virtual void  Clear ()
        {
            Type = (TYPE) WORLDOBJ; ID = (S16) ObjDisp.NewID (this);
            MiniMapColor = 0;
        }

//********************
    WORLDOBJECT* AddObject (WORLDOBJECT*e)
    {
        WORLDOBJECT* e1, *e2;
        if (e == NULL) return this;
        if (Test (e, this) <= 0)
        {
            if (e->next)
            {
                e1 = e->next, e2 = e; // e2 will eventually point to this
                                      // and this will point to e1
                while (e1 && Test (e1, this)<=0)
                {
                    e1=e1->next, e2 = e2->next;
                }
                this->next = e1;
                e2->next = this;
                return e;
            }
            else
            {
                e->next = this;
                return e;
            }
        }
        if (next == NULL)                    // assumes that
        {
            next = e;
            return this;
        }
        else
```

```
        {
            e1 = next;
            while (e1)
            {
                e->AddObject (e1);
                e1 = e1->next;
            }
            next = e;
        }
        return e;
}


//*********************

WORLDOBJECT* Remove (WORLDOBJECT*e)  // removes self (this) from list
{
        WORLDOBJECT* e1, *e2;
        if (e == NULL) return NULL;
        if (e == this) return next;

        e1 = e->next, e2 = e;
        while (e1)
        {
            if (e1->next == this) break;
            e1 = e1->next; e2 = e2->next;
        }
        if (e1 != NULL)                 // we weren't in this list
        e2->next = e1->next;
        // e1, which is this, is out of the loop
        return e;
}


//*********************

WORLDOBJECT* RemoveObject (WORLDOBJECT*e)
// removes the WORLDOBJECT pointed to
// we return a pointer in case the removed item is the head of the list
{
        WORLDOBJECT* e1 = this;
        if (e == NULL) return NULL;
        if (e == this) return next;     // remove self

        while (e1->next)
        {
            if (e1->next == e)
            {
                e1->next = e->next;  // e leaves us
                break;
            }
            e1 = e1->next;
        }
        return this;
```

```
        }
        //*********************

        WORLDOBJECT * GetNext () {return next;}

}WORLDOBJECT, *WORLDOBJECTptr, ** WORLDOBJECTlist;

//*************************************************
//*************************************************
//*************************************************
#ifdef REMOVE_NULL
#undef NULL
#undef REMOVE_NULL
#endif

#endif
```

In the headers is the #include file objdisp.h. It has a class defined as OBJECT_DISPATCHER that maintains a list of all objects created in the world. This is one of the few globals in my engine. This one is your friend. It tracks ID numbers that we talked about in the tile system.

This allows you to store ID numbers, instead of pointers, to objects in the world, which reduces memory and allows you to search through the entire list of objects. You might need to find a particular creature, or you might want to handle the interface by searching through all objects in the world to see if a player clicked on it. In any event, it is always a good idea to track all items in the game, if for nothing more than to ensure proper memory cleanup. The problem is, you might want more information on an object (info the OBJECT_DISPATCHER would maintain) than just a pointer to it.

You'll have to decide what kind of quick info you need, but remember: By going to the OBJECT_DISPATCHER and obtaining a pointer to any WORLDOBJECT, you can get its type and then get any info you might need. This is where good design can be your friend. All objects need to be derived from a common parent (WORLDOBJECT in this case), and a large list of pointers to this parent class will allow you to create and easily manipulate thousands of these objects in the game world. A virtual access routine or two could help you obtain information seamlessly within the definition of this parent class. Don't go overboard; keep the interface to the parent class as simple, yet robust, as is possible. It is a delicate decision and one that will help you or haunt you, depending on what you decide. This is one of those decisions that will affect the development cycle, so let's examine a few considerations.

All objects in the world will need a Draw function. Logically, that should go in a screen class, but it might be better to put it in WORLDOBJECT. It should be paired with an Update function, allowing any extra processing for that object (like AI and movement), but that should go in the ENTITY class described later or maybe in the WORLDOBJECT. You'll also find AddObject, Remove, and RemoveObject functions here. Based on the object's wz or elevation value, this linked list is filled in.

Here is some example code that shows how to use the WORLDOBJECT class as a linked list:

```
//****************************************

void main ()
{
        WORLDOBJECT e[10], *list = NULL;

        e[0].wz = 3;
        e[1].wz = 2;
        e[2].wz = 7;
        e[3].wz = 8;
        e[4].wz = 9;
        e[5].wz = 0;
        e[6].wz = 6;
        e[7].wz = 5;
        e[8].wz = -1;
        e[9].wz = 14;
        // 5, 8, 1, 0, 9, 7, 6, 2, 3, 4, the order of the list

        for (int i=0; i<10; i++)
        {
            e[i].ID = i;
            list = e[i].AddObject (list); this tacks the item onto the list,
            // if the item belongs at the front of the list, the item
            // is returned with "next" pointing to the list that was passed
        }

        list = e[2].Remove (list);          // 5, 8, 1, 0, 9, 7, 6, 3, 4
        // this function makes a WORLDOBJECT remove itself from the list

        list = list->RemoveObject (&e[5]);   // 8, 1, 0, 9, 7, 6, 3, 4
        // this removes the passed in item from the list.
}

//****************************************
```

Here is the FLAGS_FOR_CREATURES struct from struct.h:

```
//****************************************************
typedef struct FLAGS_FOR_CREATURES
{
        U32 ARTIFICIAL_INT:6;    // 0-5, which intelligence type 0 is none

        U32 ALIVE:1;             // 6, 1 creature is alive and can function
        U32 DYING:3;             // 7-9, 0 creature is healthy and 7 stages of
                                 // dying, if a creature is already dead, this
                                 // is the level of decay starting with
                                 // 7 and decaying to 0
        U32 PRIORITY_SETTING:5;  // 10-14, how much processing time does this
                                 // object need
        U32 WRITE_ENABLED:1;     // 15, 1-writing is possible,
                                 // certain sharing methods require
                                 // locking and unlocking of write ability
        U32 READ_ENABLED:1;      // 16, 1-reading is possible, see write above
```

18

Chapter

```
        U32 ADAPTABLE:4;              // 17-20, varying states of adaptability, 0 is
                                      // unadaptive
        U32 AGGRESSION:4;             // 21-24, aggression where 0 is docile and 15
                                      // is hostile
        U32 FULL_PATH_FOUND:1;        // 25, during the last pathing, was the full
                                      // path found
        U32 CURRENT_STATE:6;          // 26-31, 32 different states
                                      // may be replaced

        U32 BLOCKING:2;               // can walk over or through, 0-no, 1-slowly,
                                      // 2-moderate, 3-full speed
        U32 SELECTED:1;               // draw selection box
        U32 GROUP_ID:4;               // support for up to 15 groups
        U32 TIME_SINCE_BIRTH:16;      // how long have I been alive, over 30 minutes
                                      // at 30 fps, every time this rolls over, add
                                      // one experience point

        U32  EXPERIENCE:9;            // experience points. adds to chance for
                                      // hitting, damage, or intelligence

    }* FLAGS_FOR_CREATURESptr;        // 64 bits

//****************************************************
```

I'll briefly examine the various flags and variables here to help you.

The ARTIFICIAL_INT variable tells you which of 64 possible personality types this particular world object has. Most objects in the world just sit there, like trees, terrain features, or buildings. So that's one personality type for you. Then there are scouts that look around, builders whose sole purpose is to construct, resource gatherers whose sole purpose is to bring resources from one location to another, etc.

The ALIVE variable tells you if the creature is alive or dead. Since this has only two states to my way of thinking, 1 bit is enough. When processing the update cycle, it may be important for the creature to return a 0 on its update cycle, but also know that it is dead. On its next update cycle it can simply return without doing anything. Or if you decide to give it a little power, it can spawn a DYING_ ENTITY with the appropriate animation, and then kill itself by registering itself in the OBJECT_DISPATCHER to be deleted. Whatever you prefer, ALIVE is a great flag to have.

DYING tells us what state the creature is in. This can be used as a meter to show colors for life level. You might want to rename it LIFE_LEVEL, but you can use it for a colored bar over the creature to show his percentage toward death. This can be used after death as a rotting meter to tell you how far along the rotting process is. Dual purpose.

You may need to set the PRIORITY_SETTING for a creature in the world. This should affect the way you allocate time for it. Creatures visible to the player should get more processing time for managing animation, casting spells, launching missiles, and throwing rocks. Once offscreen, no processing time needs to go into changing frames of animation; just update the position. This is especially true of animated buildings; you can simply return if it isn't on screen. If you decide that isn't for you, it might be useful merely to assign certain creatures a bigger time slice based on their importance in the game. A dragon might be allowed to have more time to do whatever it does while a rocket would get very little time. All of this assumes that you will use time to limit how much a creature does during its update cycle. We will talk about ways to accomplish that later.

If you are using a multithreaded approach, WRITE_ENABLED and READ_ENABLED become necessary. Synchronization objects are great but these flags are like the same thing and much more fitting to the need. I find that a critical section requires that you block code from executing until other threads are finished with it. An event can slow the game tremendously as one section of code waits for another. A semaphore is not appropriate here. And other synchronization objects just don't fit. (These objects can be found in *Advanced Windows* by Jeffrey Richter, in case you are not familiar with synchronization.) Anyway, when a creature is modifying its own variables, it will set the READ_ENABLED flag to 0 which prevents other threads from reading its data until it is done. This isn't very likely to happen, but that is the problem with synchronization: It always happens eventually. Before some thread decides to read the value of a variable, it should set WRITE_ENABLED to 0 so that no variables will change while it is examining this world object. This method is much faster than any of the typical synchronization objects and has the same effect. It sometimes takes a little more work, but it's usually less. For simplicity, you may just want to use one of these flags since they essentially do the same thing.

ADAPTABLE can be used for a lot of things. This can be the creature's experience, the creature's adaptability, the ability of the creature to change, or just about anything else. Think of it as an extra 4 bits to play with.

A personality trait of most creatures is AGGRESSION, so I put it in the flags. This is just a variable used to determine behavior. The player should be able to modify the aggression level of the creatures under his control. You might think of this as stance or response to attack. You'll need to decide what each of the 15 different levels mean, but most games usually only have three levels.

FULL_PATH_FOUND is used in pathing (obviously) to tell us if the creature found a full set of steps to his destination. This is important only because most pathing will fall out after a certain distance or a certain amount of time. Unless the destination is close, this will rarely be set to 1.

All creatures have a current state such as resting, running, jumping, searching, attacking, dying, etc. This will be stored in CURRENT_STATE. We'll discuss state machines in great detail later.

Every world object will get these 32 bits to work with. You may want to move this structure into another class further down in the hierarchy, but I like it here because these bits can be used for a whole host of different things.

The CREATURE_FLAGS structure simply contains a FLAGS_FOR_CREATURES structure, which is a union with Value. (Value is a 64-bit value achieved by combining two 32-bit values.) This allows easy assignment from one structure to another (struct1->Value[0] = struct2->Value[0];). Normal assignment would require a copy constructor, memcpy, or variable by variable assignment, which are all much slower. Clearing the structure is easier as well by assigning the entire thing to 0. If you don't like the CREATURE_FLAGS structure, don't use it. In order to access the AGGRESSION flag in the FLAGS_FOR_CREATURES structure, you'll need to use:

```
CREATURE_FLAGS.Flag.AGGRESSION
```

That is more complex than some people prefer. Sorry, but I like this better:

```
//*******************************
typedef union  CREATURE_FLAGS
{
        BIT64                   Value;
        FLAGS_FOR_CREATURES Flag;
            //---------------------------
        CREATURE_FLAGS () {Clear ();}
        void Clear()
        {
            Value[0] = 0, Value[1] = 0;
        }
        CREATURE_FLAGS& operator = (CREATURE_FLAGS& c)
        {
            Value[0] = c.Value[0], Value[1] = c.Value[1];
            return *this;
        }
}* CREATURE_FLAGSptr;
//*******************************
```

Next we need to reexamine the SCREENOBJECT class. As I've said before, all objects needing to be drawn should be derived from SCREENOBJECT or at least contain an instance of it.

```
//*************************************************
typedef class SCREENOBJECT
{
protected:
        S16          scx, scy;              // screen position
        S16          Width, Height;

public:

        SCREENOBJECT ();
        ~SCREENOBJECT ();
            //---------------------------
        inline void  Clear ();
            //---------------------------

        //***************************
        // the following code segments are all inline code
        //***************************

        void  SetPosition (int x, int y, int w, int h)
            {scx = (S16)x, scy = (S16)y; Width = (S16)w, Height = (S16)h;}
            //---------------------------
        void  SetScreenPosition (int x, int y) {scx = (S16)x, scy = (S16)y;}
        void  SetScreenX (int x) {scx = (S16)x;}
```

```
       void   SetScreenY (int y) {scy = (S16)y;}
              //---------------------------
       void   GetScreenPosition (int& x, int& y) {x = (S16)scx, y = (S16)scy;}
       int    GetScreenX () const {return scx;}
       int    GetScreenY () const {return scy;}
              //---------------------------
       void   SetDimensions (int w, int h) {Width = (S16)w, Height = (S16)h;}
       void   SetWidth  (int w) {Width = (S16)w;}
       void   SetHeight (int h) {Height = (S16)h;}
              //---------------------------
       void   GetDimensions (int& w, int& h) {w = (S16)Width, h = (S16)Height;}
       int    GetWidth  () const {return Width;}
       int    GetHeight () const {return Height;}
              //---------------------------
       void   AddPosition (int x, int y) {scx += (S16)x, scy += (S16)y;} // offset
       void   AddX (int x) {scx += (S16)x;}
       void   AddY (int y) {scy += (S16)y;}
              //---------------------------
       bool   IsInside (int x, int y)
       {if (x>=scx && x<scx+Width && y>=scy && y<scy+Height) return 1; return 0;}
              //---------------------------
              //---------------------------
}SCREENOBJECT, * SCREENOBJECTptr, ** SCREENOBJECTlist;

//*******************************************
```

This is the actual entity class:

```
//***************************************************

class ENTITY : public WORLDOBJECT: public SCREENOBJECT
{
       GRAPHICptr        Graphic;    // assumes a single graphic
                                     // this can be used for a variety of things
                                     // including button graphics and a tree stump
       float             SizeX;
       float             SizeY;
       short             SelectEvent;

       virtual int       Update ();
       virtual void      Draw (SCREEN_STRUCT* screen);
};
//***************************************************
```

It contains all of its parent variables and a few functions that will be inherited by all of its children. A simple ENTITY has nothing to do during its update cycle so this is simply a virtual placeholder. If it has a graphic, it will be drawn at the entity's screen location, which must be calculated from world position. It will be assumed that the entity does not own this graphic, so it will never delete the memory. We have two variables, SizeX and SizeY, which define the actual world size of this object in terms of tile size (0.5 is half a tile width; 1.2 is a little larger than 1 tile width). This will allow us to easily determine when objects run into each other based on an object's "radius."

18

Chapter

Since almost every entity in the world will take up some space, this is one way to manage world space and pathing.

Most RTS/RTT games do not use a method like this. Most treat objects in the world as predefined objects that take up a fixed number of small tiles in the world. Dark Reign, Red Alert, and StarCraft all have a graphic and an associated no-pass (blocking terrain or passability) zone that is used in pathing. This method is usually much simpler to implement and it makes pathing a breeze compared to all of the trouble that Dave Pottinger had to go through to get pathing perfect for Age of Empires. Still, the method that he developed, I think, is one of the best methods in the industry. Accolades to you, Dave.

Depending on the way you structure your program, this is probably the best place to add an event ID. This is the ID number of an event that will be registered when the player clicks his mouse on this entity. This number will be fed back to the global interface manager, and hopefully icons will change and the interface will display different information. The variable is named SelectEvent. We'll initialize this stuff later, but keep it in the back of your mind for now. This was discussed in a little detail in Chapter 17.

How does this class become initialized and where are the access routines? Is that what's bugging you? Well, worry no more. This is just an intro to the real class, which is much larger. But beyond access routines, there isn't much to add to this base class. We'll need to look at specific entities for a bit more detail. The key here is to provide a consistent interface for all derived children of this class. All we have to do is begin filling functionality for the different types of derived children.

All derived children will overload the constructor, a necessity, and the function SetType. C++ now offers a mechanism for Run Time Type Identification for classes but my method is easier to test. The implementation of the overloaded SetType function will happen based on the individual classes, and much of it we'll see later in this chapter.

Here we have the base class. You can now get a rough idea about how complex even simple AI can be.

```
//**************************************************

#ifndef __ENTITY_H_
#define __ENTITY_H_

//*****************************************
//*****************************************

class ENTITY_DEFINED;
struct CREATURE_EVENT;
struct GOAL;
class GRAPHIC;
class ANIMATION_MGR;

//*****************************************
//*****************************************
```

```
#ifndef __STRUCT_H_
#include "c:/library_cur/struct.h"
#endif
#ifndef __SCREENOBJ_H_
#include "c:/library_cur/screenobj.h"
#endif
#ifndef __WORLDOBJ_H_
#include "c:/library_cur/worldobj.h"
#endif
#ifndef __QUEUE_H_
#include "c:/library_cur/queue.h"
#endif
#ifndef __ANIMATION_H_
#include "c:/library_cur/animation.h"
#endif
#ifndef __AI_SKILLS_H_
#include "c:/library_cur/ai_skills.h"
#endif

#ifndef NULL
#define REMOVE_NULL
#define NULL     0L
#endif

//*******************************************

typedef class ENTITY : public SCREENOBJECT , public WORLDOBJECT
{
public:
     ENTITY_DEFINED* Entity;

     static UNIVERSAL_ENTITY_MANAGER* Manager;
     static PATH_MANAGER* PathManager;
     static TILE_MAP* TileManager;

     void SetManager (UNIVERSAL_ENTITY_MANAGER*m) {Manager = m;}
     void SetPathManager (PATH_MANAGER*pm) {PathManager = pm;}
     void SetTileManager (TILE_MAP*tm) {TileManager = tm;}

public:
     enum TYPE {
               BASE = 0x1,
               SELECTABLE = BASE*2,
               RESOURCE = SELECTABLE*2,
               MOVING = RESOURCE*2,
               CONSTRUCTION = MOVING*2,
               RESOURCE_GATHERER = CONSTRUCTION*2,
               SOLDIER = RESOURCE_GATHERER*2,
               FLYING_UNIT = SOLDIER*2,
               TRANSPORT = FLYING_UNIT*2,
               PROJECTILE = TRANSPORT*2,
               CONSUMPTION = PROJECTILE*2,
```

```
                        EXPLOSION = CONSUMPTION*2,
                        QUEUED = EXPLOSION*2,
                        NUMTYPES = 13, ALLTYPES = 0xffff};

        enum STATE {};

protected:

        U8          CurrentAction;
        U8          PlayerID;           // if a player owns this item, it will have
                                        // an ID greater than 0
                                        // 0 means no player.

        U8          Visible;            // is it visible
        GRAPHIC*    Graphic;            // assumes a single graphic
                                        // this can be used for a variety of things
                                        // including button graphics and a tree stump

        float       SizeX;
        float       SizeY;

        U16         Dam;                // damage taken
        U16         HitPoints;          // points of damage to take, or Hit Points
        U16         Armor;
        U16         MiniMapColor;       // how does the creature appear on the minimap


        U16         SelectEvent;
        U16         SoundID;            // sound to be played when selected
                                        // you may need multiple sounds

        U16         FrameCounter;       // for keeping track of waiting, spell
                                        // length, etc, up to 4.5 years

protected:                             // functions

        bool        VerifyLiving () {return (bool) (CreatureFlag.Flag.ALIVE &
                                                    Visible);}
        virtual void    Think () {}     // this is a placeholder for the eventual
                                        // function that will be unique for every
                                        // type of creature.
                                        // this will be called from update.

        void        SendEvent (int which) {}

public:
        ENTITY() {Clear (); SetType ();}
        virtual ~ENTITY() {}

        //**************

        virtual void    Clear ()
        {
             Graphic=NULL,
```

```
        SizeX=0.0, SizeY=0.0,
        SelectEvent=0, SoundID=0, Dam = 0, HitPoints = 0, Armor = 0,
        MiniMapColor = 32767; // white
}
virtual void    SetType () {Type = BASE;}
virtual int     Die ();     // see .cpp file
                            // externally killed for whatever reason,
                            // this helps on game close or if a creature
                            // dies that sustains another such as the
                            // carriers in StarCraft

//***************

virtual int     Destination (ENTITY*, int cont) {return 0;}
                            // this function instructs
                            // the ENTITY to move to another and then perform
                            // whatever action that the entity would normally
                            // perform. The number returned is a number
                            // corresponding to the action to be performed.
                            // this is also used for an attack
                            // cont is for shift key held so this item is added
                            // to a queue
virtual int     Destination (int x, int y, int cont) {return 0;}
                            // this function instructs
                            // the ENTITY to move to a location and then perform
                            // whatever action that the entity would normally
                            // perform. The x and y are a world location, and
                            // you may need to add offsets for position on the
                            // tile.

virtual int     Damage (int amount) {return 0;}
                            // used for removing resources and attacking an
                            // opponent. An Entity will call the Damage
                            // function of another for this type of transaction.
                            // Other types of entities use this differently
virtual int     Update () {Think (); return 1;}
virtual void    DrawIcon (SCREEN_STRUCT* screen) {}  // this Graphic
virtual void    DrawAnimation (SCREEN_STRUCT* screen) {}
                            // children only, the base class has no animation
virtual bool    Spawn (int x, int y) {return 1;}
                            // try to start at this location. 1 for true, 0
                            // for false
                            // the ENTITY should be smart enough to know what to
                            // do if it is spawned on top of another entity
virtual void    SetEvent (CREATURE_EVENT*e) {}
virtual void    SetGoal (GOAL*g) {}
virtual void    Message (int type, int data1, int data2) {}
                            // respond to input
                            // keys are: type is the key 0-255
                            // data1-with shift key
                            // data2 with-ctrl key
                            // type = 256 means an interface button was pushed
```

18

Chapter

```
                                  // data1 is which button
                                  // if type high bit is set (0x80000000) mouse click
                                  // x = (type&0x7fff0000)>>16;
                                  // y = (type&0xffff);
                                  // data1 is shift key held
                                  // data2 is ctrl key held
          virtual int     Select (int x, int y, int playerID) {return 0;}
                                  // the base entity cannot be selected
          virtual int     Select (int x1, int y1, int x2, int y2, int playerID)
                                       {return 0;}

// access routines
public:
          void            SetCurrentAction (U8 action) {CurrentAction  = action;}
          U8              GetCurrentAction () {return CurrentAction;}

          void            SetPlayerID (int p) {PlayerID = p;}
          int             GetPlayerID () {return PlayerID;}

          void            SetVisible (int onoff = 1) {Visible = onoff;}
          int             GetVisible () {return Visible;}

          void            SetGraphic (GRAPHIC* g) {Graphic  = g;}
          GRAPHIC*        GetGraphic () {return Graphic;}

          // this is a radius-like size
          void            SetEntityDimensions (float x, float y) {SizeX = x,
                                               SizeY = y;}
          float           GetSizeX () {return SizeX;}
          float           GetSizeY () {return SizeY;}

          int             GetDamage () {return Dam;}       // used for health meter.
          void            SetDamage (int d) {Dam = d;}
          void            AddDamage (int d) {Dam+=d; if (Dam>HitPoints)
                                             Dam = HitPoints;}
                          // used for building as well
          void            HealDamage (int d) {Dam-=d; if (Dam<0) Dam = 0;}

          void            SetHitPoints (int p) {HitPoints = p;}
          int             GetHitPoints () {return HitPoints ;}

          void            SetArmor (int a) {Armor = a;}
          int             GetArmor () {return Armor;}

          void            SetMiniMapColor (U16 c) {MiniMapColor = c;}
          U16             GetMiniMapColor () {return MiniMapColor;}

          void            SetSoundID (U16 s) {SoundID = s;}
          U16             GetSoundID () {return SoundID;}

          U16             SetSelectEvent (U16 ID) {U16 temp = SelectEvent;
                          SelectEvent = ID; return SelectEvent;}
```

```
        int             GetType () {return Type;}
```

// these are not necessary so I only put in a few. Remember that we have public
// access to the CreatureFlag structure

```
        // these are here to simplify messing with the flags. The flags are public
        // so you can mess with them directly
        void            SetState (int s) {CreatureFlag.Flag.CURRENT_STATE = s;}
        int             GetState () {return CreatureFlag.Flag.CURRENT_STATE;}

        void            SetGroup (int g) {CreatureFlag.Flag.GROUP_ID = g;}
        int             GetGroup () {return CreatureFlag.Flag.GROUP_ID;}
        void            ClearGroup () {CreatureFlag.Flag.GROUP_ID = 0;}

        void            SetSelected (int onoff = 1)
                        {CreatureFlag.Flag.SELECTED = onoff;}
        int             GetSelected () {return CreatureFlag.Flag.SELECTED;}
        void            ClearSelected () {CreatureFlag.Flag.SELECTED = 0;}

        // relocate. often a bunch of creatures are created on the same tile and
        // this makes the ENTITY find a new home
        void            FindEmptySpot ();
}ENTITY, *ENTITYptr, **ENTITYlist;

//*******************************************
//*******************************************
//*******************************************
#ifdef REMOVE_NULL
#undef NULL
#undef REMOVE_NULL
#endif

#endif
```

Here we have the .cpp file, which only has a few items:

```
// entity.cpp

#ifndef __ENTITY_MGR_
#include "c:/library_cur/entity_mgr.h"
#endif

#ifndef __ENTITY_MGR_
#include "c:/library_cur/entity.h"
#endif


UNIVERSAL_ENTITY_MANAGER* ENTITY :: Manager = NULL;

//*************************

int    ENTITY :: Die ()
```

```
        {
                if (Manager)
                return Manager ->Kill (this);
                return 0;
        }
//***************************
// relocate. often a bunch of creatures are created on the same tile and
//          // this makes the ENTITY find a new home
void ENTITY :: FindEmptySpot ()
        {
                TILE* tile = TileManager->GetTile (wx, wy);
                if (!tile->GetObject ()) return;              // wx and wy are good
                for (int range=1; range<6; range++)
                    for (int x=-1; x<2; x++)
                        {
                                for (int y=-1; y<2; y++)
                                {
                                        tile = TileManager->GetTile (wx+x*range, wy+y*range);
                                        if (tile->GetObject ()) continue;
                                        wx += x*range, wy += y*range;
                                        return;
                                }
                        }
        }
//***************************
```

It initializes the global class variable Manager and initializes the function Die in the ENTITY class. All that Die does is remove the item from the list. This affects updates and basically makes the entity disappear. You'll see more of this in a little while. Also, the UNIVERSAL_ENTITY_MANAGER may want to introduce a dying entity to replace the entity that has died and disappeared.

Where Does an Entity Get His Default Values?

Setting default values is the hard part of initializing an entity. There are dozens of ways to handle this, from hard-coding to databases, from a big modifiable data file to individual entity files. Which way is best? All and none. They all have advantages and drawbacks.

Hard-coding the values for each creature in the game is an option. Usually hard-coding makes things easy to program but makes tweaking the game a chore, sometimes close to impossible. The programming is easy because you can test for fixed values and you always know the range of numbers. You never get freaky values because something was misread when the data was loaded. But when you start preparing for game balancing, one of the last stages before shipping, you may be pulling out your hair because of all the numbers that you will modify and all of the new code that you will have to write. When programming, hard-coding is always fastest but in the long run, it will almost always take longer to implement than any other choice.

All of the values can be loaded from a single database. Age of Empires did this by having several data files that were exported as text, loaded in as text, and then finally saved out again as a data file. Any change to the database involves many steps. Even if you streamline this process, all of the extra code for reading in a database module and then saving the values to an easier loading file can increase the size of the game somewhat significantly. Plus, there is time in loading a database, which is slow. Then there is the extra development time. Still, this method centralizes all data and makes it easy for anyone to understand. This method also makes adding extra fields and completing major changes to landscape or creatures easy.

Dark Reign uses script files for defining behavior, characteristics, weapons, etc. Script files have a lot of the advantages and disadvantages of a database, but in addition the end user can modify them, making the game a little more fun for a few players who bother to look in the install directories.

Having a "template" class that holds all of the characteristics for a particular creature is one method of storing data. One of the variables defined in the ENTITY class is ENTITY_DEFINED. You'll find this defined in entity.h. Its intent is to hold all of the values for a given creature definition. For instance, all Klingon Warbirds should start out with the same basic characteristics, and this class is an ideal way to store the data. It can store all of the animation data, base characteristics, and functionality to support your standard entity. Since it has Load and Save capabilities as well, this class serves many functions, not the least of which is its ability to be easily put into an entity editor. This allows all entities to be completely encapsulated in their own files. They only take up memory in the game if they are loaded. This further encourages expansion packs filled with new creatures and vehicles of war.

Tables can be a good solution for a purely data-driven model. Just creating a database of all creatures in the game and their basic characteristics is a sweet thing. The data is centralized and you can make quick changes. In addition, you can see the characteristics relative to one another, and game balancing (entity balancing in this case) becomes much easier.

The creatures, and all aspects of the game, must be tweakable by the designer with relative ease. This does make the difference between a good game and a bad game. It also simplifies the job (long term) for the programmers. Plus, a more data-driven model allows you to reuse your game engine in future versions of the game, so think long term. Hard-coding will often make your job harder.

However you pursue the data management, the entire game should be designed with the same paradigm. The entities, weapons, and landscape should be loaded in the same way. All things that have characteristics should be maintained the same way to keep consistency in the game and then the rest of the development team knows what to expect. Plus, you are more likely to reuse code, making the development cycle shorter. If nothing else, you'll be able to copy and paste sections of code, saving considerably on time.

Selectable Entities

Although very few items in the world can be drawn but not selected, I decided to move selection to a separate class. In Quake, all fragments flying around the screen are entities, and you'd never be able to select those. The flying polygons in Total Annihilation also are entities and cannot be selected. So I separated them for you. A SELECTABLE_ENTITY has no functionality other than this focus. All other entities will be derived from this class.

```
//****************************************************
class  SELECTABLE_ENTITY : public ENTITY      // this guy can't be drawn except
                                               // as an icon
{
public:
        SELECTABLE_ENTITY () {Clear (); SetType ();}
        void SetType () {Type = SELECTABLE;}

        int  Select (int x, int y)             // mouse selection assumes that
                                               // mouse is configured to world
                                               // coordinates
        {
            if (VerifyLiving == false) return 0;
            if (wx+SizeX>x && wx-SizeX<x && wy+SizeY>y && wy-SizeY<y)
            {
                 CreatureFlag.Flag.SELECTED = !CreatureFlag.Flag.SELECTED;
                                                          // toggle
                 return CreatureFlag.Flag.SELECTED;    // return status
            }
            return 0;
        }
        int  Select (int x1, int y1, int x2, int y2)  // click and drag selection
        {
            if (VerifyLiving == false) return 0;
            if (wx+SizeX<x2 && wx-SizeX>x1 && wy+SizeY<y2 && wy-SizeY>y1)
            {
                 CreatureFlag.Flag.SELECTED = !CreatureFlag.Flag.SELECTED;
                                                          // toggle
                 return CreatureFlag.Flag.SELECTED;    // return status
            }
            return 0;
        }
};
//****************************************************
```

Here we have two kinds of selection. Both assume that the coordinates are in world coordinates, so you'll need to make the necessary conversion to the mouse coordinates before calling either of these functions. The first is a single mouse click type of selection where the mouse clicks on the screen and the nearby entities check whether or not the mouse hit them. The second type is for click and drag where an entity quickly determines if he is fully within the boundaries of a rectangular area.

This class will probably never exist by itself but its functionality is inheritable.

Resource Entities

A resource entity is intended to be like a bank. A player sending resource gathering entities to the resource entity should be able to cut, drill, extract, or obtain some resource. A resource gathering entity can go up to a resource entity and drill by doing damage to the resource entity.

```
//****************************************************
class RESOURCE_ENTITY : public SELECTABLE_ENTITY
```

```
    {
public:
        RESOURCE_ENTITY () {Clear (); SetType ();}
        void SetType () {Type = RESOURCE;}
        int  Update () {wx = 1; return 1;}

        void DrawAnimation (SCREEN_STRUCT* screen)
// only one graphic for the RESOURCE_ENTITY
        {
                if (VerifyLiving ()== false) return;
                if (Graphic == NULL) return;
                // assuming that the screen position has been set
                Graphic->DrawAt (screen, scx, scy);
        }

        //*************

        int  Damage (int amount)
        {
                if (VerifyLiving ()== false) return 0;
                if (amount <=0) return 0;        // we limit the amount of resources
                                                 // extracted
                int ret = 1;
                     if (amount <=2) {Dam ++; }
                else if (amount <=4) {Dam += 2; ret = 2;}
                else if (amount <=6) {Dam += 3; ret = 3;}
                else if (amount <=8) {Dam += 4; ret = 4;}
                else {Dam += 5; ret = 5;}
                if (Dam > HitPoints)
                {
                     Die ();
                }
                return ret;
        }
        //*************
        bool IsEmpty ()
        {
                if (VerifyLiving ()== false) return true;
                if (Dam >= HitPoints) return true;
                return false;
        }
    };
    //*******************************************
```

The return value of the Damage function in the ENTITY class should return a
given amount of resource, and the resource entity should regulate the amount of
resource given out. Once the resource entity has full damage, it contacts the
UNIVERSAL_ENTITY_MANAGER with a message to delete itself (the resource entity,
that is). This is trivial. The RESOURCE_ENTITY kills itself after taking enough damage. Like the SOLDIER_ENTITY, the RESOURCE_GATHERER_ENTITY will do damage
to the resource entity, but before it "attacks," it will verify that the item exists. We'll

cover this later, but a resource, once all mined out, can disappear. The RESOURCE_
GATHERER_ENTITY needs to be sure that the RESOURCE_ENTITY is still valid; it can
verify that through the UNIVERSAL_ENTITY_MANAGER. We'll cover it in a while.
There is an IsValid function that every ENTITY must use before it can continue to do
whatever it is doing to a particular ENTITY. It would be bad to be mining gold from a
rock and then have the rock disappear; you'd have an invalid pointer or a pointer to a
dead object. Bad in either case.

Goals

The GOAL structure is dynamic and reminiscent of the old days of C where you never
knew exactly what values a structure had until you examined its type. This type of
dynamic structure manipulation could be better handled by a hierarchy of classes in
C++. But this is unnecessary overhead, and this structure is simple enough that creating a complex hierarchy isn't warranted. This structure is one of the keys for AI. All
creatures need to move from one goal to another. Most world creatures need direction
and they perform their assigned tasks based on goals. Even if your creatures will be
freethinking, goal-based state systems are the simplest to program and certainly the
most reliable—once you work out the bugs.

Notice that all of the destination-based goals are first. This allows for simplified
testing when you want to make sure which variables you are using. Look at the
Unions for an idea. You want to make sure that you are using the proper data.

```
//********************************
struct GOAL
{
        int  Action:6;       // 64 possibilities
        int  DT   :1;        // 0 uses target, 1 uses tile
        int  SH   :1;        // 0 uses start, 1 uses home
        int  Info :24;       // extra information, for building, tells what type
                             // can be used for anything

        enum ACTIONS   {GO_TO_DESTINATION,
                        GUARD_DESTINATION,
                        RUN_TO_DESTINATION,

                        GO_TO_TARGET,
                        ENTER_TARGET,           // ship, buildings
                        ATTACK_TARGET,
                        OBTAIN_TARGET,
                        RESOURCE_GATHERING,
                        BUILD_TARGET,
                        CAPTURE_TARGET,
                        REPAIR_TARGET,
                        BOARD_TARGET,
                        MOUNT_TARGET,
                        CHANGE_WEAPON,
                        RUN_TO_TARGET,
                        TRIGGER_TARGET,
                        GUARD_TARGET,
```

```
                        SUBDUE_TARGET,
                        WAIT,              // info for how long
                        };
        union
        {
            TILE*       Dest;
            ENTITY*     Target;
        };
        union
        {
            TILE*       Start;
            ENTITY*     Home;            // can be start location
        };
        GOAL*           next;
};
//********************************
```

Now let's look at the QUEUE:

```
// queue.h
//********************************


#if _MSC_VER >= 1000
#pragma once
#endif // _MSC_VER >= 1000


#ifndef __QUEUE_H_
#define __QUEUE_H_

// queue.h
#include <string.h>

#define FC __fastcall


//*************************************************************
//*************************************************************

template <class type>
class QUEUE
{
public:
        enum    {MAXENTRIES = 128};
protected:
        type*       array;
        int         Max, Begin, End, SearchBegin, SearchEnd;
        int         OverWriteFlag;
            // a flag to overwrite old data as new data is pushed onto the
            // queue, otherwise new data does not go on the queue until old
            // stuff is popped

        int         LastItemFlag;   // used to make the last item useful
```

```
                void        InitArray ();
                void        CleanupArray ();

        public:
                QUEUE ();
                QUEUE (int num);
                ~QUEUE ();
                //***********************
                void        FC  Push (type* obj);
                type*       FC  Pop ();
                type*       FC  Peek ();      // look at the bottom item
                type*       FC  Push ();      // get an item to use
                //************************
                void        FC  Clear ();
                //***********************
                type*       FC  GetNext ();
                type*       FC  GetFirst ();
                //***********************
                int         FC  Count ();
        };

        //*************************************************************
        //*************************************************************

        template <class type>
        QUEUE <type> :: QUEUE ()
        {
                Max = MAXENTRIES;
                InitArray ();
        }


        //************************************
        
        template <class type>
        QUEUE <type> :: QUEUE (int num)
        {
                Max = num;
                InitArray ();
        }


        //************************************

        template <class type>
        QUEUE <type> :: ~QUEUE ()
        {
                CleanupArray ();
        }
        //*************************************************************
        //*************************************************************

        template <class type>
        void  QUEUE <type> :: Push (type* obj)
```

```
{
        if (LastItemFlag == 1) return; // in case we've already used the last item
        if ((End+1 == Begin) || (End+1>=Max && Begin == 0))
                        LastItemFlag = 1;                  // do not overlap old data

        memcpy (&array[End], obj, sizeof (type));       // copy data

        // in case it changed so we don't advance the index
        if (LastItemFlag == 1) return;

        End++; if (End>=Max) End = 0;                   // the wrap around
}


//*************************************

template <class type>
type* QUEUE <type> :: Push ()                           // get an item to use
{
        if (LastItemFlag == 1) return NULL;             // in case we've already
                                                        // used the last item
        if ((End+1 == Begin) || (End+1>=Max && Begin == 0))
                        LastItemFlag = 1;                  // do not overlap old data

        /*memcpy (&array[End], obj, sizeof (type));       // copy data*/

        // in case it changed so we don't advance the index
        if (LastItemFlag == 1) return &array[End];

        End++; if (End>=Max) End = 0;                   // the wrap around
        return &array[End];
}


//*************************************

template <class type>
type* QUEUE <type> :: Pop ()
{
        if (Begin == End) return NULL;                  // no data
        int temp = Begin;                               // store this value
        Begin++; if (Begin>=Max) Begin = 0;             // advance the pointer
        LastItemFlag = 0;                               // reset flag
        return &array[temp];                            // return the queue value
}


//*************************************

template <class type>
type* QUEUE <type> :: Peek ()                           // look at the top item
{
        if (Begin == End) return NULL;                  // no top item
        return &array[Begin];                           // return the queue value
}
```

18

Chapter

```
//**************************************************************
//**************************************************************

template <class type>
type* QUEUE <type> :: GetNext ()
{
      if (SearchBegin == SearchEnd) return NULL;        // no data
      int temp = SearchBegin;                           // store this value
      SearchBegin++; if (SearchBegin>=Max) Begin = 0;   // advance the pointer
      LastItemFlag = 0;                                 // reset flag
      return &array[SearchBegin++];                     // return the queue value
}


//*************************************

template <class type>
type* QUEUE <type> :: GetFirst ()
{
      SearchBegin = Begin, SearchEnd = End;
      if (Begin == End) return NULL;                    // no data
      return &array[SearchBegin++];                     // return the queue value
}
//**************************************************************

template <class type>
void  QUEUE <type> :: Clear ()
{
      Begin = 0; End = 0; LastItemFlag = 0;
      memset (array, 0, sizeof (type)*Max);
}


//**************************************************************


template <class type>
void  QUEUE <type> :: InitArray ()
{
      array = new type[Max];
      Clear ();
}


//*************************************

template <class type>
void  QUEUE <type> :: CleanupArray ()
{
      delete array;
}


//*************************************
template <class type>
int  QUEUE <type> :: Count ()
```

```
    {
            int count = 0;
            if (Begin > End)
            {
                    count += Max-Begin;
                    count += End;
            }
            else
            {
                    count += End-Begin;
            }
            return count;
    }
    //************************************************************
    #undef FC
    #endif
    //************************************************************
```

You may remember the QUEUE call from Chapter 3; here it is again in all its glory. Because it is a template, the variable type doesn't matter, so declare it as a GOAL QUEUE. Each creature in the world that will have more than one goal assigned to it should have its own queue. The problem with this system is memory overload. If each creature has 20 goals, that's 320 bytes plus pointers to the queue, for a grand total of 324. Now if your game supports 800 creatures in the world at the same time (the type that can have queues, not trees, rocks, or rivers), you're looking at 250 K just for queues. Well, that really isn't very much memory after all. Really, go ahead and use queues. Just for the heck of it, I'd limit each creature to either 12 or 16 items in its queue. (I believe that Dark Reign has a limit of eight queued items.) Also, feel free to add an item or two to the GOAL structure. Just remember that each byte you add to the structure takes at least 9 K in the game.

I'm pretty sure Total Annihilation has a goal pool. That is, there is a huge pool of goals allocated and a creature just requests one from the pool when it needs it. This is a great paradigm that allows an almost unlimited number of queue items for any single creature. However, unless the queue is really large, you can run out of items fairly quickly. Another minor problem is looking through the pool quickly to find one that is available. Perhaps Cavedog uses something like the TAG_LIST and can check 8 bytes at a time.

Now that we have all of these items, let's look at an entity that can take orders.

Queued Entities

These poor saps do very little but use resources and create other entities. Sometimes they don't even do that much. In case the term eludes you, building entities need queues to track orders and to know which items to build next. They are any type of building construction such as houses, farms, mines, granaries, trans-warp conduits, teleporters, unit generation modules, town centers, launch pads, etc. Buildings sit there and take orders. Age of Empires and earlier RTS/RTT games had simple buildings that could only do one thing at a time. Now, all RTS/RTT games that I know of allow buildings to queue up long lists of items. Since buildings can really only do a few things, you might try the approach that Cavedog did. Instead of a queue for each item, the building has a 1-byte counter for every type of unit it can build. A left-click on a button on the interface increments the counter and a right-click decrements this same counter. Great interface idea and simple to implement.

Still, all buildings have a queue for other things like telling each unit where to go once it is built. In this section, we'll create a generic QUEUED_ENTITY and then we'll create a more specific BUILDING_ENTITY. The QUEUED_ENTITY will be used throughout the rest of the chapter as a base class since almost all future entities we discuss will require a queue.

Now to complicate issues, many buildings create new units. Also, entities that can shoot spawn the entity that flies across the screen and hits an opponent, a projectile-type entity. By that same token, the PROJECTILE entity needs to have a pointer to the entity that produced it. So at this point, it seems prudent to add a few new variables. The building will have a series of goals to use as a way of storing player input. Since this is a common thing that all entities accepting player input need, we'll derive all other entities from the QUEUED_ENTITY.

```
//***************************************************

class QUEUED_ENTITY : public SELECTABLE_ENTITY    // animation and all
{
protected:
        QUEUE<GOAL>*              Goals;
        QUEUE<CREATURE_EVENT>*    Events;
        GOAL*                     CurrentGoal;

protected:                                          // animation stuff
        ANIMATION_MGR*            Anim;
        U8                        CurrentFrame;
        U8                        Direction;
        ANIMATION_DATA :: ANIM_TYPES
                                  CurrentAnim;       // which animation sequence
        U8                        Delay;             // delay until the next frame
                                                     // of animation or movement


        //********************

protected:                                          // functions
        void ConvertStateIntoAnimState ()           // the state of the entity
            // doesn't necessarily correspond to an animation sequence
        {
            CurrentAnim = ANIMATION_DATA :: NONE;
        }
        bool IsCurrentGoalFulfilled ()
        {
            // based on CurrentGoal
            return true;
        }
        void GetNextGoal ()
        {
```

```
            CurrentGoal = Goals->Pop ();
            // here we would set animation and all
            // parameters for the completion of this goal
            // the CreatureFlags structure would be initialized with everything
      }
      void ConvertEventIntoGoal (CREATURE_EVENT* e)
      {
            // conversion code goes here, could be mouse click in the
            // world, on another creature
            // or just about anything, see ai_skills.h
      }
      bool ProcessEvents ()
      {
            CREATURE_EVENT* e = Events->GetFirst ();
            if (e == NULL) return false;
            do
            {
            ConvertEventIntoGoal (e);
            }while ((e = Events->GetFirst ()) != NULL);
            return true;
      }
      void UpdateStatus ()
      {
            // heal hit points from time
            // gain experience, etc
            // move position in the world
            // anything to do with variables or status
            ConvertStateIntoAnimState ();
            Events->Clear ();
      }


      //********************
public:
      QUEUED_ENTITY()
      {
            Goals = new QUEUE <GOAL> (12);             // up to 12 items
            Events = new QUEUE <CREATURE_EVENT> (7);  // up to 7 items per frame
            Clear (); SetType ();
      }
      ~QUEUED_ENTITY () {delete Goals; delete Events;}
      void Clear () {ENTITY :: Clear (); CurrentFrame = 0, Direction = 0,
                                          Delay = ;}
      void SetType () {Type = QUEUED;}
      void SetAnimation (ANIMATION_MGR*a) {Anim = a;}
      // this is where the new class takes over the hierarchy
      virtual void    DrawAnimation (SCREEN_STRUCT* screen)
      {
            if (VerifyLiving ()== false) return;
            if (Anim == NULL) return;
            int x = wx, y = wy;
            ConvertCoordinatesToScreenCoordinates (x, y, offx, offy); // returns
            // there needs to be a conversion here but for now this will
```

```
            // do for illustration purposes.

            Anim->SetAnimType (CurrentAnim);
            Anim->SetFrame (CurrentFrame);
            Anim->SetDirection ((ANIMATION :: DIR) Direction);
            Anim->DrawAt (screen, x, y);
            scx = screen->Width;
        }
    virtual int          Update ()
        {
            if (VerifyLiving ()== false) return 0;
            if (Delay-->0) return 0;
            ProcessEvents ();
            if (IsCurrentGoalFulfilled ()) GetNextGoal ();
            UpdateStatus ();
            // get the next frame
            Anim->SetAnimType (CurrentAnim);
            Anim->SetFrame (CurrentFrame);
            Anim->SetDirection ((ANIMATION :: DIR) Direction);
            Anim->NextFrame ();
            int x, y, z, d;
            Anim->GetOffsetData (&x, &y, &z, &d);       // get new offset data
            Delay = d;
            wx+=x, wy+=y, wz+=z;       // recalculate world position based on
                                       // requirements of the animation
            CurrentFrame = Anim->GetFrame ();
            return 1;
        }
};

//****************************************************
```

The core of the functionality for this and all children is in the new functions hidden as new protected functions. The first of these is ConvertStateIntoAnimState. It takes the entities current state and finds the correct animation to be associated with that. This will probably be unique for every type of creature in your game. However you encapsulate this, keep in mind that many times animation can be used for several different things. Attacking and mining look a lot alike, and a building animates the same no matter what it is generating, unless you deem otherwise. This is where you can use a data-driven model to link animation and actions. Also, if you use the member variable Entity (ENTITY_DEFINED*) to maintain this data, you can simply look it up.

The second new function is IsCurrentGoalFulfilled. Every update cycle, the entity in question will make sure that he hasn't completed his goal, assuming, of course, that he has goals. If he has killed his enemy, gotten to his destination, or finished building the new tank he was constructing, he will return TRUE. At that point, the entity will see what is next in his queue of things to work on. That brings us to the GetNextGoal function, which changes the CurrentGoal to whatever is on top of the queue. This could be NULL, and it often is so the entity will need to change into a waiting mode.

Our next new function is ConvertEventIntoGoal. During a frame of animation, an entity may receive a mouse click or a keyboard entry or two. The EVENT queue is set for seven items so that we can have several things happen during any single frame. Anything that may affect the status of an entity should be considered an event. The event must be stored and the entity will respond to it during the frame of animation. An alternative to the EVENT queue is to have the linked list. This allows a variable number of events and keeps memory free. There can be too many things happening during any given frame and you can run out of CREATURE_EVENT structures unless you use the ALLOCATOR class to maintain the list. This can slow things, especially if you are maintaining hundreds of events for 800 creatures. Still, it is a viable alternative and you should carefully weigh the two choices: a self-maintained queue as a memory hog and limited numbers of events or a global list which can be slower to find available items and even slower when things get busy. The CREATURE_EVENT structure is in the next section.

Our fifth new function is ProcessEvents. It is intended to convert all new events into goals or damage or healing, etc. This is a conversion process during updates. That's all.

Our last new function is UpdateStatus, which is called to change status like taking damage or any other response to events. This function should look through its event queue and heal, take damage, and so on, as appropriate. The queue will be cleared after all updating is completed.

All other changes are initialization features, implementation of these new functions, or animation related features. This class pretty much defines how all children from now on will perform.

One other function to note is a global called ConvertCoordinatesToScreenCoordinates. This will allow the object in question to be drawn at the proper location when the draw loop continues.

The Event

The CREATURE_EVENT is a variable structure. Its data members can be a wide variety of things depending on the type of event. Obscure or difficult event types were left out. The Event member stores the type of info. The other variable types can be used for a host of things. My suggestions can be found in the comments following the variables and enums.

```
//*******************************************
struct CREATURE_EVENT
{
      U8        Event;
      int       Data;
      int       Type;
      void*     Data1;      // target
      void*     Data2;      // often used for a pointer to the source of an event
                            // if a creature dies as a result of this event, he
                            // knows who to give credit to
                            // if the entity who created the event dies, he will
                            // stay in limbo for about a second, so he can still
                            // credit the player
```

```
            enum EVENT {SELECT_SELF,    // the mouse has clicked on you, change state,
                                        // or deselect. Data=1 on, Data=0 off
                       MOUSE_CLICK,     // Data is X, Type is Y, world coordinates
                       KEYBOARD_PRESS,  // Data is which key

                       SET_DESTINATION,
                       TAKE_DAMAGE,     // Data points 0-255, type is type of damage
                       TAKE_COMMAND,    // new command given, Type is event type,
                       FINISHED_GOAL,   // a Target may tell the creature that it is
                                        // done
                       SET_ACTOR,       // creature to notify when finished, type is
                                        // action mostly healing or harming
                       BECOME_HUNGRY,   // creature may notify itself to find food
                       DIE,             // creature has died and it will clean itself
                                        // up on the next update cycle.
                       LIVE,            // items in construction are told when they
                                        // can live
                       DESTINATION_REACHED, // creature can tell itself that the
                                        // destination has been reached and then grab
                                        // the next item in its queue to do.
                       MINED,           // remove an amount of whatever resource you
                                        // provide  and give it to ENTITY at Data1
                       KILLED,          // notification that the target has been killed
                                        // by you
                       CONSTRUCT        // Data=0 = at same location, Data=1 = remotely
                                        // Type=x, (int) Data1=y, (int) Data2 = z
                       };

        //CREATURE_EVENT* next;    // may be linked list, maybe not
};
//*******************************************
```

Moving Entities

Very similar to the QUEUED_ENTITY, this class is used to represent the animating entity that moves. The design changed quite a long time ago but I feel the need to leave this class in the hierarchy. Other non-animating entities like trees could still be destroyed and hence need a queue, so those are now queued entities. The only difference between moving and non-moving entities is whether or not they animate, so you may want to eliminate this class from the hierarchy or you may find another need for it. Otherwise, it is identical. The animation was moved up to the queued entity, and this structure became hidden in the design.

The only thing left here is path finding. You could move this into the queued entity, but I like it here. Path finding is dealt with in Chapter 19.

```
//*******************************************

class MOVING_ENTITY : public QUEUED_ENTITY
{
protected:
    int   PathIDNumber;
```

```
        U8    TimeSinceLastPath;              // wait at least 30 frames between
                                              // path finding
protected:
        void FindPath ();
        bool AtDestination ();                // for moving only

public:
        MOVING_ENTITY () {Clear (); SetType ();}
        void SetType () {Type = MOVING;}
        void Clear () {QUEUED_ENTITY:: Clear (); PathIDNumber = -1;}
        int  Update ();
};
```

//***

Here is the new code. It is easy to read, so go to it. AtDestination simply determines if the moving entity got to where it was going.

//*************************

```
void MOVING_ENTITY :: FindPath ()
{
        if (AtDestination ())
        {
            PathIDNumber == -1;
            Goals->Pop ();                    // get the top item off
            return;
        }
        GOAL* g = Goals->Peek ();
        int a = g->Action;
        int old = PathIDNumber;

        if (PathManager)                      // here we update the path
            // until we have found the full path
        {
            if (a == GOAL :: GO_TO_DESTINATION)
            {
                PathIDNumber = PathManager->GetPath (wx, wy,
                        g->Dest->GetWorldX (), g->Dest->GetWorldY ());
                PathManager->FreePath (old);
            }
            if (a == GOAL :: GO_TO_TARGET)
            {
                PathIDNumber = PathManager->GetPath (wx, wy,
                        g->Target->GetWorldX (), g->Target->GetWorldY ());
                PathManager->FreePath (old);
            }
        }
}
//*************************

int     MOVING_ENTITY :: Update ()
{
```

18

Chapter

```
        if (QUEUED_ENTITY :: Update () == false) return 0;
        if (TimeSinceLastPath++ >=90)           // once every 3 seconds
        {
            TimeSinceLastPath = 0;
            if (CreatureFlag.Flag.FULL_PATH_FOUND == 0)
            {
                FindPath ();
            }
        }
        return 1;
}
//**************************
//**************************
bool MOVING_ENTITY :: AtDestination ()          // for moving only
{
        GOAL* g = Goals->Peek ();               // what is the top item
        int a = g->Action;
        int dx = -2, dy = -2;
        if (a == GOAL :: GO_TO_DESTINATION)
        {
            dx = g->Dest->GetWorldX (), dy = g->Dest->GetWorldY ();
        }
        else if (a == GOAL :: GO_TO_TARGET ||
            a == GOAL :: ENTER_TARGET ||
            a == GOAL :: ATTACK_TARGET ||
            a == GOAL :: OBTAIN_TARGET ||
            a == GOAL :: RESOURCE_GATHERING ||
            a == GOAL :: BUILD_TARGET)          // etc, most goals use this
        {
            dx = g->Target->GetWorldX (), dy = g->Target->GetWorldY ();
        }
        else return true;           // not a moving destination, must be true

        // if you are within one tile, you are there
        if (dx-1<=wx && dx+1>=wx && dy-1<=wy && dy+1>=wy)
            return true;
        return false;
}
//**************************
```

Construction Entities

Now we come to something new. A factory or training center qualifies as a construction entity. Also, a peon who builds or other building units need some of the functionality here.

```
//*********************************************
class CONSTRUCTION_ENTITY : public MOVING_ENTITY
                // not all CONSTRUCTION_ENTITY's move
                // but this allows peons and buildings both to do construction
                // which is identical in scope
                // a peon will construct an entity on the map and a building
```

```
                     // will construct an entity inside of itself

{
protected:
        enum {MAX_ITEMS_BUILT = 12};              // don't make it too much larger

        QUEUE<ENTITY*>* ItemsBeingBuilt;      // pointer to items to be built
                        // these items have already been requested from
                        // the UNIVERSAL_ENTITY_MANAGER and they exist but
                        // cannot get update time because they are considered
                        // dead until this class tells it it can live.
                        // if this CONSTRUCTION_ENTITY dies while building,
                        // it will kill all of the items on the list freeing
                        // them for someone else to use.
                        // this CONSTRUCTION_ENTITY owns these items until they
                        // are finished being built.

        int  HealPoints;            // how much building can this entity do
                        // i.e. Constructing a house with 300 building points
                        // if this entity has 10 ConstPoints, he will take 30
                        // seconds to construct doing 10 points per second

        ENTITY* ConstructEntity (int type);

        void ConvertEventIntoGoal (CREATURE_EVENT* e)
        {
            // conversion code goes here, could be mouse click in the
            // world, on another creature
            // or just about anything, see ai_skills.h
            if (e->Event == CREATURE_EVENT :: CONSTRUCT)
            {

                ENTITY* ent = ConstructEntity (e->Type);
                if (e->Data == 1)
                {
                    ent->SetWorldCoordinates (e->Type,
                        (int) e->Data1,
                        (int) e->Data2);
                }
            }
        }

public:
        CONSTRUCTION_ENTITY ()
        {
            Clear ();
            SetType ();

        }
        ~CONSTRUCTION_ENTITY () {delete ItemsBeingBuilt;}
        void SetType () {Type = CONSTRUCTION;}
        void Clear ()
```

```
        {
                QUEUED_ENTITY :: Clear ();
                HealPoints = 2;
                // never more than 12 items being built at a time
                ItemsBeingBuilt = new QUEUE <ENTITY*> (MAX_ITEMS_BUILT);
        }
        int        Update ();

public:
        void SetHealPoints (int x = 2) {HealPoints = x;}
        int  GetHealPoints () {return HealPoints;}
};
//********************************************
```

First, I create a queue that holds pointers only (memory saver among other things) and I limit it to 12 items. Again, creating a huge bank of pointers and then managing queued items with a linked list is an option that I chose not to pursue. You might like the idea.

Next we have a new variable for healing or repairing called HealPoints. This building creates items from scratch so they will have hit points of 0, or the equivalent, which is full damage. HealPoints gives them a certain number of hit points per frame of animation. Pretty cool, if you ask me. This is currently set for a frame-by-frame basis but you can change it by adding a second variable for counting frames until one round of healing can occur.

This entity is similar to others but now it responds to build commands.

In the .cpp file, you'll find the following two functions. These define the essence of the CONSTRUCTION_ENTITY, which creates new creatures to be destroyed by your opponents.

```
//************************
ENTITY*  CONSTRUCTION_ENTITY :: ConstructEntity (int type)
{
        // needs to be coded according to need
        if (Manager == NULL) return NULL;
        if (ItemsBeingBuilt->Count () == MAX_ITEMS_BUILT)
            return NULL;                        // queue is full

        // spawn at my location
        ENTITY* e = Manager->Spawn (wx, wy, wz, type);
        e->SetDamage (e->GetHitPoints ());   // start with full damage
        e->CreatureFlag.Flag.ALIVE = 0;
        ItemsBeingBuilt->Push (&e);

        return e;
};


//************************

int     CONSTRUCTION_ENTITY :: Update ()
{
```

```
                    if (VerifyLiving () == false) return 0;
                    return QUEUED_ENTITY :: Update ();

                    ENTITY** e = ItemsBeingBuilt->Peek ();
                    if (e == NULL) return 1;
                    if (Manager->IsValid (e) == false)
                    {
                            ItemsBeingBuilt->Pop ();    // clear item off stack
                                                        // probably killed during construction
                            return 1;
                    }
                    (*e)->HealDamage (HealPoints);
                                                        // take item off list for construction
                    if ((*e)->GetDamage () == 0)
                            ItemsBeingBuilt->Pop ();
                                                        // now updates will mean something
                    (*e)->CreatureFlag.Flag.ALIVE = 1;
                    return 1;

            }
            //**************************
```

The ConstructEntity function relies on the UNIVERSAL_ENTITY_MANAGER to provide a new ENTITY to work with, provided that its own queue isn't already full. Then it sets the new creature to be fully ready to go by setting its damage to full. The creature won't be alive, meaning that its updates will fall out and the creature won't do anything. Drawing will also not work until the creature is alive.

The Update function does all of the normal graphics updating and then goes on to continue healing the entity that you created. Once the entity is complete, it is removed from the list, allowing the next item to be created during the next update cycle.

Note: Keep in mind that once this creature is finished being built, you'll need to give it all of the characteristics that make it unique. You are likely to have three or four types of tanks and the CONSTRUCTION_ ENTITY constructs them all the same. They would all be simply MOVING_ENTITY's; you'll need to add extra parameters to the CONSTRUCTION_ENTITY so that it knows what type of tank to start constructing.

Peon and Resource Gathering Entities

This is where we pick up things in the world, go home, and return. Everything here is related to extracting resources from one entity and carrying it to a building nearby. You'll have to code the part about finding a nearby building, but most of the rest is here. Each entity has an amount he can carry called CarryingCapacity, the current amount he is carrying called Carry, the strength with which he can extract resources called ExtractAmount, and ResourceType, which is self-explanatory.

We've added a few new functions to serve the new member variables and a few others to reflect the new functionality. This is otherwise a standard QUEUED_ENTITY.

```
//***********************************************
class RESOURCE_GATHERER_ENTITY : public MOVING_ENTITY
{
protected:
        int  CarryingCapacity;
        int  Carry;              // how much am I carrying
        int  ExtractAmount;      // how much can I extract
        int  ResourceType;

protected:
        void DumpResource ();
        ENTITY* FindHome ()       // find nearest home
        {
                return NULL;       // you'll need to code this to
                                   // be a nearby construction entity
        }
        void ConvertEventIntoGoal (CREATURE_EVENT* e);

public:
        RESOURCE_GATHERER_ENTITY () {Clear (); SetType ();}
        void SetType () {Type = RESOURCE_GATHERER;}
        void Clear ()
        {
                QUEUED_ENTITY :: Clear ();
                CarryingCapacity = 10;
                Carry = 0;
                ResourceType = 0;
        }

        int  Update ();

public:

        void SetCarryingCapacity (int cc) {CarryingCapacity = cc;}
        int  GetCarryingCapacity () {return CarryingCapacity;}

        void SetExtractAmount (int e) {ExtractAmount = e;}
        int  GetExtractAmount () {return ExtractAmount;}

        bool ArmsEmpty () {if (Carry<CarryingCapacity) return true; return
                          false;}
                                   // any amount is enough
        bool ArmsFull () {if (Carry) return true; return false;}

};
//***********************************************
```

And here are the new functions in the .cpp file:

```
//**************************
int    RESOURCE_GATHERER_ENTITY :: Update ()
```

```
           {
               if (AtDestination ())
               {
                   GOAL* g = Goals->Peek ();
                   ENTITY* t = g->Target;
                   int a = g->Action;
                   if (a > GOAL :: RUN_TO_DESTINATION)
                   {
                       if (ArmsEmpty ())
                       {
                           if (t->GetType () == RESOURCE)
                           {
                               if (Manager->IsValid ((RESOURCE_ENTITY*)t) == false
                                   || ((RESOURCE_ENTITY*)t)->IsEmpty () == true)
                               {
                                   g->Target = g->Home;
                                   g->Home = t;
                                   FindPath ();
                                   goto END;
                               }
                               if (t->GetType () == RESOURCE)
                               {
                                   Carry += ((RESOURCE_ENTITY*)t)->Damage
                                           (ExtractAmount);
                                   // we can't carry that much
                                   if (Carry>=CarryingCapacity)
                                   {
                                       // put it back
                                       ((RESOURCE_ENTITY*)t)->HealDamage
                                           (Carry-CarryingCapacity);

                                       g->Target = g->Home; // swap destinations
                                       g->Home = t;
                                       FindPath ();          // go home
                                   }
                                   goto END;
                               }
                           }
                       }
                       if (ArmsFull () && t->GetType () == CONSTRUCTION)
                               // assuming building
                       {     // simple swap  ... go back for more
                             // here we drop the resources in the player structure
                             g->Target = g->Home;
                             g->Home = t;
                             FindPath ();
                             DumpResource ();
                       }
                   }
               }
           END:
               if (MOVING_ENTITY :: Update () == 0) return 0;
```

```
                return 1;
        }
//****************************
void RESOURCE_GATHERER_ENTITY :: DumpResource ()
{
        Carry = 0;
        // here you should contact the player and give him the resource.
}
//****************************
void RESOURCE_GATHERER_ENTITY :: ConvertEventIntoGoal (CREATURE_EVENT* e)
{
        // conversion code goes here, could be mouse click in the
        // world, on another creature
        // or just about anything, see ai_skills.h
        if (e->Event == CREATURE_EVENT :: SET_DESTINATION)
        {
                GOAL* g = Goals->Push ();        // get blank goal
                if (g == NULL) return;           // uh oh
                if (e->Data1)
                {
                        // this will vary from entity to entity
                        g->Action = GOAL :: GO_TO_TARGET;
                        g->Target = (ENTITY*) e->Data1;
                        g->Home = FindHome ();
                }
                else
                {
                        // this will vary from entity to entity
                        g->Action = GOAL :: GO_TO_DESTINATION;
                        if (TileManager)
                        {
                                g->Dest = TileManager->GetTile (e->Data, e->Type);
                                g->Start = TileManager->GetTile (wx, wy);
                        }
                }
        }
}
//****************************
```

We have a little interaction here between entities as well. The Update checks to see if we are at our destination, whatever that is; if so, we proceed to check if we are ready to return to where we started. You'll notice the validation where we call the function IsValid in the Update function. A resource can be used up, destroyed, or whatever, and you'll need to make sure that the item in question is still valid. You'll always need to verify that an entity hasn't died before you proceed; there's no sense trying to extract gold from an empty mine.

Fire and Consumption Entities

These entities devour others. They can attack all directions at once, affecting multiple items. They only exist as long as something nearby exists to attack and then they disappear. For all intents and purposes, treat them like soldier entities with a limited life span.

Soldier Entities

Let's start by introducing weapons. After all, what good is a soldier without weapons? Some might argue that the heart of a soldier is all that matters, but it is awfully hard to show the heart of a soldier in a real-time strategy game.

Every weapon requires power cells, bullets, or some other means of producing the destructive force of which they are capable. These power cells have a few simple characteristics, although, if you try, you can come up with a few more.

```
//*******************************************
//*******************************************

struct POWERCELL
{
        enum ENERGYTYPE
                {
                        ELECTRICAL,
                        BULLETS,
                        PROJECTILES,
                        GELATIN,            // plasma
                        GASOLINE_GEL,       // flame thrower
                        TNT,
                        MANA,
                        OXYGEN,
                        SODIUM,
                        CHEMICAL,           // chemical container
                        BIOLOGICAL,         // biological container
                };
        ENERGYTYPE Type;
        int        Amount;
        U8         PauseBetweenBursts;  // some batteries must recharge
                                        // in between shooting
        U8         FrameCount;

        POWERCELL ()
        {
            Type = BULLETS,
            Amount = 6,
            PauseBetweenBursts = 0;
            FrameCount = 0;
        }
};

//*******************************************
```

Type is the energy type. You may not need this for your game, but it can be helpful for some. The variable Amount holds the number of bullets, the amount of electrical charges, or the amount of gas gel left. It may take a few seconds before you can fire an electrical battery again. The variable associated with this limitation is

PauseBetweenBursts. The last variable is FrameCount, which tells you the amount of time that has passed since you last fired. This is updated every frame.

These structures can be found in weapon.h.

Next, we have the weapon definition:

```
//*********************************************

struct WEAPON
{
    enum TYPE
          {
                  INCENDIARY,
                  PROJECTILE1,
                  PROJECTILE2,
                  BLAST,
                  RADIATION,
                  ENERGY1,
                  ENERGY2,
                  PLASMA,
                  LASER1,
                  LASER2,
                  FLAME_THROWER,
                  CANNON,
                  DISINTEGRATOR,
                  WAND,
                  SPELL,
                  CHEMICAL_SPRAYER,      // you need gas mask
                  BIOLOGICAL_SPRAYER,    // ditto
          };
    GRAPHIC*   Graphic;                  // icon
    float      Range;                    // how far can we shoot
    float      AOE;                      // area of effect in tiles

    U8             Type:6;               // up to 64
    U8             ShowProjectile:2;     // 1 plus filler
    U8             DiceNum, DiceSides, DiceAdd;     // points of damage done
    U8             EnergyUsagePerShot1, EnergyUsagePerShot2;

    //ANIMATION*   Animation;//          // generally not used, the animation of
                                         // the entity is usually modified, but it
                                         // may be animated in the interface
    POWERCELL Cell1, Cell2;              // some weapons require 2 energy sources

    WEAPON ()
    {
        Type = PROJECTILE1,
        Graphic = OL,
        Cell2.Amount = 0;                // cell2 is not charged.
        Range = 6.5;                     // shooting far away
        ShowProjectile = 0;              // will generate a projectile when fired.
                                         // some weapons like bullets don't show up
        EnergyUsagePerShot1 = 1, EnergyUsagePerShot2 = 1;
```

```
        }
};
```

```
//*********************************************
```

The WEAPON structure has a type that tells us the kind of weapon it is. Each weapon should have its own graphics and effects. The weapon range follows. I made it a float value to figure in half tiles or some other fractional value. It's your call. Type has 6 bits (overkill if you ask me) for storing the type of weapon. The flag ShowProjectile lets us know if this weapon generates a projectile that the player can see like an arrow, cannonball, or missile. When the SOLDIER_ENTITY fires or attacks, he then knows to try and generate a projectile.

The next five variables may seem a bit odd but they help considerably. The variables DiceNum, DiceSides, and DiceAdd all work together to generate the damage points that a weapon generates. Think in terms of rolling dice. DiceSides is the number of sides for a die, DiceNum is how many dice, and DiceAdd is any amount that you may add to raise the average. This system allows averaging. If you have a six-sided die, the odds are even that you'll roll a 1, 2, or 6 (or any other number), but that's not true of two six-sided dice. The odds of rolling a 7 are 1 in 6 but rolling a 2 is only 1 in 18. You can play with the averages all day, but the system works in your favor. It is more difficult to use (slightly) than other systems.

Now, based on the energy cell (Cell1 and Cell2), EnergyUsagePerShot1 and EnergyUsagePerShot2 tell us how much energy to use for each shot. Simply deduct that from the Cells and you are doing your record keeping like you should. Notice the Cell1 and Cell2. Most games will have just a Cell1 with unlimited energy, but maybe a small delay on firing. This structure allows you to freely upgrade a weapon by adding a new cell. If the weapon works great with a battery but even better with sodium, this is a cool way to offer these upgrades. Consider it game depth, courtesy of Mickey Kawick.

Below we have the actual soldier definition. Only a few new functions have been added, but the weapons have also been added, including a little intelligence for picking the proper weapon.

```
//*********************************************
```

```
class SOLDIER_ENTITY : public MOVING_ENTITY
{
protected:
        booL        AtDestination ();
        void        FindNearbyTarget (GOAL* g);
        ENTITY*     FindValidObjectInList (ENTITY* list);

public:
        SOLDIER_ENTITY () {Clear (); SetType ();}
        void        SetType () {Type = SOLDIER;}

        int         Update ();
        void        SetDamage (int d);
        void        AddDamage (int d);
```

```
public:
        WEAPON      Weapon[2];      // allow 2 weapons and keep them public.
                                    // No access routines needed
        U8          WeaponOfChoice; // weapon 1 or 2, 0 is bare handed
};

//********************************************
//********************************************

ENTITY* SOLDIER_ENTITY :: FindValidObjectInList (ENTITY* list)
{
        while (list)
        {
                if (list->GetPlayerID () != PlayerID &&
                        list->GetPlayerID () != 0)      // trees and general stuff
                {
                        int type = list->GetType ();

                        if (type == CONSTRUCTION || type == RESOURCE_GATHERER ||
                                type == SOLDIER || type == FLYING_UNIT ||
                                type == TRANSPORT)
                                return list;
                }
                list = (ENTITY*) list->GetNext ();
        }
        return NULL;
}


//*************************

void SOLDIER_ENTITY :: FindNearbyTarget (GOAL* g)
{
        TILE* tile;
        for (int range=1; range<6; range++)
        {
                for (int x=-1; x<2; x++)
                {
                        for (int y=-1; y<2; y++)
                        {
                                tile = TileManager->GetTile (wx+x*range, wy+y*range);
                                ENTITY* obj = tile->GetObject ();
                                if (obj)
                                {
                                        ENTITY* ptr = FindValidObjectInList (obj);
                                        if (ptr)
                                        {
                                                g->Target = ptr;
                                                g->Action = GOAL :: ATTACK_TARGET;
                                                g->DT = 0;

                                                return;
```

```
                        }
                    }
                }
            }
        }
    }

//***************************

bool SOLDIER_ENTITY :: AtDestination ()             // for moving only
{
    GOAL* g = Goals->Peek ();                        // what is the top item
    int a = g->Action;
    int dx = -60, dy = -60;
    float r = Weapon[WeaponOfChoice-1].Range;
    if (a == GOAL :: GO_TO_DESTINATION)
    {
        dx = g->Dest->GetWorldX (), dy = g->Dest->GetWorldY ();
    }
    else if (a == GOAL :: GO_TO_TARGET ||
            a == GOAL :: ENTER_TARGET ||
            a == GOAL :: OBTAIN_TARGET ||
            a == GOAL :: RESOURCE_GATHERING ||
            a == GOAL :: BUILD_TARGET)          // etc, most goals use this
    {
        dx = g->Target->GetWorldX (), dy = g->Target->GetWorldY ();
        r = 1;                                   // range test of only 1
    }
    else if (a == GOAL :: ATTACK_TARGET)
    {
        if (Manager->IsValid ((RESOURCE_ENTITY*)g) == false)
        {
            Goals->Pop ();
            g = Goals->Peek ();
            if (g == NULL)
            FindNearbyTarget (g);
        }
        dx = g->Target->GetWorldX (), dy = g->Target->GetWorldY ();
        // regular range test
    }
    else return true;           // not a moving destination, must be true


    // if you are within one tile, you are there
    if (dx-r<=wx && dx+r>=wx && dy-r<=wy && dy+r>=wy)
        return true;
    return false;
}

//***************************

int     SOLDIER_ENTITY :: Update ()
```

```
{
      MOVING_ENTITY :: Update ();
      //WEAPON weapon1, weapon2;
      return 1;
}


//*************************

void SOLDIER_ENTITY :: SetDamage (int d)
{
      AddDamage (Dam-d);
}


//*************************

void SOLDIER_ENTITY :: AddDamage (int d)
{
      // here we choose a weapon, because we are hurt
      if (Weapon[0].Cell1.Amount && Weapon[1].Cell1.Amount)
      {
           // weigh range vs. damage vs. current status
           float d = (float) Dam, hp = (float) HitPoints;
           float ratio = d/hp;                // the lower the better
           if (ratio <= 0.5F)                 // damage is more important
           {
                //DiceNum, DiceSides, DiceAdd;  // points of damage done
                int Dam1 = Weapon[0].DiceNum * Weapon[0].DiceSides *
                          Weapon[0].DiceAdd;
                int Dam2 = Weapon[1].DiceNum * Weapon[1].DiceSides *
                          Weapon[1].DiceAdd;
                WeaponOfChoice = (Dam1 > Dam2) ? 1:2;
           }
           else                                // protect our health
           {
                WeaponOfChoice = (Weapon[0].Range > Weapon[1].Range) ? 1:2;
           }
      }
      else
      {
           WeaponOfChoice = (Weapon[0].Cell1.Amount) ? 1:2;
      }
      Dam += d;
}
//*************************
//*************************
```

The function FindValidObjectInList looks through a linked list of items for a target. The objective of this function is to find something for the soldier to shoot. He begins looking around him for viable targets, avoiding anything belonging to the player who controls him and any inanimate objects. In reality, he would also avoid allies.

FindNearbyTarget begins looking up to six tiles away for any possible target. Ideally 6 would be a variable, but you'll have to decide what you want.

AtDestination is changed to test for attacking and murder. If the soldier has killed his opponent, he then begins looking for a new target. This assumes that he is completely bloodthirsty. You would want to make it player controlled.

The functions AddDamage and SetDamage have been changed to make the soldier think a little harder. If he is hurt, he'll want to use a ranged weapon if he has one; if he is healthy, he'll want to use the deadliest weapon, ranged or not. Call this intelligent, but it is a simple test and this is the place to put it so the testing is only done once in a long while.

Transport Entities

Very similar to a CONSTRUCTION_ENTITY, this entity does not construct but still holds pointers to entities.

```
//*******************************************
class TRANSPORT_ENTITY : public CONSTRUCTION_ENTITY
{
public:
        TRANSPORT_ENTITY () : CONSTRUCTION_ENTITY () {Clear (); SetType ();}
        void SetType () {Type = TRANSPORT;}
        int  Update () {CONSTRUCTION_ENTITY::Update (); return 1;}

        bool Enter (ENTITY* e)
        {
                ItemsBeingBuilt->Push (&e);
                e->SetVisible (0);
                return true;
        }
        void Empty ()
        {
                ENTITY** e = ItemsBeingBuilt->Pop ();

                while (e)
                {
                        (*e)->FindEmptySpot ();
                        (*e)->SetVisible ();
                        *e = *ItemsBeingBuilt->Pop ();
                }
        }
};
//*******************************************
```

When an entity is set to enter, that entity is set to the ENTITY array that the CONSTRUCTION_ENTITY has, and the item then disappears because the construction entity makes it invisible. That is all. It must have functions that allow other entities to board and debark. I called them Enter and Empty, but rename them as you like. This would also apply to horses that carry units.

18

Chapter

Missile Entities

Missiles are all projectiles that leave one player and hit another. The missile entity is a little tricky but still not too hard. A missile entity only needs one goal, because once it is launched, it either hits the target or it doesn't; it doesn't hang around for any length of time.

The entity that launches a PROJECTILE_ENTITY has to do all of the setup for its subject entity. Since I didn't set it up, you'll have to decide how to put it together. You should probably have a weapon own the PROJECTILE_ENTITY description, and have it create the missile. This means that the weapon should set: direction of travel, medium of locomotion, animation, damage on impact or range of damage, which is maintained in the weapon, etc. Then the ENTITY that owns it will take over as host and launch the PROJECTILE_ENTITY. If the projectile connects, the host is informed, unless he's dead, and then the player is informed directly.

```
//*********************************************

class PROJECTILE_ENTITY : public SOLDIER_ENTITY
{
        enum MEDIUM_TRAVEL {FLIGHT, SUBSPACE, WATER, UNDERGROUND};
protected:
        float MoveSpeed;
        U8    Explosive:1;          // does it create an explosion when it hits
        U8    Medium:7;             // how are we moving

protected:
        void CloseTheGap ();
        bool DoesMovementContactAnything (int startx, int starty,
                                          int endx, int endy);
        void Impact ();             // generates explosion entity when appropriate
        void SendAck ();            // tell launcher what happened, hit or miss

public:
        PROJECTILE_ENTITY ()
        {
            Clear ();
            SetType ();
        }
        void Clear ()
        {
            SOLDIER_ENTITY :: Clear ();
            MoveSpeed = 1.0;
            Goals = new QUEUE <GOAL> (1);              // only 1 goal
            Events = new QUEUE <CREATURE_EVENT> (2);   // up to 1 items per frame
            // usually, the Events won't ever matter, but just in case.
        }
        void SetType () {Type = PROJECTILE;}
        int  Update ()
        {
            if (MOVING_ENTITY :: Update () == 0) return 0;
```

```
                    // move toward opponent and verify if hit or not
                    // missiles move fast and can move through an opponent
                    // so watch for overshoot

                    return 1;
            }
    public:
    // setup for the missile
            void SetTarget (ENTITY* target);
            // for weapons that must be fired in a direction
            void SetDirection (ANIMATION :: DIR);
            // movement speed is unique to projectiles because it can vary
            // while normal motion is limited for most entities to whatever
            // the animation dictates.
            void SetLauncher (ENTITY* origin);              // who sent me
            void SetMovementSpeed (float mov) {MoveSpeed = mov;}
    };

    //*********************************************
```

Like all projectiles, a PROJECTILE_ENTITY has to travel from its launching point to a target and inflict damage. The function CloseTheGap advances the projectile towards its target, whether it is an entity or a tile, or until the rocket booster burns out. If the missile contacts something, the function DoesMovementContactAnything returns TRUE, at which point the function Impact is called.

Once the projectile travels to the target, it needs to do its damage to the target (if it hits). Then it needs to notify the entity that launched it (SetLauncher) that it killed the target; this is done through the function SendAck. Lastly, it needs to disappear, so it has to die.

All missiles should have animated engines. Take a look at StarCraft. The missiles are still frames of animation with animated thrust. This is a great alternative to full animation, considering that no one will ever see the tiny missile change shape as it rotates while moving across the screen.

Make sure that all soldiers have a limited supply of missiles, or if they don't, make the time between launches lengthy. Keep the number of projectiles down because they tend to slow the computer when 20 different creatures launch missiles simultaneously. When they do, the number of entities goes from 20 to 40.

Missile Firing Entities

Soldiers and just about any creature in your world can throw a stone, fire an arrow, or launch a missile. All you have to do is make sure that all soldiers have a launch function that sets up a missile for launch properly. The rest is handled by the missile itself.

Flying Entities

For the sake of argument, these are included here. They act like soldiers or transports, but that is about it. However, they do have simplified animation, typically, and you can save a bit of programming here by using them instead of other classes. One last consideration is pathing. Flying entities can go almost anywhere, so pathing is simplified. Other than that, just use the existing code.

Explosion Entities

Explosion entities are a great way to handle area-of-effect attacks. They are the same as a simple moving entity with animation, movement, updates, etc. The only difference is in the update. You need to do damage to anything on surrounding tiles. Making the graphics look good is important. Also make sure the sounds are appropriate.

The entity should go through 8 to 15 frames of animation before it finally kills itself and dies. Make sure you have at least three or four full explosion sequences available so that the same explosion isn't repeated so often that players become annoyed.

A Final Note on Entities

The fact is that any single hierarchy is not adequate to control all possibilities. My intent here is simply to outline functionality and to create a logical hierarchy from which any decent programmer could launch into the world of entity management and unit AI. There are plenty of different design solutions to this problem domain, most of which are a lot more complex than what we've outlined here.

The problems I did not solve for you are:

➤ I have a super dog creature that wanders the landscape in search of a player's unit to eat. Does that make him a soldier entity or something else? I suggest that you create a separate hierarchy for creatures that do not conform to the normal hierarchy. You should probably derive these classes from the existing hierarchy that you create.

➤ None of the creatures in the world are simply soldiers. What about wyrms or stormtroopers? Well, that's a dumb question. These are outlines. You might make the classes robust enough to handle any type of aggressive creature. You might derive your own classes from the hierarchy listed. In any case, this is not a complete list.

➤ How long does it take to implement the code you've put in here and fully test it within a game? About 9 to 16 months. The code and hierarchy listed here can take months just to design and implement. This should be a nice head start.

➤ How much more code will there be on the CD to help? Lots and lots.

You'll need to work long and hard to get the unit AI perfect. The hardest part will be preparing the code for your computer opponent. The unit AI is trivial by comparison. Also, plan to spend a lot of time on this portion of the game. A good design can save thousands of hours. Good luck.

Memory Management

Creating and managing hundreds, or thousands, of entities is a tricky proposal. Now comes the update cycle—how do you make sure everything gets updated properly? If you want to maintain a fast update, you might limit the update cycle to 12 milliseconds or so. How do you make sure that all creatures are updated unless you keep track of where you left off from the previous frame?

This isn't such a tough thing. First, let's look at a new memory manager. This one is dynamic and allows expansion during run time; its memory expansion is very fast. This is one of the best I've written, and I've tested it over the course of a few months. This memory manager manages lists of pointers, so when you add more items than it has space for, it simply reallocates the pointers and leaves the memory alone. This prevents most memory fragmentation (except the list of pointers) and makes memory allocation transparent. Also, when you free an element from the list, the memory is kept intact and the flag (tag) marking its availability is set. This class relies heavily on the TAG_LIST class we built on in Chapter 13. It is a template, so feel free to use any structure with it. The code can be found in entity_mgr.cpp.

Note: Do not use this class to maintain simple variable types like chars or even ints. A char takes only 1 byte. The pointers of this template take 4 bytes each (as they should) and then there is the TAG_LIST overhead. Taking more than 4 bytes to store a single char is completely unacceptable. For small amounts of memory, use some other memory management scheme. This is designed for large memory allocations, to prevent using the C++ delete function on allocated structures, and to save on time since this method beats the C++ new and delete about 20 to 1 in terms of performance (in the middle of a game).

```
#ifndef _ALLOCATOR_H_
#define _ALLOCATOR_H_

//************************************************
// allocates memory for a specific type of memory
// maintains a list of pointers which makes reallocation a breeze
// the "type" is ITEM and this template can be used for
// any variable type, including structures.
// the default size is 30 pointers and each time you need
// to allocate more ITEM's that the list can provide,
// the system allocates a new list of pointers, copies the old
// pointers on top of the old, and deletes the old list.
// incidentally, these memory allocations amount to 120 bytes at
// a time (pointer is 4 bytes times 30)
// huge pointer list becomes unwieldy, so it is better
// to have 20 lists than one big one.

template <class ITEM>
```

```cpp
class POINTER_MGR;
#define FC __fastcall

template <class ITEM>
class ALLOCATOR
{
public:              //**************************
     enum {MAX_ITEM = 30};

protected:           //************************** variables
     int      MaxItems;
     int      NumberAllocated;                    // never decrement, this is the
                                                  // number of items allocated

     ITEM**        Items;
     TAGptr        Tag;

protected:           //************************** functions

     void          FC  ReallocateList ()
     {
          int newnum = MaxItems + MAX_ITEM;    // how many new items
          ITEM** newlist = new ITEM*[newnum];  // prep new list

               // copy old list on top of new list
          memcpy (newlist, Items, sizeof (ITEM*) * MaxItems);

               // set the new pointers to NULL
          for (int i=MaxItems; i<newnum; i++)
               newlist[i] = 0L;

          MaxItems = newnum;     // store the number
          delete Items;          // delete the old list, the pointers were
                                 // copied

          Items = newlist;       // now move the new list into the old pointer

               // prep new set of tags
          TAGptr newtag = new TAG_LIST (newnum);
          Tag->Copy (*newtag);

          delete Tag;
          Tag = newtag;
     }
     //****************
     virtual
          void FC  DeleteList ()                 // derived later
     {
          if (Items)
          {
               for (int i=0; i<NumberAllocated; i++)
                    if (Items[i]) delete Items[i];
               delete Items;
```

```
        }
            Items = NULL;
    }
    //****************
    void FC  AllocateList (int num)
    {
            MaxItems = num;
            Items = new ITEM*[num];
    for (int i=0; i<num; i++) Items[i] = OL;
    Tag = new TAG_LIST (num);
    }
    //****************
    inline void IncrementCount () {NumberAllocated++;}
    inline void DecrementCount () {NumberAllocated--;}

public:          //************************* functions

    ALLOCATOR (int num = MAX_ITEM)
    {
            AllocateList (num);
            Clear ();
    }
    //****************
    //****************
    ~ALLOCATOR ()
    {
            DeleteList ();
    }
    //****************
    void Clear ()
    {
            Tag->Clear ();                // clears all, makes all available
            NumberAllocated = 0;
    }
    //****************
    //****************
    ITEM*      FC  GetNewItem ()
    {
            int which = Tag->FindOpenTag ();
            // when there are open spots in the existing list
    if (which >= 0 && which<NumberAllocated)
    {
                Tag->Set (which);
        if (Items[which] == NULL)
            {
                    Items[which] = new ITEM;
                    IncrementCount ();
            }
        return Items[which];
    }
        // we have maxed out the list
    if (NumberAllocated >= MaxItems)
```

```
        {
                ReallocateList ();
        }
    else
    {
                if (Items[NumberAllocated]) return NULL;   // abnormal
    }
    // normal operation
Tag->Set (NumberAllocated);
Items[NumberAllocated] = new ITEM;
    int num = NumberAllocated;
    IncrementCount ();
    return Items[num];
}
//***************
void      FC  ReleaseItem (ITEM* item)
{
int which = 0, Found = 0;
while (Found == 0 && which<NumberAllocated)
{
    if (Items[which++] == item) {Found = 1; break;}
    }
if (Found == 0) return;
Tag->Clear (--which);
    //DecrementCount ();         // never decrement, this is the number
                                 // of items allocated

}
//***************
void      FC  ReleaseItem (int which = 0)
{
    if (which<0 || which >= NumberAllocated) return;
    Tag->Clear (which);
    //DecrementCount ();         // never decrement, this is the number
                                 // of items allocated

}
//***************
//***************
int       FC  GetID (ITEM* item)
{
    int which = 0, Found = 0;
    while (Found == 0 && which<NumberAllocated)
    {
        if (Items[which++] == item) {Found = 1; break;}
    }
    if (Found == 0)  return -1;
    return --which;
}
//***************
ITEM* FC  GetItem (int which = 0)
{
    if (which<0 || which>= NumberAllocated) return NULL;
    Tag->Set(which);
```

```
        if (Items[which] == NULL) Items[which] = new ITEM;
        return Items[which];
}
//****************
void FC  SpinListTopToBottom ()
{
int max = NumberAllocated-1;
ITEM* top = Items[max];
int tag = Tag->Get (max);
for (int i=max; i>0; i--)
{
     Items[i] = Items[i-1];
     if (Tag->Get (i-1)) Tag->Set (i);
     else Tag->Clear (i);
}
Items[0] = top;
if (tag) Tag->Set (0);
else Tag->Clear (0);
}
//****************
void FC  SpinListBottomToTop ()
{
int max = NumberAllocated-1;
ITEM* bottom = Items[0];
int tag = Tag->Get (0);
for (int i=0; i<max; i++)
{
     Items[i] = Items[i+1];
     if (Tag->Get (i+1)) Tag->Set (i);
     else Tag->Clear (i);
}
Items[max] = bottom;
if (tag) Tag->Set (max);
     else Tag->Clear (max);
}
//****************
//****************
int      FC  CheckInUse (ITEM* item)
{
     int which = 0, Found = 0;
     while (Found == 0 && which<NumberAllocated)
{
     if (Items[which++] == item) {Found = 1; break;}
     }
     if (Found == 0) return 0;
     return Tag->Get (which);
}
//****************
int      FC  CheckInUse (int which)
{
     if (which<0 || which >= NumberAllocated) return -1;
return Tag->Get (which);
```

```
}
//****************
int        FC  GetTag (int which)
{
       if (which<0 || which >= NumberAllocated) return -1;
return Tag->Get (which);
}
//****************
//****************
int        FC  GetNumAllocated ()
{
return NumberAllocated;
}
//****************
int        FC  GetNumInUse ()
{
       int count = 0, num = NumberAllocated;
       while (num--)
       if (Tag->Get (num)) count ++;

return count;
}
//****************
//****************
int        FC  FindFirst ()
{
       return Tag->FindFirstSet ();
}
//****************
int        FC  FindNext ()
{
       return Tag->FindNextSet ();
}
//****************
//****************
int        FC  FindAvailable ()
{
       return Tag->FindOpenTag ();
}
//****************
//****************
ITEM*      FC  operator [] (int which)
{
if (which<0 || which>= NumberAllocated) return NULL;
       return Items[which];
}
//****************
//****************
};
//*************************************************
```

The following class is a derivative of the ALLOCATOR class and is designed to only maintain pointers to objects that it does not own. It does not allocate the objects; it could, but it is designed to maintain the list. If the list gets too large, the list is reallo-cated. This is used as a temporary storage device. It is helpful because it is like a stack that can't have too many items—it simply allocates space for more. We'll use this to maintain a list of creatures that have died in the past frame and it will maintain point-ers to the dying objects.

```
//**************************************************
// all items must be pointers, or this class will crash your PC

template <class ITEM>
class POINTER_MGR : public ALLOCATOR <ITEM>
{
public:           //*********************** functions

        POINTER_MGR (int num = MAX_ITEM)
        {
                MaxItems = num;
                Items = new ITEM*[num];
                for (int i=0; i<num; i++) Items[i] = 0L;
                Tag = new TAG_LIST (num);
                NumberAllocated = 0;
        }
        //***************
        //***************
        // this function is for adding items to be maintained. These items were
        // allocated elsewhere and will only be maintained here.
        bool AddNewItem (ITEM* item)
        {
                int which = Tag->FindOpenTag ();
                if (which >= 0 && which<NumberAllocated)
                {
                        Tag->Set (which);
                        if (Items[which] == NULL) Items[which] = item;
                        NumberAllocated++;
                        return true;
                }
                if (NumberAllocated >= MaxItems)
                {
                        ReallocateList ();
                }
                else
                {
                        if (Items[NumberAllocated]) return false;
                        // abnormal and strange
                }
                Tag->Set (NumberAllocated);
                Items[NumberAllocated++] = item;
                return true;
        }
        //***************
        // when items are added, and not allocated, you may call this function.
        // Do not call this function if you've allocated memory using this class.
```

```
        void ClearItems ()
        {
                for (int i=0; i<NumberAllocated; i++)
                {
                        Items[i] = NULL;
                }
                Tag->Clear ();
        }
        //***************
};

//**************************************************
```

Now how do I use this huge memory allocator? First, you'll find the ALLOCATOR class in memmgr.h. It really is sweet the way it works. It maintains a list of pointers and tags that tell it if a pointer is currently in use. It allocates new items as needed, and the list can grow dynamically without very much memory shifting or reallocation. I use it all the time.

```
        //**************************************************
        //**************************************************

        typedef class UNIVERSAL_ENTITY_MANAGER
        {
                ALLOCATOR <ENTITY>*                         Base;
                ALLOCATOR <RESOURCE_ENTITY>*                Resource;
                ALLOCATOR <CONSTRUCTION_ENTITY>*            Building;
                ALLOCATOR <MOVING_ENTITY>*                  Moving;
                ALLOCATOR <RESOURCE_GATHERER_ENTITY>*       ResourceGatherer;
                ALLOCATOR <SOLDIER_ENTITY>*                 Soldier;
                ALLOCATOR <FLYING_UNIT_ENTITY>*             FlyingUnit;
                ALLOCATOR <TRANSPORT_ENTITY>*               Transport;
                ALLOCATOR <PROJECTILE_ENTITY>*              Projectile;
                ALLOCATOR <CONSUMPTION_ENTITY>*             Consumption;
                ALLOCATOR <EXPLOSION_ENTITY>*               Explosion;
                ALLOCATOR <ENTITY>*                         List[ENTITY::NUMTYPES];
                POINTER_MGR <ENTITY*>*                      Dead;      // a list of the dead

                int WhereWeLeftOff;         // used for continuing the update cycles
                int MouseX, MouseY;
                int RectL, RectT, RectR, RectB;

                //************** private functions

                void        Draw (ALLOCATOR <ENTITY>* entity, SCREEN_STRUCT* screen);
                void        UpdateGroup (ALLOCATOR <ENTITY>* entity);
                void        UpdateGroup (int which = ENTITY :: BASE);
                ENTITY*     KillEntity (ALLOCATOR <ENTITY>* entity, ENTITY* e);

                //***************

                ENTITY*     Select (ALLOCATOR <ENTITY>* entity, int playerID);
                int         SelectInRegion (ALLOCATOR <ENTITY>* entity, int playerID);
```

```
//**************

int        Message (ALLOCATOR <ENTITY>* entity, int type, int data1, int
                    data2);

//**************
```

public:

```
//**************

UNIVERSAL_ENTITY_MANAGER ();
~UNIVERSAL_ENTITY_MANAGER ();

//**************

void       Clear ();
void       Init ();

//**************
//**************

void       Draw (SCREEN_STRUCT* screen, int which = ENTITY :: ALLTYPES);

//**************

void       Update (int TimeLimit = 2000, bool ContinueFromLastPoint =
                    true);

//**************

ENTITY*    Spawn (int x, int y, int z, int type = ENTITY :: BASE);

//**************
//**************                  // these check all items in the world

ENTITY*    Select (int x, int y, int playerID);
int        Select (int x1, int y1, int x2, int y2, int playerID);

//**************

int        Message (int type, int data1 = 0, int data2 = 0);

//**************

bool       IsValid (ENTITY* e);
bool       IsValid (RESOURCE_ENTITY* e);
bool       IsValid (CONSTRUCTION_ENTITY* e);
bool       IsValid (MOVING_ENTITY* e);
bool       IsValid (RESOURCE_GATHERER_ENTITY* e);
bool       IsValid (SOLDIER_ENTITY* e);
bool       IsValid (FLYING_UNIT_ENTITY* e);
```

```
        bool      IsValid (TRANSPORT_ENTITY* e);
        bool      IsValid (PROJECTILE_ENTITY* e);
        bool      IsValid (CONSUMPTION_ENTITY* e);
        bool      IsValid (EXPLOSION_ENTITY* e);

        //**************
        // these add kill items

        bool      Kill (ENTITY* e);

        //**************
}DADDY_MANAGER, *UNIVENTITYMGRptr;

//***************************************************
```

Here we have about 12 Allocator classes. You might be wondering why I maintain 12 lists when I could just maintain one list and create creatures dynamically. That's because I don't want dynamic allocation. Once I allocate memory for a creature, I want to use it over and over for different creatures. There is a lot of work in maintaining 12 lists and some strange casts, but this class is good at doling out the creatures that you request. It is quite handy.

The implementation is such that I'll briefly discuss its functionality because of its relative complexity.

```
        //***************************************************

UNIVERSAL_ENTITY_MANAGER :: UNIVERSAL_ENTITY_MANAGER ()
{
        Init ();
}
        //**************

UNIVERSAL_ENTITY_MANAGER :: ~UNIVERSAL_ENTITY_MANAGER ()
{
        if (Base)              delete      Base;
        if (Resource)          delete      Resource;
        if (Building)          delete      Building;
        if (Moving)            delete      Moving;
        if (ResourceGatherer)  delete      ResourceGatherer;
        if (Soldier)           delete      Soldier;
        if (FlyingUnit)        delete      FlyingUnit;
        if (Transport)         delete      Transport;
        if (Projectile)        delete      Projectile;
        if (Consumption)       delete      Consumption;
        if (Explosion)         delete      Explosion;
        if (Dead)              delete      Dead;
}
        //**************

void UNIVERSAL_ENTITY_MANAGER :: Clear ()
{
        for (int i=0; i<ENTITY :: NUMTYPES; i++)
```

```
                List[i]->Clear ();
        }

        //***************

void UNIVERSAL_ENTITY_MANAGER :: Init ()
{
        Base = new ALLOCATOR <ENTITY> (30);
            List[0] = Base;
        Resource = new ALLOCATOR <RESOURCE_ENTITY> (30);
            List[1] = reinterpret_cast <ALLOCATOR <ENTITY> * > (Resource);
        Building = new ALLOCATOR <CONSTRUCTION_ENTITY> (30);
            List[2] = reinterpret_cast <ALLOCATOR <ENTITY> * > (Building);
        Moving = new ALLOCATOR <MOVING_ENTITY> (30);
            List[3] = reinterpret_cast <ALLOCATOR <ENTITY> * > (Moving);
        ResourceGatherer = new ALLOCATOR <RESOURCE_GATHERER_ENTITY> (30);
            List[4] = reinterpret_cast <ALLOCATOR <ENTITY> * > (ResourceGatherer);
        Soldier = new ALLOCATOR <SOLDIER_ENTITY> (30);
            List[5] = reinterpret_cast <ALLOCATOR <ENTITY> * > (Soldier);
        FlyingUnit = new ALLOCATOR <FLYING_UNIT_ENTITY> (30);
            List[6] = reinterpret_cast <ALLOCATOR <ENTITY> * > (FlyingUnit);
        Transport = new ALLOCATOR <TRANSPORT_ENTITY> (30);
            List[7] = reinterpret_cast <ALLOCATOR <ENTITY> * > (Transport);
        Projectile = new ALLOCATOR <PROJECTILE_ENTITY> (30);
            List[8] = reinterpret_cast <ALLOCATOR <ENTITY> * > (Projectile);
        Consumption = new ALLOCATOR <CONSUMPTION_ENTITY> (30);
            List[9] = reinterpret_cast <ALLOCATOR <ENTITY> * > (Consumption);
        Explosion = new ALLOCATOR <EXPLOSION_ENTITY> (30);
            List[10] = reinterpret_cast <ALLOCATOR <ENTITY> * > (Explosion);

        Dead = new POINTER_MGR <ENTITY*> (30);
        // used for items to be taken out of service

        WhereWeLeftOff = 0;

}


        //***************
```

The first few lines are obvious where we allocate memory and the destructor cleans it up. This is no biggie. The Clear function clears all of the ALLOCATOR's.

Then the code gets a little trickier. The Draw function takes a pointer to an ALLOCATOR <ENTITY>. We can cast all of the ALLOCATOR's to this and they will draw properly. They all know what type they are, even if this function does not. This is inheritance at its simplest and one of the fortes of C++.

```
        //*************** private functions
void UNIVERSAL_ENTITY_MANAGER :: Draw (ALLOCATOR <ENTITY>* entity,
                                    SCREEN_STRUCT* screen)
{
        ENTITY* item = NULL;
        int num = entity->GetNumAllocated ();
        for (int i=0; i<num; i++)
        if (entity->CheckInUse (i))  // is it actually in use, not just allocated
        {
```

18

Chapter

```
                        item = entity->GetItem (i);
                        item->DrawAnimation (screen);
                }
        }
        //***************
void UNIVERSAL_ENTITY_MANAGER :: UpdateGroup (ALLOCATOR <ENTITY>* entity)
{
        ENTITY* item = NULL;
        int num = entity->GetNumAllocated ();
        for (int i=0; i<num; i++)
        if (entity->CheckInUse (i))  // is it actually in use, not just allocated
        {
                item = entity->GetItem (i);
                item->Update ();
        }
}
        //***************
void UNIVERSAL_ENTITY_MANAGER :: UpdateGroup (int which)
{
        if (which & ENTITY :: RESOURCE)
            UpdateGroup (reinterpret_cast <ALLOCATOR <ENTITY> * > (Resource));

        if (which & ENTITY :: CONSTRUCTION)
            UpdateGroup (reinterpret_cast <ALLOCATOR <ENTITY> * > (Building));

        if (which & ENTITY :: MOVING)
            UpdateGroup (reinterpret_cast <ALLOCATOR <ENTITY> * > (Moving));

        if (which & ENTITY :: RESOURCE_GATHERER)
            UpdateGroup (reinterpret_cast <ALLOCATOR <ENTITY> * >
                    (ResourceGatherer));

        if (which & ENTITY :: SOLDIER)
            UpdateGroup (reinterpret_cast <ALLOCATOR <ENTITY> * > (Soldier));

        if (which & ENTITY :: FLYING_UNIT)
            UpdateGroup (reinterpret_cast <ALLOCATOR <ENTITY> * > (FlyingUnit));

        if (which & ENTITY :: TRANSPORT)
            UpdateGroup (reinterpret_cast <ALLOCATOR <ENTITY> * > (Transport));

        if (which & ENTITY :: PROJECTILE)
            UpdateGroup (reinterpret_cast <ALLOCATOR <ENTITY> * > (Projectile));

        if (which & ENTITY :: CONSUMPTION)
            UpdateGroup (reinterpret_cast <ALLOCATOR <ENTITY> * > (Consumption));

        if (which & ENTITY :: EXPLOSION)
            UpdateGroup (reinterpret_cast <ALLOCATOR <ENTITY> * > (Explosion));

        if (which & ENTITY :: BASE)
            UpdateGroup (Base);
```

```
}
    //**************

ENTITY*    UNIVERSAL_ENTITY_MANAGER :: KillEntity (ALLOCATOR <ENTITY>* entity,
ENTITY* e)
{
    ENTITY* item = NULL;
    int num = entity->FindFirst ();
    if (num == -1) return NULL;
    do
    {
        item = entity->GetItem (num);
        if (item == e) {entity->ReleaseItem (num); return item;}
    }while ((num = entity->FindNext ()) != NULL);
    return NULL;
}


    //**************
    //**************
ENTITY*    UNIVERSAL_ENTITY_MANAGER :: Select (ALLOCATOR <ENTITY>* entity, int
playerID)
{
    ENTITY* item = NULL;
    int num = entity->GetNumAllocated ();
    for (int i=0; i<num; i++)
    if (entity->CheckInUse (i))  // is it actually in use, not just allocated
    {
        item = entity->GetItem (i);
        if (item->Select (MouseX, MouseY, playerID)) return item;
    }
    return NULL;
}
    //**************
int    UNIVERSAL_ENTITY_MANAGER :: SelectInRegion (ALLOCATOR <ENTITY>* entity,
int playerID)
{
    ENTITY* item = NULL;
    int num = entity->GetNumAllocated ();
    for (int i=0; i<num; i++)
    if (entity->CheckInUse (i))  // is it actually in use, not just allocated
    {
        item = entity->GetItem (i);
        item->Select (RectL, RectT, RectR, RectB, playerID);
        // we can select multiple items
    }
    return (item)? 1:0;
}
    //**************
    //**************
int    UNIVERSAL_ENTITY_MANAGER :: Message (ALLOCATOR <ENTITY>* entity, int type,
int data1, int data2)
{
```

18

Chapter

```
            ENTITY* item = NULL;
            int num = entity->GetNumAllocated ();

            for (int i=0; i<num; i++)
            if (entity->CheckInUse (i))  // is it actually in use, not just allocated
            {
                item = entity->GetItem (i);
                if (item->GetSelected ())
                    item->Message (type, data1, data2);
            }
            return (item)? 1:0;
    }

    //***************

void UNIVERSAL_ENTITY_MANAGER :: Draw (SCREEN_STRUCT* screen, int which)
{
        int num = 0;
        if (which & ENTITY :: RESOURCE)
            Draw (reinterpret_cast <ALLOCATOR <ENTITY> * > (Resource), screen);

        if (which & ENTITY :: CONSTRUCTION)
            Draw (reinterpret_cast <ALLOCATOR <ENTITY> * > (Building), screen);

        if (which & ENTITY :: MOVING)
            Draw (reinterpret_cast <ALLOCATOR <ENTITY> * > (Moving), screen);

        if (which & ENTITY :: RESOURCE_GATHERER)
            Draw (reinterpret_cast <ALLOCATOR <ENTITY> * > (ResourceGatherer),
                screen);

        if (which & ENTITY :: SOLDIER)
            Draw (reinterpret_cast <ALLOCATOR <ENTITY> * > (Soldier), screen);

        if (which & ENTITY :: FLYING_UNIT)
            Draw (reinterpret_cast <ALLOCATOR <ENTITY> * > (FlyingUnit), screen);

        if (which & ENTITY :: TRANSPORT)
            Draw (reinterpret_cast <ALLOCATOR <ENTITY> * > (Transport), screen);

        if (which & ENTITY :: PROJECTILE)
            Draw (reinterpret_cast <ALLOCATOR <ENTITY> * > (Projectile), screen);

        if (which & ENTITY :: CONSUMPTION)
            Draw (reinterpret_cast <ALLOCATOR <ENTITY> * > (Consumption), screen);

        if (which & ENTITY :: EXPLOSION)
            Draw (reinterpret_cast <ALLOCATOR <ENTITY> * > (Explosion), screen);

        if (which & ENTITY :: BASE)
            Draw (Base, screen);
    }
    //***************
```

```
void UNIVERSAL_ENTITY_MANAGER :: Update (int TimeLimit, bool
ContinueFromLastPoint)
{
      int num = 0, i;
      int oldpos = WhereWeLeftOff;
      int item = Dead->FindFirst ();
      if (item != -1)                          // clean up the dead
      {
            do
            {
                  for (int i=0; i<ENTITY :: NUMTYPES; i++)
                  if (KillEntity (List[i], *Dead->GetItem (item)) != NULL) return;
            }while ((item = Dead->FindNext ()) != -1);
      }
      Dead->ClearItems ();
      // begin update
      long time1 = timeGetTime (), time2;

      if (ContinueFromLastPoint)
      {
            for (i=WhereWeLeftOff; i<ENTITY :: NUMTYPES; i++)
            {
                  UpdateGroup (1<<i);
                  time2 = timeGetTime ();
                  if (time2-time1 >= TimeLimit) return;
            }
            if (oldpos == 0) return;        // we cycled through everything
            for (i=0; i<oldpos; i++)
            {
                  UpdateGroup (1<<i);
                  time2 = timeGetTime ();
                  if (time2-time1 >= TimeLimit) return;
            }
            return;
      }
      for (i=0; i<ENTITY :: NUMTYPES; i++)
      {
            UpdateGroup (1<<i);
            WhereWeLeftOff = i;
            time2 = timeGetTime ();
            if (time2-time1 >= TimeLimit) return;
      }
}

//***************
```

UpdateGroup is the same way. We will be calling it with a pointer to each of our ALLOCATOR's and letting C++ do most of the work for us. Look at the function immediately below UpdateGroup. It is also called UpdateGroup. It calls the first function once for each type of ALLOCATOR in the UNIVERSAL_ENTITY_MANAGER class. This implementation is rather sweet, easy to use, and a pain to program. But you saw it here, so help yourself. The rest of the class is based on this same paradigm.

The Spawn function is where you get new entities from. Call this function with coordinates and an ENTITY type, and it'll generate a new entity for you. The types are in all caps in the switch statement.

```
//***************
ENTITY*      UNIVERSAL_ENTITY_MANAGER :: Spawn (int x, int y, int z, int type)
{
      ENTITY* e = NULL;
      switch (type)
      {
      case ENTITY :: RESOURCE:
           e = Resource->GetNewItem ();
           break;
      case ENTITY :: CONSTRUCTION:
           e = Building->GetNewItem ();
           break;
      case ENTITY :: MOVING:
           e = Moving->GetNewItem ();
           break;
      case ENTITY :: RESOURCE_GATHERER:
           e = ResourceGatherer->GetNewItem ();
           break;
      case ENTITY :: SOLDIER:
           e = Soldier->GetNewItem ();
           break;
      case ENTITY :: FLYING_UNIT:
           e = FlyingUnit->GetNewItem ();
           break;
      case ENTITY :: TRANSPORT:
           e = Transport->GetNewItem ();
           break;
      case ENTITY :: PROJECTILE:
           e = Projectile->GetNewItem ();
           break;
      case ENTITY :: CONSUMPTION:
           e = Consumption->GetNewItem ();
           break;
      case ENTITY :: EXPLOSION:
           e = Explosion->GetNewItem ();
           break;

      default:
           e = Base->GetNewItem ();
      }

      e->Clear ();
      e->SetWorldCoordinates (x, y, (z>-1) ? z:3);
      return e;
}
//***************
```

When you drag the mouse over a region on the map, or you simply click on the map, we go through all of the creatures to see if that click was on one of the entities of the world. This test should be done after you first verify that the player has clicked on the map. These functions can be speeded up significantly if the UNIVERSAL_ENTITY_MANAGER is made aware of the map. It can simply test the few tiles on the screen for mouse clicks, although click and drag isn't helped much. You can still drag offscreen.

Finally there is a section for validation of each type of entity. This is here to make sure that you have a valid pointer before you go making function calls to that entity.

```
//***************              // these check all items in the world

ENTITY*    UNIVERSAL_ENTITY_MANAGER :: Select (int x, int y, int playerID)
{
      MouseX = x, MouseY = x;
      int num = 0;
      ENTITY* item = NULL;

      for (int i=0; i<ENTITY :: NUMTYPES; i++)
      {
            item = Select (List[i], playerID);
            if (item) return item;
      }
      return item;
}

//**************

int UNIVERSAL_ENTITY_MANAGER :: Select (int x1, int y1, int x2, int y2, int
playerID)
{
      RectL = x1, RectT = y1, RectR = x2, RectB = y2;
      int item = 0;

      for (int i=0; i<ENTITY :: NUMTYPES; i++)
      {
            item += SelectInRegion (List[i], playerID);
      }
      return item;
}

//**************
//**************

int    UNIVERSAL_ENTITY_MANAGER :: Message (int type, int data1, int data2)
{
      int ret = 0;

      for (int i=0; i<ENTITY :: NUMTYPES; i++)
      {
            ret = Message (List[i], type, data1, data2);
```

```
                if (ret) return ret;
            }
        return ret;
    }

//***************
//***************

bool UNIVERSAL_ENTITY_MANAGER :: IsValid (ENTITY* e)
{
        int ret = Base->CheckInUse (e);
        if (ret == -1) return false;          // not valid
        return (ret)? true:false;
}
//***************

bool UNIVERSAL_ENTITY_MANAGER :: IsValid (RESOURCE_ENTITY* e)
{
        int ret = Resource->CheckInUse (e);
        if (ret == -1) return false;          // not valid
        return (ret)? true:false;
}
//***************

bool UNIVERSAL_ENTITY_MANAGER :: IsValid (CONSTRUCTION_ENTITY* e)
{
        int ret = Building->CheckInUse (e);
        if (ret == -1) return false;          // not valid
        return (ret)? true:false;
}
//***************

bool UNIVERSAL_ENTITY_MANAGER :: IsValid (MOVING_ENTITY* e)
{
        int ret = Moving->CheckInUse (e);
        if (ret == -1) return false;          // not valid
        return (ret)? true:false;
}
//***************

bool UNIVERSAL_ENTITY_MANAGER :: IsValid (RESOURCE_GATHERER_ENTITY* e)
{
        int ret = ResourceGatherer->CheckInUse (e);
        if (ret == -1) return false;          // not valid
        return (ret)? true:false;
}
//***************

bool UNIVERSAL_ENTITY_MANAGER :: IsValid (SOLDIER_ENTITY* e)
{
        int ret = Soldier->CheckInUse (e);
        if (ret == -1) return false;          // not valid
```

```
            return (ret)? true:false;
      }
      //**************

      bool UNIVERSAL_ENTITY_MANAGER :: IsValid (FLYING_UNIT_ENTITY* e)
      {
            int ret = FlyingUnit->CheckInUse (e);
            if (ret == -1) return false;          // not valid
            return (ret)? true:false;
      }
      //**************

      bool UNIVERSAL_ENTITY_MANAGER :: IsValid (TRANSPORT_ENTITY* e)
      {
            int ret = Transport->CheckInUse (e);
            if (ret == -1) return false;          // not valid
            return (ret)? true:false;
      }
      //**************

      bool UNIVERSAL_ENTITY_MANAGER :: IsValid (PROJECTILE_ENTITY* e)
      {
            int ret = Projectile->CheckInUse (e);
            if (ret == -1) return false;          // not valid
            return (ret)? true:false;
      }
      //**************

      bool UNIVERSAL_ENTITY_MANAGER :: IsValid (CONSUMPTION_ENTITY* e)
      {
            int ret = Consumption->CheckInUse (e);
            if (ret == -1) return false;          // not valid
            return (ret)? true:false;
      }
      //**************

      bool UNIVERSAL_ENTITY_MANAGER :: IsValid (EXPLOSION_ENTITY* e)
      {
            int ret = Explosion->CheckInUse (e);
            if (ret == -1) return false;          // not valid
            return (ret)? true:false;
      }
      //**************
      bool UNIVERSAL_ENTITY_MANAGER :: Kill (ENTITY* e)
      {
            Dead->AddNewItem (&e);
            return false;
      }


      //**************
      //***********************************************
```

Calculating Screen Position Based on World Position

We added a global function to the QUEUED_ENTITIES struct called:

> void ConvertCoordinatesToScreenCoordinates (int& x, int& y, int offx, int offy).

These conversions are generally easy, but converting to screen coordinates is a slightly different matter. Refer to Figures 16.23 and 16.24 for examples of tile coordinates in a world system.

To establish conversions, we need a global system of maintaining screen offset into the world. Back in Chapter 8, all of the minimaps had a little rectangle that represented where the screen rendering was in relation to the rest of the map. The way we do this is to have a global variable called something like ScreenOffsetX and ScreenOffsetY. When you go to render a frame, all tiles partially within the range of the screen will be rendered and clipped against the drawing region. This is an example of how a map might be rendered:

```
//*************************************************
extern SINGLE_TILEptr tiles;
extern int NumTiles;

extern int ScreenOffsetX, ScreenOffsetY;

// the dimensions of the render area in relation to screen coordinates
extern int RenderMapX, RenderMapY;
extern int RenderMapWidth, RenderMapHeight;

//*************************************************

void RenderMap (SCREEN_STRUCT* screen)
{
        RECTANGLE r (RenderMapX, RenderMapY, RenderMapWidth, RenderMapHeight);

        // set global clipping for rendering
        // this clipping will apply to all rendering
        tiles->GetGraphic ()->SetClipRectangle (r);

        for (int i=0; i<NumTiles; i++)
        {
            int x = tiles[i].GetWorldX ();                      // worldcor.h
            int y = tiles[i].GetWorldY ();
            // int z = tiles[i].GetWorldZ ();                   // ignoring height
            int w = tiles[i].GetGraphic ()->GetWidth ();        // screenobj.h
            int h = tiles[i].GetGraphic ()->GetHeight ();

            // we want to render if any portion of the
            // tile is showing, even one pixel.
            if (x < RenderMapX+RenderMapWidth &&
                x+w > RenderMapX &&
                y < RenderMapY+RenderMapHeight &&
                y+h > RenderMapY)
            {
```

```
                         // offset the position
                         tiles[i].Draw (screen, x-ScreenOffsetX, y-ScreenOffsetY);
             }
         }
}
//**************************************************
```

However, this method is somewhat inefficient. If you have a 200x200 map, that is 40,000 tests even though you'll probably render only 20x20, or 400, tiles. Better to hard-code offsets like the following code in TILE_MAP (the entire code is in tile.h):

```
//**************************************************
void  TILE_MAP :: Draw (SCREEN_STRUCT* screen)
       // use scx, scy, Width, and Height for determining clipping plane
       // since the world coordinates translate exactly into world coordinates
       // with an offset
{
       int startx = UpperX/64-1;
       if (startx<0) startx = 0;

       int endx = screen->Width/64+1 + startx;
       if (endx>DimX) endx = DimX;

       int starty = UpperY/32-1;
       if (starty<0) starty = 0;

       int endy = screen->Height/32+1 + starty;
       if (endy>DimY) endy = DimY;

       int scrx = UpperX-startx*64, scry = UpperY-starty*32;

       for (int i=startx, x=scrx; i<endx; i++, x+=64)
           for (int j=starty, y=scry; j<endy; j++, y+=32)
           {
                Map[i][j].Draw (screen, x, y);
           }
}
//**************************************************
```

The starting position in the map is precalculated. Many of the variables are member variables. The tiles in this case are 64x32, in case you hadn't guessed from the code.

The variable Map is of type TILE. The Draw function automatically clips. This code is about 100 times more efficient but it makes assumptions. It relies on the clipping rectangle to already be set and all of the dimensions to be set. Also, the code is not in any way generic, relying on the TILE class. That is the trade-off. Anyway, it is very easy code to use and hopefully understand.

Resources and Gathering

The big difference between real-time strategy and real-time tactical games is resources and gathering. The resource entity is the type of creature that exists to give away things. It typically doesn't do anything more. However, in Age of Empires, there were free-roaming creatures that ran away when attacked, but became food resources once killed. So some types of resources can do more than sit there. These entities should have very short update cycles. If a resource entity has nobody around it, then other than graphics and animation changes, it should automatically return immediately from a call to its Update function. If a resource gathering entity is extracting resources from a resource entity, then the resource entity Update function would process a message received from the "extractor" like "EXTRACT_RESOURCE." The resource uses Hip Points to be resource points that represent its total resource value. The resource would respond by subtracting some "health" from itself, and then return a message to the extractor of type "RESOURCE_EXTRACTED" and the amount given away.

Resource gathering entities should be limited in the types of resources they can carry and how much they can carry. A person cannot easily carry 100 pounds of anything, let alone gold. He would need a wheelbarrow or a truck. Regardless of the weight, carrying wood or timbers is utterly ridiculous. They are way too cumbersome. A wagon might be able to carry them, but no person could ever hope to. Keep these things realistic. Most games do well at this, but Age of Empires has guys carrying enough wood to equal half a house, which is utterly ridiculous, and other guys carrying huge amounts of gold and stone. Tools for carrying, like donkeys and wheelbarrows, would go a long way toward realism. Just try to be realistic in your design choices. StarCraft took the high road and provided a kind of resource—crystals—that we've never seen before and so we don't know what it's worth or what it weighs. So it is easy to do whatever you want with such a resource.

Storage pits and places to put things are important. No storehouse can hold everything. Total Annihilation does a good job of emphasizing this by allowing the player to build storage centers for energy and metal. Most RTS/RTT games let players store as much material as they can collect, and although this helps keep the focus of the game on other things like fighting, it destroys the realism of the experience. Warehousing is one of the biggest industries in the United States, and lots of big companies rely on warehouse companies for storage. It should be at least somewhat important in a RTS/RTT game.

Area and Build Area

Deciding how big a creature or building should be relative to other objects in your world is tricky. Most games have humans or trucks that appear giant when compared to the size of the buildings. Keeping buildings truer to real size relative to the creatures in the game is tough. Generally, the buildings need to be really big or the creatures are too small to see. It is usually better to have buildings be iconic rather than real size. Maybe three to four times the size of a creature that they produce is about right. Plus, when you consider the size of most factories in the real world, your production facilities would take about one-fourth of a really big map, and that doesn't make for a very fun game. You could only put four buildings on the whole map and then where do your creatures fit in?

The "blocking area" that a creature has is its map size. Think of this map size as the space required around a creature or unit. You can't walk through a tree—you have to go around. That area around the tree is its map size. This is usually measured in tiles or fractional tiles. It is doubtful that you will make a humanoid creature the size of a full tile, so consider making this map size a fractional or float value. Games like StarCraft can get away with making all of their world object's map sizes in whole numbers because they have very small tiles and they use the supertile concept. If you go this route, this will simplify your life at the expense of some flexibility.

Another trait of map size is its rectangular nature. Most objects, in the interest of simplicity, should be rectangular in their map sizes. This does not mean square; notice that most trucks aren't nearly as wide as they are long. So you'll need two variables to represent these two values.

Getting around these map sizes when pathing is a tricky issue. You need only to make sure that enough room exists on both sides of an object for it to pass between two other objects. This is a simple comparison once you know the creature's map size width; you just path toward the destination, comparing spacing between objects to the creature's width as you calculate the path. The tricky part comes when the creature can rotate, changing its facing, and therefore squeeze into spaces where it may not have been able to fit otherwise. This can make pathing a lot more work... good luck.

18

Chapter

Chapter 19

Pathing

Easy and yet difficult at the same time, pathing can be a good challenge for any programmer. Good pathing is hard to come by. *Path finding* is the algorithmic solution of getting a creature to move across the map. In the real world, this applies to robots moving around or an Internet application finding the fastest route to a Web site. There are many different methods of pathing, including such things as a traveling salesman who has seven cities to visit and wants to find the shortest way to see them all without returning to any. Then there's the greedy first search where you look around your starting position for the best way to begin your path to your destination. This is a little narrow-minded and creatures tend to get stuck. The problem of path finding is an old one, and many different methods exist to accomplish this goal.

The purpose of path finding is getting from point A to point B. This is trivial on a simple flat map. You simply find a line between two points or you can even have the creature calculate in real time where he is going. But how do you get around the wall in the middle of the map or across the land bridge? Then there's the question of group path finding. Creatures pathing toward the other side of the map in a group must cooperate so that they don't run into each other. We'll talk about all of these issues and many more before we're done. We'll cover the basics here and then we'll discuss ways of improving performance.

Simple Terrain

Say we have an open map. Nothing in the way—no trees, no buildings, and no other creatures. Sounds pretty boring, right? In fact, why would you ever need to find a path across a map that has nothing on it? That being said, let's start our discussion with the simplest of all cases.

In Figure 19.1, Joe needs to go across the map, represented here as a grid, to his destination, which is marked with an X.

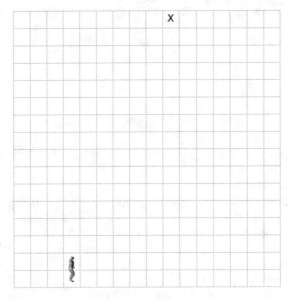

Figure 19.1
*X marks the
spot where Joe
needs to go*

Here we have Joe and his destination, an X.

Using Bresenham's line drawing algorithm, we end up with a path similar to that in Figure 19.2.

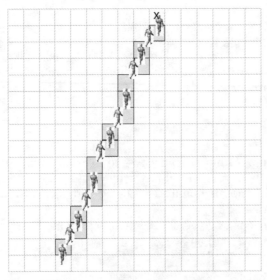

Figure 19.2
*This is a more
direct path, but
it requires too
many graphics.*

Joe's path forces him to change his facing too often and it can look odd. I have placed a graphic for every time Joe changes the direction he is facing. We can improve this.

Rather than zigzagging across the map and causing Joe to constantly change the direction he is facing, we can make him go in the same direction until he has a straight shot to his goal and then change directions, as in Figure 19.3.

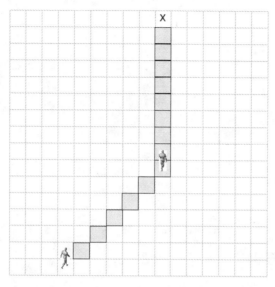

Figure 19.3
Using a more natural path to the destination

Now Joe is much happier on his much more natural path. No zigzagging and he should be able to still get to his destination provided that nothing pops up in his way.

This creates a more continuous motion but players may wonder why a creature doesn't head straight for his destination. By reducing the size of the grid, increasing the number of animation directions to 16, and forcing the creature to stay facing the same direction, you get a much more fluid pathing. See Figure 19.4.

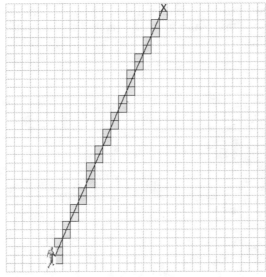

Figure 19.4
*Using smaller
tiles means the
path is more
natural and
requires fewer
graphics*

Even better is a grid of smaller tiles. Blocking tiles are smaller and easier to get around. The creature can pretty much path to his destination without changing his facing, and the path is really smooth.

This is a bit of overkill but creates the best results. The boys at Blizzard did this for StarCraft, which has a tiny tile size and 16 facings for all animated creatures.

Keeping the terrain simple is the best way to ensure that your pathing is fast and reliable. Take a look at StarCraft, Warcraft, Command and Conquer, and Seven Kingdoms. Their landscapes are super simple and unchanging for the most part. Simple landscapes are easy to path around and rely on. A grove of trees shaped like the letter U is easy to path around except from the top. Stick to simple curves of blocking terrain and avoid creating areas that can be partially or wholly enclosed. This is mostly controlled in the map editing process, so tell your level designers to avoid making them.

Rounded blocking sections can be the best way to control the problem, like big circles of objects. Another solution is to keep blocking sections small like tiny groves of trees. The hardest part of this problem is changing terrain. A creature mining crystals will change which landscape is passable and which is not. But we'll talk about this phenomenon in the next section.

If you really want that much realism, make your game 3-D and ignore tiles completely. Pathing using this method involves ray casting. A creature casts an invisible ray toward his destination in an attempt to "see" his destination. If he sees his destination, he paths immediately toward it, costing almost nothing computationally. If he hits something, he casts a ray in a different direction close to his original attempt. If that ray goes much farther than his previous attempt, then he'll path on that ray to just past the original blockage. Then he'll path from that point to his old destination. This ray casting continues until he cannot "see" a way out of where he is or until he finds an opening. This method is described briefly in the "Ray Cast Pathing" section in this chapter. This method can work well in a tile-based game or in games like Quake. Its complexity is high and there are many caveats, but it is one of the most effective methods for pathing that I have found.

Note: I use ray casting as an alternative to A*. (We'll cover A*—called "A star"—later in this chapter.) It doesn't always find the path like A*, but most of the time ray cast pathing finds a path equally fast and most of the time on fairly simple maps, it'll beat A* by over 30 percent in speed on average. Consider it a 30 percent performance boost on simple maps. When you can't find a path using ray casting, then fall back to A*.

Blocking Terrain

Most RTS/RTT games have a few things on the map other than a single creature; this is what makes them interesting to play. The things that can block your way include rivers, trees, buildings, other creatures, mountains, etc. Blocking terrain is tiles that have too much stuff on them to walk across. You may decide that creatures can walk through tiles with trees on them because trees are usually easy to walk under. Of course, drawing the tree and creature superimposed on it properly might be tough, but it does allow a player to hide units in the forest. Blocking terrain may also have piles of gold, mining facilities, or be force-field-protected. To further complicate issues, terrain can be partially blocking. This means a house may occupy only part of a tile, or the land may be marshy, making traversal difficult. Elevation can also make a creature want to go around.

In terms of pathing, you should avoid including movable creatures in your paths, particularly for long distance. Those creatures are likely to move out of the way at some point, and you'll need to plan on having waypoints as a means around the changing landscape anyway.

How does a virtual creature like Joe get around obstacles? Well, much like you or I do: We look for a way around. Say you are looking at a wall in front of you. You want to get to the other side of the wall, but you've never been on the other side nor can you see beyond the wall. Which direction do you go? Probably the most obvious and shortest route, right? Not necessarily. Once you get around the shortest side of the wall, you may find that you have a dead end in front of you or a fence blocks your way, and you discover that going the other way would have been much easier and shorter.

These problems are the same ones we face as programmers trying to move creatures from one side of the game map to the other. What happens if a creature gets trapped? What happens if the path Joe is taking is blocked by a small army? Should Joe figure out his complete path before beginning his journey or should he figure it out as he moves across the map, like we do?

19

Chapter

You'll have to gauge the best approach, but here are a few simple guidelines to make your coding life a lot easier. These are briefly discussed and you will understand them better as you move through the rest of this chapter.

➤ Never allow your map designers to make C-shaped areas of blocking terrain. It is too easy for creatures to get trapped and dramatically slows the game while the creature searches for a way out. Circular areas should also be avoided unless creatures cannot enter them.

➤ Make sure that the terrain doesn't have huge sections of walls or maze-like areas. The pathing routines will find their way through, but at a huge computational cost.

➤ Find a path all the way across to the destination. The reason to try going all the way across is to make sure that the path the creature is starting goes to his destination. While we humans can get reoriented if we get lost or take a wrong turn, a creature getting lost makes the game somewhat unplayable. If the destination is too far away, this can be too computationally intensive. I find that more than 60 tiles is too far, but you might want to try going all the way anyway.

➤ Set waypoints. These are what military aircraft use to set intermediate destinations when trying to reach a final destination. They are also used to set patrol paths where a plane may move between three or four points over a period of time on patrol. These waypoints help if something gets in the way because your path is now a lot shorter, and so pathing around your new obstacle doesn't take much time.

There are lots of ways to make your job easier but the above seem to have the most significant impact on performance and the ability to find a path. Still, sometimes you just can't find a path to your destination. Blocking terrain can be completely blocking. What do you do? The creature must give up. A creature should path as close as is possible to its destination and then stop. This means walking to the edge of the river or the edge of the forest before stopping.

Also, a creature will have to know if something is going to move before it gives up. If you have a group of 20 creatures moving at the same time across the map to the same destination, they are bound to run into each other when you get to the land bridge where only one can cross at a time. If a creature in the back stops pathing when he runs into just anything, he'll never make it across. In fact, out of 20 creatures, only three on average will make it across. What I'm saying is that blocking terrain isn't just blocking. It may be temporarily blocking which means that creatures will need to be put in a wait state for the amount of time it takes for another creature to move out of the way.

Blocking terrain can be avoided, and that is what path finding is all about. We'll be discussing the actual path finding at length in the next few sections.

Tough Terrain

Crescent-shaped sections can be difficult to path around. They are easy from five of eight directions but the three directions leading into the opening of the crescent-shaped area can add a woeful amount of time for a pathing routine, slowing the over-all game performance. If you only have one crescent on a map, you probably will never see the speed difference. But when you begin putting them all over the map, your game's performance will nose-dive. The worst shape, by far, is an O-shaped obstacle with a way into the middle through a really small opening. Just getting out of this predicament is tricky, but pathing into and then out of and around such a structure is highly unlikely. You will need to make sure that your map does not have any of these and that they cannot be easily created.

Let's say a creature fetching wood chops a hole into a rounded section of woods. Once he finishes chopping down the tree and bringing the wood back to the village, he'll look for another tree close by. He should return to where he just chopped down the tree. Then he needs to make a small list of trees nearby.

Maze-like conditions can kill the speed of a pathing routine, although usually they are not terrible. Don't expect any pathing routine to reasonably find its way through a maze in a fast way.

Moving terrain and changing landscape create a new dynamic for pathing routines. What do you do when you can't get across the drawbridge anymore? How do you get through a force field that wasn't there before? What about that new hole through the forest—should you take advantage of it?

These issues are best answered with partial paths and waypoints, which we'll discuss a little later.

The Destination

Defining a destination may not be as simple as it sounds. A destination can be a tile on the map. That's fair enough and certainly simple. Most of your destinations assigned by players will probably be tiles for purposes of moving units around the map. Moving creatures into tactical positions on the map will involve sending creatures to a destination, a tile on the map. But as the player assigns its creatures to attack, all of the destinations will be world objects. Most creatures, once they arrive at their destinations and find that the target has moved, must path themselves once they see an enemy unit. So ultimately, most pathing will be toward an object that will always be fairly close. Pathing to a point on the map is straightforward and doesn't change much once started. Pathing to a creature all the way across the map should be treated exactly the same until the creature arrives at the destination and sees that the target creature has moved on.

So now comes the problem: What happens if the target moves? This can be further complicated by distance. On a map where the players can see the whole map, telling a unit to move across the screen and attack a unit becomes an odd venture. Does the creature path across the entire map until it sees its target and then walk toward the target on a tile-by-tile basis? What happens if the creature gets across the map and his target has moved? What's even worse is if the target has moved toward your creature and your creature walks by his target on the way to his destination. But you can't have constantly moving destinations, can you?

If I can't see my target, but I know where he is, I will go to where I know he is. If I get to where I thought he was and he has moved (like my car keys that seem to move on occasion), I'll start looking around for my target. If the person I was supposed to meet or attack has died, I'll just wait around until reassigned to do something else. If I see my target at any time, within visual range, I will move to intercept, not allowing him to simply walk by me. This is exactly how your pathing routines should work, but there are some decisions here that could be different. You and the game designer will have to decide if you want the behavior to be slightly different.

If a creature is fairly close to his target, pathing can be simple. You probably won't even need real pathing routines. If things are in the way, then you'll need to have simplified pathing routines but not the full-blown pathing routine. But otherwise, simply moving toward your target may be enough. Pathing can be really simple when you don't need to avoid hitting things.

Getting to a moving target is tricky since you can never truly arrive. A creature moving across the map continues to move and if your creature has targeted it, then how does your creature ever get to his destination? Every time your creature arrives, the target creature keeps moving. Since most of the time when you click on an opponent's unit as a target you mean to attack that creature, it is probably best to move the pathing creature to attack distance, attack, and then path to attack distance again. Attacking usually means attacking until your opponent (target) is dead, so the creature assigned to attack a target should keep attacking until it gets new orders, dies, or kills the target creature. Another possibility is to assign your creatures to follow one another so you click on one of your own creatures as a target. The pathing creature should follow the target creature until it is dead, stopping only to attack opposing creatures. This allows you to assign groups to patrol between a few points on the map. Pathing creatures should have a pointer to a destination world object so that they can grab location information and path toward that world object.

Of course, the biggest issue for pathing and then repathing is the performance issue. There would be no problem in simply recomputing the path at every step a creature takes other than the demand on the CPU. Even the very simple code in this can be very slow under certain circumstances such as when the map is big or there are a lot of obstacles. If you are planning on supporting repathing, as well you should, you should only repath once a creature has moved at least one tile away from the last point where he last searched for a path. More likely, you should only recalculate the path once the creature is fairly close to its destination and it can see that its target is no longer where it used to be.

Waypoints along the path will help reduce repath time by offering intermediate stages along the path. This way, you won't need to have the pathing routine recalculate the path all the way across the map, but just a short distance. This saves huge amounts of CPU time and allows a creature to easily walk around objects that appear in its way on a longer path.

But once you get close to the destination, say within 20 tiles, pathing more often is possible and useful. This is especially true if the pathing creature moves across the map quickly. Fast-moving creatures move along their paths quickly (by definition) and you might want to wait for the creature to travel two tiles before repathing. This reflects the fact that a fast-moving creature is likely to move too fast to easily compensate for, even perhaps overshooting his target.

The point is, try to keep repathing to a minimum.

What if you have ranged weapons? When do you arrive at your destination if told to attack a target but you have a ranged weapon? Provided that a creature "knows" that the target is to be destroyed, this type of pathing is simple. The creature needs a full path to its target. Once he has the path, he will follow that path until in range. Since he "knows" he has to destroy his target, he will repath once his target moves, just like in our previous example. However, what happens if the target moves closer? Let's say you have a mobile rocket launcher firing on an enemy tank and the tank approaches. Depending on your game design, the rocket launcher could just sit there, try to find a direction to move to get away from the tank, retreat, move out of the tank's range, etc. Maybe the rocket launcher has a minimum range and a maximum range for its rockets, say no more than eight tiles away and no less than two. If an enemy unit moves within two tiles, it moves away. But pathing away is relatively easy.

First, to look for a path away, look for an open spot on the map that you can get to that is the correct range from the target. The simplest approach is to pick a random spot within four or five tiles' distance, see if it is about the correct distance, and path to it. Another approach is to take the required distance and the target's world position, and sweep around the creature at that distance using sin/cos functions until you find an open tile and path to it. Think of this method as a radar dish sweeping the terrain for an empty tile.

What do you do once you get there? That comes with the interface and telling units what to do. You will have to have a method of assigning tasks to creatures, like build, attack, move to, repair, etc.

Finding Your Way

Pathing can be done in so many ways, it is almost unimaginable. But for tile games, there are a few standard ways to manage the path.

BFS

Breadth First Search is the most exhaustive search. It works by taking a direction, calculating the distance to the destination, and taking the shortest path. If a couple directions are the same distance, then they will all need to be explored. This can quickly become exponential as more and more paths that are roughly the same distance are explored. If you need to find a path across the map, this can easily become millions of calculations, and as fast as optimized path finding is, it simply will slow down the computer way too much in this case.

An optimization to this method is simply to allow only one path, no matter if two directions are equal or not. This changes exponential branching and speeds up the entire process by about $3n$ where n is the number of tiles between a creature and its destination. The exact number depends on a lot of factors but the multiplier can easily be between 1.3 and 4; 3 is the most common.

If you were to try to find the way to a destination only 20 tiles away using only Breadth First Search, you'd have about 3,486,784,401 calculations. If you were wise and performed optimization by only calculating each tile once and storing the values in some 2-D array like the map, that could be reduced to exactly 100 distance calculations. Then you need more memory for distance calculations equivalent to 4 bytes per tile, being a float value. That would dramatically speed things, but even ignoring the calculations, you still have distance comparisons to make, and the number 3,486,784,401 cannot be changed there. How long does it take your PC to do that many cycles? Well, on a 600 MHz PC, you're looking at about 6 seconds, assuming 1 cycle per operation. A test typically takes a loop, an index, an offset, a comparison, a branch, and, if highly optimized, about 6 cycles per calculation. So with 3,486,784,401 calculations, you're looking at about 30 seconds or more. That is for a single creature to find a path to something 20 tiles away. Ridiculous. We need a different approach.

Estimating Distance Remaining

Many books containing pathing routines rely on distance remaining to provide a benchmark when picking a path. You have an estimate of the distance remaining that is slightly smaller than the actual distance remaining, and everywhere you look you compare to that distance. The spot that is closest to that remaining distance approximation is chosen. Then you move to the spot and choose an estimation of distance remaining (maybe subtracting the distance you just traveled). Then you begin again. This works fine but requires too much work. Why not just choose the shortest path at any given point?

DFS

Depth First Search is great when there are a limited number of nodes or steps to getting to your destination. It starts along a path and continues following that line of thinking until it gets to its destination. That path is essentially chosen at random. Then it runs another random direction until it arrives. It is indiscriminate about choosing a path as long as it seems to head toward the destination. When it hits a wall, it backs up a node (tile in this case) and tries different directions. We'll be using this method in conjunction with BFS to perform an optimal search, which is A*.

A* Described

The idea behind A*, or "A star," is to look for the shortest possible route to your destination. Actually, that is true of all optimal path searches. The problem with Breadth First Search is that you try all directions for the shortest path, and then continue trying all directions. This can lead to an explosion of attempts, culminating in billions of tests and possible paths. The problem with Depth First Search is that you don't explore any other possibilities in an effort to simply find some path. In order to find the shortest, you'll need to compare a few options to discover which is the shortest using the best of BFS and DFS.

Now, instead of exploring tons of different paths simultaneously, like in BFS, we will be exploring one path fully, like in DFS. Unlike DFS, we will compare all possible directions at a given point, like BFS. This combination yields a good working path finding routine.

Let's go step by step and examine how an optimal search might work. Keep in mind that dozens of path finding methods exist and I am only highlighting one of those here.

Note: Dave Pottinger described this method to me (with a few differences) a few years ago. This method is much better than many others I know. Dave is a great AI programmer who works at Ensemble Studios on games such as Age of Empires. He is one of the better AI programmers I have met.

Take a look at Figure 19.5.

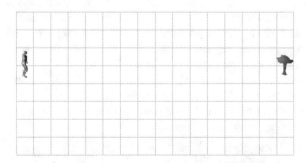

Here we have a peon who is assigned to path over to the tree. This could be simple enough because there is nothing in the way and it is a straight line. Just about anyone could write code to do this. Still, think about how you might manage this procedurally.

Everything is perfect here. The man is facing the right direction, there is nothing in the way, the tiles are flat...

This tile grid represents either a rectangular grid or a diamond grid. It doesn't matter that they are square, because all tiles are considered square for purposes of calculating distance anyway, except hex.

Figure 19.5
A simple world with no blocking terrain between the creature and its destination

This is the simplest world possible, unless you remove the guy, the tree, and the tiles, but that wouldn't be much of a world, would it? There is nothing in the way and all of the tiles are square for purposes of calculating distance. When visible in the game, tiles can be any shape, but you should consider hex-, rectangular-, or diamond-shaped tiles for purposes of simplicity. The methods learned here can apply to any tile-based system and even a few non-tile-based systems.

Walking to the tree is pretty straightforward. Still, understanding it procedurally will help us in solving the problems that we'll be encountering later. So we'll break it down. This method of pathing is on a tile-by-tile basis. There is no gestalt where the program assesses the entire situation and makes a decision. There are simply too many variables and too much work to do to find the absolute best path. This method will find a very good path but it may miss an obvious easier path due to its "ant-like" search method.

This method requires that you feel your way toward your goal like an ant. Unlike an ant, you always know your final destination and the "feeling around" is guided by tests. But this is still like feeling your way around while working toward your goal and you move until you can't move forward and then back up and try again. Even with this simplistic approach, given enough time, A* will always find a path—if one exists.

The problem with feeling your way around is you don't have all the time in the world. Giving a lot of time to find the path can dramatically slow the game at certain times or if the terrain is difficult. I artificially limit the number of steps in the pathing routine to 80, meaning that the pathing code will get as close as it can in 80 steps or fewer. If the distance is 100 steps, the pathing will not reach the destination, but the creature will simply repath once he reaches the end of the 80 steps. He will get there eventually. If a creature runs into a wall and has to back up, that counts as two steps. The idea here is to limit the amount of time spent pathing. Luckily, almost all pathing is close range such as in combat. This is between 80 and 90 percent of the game. The other 10 to 20 percent of the time, the game needs to calculate the full distance and then drop out of the loop after 80 attempts.

In our example, there are 14 empty tiles from the creature (Joe) to our target (the tree). This falls well below our limit of 80 steps, and even with walls, Joe can easily find his way to the tree. Only maze-like conditions or large enclosed areas could cause enough problems to surpass the 80 limit. We'll discuss the 80-step limit later.

Looking at Figure 19.6, we see that we are testing to check if the tile is open.

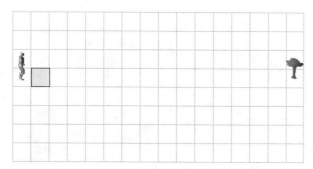

The procedure goes something like this:
Is the tile in front of me open? If so, I'll plan on moving there.

I am assuming a lot here. What does "in front of me" mean?
Which way should I walk?

We'll resolve these later.

Figure 19.6
Testing the first tile to see if it is open

This can be tricky if the object does not take a full tile, but for purposes of easy testing, we'll limit the pathing to full tile boundaries. If a tile is partially blocked, then we treat it as impassable. You'll have to play with the code for partially passable paths. The darkened tile is the first tile we'll test. It has nothing on it, so we can store the location as part of the eventual path, and test the next tile. If it had been blocked, we could have tried going in a different direction. This is very simplified pathing. We'll describe smarter pathing in a little while.

Note: Before the creature takes his first step, we calculate the path he'll take. When I talk about the creature taking a step or moving, this is figuratively. The motion doesn't start until the entire path is calculated.

Now that we're at a new tile for testing, we see that the next tile is open as well, as shown in Figure 19.7.

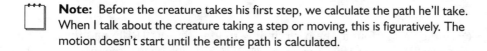

19

Chapter

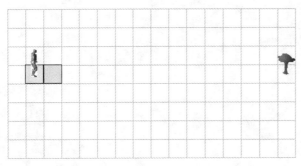

Figure 19.7
*At each tile, the
creature tests to
see if the next
tile is open*

Now we do the same thing until we get there.

By repeating this method over and over, we get to our target, as seen in Figure 19.8.

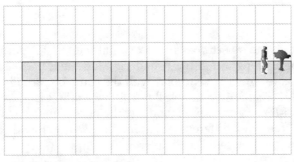

Figure 19.8
*Eventually Joe
arrives at his
destination*

We have arrived in this simple world.

Once the path is found, the path finding routine returns TRUE, and the creature gets the path ID number from the PATH_MANAGER, which we'll see in a bit. Now the creature essentially has a pointer to a path and he can simply say "give me the next world position on path 121" or something like this. The path stores all of the individual steps in an array of PATH_STEP structs. Here you see the simplicity of the structure. x and y can hold almost any value, within reason, and certainly within the realm of a 200x200 map.

```
//***************************************************

class PATH_STEP_MGR;

//***************************************************

typedef struct    PATH_STEP
{
      S16         x, y;              // -32768 to 32767

      //************************

      PATH_STEP (int x1 = 0, int y1 = 0) {x = x1, y = y1;}
```

```
        ~PATH_STEP ();
        void Clear () {x = 0, y = 0;}

        //************************

        void Set (int x1 = 0, int y1 = 0) {x = x1, y = y1;}
        void Set (PATH_STEP& step) {x = step.x, y = step.y;}

        //************************

        void Get (int& x1, int& y1) {x1 = x, y1 = y;}
        void Get (PATH_STEP& step) {step.x = x, step.y = y;}

}PATH_STEP, *PATH_STEPptr, **PATH_STEPlist, STEP, *STEPptr;

//*****************************************************
```

Since all it stores are two shorts (S16 is the same as a signed short), the structure size is rather small, only 4 bytes. Changing the S16 to a U16 (unsigned short) will double the number of possible map locations but you probably won't need that. If you are storing tile locations, then a U8 (unsigned char) will probably be large enough to store the entire map, which reduces this structure to 2 bytes. Actually, with 4 bytes, 1,000 paths of 80 steps only takes about 320 K, and you'll never want 1,000 paths at the same time anyway. Besides, your computer will slow to a crawl. More likely, you'll want to limit the total number of active paths to 300 or so, reducing this number to about 96 K. You could even add more data, allowing a faster path perhaps. Anyway, this gives you a rough idea as to the memory footprint that pathing will take.

There are a few access routines provided to help with easy assignment and to help with encapsulation, but they aren't necessary unless you change this structure into a class. For our next amazing trick, we have a class defined strictly to encapsulate functionality. There are no variables, just functions, and since we only need functionality, they are all static functions. Actually, you can use many of these functions for a variety of things, but they have particular appeal in the path finding arena.

```
        //*****************************************************
        // a class for functionality only
        class PATH_TOOLS
        {
        public:             // these numbers are used for testing
                enum {A_BIG_NUMBER = 0x7fffffff, A_SMALL_NUMBER = 0};
        public:
                static int      GetLargestNumber (int* array, int num);
                static int      GetSmallestNumber (int* array, int num);

                static int      GetDist (int x1, int y1, int x2, int y2);
                static int      GetDist (STEP_ref step1, STEP_ref step2);

                static double   GetRealDist (int x1, int y1, int x2, int y2);
                static double   GetRealDist (STEP_ref step1, STEP_ref step2);

                static int      GetMapPassability (int x, int y);
```

```
// the following functions allow you to test a range. for
// pathing purposes, this allows you to check a direction
static int      GetLargestNumber (int* array, int num, int begin, int
                        end);
static int      GetSmallestNumber (int* array, int num, int begin, int
                        end);
};
//****************************************************
```

The first GetLargestNumber function takes an int array and finds the largest element of the array. The parameter num is the number of items in the array. The function GetSmallestNumber does the same but finds the smallest element of the array. This will help us as we calculate distances to our target and then search for the shortest distance. At the end of the class declaration, you'll find another instance of GetLargestNumber and GetSmallestNumber. These functions examine the array but only in a range. Say you want to only compare elements 6 to 10 in an array of 0 to 100. These would only search in that range.

GetDist is a common function and its functionality has been centralized here for easy change. The distance formula I use is:

```
dist = ((x2-x1)^2) + ((y2-y1)^2)
```

Normally, you would take the square root of the result, but I only need this value for comparing the value of one tile over another, so relative distance is good enough, especially when one square root operation is 70 clock cycles. There are two types of GetDist, which take different parameters but yield the same result. The GetRealDist functions return the true distance if you need it, using the standard distance formula from algebra.

The last function is GetMapPassability, which takes tile coordinates and returns a 0 for not passable or 1 for passable. The code for this is based on a char array of passable/non-passable values. In real games, you look at the tiles on the map and return an appropriate value based on what the tile has on top of it.

These PATH_TOOLS should help you greatly.

The next thing we need to talk about is blocking terrain. Starting with Figure 19.9, we can easily see that getting to our destination won't be hard, but it also won't be a straight line. There is a blocked tile marked by an X and a darkened tile in the middle of the map. How do you get around it? Easy as pie. By the way, the tree is still Joe's destination.

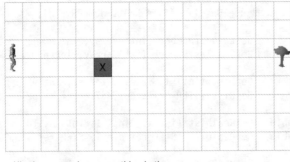

Figure 19.9
An obstacle blocks the path to Joe's destination

Uh oh, now we have something in the way.

Like before, we path as far as possible. Figure 19.10 shows Joe running into the block. You can't do anything but stop or move around it.

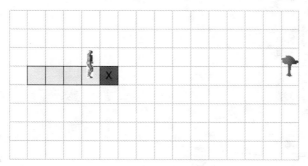

Figure 19.10

Joe runs into the obstacle

We path just the same way we were doing up to the point where there is a block. This is done by only looking ahead one tile at a time. Once we hit something, we have to find a way around.

If you look at Joe's position on the map, he only has one blocked tile around him, and that is to the right. All other tiles are open to him to move to, as shown in Figure 19.11.

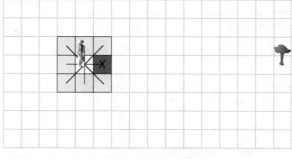

Figure 19.11

Joe has several choices to find his way around the obstacle

The shaded squares show possible tiles that we can go to other than the blocked tile. How do we pick the next one?

19

Chapter

Joe has seven choices of where to move next. He needs to make a good choice; after all, picking a tile behind him might be bad since he would go backward, and then probably forward again, caught in an endless loop. So he needs to compare his seven choices to one another and then make a decision. The best tile choice is one that will get him there the fastest, so a simple distance calculation of each possible tile compared to his destination will yield a bunch of distance calculations that we can use to make that decision.

So we go through all seven tiles and store the distances in an array, and then we use the PATH_TOOLS function GetSmallestNumber to find out which of the tiles is closest to our destination. See Figure 19.12.

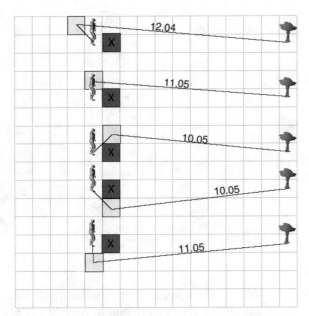

Simple, we test distance. A few of the distances are listed here. The shortest one is the one we will use to make sure that we are heading in the right direction. I didn't illustrate all possibilities because of space. You can pick either of the 10.05 distances and that will be just fine. The distance formula in case you forgot is:

```
dist = sqrt (((x2-x1)^2) + ((y2-y1)^2))
```

On a Pentium, the sqrt function takes 70+ clock cycles. And since we are trying to compare distance, and not use the distance value for something else, let's not use the sqrt and just use:

Figure 19.12
Calculating the
shortest path

```
dist = ((x2-x1)^2)+((y2-y1)^2))
```

This formula makes pathing three to four times faster.

Because of our angle, several of the tiles have the same distance, which is less common in a real game. We would just go with the first one that appears shortest; since we test clockwise, that would be to the upper right, although it really makes no difference at all. Now that we have a valid space to move to, we move and continue with the path, which yields Figure 19.13.

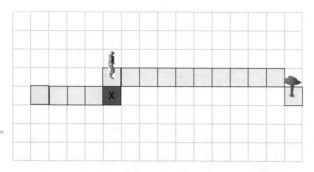

Figure 19.13
Choosing a new tile and continuing to the destination

I chose the top tile, just because it was close. Now that we are here, we continue testing distance at each tile. The highlighted path shows the result.

At this stage we'd return a TRUE value and the creature would begin walking.

In fact, this is the best way to find the path in general. The code is written so that every time a creature goes to a new tile, he must compare all of the tiles around him to find which one would be the best for his next tile until he finally arrives at his destination. This makes the code exceedingly simple. The main loop of the pathing code simply goes along, choosing the open tile closest to home from his current map position. This is almost all there is to it, and this is all you need for really simple terrain. The problem is that this method of pathing doesn't always work. This method is similar to what was used in Warcraft where way too many orcs got trapped in C-shaped tree formations.

Before we go any further, let's cover another optimization (the first being the simplified distance calculation). In our last example, we tested seven directions and found one that was shortest. For simplicity, you would always test eight directions, and any blocked tiles would not be figured into the list of possible directions for travel. But by testing only the three most likely directions of travel, we can reduce the amount of distance calculations and comparisons. See Figure 19.14.

19

Chapter

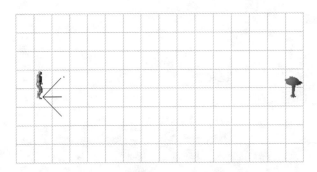

Normally, in order to conserve time, you really only need to try the three closest directions. This is sometimes considered an optimization.

Figure 19.14
Testing only the three most likely directions of travel reduces the amount of calculations and comparisons

First, we treat the pathing character normally for the first step, letting it try all eight directions. This is for finding which of eight directions he should start going. Then we face him in the closest direction.

From then on, in this example, we always try the direction directly in front, to the front-left, and to the front-right. So then we are always only comparing three directions instead of gathering data on eight directions and comparing them. This is over twice as fast as testing eight directions.

When we begin finding a path, at the very first tile we test eight directions because we do not know the most likely direction to travel. After that, the most likely direction is the same direction you chose last. Then we allow for going around corners and the possibility that a diagonal direction may yield a closer tile to the destination. We kind of "shine a flashlight" in the general direction of the destination and it works almost all of the time.

Difficulty with this method comes when we walk straight into a wall like in Figure 19.15.

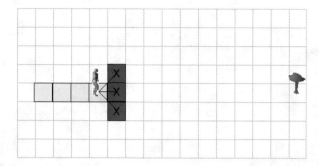

The problem comes when we come to a wall. What do we do?
This is where a second array of tags to tell us where we've
already been helps.

Here is an example of an array below. This array holds nothing
but tags telling us where we've been so that we don't go there
again. We'll be backing up one. The tags act like a wall, telling
us which tiles we've already tried.

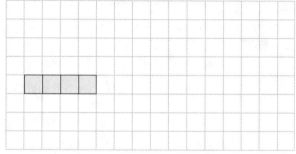

Figure 19.15
*A wall blocks the
creature's path*

19

Chapter

We'll discuss it more in a while, but you can see how this might be a problem
since all three directions are blocked. We'll need to add the ability to back up if we are
to restrict motion to the three most likely directions. I also want to point out that we
not only want a path, but we want a good path. Take a look at Figures 19.16 and
19.17.

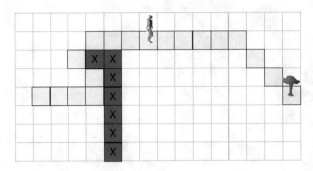

This is a bad path. Look at the roundabout way that Joe has to go. This looks bad and no human would ever walk that way around an obstacle. Most animals could do better.

Joe found this path by testing eight directions at every point and not backtracking at all. This is perfectly acceptable as a means of pathing, but it's not very natural looking, slow for Joe to traverse, and kind of kludgy.

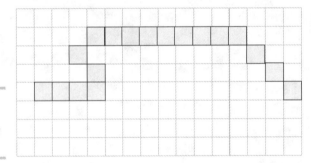

Figure 19.16
An acceptable but not optimal path

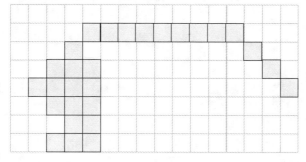

This is a better path. The "already tried" array below shows that a little more work was done, but by allowing only three directions and then allowing backing up, you get a lot smoother path that looks a lot more natural. Joe can also get to his destination quicker.

You might think that the extra work that it takes (see below) might take longer, but since you are only testing three directions rather than eight at every point, there would only be 84 total comparisons rather than 136 like in Figure 19.16.

Figure 19.17
A great path but difficult to achieve

Figures 19.16 and 19.17 show a good comparison of moving by eight-direction testing and three-direction testing. Three-direction testing is a lot faster and can get a lot more efficient paths as a result. It also finds the path in about half the time. The problem of this method can come when backing up. If there are traps or other difficult terrain, the three-direction optimization can be 50 percent slower than eight-direction testing. But its paths are still better, so it's a trade-off.

In Figure 19.18, we see that at every tile, we test three directions. The direction to the right is always the closest so we move there. Eventually we hit the block, but since we are testing three directions at every step, either of the other two is available, so we simply choose one of those.

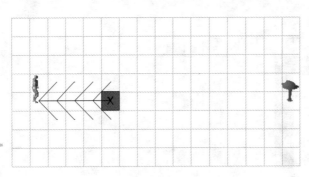

Figure 19.18
Three directions are tested at each tile, and the creature moves to the closest one

Back to our earlier problem. Since we are always testing three directions, once we get to the barrier, we know that we can't go there, so we simply choose one of the other directions and keep going in the general direction of our destination, the tree.

See how easy this is?

The creature heading must change, however, as in Figure 19.19.

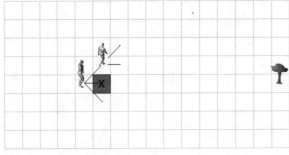

Figure 19.19
Each time the creature changes directions, the creature graphic must change

Once we go a different direction, we change our main creature's heading. This will change the three directions that we will test for closeness, or proximity, next.

This means that the three most likely directions have changed slightly.

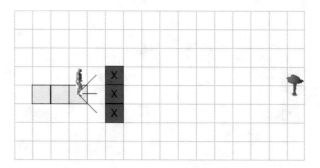

When he continues looking for a path, in front is just like a wall
because of the blocked tile diagram below. So he won't look there
again. Now he looks to the front left and starts looking for a free
tile to move to.

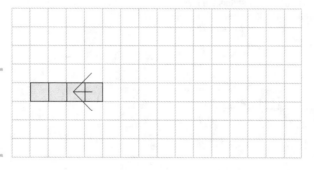

Figure 19.20
Testing three
directions when
the creature
runs into a wall

The heading continually changes as Joe moves in different directions and this
affects which three directions we test at any given point.

These map examples are rather trivial, so let's turn it up a bit. Figure 19.15 shows
a wall blocking the creature's path. This will allow us to expand our algorithm and
demonstrate how to properly path using the three-likely-directions rule. We don't
want a path like in Figure 19.16. We're shooting for something better, such as the path
in Figure 19.21.

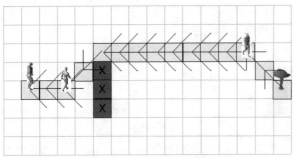

Joe continues like before on the path like above. Notice how the traversed part of the map fills in and how clean the path to the destination finally looks.

Something to keep in mind is that the path is precalculated. None of the work we have done thus far is done on the fly. When you make a request for a creature to move across the map, first he calculates the path, and then he starts down that path, one tile at a time. This path is stored and deleted once he reaches his destination or he gets new instructions.

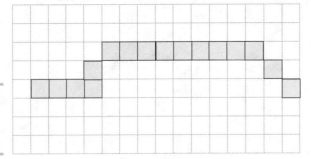

Figure 19.21
A path around the wall to the destination

So following Figure 19.21, we end up facing a wall. Now what do we do?

Before we discuss that, look at the bottom part of Figure 19.21. This is our tool for determining whether or not we've been to a tile. We need to show you how to implement one of these. Later in this chapter, look for the class called TAG_LIST_2D. It holds a 2-D bit array. All you do is set bits (or tags, which is what I call them) as you move along, passing x,y coordinates to the Set function and using Get to determine whether or not a flag is set. This class is efficient like the TAG_LIST class; a map that is 200x200 tiles (huge by most RTS game standards) takes less than 5 K of RAM. This class has exceedingly fast access. If you've forgotten how the TAG_LIST works, here it is again. We'll need it as well for maintaining a list of paths.

Our 2-D tag list tells us where we've been and therefore gives us clues as to where we shouldn't try going again. This could be thought of as painting an invisible trail behind Joe as he moves. Any area painted with "bread crumbs" he'll know not to walk on again. This tool will make our pathing quite efficient. We'll treat invisible trails like walls and not walk on them. Let's reintroduce the TAG_LIST and then continue with our discussion. You will gain a better perspective on how we track items and how efficient the TAG_LIST family really is. TAG_LIST_2D is described at the end of the chapter.

The TAG_LIST Again

Although you've seen it before, here is the TAG_LIST class implementation again. I put it here again for reference. It'll help us when picking an open path. This is much like the Standard Template Library class bitset. Bitset is somewhat different and limited so I chose to reimplement it myself. This class is great for managing a bunch of on/off switches and it has enough bells and whistles to make it super to use. Say you have a list of items and you need to track which ones are in use. You'd use this class with switches to monitor the state of each. Another nice thing about this class is its size. It has two pointers and four int's, making it 24 bytes. When the class is initialized to 100 switches, it will occupy only 57 bytes in RAM. When you have 1,000 switches, it takes 157 bytes, coincidentally (the 57 is coincidental). That's not very large when you think that it is storing a simple state for all 1,000 items. Most people might use an int, taking at least 4,000 bytes, while some might optimize and use a byte per item for 1,000 bytes.

In any case, this class is super powerful and much of it I use on a daily basis. The main functions that you should stick to are Clear, Set, Get, and Flip. There are also assignment operators and FindOpenTag, which finds the first available bit not used, but most of the time you won't need these. Clear, without parameters, clears the entire array, turning off the entire set of bits. If you need to turn on the entire array, use the following code:

```
TAG_LIST tag (1000);
tag.Clear ();
tag = ~tag;
```

That will flip all of the bits on. Set turns on a bit. Flip changes the state of a bit to the opposite of its current state: TRUE becomes FALSE, off becomes on. Get gets the state of the bit. All three functions take an integer as a parameter which tells the TAG_LIST which bit to access. All parameters passed to these functions are bounds checked. This class is so versatile and useful that you might want to use it in just about everything you do. The best part is if you have a list of objects and you need a free object to do some task, this class can look up and find an available one quickly. It also has some bit manipulation schemes to allow AND'ing and OR'ing and other various bit shifts and so on.

```
// taglist.h


#if _MSC_VER >= 1000
#pragma once
```

```
#endif                                          // _MSC_VER >= 1000


#ifndef __TAG_LIST__
#define __TAG_LIST__

#include <string.h>
#ifndef __STRING_H_
#include "struct.h"
#endif

#define FC __fastcall

//*************************************************
//*************************************************
//*************************************************

typedef class  TAG_LIST
{

private:

        enum {MAX_LIST = 64, BIT_SHIFT = 3, DIVIDE = 8, WHICH_BIT = 7,
              FULL = (1<<DIVIDE)-1};

        int            ListLength;       // number of items in list
        int            Current;          // the current byte we are using
        int            Last;             // stores last find position
        int            CountOn;
        U8ptr          Tag;
        U8ptr          BitMask;

        //**********************
        void IncCountOn () {CountOn ++;}
        void DecCountOn () {CountOn --;}

public:

        //**********************

        TAG_LIST (int num = MAX_LIST)
        {
            // init the BitMask list
                BitMask = new U8[8];
//      U8    bits[8] = {1,2,4,8,16,32,64,128};

            for (int i=0; i<8; i++)
                BitMask[i] = 1<<i;

            if (num == 0) ListLength = MAX_LIST;
            else ListLength = num;
            Tag = new U8 [(ListLength>>BIT_SHIFT)+1];      // 8 bits
```

```
        Clear ();
}
//**********************
TAG_LIST (TAG_LIST & TL)
{
    // init the BitMask list
        BitMask = new U8[8];
    for (int i=0; i<8; i++)
        BitMask[i] = 1<<i;

    ListLength = TL.ListLength;

    Tag = new U8 [(ListLength>>BIT_SHIFT)+1];        // 8 bits
    Clear ();
    Current = TL.Current;
    CountOn = TL.CountOn;
    memcpy (Tag, TL.Tag, (ListLength>>BIT_SHIFT)+1);
}
//***********************
~TAG_LIST ()
{
    delete Tag;
    if (BitMask) delete BitMask;
    BitMask = 0L;
}
//***********************
void FC  Copy (TAG_LIST& copy)
{
    // make sure that we have the space for copying
    if (ListLength > copy.ListLength)
    {
        if (copy.Tag) delete copy.Tag;
        copy.Tag = new U8 [(ListLength>>BIT_SHIFT)+1];
        copy.ListLength = ListLength;
        // Clear ();
    }
    copy.Current = Current;
    copy.CountOn = CountOn;
    memcpy (copy.Tag, Tag, (ListLength>>BIT_SHIFT)+1);
}
//***********************
void FC  Clear ()
{
    memset (Tag, 0, (ListLength>>BIT_SHIFT) + 1);
    Current = 0, Last = 0, CountOn = 0;
}
//***********************
//***********************
int  FC  GetTag (int i)
{
    if (i>=0 && i<ListLength)
    return  Tag[i / DIVIDE] & BitMask[i & WHICH_BIT];
```

```
        return 0;
    }
//***********************
void FC  SetTag (int i)
{
    if (i>=0 && i<ListLength)
    {                                               // set on
        if (! (Tag[i / DIVIDE] & BitMask[i & WHICH_BIT])) IncCountOn ();
        Tag[i / DIVIDE] |= BitMask[i & WHICH_BIT];
    }
}
//***********************
void FC  ClearTag (int i)
{
    if (i>=0 && i<ListLength)
    {                                               // set off
        if (Tag[i / DIVIDE] & BitMask[i & WHICH_BIT]) DecCountOn ();
        Tag[i / DIVIDE] &= ~ (BitMask[i & WHICH_BIT]);
        Current = i>>BIT_SHIFT;
    }
}
//***********************
int  FC  OnOffTag (int i)                        // simple test
{
    return (Tag[i / DIVIDE] & BitMask[i & WHICH_BIT]);
}
//***********************
int  FC  FlipTag (int i)
{
    if (OnOffTag (i))
        ClearTag (i);
    else SetTag (i);
    return Tag[i / DIVIDE] & BitMask[i & WHICH_BIT];
}
//***********************
//***********************
int  FC  Get (int i)
{
    return GetTag (i);
}
//***********************
void FC  Set (int i)
{
    SetTag (i);
}
//***********************
void FC  Clear (int i)
{
    ClearTag (i);
}
//***********************
int  FC  Test (int i)
```

```
{
     return OnOffTag (i);
}
//***********************
int   FC  Flip (int i)
{
     return FlipTag (i);
}
//***********************
//***********************
int   FC  FindOpenTag ()              // uses the Current pointer to start,
                                      // remember to call FindOpenTag in
                                      // continuous succession if you need
                                      // this functionality.
{
     int NumBytes = (ListLength>>BIT_SHIFT)+1;
     int StartByte = Current;
     while (Tag[Current] == FULL && Current < NumBytes)        // full
          {Current++;}
     if (Current >= NumBytes)
     {
          Current = 0;              // none available
          while (Tag[Current] == FULL && Current < StartByte)  // full
               {Current++;}
          if (Current >= StartByte) return -1;      // none available
     }

     // go bit by bit to find an available one
     int WhichBit = Current<<BIT_SHIFT;
     for (int i=0; i<DIVIDE; i++, WhichBit++)
     {
          if (GetTag (WhichBit) == 0) return WhichBit;
     }

     return -1;                     // nothing available
}
//***********************
int   FC  FindFirstSet ()
{
     Last = 0;
     while (Last<ListLength)
     {
          if (GetTag (Last)) break;
     }

     if (Last >= ListLength) return -1;
     return Last++;
}
//***********************
int   FC  FindNextSet ()
{
     while (Last<ListLength)
```

```
            {
                if (GetTag (Last)) break;
            }

        if (Last >= ListLength) return -1;
        return Last++;
}
//***********************
//***********************
int   FC  CountSet ()
{
        return CountOn;
}
//***********************
//***********************
TAG_LIST& FC  operator = (const TAG_LIST& TL)
{
        if (TL.ListLength != ListLength)
        {
            if (Tag) delete Tag;
            ListLength = TL.ListLength;
            Tag = new U8 [(ListLength>>BIT_SHIFT)+1];        // 8 bits
        }
        Clear ();
        Current = TL.Current;
        CountOn = TL.CountOn;
        memcpy (Tag, TL.Tag, (ListLength>>BIT_SHIFT) +1);
        return *this;
}
//***********************
bool FC  operator == (const TAG_LIST& TL) const
{
        if (ListLength != TL.ListLength) return false;
        int t = (ListLength>>BIT_SHIFT) +1;
        for (int i=0; i<t; i++)
        {
                if (Tag[i] == TL.Tag[i]) return false;
        }
        return true;
}
//***********************
bool FC  operator != (const TAG_LIST& TL) const
{
        return (! (*this == TL));
}
//***********************
int   FC  operator [] (int which)
{
        if (which<0 || which>=ListLength) return 0;
        int val = GetTag (which);
        return val;
}
```

```
//************************
//************************
TAG_LIST& FC  operator <<= (int num)          // num must be less than DIVIDE
{
     if (num<0) return (*this >>= num);

     int n = ListLength;

     while (n--)
     {
          if (GetTag (n-num)) SetTag (n);
          else ClearTag (n);
     }
     return *this;
}
//******
TAG_LIST  FC  operator << (int num)
{
     return (TAG_LIST (*this) <<= num);
}
//***********************
TAG_LIST& FC  operator >>= (int num)          // must be less than DIVIDE
{
     if (num<0) return (*this <<= num);

     int n = ListLength;

     for (int i=0; i<n; i++)
     {
          if (GetTag (i+num)) SetTag (i);
          else ClearTag (i);
     }
     return *this;
}
//******
TAG_LIST  FC  operator >> (int num)
{
     return (TAG_LIST (*this) >>= num);
}
//***********************
TAG_LIST& FC  operator |= (TAG_LIST& TL)
{
     int len = (ListLength>>BIT_SHIFT) +1;
     int testlen = (TL.ListLength>>BIT_SHIFT) +1;
     if (testlen < len) len = testlen;    // take the shorter of the 2
     for (int i=0; i<len; i++)
     {
          Tag[i] |= TL.Tag[i];
     }
     return *this;
}
//******
```

```
TAG_LIST FC  operator | (TAG_LIST& TL)
{
     return (TAG_LIST (*this) |= TL);
}
//**********************
TAG_LIST& FC  operator &= (TAG_LIST& TL)
{
     int len = (ListLength>>BIT_SHIFT) +1;
     int testlen = (TL.ListLength>>BIT_SHIFT) +1;
     if (testlen < len) len = testlen;    // take the shorter of the 2

     for (int i=0; i<len; i++)
     {
          Tag[i] &= TL.Tag[i];
     }
     return *this;
}
//******
TAG_LIST& FC  operator & (TAG_LIST& TL)
{
     return (TAG_LIST (*this) &= TL);
}
//**********************
TAG_LIST& FC  operator ^= (TAG_LIST& TL)
{
     int len = (ListLength>>BIT_SHIFT) +1;
     int testlen = (TL.ListLength>>BIT_SHIFT) +1;
     if (testlen < len) len = testlen;    // take the shorter of the 2

     for (int i=0; i<len; i++)
     {
          Tag[i] ^= TL.Tag[i];
     }
     return *this;
}
//******
TAG_LIST FC  operator ^ (TAG_LIST& TL)
{
     return (TAG_LIST (*this) ^= TL);
}
//**********************
//**********************
TAG_LIST  FC  operator ~ ()
{
     TAG_LIST t (*this);
     int len = (ListLength>>BIT_SHIFT) +1;

     for (int i=0; i<len; i++)
     {
          t.Tag[i] = ~t.Tag[i];
     }
     return t;
```

```
        }

        //**********************
}*TAGptr, **TAGlist;

//*************************************************
//*************************************************
//*************************************************
```

A* Described Continued...

The 2-D version of the TAG_LIST class allows bit setting and retrieval based on x,y coordinates. Otherwise, it is nearly identical to the TAG_LIST we just saw. This class provides us the means to easily keep track of where we've been on our map and I use it for lots of different things. The TAG_LIST is also used by the PATH_MANAGER, which we'll see in a little while, to tell which paths are still in use. Now that you've seen this class in all its glory, we'll get back to the task at hand.

The code design is a bit tricky. We'll discuss the full implementation later, but remember that like any bit of code, the design can be built in a myriad of ways. I choose a design that puts a creature in charge. He calls the PATH_MANAGER with a path request. The PATH_MANAGER has allocated a bunch of PATH_SIMPLE classes which each maintain a path. If a PATH_SIMPLE is available to be used, the PATH_MANAGER will return a pointer to it and the creature can get under way.

This implementation works well but is rather limited. The PATH_SIMPLE class has a limit of 80 steps. A better implementation is on the CD in the path.h file. Look for the PATH_DYNAMIC class and the PATH_MANAGER_DYNAMIC class. This has the three-direction optimization, and they have dynamic path lengths because they use a doubly linked list for maintaining path steps. The complexity in managing a doubly linked list coupled with path management might take a whole chapter beyond this one, but if you understand the basics of the Standard Template Library, you'll be ready for it. Otherwise, stick to PATH_SIMPLE because it is an order of magnitude easier to use. It's not optimal in terms of memory handling, but it will almost always find a path.

Returning to Figure 19.15, here we sit facing the wall. All three of our preferred directions are blocked. Since we are not actually moving but calculating a path, we can back up, making sure that we don't ever store the location where we just were. So Joe backs up one step by grabbing the previous step, decrementing the number of steps he has stored, and continuing with the path from there. Since he stores a tag in the TAG_LIST_2D as he moves along that tells us where he's been, we know to never try to move in the same direction that we just moved. Referring to Figure 19.21, we see that Joe's path has been shortened by moving backward, but the tags in the lower part of the diagram tell us that he can't move to the right anymore. We can choose either upper right or lower right and nothing else; if those directions are exhausted, then we back up again. Luckily, backing up once has given us a direction to go.

Going to the upper right, which is Joe's front left, we follow the path to its conclusion, shown previously in Figure 19.21. I put the three preferred directions here at every step to illustrate how they change based on the last direction Joe moved. The path is smooth and natural. The time it takes to find this path is about 500 clock cycles. On a P200, this amounts to about 2 microseconds. That means that you could find this path about 500 times per millisecond. This is a short path, but it illustrates that the code is sufficiently fast for you to focus on other things in terms of code optimization.

We can make life tougher for Joe, and this is where simpler pathing code begins to fail. See Figure 19.22.

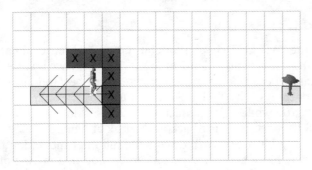

Now things get a little complicated. We can't just go around the top. Also, remember when we had to back up in Figure 19.15? Well, when we do that, we need to keep track of that point where we continued. Now here we are just like in Figure 19.15.

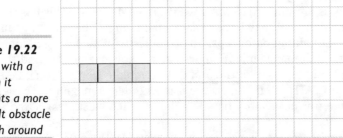

Figure 19.22
A wall with a cap on it presents a more difficult obstacle to path around

We have a wall like before but with a cap on the top portion. Joe cannot easily go over the top (upper right) of this blocking terrain, so we can assume that Joe will go around the lower part of the wall, which is to the lower right. Unfortunately for our algorithm, Joe will have to discover this by trial and error.

First he walks straight up to the wall in front of him and discovers that he can't go any farther forward, as shown above. Just like before, he backs up and looks around for another direction to go, as in Figure 19.23.

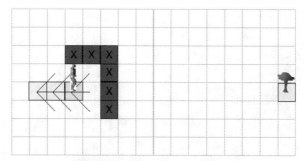

We back up just like before. This is the tile where we will start looking in different directions. It is shown here in a darker shade.

Since we are trying three directions when moving toward our goal, we try to Joe's left next. If this doesn't pan out, we'll back up again.

We'll advance into the corner and end up right back at this spot when we back up.

Figure 19.23
Joe backs up and looks for another direction to go when he finds that he cannot go forward

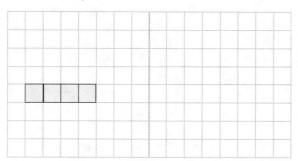

19

Chapter

The upper right (his forward left) is open, as is the lower right (his forward right). He will choose his left side, which puts him in the corner of the blocking terrain; see Figure 19.24.

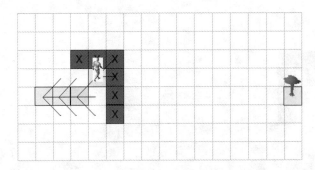

Well, we aren't going anywhere in this direction. You would
never be able to go in any of these three directions, so you
back up to the last tagged tile.

Notice the traversed tiles below. This really does help you keep
track of the tiles you have visited and so you don't need to
memorize which directions you have already gone. This tile tag
list tells you all you need to know.

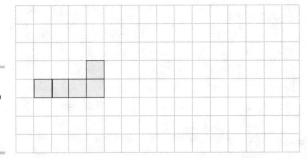

Figure 19.24
*Joe continues to
test directions
to find a valid
path*

You can see how TAG_LIST_2D is filling in the bottom portion of our diagram.
Next time we try going back one tile, we can only go to the bottom or back up
another tile. We'll go to the bottom right (Joe's forward right) and we'll complete the
path as shown in Figure 19.25.

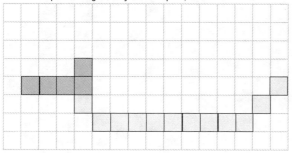

Here we back up again. Looking around for a place to go, and relying on our tags in the diagram below, we find that the only acceptable direction is to the lower-right, so Joe progresses from there to his destination.

The tags below reflect everywhere that Joe has been. The darker tags below indicate the state of the tags before Joe made the decision to turn to the lower-right.

Joe ends up following a really smooth path, as shown above.

Figure 19.25
Joe finds a path around the blocking terrain to his destination

19

Chapter

This much more difficult blocking terrain cost us one more move forward and one more retreat than the simple wall. This is an additional cost of 40 clock cycles or so. Look at Figure 19.26 for one more example.

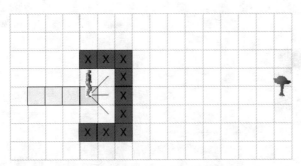

Here, our situation has gotten worse. It's going to force us to back up even more. I show below that we have already tried three directions to no avail. Each time we have backed up to our current position. Now we're forced to back up again.

If we had decided to go a different direction, we would still have five directions left to try and then the path will look jerky and zigzaggy. Better to have a smooth path. So we back up to the start if necessary. Only then will we look in more than three directions.

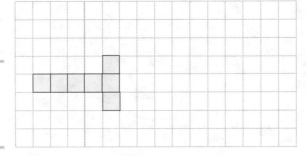

Figure 19.26
A C-shaped obstacle presents some difficulty for Joe

Joe has moved into the wall, backed up, moved to the upper right, found the corner, backed up, moved to the lower right, found the corner, and backed up. Is Joe really trapped? No, because the algorithm simply backs up again. This method of trying every direction and backing up when necessary continues, as shown in Figure 19.27, until a way around is found.

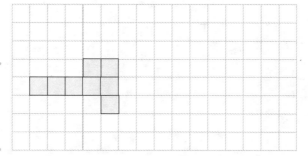

So we have backed up again. Here we see Joe, having moved into the upper right tile, looking in three directions. Using cardinal directions, to the north is blocked, to the northeast is blocked, and referring to the tags below, Joe has already been to the east. This tile is a dead end so he tries the same at the lower position that I have marked with a P. He finds the same thing and backs up.

With nowhere left to turn, he backs up again.

Figure 19.27
Joe tries each of three directions and backs up when necessary

Ultimately, Joe finds his way to the tree by filling in tags in the tag list in the lower part of the diagram. These act like walls, restricting him from taking these wayward directions, and he uses them to guide him around areas he's already checked. It is all trial and error and there are occasionally odd paths that the algorithm will find, but overall, it is efficient and very fast. Figure 19.28 shows the path around the obstacle.

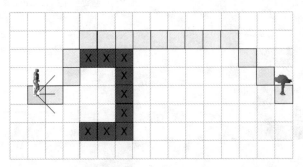

Now that we're back at the start, we can go quite nicely around our obstacle and create a path that will have people thinking that you are a genius pathing programmer. Of course, the path was found by trial and error, but they will see it and praise you.

If you had tried forward, forward-left, and forward-right from the start position, then you would need to start trying different directions other than the three preferred. Pathing can be done in better ways, but this defines most of it.

Figure 19.28
Joe ultimately finds his way around the obstacle by trying each of three directions and backing up when necessary

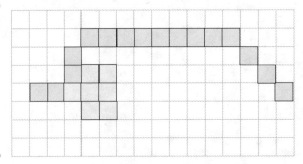

This method isn't flawless. A maze will slow it down and certain other contraptions will slow it to a crawl. Figure 19.29 shows a difficult situation, but actually this isn't too bad. You'd lose about 400 clock cycles, but on a 450 MHz machine, you probably won't even notice that. Still, it is something Joe can't easily get through. Better to not have this type of terrain anywhere in the game.

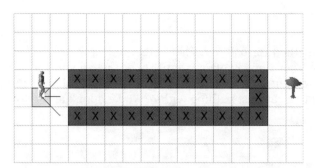

Figure 19.29
This blocking terrain is a real obstacle for the creature to path around

Of course, we can have an impossible situation. I sure hope that you don't have many of these in your game. This is dreadfully time consuming. Joe has to go all the way to the end and backtrack completely to the starting point and then choose a different direction entirely. This is where ray casting might help. If he immediately tries to see his destination without doing the pathing bit, then he can save a few steps by knowing that he either can get there directly or not. Then he can search for a way around if he needs to.

Worse yet is the situation in Figure 19.30.

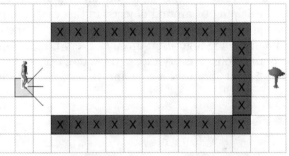

Figure 19.30
This type of obstacle takes too much time to figure out. It's best not to have something like this in your game.

This is even worse. This guy would be stuck for a very long time bouncing off of walls until he found a way out. This might slow down the game somewhat. Especially if you have a group of 20 or so Joes.

This is a 1,600 clock cycle pit. Joe has to spend way too much time just figuring out where he can't go. After all of that work, he can finally find his path, which is only 16 steps. A lot of work for such a short path, eh? Make sure that your maps don't have these kinds of traps, and the pathing code will do just fine.

Ray Cast Pathing

This is a very fast method for pathing. There are a few problems with the following diagrams, however. They don't explain what happens when you get to an edge of the map nor can they account well for changing terrain. But these problems are easily fixed by supplementing ray cast pathing with A*. Take a look at the following figures.

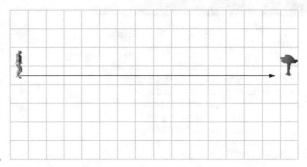

Figure 19.31
Ray cast pathing

The creature needs to calculate the angle in ray cast pathing. Here, it is 0° and there are no obstacles.

The first thing you do is calculate the angle (arctan or atan), which is 0° in this case. This angle is key to helping us around objects. In this case, the path is clear. The cast simply uses the angle to set a destination, the arrow head in the above diagram, and then steps like a line drawing algorithm through every tile, making sure that it is empty. There are no comparisons at every tile, and we don't try to feel our way to the goal; we try to make a straight shot to the goal and very often, especially at close distances, this is the best approach.

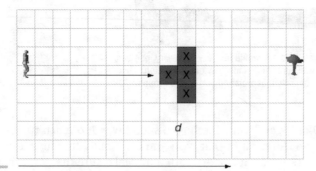

Figure 19.32
The ray runs into an obstacle

When the ray runs into something, we need to trace into the blocked terrain and figure out its thickness until we hit non-blocking terrain.

When the ray runs into an obstacle, we trace into the blocked terrain and figure out its thickness (the distance until we hit non-blocking terrain). This is 2 in the previous diagram. Add this thickness to the distance up to the blocking terrain, which is seven tiles from Joe to the first blocking terrain. The total is 9, to which we add 1 and then multiply the whole lot by 1.13. (This number seems rather arbitrary, but it works a lot better than 1.1 or 1.2; I'm not sure why.) The result is 11.3. This number is our test distance. The arrow at the bottom of the figure shows this length.

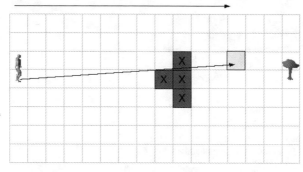

Figure 19.33
Casting a different path to avoid the obstacle

We cast out at an angle to our original angle of 0° in this figure.
Then we find the endpoint (shown shaded here).

The ray at the top of the diagram is about 11.3 tiles long. Now we cast out at an angle to our original angle of 0°. I chose 4° as an offset angle. Then we find the endpoint (the shaded tile). Here is the math:

x = cos (angle) * 11.3 + startx

y = sin (angle) * 11.3 + starty

The math is fairly fast, but it can be speeded up by a lookup table. startx and starty are Joe's starting position.

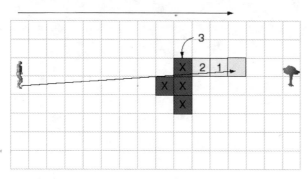

Figure 19.34
Tracing back to see if the ray hit an obstacle

We trace backwards along the ray to see if we hit anything, testing each tile from the endpoint back until we hit something. We fall out and try another direction.

The next step is tracing back to see if the ray hit anything. We go backwards along the ray, first testing the end. It's clear; so far, so good. Then we step back one (the tile labeled 1); this tile is also clear. We continue until we hit something or arrive at the starting point. In the above example, we hit something on the tile marked 3. We fall out and test in another direction.

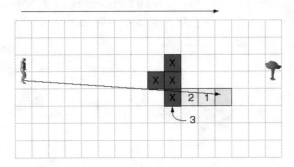

Figure 19.35
Using a different angle

We try testing on the opposite side, using −4°. If this doesn't find a clear path, we return to the +4° side and add another 4°.

We perform the same testing on the opposite side from the original ray, using −4°. We find a destination tile and backtrack, with the same results as before. In a real situation, this might never happen. Like a human trying to find the best way around a wall to a tennis court, you look at the wall straight on and try to figure out which direction is shortest. You compare relative distance both ways, and when you think you have a clear shot you go for it. This particular round of ray casting didn't get us anywhere, so we return to the +4° side and add another 4°.

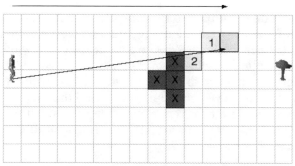

We use 8° and trace backwards again. This is unsuccessful, so we try –8°.

Here is the "already tried" array that keeps us from testing the same tile twice.

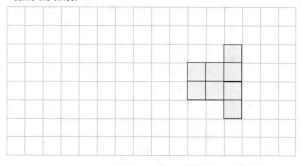

Figure 19.36
Using a different angle

Provided that we keep a filled array, as in A* pathing, this time we fall out at two steps. Otherwise, we fall out in three steps. We repeat this test at –8° and get the same results. In a real-world scenario, you will almost always get different results based on the side and usually by now you will have an open path, but not at short distances. Notice in the bottom of the figure, the "already tried" array; this keeps us from testing the same tile twice.

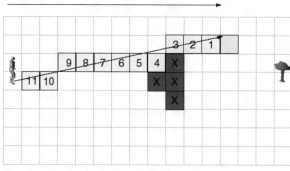

Figure 19.37
Choosing yet another angle in ray cast pathing

Once we are at the destination, the lightly shaded tile, we use it as a waypoint and start the process all over from that position. Our final destination is still the tree.

19
Chapter

Using 12° gives us a different path to the same destination. This is a good path and is open, so we go for it. We treat the destination as a waypoint and start the process all over from the new position. When we are really close, within five tiles, straight pathing, such as a line drawing algorithm, is easier—as long as nothing is in the way. If we had failed to find a path at 12° and at –12°, we would increase the change in angle from 4° to 6° as we work our way around the circle.

Ray cast pathing can be slower for very complex terrain, and it has its own weakness based on the depth calculation, but for relatively simple terrain, it is much faster than A*.

Managing Multiple Paths Simultaneously

BFS means managing multiple paths. The idea is to branch out from every node on the path to new paths that lead to the destination. Unfortunately, that means eight branches at every step of the way. This quickly gets out of hand, making multiple paths impossible. BFS works great when the number of nodes at any point is somewhat limited but given that every tile connects to at least three others in a corner, five others on the edges of the map, and eight others anywhere but the edges, the possibilities are nearly endless. And maintaining a list of all the paths that reach the destination is still a daunting task. You need a directed search, which DFS gives us.

Even with this, you can still end up with several possibilities. Any given tile may have two neighbors that are both equidistant from the destination. Refer back to Figure 19.12 for an example. Then which way is really shorter? It might be best to explore both possibilities. Here's what you do:

First, you need a way to hold a list of paths. Make it a maximum of 10 items or so. First, get an empty path, that is, a path that is not being used. Then, copy the path that you are currently working on into the new path. Set one of your allocated pointers to the new path and follow the path to its conclusion. Now continue with the second path, but make sure that it shares the TAG_LIST_2D from the path that just finished. That way you can be sure that the two paths do not share any of the same path nodes and are thus unique. At the end, simply verify that both paths reach the destination and then compare the number of steps required for each. Choose the shortest.

Adding Elevation to the Mix

Finding your way around a rock formation is relatively easy since you really can't walk through it anyway and climbing over it takes much longer than simply walking around. But adding elevation into the distance calculation can make life a little more difficult. First of all, just being at a higher elevation is not any more difficult than being at a lower elevation, unless you are over 4,000 meters above sea level where the air begins to thin. Not many games feature air pressure changes, and there may never be an RTS game that takes elevation into account. So when does elevation count?

Elevation only matters when traveling between elevations. Let's say you design a world with 12 levels of height. A creature walks along at an elevation of 3, which is sea level. The creature is told by his commander in chief (the player) to go to the top of a small hill and attack the death ray gun at the top. The creature moves toward the bottom of the hill at his normal speed of one tile per second. As soon as he starts walking up the hill, he slows to two-thirds of a tile per second. If he'd gone a few tiles around to the side of the hill, he could have gone full speed, but this frontal attack will make him too slow and he'll be cannon fodder in the clutches of the death ray gun.

All of the numbers in the above example are open to argument; you'll have to decide the true numbers for your game. The fact is, a straight line may not be the best approach. Then again, it may be the only approach. The best way to handle this is to add a small amount to the distance calculation. When figuring out which direction to go, if there is an incline change or an elevation change, add a little distance. When the elevation is lower, like going down a hill, subtract a little. What we want to do is influence the direction that a creature takes, but not completely change it.

So when you calculate the path, add between 0.2 and 0.8 tiles to the distance calculation before the squaring. Just add that much to the x and y directions. The higher the number, the more likely a creature will try to find a way around.

Another gimmick is to make a creature look for a way around. He can compare his current elevation to the destination elevation and if they are the same, he should try extra hard to find a way around a hill.

Simple A* Implementation

A* is a highly simplified path finding routine. All of the basics are covered here but don't expect bells and whistles. We'll get to some more difficult issues later. This code does not back up, nor does it use only three directions. It is meant for simple worlds and to introduce you to the structure of a path finding routine. The creatures in the map will find a path to the destination in almost every instance using the following code. This code is not robust, so if you change the map so that no path to the destination exists, the program will hang forever. Keep it simple for now.

Path finding was never considered a terribly easy task and the amount of code involved may seem daunting. But a cursory look at the code shows you how little code is really there. I designed it with simplicity and extensibility in mind, and break it up nicely. For purposes of testing, I have created a simplified method of map management. Clearly, this is not how a map should be managed. However, having a char array of blocked and open tiles can dramatically speed up the pathing process. That array would need to be maintained and modified as trees are chopped down, buildings erected, and creatures moved. The map manager should create and maintain this array for visibility, regions, kingdoms, elevation, and other things that need quick evaluation or could be displayed for player info.

So at the beginning of the first section of code in the main.cpp here, we have a "map" defined that contains the simple info of blocked or not blocked. In a real game, this type of array may be much more complex, but it serves our purposes here. The 1's and 0's can easily be changed to allow simple testing. The output is in text and appears in a DOS window. Hence, the next function outputs a bunch of X's and periods so that you can see what the final map might look like.

```cpp
// main.cpp

//#include "taglist.h"
#include "path.h"
#include <iostream.h>
#include <conio.h>


//****************************************************
int    MapWidth = 15, MapHeight = 10;
int    NumTiles = MapWidth * MapHeight;
U8
map []= {  0, 0, 0, 0, 0, 0, 0, 0, 0, 0, 0, 0, 0, 0, 0,
           0, 0, 0, 0, 0, 0, 0, 0, 0, 0, 0, 0, 0, 0, 0,
           0, 0, 0, 0, 1, 0, 0, 0, 0, 0, 0, 0, 0, 0, 0,
           0, 0, 0, 0, 1, 0, 0, 0, 0, 0, 0, 0, 0, 0, 0,
           0, 0, 0, 0, 1, 0, 0, 0, 1, 0, 0, 0, 0, 0, 0,
           0, 0, 0, 0, 1, 0, 0, 0, 1, 0, 0, 0, 0, 0, 0,
           0, 0, 0, 0, 1, 0, 0, 0, 1, 0, 0, 0, 0, 0, 0,
           0, 1, 1, 1, 1, 0, 0, 0, 1, 0, 0, 0, 0, 0, 0,
           0, 0, 0, 0, 0, 0, 0, 0, 1, 0, 0, 0, 0, 0, 0,
           0, 0, 0, 0, 0, 0, 0, 0, 1, 0, 0, 0, 0, 0, 0,
};
//****************************************************
void OuputMap ()
{
        cout<<"Map:"<<endl;
        for (int j=0; j<MapHeight; j++)
        {
                for (int i=0; i<MapWidth; i++)
                {
                        if (map[i+MapWidth*j]) cout<< "X ";
                        else cout <<". ";
                }
                cout<<endl;
        }
        cout<<endl;
        cout<<endl;
}
//**********************
void main ()
{
        PATH_MANAGER PathMgr (40);
        PATH_SIMPLEptr path;
        bool ret = PathMgr.GetPath (0, 0, 9, 14);
        OuputMap ();
        path = PathMgr.GetCurrentPath ();
        path->DisplayPath ();
```

```
        getch ();
}
```

```
//***************************************************
```

The main function is simplicity itself. The first thing I do is declare the maximum number of creatures that will need a path at the same time during the game. I doubt that any game would limit the total number of paths used at any given time to 40, but what the heck, here it is. This class is fixed, so don't underestimate or a lot of creatures will wait until other paths are cleared. I would allot about 40 paths per player in the game, give or take a dozen. Anytime a player has over 60 creatures moving at once, things get a little complicated for most people to manage. Still, when an advanced player needs to move a few small armies across the map, he doesn't want excuses from the game programmer like "I didn't allot enough paths to move that many creatures at once." That's where group pathing comes into play. The likelihood of a player being able to manage pathing 60 separate creatures across the map at once seems difficult to imagine. That's why 40 per player is a good rough estimate. Of course, computer opponents can manage more without any difficulty, so that number may need to be revised.

Then I declare a pointer to a PATH_SIMPLE named path, which we'll use to get a pointer to a path to hand off to a creature. The creature can then use it to find his destination. More likely, a creature would receive a command to go somewhere and would obtain his own path. The next thing we do is find a path to our destination. The return value is 1 (TRUE) for a good path, 0 (FALSE) for no path found, and –1 for an error like out of bounds or no paths available. No paths available means that you have passed the artificial limit of 40 paths that we passed to the constructor. We could just as easily declare 4,000 to be the standard number, but this is a simple example with limited code.

I know that a path will be found (if one exists, almost every time it will find the path), so I output the map no matter what. Nothing bad will happen if a path is not found.

The numbers passed to the GetPath member function of the PATH_MANAGER class are start location x,y and destination x,y. In order to do anything with the path, we have to get the resultant path. The return value from GetPath just tells us if the path finding was successful but does not return a pointer to the path. For a pointer to the path, we need to call GetCurrentPath if the result of GetPath is TRUE. What we get back is a pointer to a PATH_SIMPLE. It contains a step-by-step description of how to get from point A to point B. For testing purposes, I provided a function called DisplayPath which uses cout to print text displaying a line-by-line representation of what the path looks like. This way you can test the code without having to write some large convoluted program.

First, we have the header; the .cpp file will come a little later.

```
// path.h
```

```
#if _MSC_VER >= 1000
#pragma once
```

19

Chapter

```
#endif                                    // _MSC_VER >= 1000


#ifndef __PATHS_H_
#define __PATHS_H_


#ifndef      __TAG_LIST__
#include "c:/library_cur/taglist.h"
#endif

class PATH_STEP_MGR;

//****************************************************
//****************************************************
//****************************************************

typedef struct    PATH_STEP
{
     static PATH_STEP_MGR* PathPool;
     S16       x, y;                  //-32768 to 32767

     PATH_STEP (int x1 = 0, int y1 = 0) {x = x1, y = y1;}
     ~PATH_STEP ();
     void Clear () {x = 0, y = 0;}
}PATH_STEP, *PATH_STEPptr, **PATH_STEPlist, STEP, *STEPptr;


// total size is 4 bytes

//****************************************************
//****************************************************
//****************************************************

// direction is a specialty structure. It needs to know the actual
// distance traveled when you go any cardinal direction from tile to tile.
// This is especially important in certain tile games where the tiles may have
// odd alignment
// the numbers here for direction represent a simple tile system
struct DIRECTION
{
     enum DIR {N, NE, E, SE, S, SW, W, NW, BAD = -1};
     char x, y;
     DIRECTION (DIR dir = N)
     {
          SetDir (dir);
     }
     void SetDir (DIR dir = N)
     {
          switch (dir)
          {
          case N:    x = 0, y =-1; break;
```

```
                case NE:   x = 1, y =-1; break;
                case E:    x = 1, y = 0; break;
                case SE:   x = 1, y = 1; break;
                case S:    x = 0, y = 1; break;
                case SW:   x =-1, y = 1; break;
                case W:    x =-1, y = 0; break;
                case NW:   x =-1, y =-1; break;
                default:   x = 0, y = 0;
                }
        }
        DIR GetDir (int cx, int cy, int dx, int dy)
        {
            if (cx>dx)
            {
                if (cy>dy) return NW;
                else if (cy<dy) return SW;
                return W;
            }
            else if (cy>dy)
            {
                if (cy>dy) return NE;
                else if (cy<dy) return SE;
                return E;
            }
            else
            {
                if (cy>dy) return N;
                else if (cy<dy) return S;
                return BAD;
            }
        }
        float GetDist (DIR d, float posx = 0.0, float posy = 0.0)
        {
            if (d==N || d==E || d==S || d==W)
            return 1.0F;            // for our purposes, all cardinal directions
            // have the same value
            // this may be different for different tile systems.
            // diagonals are the square root of 2. Look at a right triangle
            // with the 2 sides that have a value of 1.
            //    1^2 + 1^2 = 2^2
            //    so the answer is square root of 2 or 1.414213562373;
            return 1.414F;          // close enough
        }
};


//****************************************************
//****************************************************
//****************************************************
// a class for functionality only
class PATH_TOOLS
{
public:                             // these numbers are used for testing
```

19

Chapter

```
            enum {A_BIG_NUMBER = 0x7fffffff, A_SMALL_NUMBER = 0};
public:
        static int      GetLargestNumber (int* array, int num);
        static int      GetSmallestNumber (int* array, int num);

        static int      GetDist (int x1, int y1, int x2, int y2);
        static int      GetDist (STEP_ref step1, STEP_ref step2);

        static double   GetRealDist (int x1, int y1, int x2, int y2);
        static double   GetRealDist (STEP_ref step1, STEP_ref step2);

        static int      GetMapPassability (int x, int y);

        // the following functions allow you to test a range. for
        // pathing purposes, this allows you to check a direction
        static int      GetLargestNumber (int* array, int num, int begin, int end);
        static int      GetSmallestNumber (int* array, int num, int begin, int end);
};

//****************************************************
//****************************************************
```

This is the simple program we are emphasizing here. The more "professional" version is in the code on the CD and will not be discussed here. The more advanced version yields the same paths at about the same speed, but it does it dynamically using linked lists for storing paths rather than a fixed array, which slows it down. Of course, fixed arrays will be faster, but for better memory management, use PATH_MANAGER_DYNAMIC. This will allow a pool of PATH_STEP's stored in DOUBLE_LINK's. These links can be found in link_obj2.h.

One special thing of note: The purpose of the DIRECTION structure is to provide an easy way to manipulate distances and directions of movement on the map. Should you decide to do a hex-based game or maybe a triangle-based game, you should start by changing this class. I only use it here for figuring which direction to go and which direction I just went. We'll discuss this a little later when you see it in code, but it is a very useful encapsulation of all of its information.

The PATH_SIMPLE class works with blocks of preallocated paths of fixed length. PATH_SIMPLE simply is designed to maintain x,y positions on a map for retrieval. These are encapsulated in the PATH_STEP class. All of the other code and variables in this class exist to support this single functionality.

```
//****************************************************

typedef class PATH_SIMPLE
{
public:
        enum {MAXSTEPS = 80};
private:
        PATH_STEP* Steps;
        U16     MaxSteps;       // cannot have more than this many
        U16     NumSteps;       // number in the most recent path found
```

```
        U16        CurrentStep;    // out of the NumSteps, which one I am on.
    starts at 0

        int   Find (PATH_STEPptr ptr)
        {
            for (int i=0; i<MaxSteps; i++)
                if (ptr == &Steps[i]) return i;
            return -1;
        }

    public:

        PATH_SIMPLE (int num = MAXSTEPS);
        ~PATH_SIMPLE ();

        void Clear ();

        // these are for the entity when he is following the path
        PATH_STEPptr    GetFirstStep ();                // always the start location
        PATH_STEPptr    GetNextStep ();
        PATH_STEPptr    GetNextStep (PATH_STEPptr); // get step following this
                                                    // pointer
        PATH_STEPptr    GetStep (int which);
        PATH_STEPptr    GetLastStep ();

        // the next 2 functions are for the PATH_MANAGER_DYNAMIC
        bool StoreStep (PATH_STEPptr step);  // true means everything is OK,
                                             // false means that there is no
                                             // more room, or some other problem
                                             // this function stores the variables
                                             // and advances the pointer
        bool StoreStep (int x, int y);       // simple location
        void RemoveLastStep ();              // from the top of the stack.

        // maintainence
        bool InUse ();                       // true is used, false is avail
        int  GetDistTravelled ();
        int  GetNumSteps ();

        void DisplayPath ();

    }PATH_SIMPLE, *PATH_SIMPLEptr, **PATH_SIMPLElist;

    //****************************************************
```

The PATH_MANAGER class holds a list of PATH_SIMPLE's and fills one in with the path between two points once it receives a request. The PATH_MANAGER does all of the path finding and storage using the PATH_SIMPLE interface to store map positions and removing them when a creature goes into a corner and needs to back up a bit. To advance the path, the PATH_MANAGER calls the function StoreStep of PATH_SIMPLE; when it needs to back up one, it calls RemoveLastStep. The interface of this class is rather clean as you can see.

An entity, once it has a path, will use the functions GetFirstStep, GetNextStep, GetNextStep (PATH_STEPptr), GetStep (int which), and GetLastStep. Mostly, an entity will stick to GetFirstStep and GetNextStep. The rest is just in case. Again, this is mostly a container class with a fixed amount of steps.

Here we have the PATH_MANAGER, which receives requests for paths, finds an available path in its list, goes step by step from the origin to the destination, and returns the path number, or ID, to the caller:

```
//****************************************************

class PATH_MANAGER
{
public:
      enum {MAXPATHS = 20, MAX_STEPS_ALLOWED = 80};
private:                            // variables
      PATH_SIMPLEptr  Path;
      TAGptr          Tags;   // for determining which paths are already taken
      int             MaxPaths;
      TAG_LIST_2D*TestMap;        // used for tracking progress
      int             CurrPath, StartX, StartY, CurrX, CurrY, DestX, DestY;
      U8              LastDir;  // for optimization, start with the last
                                // direction when we are
                                // are checking distances

      DIRECTION* Dir;

   private:                            // functions

      // usage functions
      void PrepTestMap ();
      int  GetDist (int x, int y);
      int  GetAvailablePath (); // returns -1 if none avail, 0+ for index
      floatGetMapPassability (int x, int y);    // simple test 0.0 is not
                                    // passable while 1.0 is wide open
      bool IsValidLocation (int x, int y);
      void SetLocationBlocked (int x, int y);
      bool StoreLocation (int x, int y);        // store the values in the Path

      // pathfinding functions
      int  FindFirstDirection ();
      bool FindNextLocation ();
      bool GoToPreviousLocation ();
      bool FindPath ();


   public:

      PATH_MANAGER (int num = MAXPATHS);        // max number of paths
      ~PATH_MANAGER ();

      void Clear ();
      int  GetPath (int startx, int starty, int destx, int desty);
      PATH_SIMPLEptr GetPath (int which);
```

```
        void FreePath (int which);
        PATH_SIMPLEptr GetCurrentPath ();

};

//**************************************************
//**************************************************
//**************************************************
#endif
```

Normally, requests for paths will come from an entity on the map, which has a directive to move across the map either from the player who controls it or from its AI telling it to fulfill some need. The path finding is all internal and hidden. The programmer should not need to worry about any of the implementation, only the function call to the interface, which is totally easy to use.

There are two functions named GetPath. The first GetPath takes four parameters, which are the starting coordinates and destination coordinates defined in tile/world coordinates. The return value is –1 in the case of an error like no path available, or an index number of the path. When later requesting direct access to the path using the other GetPath function, you pass the index number and a path is returned. You can then do whatever you want with the path; just don't delete it. The three other functions—Clear, FreePath (which takes an index number and frees the path for future use), and GetCurrentPath (which returns a pointer to the path that the PATH_MANAGER is working on)—all are an important part of making the interface complete. Their names are self-explanatory.

Now I use some global variables to define an artificial map, a char array really, with some global variables defining the map dimensions. Take a look back at our main function a few pages ago. These will need to be replaced by a real map or by access routines into the real map. The only code you should have to modify in the pathing code to get it to work is the function GetMapPassability, which looks directly at the map to determine if a tile is passable. You'll probably want to make modifications such as "from which other tile" and "how big an area do you need to get by" to this function but that will be your own game design. Besides that, there isn't much to know. This class is designed to be simple.

Here is the .cpp file that contains all of the code necessary for simple path finding:

```
// path.cpp

#include "c:/library_cur/path.h"
#include <string.h>
#include <iostream.h>
#include <math.h>


#ifndef SQR
#define SQR(a) ((a)*(a))
#endif
#ifndef STRAIGHTDIST
#define STRAIGHTDIST (a,b) (SQR (a) + SQR (b))
```

19

Chapter

```
        #endif

        #define EXT        extern

        EXT    int         MapWidth, MapHeight;
        EXT    int         NumTiles;
        EXT    U8          map[];

        //*******************************
        //*******************************

        int    PATH_TOOLS :: GetLargestNumber (int* array, int num)
        {
             int index = -1, largest = A_SMALL_NUMBER;
             for (int i=0; i<num; i++)
             {
                  if (array[i] > largest) {largest = array[i]; index = i;}
             }
             return index;
        }
        //*******************************
        // the parameter end must be equal to the last item in the array,
        // not one greater
        int    PATH_TOOLS :: GetLargestNumber (int* array, int num, int begin, int end)
        {
             int index = -1, largest = A_SMALL_NUMBER, val;
             if (num == 8)                      // optimization
             {
                  for (int i=begin; i<=end; i++)
                  {
                       val = i & 7;             // just the remainder
                       if (array[val] > largest) {largest = array[val]; index = val;}
                  }
             }
             else
             {
                  for (int i=begin; i<=end; i++)
                  {
                       val = i;
                       if (val >= num)          // beyond the end of the array
                            val %= num;         // just the remainder
                       if (array[val] > largest) {largest = array[val]; index = val;}
                  }
             }
             return index;
        }
        //*******************************

        int    PATH_TOOLS :: GetSmallestNumber (int* array, int num)
        {
             int index = -1, smallest = A_BIG_NUMBER;
             for (int i=0; i<num; i++)
```

```
        {
            if (array[i] < smallest) {smallest = array[i]; index = i;}
        }
        return index;
}
//*******************************
// the parameter end must be equal to the last item in the array, not one
// greater
int     PATH_TOOLS :: GetSmallestNumber (int* array, int num, int begin, int end)
{
        int index = -1, smallest = A_BIG_NUMBER, val;
        if (num == 8)                      // optimization
        {
            for (int i=begin; i<=end; i++)
            {
                val = i & 7;            // just the remainder
                if (array[val] < smallest) {smallest = array[val]; index = val;}
            }
        }
        else
        {
            for (int i=begin; i<=end; i++)
            {
                val = i;
                if (val>=num)           // beyond the end of the array
                    val %= num;         // just the remainder
                if (array[val] < smallest) {smallest = array[val]; index = val;}
            }
        }
        return index;
}

//*******************************

int     PATH_TOOLS :: GetDist (int x1, int y1, int x2, int y2)
{
        int distx = (x2-x1);
        int disty = (y2-y1);
        int ret = STRAIGHTDIST (distx, disty);
        return ret;
}

//*******************************

int     PATH_TOOLS :: GetDist (STEP_ref step1, STEP_ref step2)
{
        return GetDist (step1.x, step1.y, step2.x, step2.y);
}

//*******************************
double PATH_TOOLS :: GetRealDist (int x1, int y1, int x2, int y2)
{
```

```
        int distx = (x2-x1);
        int disty = (y2-y1);
        int ret = STRAIGHTDIST (distx, disty);
        return sqrt (ret);
}


//*******************************

double PATH_TOOLS :: GetRealDist (STEP_ref step1, STEP_ref step2)
{
        return GetRealDist (step1.x, step1.y, step2.x, step2.y);
}


//*******************************

int     PATH_TOOLS :: GetMapPassability (int x, int y)
{
        if (x<0 || y<0) return 0;
        if (x>=MapWidth || y>=MapHeight) return 0;
        int pass = map[x+y*MapWidth];        // get the map value
        if (pass) return 0;
        return 1;
}


//*******************************
//*******************************
PATH_STEP :: ~PATH_STEP ()
{}
//*****************************************************
```

This file contains all of the PATH_TOOLS code, the code for the PATH_SIMPLE class, and the path finding class PATH_MANAGER. In addition, it contains the PATH_DYNAMIC that dynamically allocates steps for the path from a pool, and the PATH_MANAGER_DYNAMIC class that does the path finding for that class. The PATH_MANAGER_DYNAMIC class is very similar to the PATH_MANAGER class in functionality and structure, with only minor differences. I considered making PATH_MANAGER_DYNAMIC derive from PATH_MANAGER, but it was too much work for code that rarely changes and needs little maintenance. Plus, path finding is somewhat unique to every tile-based game, so this code will always need tweaking anyway.

We begin with a few #include files. You can eliminate the iostream.h include, which was placed there to output the text of the found path based on the main.cpp file that we discussed a little earlier. Once you put this code into a game, you won't have much need for this but it is a useful debugging tool. The other #include files are all necessary. Then we define a few macros. These can be found in struct.h, but rather than include it here, I simply redefine the macros for clarity.

I defined a few external global variables that should appear in main.cpp. These will eventually be replaced by access routines or direct access to the map itself. For illustrative purposes, I have left this here, and in the interest of simplicity, I have made these variables of simple types.

Our first section of code involves the PATH_TOOLS code; it is straightforward code to help with array handling and distance calculations. Some of these can be found in the Standard Template Library, but I put them here in case your compiler doesn't have access to the STL. I centralized it all into this single class for ease of use and good encapsulation. A cursory look at the code will reveal its simplicity.

Here is the implementation of the PATH_SIMPLE class:

```
//****************************************************
PATH_SIMPLE :: PATH_SIMPLE (int num)
{
        MaxSteps = num;
        Steps = new PATH_STEP[num];
        Clear ();
}

//*******************************
PATH_SIMPLE :: ~PATH_SIMPLE ()
{
        if (Steps) delete[] Steps;
}

//*******************************
void PATH_SIMPLE :: Clear ()
{
        memset (Steps, 0, sizeof (PATH_STEP) * MaxSteps);
        NumSteps = 0;
        CurrentStep = 0;
}

//****************************************************
PATH_STEPptr PATH_SIMPLE :: GetFirstStep ()        // always the start location
{
        CurrentStep = 0;
        return &Steps[0];
}

//*******************************
PATH_STEPptr PATH_SIMPLE :: GetNextStep ()
{
        if (CurrentStep >= MaxSteps) return NULL; // error
        if (CurrentStep >= NumSteps) return &Steps[CurrentStep]; // keep sending
                                                                 // the last step
        return &Steps[CurrentStep++];
}

PATH_STEPptr PATH_SIMPLE :: GetNextStep (PATH_STEPptr ptr)
{
```

```
        int x = Find (ptr);
        if (x>-1) return &Steps[x];
        return NULL;
}
//********************************

PATH_STEPptr PATH_SIMPLE :: GetStep (int which)
{
        if (which >= MaxSteps) return NULL;                 // error
        if (which >= NumSteps) return &Steps[NumSteps-1];   // keep sending the
                                                            // last step

        return &Steps[which];
}


//********************************

PATH_STEPptr PATH_SIMPLE :: GetLastStep ()
{
        if (NumSteps == 0) return NULL;
        return &Steps[NumSteps-1];
}
//********************************

bool PATH_SIMPLE :: StoreStep (PATH_STEPptr step)
                // true means everything is OK,
                // false means that there is no more room, or some other problem
                // this function stores the variables and advances the pointer
{
        if (NumSteps >= MaxSteps) return false;
        int which = NumSteps++;
        Steps[which].Set (*step);
        return true;
}

bool PATH_SIMPLE :: StoreStep (int x, int y)      // simple location
{
        if (NumSteps >= MaxSteps-1) return false;
        int which = NumSteps++;
        Steps[which].Set (x, y);
        return true;
}
//********************************

void PATH_SIMPLE :: RemoveLastStep ()                 // from the top of the stack.
{
        if (NumSteps == 0) {Steps[0].Clear (); return;}
        Steps[--NumSteps].Clear ();
}


//********************************

bool PATH_SIMPLE :: InUse ()
```

```
      {
            if (NumSteps) return true;
            return false;
      }

//*******************************

int  PATH_SIMPLE :: GetDistTravelled ()
{
      int x1 = Steps[0].x, y1 = Steps[0].y;
      int x2, y2;
      if (NumSteps>0) x2 = Steps[NumSteps-1].x, y2 = Steps[NumSteps-1].y;
      else return 0;

      return PATH_TOOLS :: GetDist (Steps[0], Steps[NumSteps-1]);
}

//*******************************

int     PATH_SIMPLE :: GetNumSteps ()
{
      return NumSteps;
}
//*******************************
void PATH_SIMPLE :: DisplayPath ()
{
      cout<< "Path:"<<endl;
      char* array = new char[NumTiles];
      memset (array, 0, NumTiles);
      for (int i=0; i<NumSteps; i++)
      {
            array[Steps[i].x+Steps[i].y*MapWidth] = 1;
      }

      for (int j=0; j<MapHeight; j++)
      {
            for (int i=0; i<MapWidth; i++)
            {
                  if (array[i+MapWidth*j]) cout<<1<<" ";
                  else cout<< ". ";
            }
            cout<<endl;
      }
      delete array;
}

//****************************************************
```

Again, its main function is maintenance of the path. It contains 80 instances of PATH_STEP (the default value) in a dynamically allocated array. The PATH_STEP structure simply holds x,y coordinates, making PATH_SIMPLE very simple to maintain. All functions work in some way to store, remove, or access steps along the path that will be created by the PATH_MANAGER. The functions GetFirstStep and GetNextStep are meant for an entity to use as it moves tile by tile through the map toward its eventual destination.

As the PATH_MANAGER finds open tiles, it calls the StoreStep function to store map locations in the instance of the PATH_SIMPLE class it is working on. If it moves into a corner, it backs up by repeatedly calling RemoveLastStep until it gets to a place where it can move around the obstruction.

The function InUse is used to determine quickly if a path is available. Once an entity finishes with a path, i.e., it reaches its destination or gets a different order, the entity calls the Clear function, which makes this instance of the PATH_SIMPLE class available again to be used by the PATH_MANAGER relying on the InUse function. In truth, the entity should relinquish control of the PATH_SIMPLE pointer it has by calling the function in PATH_MANAGER called FreePath. I use the TAG_LIST, but this isn't necessary. I have allowed the user to simply clear the path using Clear. If the PATH_MANAGER cannot find an open tag (unused path) in its TAG_LIST, then it performs a search on the individual PATH_SIMPLE's to try and find one.

Lastly, the DisplayPath function is used to display, in text, the resultant path. This can be eliminated for the final game but is great when testing.

Below is PATH_MANAGER. This is where the pathing takes place. You already know how it works as described in the section "A* Described." However, we'll cover this a bit better in depth here.

```
//****************************************************
//****************************************************
PATH_MANAGER :: PATH_MANAGER (int num)
{
        MaxPaths = num;
        Tags = new TAG_LIST (num);
        Path = new PATH_SIMPLE [num];
        TestMap = NULL;

        LastDir = 0, CurrPath = 0;
        StartX = 0, StartY = 0, CurrX = 0, CurrY = 0, DestX = 0, DestY = 0;

        Dir = new DIRECTION[8];
        Dir[0].SetDir (DIRECTION:: NW);
        Dir[1].SetDir (DIRECTION:: N);
        Dir[2].SetDir (DIRECTION:: NE);
        Dir[3].SetDir (DIRECTION:: E);
        Dir[4].SetDir (DIRECTION:: SE);
        Dir[5].SetDir (DIRECTION:: S);
        Dir[6].SetDir (DIRECTION:: SW);
        Dir[7].SetDir (DIRECTION:: W);
}


//******************************------

PATH_MANAGER :: ~PATH_MANAGER ()
{
        if (Tags) delete Tags;
```

```
        if (Path) delete[] Path;
        if (TestMap) delete TestMap;
        if (Dir) delete[] Dir;
}


//*****************************

void PATH_MANAGER :: Clear ()
{
        for (int i=0; i<MaxPaths; i++)
            Path[i].Clear ();
        Tags->Clear ();
        CurrPath = 0;
        StartX = 0, StartY = 0, CurrX = 0, CurrY = 0, DestX = 0, DestY = 0;
}


//*****************************************************
```

First, let me say that this class is not perfect. There are ways to trap this class, albeit just a few. It keeps trying to get to its destination until its 120 attempts run out, meaning that if a path doesn't exist to the destination it'll keep looking, even if it somehow ends up farther away. You should add the ability to store multiple sized paths, such as short paths of 10 tiles or fewer, medium sized paths of 30 or fewer, and long paths of 80 tiles. This allows more efficient use of memory and resources.

The constructor does a lot. It sets the number of paths available for usage and initializes all of the member variables except TestMap. That is because the dimensions of the map may be undecided when this class is created, so it waits until it needs to make a path for the first time before relying on these global values. Now that's good thinking...

There is the initialization of the Dir variable. This is one of the integral factors of the path finding. We will rely on this class for offsets. When I want to go in the north direction, I look at the setting of x and y of Dir[0]. The function SetDir sets up these variables for each compass direction. When comparing tile distances to our destination, we want to grab each tile in turn. So I take the current tile coordinates, say tile 10,10, and add these offset values (x and y) to find out which tile I want to access next. We'll see it in action in a few pages in FindFirstDirection and FindNextLocation.

The destructor cleans up all of the memory that we've allocated. It is worth noting that I still test the values of these variables to make sure that the memory allocated correctly. Standard C++ now states that this is not necessary; however, my experience with Microsoft compilers shows they aren't completely C++ compliant. There are a few things that they still lack. I have had a problem before with deleting a NULL pointer value in Visual C++ 5.0, so better safe than sorry. The Clear function, as usual, clears everything and makes the class fresh as a baby's bottom.

The main interface to the class follows. This is where most of what the outside world sees takes place.

```
//*****************************************************
int    PATH_MANAGER :: GetPath (int startx, int starty, int destx, int desty)
{
        PrepTestMap ();
```

19

Chapter

```
        if (IsValidLocation (destx, desty) == false) return -1;
        if (IsValidLocation (startx, starty) == false) return -1;
        if (startx == destx && starty == desty) return -1; // we are already there
        StartX = startx, StartY = starty, CurrX = startx, CurrY = starty,
            DestX = destx, DestY = desty;

        return (FindPath ());
}

//*******************************

PATH_SIMPLEptr PATH_MANAGER :: GetCurrentPath ()
{
        return &Path[CurrPath];
}

//*******************************

PATH_SIMPLEptr PATH_MANAGER :: GetPath (int which)
{
        if (which<0 || which>=MaxPaths) return NULL;
        Tags->Set (which);
        return &Path[which];
}

//*******************************

void    PATH_MANAGER :: FreePath (int which)
{
        if (which<0 || which>=MaxPaths) return;
        Tags->Clear(which);
        Path[which].Clear ();
}

//*******************************

void PATH_MANAGER :: PrepTestMap ()              // also clears memory
{
        if (TestMap == NULL) TestMap = new TAG_LIST_2D (MapWidth, MapHeight);
        TestMap->Clear ();
}

//*******************************************************
```

GetPath takes four parameters—start positions and destination positions—and returns an index to a path, or –1 in the case where a path is not currently available for use (as we'll see later) or because some of the passed parameters are bad. The first thing the function does is call PrepTestMap, which allocates TestMap if necessary and then clears its memory. We use this TAG_LIST_2D to track where we've been as described in the section "A* Described." Next, we verify that the destination and start locations are valid map locations. Then we make sure that we aren't pathing from a start location that is the same as the destination. If everything checks out, we initialize a few local variables and call FindPath to take care of the rest.

After using GetPath, rather than relying on the return value, you can call GetCurrentPath to return a pointer to the last found path. This can be helpful. The function GetPath, taking a single index value, returns a pointer to the specified path. This is useful after calling GetPath to find the path to the destination. Our last interface function, FreePath, releases a path after use to be used again.

The administration of the path finding happens here in FindPath:

```
//*****************************************************
bool PATH_MANAGER :: FindPath ()
{
        CurrPath = GetAvailablePath ();
        if (CurrPath == -1) return false;
        int NumSteps = 0;
        int MaxSteps = MAX_STEPS_ALLOWED+ MAX_STEPS_ALLOWED/2;
        bool Found = false;

        LastDir = FindFirstDirection ();
        if (LastDir == -1) return false;

        while (NumSteps++ < MaxSteps && Found == false)
        {
            if (FindNextLocation () == false)     // we need to back up one
            {
                // we have tried to go to far, we're out of storage
                if (Path[CurrPath].GetNumSteps () == MAX_STEPS_ALLOWED)
                    return false;
                GoToPreviousLocation ();
            }
            if (CurrX == DestX && CurrY == DestY) Found = true;
        }
        if (Found == false) return false;    // this means NumSteps = MaxSteps

        return true;
}

//*****************************************************
```

First we attempt to find an available PATH_SIMPLE in the preallocated list. If one is not available, we return a –1 value, which ultimately makes it back to the entity that requested the path in the first place. NumSteps is initialized to 0 so we can track how many steps we've taken toward our goal. This number will include steps back when we are trapped, so the count will either run out of steps or find the path. We set the value MaxSteps to 50 percent more than the enumerated value because when we set the enumeration, we rarely guess right and 80 probably isn't enough when you consider retracing your steps. This is up to you as the game implementer. Just remember that most pathing is less than 20 tiles away and that a group of creatures should share a single long path, further cutting down the worry that all your processor time will be used for pathing. A path 15 to 20 tiles away with retracing your steps takes about 0.3 milliseconds (on a P233), or about 1 percent of the time for a single rendered game frame. This means that you could find 30 different paths for 30 different creatures during a second of game time that would take about 1 percent of your total CPU time. If you balance path finding by limiting it to four paths per game frame, then all requests could probably be met within a frame or two of the original request. No player would ever see the difference and it keeps the time in the game balanced.

Note: Most gamers use 30 frames per second as the standard benchmark for measuring game performance. If you dip below that, you need to optimize something. Some games run fine at 20 fps, especially RTS/RTT games that don't need split-second timing like Quake II, Sin, Half Life, or some flight sims. Don't ever allow your game to go below 20 fps or the game magazines will criticize its performance. At 30 fps, you have 33 milliseconds to perform all of the updating which includes network handling, interface management, redraw, AI, player updates, entity updates, and pathing, among other things. At 20 fps you have 50 milliseconds, which is a lot more time. On a 400 MHz Pentium at 30 fps you have 13 million clock cycles to complete your task, while at 20 fps you have 20 million cycles. That's a lot more horsepower for your tasks.

Then we set the Found variable to FALSE as we begin searching for a way to our destination. Now, as part of our three-direction optimization, we find our beginning compass direction. We store that value in the member variable LastDir which will guide us in our quest for the destination. We rely on this variable a great deal as we head for the destination because it is the facing that we spoke of in the section "A* Described." If it has a –1 value when it is assigned, the tile is completely enclosed and there is no way out. This is extremely rare, so you can comment this out in your game and things will be fine.

The main loop begins here. This is where we do a step-by-step search for the destination. Our while loop breaks when we get to the destination or when NumSteps exceeds our limit. Pretty simple, actually.

Then comes the first function call to FindNextLocation, which moves the CurrX and CurrY to a tile closer to the destination and returns a value of TRUE, unless it's blocked by blocked terrain or a previous path at which point it returns FALSE. If it can't move forward, then we back up one with the function GoToPreviousLocation, which is still counted by NumSteps. Then we test to see if we are there yet. This is a very simple loop, as it should be.

The last thing this function does is return FALSE if the routine never reached its destination or TRUE if it got there. These values are passed back to the entity that requested the path.

Here we have the heart and soul of path finding:

```
//****************************************************
int    PATH_MANAGER :: FindFirstDirection ()
{
        int DistArray[8];
        for (int i=0; i<8; i++)
```

```
        {
            DistArray[i] = PATH_TOOLS :: A_BIG_NUMBER;
            int x = CurrX + Dir[i].x, y = CurrY + Dir[i].y;
            if (GetMapPassability (x, y) == 0.0) continue;
            DistArray[i] = PATH_TOOLS :: GetDist (x, y, DestX, DestY);
        }
        int which = PATH_TOOLS :: GetSmallestNumber (DistArray, 8);
        if (which == -1) return -1;

        // LastDir = which;

        SetLocationBlocked (CurrX, CurrY);   // so we don't retrace our steps
        return which;
    }
//********************************
```

FindFirstDirection and FindNextLocation (described next) are virtually identical and they do the same thing anyway, but FindNextLocation only tests three directions, part of our path optimization. The idea is to gather data about all of the tiles bordering the CurrX, CurrY tile to find out which is closest to the destination. All blocked tiles, by terrain or by prior pathing, are ignored. Once the data about all of the bordering tiles is gathered, the array containing that information is passed to a function that will tell us which of the distances is shortest. Lastly, we set the tile as blocked so that we never retrace our steps on the same tile.

We start by declaring the DistArray for storing distances, and then start a loop for eight different directions. Then we set the *i*th value in the DistArray to a very big number that you'll find enum'd in path.h. This will make it a huge value beyond consideration when we start comparing relative distances. If a tile is off limits, such as off the edge of the map or impassable, it never gets assigned a smaller value. Later in this function when we call GetSmallestNumber, it'll never be close to the smallest number, so we'll never attempt to go in that direction.

We'll be relying on the Dir array to give us offset values resulting in new tile coordinates for testing. We set temporary x,y values based on the current map x,y position plus a directional offset controlled by the DIRECTION class. We set these values in the constructor. These temporary x,y coordinates refer to the coordinates of a tile; before we do anything with that tile, we need to make sure it is free to walk on and that we haven't already pathed onto this tile before. The function GetMapPassability returns 1.0 for every tile we can tread on and 0.0 otherwise. That means that invalid tiles never reassign the DistArray values. After verifying that the coordinates we are testing are valid, we calculate the distance to the destination and store that value in the DistArray to be compared later.

Once we've accumulated all of the distances, we'll compare them. It might be noted that we could have done the comparison as we accumulate data, which could be somewhat faster. However, it is tougher to explain and the speed difference is very small. The comparison is done in the PATH_TOOLS function GetSmallestNumber which returns –1 if none of the numbers is smaller than PATH_TOOLS :: A_BIG_NUMBER. Then we block the tile at our current location from being "stepped on" again by calling the function SetLocationBlocked. Then we return the direction.

This function could be simplified by just getting the general direction of the destination, but in an effort to remain consistent, I kept the same paradigm used by the FindNextLocation function. You'll notice how similar they are.

There are only a few differences between FindFirstDirection and FindNextLocation, so I will briefly explain the differences and leave the rest as previously explained.

```
//*******************************
bool PATH_MANAGER :: FindNextLocation ()      // based on CurrX and CurrY
{
        int DistArray[8];
        if (CurrX == DestX && CurrY == DestY) return true;
        bool found = false;
        // only 3 directions

        if (LastDir == DIRECTION :: BAD) FindFirstDirection ();
        for (int i=LastDir-1; i<=LastDir+1; i++)
        {
            int ILimit = i&7;
            DistArray[ILimit] = PATH_TOOLS :: A_BIG_NUMBER;
            int x = CurrX + Dir[ILimit].x, y = CurrY + Dir[ILimit].y;
            if (GetMapPassability (x, y) == 0.0F) continue;
            DistArray[ILimit] = PATH_TOOLS :: GetDist (x, y, DestX, DestY);
            found = true;
        }
        if (found == false) {return false;}
        int which = PATH_TOOLS :: GetSmallestNumber (DistArray, 8, LastDir-1,
            LastDir+1);
        if (which == -1) return false;

        CurrX += Dir[which].x, CurrY += Dir[which].y;

        if (StoreLocation (CurrX, CurrY) == false) return false;
        SetLocationBlocked (CurrX, CurrY);    // so we don't retrace our steps

        return true;

}
//*******************************
```

If we have arrived at the destination, we return with a TRUE value. We then test to make sure that LastDir is valid. It could be a –1, meaning that we need to find a new direction to go; this is rather rare however.

Our loop only needs three directions instead of eight. We want to go the same direction as our LastDir—to the forward left and to the forward right. The direction is expressed as a number between 0 and 7, 0 being North, like we declared in the constructor, and goes clockwise with 7 being Northwest. So we start to the left of LastDir (LastDir–1) and we go to the right of LastDir (LastDir+1). There is a small problem with this: We only have eight directions and if LastDir is 0, then LastDir–1 is –1. Anything based on that value, like array access, might cause problems. On the other end of this problem is when LastDir equals 7 and LastDir+1 is 8, beyond the end of our array.

The solution to this is simple. We declare another variable to AND the loop value *i* with 7. This has the same effect of using i%7 but at 19 times the speed. Anyway the result turns any –1 into a 7 (going around the circle) and any 8 into a 0 (going the other way around the circle). Most convenient.

We call a different GetSmallestNumber function so that we can limit the range of items being tested. Other than that, it is identical. Our last difference is the call to StoreLocation, which puts the current location into the resultant path that the entity will use.

That concludes the majority of the functionality regarding path finding. Still, we need to talk about retracing our steps and a few other basic functions.

Once we back into a corner, we need to back out and try a different direction. GoToPreviousLocation does just that.

```
//*******************************
bool PATH_MANAGER :: GoToPreviousLocation ()
{
        // if we are at the beginning
        if (Path[CurrPath].GetDistTravelled () == 0) return false;

        Path[CurrPath].RemoveLastStep ();      // go back a step in the path,
                                               // ptr is no longer valid
        PATH_STEPptr ptr = Path[CurrPath].GetLastStep ();

        if (ptr)
        {
            DIRECTION dir;
            int d = dir.GetDir (ptr->x, ptr->y, CurrX, CurrY);
            CurrX = ptr->x, CurrY = ptr->y; // store position of previous step
            LastDir = d;                    // restore previous direction
        }
        return true;
}
//*******************************
```

First, if we have not moved at all, then we forget the whole deal and return without finding a path. Second, we remove the last stored step, the one where we've stored CurrX and CurrY. Next we retrieve a pointer to the step before that one, and if the pointer is valid, which is almost always the case, then we change CurrX and CurrY to be the last position and we change LastDir to be the direction traveled before that last step. Then we return TRUE.

GetDist simply provides a local function referring to the PATH_TOOLS function. It really doesn't need to be here, but I left it anyway.

```
//****************************************************
int    PATH_MANAGER :: GetDist (int x, int y)
{
        return PATH_TOOLS :: GetDist (x, y, CurrX, CurrY);
}
//*******************************
int  PATH_MANAGER :: GetAvailablePath ()
{
```

19

Chapter

```
            int val;
            val = Tags->GetNextAvailable ();
            if (val >-1) return val;
            for (int i=0; i<MaxPaths; i++)
                if (Path[i].InUse () == false) return i;
            return -1;
    }
    //******************************

    float   PATH_MANAGER :: GetMapPassability (int x, int y)
    {
            int which = x+y*MapWidth;
            // we test our internal map first, we may have already declared this
            // map position impassable
            if (IsValidLocation (x, y) == false) {return 0.0F;} // blocked or invalid

            int pass = map[which];                            // get the map value
            if (pass) {TestMap->Set (x,y); return 0.0F;}      // blocked
            else return 1.0F;                                 // wide open
    }


    //******************************

    bool    PATH_MANAGER :: StoreLocation (int x, int y)
    {
            if (IsValidLocation (x, y) == false) return false;

            return Path[CurrPath].StoreStep (x, y);
    }


    //******************************

    void    PATH_MANAGER :: SetLocationBlocked (int x, int y)
    {
            if (IsValidLocation (x, y) == false) return;
            TestMap->Set (x,y);
    }


    //******************************

    bool    PATH_MANAGER :: IsValidLocation (int x, int y)
    {
            if (TestMap->Get (x,y) != 0) return false;
            return true;
    }
    //****************************************************
    //****************************************************
    //****************************************************
```

The function GetAvailablePath looks for a path not being used by any entity and returns an index number. If the Tags variable is not up to date, which can happen if the entities clear the paths but do not call the PATH_MANAGER member function

FreePath, then it does a meticulous search through every path to see if it is in use. If it finds one, it returns the index number. Otherwise, it returns –1, meaning nothing is available.

The function GetMapPassability will have to be modified to allow for real map access and the passability factor will need to be modified to approximate how your game handles it. Other than this, you can see how the function works.

StoreLocation puts the current map location into storage in whichever PATH_SIMPLE is the currently selected one, after doing a last-second verification that the x,y coordinate is valid. This coordinate gets stored and becomes part of the eventual path that the entity will follow.

SetLocationBlocked stores the passed-in x,y coordinates as a blocked tile in the TestMap, meaning that we cannot path onto this tile again. The last function in this class, IsValidLocation, relies on the TestMap (TAG_LIST_2D) to return 1 if any value is beyond map boundaries or if we have "stepped" on this tile before.

That explains it. Hopefully it's easy enough to understand. Refer to the section "A* Described" for a thorough explanation as to the theory on how this code works.

Waypoints and Partial Paths

Waypoints and partial paths can dramatically improve pathing performance. They also provide keys to allowing players to designate complex paths. A partial path is an incomplete path. On a 100x100 map, a creature on one side of the map needing to path to the other side could never do it in 80 steps or fewer. An entity at the end of a path will need to see if he has met his goal of getting to an x,y map location. If so, he clears the path and then does whatever he was told to do next. But if not, he'll need to path to the end of his 80 steps, free his current path for reuse, and request a path for the remaining distance. Even with limited length paths, partial paths provide the solution to moving across huge maps.

Waypoints are much like partial paths in that they solve a big problem by breaking it into many smaller parts. There are two kinds of waypoints: "player-assigned" waypoints and "broken path" waypoints.

Player-assigned waypoints allow players to assign complex paths to a creature. They do not tell creatures to go to the town center, heal the morpho-matic machine, go to the forest, attack the castle there, and return home. These are goals and should be treated as such, not waypoints. Waypoints are used strictly in pathing. A player should be able to tell a creature to go to this spot on the map, then this spot, and then this spot. But since these fall into the realm of goals, leave the paradigm as it is. It works better that way.

Broken path waypoints are a great way to help with repathing. Say that you need a creature to move 80 tiles away. On the way, he runs into a new magical forest that has grown there since he first got directions to his destination, only 20 tiles away. Should he throw away his old path and start over? That would lose quite a bit of pathing.

By breaking the path into sections and setting those locations as goals, a repath is a small undertaking. Say that the 80-step path described is broken into four equal parts of 20 tiles. The entity now has a small path that is only 20 tiles long and four waypoints, including his eventual destination. The rest of the path is kept, but at any time, things getting in the way are pathed around. It is the next waypoint, not the destination, that is the goal. This method can save a lot of processing time on really long paths but should be avoided in any path shorter than 40 tiles. Think of these waypoints as an optimization.

Sources

The following resources are available for pathing techniques. All of these were valid at this writing:

Theory:
> http://theory.stanford.edu/~amitp/GameProgramming/PathFinders.html

Pathing techniques:
> http://www.michaelross.com/~steveg/cs450/search.html

Theory and ideas:
> http://people.mw.mediaone.net/markeverson/map_ai.htm

Internet but good:
> http://aif.wu-wien.ac.at/usr/geyers/archive/iagents/vo/u5/unitflat/unit.html

A great home page:
> http://home.sol.no/~johncl/spath/modspan.htm and
> http://home.sol.no/~johncl/shorpath.htm

Very technical:
> http://joda.cis.temple.edu/~ingargio/cis587/readings/search.html

Broad discussion personal page:
> http://www.mat.uc.pt/~eqvm/OPP/shortestpath.html

Groups

How to manage groups raises difficult questions. Should they be doubly linked to each other? Should they all have a group ID number like in the CREATURE_FLAGS structure in struct.h? In terms of pathing, the behavior should follow one of a few different varieties.

Let's discuss waiting for clearing before we talk about different methods. An entity on a particular path should follow that path to its conclusion, but what happens when somebody else steps in his way? Should he give up and repath immediately? Probably not, because repathing would eat up all available CPU time when you path a group across the map. It is better for a creature to wait for clearing. This is especially true if he can look at the group ID number of the creature blocking the way and see that they are in the same group. That means that the creatures are likely headed in the same direction and that a creature trying to get onto its path should be polite and wait.

Of course, a blocked creature could path around. This still requires some pathing time and requires some support for the waypoint idea, or at least something very similar, but it should be considered. A creature, upon seeing that his path is blocked, could immediately request another path to some point along the way to the destination or to some waypoint on the path. This isn't usually much better than waiting and is often worse. You usually end up with the same path a second time or something too close to make any real performance difference.

So then the question becomes: How long should a creature wait? That is a preference issue but I don't want to sound trite when I say "as long as it takes." The problem may be that a group of creatures pathing to their destination may come to a pass where only one can enter at a time. Some creatures may have to wait until the end before they can path into the pass. Basically a creature in a group told to go somewhere should wait indefinitely for other members of its group to move out of its way. It should also verify that the other creatures in its way have the same goal. Otherwise it should path around; after all, it could be assigned to a group but get an individual command to go somewhere.

Each creature receiving a path command could find its own path to the destination. This can be tough, especially if you have large groups of creatures, but it makes group pathing easier. However, the processing time might be quite long. It is better for them to all share a path, but if paths are short, this might be an option.

Creating a single path for a group and making all members go toward that path is one way that many game developers solve this problem. Basically, all members of an assigned group go single file toward their destination. It works well and is easy to implement. Just make every creature walk toward the path and then follow it. Each creature will wait for others in its group to get out of the way. Most RTS/RTT games use this method.

Then you could create a single path for the group where each creature in the group tries to maintain his original distance from others in the group. Basically, each creature in the group follows the resultant path at a distance equal to its starting distance from the path. This keeps the creatures from bumping into each other and is good for the support of formations. Constrictions caused by terrain break this but overall it works well. You can see this in Age of Empires. Formation moving can look odd at times, however. Say you have two creatures five tiles apart and you select them and tell them to move 20 tiles away. They will try to stay apart from each other and arrive in that same formation 20 tiles away. You would expect them both to go to the same tile if possible.

A hybrid of this would be to path toward the middle when able and otherwise keep distance. Basically, the members of a group are always trying to move toward the middle but still always following the path. This eliminates single-file movement and allows a group to arrive at its destination in force without some of the odd behavior that you see in formation moving.

19

Chapter

The Entities-Trying-to-Get-Around-Each-Other Problem

This problem is much too common to ignore. Two friendly creatures (as opposed to enemies that might attack each other) meet head-on trying to get past each other. One moves a little, and then the other moves a little and they sit there in a little dance. This is easy to witness in Total Annihilation. Age of Empires solved this by making one of the creatures wait a second while the other one made a brief excursion around. Again, credit goes to Dave Pottinger at Ensemble Studios for a great solution to an obviously thorny problem.

The problem is caused by a few factors. First, the creatures need to know why they can't move onto the next tile. Just knowing that another creature is there isn't enough because then they both just do a quick detour and run into each other again. Once they know that another creature is in the way, one needs to wait while the other does the excursion, meaning that a little communication must exist between the two in order for this to happen or the main program must make this decision for them (like God intervening). Deciding who goes and who waits can be decided at random; it really doesn't matter.

How to Keep Track of Paths Passed

The third class listed in taglist.h is explained below. This TAG_LIST_2D class keeps tracks of paths that have already been used.

```
//***************************************************
//***************************************************
typedef class   TAG_LIST_2D
{

private:

    enum {MAX_LIST = 64, BIT_SHIFT = 3, DIVIDE = 8, WHICH_BIT = 7, FULL =
        (1<<DIVIDE)-1};

        int       ListLength;      // number of items in list
        int       Current;         // the current byte we are using
        int       Last;            // stores last find position
        int       CountOn;
        U8ptr     Tag;
        U8ptr     BitMask;
        int       Width, Height;

        //**********************
        void IncCountOn () {CountOn ++;}
        void DecCountOn () {CountOn --;}

    public:

        //**********************
```

```
TAG_LIST_2D (const int w, const int h)
{
    Width = w, Height = h;
    int num = Width*Height;
    // init the BitMask list
        BitMask = new U8[8];
//  U8   bits[8] = {1,2,4,8,16,32,64,128};
    for (int i=0; i<8; i++)
        BitMask[i] = 1<<i;

    if (num == 0) ListLength = MAX_LIST;
    else ListLength = num;
    Tag = new U8 [(ListLength>>BIT_SHIFT)+1];        // 8 bits
    Clear ();
}
//***********************
TAG_LIST_2D (const TAG_LIST_2D & TL)
{
    Width = TL.Width, Height = TL.Height;
    // init the BitMask list
        BitMask = new U8[8];
    for (int i=0; i<8; i++)
        BitMask[i] = 1<<i;

    ListLength = TL.ListLength;

    Tag = new U8 [(ListLength>>BIT_SHIFT)+1];         // 8 bits
    Clear ();
    Current = TL.Current;
    CountOn = TL.CountOn;
    memcpy (Tag, TL.Tag, (ListLength>>BIT_SHIFT) +1);
}
//***********************
~TAG_LIST_2D ()
{
    delete Tag;
    if (BitMask) delete BitMask;
    BitMask = 0L;
}
//***********************
void FC  Copy (TAG_LIST_2D& copy) const
{
    // make sure that we have the space for copying
    if (ListLength > copy.ListLength)
    {
        if (copy.Tag) delete copy.Tag;
        copy.Tag = new U8 [(ListLength>>BIT_SHIFT)+1];
        copy.ListLength = ListLength;
        // Clear ();
    }
    copy.Width = Width, copy.Height = Height;
    copy.Current = Current;
```

19

Chapter

```
            copy.CountOn = CountOn;
            memcpy (copy.Tag, Tag, (ListLength>>BIT_SHIFT) +1);
}
//***********************
void FC  Clear ()
{
    // num is the number of vertices
    memset (Tag, 0, (ListLength>>BIT_SHIFT) +1);
    Current = 0, Last = 0, CountOn = 0;
}
//***********************
//***********************
int       FC  GetTag (const int i) const
{
    if (i>=0 && i<ListLength)
        return  (Tag[i / DIVIDE] & BitMask[i & WHICH_BIT])?1:0;

    return 0;
}
//***********************
void FC  SetTag (const int i)
{
    if (i>=0 && i<ListLength)
    {
        if (! (Tag[i / DIVIDE] & BitMask[i & WHICH_BIT])) IncCountOn ();
        // set on
        Tag[i / DIVIDE] |= BitMask[i & WHICH_BIT];
    }
}
//***********************
void FC  ClearTag (const int i)
{
    if (i>=0 && i<ListLength)
    {
        if (Tag[i / DIVIDE] & BitMask[i & WHICH_BIT]) DecCountOn ();
        // set off
        Tag[i / DIVIDE] &= ~(BitMask[i & WHICH_BIT]);
    }
}
//***********************
int  FC  OnOffTag (const int i) const      // simple test
{
    return (Tag[i / DIVIDE] & BitMask[i & WHICH_BIT]);
}
//***********************
int  FC  FlipTag (const int i)
{
    if (OnOffTag (i))
        ClearTag (i);
    else SetTag (i);
    return Tag[i / DIVIDE] & BitMask[i & WHICH_BIT];
}
```

```
//*********************
//*********************
int  FC  Get (const int i) const
{
     return GetTag (i);
}
//*********************
void FC  Set (const int i)
{
     SetTag (i);
}
//*********************
void FC  Clear (const int i)
{
     ClearTag (i);
}
//*********************
int  FC  Test (const int i) const
{
     return OnOffTag (i);
}
//*********************
int  FC  Flip (const int i)
{
     return FlipTag (i);
}
//*********************
//*********************
int  FC  FindOpenTag ()
// uses the Current pointer to start, remember to call
// FindOpenTag in continuous succession if you need this functionality.
{
     int num = (ListLength>>BIT_SHIFT) +1;
     while (Tag[Current] == FULL && Current < num)   // full
          {Current++;}
     if (Current >= num) return -1;                  // none available

     int which = Current<<BIT_SHIFT;
     for (int i=0; i<DIVIDE; i++, which++)
     {
          if (Get (which) == 0) return which;
     }

     return -1;                                      // nothing available
}
//*********************
int  FC  FindFirstSet ()
{
     Last = 0;
     while (Last<ListLength)
     {
          if (Get (Last)) break;
```

19

Chapter

```
            }

            if (Last >= ListLength) return -1;
            return Last++;
        }
//***********************
int   FC  FindNextSet ()
{
        while (Last<ListLength)
        {
              if (Get (Last)) break;
        }

        if (Last >= ListLength) return -1;
        return Last++;
}
//***********************
//***********************
int   FC  CountSet ()
{
        return CountOn;
}
//***********************
//***********************
        TAG_LIST_2D& FC  operator = (const TAG_LIST_2D& TL)
{
        if (Tag) delete Tag;

        ListLength = TL.ListLength;
        Width = TL.Width, Height = TL.Height;

        Tag = new U8 [(ListLength>>BIT_SHIFT)+1];        // 8 bits
        Clear ();
        Current = TL.Current;
        CountOn = TL.CountOn;
        memcpy (Tag, TL.Tag, (ListLength>>BIT_SHIFT) +1);
        return *this;
}
//***********************
bool FC  operator == (const TAG_LIST_2D& TL) const
{
        if (ListLength != TL.ListLength) return false;
        int t = (ListLength>>BIT_SHIFT) +1;
        for (int i=0; i<t; i++)
        {
              if (Tag[i] == TL.Tag[i]) return false;
        }
        return true;
}
//***********************
bool    FC  operator != (const TAG_LIST_2D& TL) const
    {
```

```
        return (! (*this == TL));
}
//***********************          // only used for getting a value
int  FC  operator [] (const int which)
{
        if (which<0 || which>=ListLength) return 0;
        int val = GetTag (which);
        return val;
}
//***********************
// here are the main interface elements that we'll be using
// most of the operator overloading didn't make much sense
// so I eliminated them
//***********************
int  FC  Get (const int x, const int y) const
{
        if (x<0 || x>=Width) return 1;        // outside boundaries is tagged
        if (y<0 || y>=Height) return 1;       // outside boundaries is tagged
        return GetTag (y*Width+x);
}
//***********************
void FC  Set (const int x, const int y)
{
        if (x<0 || x>=Width) return;          // outside boundaries
        if (y<0 || y>=Height) return;         // outside boundaries
        SetTag (y*Width+x);
}
//***********************
void FC  Clear (const int x, const int y)
{
        if (x<0 || x>=Width) return;          // outside boundaries
        if (y<0 || y>=Height) return;         // outside boundaries
        ClearTag (y*Width+x);
}
//***********************
int  FC  Test (const int x, const int y) const
{
        if (x<0 || x>=Width) return 1;        // outside boundaries
        if (y<0 || y>=Height) return 1;       // outside boundaries
        return OnOffTag (y*Width+x);
}
//***********************
int  FC  Flip (const int x, const int y)
{
        if (x<0 || x>=Width) return 1;        // outside boundaries
        if (y<0 || y>=Height) return 1;       // outside boundaries
        return FlipTag (y*Width+x);
}
//***********************
//***********************
void FC    SetColumn (const int x)
{
```

```
            for (int i=0, loc=x; i<Height; i++, loc+=Width)
            {
                    SetTag (loc);
            }
    }
    //***********************
    void FC    ClearColumn (const int x)
    {
            for (int i=0, loc=x; i<Height; i++, loc+=Width)
            {
                    ClearTag (loc);
            }
    }
    //***********************
    void FC    FlipColumn (const int x)
    {
            for (int i=0, loc=x; i<Height; i++, loc+=Width)
            {
                    FlipTag (loc);
            }
    }
    //***********************
    void FC    SetRow (const int y)
    {
            for (int i=0, loc=y*Width; i<Width; i++, loc++)
            {
                    SetTag (loc);
            }
    }
    //***********************
    void FC    ClearRow (const int y)
    {
            for (int i=0, loc=y*Width; i<Width; i++, loc++)
            {
                    ClearTag (loc);
            }
    }
    //***********************
    void FC    FlipRow (const int y)
    {
            for (int i=0, loc=y*Width; i<Width; i++, loc++)
            {
                    FlipTag (loc);
            }
    }
    //***********************
    //***********************
    void FC    SetAll ()
    {
        int num = Width*Height;
        int t = (ListLength>>BIT_SHIFT) +1;
        for (int i=0; i<t; i++)
```

```
        {
                Tag[i] = 255;
        }
        CountOn = num;
}
//**********************
void FC    ClearAll ()
{
        Clear ();
}
//**********************
void FC    FlipAll ()
{
        int num = Width*Height;
        for (int i=0; i<num; i++)
        {
                FlipTag (i);
        }
}
//**********************
}*TAG2Dptr, **TAG2Dlist;

//****************************************************
//****************************************************
```

This class nearly identical to the TAG_LIST described earlier but it works in 2-D. There are a bunch of new access routines added at the end of the class definition. They work like the 1-D version (1-D meaning single-dimensional, sometimes called a vector). The new functions include: Get (int x, int y), Set (int x, int y), Clear (int x, int y), Test (int x, int y), Flip (int x, int y), SetColumn (int x), ClearColumn (int x), FlipColumn (int x), SetRow (int y), ClearRow (int y), FlipRow (int y), SetAll, ClearAll, and FlipAll.

You'll notice that many of the functions require x,y position rather than just a single position. There you go. In addition, code for rows and columns exists to block off portions of the map from pathing, maybe unexplored portions of the map. The last few functions allow you to clear, set, or invert all positions on the map. I can think of several more functions you could add, but we'll leave it as it is.

This class requires dimensions at constructor time. These values are used to set the size of the bit array. One thing of note: The array is still a single-dimensional string but all of the Get, Set, Flip, Clear, and Test functions have been modified to do the math, treating the single-dimensional array as if it were 2-D.

This class is just as easy as the TAG_LIST and you won't find anything like it (or really very similar) in the Standard Template Library. Also note the column and row functions are actually quite fast. These functions call the functions SetTag, ClearTag, etc., because these functions track counts of how many bits are set, in case you need that. You can always simplify the class by eliminating these counts.

Most maps will probably average 120 tiles by 120 tiles; the memory for this puppy (TAG_LIST_2D) takes only 1,840 bytes to track an entire map. It might be worth allocating an array like this for each path of the PATH_MGR since you'll probably never

19

Chapter

need over 200 paths at any given time since most creatures just stay put most of the time anyway. The memory footprint for all of that plus the paths is under 400 K; in a 64 MB game, that accounts for 0.625 percent of the memory available. The reason to keep these TAG_LIST_2D's allocated is to ensure that a creature remembers where it is going, especially when it calculates a path but only gets about halfway before it runs out of time or the path is longer than the pathing limit.

This class is very similar to TAG_LIST except that it tracks width and height. If you try to go outside that range, it returns a blocked value. This means that there is an artificial wall around the entire map that prevents creatures from trying to path outside of it. Nice, huh?

As before, there are the bitwise operators, so good luck playing with those. The reason I didn't derive this class from the TAG_LIST is that it has too many subtle differences. There are a lot of similarities, but these two are better separate.

Chapter 20

DirectSound

Just behind gameplay, graphics, interface, and game depth is the next most important thing: sound. Hiring a full-time sound guy can keep your game out of the "Good gameplay but cheesy sound makes this a second-rate game" category. You don't want to be in that ballgame. Sound is very important to the success of your game, and a good RTS/RTT game needs great sound. But just like this chapter, it is usually an afterthought and always comes late in the development cycle. You should expect to pay a full-time sound engineer for about a year to create all of the sound effects for your game and write five or six tunes to play in the background.

I was not planning to include a chapter on DirectSound. It is so trivial that even the most junior programmer can implement it. However, after looking over the documentation on DirectSound for DirectX 6.0, I figured that it might be a good idea to include this chapter. What was once easy and clear Microsoft has obscured once again. The sample code is bad, and the help files are no longer online help. The help files have their usual helpful character (for better or worse), but many of the great Direct-Sound samples have been eliminated. It's hard to figure out just from their samples what you need and what you don't based on the files that come with DirectX 6.0, so here is a pretty good implementation.

The ALLOCATOR Class

The ALLOCATOR class is back again from Chapter 18 in all its glory. This really is a great class. We'll be using it to manage sounds and override it to maintain the Direct-Sound interface. First, let's look at how the class is used in implementation and how we load and use the sounds themselves. Then we'll examine the classes in detail.

Below is an example of loading three different sounds and then playing two of them:

```
void InitSoundSystem (HWND WindowHandle)
{
        int Array[3];
        SOUND_MGR sound (WindowHandle);

        STRINGC filename = "c:/sounds/bang.wav";
        Array[0] = sound.LoadSound (filename);
        filename = "c:/sounds/gun.wav";
```

```
Array[1] = sound.LoadSound (filename);
Array[2] = sound.LoadSound ("c:/sounds/fire.wav");

sound.PlaySound (Array[0]);

SOUND* ptr = sound.GetSound (Array[1]);
ptr->SetVolume (SOUND :: LOUD);
ptr->SetPan (SOUND :: RIGHTCENTER);
ptr->SetFrequency (SOUND :: MEDLOW_FREQ);
ptr->Play ();
}
```

We start with a storage array for storing indices into a list of sounds. In all likelihood, these indices will be 0, 1, and 2, but I put the array here for illustrative purposes. You do need to save the index if you want to play the sound later. After loading a sound, this index is your only way to play the sound. Next we declare an instance of the SOUND_MGR that needs a window handle to initialize the DirectSound system. Once all of this is performed, you can start loading sounds. I have prepared a string with a file path and then I call the function LoadSound. I pass the STRINGC parameter to this function, which then loads the sound, prepares it to be played, and returns an index into the SOUND_MGR telling us which ID number to play. You can also pass a char array for loading as in the last load for Array[2].

We have now loaded three sounds. You can verify that the sounds loaded correctly by the return value, which will be –1 if a problem exists. Now playing the sounds can be done in two different ways. We can call the SOUND_MGR function PlaySound, passing the index, and the sound plays normally. We can also obtain a pointer to the SOUND by calling GetSound and passing an index. This allows us to change sound factors like volume, panning, and frequency. Then we simply call the Play function. This class encapsulates everything and makes your life quite easy. It only loads .wav files, but those are pretty standard these days, so no big deal. If you want to support MP3, you'll have to write your own interpreter.

Header Files

Here we have the header file containing the declaration of the SOUND class and the SOUND_MGR class, which is derived from ALLOCATOR in Chapter 18:

```
// dsound.h

#if _MSC_VER >= 1000
#pragma once
#endif                        // _MSC_VER >= 1000

#ifndef __DIRSOUND_H_
#define __DIRSOUND_H_
#define FC __fastcall

#ifndef __STRUCT_H_
#include "c:/library_cur/struct.h"
```

```
        #endif

        #ifndef __STRINGC_H_
        #include "c:/library_cur/stringc.h"
        #endif

        #ifndef __MEMMGR_H_
        #include "c:/library_cur/memmgr.h"
        #endif

        #ifndef __DSOUND_INCLUDED__
        #include <dsound.h>
        #endif

        #ifndef _WINDOWS_
        #include <windows.h>
        #endif

        //****************************************
        //****************************************

        class SOUND
        {
        public:
                // this variable is safe here because only one buffer at a time
                // will be loaded. This 18 bytes is useless after the buffer is
                // initialized, so we might as well make this available to all
                // instantiations of this class.

                static WAVEFORMATEX Format;

                // this is a bigger structure and is only used during loading.
                // might as well make it available to all
                static DSBUFFERDESC  BufferDescription;

                // quite a few enumerations, when setting volume, pan, and freq
                // stick to these standard values unless you know what you're doing
                enum {STD_VOL = 0, STD_PAN = 0, STD_FREQ = 11025};
                        // 11025 is a standard sound frequency
                enum STATUS {BAD = 0, GOOD = 1};
                enum VOLUME {LOUDEST, LOUD, REGULAR, QUIET, VERYQUIET};
                enum PAN {LEFT, LEFTCENTER, CENTER, RIGHTCENTER, RIGHT};
                enum FREQ {LOW_FREQ, MEDLOW_FREQ, MED_FREQ, MEDHIGH_FREQ, HIGH_FREQ};

        protected:
                int     Vol;    // 0 (normal volume) to -10,000 (silent)
                int     Pan;    // -10,000 (left) to 10,000 (right)
                int     Freq;   // 100 (low) to 100000 (ultra high)
                STATUS  Status;

                LPDIRECTSOUNDBUFFER SoundBuffer;
```

20

Chapter

```
    //**************

protected:                    // functions

        bool LoadFile (STRINGC& filename, U8ptr* Buffer, int& BufferSize);

public:
        SOUND ();
        ~SOUND ();
        void Init (LPDIRECTSOUND SoundObj, STRINGC& filename);
        void Play ();
        void Stop ();
        void Release ();        // do not call directly, management only

    //**************

        void SetVolume (VOLUME v);
        void SetPan (PAN p);
        void SetFrequency (FREQ f);

        void SetVolume (int v) {Vol = LIMIT (v, -10000, 10000);}
        void SetPan (int p) {Pan = LIMIT (p, -10000, 10000);}
        void SetFrequency (int f) {Freq = LIMIT (f, 100, 100000);}

    //**************

        void RaiseVolume (int amount = 200);
        void LowerVolume (int amount = 200);

        void PanLeft (int amount = 200);
        void PanRight (int amount = 200);

        void RaiseFrequency (float amount = 16.667);    // a whole note
        void LowerFrequency (float amount = 16.667);    // a whole note

    //**************
        STATUS    GetStatus () {return Status;}
    };

    //****************************************
```

The SOUND_MGR class is in charge here and initializes the DirectSound system. It does require a valid HWND in the constructor to initialize the sound system.

Note: I don't understand this. Of what significance is the HWND in initializing the sound system? This seems like a network service or maybe like using the hard drive. Probably, in an effort to keep the paradigm consistent, they require an HWND parameter, even though there doesn't seem to be any need for it. One thing it does give you is sound control. If your program is in the foreground and in exclusive sound mode, then you have control. DirectSound can tell that and it turns off sound to other programs. But if the program is in the foreground, background processes get very little processor time anyway, so this benefit is very small.

We have a lot of the standard header stuff at the beginning and then the class declaration of SOUND. The class has a simple interface that allows a lot of basic control to the user. You can initialize the sound, play it, stop it, or change the frequency, volume, and panning in a few different ways. It has an internal, hidden function called LoadFile but that is about as complex as it gets. It has five member variables including SoundBuffer, which is its interface to DirectSound that will be used to play the sound.

During the loading process, a few other variables are used that need some persistence, so I made them global to the class. They are Format and BufferDescription. These hold values for the loading buffer until the buffer is created, and then the values are no longer needed. They are also here in case you need to take a bunch of .wav files and put them in some huge sound file that has all of the sounds for your game. These data need to be stored in that file to play the sounds right.

Here we have the controlling class:

```
//****************************************
class SOUND_MGR : public ALLOCATOR <SOUND>
{
        enum STATUS {NOT_WORKING, WORKING};

        LPDIRECTSOUND   SoundObj;
        HWND            WindowHandle;
        DSCAPS          SoundCardCapabilities;
        int             MaxBuffers;
        int             Status;

public:
        SOUND_MGR (HWND);
        ~SOUND_MGR ();

        void    Clear ();                       // stops playing sounds
        void    ReleaseAll ();                  // clears all buffers

        int     LoadSound (STRINGC& file); // returns index
        int     LoadSound (char* file) {return LoadSound (STRINGC (file));}
                                                // returns index
        void    PlaySound (int index);

        SOUND*  GetSound (int which) {return GetItem (which);}
};

//****************************************
//****************************************

#endif
```

20

Chapter

The SOUND_MGR maintains a list of sounds, expands the list if you exceed the default number of 400, initializes direct sounds, and plays sounds by index number. This class then cleans up all the sound files and DirectSound upon deletion. Pretty complete. It has five member variables. The first is SoundObj, which is the Direct-Sound interface pointer. Sounds can only go into the sound card through this interface. It has a WindowHandle in case I need it for future expansion. The variable SoundCardCapabilities allows us to verify that a sound buffer is available at any given time for playing. Most sound cards these days can play 22 sounds at a time minimum. Mine can play up to 128 simultaneous sounds. (That would be a very noisy game.) I don't bother checking anymore and you may want to eliminate this rather large structure, although you will only have one instance of this class in a game at a time, so a few extra bytes isn't a big deal. MaxBuffers is also used to test the card, but you may eliminate it, too. These two variables are in the function PlaySound and can be used to make sure that the sound is able to play. The last variable is Status. This tells us if everything initialized properly or not. You don't want to have your program crash if the sound system doesn't initialize properly.

Note: I recently installed a new sound card from NewCom called the NewClear 128 which had bad DirectX drivers, verified from the DirectX control panel. The DirectX control panel crashed when I tried to view the DirectSound driver settings. This panel is only available if you install the debug version of the drivers from the DirectX CD. I had to manually delete the directory containing the drivers to fix my system, which is now relatively stable. Anyway, every game on my PC still ran and even had sound, but they used the Windows PlaySound function or some other workaround. The only game, out of a dozen or so, that didn't work was Total Annihilation, and I was sorely disappointed because it's my favorite. The game wouldn't run or even initialize until I had removed the faulty drivers.

The interface and structure to this class is very basic. Having no private or protected functions simplifies this class further. Of course, this class inherits all of the functionality from its parent, which makes a lot of functionality available while keeping this class apparently simple. It has a constructor, a destructor, LoadSound functions requiring file path information, a PlaySound function requiring an index to a sound it will play, a GetSound function to make access to sounds in the list easier, and a few different clearing functions. Clear stops all sounds that are playing, while ReleaseAll invalidates all sounds and you'll need to reload all of them.

Implementation

The only complicated thing about this .cpp file is the file loading. The rest of this is very basic, like I designed it to be.

```
// dirsound.cpp

#ifndef _WINDOWS_
#include <windows.h>
#endif

#ifndef _INC_MMSYSTEM
#include <mmsystem.h>
#endif
#include "c:/library_cur/dirsound.h"
#include "c:/library_cur/fileobj.h"

//********************************************
//********************************************

WAVEFORMATEX SOUND :: Format = {0, 0, 0, 0, 0, 0};
DSBUFFERDESC SOUND :: BufferDescription = {0, 0, 0, 0, 0};

//********************************************
```

Below the #include files, you'll find our initialization of the two global member structures belonging to the SOUND class. You could just as well eliminate the initialization with 0's. Your choice, but my initialization is more complete.

Here we have the initialization of the SOUND class:

```
//********************************************

SOUND :: SOUND ()
{
        SoundBuffer = NULL;
        Status = BAD;
        Vol = STD_VOL;
        Pan = STD_PAN;
        Freq = STD_FREQ;
}

//***************

void SOUND :: Init (LPDIRECTSOUND SoundObj, STRINGC& filename)
{
        if (SoundObj == NULL) return;

        U8ptr     Buffer; int BufferSize;
        U32       Offset = 0;
        VoidPtr   dest1, dest2;
        U32       BytesToBeWritten1, BytesToBeWritten2;
        HRESULT   res;

        if (LoadFile (filename, &Buffer, BufferSize) == false)
            {goto BAD_RETURN;}
        // setup buffer description
        memset (&BufferDescription, 0, sizeof (DSBUFFERDESC));
        BufferDescription.dwSize = sizeof (DSBUFFERDESC);
```

```
BufferDescription.dwFlags = DSBCAPS_CTRLALL;
BufferDescription.dwBufferBytes = BufferSize;

// 8.0 kHz, 11.025 kHz, 22.05 kHz, 44.1 kHz
Freq = Format.nSamplesPerSec;

// after LoadFile, should have a value for Format
BufferDescription.lpwfxFormat = &Format;

// create buffer
res = SoundObj->CreateSoundBuffer (&BufferDescription, &SoundBuffer, NULL);
if (res != DS_OK) {goto BAD_RETURN;}

// prep to move data into buffer
res = SoundBuffer->Lock (Offset, BufferSize, &dest1,
        &BytesToBeWritten1, &dest2, &BytesToBeWritten2, 0);
if (res != DS_OK) {goto BAD_RETURN;}

// move data into buffer
memcpy (dest1, Buffer, BytesToBeWritten1);
if (BytesToBeWritten2 != 0)
memcpy (dest2, Buffer+BytesToBeWritten1, BytesToBeWritten2);

// make usable
res = SoundBuffer->Unlock (dest1, BytesToBeWritten1, dest2,
        BytesToBeWritten2);
if (res != DS_OK) {goto BAD_RETURN;}

        Status = GOOD;
        delete Buffer;
        return;
BAD_RETURN:
        Status = BAD;
        if (Buffer) delete Buffer;
        return;
}


//*********************************
```

The class is prepared with a few standard values. The Status is set to BAD in case a user tries to play a sound that hasn't been loaded; this will cause the class to immediately return instead of playing. The SoundBuffer is not initialized here. We want this class to be valid and then we load the sounds. This means that we can clear the sound buffer and still maintain a valid pointer to any instance of the SOUND class. We don't want to have to delete any SOUND class pointer just to clear the buffer, so we initialize the buffer from a second function to initialize the sound and load it. So we come to Init.

Init takes two parameters—a pointer to the DirectSound system that it needs for initializing the SoundBuffer and a filename. This is all the information needed to load the file. A few local variables are initialized and we are ready to begin. Looking at our variables here, we first come to Buffer. The Buffer variable will hold the sound information from the file once it is loaded. Then BufferSize will tell us how much memory was used to store Buffer. DirectSound allows us to initialize a buffer starting at any point in the data (sound data), so we have an Offset variable. Our sounds will always load at the beginning of the sound file, so this value is set to 0. You should be aware of this value and you may wish to change it, in case you have a sound that wasn't recorded properly with extra time at the beginning of the file.

Note: You really should make sure that your sound engineer does his job and that all of your sounds are the way you want them to be before you try to fit them into the game. There is nothing more tedious than spending all of your time hacking at sounds to try and get something perfect that somebody else should have done. This actually goes for all aspects of the game where you spend your time working on something somebody else should have done as his job.

The next few variables are a bit complicated. Say you have a sound file that is 1 MB. On many sound cards, that file won't fit into the sound card memory, at least not into a single sound buffer (buffers can be just about any arbitrary size, but few go as high as 1 MB). So a mechanism exists for you to store a sound file in two different sound buffers and link them together. The next four variables allow us to work with this mechanism with two pointers to different buffers and their various sizes. The last variable will be used to track return values from DirectSound function calls.

The first thing this function does is verify the validity of the SoundObj being passed to the function. Next we load our file. We'll cover those details later, but suffice to say that when it returns, we either have an error or Buffer is full and it has Buffer-Size bytes in its array of allocated space. Also, SOUND has a static member variable called Format that has valid values set during the load. Then we clear BufferDescription and initialize it with a few values so that SoundBuffer will do what we want including allowing us to modify all of the pan, frequency, and volume values. Then we store Frequency based on what the loaded file value is.

Note: We have no other way to know this value other than from the Format structure. Guessing is fine, but the recording process has so many variables. If the sound is a whistle, you would probably want to use 44.1 kHz to capture the high quality whistle. An explosion doesn't need high quality and you can probably use a lower frequency like 8 kHz. The lower the frequency value, the less data is stored and the more memory is saved. That is why you would really care about using the right sound frequency for the job—memory vs. quality. This should be on your mind throughout every aspect of planning your game anyway.

Now we create SoundBuffer using SoundObj and we pass it two variables: BufferDescription to tell DirectSound what kind of SoundBuffer we want and the variable SoundBuffer that will store a pointer to our DirectSound sound so that we can play it. A bad return value clears the loaded buffer and returns with an error.

Before we can move the loaded sound data into SoundBuffer, we need to lock it. Locking it retrieves two valid memory pointers: dest1 and dest2. Generally dest2 will be NULL unless your sound file is huge. Now you can copy your data into Sound-Buffer. We memcpy Buffer into dest1 with as many bytes as it will allow. This number is generally the entire number of bytes, but it can be fewer, so we have another memcpy just in case below this function call. Our last order of business is to unlock SoundBuffer, delete the memory allocated in the LoadFile function, and return with a GOOD status. If you leave SoundBuffer locked, you will not be able to do anything with sound at all, so always unlock it.

That's it for initializing the SOUND class.

The destructor releases SoundBuffer, making it invalid, which releases all memory associated with SoundBuffer:

```
//*********************************

SOUND :: ~SOUND ()
{
        if (SoundBuffer) SoundBuffer->Release ();
}


//*********************************
```

Here is the only real complexity in the class. It is well commented, but we'll still go through it step by step to clarify:

```
//*********************************

bool SOUND :: LoadFile (STRINGC& filename, U8ptr* Buffer, int& BufferSize)
{
        HMMIO      hmmio;                // file handle for open file
        MMCKINFO   ParentChunk;          // parent chunk information
        MMCKINFO   SubChunk;             // subchunk information structure
        int        FMTSize;              // size of "FMT" chunk

        if (! (hmmio = mmioOpen (filename.GetString (), NULL, MMIO_READ |
            MMIO_ALLOCBUF)))
          return false;                  // failed to open file

        // make sure the file is a "wav" file.
        ParentChunk.fccType = mmioFOURCC ('W', 'A', 'V', 'E');
        if (mmioDescend (hmmio, (LPMMCKINFO) &ParentChunk, NULL,
            MMIO_FINDRIFF))
        {
             mmioClose (hmmio, 0);
        return false;                    // this is not a wav file
        }

        // Find the "FMT" chunk which must be a subchunk of the "RIFF" chunk.
     SubChunk.ckid = mmioFOURCC ('f', 'm', 't', ' ');
        if (mmioDescend (hmmio, &SubChunk, &ParentChunk, MMIO_FINDCHUNK))
        {
```

```
            mmioClose (hmmio, 0);      // wav file has no "FMT" chunk
            return false;
    }

    // Get the size of the "FMT" chunk and allocate memory for it
    FMTSize = SubChunk.cksize;      // This will be filled with
    // all but the last 2 bytes of the 18 byte structure.
    // should be 16 bytes, older formats may vary so
    // we don't know exactly how many bytes to read until we get
    // the amount from the file.

    // Read the "FMT" chunk which contains file format info like
    // record quality (sample rate) and stereo/mono setting
    if (mmioRead (hmmio, (HPSTR) &Format, FMTSize) != FMTSize)
    {
            mmioClose (hmmio, 0);      // failed to read format chunk
    return false;
    }

    // Ascend out of the "FMT" subchunk.
    mmioAscend (hmmio, &SubChunk, 0);

    // Descend to locate the data chunk
    SubChunk.ckid = mmioFOURCC ('d', 'a', 't', 'a');
    if (mmioDescend (hmmio, &SubChunk, &ParentChunk, MMIO_FINDCHUNK))
    {
            mmioClose (hmmio, 0);      // wav file has no data chunk
            return false;
    }
    // Get the size of the data subchunk or the actual sound data
    BufferSize = SubChunk.cksize;
    if (BufferSize == 0L)
    {
            mmioClose (hmmio, 0);      // The data chunk contains no data
            return false;
    }

    *Buffer = new U8[BufferSize];
    // this is a pointer to a buffer so this memory can be returned.

    // Read the waveform-audio data subchunk.
    if (mmioRead (hmmio, (HPSTR) *Buffer, BufferSize) != BufferSize)
    {
            mmioClose (hmmio, 0);      // Failed to read data chunk
    return false;
    }

    // Close the file.
    mmioClose (hmmio, 0);
    return true;
}

        //********************************
```

Microsoft has defined this big MMSYSTEM thing which involves multimedia. Wave files fall into this category for some reason, and hence all of the special variables here have MM in their names. The functions for multimedia support all start with mm. A lot of the parameters passed to these functions start with MM.

We declare a few variables that we will use during loading. hmmio is like a file handle (FILE*) but it is a long pointer, not an int pointer. Multimedia files are divided into sections, or chunks, that have names and text values associated with them. You'll see this in a moment. Anyway, these chunks have info that we need and so we'll store that info in the local variables ParentChunk and SubChunk.

Then we open the .wav file using the function mmioOpen. Hopefully the filename is valid; if it isn't, we'll get a non-zero value returned from this function and we return an error. Then we verify that it is truly a .wav file, not just one with the proper extension. The Descend function is basically a search function that searches a file for a particular value. We have told it to look for the 'W', 'A', 'V', 'E' section, and the parameter MMIO_FINDRIFF forces the function to look at the first 4 bytes of the file to verify that their values are "RIFF." This is the way to verify a .wav file.

We then look for the next section, which contains the sound file format information. The name of the section is 'f', 'm', 't', ' '. Once we get a little info on the size of the format information (older versions have varying format sizes), we then load the format info. Now we know enough about the sound data to load and play the info. We exit the last section by calling the Ascend function.

Now, we find the 'd', 'a', 't', 'a' section containing sound information. We find out the size of the buffer required to hold all of the sound data, allocate memory for it, and then load the sound data. This allocated memory will make its way back to the function that called LoadFile in the Buffer variable passed to this function. We don't need to ascend to get out of this file, just close it. That's it.

Now we play the loaded sound:

```
//**********************************

void SOUND :: Play ()
{
        if (Status == BAD) return;
        HRESULT res = SoundBuffer->SetFrequency (Freq);
        res = SoundBuffer->SetPan (Pan);
        res = SoundBuffer->SetVolume (Vol);
        res = SoundBuffer->SetCurrentPosition (0);     // reset to beginning
        res = SoundBuffer->Play (0, 0, 0);
        if (res != DS_OK)
        res = SoundBuffer->Restore ();
}


//**********************************
```

If the sound is valid, we set all of its values and then play the sound. This is really very simple. The SetCurrentPosition function resets the sound to play from the beginning; consider it a rewind button. After you play a sound, the buffer is at the end of the file and must be reset. The SoundBuffer->Play (0, 0, 0) call tells the SoundBuffer to play the entire sound. These parameters are mostly reserved and mostly meaningless. Ignore them for now.

If you need to interrupt a sound, use this:

```
//*******************************

void SOUND :: Stop ()
{
        if (Status == BAD) return;
        HRESULT res = SoundBuffer->Stop ();
}


        //*******************************
```

The Release function is intended to be used strictly by the SOUND_MGR. You should never call this function directly.

```
        //*******************************

void SOUND :: Release ()          // do not call directly, management only
{
        HRESULT res = SoundBuffer->Release ();
        SoundBuffer = NULL;
        Status = BAD;

}


        //*******************************
```

The next few functions allow you to modify the sound controls. Play with them to see how they work. The frequency setting should only be changed once during the game, given the nature of its modifications to the Freq variable. The comments make the variable setting quite clear.

```
        //*******************************

void SOUND :: SetVolume (VOLUME v)
{
        // 6 db is equivalent to doubling the distance
        // between you and the sound source. Volume is
        // measured in 100ths of a db so I reduce volume
        // by 600 "ticks" to make the distance 2x. Any
        // other measurement is equally valid.
        // Difference of less than 2 db is not normally
        // discernable by humans
        switch (v)
        {
        case LOUDEST: Vol = 0;
            break;
        case LOUD: Vol = -600;
            break;
        case REGULAR: Vol = -1200;
            break;
        case QUIET: Vol = -1800;
```

```
            break;
    case VERYQUIET: Vol = -2400;
            break;
    }
}
                //********************************

void SOUND :: SetPan (PAN p)
{
    // these are pretty rough values. They do create
    // very distinct and audible differences between
    // the speakers. For a more subtle difference, use
    // SetPan (int) with values.
    switch (p)
    {
    case LEFT: Pan = -10000;
        break;
    case LEFTCENTER: Pan = -5000;
        break;
    case CENTER: Pan = 0;
        break;
    case RIGHTCENTER: Pan = 5000;
        break;
    case RIGHT: Pan = 10000;
        break;
    }
}

                //********************************

void SOUND :: SetFrequency (FREQ f)
{
    // an octave is defined by doubling the frequency of
    // a base value. Each of these settings is an octave
    // change from the standard frequency which is 440 Hz
    // or a setting of 4400.

    switch (f)          // 8.0 kHz, 11.025 kHz, 22.05 kHz, 44.1 kHz
    {
    case LOW_FREQ: Freq = 8000;
        break;
    case MEDLOW_FREQ: Freq = 11025;
        break;
    case MED_FREQ:
        break;
    case MEDHIGH_FREQ: Freq = 22050;
        break;
    case HIGH_FREQ: Freq = 44100;
        break;
    }
}
```

```
                //********************************
                //********************************

void SOUND :: RaiseVolume (int amount)
{
        Vol = LIMIT (Vol+amount, 0, -10000);
}
void SOUND :: LowerVolume (int amount)
{
        Vol = LIMIT (Vol-amount, 0, -10000);
}


                //********************************

void SOUND :: PanLeft (int amount)
{
        Pan = LIMIT (Pan-amount, -10000, 10000);
}
void SOUND :: PanRight (int amount)
{
        Pan = LIMIT (Pan+amount, -10000, 10000);
}


                //********************************
void SOUND :: RaiseFrequency (float amount)      // a whole note
{
        float val = static_cast <float> (Freq);
        val += val*amount;
        Freq = static_cast <int> (LIMIT (val, 100, 100000));
}
void SOUND :: LowerFrequency (float amount)      // a whole note
{
        float val = static_cast <float> (Freq);
        val -= val*amount;
        Freq = static_cast <int> (LIMIT (val, 100, 100000));
}

//*******************************************
```

That does it for this class. Quite simple.
Here is the last implementation detail, the sound manager:

```
//*******************************************

SOUND_MGR :: SOUND_MGR (HWND hwnd) : ALLOCATOR <SOUND> (400)
{
        WindowHandle = hwnd;
        HRESULT res = DirectSoundCreate (NULL, &SoundObj, NULL);
        if (res != DS_OK) {Status = NOT_WORKING; return;}

        res = SoundObj->SetCooperativeLevel (WindowHandle, DSSCL_EXCLUSIVE);
        if (res == DS_OK)    Status = WORKING;
        else Status = NOT_WORKING;
```

20

Chapter

```
        }

                        //*******************************

SOUND_MGR :: ~SOUND_MGR ()
{
        DeleteList ();
        if (SoundObj) SoundObj->Release ();
}

                        //*******************************
```

It needs the HWND (window handle) to initialize the sound system. Once it runs, it takes over the sound of your computer with the DSSCL_EXCLUSIVE variable. That is all that the constructor does. The destructor cleans up everything including memory and all of the sound buffers.

The following functions are also useful:

```
                        //*******************************

void SOUND_MGR :: Clear ()
{
        if (Items)
    {
            for (int i=0; i<NumberAllocated; i++)
                if (Items[i]) Items[i]->Stop ();

    }

                        //*******************************

void   SOUND_MGR :: ReleaseAll ()        // clears all buffers
{
        if (Items)
    {
            for (int i=0; i<NumberAllocated; i++)
                if (Items[i]) Items[i]->Release ();
    }
}

                        //*******************************
```

The Clear function stops all sounds that are playing. You might need this for the end of the game or when the interface changes. The ReleaseAll function clears all sounds and resets them. You cannot play any sound after this unless you reload them all.

These last two functions do exactly what their names say:

```
                        //*******************************

int    SOUND_MGR :: LoadSound (STRINGC& file)    // returns index
{
        if (Status == NOT_WORKING) return -1;      // error
```

```
         SOUND* sound = GetNewItem ();
         if (sound == NULL) return -1;
         sound->Init (SoundObj, file);
         if (sound->GetStatus () == SOUND:: BAD)
         {
               ReleaseItem (sound);
               return -1;
         }
         return GetID (sound);
}


         //*********************************

void SOUND_MGR :: PlaySound (int which)
{
         // is there is an error, then we'll have a -1 value for which
         if (which<0 || which>=NumberAllocated) return;
         if (CheckInUse (which) == 0) return;
         // memset (&SoundCardCapabilities, 0, sizeof (DSCAPS));
         // SoundCardCapabilities.dwSize = sizeof (DSCAPS);
         // SoundCardCapabilities.dwFlags = DSCAPS_PRIMARYSTEREO |
         // DSCAPS_SECONDARYSTEREO;

         // HRESULT res = SoundObj->GetCaps (&SoundCardCapabilities);
         // MaxBuffers = SoundCardCapabilities.dwMaxHwMixingAllBuffers;

         Items[which]->Play ();
}
//*******************************************
//*******************************************
```

LoadSound verifies that the system is working, finds an available sound in the
Items array, and loads sounds into it. One thing it doesn't do is verify uniqueness. A
file "Bop.wav" requested to be loaded three times will be loaded three times. This is
an advantage of the graphic manager described a few chapters ago which ensures that
all files loaded are unique and returns a pointer to an already loaded file if necessary.
You might want to make the modifications to this function for uniqueness verification.

The last function plays the loaded sound. If verifies that the sound is valid and
plays it. It really is that simple. The code that is commented out can be used to verify
that a sound buffer is available, if necessary, for playing. Like I said before, most cards
support so many simultaneous sounds that this is almost useless.

That's it. That is all the code you need to manage the entire sound system. You'll
probably just need to include these files in your project and use the code in the first
function in this chapter, InitSoundSystem, to play your sounds. The details listed
herein aren't important unless you want to know how the system works. Good luck.

20

Chapter

Index

2-D, 432
3D, 432
3-D art packages, 382
8-bit color, 165-166
15-bit color, 166-167, 170
16-bit color, 167, 170
24-bit color, 167-168
    converting to 16-bit, 303-305
32-bit color, 168-169

A

A* description, 612-629, 637-645
A* implementation, 651-675
ABS, 87-88
actions, 526
Age of Empires, 127-134
AI, 540-546
ALLOCATOR, 579-585
alphabet, 245-246
    characteristics, 246
ALPHABET_MANAGER, 247-450
ambience, 434-435
ANGLE, 88
ANIM_TYPES, 393
animating
    backgrounds, 405-408
    buildings, 414-415
    death, 416-419, 482
    directions, 381, 400-405
    entities, 410-411
    landscape, 478
    overlays, 415-416
    reaction, 409
animation, 379-420
    basics, 385-386
    cycle, 380
    data, *see* ANIMATION_DATA
    delay, *see* OFFSET_DATA
    offset, *see* OFFSET_DATA

    preparation, 409-410
    screen position, *see* ANIMSCREEN_POS
    sequence, 380
    types, *see* ANIM_TYPES
ANIMATION, 400-405
ANIMATION_DATA, 391-395
ANIMSCREEN_POS, 396-398
API, 5
application programming interface, *see* API
art, 380-382
art packages, 382
artificial intelligence, *see* AI
AssembleColor, 280, 284-285
assets, 385
AVG, 89

B

back buffer, 164
backgrounds, animating, 405-408
backing up, 81-82
basic program, *see* WinMain
beginning game, 4
BFS, *see* Breadth First Search
BIT128, 90
BIT64, 90
BITMAP_FLAGS, 97
blending color, 419-420
blit optimization, 268-270
BlitGraphic, 268, 305
BlitGraphicClipped, 271-275
blitting, 164, 262-270
blocking area, 601
blocking terrain, 459-460, 607-608
braces, 40
Breadth First Search, 611-612
Bresenham's algorithm, 222-224, 242-244
buffer,
    back, 164
    offscreen, 164, 352-353

buffering, double, 163
build area, 600
build location, 13
buildings, 430
    animating, 414-415
buttons, 497-498, 516-517

C

C/C++, 33-39 *see also* Visual C++
calculator, 108
characters, 246-247
classes, 306
Clear, 57-58
ClearBackBuffer, 199-200
ClearScreen, 279, 283
cliffs, 457-458
clipping,
    graphics, 270-275
    line, 224-226, 236-242
    rectangle, 236-239
    text, 275-276
CMYK color model, 169
code design, 19-31, 75-77
code listings
    alphabet.h, 248-249
    dirdraw.cpp, 177-187
    dirdraw.h, 172-174
    dsound.h, 688-690
    entity.cpp, 545-546
    graphic.cpp, 312-331
    graphic.h, 309-312
    GraphicSequence.h, 398-400
    header.h, 158-159
    loops.cpp, 208-209, 211-212, 267,
      286-287, 305-306
    main.cpp, 445-453, 464-465, 652-653
    message.cpp, 206-208
    path.cpp, 659-662
    path.h, 653-656
    queue.h, 59-63, 551-555
    screen.h, 277-281
    stringc.h, 294-297
    struct.h, 86-87, 88-89, 90-103
    struct3d.h, 99-103
    taglist.h, 629-637
    WinMain, 285-286

    winmain.cpp, 46-50
    winshell.cpp, 205-206
    winshell.h, 203-204
    worldobj.h, 531-534
code reusability, 78-79
code sharing, *see* source control
coding environment, 43-45
coding style, 39-43
cohesion, 22
color, 214-216
    blending, 419-420
    modes, 165-169
    models, 169-171
    setup, 108-110
ColorType, 174-175
comments, 42
competition, 81
compiler, 7
compression, 357-369
constants, 85-87
construction entity, 562-565
consumption entity, 568-570
coupling, 22
CreateDirectDraw, 180, 190-196
CreateGraphic, 265, 289-290
CreateMainWindow, 178, 187-189
creature
    definition, 528-546
    identification, 13
CREATURE_EVENT, 559-560
CREATURE_FLAGS, 537-538
creatures, 430, *see also* entities
CUBE, 87-88
cursors, 496-497

D

D80, 90
damage, *see* landscape damage
Dark Omen, 135-138
Dark Reign, 139-143
data driven, 22
data types, 89-103, 159-162
DDObject, 173
DDObjectNew, 173
ddraw.lib, 114
DDSCAPS, 162

DDSURFACEDESC, 160
DDSURFACEDESC2, 161
death, animating, 413, 416-419, 482
debug mode, 114
decorations, 430
default entity values, *see* entity defaults
DEG120, 86
DEG30, 86
DEG45, 85-86
DEG60, 86
DEG90, 86
DEGtoRAD, 86-87
delay, *see* OFFSET_DATA
deleting files, 121-122
Depth First Search, 612
design document, 65-68
design examples, 123-154
desktop color, *see* color setup
desktop setup, 107-108
destination, 609-611
development, 71-83
development cycle, 31-33, 73-75
DFS, *see* Depth First Search
DirectDraw, 5, 155
　　file structure, 158-159
　　layers, 156-157
DIRECT_DRAW_MANAGER, 171-210
Direct3D, 6, 421-422
DirectInput, 6
DIRECTION, 654
directions, 381, 400-405
DirectPlay, 6
DirectSound, 6, 687-703
DirectX, 5-6, 106, 155-156
DisassembleColor, 280
DIST, 88
distance formula, 620
distance remaining, 612
documents, 65-70
double buffering, 163
Draw, 213-216, 220-222, 244-245, 267-268,
　　271-272, 288-289, 314, 492
DrawAt, 314
DrawBitmap, 279, 284
DrawClippedLetter, 275-276

DrawFrame, 185, 197-199
drawing
　　graphics, 305-306
　　letters, 260-262
　　lines, 216-222
　　rectangles, 233-236
DRAWING_MANAGER, 277-290
DrawLetter, 256-257, 261-262
DrawLLECompressed_Clipped16Bit, 328-331,
　　372-378
DrawLLECompressed16Bit, 327-328, 369-372
DRAWSTRUCT, 90-91
drop shadow, *see* shadow
dsound.lib, 114
dxguid.lib, 114
dynamic-link libraries, 43

E
effects, 415
elevation, 12, 436-455, 650-651
encoding, 361
end game, 5
engine, 33
engine design, 77-78
entities, 521-602
　　and design, 524-525
　　animating, 410-44
　　pointers to, 466-467
　　types, 547-550, 555-559, 560-578
entity, 521
　　actions, 526
　　characteristics, 525-528
　　communication, 527, 678
　　defaults, 546-547
　　selection, 547-548
　　thinking, 527-528
ENTITY, 539, 541-546
EVEN, 87-88
EVENT, 54-55
EVENT_QUEUE, 55-57
expectations, 80
explosion entity, 578

F
F32, 90
feedback, 487-488

file conversion, 303-305
file list, *see* recent files
FILE_MASTER, 291-292
filenames, 308-309
files, deleting, 121-122
FillRect, 280, 284
fire entity, 568-569
FLAGS_FOR_BITMAPS, 96-97
FLAGS_FOR_CREATURES, 98, 535-537
flipping, 165
flying entity, 577-578
fog of war, 468
font, 245 *see also* alphabet
FRAME, 388-391
FrameRect, 280, 284
frames, skipping, 411-412
framework, 30-31
functions, naming, 39-40

G
game design, 9, 16-20
game examples, 123-154
game stages, 4-5
gameplay issues, 9-14
GDI, 165
GOAL, 550-551
GRAPHIC, 309-312
GRAPHIC_MGR, 387-388
GRAPHIC_SEQUENCE, 398-400
graphics,
        blitting, 262-270
        clipping, 270-275
        drawing, 305-306
        loading, 291-301
        maintenance, 386-387
        overlays, 458-459
        storage, 301-302, 306
graphical device interface, *see* GDI
group behavior, 525
group pathing, 676-677

H
hardware considerations, 79-80
hardware layer, *see* layers
headers, 119-121, 158-159
height, *see* elevation

hexagonal tiles, 423, 438, 439
HI_BYTE, 88
horizontal line
        clipping, 224-225
        drawing, 216-218
HorizontalLine, 218, 224-225, 227-230
hot keys, 106-107
hot points, 479
HSV color model, 169-170
HSVfloat, 96

I
impassable terrain, 436
indexing, 466
InitSoundSystem, 687-688
installation, 105-106
interface, 485-520
        appearance, 486
        color, 519
        elements, 497-498
        messages, 488-495
        purpose, 485
        utility, 486-487
INTERFACE, 502-515
INTERFACE_MGR, 488-495
internetworking, 518
InterruptFrame, 185, 197
isometric tiles, 423, 437, 439-441

K
kingdom, *see* regions

L
landscape, 421-482
        considerations, 477-482
        damaging, 431
        elevation, 436-455
        rendering, 455-457
        types, 429-430
layers, 156-158
letters,
        clipping, 275-276
        drawing, 260-262
Letters, 251
lib files, 114
library, 43
library files, 114

LIMIT, 88
line
    clipping, 224-226, 239-242
    drawing, 216-222 *see also* Bresenham's
      algorithm
    optimizing, 227-232
Line, 222-223, 242-243, 279, 284
linked list, 498
LLE, 357-378
    clipping with, 372-378
    compression, 357-369
    drawing with, 369-372
    format, 361-369
LLECompression16Bit, 365-367
LLECompressSingleLine16Bit, 326-327,
  362-363
loading graphics, *see* graphics, loading
LoadTGA, 300-305, 331-333

M
macros, 41, 85-103
Main, *see* WinMain
map coordinate system, 474-477 *see also*
  world coordinate system
map size, 467-468
maps, 460-463
MAX, 87-88
memcpy16BitBackwards, 384
memory management, 579-597
message, 490
MessageHandler, *see* WinMain
MessageLoop, 206-208, *see also* WinMain
messages, *see* interface messages
mid game, 5
MIN, 87-88
mines, 478
minimap, 467
minimum hardware, *see* hardware
  considerations
mirroring, 382-385
missile entity, 576-577
missile firing entity, 577
mood, 11, 422
mouse, 516
moving entity, 560-562
multiple paths, 650

N
networking, 518
new project, creating, 111-113
NOT, 88

O
OBJECT_DISPATCHER, 534
objects, *see* entities
ODD, 87-88
offscreen buffer, 164, 352-353
OFFSET_DATA, 395
OffSurfaces, 200-202
OffX, *see* OFFSET_DATA,
  WORLDCOORDINATE
OffY, *see* OFFSET_DATA, WORLDCOORDINATE
OffZ, *see* OFFSET_DATA,
  WORLDCOORDINATE
old files, *see* recent files
optimization,
    blit, 268-270
    letter drawing, 260-262
    line drawing, 227-232
orthogonal tiles, *see* isometric tiles
overdraw, 455-457
overlays, 415-416, 458-459, 480

P
Paint Shop Pro, 306
PaintText, 186-187, 202-203
PARTICLE, 91, 354
particle systems, 353-354
passable terrain, 436
path choice, 650
path finding, *see* pathing
PATH_MANAGER, 657-659, 666-675
PATH_SIMPLE, 656-657, 663-665
PATH_STEP, 616-617
PATH_TOOLS, 617-618, 660-663
pathing, 459-460, 603-686
    destination, 609-611
    methods, 611-650
paths,
    multiple, 650
    partial, 675-676
peons, 565-568
PI, 85-86

PI2, 85-86
PIdiv2, 85-86
PItimes2, 86
PIover2, 85-86
PIx2, 86
pixels, 212-213
player colors, 519-520
Plot, 213-214
POINTER_MGR, 585-586
pointers, 466-467
POLY3D, 100-101
POLY3D_GROUP, 101
POWERCELL, 569
preparation, 71-73
PrepFrame, 185, 196-197
PrintASCIIchr, 255-256
PrintNumber, 253-254
PrintText, 253-254
profiling, 105
programming style, 33-39
programming tools, 79
project, 111-118
    creating, 115-118
    settings, 113-115
    starting, 111-113
    types, 112

Q
queue, 54
QUEUE, 551-555
queued entity, 555-559

R
RADtoDEG, 57, 87
random maps, 460-463
random starting locations, 463-465
ray cast pathing, 646-650
ray casting, 606-607
reaction, 409
real-time strategy, 2-3
real-time tactical, 2-3
recent files, 110
RECIP, 87-88
RECTA, 91
RECTANGLE, 91
RectangleFill, 233

RectangleFrame, 234
rectangles, 233-234
    clipping, 236-239
    drawing, 234-236
    filling, 232-234
rectangular tiles, 423, 438-440, 442-443
reflection, *see* mirroring
regions, 480-481, *see also* update regions
release mode, 115
resource entity, 548-550
resource gathering entity, 565-568
RESOURCE_ENTITY, 413-414
resources, 413, 430, 432-434
    gathering, 600
reusability, 78-79
RGB color model, 169
RGBfloat, 96
RGBVal, 92-95
RLE, 355
rotation, 412-413
ROUND, 87-88
RTS, *see* real-time strategy
RTT, *see* real-time tactical

S
S16, 90
S32, 90
S8, 90
sales, 81
scheduling, 31, 80
screen position, 598-599
SCREENOBJECT, 307-308, 538-539
SCREEN_STRUCT, 91
scrolling, 496
scx, 538
scy, 538
secondary storage, *see* backing up
SELECTABLE_ENTITY, 548
selecting, 495-496, 517-518
    entities, 547-548
SetClippingRect, 280, 285
SetDestColor, 280, 284
SetScreenPosition, 538
SetScreenX, 538
SetScreenY, 538
SetVal, 95

SetWorldX, *see* WORLDCOORDINATE
SetWorldY, *see* WORLDCOORDINATE
Seven Kingdoms, 124-126
SGN, 87-88
shadow, 247
sharing code, *see* source control
simple terrain, 603-607
SINGLE_TILE, 425-429
SKILLS, 521-523
skipping frames, 411-412
SL, 90
software layer, *see* layers
soldier entity, 569-575
SOUND, 689-690, 693-701
SOUND_MGR, 691, 701-703
source control, 82-83
span list, 334-336, 344-352
SPAN_GROUP, 344-345
SPAN_LIST, 346-352
special effects, 415
specialized devices, 479
SQR, 87-88
stack, 54
standard data types, *see* data types
standard macros, *see* macros
StarCraft, 144-147
strategy, 3, 9-10
STRINGC, 293-300
SUM, 88
supertile, 460
SWAP, 87-88
symbols, 430

T
tactics, 3-4, 10-11
TAG_LIST, 336-343, 629-637
TAG_LIST_2D, 678-686
tags, *see* TAG_LIST
Targa, 292-293, 300-302
TARGA_HEADER, 293
technical design document, 68-70
templates, 41
terrain, 12-13, 603-609
    blocking, 607-608
    features, 430
    impassable, 436

passable, 436
simple, 603-607
tough, 609
test bed, 118-119
text,
    clipping, 275-276
    drawing, 260-262
TEXTURE, 99
thinking, *see* entity thinking
threads, 21
tile
    coordinate system, *see* world coordinate
        system
    diagram, 444-445
    dimensions, *see* tile size
    grouping, 469-471
    size, 472
tiles, 422-429
TILE_TYPE_DEFINED, 429, 469-471
TILEFLAGS, 425, 469
TODEG, 89
tools, 7, 79
TORAD, 89
Total Annihilation, 148-154
tough terrain, 609
transport entity, 575
traps, 478
trenches, 481-482
triggers, 430, 479
TRUNC, 87-88
turning sequence, 412-413

U
U16, 90
U16ptr, 90
U32, 90
U32ptr, 90
U8, 90
U8ptr, 90
UL, 90
UNIVERSAL_ENTITY_MGR, 586-597
update cycle, 482-484, 590, 593
update regions, 353

V
variables, naming, 40

VECTOR, 100-103
VERT2D, 99-100
VERT3D, 100
vertical line
    clipping, 226
    drawing, 219-222
VerticalLine, 219, 226, 231-232
video card layer, 157
video modes, *see* color modes
video surfaces, 356
Visual C++, *see also* C/C++
    installation, 105-111
volatility, 21-22

W
walls, 481-482
waypoints, 675-676
WEAPON, 570-571
whitespace, 41-42
WindowHandle, 173
windows, 497-498
WinMain, 45-54, 205-206, 266, 285-286
Winmm.lib, 114
WM_ACTIVEAPP, 53

WM_CREATE, 53
WM_DESTROY, 53
WM_KEYDOWN, 53
WM_KEYUP, 53
WM_LBUTTONDOWN, 53
WM_MOUSEMOVE, 53, 495
WM_RBUTTONDOWN, 53
WM_USER, 488
world coordinate system, 472-473, *see also*
    map coordinate system
world position, 530, 598-599
world size, *see* map size
WORLDCOORDINATE, 423-425, 529-530
WORLDOBJECT, 531-534
WPOINT, 90
wx, *see* WORLDCOORDINATE
wy, *see* WORLDCOORDINATE
wz, *see* WORLDCOORDINATE

X
XOR, 88

Y
YUV color model, 169

The Wordware Computer Game Developer's Library

Delphi Developer's Guide to OpenGL

Jon Jacobs

Delphi Developer's Guide to OpenGL is a step-by-step review of OpenGL graphics programming with any 32-bit version of Delphi including Delphi 3 and 4 and future versions of Delphi in 1999. It is the only book on the market that explains how to connect OpenGL with 32-bit versions of Delphi. Intermediate and advanced Delphi developers will learn to use the powerful multi-platform 3-D graphics library known as OpenGL, which has become a standard among graphics programmers and developers.

600 pp. • 7½ x 9¼ • May 20, 1999 • includes CD
1-55622-657-8 • **$59.95** US
$113.95 AUS. • $92.95 CAN.

level: intermediate to advanced Delphi 32-bit programmers and developers
category: Delphi/OpenGL/graphics programming

Squirrel's Computer Game Development in C

Brian "Squirrel" Eiserloh

This book is ideally suited for the introductory or intermediate C programmer who wants to know more about the computer game development environment. Currently, there are no directly competitive titles to *Squirrel's Computer Game Development in C*, which is part of the Wordware Computer Game Developer's Library. Eiserloh's title provides a concise tutorial to game programming in C suitable for beginners and includes a complete coding sample of a computer game.
Brian Eiserloh is a highly experienced computer game programmer in Dallas, Texas, and is also a lead programmer for Ion Storm, one of the most innovative computer game companies in the industry.

500 pp. • 7½ x 9¼ • August 20, 1999 • includes CD
1-55622-664-0 • **$49.95** US
$94.95 AUS. • $77.95 CAN.

level: introductory to intermediate C programme
category: computer game programming/C programming

Developer's Guide to Computer Game Design

John Scott Lewinski

Computer game design from a creative perspective is one of the most important features of a successful computer game that developers and programmers must master before any code is ever written. The plot, the strategy, and the characterizations are components of any successful game, and these components must be developed well ahead of any code. Lewinksi, one of the computer game industry's foremost designers, provides a distinctive review of the game design process for other designers, programmers, and developers in this industry. One of the book's most competitive features is the many interviews with top game designers, providing insight into how they have designed award-winning computer games.
John Scott Lewinksi co-wrote Virgin Interactive's "Command and Conquer—Red Alert," which sold more than 3 million copies worldwide and appeared on the Best Games of the Year list in several national industry publications.

300 pp. • 7½ x 9¼ • June 20, 1999 • includes CD
1-55622-667-5 • **$49.95** US
$94.95 AUS. • $77.95 CAN.

level: intermediate to advanced computer game developers and designers
category: computer game design

Delphi Graphics and Game Programming Exposed with DirectX 6.0

John Ayres

This text is a concise, detailed tutorial and reference describing high-performance graphics and game programming techniques in the Delphi development environment that until now have only been in the domain of C programmers.
This book takes the reader from the most basic sprite movement through tile-based scrolling map engines, voxel engines, texture mapping, and 3-D first-person shooter engines. All techniques are demonstrated using both standard Windows programming techniques and Microsoft's DirectX game development environment. The CD includess all of the projects and example code found in the book, plus bonus programs, shareware, and freeware games written in Delphi; sounds; and music for use in custom games; evaluation versions of Delphi game components and graphics software; and other retail software products.
John Ayres is the lead author of the best-selling *The Tomes of Delphi 3: Win32 Core API* (1-55622-556-3) and *The Tomes of Delphi 3: Win32 Graphical API* (1-55622-610-1).

650 pp. • 7½ x 9¼ • August 20, 1999 • includes CD
1-55622-637-3 • **$54.95** US
$104.95 AUS. • $85.95 CAN.

level: intermediate/advanced
category: Delphi/DirectX/games and graphics programming

Visit our web site at **www.wordware.com**

About the CD

The companion CD contains all the code discussed in the book, plus a few extras. The code is organized in a number of directories that correspond to individual chapters. In addition, there is an Alphabet editor, a tile system example, and the library. The library contains all of the base files for the book and a daunting amount of code. It is mostly readable and fairly well-documented. Be sure to copy the Library directory to your C drive as C:\Library. All of the code refers to it being in that base directory.

 Notice: Opening the CD package makes this book nonreturnable.